MARK TWAIN

Selected Writings of an American Skeptic

Edited by Victor Doyno
Foreword by Leslie Fiedler

Prometheus Books
59 John Glenn Drive
Amherst, NewYork 14228-2197

Published 1995 by
Prometheus Books
59 John Glenn Drive, Amherst, New York 14228-2197,
716-691-0133. FAX: 716-691-0137.

Library of Congress Card Catalog No. 82-60382
ISBN 0-87975-972-0

Printed in the United States of America

I praise generations of collectors, librarians, and scholars who have patiently gathered and explored Twain's works. I dedicate this volume to those who will have moments of thrilling shock as they read and discuss Twain's inventive, surprising mind.

Wouldn't it assist *the work, if you dropped out of harness & routine for a day or two & have that sort of revivification which comes of a holiday-forgetfulness of the workshop? I can always work after I've been to your house; & if you will come to mine, now, & hear the club toot their various horns over the exasperating metaphysical question which I mean to lay before them in the disguise of a literary extravaganza, it would just brace you up like a cordial.*

—Mark Twain, in a letter to William Dean Howells dated January 18, 1876

Contents

Acknowledgments

Several people have generously helped make this volume possible. I am particularly indebted to Robert Hirst, Victor Fischer, W. W. Howells, Milton Meltzer, the University of California Press, Harvard University Press, Harper & Row, and the trustees of the Mark Twain Foundation.

FOREWORD

Subversive Mark Twain

Readers of newspapers earlier this year followed the controversy initiated when a school administrator in Fairfax County, Virginia, urged the dropping from the English curriculum of Mark Twain's *Huckleberry Finn.* The ironies implicit in the case were multiple enough to have delighted Twain himself, since the book recommended for banning is recognized by critical consensus as not only the greatest but the most authentically American of all books ever written in this country—and the most seminal as well. All subsequent American fiction, Hemingway once suggested (and scarcely anyone has ever demurred), came out of that single remarkable book. Moreover, the school involved in this case was, like so many others up and down this land, called after Mark Twain, who even to those who have never read him—learning of him from the movies, television, comic books, or simply word of mouth—is a Great American Hero.

The reasons given by the would-be censor from Virginia for keeping *Huckleberry Finn* out of the hands of children were, according to the values of present-day enlightened liberalism, unimpeachable. It is a novel, the offended administrator argued, that "ridicules blacks" and is therefore particularly difficult for "black youngsters" to handle, allegedly subjecting them to "mental cruelty, harassment, and outright intimidation." If this sounds rather like the plea of a lawyer for the plaintiff in a divorce case, that is fair enough in light of the fact that the relationship between Twain and the American reading public seemed once like an old-fashioned marriage, promising to survive till death did them part.

But, as such a plea might be, the case against *Huckleberry Finn* is based on misunderstanding, if not downright mirepresentation; because, after all, disinterested readers would agree that Twain created in Nigger Jim one of the most noble and sympathetic of all fictional American characters, black or white. And yet, counsel for the plaintiff responds, he is called *Nigger,* and that epithet, taboo these days (at least among whites), is repeated over and over again in the book until it seems a kind of litany: nigger, nigger, nigger, nigger . . . To which the defendant pleads in surrebuttal that "realism" requires it: there was no other word used for blacks by the kind of characters the book portrays, inhabitants of the antebellum South and Midwest.

But perhaps, it occurs to me, the whole forensic debate is beside the point, dealing as it does only with the overt, the conscious, the ostensible arguments for banning *Huckleberry Finn,* which those of us with long memories are aware has been forbidden before, sometimes at the urging of downright, unreconstructed "nigger-haters." There must be, this suggests, deeper, less conscious reasons—reasons whispered in the inner darkness of our heads rather than spoken aloud in public forums—why *Huckleberry Finn* has been banned over and over again; indeed, reasons why many if not all of us, whatever our avowed values, have found and continue to find not just this novel but much of Twain's other fiction (most notably *Pudd'nhead Wilson* and *A Connecticut Yankee*) disturbing, dangerous, somehow subversive.

Let us look at the historical record. Long before the brouhaha in Fairfax, Virginia, critics on the left had argued that Twain's great novel was "racist" and should be kept out of the hands of schoolchildren. There was a parallel case only two or three years ago in a fashionable suburb of Chicago; and long before that, at least as early as the fifties, with the emergence of the civil-rights movement, it was banned in certain high schools and colleges, chiefly in and around New York City.

But long before the cry "Black is beautiful!" was heard in our land, spokesmen for the moderate and genteel Center had begun to attack *Huckleberry Finn.* Almost immediately after its publication in 1885, it was removed from the shelves of the library in Concord, Massachusetts, of all places, the Cradle (once more there is a Twain-like turn of the ironic screw) of American Liberty and the birthplace of the notion of civil disobedience. The ostensible grounds this time were religious, based on the fact that Twain had glorified a boy who shamelessly decides to "go to Hell" for the sake of his black friend. And other good Christians followed suit in the genteel decades ahead, condemning the book for (as Lionel Trilling summarized it) "the endemic lying, the petty thefts, the denigrations of respectability and religion, the bad language and the bad grammar."

Nor was the political Right far behind. Quite early in this century, for example, a congressman called Joseph Shannon demanded that all public honors be denied Twain, not so much for anything he had written as because he had been "a foresaker of the south, a coward and a deserter." That Twain had, indeed, been a deserter cannot be denied; but we should be aware, too (especially those of us whose allegiances are different from those of Congressman Shannon), of which army Twain had deserted. The only American author to serve in the Civil War, Twain had volunteered for service with the Confederacy; i.e., before he became a deserter, he was already a rebel against his own country. And it was perhaps a dim sense of this that impelled a much more renowned member of Congress, the infamous Senator Joseph McCarthy, in the heyday of his crusade against the Red Menace, to denounce *Huckleberry Finn*—presumably as a Communist propaganda *ante lettera.*

As early as 1959, in fact, such semi-official attempts to bar access to *Huckleberry Finn* had become so notorious worldwide that an anti-American article in the *Moscow Literary Gazette* was able self-righteously to scold our country for having rejected its most eminent author, quoting Theodore Dreiser (at that point a Communist sympathizer) to the effect that, like the "few other authentically great thinkers" the capitalist United States had somehow managed to produce, Twain was "under ban" in his native country. But that was, of course, only half of a complex truth, since Twain would never have come under fire at all except for the fact that he had in the first place come to be required reading in our schools. But this prior canonization of Twain in the citadels of high culture seems to me an even greater irony than his subsequent banning. After all, Twain had stated quite unequivocally in 1899, "I have never tried in even one single instance, to help cultivate the cultivated class . . . I . . . always hunted for bigger game—the masses. I have seldom deliberately tried to instruct them, but have done my best to entertain them."

Clearly, however, this is not the whole truth either; since, though Twain did not in any *positive* way try to educate Americans, old or young, he did, whether deliberately or not, attempt to challenge, undercut, subvert (as Victor Doyno convincingly argues, and as the texts he has assembled here demonstrate) many of the values the school system sought to instill in the young—including a respect for polite letters. This he scarcely tried to keep secret, any more than he did his profound distrust of the larger ideals of Christian humanism—indeed, of everything that Huck contemptuously calls "civilization." What Twain did seek to conceal from his contemporaries (especially, it would seem, his mother, his wife, and his daughters) was his conviction—confessed in texts that he ordered be kept under lock and key for a hundred years—that the Judeo-Christian God was dead.

How then was he ever accepted into the curriculum (continually challenged, but always in the end reinstated) of the educational establishment from which he himself had escaped at age twelve and continued to mock for ever after? It is, in part, I suppose, because he was in many quarters never taken seriously—coming on in the guise of an entertainer, a "phunny pheller," a clown, willing to say or do anything for a laugh. But surely also it is because of the divided minds of the popular audiénce itself, longing for someone to give voice to their otherwise unconfessed inner doubts about the values they publicly espouse.

He was, moreover, as divided in himself as the American masses who loved him. Despite his disavowal of some of the articles of faith by which they lived, others he subscribed to as devoutly as any of them, believing, for instance, in the innocence of childhood, the purity of women, the benignness of technology, the sweetness of success. Nor was he immune to all the prejudices of his time and place. Though he demurred from popular contempt for blacks and Jews, he hated Indians and half-breeds, feared sex, and considered the French a disgustingly immoral people. Moreover, even toward certain of the standard received beliefs he disavowed, he betrayed a considerable margin of ambivalence.

It is to the positive underside of some of his most negative convictions that his most sophisticated as well as his most naive readers (not least of all, perhaps, children) respond, sensing a joyous affirmation beneath his bleakest nihilism. Many *half*-sophisticated readers, however, who include in their numbers the would-be banners of his books, either miss that underside completely or take it as evidence of unworthy duplicity verging on downright hypocrisy. Certain apparent contradictions between his work and his life, between what he said and what he did, seem to bear this out. After all, he did not light out for the territory like Huck, but instead grew rich and famous writing about it. Similarly, despite his declared skepticism about elite higher education, he rejoiced in the honorary degree bestowed on him by Oxford University; just as in contempt of his own bitter criticism of the Robber Barons and their greed, he himself attempted to be a capitalist entrepreneur, counting among his best friends Andrew Carnegie and Henry H. Rogers, a vice-president of Standard Oil. Moreover, though he was a lifelong mocker of Christian chivalry and the ethos of patriotic war, his two greatest heroes were Joan of Arc and General Ulysses S. Grant.

No wonder he has always seemed dangerous to the self-righteous few who believe that there is a single correct way to do everything and that that is the one they practice, meanwhile pleasing the muddled many who live by ambivalence without even knowing its highfalutin' name. Yet, finally, perhaps even more than his implicit ambivalence, it is Twain's explicit skepticism, that total skepticism even of skepticism itself, that had made him seem to the Great Audience one of their own, a sympathetic fellow rather than the alienated outsider he sometimes thought of himself as being. To be sure, sometimes especially toward the embittered end of his life, he liked to assume the posture of the lonely satirist attacking the Idols of the Tribe in the name of sweet reason and a higher truth revealed only to him. And if this was all there was to him, he might have turned himself a provincial cynic, a village atheist like Robert Ingersoll or his own Pudd'nhead Wilson.

But he was able to identify not only with such a proud doubter of everything as Pudd'nhead, but also with the humble, credulous Huck, who is deceived by everyone yet somehow never deceives himself. In the end, therefore, Twain's satire, like the skepticism that underlies it, dissolves into something higher and more inclusive: a kind of absolute irony, which responds to the human condition, the unbridgeable gap between what we dream we might be and what we know we are, not with contempt or anger or even tears, but the sort of laughter indistinguishable from love.

Leslie A. Fiedler

Buffalo, New York
June 3, 1982

INTRODUCTION

Mark Twain, American Doubter

Many Americans feel a natural and easy identification with Mark Twain, who was praised by his contemporaries as "the people's author" and "the laughing philosopher." His humor, his wit, his insights, his social concern—and perhaps even his pose of anti-intellectualism—endear him to countless Americans who think of him as somehow their own, one of them.

Twain was able to deal perceptively and humorously with what ordinary people consider philosophical topics, such issues as religion, politics, belief, justice, prejudice, child rearing, human nature, love, and death. My purpose has been to assemble, from a wide range of sources, a comprehensive selection of Twain's writings that reveals his practical and philosophical skepticism. Naturally, this gathering includes selections from his fiction, travel literature, essays, and letters, and places them in a philosophical context.

For the general reader this volume should provide an introduction to Mark Twain's philosophy of life. It should also serve as a convenient resource and a spark for many debates. Moreover, it should convince specialists in American Literature that Mark Twain was, although not a systematic philosopher, a skeptic for most of his lifetime. Twain's importance in the history of skepticism demands some explanation. He need not be valued as an original or as a systematic, consistent thinker. Indeed, he contradicts many of his own positions. But he should be valued for the conciseness, wit, and phrasing of his philosophical statements. Many people will discover that their own thoughts or reactions have been shared with Mark Twain. For example, Kurt Vonnegut testifies, "I was confirmed in my skepticism by Mark Twain during my formative years, and by some other good people, too." Sam Clemens/Mark Twain was not formally educated, but many details in his wide, rich life experience were carefully, thoughtfully considered. He serves as a prime example of a prototypical American thinker—independent, self-educated, vitally involved, a prismatic American Adam, a natural innocent, a man of goodness and intelligence.

Twain had the ability to present common or age-old philosophical problems in memorable, imaginatively phrased ways. Although not a professional philosopher, he presents these issues in fictional or personal form. Accordingly, this philosophy is easy to read and to understand. Most of us have had the experience of laboring through a philosophical discourse only to have the thought, upon reflection, evaporate. Moreover, much professional philosophical writing has become so specialized or abstract that it has little apparent relevance to the ordinary person's day-to-day life. With the writings of Mark Twain one has the opposite experience: the reader may need to pause in the midst of enjoyable reading to reflect upon the philosophical seriousness of the issues under discussion, clothed as it is in the accessible prose of fiction or personal commentary.

One current widespread view of Mark Twain holds that his scathing skepticism and acid pessimism were caused by the many personal tragedies of his life. Clearly the man behind the mask, Sam Clemens (1835–1910), suffered great sorrow. He buried his first-born, a son (1870). His lively daughter, Susy, his "favorite," died when Sam was abroad (1896). His wife, Livy, was often sickly and died in 1904 after a long, draining illness. Another daughter died of an epileptic fit on Christmas Eve morning in 1909. He could not bring himself to attend the funeral. Anyone who reads about these events in his letters may feel the enormous sorrow and rage that shook him. His frequent financial difficulties and his bankruptcy in 1894 also may have contributed to his disillusionment with conventional wisdom.

But another, more thorough view of the man and his work would transcend this simple biographical explanation. As this book demonstrates, Mark Twain's skepticism is found throughout his published works, early to late. It is an oversimplification—and finally disrespectful to the man and his mind—simply to say that personal difficulties caused his skepticism. A wider perspective reveals that his background, his experience, his journalistic ability to be objective and to see only what is there, his reading, and, most of all, his intellectual acuity contributed to the shape of his thought.

Among the many influences that shaped Sam Clemens's philosophy of life, his family is primary.[1] According to family legend his father, John Marshall Clemens, was named after the famous jurist. As a boy, Sam must have observed his father's principled behavior and heard his agnostic and free-thinking philosophy. Before Sam was born, John Marshall Clemens had shown his impatience with a visiting minister—who had failed to make an announcement for Clemens from his pulpit—by shouldering him aside to report to the assembled congregation that his cow was missing. The child of such a father is unlikely to consider religious ritual as sacrosanct. But this pragmatic action was not typical of the father, who was, in many ways, a dreamer, a gentleman of slender income gradually growing poorer. He was called "Judge," in the Southern fashion; and, although he was temperamentally taciturn, his infrequent comments were occasionally blistering. The father's marginal role in the economy of Hannibal, Missouri, may have also set a foundation for his son's nonestablishment thinking. The family's frequent moves, usually to shabbier housing, may have affected both the father's pride and the son's sense of security.

Sam's mother, Jane Lampton Clemens, often contradicted her husband's views, creating for Sam a possibility of independence that most consistent child-rearing practices of that era did not permit. Jane Clemens was a believer, and she combined traditional religious beliefs with tinges of Spiritualism. She believed in dreams, visions, omens, and other supernatural events. When Sam became a sleepwalker and when he plucked at a coverlet (supposedly foretelling death) his mother concluded that he had the "gift" or the "power." How would a boy react to this? He might develop a sense of his own specialness and a suspicion of those who are too quick to believe.

Mrs. Clemens apparently had a sympathetic heart and frequently took the side of the underdog. A family amusement involved the conspirators criticizing Satan, and Jane was lured into defending him, excusing and explaining his behavior. She was apparently also a brave woman and once stepped forth to protect a woman who was being beaten.

Jane Clemens was a witty person, a woman who could imitate a cousin's mannerisms, sass a friend, and ironize about a custom. Dixon Wecter, the author of *Sam Clemens of Hannibal,* the book offering the best treatment of Mark Twain's childhood, calls Jane Clemens "a connoisseur—rather than a convert—of religious cults." Her ready, inventive, open-minded intelligence undoubtedly contributed to Sam's individuality.

Sam's oldest brother, Orion, also must have had an influence, but as a negative example. Orion seems to have been both fervent and unrealistic, a naive, foolish, enthusiastic bumbler. Whatever he touched turned to dust; numerous projects fizzled. Late one night Orion returned to Hannibal from St. Louis and, forgetting that the family had moved, entered the wrong house, undressed, and crawled into bed with an elderly maiden.

When Sam worked for Orion on the Hannibal newspapers, he developed a greater knowledge of his brother's failings. Orion's adult life included frequent changes in belief and opinion, as well as frequent schemes for success. Sam thought Orion's life so extraordinary that he once asked Orion to write an account of it. Sam himself tried to tell Orion's story, calling it "Autobiography of a Damned Fool." Sam had, in Orion, a constant and proximate model of the folly of credulous innocence.

Similarly, one of Sam's sisters, Pamela, was a sincere, devout, somewhat simple woman. It was necessary for family members to explain to her when someone was joking. Later in life Pamela became an advocate of the temperance movement, and it is known that she urged Sam not to make fun of religion.

Miss Newcomb, the teacher who taught Sam how to read, was for a while a boarder in the Clemens's home. We may surmise that her presence was a factor reinforcing Sam's learning.

Although Mark Twain has written inimitably about Sam Clemens's adventures in the small school in Hannibal, one part of his education requires emphasis for our purposes. Sam's father insisted on subscribing to various children's magazines, apparently in hopes that his children would benefit. The influence proved invaluable—but contrary to expectation. Young Sam apparently learned to doubt the validity of this moralizing material. In a typical story, a poor and honest good boy finds a lost valuable and returns it. As a result, he is offered a job in a bank and, ultimately, the hand in marriage of the banker's lovely daughter. Such material seemed appropriate to parody to Mark Twain, because he wrote a matching pair, "The Story of the Bad Little Boy" (1865) and "The Story of the Good Little Boy" (1870). (See Part 2 of this book.) In these stories the bad boy becomes a congressman and the good boy is dynamited. Much of Sam Clemens's life and Mark Twain's career was devoted to posing as a brash, decent-hearted bad little boy, an interloper, an outsider, a Westerner in the East, or an American in Europe.

Young Sam went to the Methodist Sunday School of the Old Ship of Zion Church, where apparently the emphasis was on memorization. Clemens later claimed that he had won prizes by memorizing and repeating the same five Bible verses Sunday after Sunday. The story, whether true or not, makes a nice contrast between the boy's memory and the teacher's forgetfulness. Similarly, Clemens recounts a story of praying for a piece of gingerbread, and suddenly seeing a fellow student's piece lying unprotected. But, later, equally pragmatic prayers did not succeed.

In 1843 Jane Clemens became a Presbyterian, and all of the members of the family followed—except her husband, who Sam claimed attended a church only once, and never again. This shift in loyalty may well have loosened some of Sam's convictions.

But John Marshall Clemens's anti-clericalism was not typical of Hannibal. Camp meetings and revivals were welcome activities. A Twain note, now in the Buffalo Historical Society, remarks on a Campbellite revival that claimed many souls—"all but me"—and observes that they were "all sinners again in a week." Similarly, Sam's memories included a group of apocalyptic Millerites who awaited the end of the world and were disappointed. Spiritualism enjoyed some credence in Hannibal, although there were many hoaxes. Sam claimed that a young girl fashioned a spirit out of some dough that so terrified a local woman that she was put in an asylum.

Undoubtedly much of Sam's Calvinist conscience, religious skepticism, and fascination with predestination came from the formative influences of this period. He claimed that he had read the Bible completely by the age of fifteen and that its impurity had soiled his mind.

During several summer vacations, young Sam stayed on the farm of his uncle, John Quarles, a Universalist. This man's religion held that all people could be saved; this view, of course, offended the notion of exclusive salvation of most other religions. The Universalist sect was quite small and had been subjected to persecution. Later, Clemens was to recall that he never knew a better man than John Quarles, and in his late fragmentary fiction Twain rehearses some of the arguments about universal salvation for animals, germs, and vitamins.

Hannibal's location on the Mississippi provided a constant contrast between small-town life and the larger world floating past. The steamboat culture was, by Hannibal's standards, dazzlingly sophisticated. One of Twain's earliest national publications creates a contrast between a traveling dandy and a local squatter. This constant contrast may have encouraged Sam Clemens's development as a cultural amphibian, able to become immersed and successful in a culture while also remaining objective and critical of it.

The idyllic aspects of Sam Clemens's childhood are widely known, but the contrasting, terrorizing elements need to be mentioned. The Clemens family lost three children. In May 1842, when Sam was six, his older brother Benjamin died, and Sam must have faced the uncertainty of life. Five months later his home was offered at a public sale to settle debts. The family's one slave asked to be sold, perhaps in the hope that another owner would be more prosperous.

Of course, violence also pervaded Hannibal; a man hit a slave with a piece of slag, killing him. Once Sam came upon a corpse in his father's office. Shootings and attempted shootings were deplored, but not extraordinary.

After John Marshall Clemens died, when Sam was eleven, the boy apparently watched a portion of the post-mortem examination. During this period of stress, Sam reverted to sleepwalking, startling his recently widowed mother.

The death of his father must have had a complex effect upon the boy. Psychologically, the dominant male influence was gone at a crucial time. Economically, the loss of the father hurt the already poor family. Probably Sam began to work part-time. He later dropped out of school and became apprenticed to a local printer. But his education actually continued as he set "acres" of print. He was an autodidact. His later thinking accordingly seems a bit peculiar: enthusiastic, spotty, contradictory. It is probable that for quite a while, approximately between the ages of twelve and twenty-three, Sam read and set type as if he hoped one day to happen upon a piece of writing that would explain life, reveal an explanation of its secrets.

One May, perhaps in 1850, when Sam was fourteen, he volunteered to be the subject for a mesmerizer. Sam claimed that he was motivated by envy of a person named, paradoxically, Urban Hicks, who had proved himself to be a good subject and received a good deal of attention because of it. Sam apparently vowed to surpass Hicks. A Dr. Humphrey Peake had a good reputation as a skeptic about hypnotism. When Sam was pretending to be mesmerized he told details he had overheard about Dr. Peake's previous residence, and thereby convinced the doctor of his powers. Such an experience, deliberately fooling the respected unbeliever into a state of credulity, must have affected Sam.

Did he lose respect for the person he had hoaxed? Would Sam be less easily fooled thereafter?

Dixon Wecter places in Sam's early printing-house experience his exposure to the compositors' form of "sarcastic applause," made by sawing their boxes with a composing stick, making "an urgent and strenuous and hideous sound and when an expert makes it it shrieks out like the braying of a jackass." The witness of such sarcastic approval will not desire such attention for himself.

During the years 1853–1857 Sam Clemens was day by day, unknowingly, making the transition from a rural youth skilled at typesetting to an experienced traveler seeing America. His journey included St. Louis, New York, Philadelphia, Washington, Keokuk, and Cincinnati. Throughout his life, his worldly experiences may have led him to doubt the possibility of certainty. Numerous exposures to shams educated Sam.

For many American authors—from Franklin and Twain to Crane and Hemingway—the printing shop ("the poor boy's college") and journalism have provided alternative methods of education. Twain earned his living as a journeyman, a traveling typesetter who sets good, bad, and indifferent writing in print. It may be observed that a printer is likely to take a less than honorific view of a writer's text, knowing that it is, after all, only a product of a tedious manual process, subject to error and accidental influences. The printed word held, for Sam, little mystical authority.

Sam also made money by writing "travel letters" for rural newspapers, explaining in comic dialect the adventures of a country bumpkin in a big city. Irony and social criticism permeate this form, which can vary from the objective reporting of information to imaginative invention, and these letters appealed to Twain throughout his career. In various ways, his letters from Thomas Jefferson Snodgrass, from *The Innocents Abroad,* from Huckleberry Finn, from a newly arrived Chinese immigrant, and from a fallen angel about human foibles are all extensions of this genre, combining elements of a naive narrator and social criticism.

In August 1856, Sam was considering a trip to South America to make his fortune. He wrote to his brother Henry that he was leading Orion to believe that he would stop in New York or New Orleans and let Ward, his companion, survey the situation on the southern continent alone. Sam revealed to Henry, "But that don't suit me. My confidence in human nature does not extend quite that far. I won't depend upon Ward's judgment or anybody else's. I want to see with my own eyes and form my own opinion." Sam had, at twenty, already formed a strong foundation of individualistic skepticism. He would not easily accept second-hand opinions or conventional dogmatism.

One chance meeting had a significant impact on Sam, partly for confirming past thoughts and partly for giving an intellectual framework to what had probably been inchoate, disparate experience. During the winter of 1857 in Cincinnati, Sam, aged twenty-two, stayed in a boarding house where a dour, talkative, self-educated Scot named Macfarlane talked of his philosophy.

Twain had recently read Tom Paine's *The Rights of Man* and *The Age of Reason*.

To this base Macfarlane probably added the then startling insights that all animal life had gradually evolved through different forms until man was reached. Thenceforth, the ascent turned into a descent. Macfarlane was quite definite about man's degradation of nature and intellect in his selfishness. The fact that Macfarlane knew the dictionary and the Bible, seemingly perfectly, lent added weight to his opinions. The traces of scientific evidence also must have impressed Sam. Later Twain would write repeatedly about man's descent from the other animals.

Another significant influence upon Twain's skepticism involves a peculiar form of American humor, the tall tale.[2] Clemens heard many tall tales as a child and as an author retailed several hundred of them. In this type of humor the story-teller begins an apparently reasonable story but gradually slips in increasingly impossible elements. The dynamic of this humor includes the deadpan story-teller watching the listener's face for flickers of doubt or disbelief. Should doubt flash across the listener's face or should there be a suspicious question, the teller simply supplies more realistic, plausible details, until the listener is once more unsuspecting. The listener who hears the story to the end, thereby revealing himself to be credulous, is shamed. Any naive questions asked by the listener are repeatedly thrown up to him as evidence of his astonishing stupidity. The dynamic of this humor includes the teller of the tall story and any witnesses taunting the believer by quoting him. Most people who are victims of tall tales feel utterly humiliated when their credulity is mockingly quoted. The daunted believers simply appear to be powerless. Of course Sam Clemens was occasionally the victim, frequently the knowing on-looker, and often the spinner of the tall tale. It seems reasonable to suggest that this exposure and experience could well have pushed Twain toward a wide-ranging skepticism.

Other aspects of oral humor and frontier male conversation, such as exaggeration, bravado, joshing, and the long, pointless narratives of shaggy dog stories undoubtedly also contributed to Twain's skepticism. The initiation of a rookie or a greenhorn, the arrival of a newcomer, or merely an idle few minutes could be the occasion for some variety of oral humor. Sam Clemens also apparently had an extraordinary ability to perpetuate hoaxes, some played on people, some printed as stories. And Twain frequently suffered—or claimed to have suffered—the artistic exaltation and humiliation of having his hoaxes taken seriously. Although the artist may be pleased by the compliment on his writing, the man may feel disillusioned with his audience, or skeptical about the audience's credulity.

In contrast, Sam's early experience in reporting for small-town newspapers probably influenced him to observe the facts closely when he wanted to; if he varied significantly from the facts, a local observer might contradict, attacking his credibility. Some of Sam's colleagues on the small Nevada *Territorial*

Enterprise, especially newspapermen like Rollin M. Daggett and Steve Gillis, exemplified courageous journalism.

In Carson City, on February 2, 1863, Sam Clemens sent a dispatch to the *Enterprise,* signing it with a new pen name—"Mark Twain." Perhaps because of his ability to observe objectively, decide independently, and write scathingly, he acquired a following first in the mining areas, then in California, and then across the country. He could write both frontal sarcastic attacks and subtle or blatant hoaxes. He had and would continue to have enough journalistic and literary battles to keep his skills sharp.

His western experience included the mining towns and the newspaper offices. Saloons, campfires, and "bull sessions" were occasions for oral education and performance. In San Francisco, the theaters, saloons, police stations, and the morgue (and, according to an attacker, the brothels) gave him an education in the ways of the world. At one point, in 1866, he considered suicide, and even put a gun to his head. Late in life he reflected "Many times I have been sorry I did not succeed, but I was never ashamed of having tried."

The reporter's need for objectivity was held in uncertain balance with the story-teller's need for an individual perspective. His trip to Hawaii and his subsequent voyage to Europe and the Middle East confirmed his ability to write entertaining travel letters, and he was paid handsomely for his skills. His observations on his European journey smashed any remaining veneration for conventional culture. As *Innocents Abroad* demonstrates, Twain's disbelief and lack of awe created his individual voice. Moreover, Twain, now a world traveler, gradually gained the self-confidence to state his opinions forcefully and the literary skill to express his thoughts memorably.

In October 1865, Sam Clemens/Mark Twain wrote to Orion and his wife Mollie that he wished to be a preacher or a river-boat pilot but that the first choice was impossible because he didn't have the "necessary stock in trade—*i.e.* religion." However, his books and his public platform would become his pulpit. Much later, looking back at his career, Twain stated: "Humor must not professedly teach and it must not professedly preach, but it must do both if it would live forever. By forever I mean thirty years." In an 1898 essay Twain says: "Do I seem to be preaching? It is out of my line: I only do it because the rest of the clergy seem to be on vacation." This ability to teach and preach and entertain, in rare combination, has far surpassed Twain's limited temporal expectations, pleasing generations of readers. Although Sam Clemens died in 1910, Mark Twain continues to live.

Sam Clemens made his readers and listeners familiar with his life, cleverly blending the real and the fictional, creating the personality of Mark Twain, whom Americans recognized and loved. This deliberate self-transformation, or re-creation of the self, is a quintessential American myth. The public knowledge of Mark Twain's "life" fit certain stereotypic patterns. The story involved a young boy born in obscure circumstances, maturing with a series of idyllic and terrorizing moments. The youthful hero ventures into strange and distant lands, receives popular acclaim, marries a beautiful heiress, and earns worldly success and fame. The victory over problems of adulthood, such as bankruptcy, only adds to the glory of the legendary life.

Because the story is mythic, Twain has assumed a prismatic role in American popular culture. Because the executors of his estate preferred a proper—and profitable—image, the notion of Mark Twain as the genial, avuncular joker remained popular; it was what could be considered a Walt Disney or Norman Rockwell version, appropriate for a vague nostalgia. But recent biographical and critical studies indicate, as does this volume, the author's complexity.

Two literary fashions were dominant in polite American culture, but Twain usually reacted against both.[3] Most earlier esteemed writers characteristically used a highly polysyllabic, Latinate vocabulary, often with involuted sentence structure. Twain managed to write in a common language, and he made this ordinary style esteemed. His achievement—creating timeless art in the vernacular—helped advance American cultural independence and diversity.

A second dominant literary fashion was the doctrine of associationalism. This view held that the writing about a famous or holy place should be a combination of a physical description and an emotional, imaginative recounting of the significant events that *might* have occurred in the past. For example, a tourist to the Holy Land would read in guide books a description of the path of Christ carrying the cross followed by a rapture, e.g., "Here the feet of Christ stumbled, here the humble servant girl hurried past, here the brave Crusader fought, and here the pious pilgrim knelt." The manufacturing of these elevating "associations" was one way to expand a meager description to greater length. But Twain denied many of the expectations of "associationalism," especially in *The Innocents Abroad.* He claimed, instead, to see what the reader would see if unhindered by the guidebook emotion. Thus he mocks, denying the likelihood of a Second Coming on the grounds that anyone who had seen this parched area once would not come back.

The leading critic of that era, William Dean Howells, praised Twain's "ethical intelligence, which underlies his humor" and lauded his "certain intensity of common sense" and "passionate love of justice." The insight was accurate. Twain read carefully and marked laboriously and contentiously a two-volume study by W. E. H. Lecky, *History of European Morals from Augustus to Charlemagne.*[4] Lecky describes two kinds of moralists: one group holds that people act morally because of an innate intuitive preference for virtue, while the other group forms morality based on a selfish perception of happiness or pain. Although Lecky cast his authorial bias with the intuitionalist school, Twain conducted a fierce marginal debate. This ethical debate underlies his masterpiece, *Adventures of Huckleberry Finn.* Increasingly, Twain wrote from the deterministic view, as in *Connecticut Yankee.* During most of his career, he noticed the human ability to rationalize in a self-advantageous way, just as he had a keen ear for humbug and a sharp eye for sham.

Other areas of increased information contribute to our new, complex understanding. For example, a knowledge of Twain's reading, and of the influence of authors like Paine, Mill, and Carlyle on his thinking, reveals the deceptiveness of the Mark Twain persona of a naive, ignorant, amiable native genius.[5] Recently, critics and scholars have offered a superb series of carefully edited texts that clarify the issues.[6] Another transformation is currently underway, as readers gradually realize that Twain is an author of almost Shakespearean dimension and complexity.

His distinctive lecture style—the slow-paced delivery, the deadpan expression, and the occasional air of incomprehension—actually empowered his audience. The group became, in the dynamics of the lecture situation, apparently more perceptive than the performer; yet Twain the performer obviously shaped and controlled the entire interaction. The lectures and public readings thus became, in Twain's case, a democratic art form as well as an exercise in enjoyable, mutually recognized artistic deception.

Readers are advised to read all of Twain's writings skeptically; one must remain ever alert for a shift of tone, a modification from praise to sarcasm. The proper way to read Twain involves maintaining a state of continuous enjoyment and doubtfulness. Here is an author who will engage your trust only to test your ability to detect a sham. Twain is hence a liberating author, freeing you of preconception and even from over-reliance on the author.

Several incidents of nonskeptical behavior may qualify any reader's belief that Clemens/Twain was utterly consistent. For example, Sam wrote from New Orleans to Orion on February 6, 1861, about his visit to a well-known clairvoyant, Madame Caprell. She gave him a remarkable reading despite his sarcastic interjections, and he vowed to visit her again, in disguise, to test her powers of perception. Similarly, he visited a phrenologist. And once he urged his wife to consult mind-curists (hypnotists) for medical treatment. He was open-minded enough to explore.

Moreover, Twain varied from his characteristic skepticism by attempting religious reforms—repeatedly. On his first voyage to Europe he once led the evening devotions. Later, when courting Livy, he tried manfully to immerse himself in religion, but his devotion was more to Livy than to God. And after marriage he once surprised an old friend by saying grace before a meal. But the attempts failed, and he gradually converted Livy to his way of thinking. He genuinely tried to swear less—or less blasphemously—for her sake. After his daughter Susy died he tried to contact her several times, through Spiritualists, but realized that the attempts failed. Later in life, when Livy was dying, Sam persuaded her that he did believe in the possibility of an afterlife, a gesture of loving support and nurturative continuance.

What kind of philosophy of life did he develop? Twain wrote of himself, "Born irreverent, like all other people I have ever known or heard of—I am hoping to remain so while there are any reverent irreverences left to make fun of." As a child, Sam was given totalistic, usually religious, explanations of life, but the explanations frequently were contradicted by experience. As he matured,

Sam read voraciously, as if he hoped to find ultimate explanations if he could only find the right book. Increasingly he became a skeptic willing to try a new system, but cautious about lending it belief. His increasing range of experience by its very diversity confirmed the skeptical position. He became a highly skillful debater.

His marriage and his love for his family provided one sustaining value in his life. Sam apparently remained devoted to Livy and, to varying degrees, to his children. "Love seems the swiftest, but it is the slowest of all growths. No man or woman really knows what perfect love is until they have been married a quarter of a century." Although recent scholarly work reveals a surprisingly high level of absence and of tension, his family remained one unquestioned good. Sam must have been, from a modern perspective, a difficult, doting, loving husband and father. In contrast, a high proportion of his friendships ended badly, with Sam usually feeling cheated or betrayed. The few friendships that endured, with Howells, Joe Twitchell, and Henry H. Rogers, were unusual.

In his maturity Sam Clemens came to doubt that the universe had a purpose or meaning. Later in his life, around 1889, he adopted a philosophy of determinism, a rather elaborate application of what we would call a combination of heredity, environment, conditioning, and chance, the belief that humans had no choice to be anything other than what they are. Such a philosophy was obviously opposed to the traditional religions of his era. These thoughts became increasingly consoling to the author because they relieved him from the bruises of life.

His writing provided a chance to test out, to dramatize his ideas. And in some of his later, extraordinarily bleak, fragmentary writings Twain would repeatedly tell stories in which a loving, respected father either loses all his money or loses and then reunites with his children. These late fictions—attempts to reconstitute his world—are heartbreaking.

He once stated: "When a man stands on the verge of seventy-two you know perfectly well that he never reached that place without knowing what this life is—heartbreaking bereavement. And so our reverence is for our dead. We do not forget them; but our duty is toward the living; and if we can be cheerful, cheerful in spirit, cheerful in speech and in hope, that is a benefit to those who are around us." He continued to be a public figure, always entertaining and philosophizing.

He repeatedly toyed with the idea that all of life was a dream, that all the human emotions and experiences were delusions. Similarly, he explored the common notion of infinite macro- or microscopic worlds, that we are mere germs in the bloodstream of a massive creature, that the planets are mere particles of dust in some larger universe, or that microscopic worlds replicate aspects of our existence. Death became a wished-for event, as in his short story "The Five Boons of Life."

Sam Clemens's life ultimately included a kaleidoscopic variety: printer, riverboat pilot, prospector, reporter, travel writer, newspaper owner, humorist, novelist, husband, father, inventor, investor, publisher, public speaker, shaper of public opinion, lavish host, bankrupt, favorite of financiers and of the common people. The range of his opinions is appropriately large and contradictory, as the range of his felt emotions covers the spectrum from sheer joy to shattering despair and rage. His overall life experience led Sam Clemens/Mark Twain to know that this life, this earth, is all we know of heaven—and all we need to know of hell.

This selection of texts to reveal the range and depth of Twain's skepticism could easily be three times as long. But a deliberate decision has been made to decrease the emphasis upon Twain's skepticism about monarchy, nobility, and hierarchical government. When he wrote, there were over thirty-five crowned heads of state reigning on the planet. Although monarchy is now less prevalent, and therefore a less compelling target for skepticism, the number of authoritarian regimes is immense. Twain would undoubtedly apply the same satiric thrusts to most absolute dictators, whether they cloak their claims to power in religious robes or military uniforms. But, because his doubts about dictatorial monarchs may seem dated to many readers, I have given that material less emphasis.

The concluding section offers suggestions for further reading in the primary texts and in the scholarship.

Selected illustrations are included from the first editions of *The Innocents Abroad, Life on the Mississippi,* and *A Connecticut Yankee in King Arthur's Court.* The illustrations indicate what impressions Twain's earliest readers would form. In addition, one illustration from *Life on the Mississippi* has special interest because the picture of Sam Clemens's face surrounded by flames, which was placed at the end of a chapter on cremation, bothered Livy so much that Twain had it removed. The illustrator for *Connecticut Yankee,* Dan Beard, by picturing contemporary people, added to the social criticism of the nineteenth century. For example, Beard, a socialist, drew the face of J. Gould as the slave driver. The drawings extended the written criticism in a surprisingly topical fashion.

NOTES

1. In this introduction to the life of Sam Clemens/Mark Twain I rely upon his autobiographical writings and letters. I draw heavily upon Dixon Wecter's description of the family and childhood in *Sam Clemens of Hannibal* (Boston, 1952). Similarly, this account also utilizes the insights and information presented by William Dean Howells in *My Mark Twain* (New York, 1910), by Justin Kaplan in *Sam Clemens and Mark Twain* (New York, 1966), and by Hamlin Hill in *God's Fool* (New York, 1973).

2. Walter Blair's *Native American Humor* and Walter Blair and Hamlin Hill's *American Humor* (New York, 1978) provide a range of relevant material.

3. Henry Nash Smith's *Mark Twain, The Development of a Writer* deals with both the inclusion of vernacular in literature and the role of associationalism.

4. See Walter Blair's definitive study *Mark Twain and Huck Finn* (Berkeley, 1960).

5. Alan Gribben's landmark two-volume *Mark Twain's Library: A Reconstruction* (Boston: G. K. Hall, 1980) will disabuse anyone who fondly believes that Twain was not a reader.

6. The Mark Twain Papers, published by the University of California Press, have set a valuable standard of meticulous editing.

I

Early Writings and Travel Literature

Juvenilia and Early Journalism

When Sam Clemens was seventeen he wrote "Historical Exhibition—A No. 1 Ruse" for the Hannibal Journal *of September 16, 1852. The story has the weakness of* juvenilia: *it is too long, and the comic points are hammered to strike even dull readers. But the tale reveals how early the author was dealing with stories of deception and credulity. In addition, the early piece shows the author's concern with the contrast between elaborate, stately, deceptive language and short, vivid, realistic language. Clemens published this piece under the pseudonym of "W. Epaminondas Adrastus Blab." Although the piece is far from perfect, it is beyond the reach of most seventeen-year-old authors.*

The second selection is unusual. Edgar Branch and Robert Hirst, the editors of Twain's Early Tales and Sketches, *identify this sketch of boarding-house life as an item attributed to Twain. We cannot prove conclusively in the conventional ways that the story is Twain's, but a thorough knowledge of his works convinces one that, though imperfect, it is indeed his. The characterizations are confusing, but the topics are typical. It is apparent that the young author, aged twenty, was exploring, not controlling, the art of the deadpan ending.*

Twain wrote the "Petrified Man" for publication in October 1862. He probably intended to mock both Justice Sewell and the fad of petrification stories. A number of newspapers reprinted the story as if it were true. Twain probably exaggerated the number of editors who were fooled. But any skeptical reader who would imitate the pose would soon be aware of the hoax.

The last selection, "New Year's Day," was written for publication on January 1, 1863. We begin to see the tolerant acceptance of humanity balanced by the sharp attention to hypocrisy.

The texts are taken from Early Tales and Sketches, *vol. 1, 1851–1864, edited by Edgar M. Branch and Robert H. Hirst (University of California Press, Berkeley, 1979).**

Historical Exhibition—A No. 1 Ruse

A young friend gives me the following yarn as fact, and if it should turn out to be a double joke, (that is, that he imagined the story to fool me with,) on his own head be the blame:

It seems that the news had been pretty extensively circulated, that Mr. Curts, of the enterprising firm of Curts & Lockwood, was exhibiting at their store, for the benefit of the natives, a show of some kind, bearing the attractive title of "Bonaparte crossing the Rhine," upon which he was to deliver a lecture, explaining its points, and giving the history of the piece, the price being "one dime per head, children half price." Well, the other day about dusk, a young man went in, paid his dime, "saw the elephant," and departed, apparently "with a flea in his ear," but the uninitiated could get nothing out of him on the subject; he was mum—had seen the varmint, and that was the full extent of the information which could be pumped out of him by his enquiring friends.

Well, everybody who saw the sight seemed seized with a sudden fit of melancholy immediately afterwards, and dimes began to grow scarce. But pretty soon Jim C——, with a crowd of eager boys at his heels, was seen coming down the street like half a dozen telegraphs. They arrived at the store, gasping and out of breath, and Jim broke out with:

"Mr Curts—want—to see—that—show! What's—price!"

"Oh, we let boys see it at half price—hand out your five cents."

Jim had got done blowing by this time, and threw down his money in as great a hurry as if life and death depended upon the speed of his movements, saying:

"Quick! Mr. Curts, I want to see it the worst kind."

"Yes, Oh yes; you want to see 'Bonaparte crossing the Rhine,' do you," said Abram, very deliberately.

"Yes, that's it—that's what I want to see," said Jim, who was so anxious to see the show that he could scarcely stand still.

"Well, you shall see it," said the worthy exhibitor, with a wise look, at the same time dropping the five cents into the money drawer, "and I hope by this show to impress upon your young minds, this valuable piece of history, and illustrate the same in so plain a manner that the silliest lad amongst you will readily comprehend it."

The juvenile audience was now breathless with expectation, and crowded around with eager looks, and not the slightest movement on the part of the learned lecturer was overlooked by them, as he drew from a drawer a piece of bone about three inches long, and holding it up before the wondering boys, he slowly and deliberately commenced his lecture, or explanation:

"My young friends, you now perceive——"

"Yes sir," interrupted Jim with mouth, eyes and ears wide open.

"As I was saying," continued Mr. Curts, "you now see before you the 'Bonaparte'—the *'Bony-part,'* you understand, the *'bony part'* of a hog's leg (house shakes with laughter from the crowd which had now assembled, but Jim did not join in the general merriment, but looked very sober, seeming to think there was very little about it to laugh at, at least on his side) yes, boys," said Abram, as grave and solemn as a judge about to pass sentence, "this is the bony-part of a hog's leg."

"Is-is a-a-that all!" gasped poor Jim, beginning to look blue about the gills.

"Oh no," said the lecturer, "this is merely a part of the exhibition," and he took from a shelf a piece of meat skin about as large as a piece of paper i.e. the size of a dollar bill, and presenting it to view he proceeded with the lecture.

"Now, my young hearers, this you see is the 'Rhine'—yes," he continued, as solemnly as before, "this is the 'Rhine,'—properly speaking, the hog's rind—a piece of hog's rind."

When the laugh had subsided, Mr. C. again went on with the explanation:

"Now, young gentlemen, draw near and give me your attention a moment, for this is the most interesting part of the exhibition," and old Abram looked and spoke, if possible, still more wise and solemn than before; then slowly passing the piece of bone back and forth across the skin, he said, "you see, boys this is the 'bony part crossing the rind,' very lucidly explained—yes, (drawing his bone across again with the most imperturbable gravity imaginable, amid the roars of laughter) this sir, is, I may be allowed to say, a *very* apt illustration of that noted event in history, 'Napoleon crossing the Rhine.' You have now learned a valuable lesson——"

"Yes!" broke in Jim "I have that, but it's the last one you'll ever learn me—(laughter) you're nothing but an old swindler, anyhow—(renewed laughter, which somewhat riled our hero) yes, this is a swindling shop and a swindling show, and you don't do nothing but swindle people."

The laugh now became so universal, that poor Jim had to force a laugh and a "don't care" look, as he continued:

"I don't care, laugh, jest as much as you please—I ain't particular about the money, nohow; I know'd it was a swindle, 'fore I come down (a piece of knowledge which Jim, in the excitement had before unfortunately forgotten that he ever possessed,) yes I knowed it, and I jest come down for devilment—but I don't care, you can keep the money, I ain't particular about it (Jim seemed particularly anxious to impress this important fact upon the mind of the lecturer)—cause I know you need it worse'n I do, when you can swindle a feller out of it that way."

The crowd now laughed till they were completely exhausted, and Jim's face slowly relaxed from the ludicrous expression it had worn for a time. He now looked as if he had been suddenly bereft of every relation he had in the world—his face became lengthened to an alarming extent, and upon the said countenance the most woe-begone look settled, mingled with a most "sheep-stealing" expression; he was now in a profound reverie, seemingly entirely unconscious of the jeers cast at him by the company. But Abram now broke in upon his meditations, and although he too had been enjoying his joke with a hearty laugh, he immediately assumed his former solemn look and grave tone, and thus addressed the cheap-looking "seeker after knowledge under difficulties."

"Young man, you have now learned an important historical lesson, and are no doubt well pleased with it. I am anxious, however—ahem!—I am anxious, as I before remarked, that you should be entirely satisfied with the exhibition—if you did not understand it in its minutest details—if the illustration was not sufficiently lucid, and everything had not been exhibited to your entire satisfaction, I beg of you, my friend, to make it known; and if it has met with favor in your eyes, I shall hold myself under the greatest of obligations, (with a profound bow,) if you will use your influence in forwarding the cause of learning and knowledge, (another bow,) by inviting your friends to step in when they pass this way. What, may I ask, is your opinion of the exhibition?"

Poor Jim! He seemed not to have heard a word that had been spoken; but, with his eyes bent steadfastly upon some object that wasn't there, he moved not a muscle for the space of a minute, when, opening his lips, he slowly ejaculated the few, but significant words "Sold!—cheap---as---dirt!"

And striding out of the house he marched down the street in a profound fit of mental abstraction.

Since the above occurrence, if any one speaks to Jim, or asks him a question, he merely mutters "Bonaparte crossing—sold!"

Mr. Curts told one of Jim's companions to say to him, that his exhibition was merely an agency—that a noted wholesale firm of this city were the proprietors of the concern, that the apparatus belonged to them, that if Jim did not think his money well spent, they would in all probability refund it—but that being himself merely an agent, he did not feel authorized to do so.

W. EPAMINONDAS ADRASTUS BLAB.

CINCINNATI BOARDING HOUSE SKETCH

CINCINNATI, O., Nov. 8th, 1856.

MESSRS. EDITORS:—I propose now to show you the inside of our boarding house, remarking at the outset, that our boarding house is like all other boarding houses. The scene is the front parlor, this frosty Sunday morning, the 8th day of November, and a number of chairs are drawn up in a semi-circle round a coal fire, snapping and sputtering, in the grate. Breakfast is just over. During the few minutes silence which follows, and which time is employed by these gentlemen in picking their teeth, I'll point out the principal characters.

In the chair next the stove, sits an "old residenter," entirely bald, with the exception of a fringe of hair commencing at the top of his forehead and running clear round the head, giving that otherwise bare but shining organ something of the appearance of the moon in a dim halo. This is Mr. Luculus (or, as he is sometimes called, "Sir Oracle") Cabbage, and his remarks and decisions are always received with the utmost reverence.

Not far from him sits his first born Mr. Jonas Cabbage, whose name has gone through several modifications, commencing with Jones; then Jone; then Jack, and finally Jack-*ass*. (The latter probably the most appropriate.) He, too, has lost the hair from the top of his youthful head—which has the soft appearance of mush done up in a cotton rag, with a dent here and there—but he has an abundance of red whiskers and moustachios to make amends for the bereavement. He knows when the laugh comes in after an anecdote, by watching the faces of his neighbors.

Mr. Blathers sits next to him. He is rashly fond of an argument, and his eternal misfortune is to get the whole house arrayed against him. He is a long, lank Irishman.

The other gentlemen of importance are Mr. Pottery, Mr. Doodle and Mr. Toploftical. Discussion opens.

Doodle. Have you heard of the homicide in Philadelphia the other day, where a clerk killed his employer, on account of improper intimacy between the latter and the former's wife?

Pottery. Is that so! Served him right.

Toploftical. Be not too hasty. Killing is a terrible thing.

Blathers. Did serve him right. A man who would treat a dependant in such a manner, has no more soul than a horse.

D. Hold on. I spose you think a horse has got no soul.

B. I *know* it hasn't.

T. Wait a moment, Mr. B. Human beings, poor worms, can't *know* of the existence of anything which they cannot *see,* and you cannot see the soul.

B. Tut, tut. I'm *not* obliged to see a thing in order to know it. Now there's that bloody murder sometime ago. I knew that deed was done, but I didn't see it, and I know the man that done it richly deserved hanging, but was cleared, and left the country, but I didn't see him.

Cabbage Senior. Ah, Mr. Blathers, you shouldn't say the man deserved hanging till you know something more about the matter. Some men are born to be murderers and they ain't responsible for their natures.

B. It's no difference, Mr. Cabbage, you know, how a man is born—if he's brought up right he won't be a murderer. However yours is a knotty proposition, I must admit.

C. No. 1. Well, but I tell you bringin' up has got nothing to do with it. Individuals and even nations are born murderers.

C. No. 2. That's so, dad! Look at the Injins, darn 'em. Don't they kill people from June till January, and who teaches *them?* Some of 'em, too, is as intelligent as *we* are.

(Voice.) Amen!

B. Bah! Their fathers taught them. (Silence of two minutes.)

C. No. 2. The devil they did! Who taught their fathers! He! he! he!

(Voice.) D——d fool. (Aside.)

B. *Their* fathers—and so on, from generation to generation back to the days when idiots kept their mouths closed.

(No. 2 who thinks B. "soaked it" to T. that time, enjoys the joke exceedingly; but not seeing any good opening to begin his argument again, goes partially asleep.)

P. What was that about the intelligence of this assemblage?

No. 2. I didn't say anything about the intelligence of this assemblage. I meant the—ah,—the—country. Yes, the country—United States. I meant to say that we—that is,—the United States—as a people—ah—is more intellectually developed—in developed in—an intellectual extent of capacity than—that is to say—the intellectual powers is more strong in the development of—of the United States as a people—that is, the intellectuality of the whole country. (Dern this argerin.)

B. Well, well, well. If I've a soul to be saved—

T. Soul, again? How do you know you've got a soul?

B. How do I know I've got a soul? Why, how do I know there is a God?

C. No. 1. Well, how *do* you know there is a God? You can't see him, you can't feel him, you can't hear him. Come—don't hesitate.

Everybody. Out with it! Out with it!

B. Well, upon my soul. Now you are confounding finite matters with the infinite. Listen, gentlemen. I know that there is a God, by the works of his hands—the gorgeous sun—the gentle moon—the twinkling stars that bespangle the blue dome above our heads. Yea, the vast rivers and the trackless—

No. 1. Oh! dam nonsense. That is nothing but the belief, the faith imparted by imagination. There is a great difference between knowledge and belief.

No. 2. The old man let him have it that time. That cabbage is a knowin' old vegetable. Why, of course the twinkling sun, and gorgeous stars, and the—the vast area—and the—rivers—vastly spangled with—with—water—why *that* ain't no evidence—*that* don't prove—prove—don't prove—pap, what the devil *was* he tryin to prove!

No. 1. The existence of a Deity, my son. Don't exert yourself.

B. Nonsense, yourself. Faith and belief *is* knowledge. If a man isn't to know anything but what comes under his personal observation, what's the use of having courts of law, where men are sworn?

T. Why, in that case, a man believes a witness—but his belief won't amount to knowledge—absolute knowledge, my dear sir.

B. There you are, confounding the finite with the infinite, again. Now, *don't* I know that James Buchanan is elected President of these United States?

Several voices. No Sir! You don't know any such thing. If you think so, you'll be about as badly fooled as that old man Doodle tells about.

Others. Tell it, Doodle. Hurrah for the yarn.

D. Well, it was about this way. An old farmer had a big buck ram which would invariably chase him out of one of his fields every time he went into it; and one day, as he stood on the stile, bowing and smirking with excessive politeness to some ladies passing by, the ram took a stand about twenty yards behind him, and then measuring his distance and his target with a knowing eye, he darted forward, planted his head with tremendous force just beneath the old man's short coat tail, and sent him heels over head into a hog-wallow on the other side. The old gentleman swore vengeance; and after thinking over divers plans, he at last hit upon this one: He got an old wooden chair seat and filled one side of it with sharp-pointed nails, allowing them to project about half an inch. Went to the meadow—knelt down near the stile, and placed the board against his wounded seat of honor, but through some mistake, turned the nail side next himself.

No. 2. Oh! ha! ha! ha!—that was a good one!—tell us another.

Others. Dry up—dry up—the yarn ain't finished.

Doodle. In about three seconds the old enemy sent his head against that board like a battering ram, driving the nails home so effectually that the old man says he felt like a sieve for three weeks afterwards.

Everybody. Ha! ha! Served him right.

No. 2. Yes, served him right, but then what the devil did he turn the nails *in* for?

T. Well, that reminds me of an old ram that once got into a man's cellar one dark night. The servant maid went down and come up frightened to death at the *devil* she had seen. Then the old man went down, and finally the oldest son, all seeing the devil. Then they sent for the parson, and he went down, wrapped in his cloak, and kneeling on the ground, began to pray. The ram came up behind and butted him clear across the cellar. "Save yourselves, brethren," said he, "for the devil's got my cloak."

Doodle looks vacantly at Pottery; Pottery looks at the elder Cabbage, and the younger vegetable gazes into everybody's faces. There's a damper on that conversation! No man knowing whether the anecdote was intended to be funny or serious; they are afraid to risk a laugh, so the company assumes a grave air, and one by one they leave, until finally the room is deserted—a conversation murdered by a pointless anecdote.

Yours.

L.

Petrified Man

A petrified man was found some time ago in the mountains south of Gravelly Ford. Every limb and feature of the stony mummy was perfect, not even excepting the left leg, which has evidently been a wooden one during the lifetime of the owner—which lifetime, by the way, came to a close about a century ago, in the opinion of a savan who has examined the defunct. The body was in a sitting posture, and leaning against a huge mass of croppings; the attitude was pensive, the right thumb resting against the side of the nose; the left thumb partially supported the chin, the fore-finger pressing the inner corner of the left eye and drawing it partly open; the right eye was closed, and the fingers of the right hand spread apart. This strange freak of nature created a profound sensation in the vicinity, and our informant states that by request, Justice Sewell or Sowell, of Humboldt City, at once proceeded to the spot and held an inquest on the body. The verdict of the jury was that "deceased came to his death from protracted exposure," etc. The people of the neighborhood volunteered to bury the poor unfortunate, and were even anxious to do so; but it was discovered, when they attempted to remove him, that the water which had dripped upon him for ages from the crag above, had coursed down his back and deposited a limestone sediment under him which had glued him to the bed rock upon which he sat, as with a cement of adamant, and Judge S. refused to allow the charitable citizens to blast him from his position. The opinion expressed by his Honor that such a course would be little less than sacrilege, was eminently just and proper. Everybody goes to see the stone man, as many as three hundred having visited the hardened creature during the past five or six weeks.

New Year's Day

Now is the accepted time to make your regular annual good resolutions. Next week you can begin paving hell with them as usual. Yesterday, everybody smoked his last cigar, took his last drink, and swore his last oath. To-day, we are a pious and exemplary community. Thirty days from now, we shall have cast our reformation to the winds and gone to cutting our ancient shortcomings considerably shorter than ever. We shall also reflect pleasantly upon how we did the same old thing last year about this time. However, go in, community. New Year's is a harmless annual institution, of no particular use to anybody save as a scapegoat for promiscuous drunks, and friendly calls, and humbug resolutions, and we wish you to enjoy it with a looseness suited to the greatness of the occasion.

The Innocents Abroad

The Innocents Abroad *(1869) offers Twain's reactions to a tour of Europe and the Middle East. He had originally tried to go on the trip as a religious correspondent, but that disguise was almost immediately discarded. He went, instead, as a newspaper correspondent, reporting in a series of travel letters to the* San Francisco Daily Alta California *and the* New York Tribune *audiences about the foreign landscape, customs, and sights, as well as about the reactions of American travelers, most of whom were pious elderly "pilgrims" and only a few of whom were "sinners" (his friends). Twain considered the captain a model hypocrite, an "animated flatulence."*

The trip, which Twain later described as "a funeral without a corpse," offered a range of opportunity. Twain offered his thoughts on human hypocrisy, traditional credulity in religion, and the easy belief in religious relics or in "authoritative" guide books. No target was safe from his sarcasm.

Twain was also shaping his attitude toward the Old World, and most of his attitude is critical. Twain and his cronies claim to address all the guides as Ferguson; the "sinners" repeatedly question the unfortunate guides about a painting, a bust, or an object associated with the past by saying "is he—is he—is he dead?" That is the vigorous vital Americans' mockingly timorous response to being asked to venerate something from the past.

The only topic that consistently provoked greater contempt was the reliance of Twain's fellow Americans upon guide books for feelings, interpretations, descriptions, and attitudes toward the sights. In fact, as Twain says in his Preface, his purpose was to see *what was really* there, *not what the guide books encouraged the credulous pilgrims to become ecstatic about.*

At the time Twain was writing, it was a standard technique for a travel writer to practice associationalism. After a brief description of the scene or building, the writer would launch into a catalogue of thoughts or feelings associated with the subject. Although occasionally falling victim to this contagion, Twain characteristically mocks it.

The credulity of the Americans—including their dependency upon the guide book for associationalist emotions—is matched by the credulity of the believers—their uncritical acceptance of the relics and the myths. Frequently Twain mocks the believing process—saying that he believed because he himself saw the rock, or because he had not heard anyone disprove the story. For example, he observed enough nails from Christ's cross to make up a keg.

But Twain was much more than an irreverent mocker in The Innocents Abroad. *He was, foremost, a writer mastering his craft, and a thinker asserting his independence, his skepticism, his ability to determine on his own.*

Further information about this formative journey and about Twain's revision of the original travel letters to form the book can be conveniently found in

Dewey Ganzel's Mark Twain Abroad *(Chicago University Press, 1968). The text and selected illustrations are taken from the 1869 edition.*

Preface

This book is a record of a pleasure-trip. If it were a record of a solemn scientific expedition, it would have about it that gravity, that profundity, and that impressive incomprehensibility which are so proper to works of that kind, and withal so attractive. Yet notwithstanding it is only a record of a pic-nic, it has a purpose, which is, to suggest to the reader how *he* would be likely to see Europe and the East if he looked at them with his own eyes instead of the eyes of those who travelled in those countries before him. I make small pretence of showing any one how he *ought* to look at objects of interest beyond the sea—other books do that, and therefore, even if I were competent to do it, there is no need. . . .

Chapter 4

. . . There were those among the unregenerated who attributed the unceasing head-winds to our distressing choir-music. There were those who said openly that it was taking chances enough to have such ghastly music going on, even when it was at its best; and that to exaggerate the crime by letting George help, was simply flying in the face of Providence. These said that the choir would keep up their lacerating attempts at melody until they would bring down a storm some day that would sink the ship.

There were even grumblers at the prayers. The executive officer said the Pilgrims had no charity:

"There they are, down there every night at eight bells, praying for fair winds—when they know as well as I do that this is the only ship going east this time of the year, but there's a thousand coming west—what's a fair wind for us is a *head* wind to them—the Almighty's blowing a fair wind for a thousand vessels, and this tribe wants him to turn it clear around so as to accommodate *one,*—and she a steamship at that! It ain't good sense, it ain't good reason, it ain't good Christianity, it ain't common human charity. Avast with such nonsense!"

Chapter 6

. . . It is in communities like this that Jesuit humbuggery flourishes. We visited a Jesuit cathedral nearly two hundred years old, and found in it a piece of the veritable cross upon which our Saviour was crucified. It was polished and hard, and in as excellent a state of preservation as if the dread tragedy on Calvary had occurred yesterday instead of eighteen centuries ago. But these confiding people believe in that piece of wood unhesitatingly.

In a chapel of the cathedral is an altar with facings of solid silver—at least they call it so, and I think myself it would go a couple of hundred to the ton (to speak after the fashion of the silver miners,) and before it is kept forever burning a small lamp. A devout lady who died, left money and contracted for unlimited masses for the repose of her soul, and also stipulated that this lamp should be kept lighted always, day and night. She did all this before she died, you understand. It is a very small lamp, and a very dim one, and it could not work her much damage, I think, if it went out altogether.

The great altar of the cathedral, and also three or four minor ones, are a perfect mass of gilt gimcracks and gingerbread. And they have a swarm of rusty, dusty, battered apostles standing around the filagree work, some on one leg and some with one eye out but a gamey look in the other, and some with two or three fingers gone, and some with not enough nose left to blow—all of them crippled and discouraged, and fitter subjects for the hospital than the cathedral.

The walls of the chancel are of porcelain, all pictured over with figures of almost life size, very elegantly wrought, and dressed in the fanciful costumes of two centuries ago. The design was a history of something or somebody, but none of us were learned enough to read the story. The old father, reposing under a stone close by, dated 1686, might have told us if he could have risen. But he didn't. . . .

Chapter 17

. . . I have not been to church so often in a long time as I have in the last few weeks. The people in these old lands seem to make churches their specialty. Especially does this seem to be the case with the citizens of Genoa. I think there is a church every three or four hundred yards all over town. The streets are sprinkled from end to end with shovel-hatted, long-robed, well-fed priests, and the church bells by dozens are pealing all the day long, nearly. Every now and then one comes across a friar of orders gray, with shaven head, long, coarse robe, rope girdle and beads, and with feet cased in sandals or entirely bare. These worthies suffer in the flesh, and do penance all their lives, I suppose, but they look like consummate famine-breeders. They are all fat and serene.

PRIEST AND FRIAR.

The old Cathedral of San Lorenzo is about as notable a building as we have found in Genoa. It is vast, and has colonnades of noble pillars, and a great organ, and the customary pomp of gilded moldings, pictures, frescoed ceilings, and so forth. I can not describe it, of course—it would require a good many pages to do that. But it is a curious place. They said that half of it—from the front door half way down to the altar—was a Jewish Synagogue before the Saviour was born, and that no alteration had been made in it since that time. We doubted the statement, but did it reluctantly. We would much rather have believed it. The place looked in too perfect repair to be so ancient.

The main point of interest about the Cathedral is the little Chapel of St. John the Baptist. They only allow women to enter it on one day in the year, on account of the animosity they still cherish against the sex because of the murder of the Saint to gratify a caprice of Herodias. In this Chapel is a marble chest, in which, they told us, were the ashes of St. John; and around it was wound a chain, which, they said, had confined him when he was in prison. We did not desire to disbelieve these statements, and yet we could not feel certain that they were correct—partly because we could have broken that chain, and so could St. John, and partly because we had seen St. John's ashes before, in another Church. We could not bring ourselves to think St. John had two sets of ashes.

They also showed us a portrait of the Madonna which was painted by St. Luke, and it did not look half as old and smoky as some of the pictures by Rubens. We could not help admiring the Apostle's modesty in never once mentioning in his writings that he could paint.

But isn't this relic matter a little overdone? We find a piece of the true cross in every old church we go into, and some of the nails that held it together. I would not like to be positive, but I think we have seen as much as a keg of these nails. Then there is the crown of thorns; they have part of one in Sainte Chapelle, in Paris, and part of one, also, in Notre Dame. And as for bones of St. Denis, I feel certain we have seen enough of them to duplicate him, if necessary.

I only meant to write about the churches, but I keep wandering from the subject. I could say that the Church of the Annunciation is a wilderness of beautiful columns, of statues, gilded moldings, and pictures almost countless, but that would give no one an entirely perfect idea of the thing, and so where is the use? One family built the whole edifice, and have got money left. There is where the mystery lies. We had an idea at first that only a mint could have survived the expense. . . .

Chapter 18

. . . This was good St. Charles Borroméo, Bishop of Milan. The people idolized him; princes lavished uncounted treasures upon him. We stood in his tomb. Near by was the sarcophagus, lighted by the dripping candles. The walls were faced with bas-reliefs representing scenes in his life done in massive silver. The priest put on a short white lace garment over his black robe, crossed himself, bowed reverently, and began to turn a windlass slowly. The sarcophagus separated in two parts, lengthwise, and the lower part sank down and disclosed a coffin of rock crystal as clear as the atmosphere. Within lay the body, robed in costly habiliments covered with gold embroidery and starred with scintillating gems. The decaying head was black with age, the dry skin was drawn tight to the bones, the eyes were gone, there was a hole in the temple and another in the cheek, and the skinny lips were parted as in a ghastly smile! Over this dreadful face, its dust and decay, and its mocking grin, hung a crown sown thick with flashing brilliants; and upon the breast lay crosses and croziers of solid gold that were splendid with emeralds and diamonds.

How poor, and cheap, and trivial these gew-gaws seemed in presence of the solemnity, the grandeur, the awful majesty of Death! Think of Milton, Shakspeare, Washington, standing before a reverent world tricked out in the glass beads, the brass ear-rings and tin trumpery of the savages of the plains!

Dead Bartoloméo preached his pregnant sermon, and its burden was: You that worship the vanities of earth—you that long for worldly honor, worldly wealth, worldly fame—behold their worth!

To us it seemed that so good a man, so kind a heart, so simple a nature, deserved rest and peace in a grave sacred from the intrusion of prying eyes, and believed that he himself would have preferred to have it so, but peradventure our wisdom was at fault in this regard. . . .

The priests showed us two of St. Paul's fingers, and one of St. Peter's; a bone of Judas Iscariot, (it was black.) and also bones of all the other disciples; a handkerchief in which the Saviour had left the impression of his face. Among the most precious of the relics were a stone from the Holy Sepulchre, part of the crown of thorns, (they have a whole one at Notre Dame,) a fragment of the purple robe worn by the Saviour, a nail from the Cross, and a picture of the Virgin and Child painted by the veritable hand of St. Luke. This is the second of St. Luke's Virgins we have seen. Once a year all these holy relics are carried in procession through the streets of Milan. . . .

Chapter 19

. . . Afterward we walked up and down one of the most popular streets for some time, enjoying other people's comfort and wishing we could export some of it to our restless, driving, vitality-consuming marts at home. Just in this one matter lies the main charm of life in Europe—comfort. In America, we hurry—which is well; but when the day's work is done, we go on thinking of losses and gains, we plan for the morrow, we even carry our business cares to bed with us, and toss and worry over them when we ought to be restoring our racked bodies and brains with sleep. We burn up our energies with these excitements, and either die early or drop into a lean and mean old age at a time of life which they call a man's prime in Europe. When an acre of ground has produced long and well, we let it lie fallow and rest for a season; we take no man clear across the continent in the same coach he started in—the coach is stabled somewhere on the plains and its heated machinery allowed to cool for a few days; when a razor has seen long service and refuses to hold an edge, the barber lays it away for a few weeks, and the edge comes back of its own accord. We bestow thoughtful care upon inanimate objects, but none upon ourselves. What a robust people, what a nation of thinkers we might be, if we would only lay ourselves on the shelf occasionally and renew our edges!

I do envy these Europeans the comfort they take. When the work of the day is done, they forget it. Some of them go, with wife and children, to a beer hall, and sit quietly and genteelly drinking a mug or two of ale and listening to music; others walk the streets, others drive in the avenues; others assemble in the great ornamental squares in the early evening to enjoy the sight and the fragrance of flowers and to hear the military bands play—no European city being without its fine military music at eventide; and yet others of the populace sit in the open air in front of the refreshment houses and eat ices and drink mild beverages that could not harm a child. They go to bed moderately early, and sleep well. They are always quiet, always orderly, always cheerful, comfortable, and appreciative of life and its manifold blessings. One never sees a drunken man among them. The change that has come over our little party is surprising. Day by day we lose some of our restlessness and absorb some of the spirit of quietude and ease that is in the tranquil atmosphere about us and in the demeanor of the people. We grow wise apace. We begin to comprehend what life is for. . . .

Chapter 21

. . . We saw interior Italy, now. The houses were of solid stone, and not often in good repair. The peasants and their children were idle, as a general thing, and the donkeys and chickens made themselves at home in drawing-room and bed-chamber and were not molested. The drivers of each and every one of the slow-moving market-carts we met were stretched in the sun upon their merchandise, sound asleep. Every three or four hundred yards, it seemed to me, we came upon the shrine of some saint or other—a rude picture of him built into a huge cross or stone pillar by the road-side.—Some of the pictures of the Saviour were curiosities in their way. They represented him stretched upon the cross, his countenance distorted with agony. From the wounds of the crown of thorns; from the pierced side; from the mutilated hands and feet; from the scourged body—from every handbreadth of his person streams of blood were flowing! Such a gory, ghastly spectacle would frighten the children out of their senses, I should think. There were some unique auxiliaries to the painting which added to its spirited effect. These were genuine wooden and iron implements, and were prominently disposed round about the figure: a bundle of nails; the hammer to drive them; the sponge; the reed that supported it; the cup of vinegar; the ladder for the ascent of the cross; the spear that pierced the Saviour's side. The crown of thorns was made of real thorns, and was nailed to the sacred head. In some Italian church-paintings, even by the old masters, the Saviour and the Virgin wear silver or gilded crowns that are fastened to the pictured head with nails. The effect is as grotesque as it is incongruous.

WAYSIDE SHRINE.

Here and there, on the fronts of roadside inns, we found huge, coarse frescoes of suffering martyrs like those in the shrines. It could not have diminished their sufferings any to be so uncouthly represented. We were in the heart and home of priestcraft—of a happy, cheerful, contented ignorance, superstition, degradation, poverty, indolence, and everlasting unaspiring worthlessness. And we said fervently, It suits these people precisely; let them enjoy it, along with the other animals, and Heaven forbid that they be molested. *We* feel no malice toward these fumigators.

We passed through the strangest, funniest, undreampt-of old towns, wedded to the customs and steeped in the dreams of the elder ages, and perfectly unaware that the world turns round! And perfectly indifferent, too, as to whether it turns around or stands still. *They* have nothing to do but eat and sleep and sleep and eat, and toil a little when they can get a friend to stand by and keep them awake. *They* are not paid for thinking—*they* are not paid to fret about the world's concerns. They were not respectable people—they were not worthy people—they were not learned and wise and brilliant people—but in their breasts, all their stupid lives long, resteth a peace that passeth understanding! How can men, calling themselves men, consent to be so degraded and happy. . . .

PEACE AND HAPPINESS.

CHAPTER 23

. . . We see the ladies go out shopping, in the most natural way, and flit from street to street and from store to store, just in the good old fashion, except that they leave the gondola, instead of a private carriage, waiting at the curbstone a couple of hours for them,—waiting while they make the nice young clerks pull down tons and tons of silks and velvets and moire antiques and those things; and then they buy a paper of pins and go paddling away to confer the rest of their disastrous patronage on some other firm. And they always have their purchases sent home just in the good old way. Human nature is *very* much the same all over the world; and it is *so* like my dear native home to see a Venetian lady go into a store and buy ten cents' worth of blue ribbon and have it sent home in a scow. Ah, it is these little touches of nature that move one to tears in these far-off foreign lands. . . .

. . . We enjoy it thoroughly. Very many of the young women are exceedingly pretty and dress with rare good taste. We are gradually and laboriously learning the ill-manners of staring them unflinchingly in the face—not because such conduct is agreeable to us, but because it is the custom of the country and they say the girls like it. We wish to learn all the curious, outlandish ways of all the different countries, so that we can "show off" and astonish people when we get home. We wish to excite the envy of our untraveled friends with our strange foreign fashions which we can't shake off. All our passengers are paying strict attention to this thing, with the end in view which I have mentioned. The gentle reader will never, never know what a consummate ass he can become, until he goes abroad. I speak now, of course, in the supposition that the gentle reader has not been abroad, and therefore is not already a consummate ass. If the case be otherwise, I beg his pardon and extend to him the cordial hand of fellowship and call him brother. I shall always delight to meet an ass after my own heart when I shall have finished my travels.

On this subject let me remark that there are Americans abroad in Italy who have actually forgotten their mother tongue in three months—forgot it in France. They can not even write their address in English in a hotel register. I append these evidences, which I copied *verbatim* from the register of a hotel in a certain Italian city:

> "John P. Whitcomb, *Etats Unis.*
> "Wm. L. Ainsworth, *travailleur* (he meant traveler, I suppose,) *Etats Unis.*
> "George P. Morton, *et fils, d'Amerique.*
> "Lloyd B. Williams, *et trois amis, ville de* Boston, *Amerique.*
> "J. Ellsworth Baker, *tout de suite de France, place de naissance Amerique, destination la Grand Bretagne.*"

I love this sort of people. A lady passenger of ours tells of a fellow-citizen of hers who spent eight weeks in Paris and then returned home and addressed his dearest old bosom friend Herbert as Mr. "Er-bare!" He apologized, though, and said, " 'Pon my soul it is aggravating, but I cahn't help it—I have got so used to speaking nothing but French, my dear Erbare—damme there it goes again!—got so used to French pronunciation that I cahn't get rid of it—it is positively annoying, I assure you." This entertaining idiot, whose name was Gordon, allowed himself to be hailed three times in the street before he paid any attention, and then begged a thousand pardons and said he had grown so accustomed to hearing himself addressed as M'sieu "Gor-r-*dong,*" with a role to the r, that he had forgotten the legitimate sound of his name! He wore a rose in his button-hole; he gave the French salutation—two flips of the hand in front of the face; he called Paris *Pairree* in ordinary English conversation; he carried envelopes bearing foreign postmarks protruding from his breast-pocket; he cultivated a moustache and imperial, and did what else he could to suggest to the beholder his pet fancy that he resembled Louis Napoleon—and in a spirit of thankfulness which is entirely unaccountable, considering the slim foundation there was for it, he praised his Maker that he was *as* he was, and went on enjoying his little life just the same as if he really *had* been deliberately designed and erected by the great Architect of the Universe.

Think of our Whitcombs, and our Ainsworths and our Williamses writing themselves down in dilapidated French in foreign hotel registers! We laugh at Englishmen, when we are at home, for sticking so sturdily to their national ways and customs, but we look back upon it from abroad very forgivingly. It is not pleasant to see an American thrusting his nationality forward *obtrusively* in a foreign land, but Oh, it is pitiable to see him making of himself a thing that is neither male nor female, neither fish, flesh, nor fowl—a poor, miserable, hermaphrodite Frenchman! . . .

. . . We have seen famous pictures until our eyes are weary with looking at them and refuse to find interest in them any longer. And what wonder, when there are twelve hundred pictures by Palma the Younger in Venice and fifteen hundred by Tintoretto? And behold there are Titians and the works of other artists in proportion. We have seen Titian's celebrated Cain and Abel, his David and Goliah, his Abraham's Sacrifice. We have seen Tintoretto's monster picture, which is seventy-four feet long and I do not know how many feet high, and thought it a very commodious picture. We have seen pictures of martyrs enough, and saints enough, to regenerate the world. I ought not to confess it, but still, since one has no opportunity in America to acquire a critical judgment in art, and since I could not hope to become educated in it in Europe in a few short weeks, I may therefore as well acknowledge with such apologies as may be due, that to me it seemed that when I had seen one of these martyrs I had seen them all. They all have a marked family resemblance to each other, they dress alike, in coarse monkish robes and sandals, they are all bald headed, they all stand in about the same attitude, and without exception they are gazing heavenward with countenances which the Ainsworths, the Mortons and the Williamses, *et fils,* inform me are full of "expression." To me there is nothing tangible about these imaginary portraits, nothing that I can grasp and take a living interest in. If great Titian had only been gifted with prophecy, and had skipped a martyr, and gone over to England and painted a portrait of Shakspeare, even as a youth, which we could all have confidence in now, the world down to the latest generations would have forgiven him the lost martyr in the rescued seer. I think posterity could have spared one more martyr for the sake of a great historical picture of Titian's time and painted by his brush—such as Columbus returning in chains from the discovery of a world, for instance. The old masters did paint some Venetian historical pictures, and these we did not tire of looking at, notwithstanding representations of the formal introduction of defunct doges to the Virgin Mary in regions beyond the clouds clashed rather harshly with the proprieties, it seemed to us.

ST. MARK, BY THE OLD MASTERS.

ST. MATTHEW, BY THE OLD MASTERS.

ST. JEROME, BY THE OLD MASTERS.

But humble as we are, and unpretending, in the matter of art, our researches among the painted monks and martyrs have not been wholly in vain. We have striven hard to learn. We have had some success. We have mastered some things, possibly of trifling import in the eyes of the learned, but to us they give pleasure, and we take as much pride in our little acquirements as do others who have learned far more, and we love to display them full as well. When we see a monk going about with a lion and looking tranquilly up to heaven, we know that that is St. Mark. When we see a monk with a book and a pen, looking tranquilly up to heaven, trying to think of a word, we know that that is St. Matthew. When we see a monk sitting on a rock, looking tranquilly up to heaven, with a human skull beside him, and without other baggage, we know that that is St. Jerome. Because we know that he always went flying light in the matter of baggage. When we see a party looking tranquilly up to heaven, unconscious that his body is shot through and through with arrows, we know that that is St. Sebastian. When we see other monks looking tranquilly up to heaven, but having no trade-mark, we always ask who those parties are. We do this because we humbly wish to learn. We have seen thirteen thousand St. Jeromes, and twenty-two thousand St. Marks, and sixteen thousand St. Matthews, and sixty thousand St. Sebastians, and four million of assorted monks, undesignated, and we feel encouraged to believe that when we have seen some more of these various pictures, and had a larger experience, we shall begin to take an absorbing interest in them like our cultivated countrymen from *Amerique.*

ST. SEBASTIAN, BY THE OLD MASTERS.

ST. UNKNOWN, BY THE OLD MASTERS.

Now it does give me real pain to speak in this almost unappreciative way of the old masters and their martyrs, because good friends of mine in the ship—friends who do thoroughly and conscientiously appreciate them and are in every way competent to discriminate between good pictures and inferior ones—have urged me for my own sake not to make public the fact that I lack this appreciation and this critical discrimination myself. I believe that what I have written and may still write about pictures will give them pain, and I am honestly sorry for it. I even promised that I would hide my uncouth sentiments in my own breast. But alas! I never could keep a promise. I do not blame myself for this weakness, because the fault must lie in my physical organization. It is likely that such a very liberal amount of space was given to the organ which enables me to *make* promises, that the organ which should enable me to keep them was crowded out. But I grieve not. I like no half-way things. I had rather have one faculty nobly developed than two faculties of mere ordinary capacity. I certainly meant to keep that promise, but I find I can not do it. It is impossible to travel through Italy without speaking of pictures, and can I see them through others' eyes?

If I did not so delight in the grand pictures that are spread before me every day of my life by that monarch of all the old masters, Nature, I should come to believe, sometimes, that I had in me no appreciation of the beautiful, whatsoever.

It seems to me that whenever I glory to think that for once I have discovered an ancient painting that is beautiful and worthy of all praise, the pleasure it gives me is an infallible proof that it is *not* a beautiful picture and not in any wise worthy of commendation. This very thing has occurred more times than I can mention, in Venice. In every single instance the guide has crushed out my swelling enthusiasm with the remark:

"It is nothing—it is of the *Renaissance.*"

I did not know what in the mischief the Renaissance was, and so always I had to simply say,

"Ah! so it is—I had not observed it before."

I could not bear to be ignorant before a cultivated negro, the offspring of a South Carolina slave. But it occurred too often for even my self-complacency, did that exasperating "It is nothing—it is of the *Renaissance.*" I said at last:

"*Who* is this Renaissance? Where did he come from? Who gave him permission to cram the Republic with his execrable daubs?"

We learned, then, that Renaissance was not a man; that *renaissance* was a term used to signify what was at best but an imperfect rejuvenation of art. The guide said that after Titian's time and the time of the other great names we had grown so familiar with, high art declined; then it partially rose again—an inferior sort of painters sprang up, and these shabby pictures were the work of their hands. Then I said, in my heat, that I "wished to goodness high art had declined five hundred years sooner." The Renaissance pictures suit me very well, though sooth to say its school were too much given to painting real men and did not indulge enough in martyrs.

The guide I have spoken of is the only one we have had yet who knew any thing. He was born in South Carolina, of slave parents. They came to Venice while he was an infant. He has grown up here. He is well educated. He reads, writes, and speaks English, Italian, Spanish, and French, with perfect facility; is a worshipper of art and thoroughly conversant with it; knows the history of Venice by heart and never tires of talking of her illustrious career. He dresses better than any of us, I think, and is daintily polite. Negroes are deemed as good as white people, in Venice, and so this man feels no desire to go back to his native land. His judgment is correct. . . .

Chapter 24

. . . The peculiar devotional spirit of the olden time, which placed a higher confidence in outward forms of worship than in the watchful guarding of the heart against sinful thoughts and the hands against sinful deeds, and which believed in the protecting virtues of inanimate objects made holy by contact with holy things, is illustrated in a striking manner in one of the cemeteries of Pisa. The tombs are set in soil brought in ships from the Holy Land ages ago. To be buried in such ground was regarded by the ancient Pisans as being more potent for salvation than many masses purchased of the church and the vowing of many candles to the Virgin. . . .

Chapter 25

. . . But it is an ill-wind that blows nobody good. A year ago, when Italy saw utter ruin staring her in the face and her greenbacks hardly worth the paper they were printed on, her Parliament ventured upon a *coup de main* that would have appalled the stoutest of her statesmen under less desperate circumstances. They, in a manner, confiscated the domains of the Church! This in priest-ridden Italy! This in a land which has groped in the midnight of priestly superstition for sixteen hundred years! It was a rare good fortune for Italy, the stress of weather that drove her to break from this prison-house.

They do not call it *confiscating* the church property. That would sound too harshly yet. But it amounts to that. There are thousands of churches in Italy, each with untold millions of treasures stored away in its closets, and each with its battalion of priests to be supported. And then there are the estates of the Church—league on league of the richest lands and the noblest forests in all Italy—all yielding immense revenues to the Church, and none paying a cent in taxes to the State. In some great districts the Church owns *all* the property—lands, watercourses, woods, mills and factories. They buy, they sell, they manufacture, and since they pay no taxes, who can hope to compete with them?

Well, the Government has seized all this in effect, and will yet seize it in rigid and unpoetical reality, no doubt. Something must be done to feed a starving treasury, and there is no other resource in all Italy—none but the riches of the Church. So the Government intends to take to itself a great portion of the revenues arising from priestly farms, factories, etc., and also intends to take possession of the churches and carry them on, after its own fashion and upon its own responsibility. In a few instances it will leave the establishments of great pet churches undisturbed, but in all others only a handful of priests will be retained to preach and pray, a few will be pensioned, and the balance turned adrift.

Pray glance at some of these churches and their embellishments, and see whether the Government is doing a righteous thing or not. In Venice, to-day, a city of a hundred thousand inhabitants, there are twelve hundred priests. Heaven only knows how many there were before the Parliament reduced their numbers. There was the great Jesuit Church. Under the old regime it required sixty priests to engineer it—the Government does it with five, now, and the others are discharged from service. All about that church wretchedness and poverty abound. At its door a dozen hats and bonnets were doffed to us, as many heads were humbly bowed, and as many hands extended, appealing for pennies—appealing with foreign words we could not understand, but appealing mutely, with sad eyes, and sunken cheeks, and ragged raiment, that no words were needed to translate. Then we passed within the great doors, and it seemed that the riches of the world were before us! Huge columns carved out of single masses of marble, and inlaid from top to bottom with a hundred intricate figures wrought in costly verde antique; pulpits of the same rich materials, whose draperies hung down in many a pictured fold, the stony fabric counterfeiting the delicate work of the loom; the grand altar brilliant with polished facings and balustrades of oriental agate, jasper, verde antique, and other precious stones, whose names, even, we seldom hear—and slabs of priceless lapis lazuli lavished every where as recklessly as if the church had owned a quarry of it. In the midst of all this magnificence, the solid gold and silver furniture of the altar seemed cheap and trivial. Even the floors and ceilings cost a princely fortune.

Now, where is the use of allowing all those riches to lie idle, while half of that community hardly know, from day to day, how they are going to keep body and soul together? And, where is the wisdom in permitting hundreds upon hundreds of millions of francs to be locked up in the useless trumpery of churches all over Italy, and the people ground to death with taxation to uphold a perishing Government?

As far as I can see, Italy, for fifteen hundred years, has turned all her energies, all her finances, and all her industry to the building up of a vast array of wonderful church edifices, and starving half her citizens to accomplish it. She is to-day one vast museum of magnificence and misery. All the churches in an ordinary American city put together could hardly buy the jeweled frippery in one of her hundred cathedrals. And for every beggar in America, Italy can

THE CONTRAST.

show a hundred—and rags and vermin to match. It is the wretchedest, princeliest land on earth.

Look at the grand Duomo of Florence—a vast pile that has been sapping the purses of her citizens for five hundred years, and is not nearly finished yet. Like all other men, I fell down and worshipped it, but when the filthy beggars swarmed around me the contrast was too striking, too suggestive, and I said,

"O, sons of classic Italy, *is* the spirit of enterprise, of self-reliance, of noble endeavor, utterly dead within ye? Curse your indolent worthlessness, why don't you rob your church?"

Three hundred happy, comfortable priests are employed in that Cathedral.

And now that my temper is up, I may as well go on and abuse every body I can think of. They have a grand mausoleum in Florence, which they built to bury our Lord and Saviour and the Medici family in. It sounds blasphemous, but it is true, and here they *act* blasphemy. The dead and damned Medicis who cruelly tyrannized over Florence and were her curse for over two hundred years, are salted away in a circle of costly vaults, and in their midst the Holy Sepulchre was to have been set up. The expedition sent to Jerusalem to seize it got into trouble and could not accomplish the burglary, and so the centre of the mausoleum is vacant now. They say the entire mausoleum was intended for the Holy Sepulchre, and was only turned into a family burying place after the Jerusalem expedition failed—but you will excuse me. Some of those Medicis would have smuggled themselves in sure.—What *they* had not the effrontery to do, was not worth doing. Why, they had their trivial, forgotten exploits on land and sea pictured out in grand frescoes (as did also the ancient Doges of Venice) with the Saviour and the Virgin throwing bouquets to them out of the clouds, and the Deity himself applauding from his throne in Heaven! And who painted these things? Why, Titian, Tintoretto, Paul Veronese, Raphael—none other than the world's idols, the "old masters."

Andrea del Sarto glorified his princes in pictures that must save them for ever from the oblivion they merited, and they let him starve. Served him right. Raphael pictured such infernal villains as Catherine and Marie de Medicis seated in heaven and conversing familiarly with the Virgin Mary and the angels, (to say nothing of higher personages,) and yet my friends abuse me because I am a little prejudiced against the old masters—because I fail sometimes to see the beauty that is in their productions. I can not help but see it, now and then, but I keep on protesting against the groveling spirit that could persuade those masters to prostitute their noble talents to the adulation of such monsters as the French, Venetian and Florentine Princes of two and three hundred years ago, all the same.

I am told that the old masters had to do these shameful things for bread, the princes and potentates being the only patrons of art. If a grandly gifted man may drag his pride and his manhood in the dirt for bread rather than starve with the nobility that is in him untainted, the excuse is a valid one. It would excuse theft in Washingtons and Wellingtons, and unchastity in women as well.

But somehow, I can not keep that Medici mausoleum out of my memory. It is as large as a church; its pavement is rich enough for the pavement of a King's palace; its great dome is gorgeous with frescoes; its walls are made of—what? Marble?—plaster?—wood?—paper? No. Red porphyry—verde antique—jasper—oriental agate—alabaster—mother-of-pearl—chalcedony—red coral—lapis lazuli! All the vast walls are made wholly of these precious stones, worked in, and in and in together in elaborate patterns and figures, and polished till they glow like great mirrors with the pictured splendors reflected from the dome overhead. And before a statue of one of those dead Medicis reposes a crown that blazes with diamonds and emeralds enough to buy a ship-of-the-line, almost. These are the things the Government has its evil eye upon, and a happy thing it will be for Italy when they melt away in the public treasury.

And now—. However, another beggar approaches. I will go out and destroy him, and then come back and write another chapter of vituperation.

Having eaten the friendless orphan—having driven away his comrades—having grown calm and reflective at length—I now feel in a kindlier mood. I feel that after talking so freely about the priests and the churches, justice demands that if I know any thing good about either I ought to say it. I *have* heard of many things that redound to the credit of the priesthood, but the most notable matter that occurs to me now is the devotion one of the mendicant orders showed during the prevalence of the cholera last year. I speak of the Dominican friars—men who wear a coarse, heavy brown robe and a cowl, in this hot climate, and go barefoot. They live on alms altogether, I believe. They must unquestionably love their religion, to suffer so much for it. When the cholera was raging in Naples; when the people were dying by hundreds and hundreds every day; when every concern for the public welfare was swallowed up in selfish private interest, and every citizen made the taking care of himself his sole object, these men banded themselves together and went about nursing the sick and burying the dead. Their noble efforts cost many of them their lives. They laid them down cheerfully, and well they might. Creeds mathematically precise, and hair-splitting niceties of doctrine, are absolutely necessary for the salvation of some kinds of souls, but surely the charity, the purity, the unselfishness that are in the hearts of men like these would save their souls though they were bankrupt in the true religion—which is ours.

One of these fat bare-footed rascals came here to Civita Vecchia with us in the little French steamer. There were only half a dozen of us in the cabin. He belonged in the steerage. He was the life of the ship, the bloody-minded son of the Inquisition! He and the leader of the marine band of a French man-of-war played on the piano and sang opera turn about; they sang duets together; they rigged impromptu theatrical costumes and gave us extravagant farces and pantomimes. We got along first-rate with the friar, and were excessively conversational, albeit he could not understand what we said, and certainly he never uttered a word that we could guess the meaning of. . . .

Chapter 26

. . . The Appian way is here yet, and looking much as it did, perhaps, when the triumphal processions of the Emperors moved over it in other days bringing fettered princes from the confines of the earth. We can not see the long array of chariots and mail-clad men laden with the spoils of conquest, but we can imagine the pageant, after a fashion. We look out upon many objects of interest from the dome of St. Peter's; and last of all, almost at our feet, our eyes rest upon the building which was once the Inquisition. How times changed, between the older ages and the new! Some seventeen or eighteen centuries ago, the ignorant men of Rome were wont to put Christians in the arena of the Coliseum yonder, and turn the wild beasts in upon them for a show. It was for a lesson as well. It was to teach the people to abhor and fear the new doctrine the followers of Christ were teaching. The beasts tore the victims limb from limb and made poor mangled corpses of them in the twinkling of an eye. But when the Christians came into power, when the holy Mother Church became mistress of the barbarians, she taught them the error of their ways by no such means. No, she put them in this pleasant Inquisition and pointed to the Blessed Redeemer, who was so gentle and so merciful toward all men, and they urged the barbarians to love him; and they did all they could to persuade them to love and honor him—first by twisting their thumbs out of joint with a screw; then by nipping their flesh with pincers—red-hot ones, because they are the most comfortable in cold weather; then by skinning them alive a little, and finally by roasting them in public. They always convinced those barbarians. The true religion, properly administered, as the good Mother Church used to administer it, is very, very soothing. It is wonderfully persuasive, also. There is a great difference between feeding parties to wild beasts and stirring up their finer feelings in an Inquisition. One is the system of degraded barbarians, the other of enlightened, civilized people. It is a great pity the playful Inquisition is no more.

I prefer not to describe St. Peter's. It has been done before. The ashes of Peter, the disciple of the Saviour, repose in a crypt under the *baldacchino*. We stood reverently in that place; so did we also in the Mamertine Prison, where he was confined, where he converted the soldiers, and where tradition says he caused a spring of water to flow in order that he might baptize them. But when they showed us the print of Peter's face in the hard stone of the prison wall and said he made that by falling up against it, we doubted. And when, also, the monk at the church of San Sebastian showed us a paving-stone with two great footprints in it and said that Peter's feet made those, we lacked confidence again. Such things do not impress one. The monk said that angels came and liberated Peter from prison by night, and he started away from Rome by the Appian Way. The Saviour met him and told him to go back, which he did. Peter left those footprints in the stone upon which he stood at the time. It was not stated how it was ever discovered whose footprints they were, seeing the interview occurred secretly and at night. The print of the face in the prison was that of a man of common size; the footprints were those of a man ten or twelve feet high. The discrepancy confirmed our unbelief. . . .

Chapter 27

. . . In this place I may well jot down a chapter concerning those necessary nuisances, European guides. Many a man has wished in his heart he could do without his guide; but knowing he could not, has wished he could get some amusement out of him as a remuneration for the affliction of his society. We accomplished this latter matter, and if our experience can be made useful to others they are welcome to it.

Guides know about enough English to tangle every thing up so that a man can make neither head or tail of it. They know their story by heart—the history of every statue, painting, cathedral or other wonder they show you. They know it and tell it as a parrot would—and if you interrupt, and throw them off the track, they have to go back and begin over again. All their lives long, they are employed in showing strange things to foreigners and listening to their bursts of admiration. It is human nature to take delight in exciting admiration. It is what prompts children to say "smart" things, and do absurd ones, and in other ways "show off" when company is present. It is what makes gossips turn out in rain and storm to go and be the first to tell a startling bit of news. Think, then, what a passion it becomes with a guide, whose privilege it is, every day, to show to strangers wonders that throw them into perfect ecstasies of admiration! He gets so that he could not by any possibility live in a soberer atmosphere. After we discovered this, we *never* went into ecstacies any more—we never admired any thing—we never showed any but impassible faces and stupid indifference in the presence of the sublimest wonders a guide had to display. We had found their weak point. We have made good use of it ever since. We have made some of those people savage, at times, but we have never lost our own serenity.

The doctor asks the questions, generally, because he can keep his countenance, and look more like an inspired idiot, and throw more imbecility into the tone of his voice than any man that lives. It comes natural to him.

The guides in Genoa are delighted to secure an American party, because Americans so much wonder, and deal so much in sentiment and emotion before any relic of Columbus. Our guide there fidgeted about as if he had swallowed a spring mattress. He was full of animation—full of impatience. He said:

"Come wis me, genteelmen!—come! I show you ze letter writing by Christopher Colombo!—write it himself!—write it wis his own hand!—come!"

He took us to the municipal palace. After much impressive fumbling of keys and opening of locks, the stained and aged document was spread before us. The guide's eyes sparkled. He danced about us and tapped the parchment with his finger:

"What I tell you, genteelmen! Is it not so? See! handwriting Christopher Colombo!—write it himself!"

We looked indifferent—unconcerned. The doctor examined the document very deliberately, during a painful pause.—Then he said, without any show of interest:

"Ah—Ferguson—what—what did you say was the name of the party who wrote this?"

"Christopher Colombo! ze great Christopher Colombo!"

Another deliberate examination.

"Ah—did he write it himself, or—or how?"

PENMANSHIP.

"He write it himself!—Christopher Colombo! he's own hand-writing, write by himself!"

Then the doctor laid the document down and said:

"Why, I have seen boys in America only fourteen years old that could write better than that."

"But zis is ze great Christo—"

"I don't care who it is! It's the worst writing I ever saw. Now you musn't think you can impose on us because we are strangers. We are not fools, by a good deal. If you have got any specimens of penmanship of real merit, trot them out!—and if you haven't, drive on!"

We drove on. The guide was considerably shaken up, but he made one more venture. He had something which he thought would overcome us. He said:

"Ah, genteelmen, you come wis me! I show you beautiful, O, magnificent bust Christopher Colombo!—splendid, grand, magnificent!"

He brought us before the beautiful bust—for it *was* beautiful—and sprang back and struck an attitude:

"Ah, look, genteelmen!—beautiful, grand,—bust Christopher Colombo! beautiful bust, beautiful pedestal!"

The doctor put up his eye-glass—procured for such occasions:

"Ah—what did you say this gentleman's name was?"

"Christopher Colombo!—ze great Christopher Colombo!"

"Christopher Colombo—the great Christopher Colombo. Well, what did *he* do?"

"Discover America!—discover America, Oh, ze devil!"

"Discover America. No—that statement will hardly wash. We are just from America ourselves. We heard nothing about it. Christopher Colombo—pleasant name—is—is he dead?"

"Oh, corpo di Baccho!—three hundred year!"

"What did he die of?"

"I do not know!—I can not tell."

"Small-pox, think?"

"I do not know, genteelmen!—I do not know *what* he die of!"

"Measles, likely?"

"May be—may be—I do *not* know—I think he die of somethings."

"Parents living?"

"Im-posseeble!"

"Ah—which is the bust and which is the pedestal?"

"Santa Maria!—*zis* ze bust!—*zis* ze pedestal!"

"Ah, I see, I see—happy combination—very happy combination, indeed. Is—is this the first time this gentleman was ever on a bust?"

ON A BUST.

That joke was lost on the foreigner—guides can not master the subtleties of the American joke.

We have made it interesting for this Roman guide. Yesterday we spent three or four hours in the Vatican, again, that wonderful world of curiosities. We came very near expressing interest, sometimes—even admiration—it was very hard to keep from it. We succeeded though. Nobody else ever did, in the Vatican museums. The guide was bewildered—non-plussed. He walked his legs off, nearly, hunting up extraordinary things, and exhausted all his ingenuity on us, but it was a failure; we never showed any interest in any thing. He had reserved what he considered to be his greatest wonder till the last—a royal Egyptian mummy, the best preserved in the world, perhaps. He took us there. He felt so sure, this time, that some of his old enthusiasm came back to him:

"See, genteelmen!—Mummy! Mummy!"

The eye-glass came up as calmly, as deliberately as ever.

"Ah,—Ferguson—what did I understand you to say the gentleman's name was?"

"Name?—he got no name!—Mummy!—'Gyptian mummy!"

"Yes, yes. Born here?"

"No! *'Gyptian* mummy!"

"Ah, just so. Frenchman, I presume?"

"No!—*not* Frenchman, not Roman!—born in Egypta!"

"Born in Egypta. Never heard of Egypta before. Foreign locality, likely. Mummy—mummy. How calm he is—how self-possessed. Is, ah—is he dead?"

"Oh, *sacre bleu,* been dead three thousan' year!"

The doctor turned on him savagely:

"Here, now, what do you mean by such conduct as this! Playing us for Chinamen because we are strangers and trying to learn! Trying to impose your vile second-hand carcasses on *us!*—thunder and lightning, I've a notion to—to—if you've got a nice *fresh* corpse, fetch him out!—or by George we'll brain you!"

We make it exceedingly interesting for this Frenchman. However, he has paid us back, partly, without knowing it. He came to the hotel this morning to ask if we were up, and he endeavored as well as he could to describe us, so that the landlord would know which persons he meant. He finished with the casual remark that we were lunatics. The observation was so innocent and so honest that it amounted to a very good thing for a guide to say.

There is one remark (already mentioned,) which never yet has failed to disgust these guides. We use it always, when we can think of nothing else to say. After they have exhausted their enthusiasm pointing out to us and praising the beauties of some ancient bronze image or broken-legged statue, we look at it stupidly and in silence for five, ten, fifteen minutes—as long as we can hold out, in fact—and then ask:

"Is—is he dead?"

That conquers the serenest of them. It is not what they are looking for—especially a new guide. Our Roman Ferguson is the most patient, unsuspecting, long-suffering subject we have had yet. We shall be sorry to part with him. We have enjoyed his society very much. We trust he has enjoyed ours, but we are harassed with doubts. . . .

. . . In the catacombs were buried St. Cecilia, St. Agnes, and several other of the most celebrated of the saints. In the catacomb of St. Callixtus, St. Bridget used to remain long hours in holy contemplation, and St. Charles Borroméo was wont to spend whole nights in prayer there. It was also the scene of a very marvelous thing.

> "Here the heart of St. Philip Neri was so inflamed with divine love as to burst his ribs."

I find that grave statement in a book published in New York in 1858, and written by "Rev. William H. Neligan, LL.D., M.A., Trinity College, Dublin; Member of the Archaeological Society of Great Britain." Therefore, I believe it. Otherwise, I could not. Under other circumstances I should have felt a curiosity to know what Philip had for dinner.

This author puts my credulity on its mettle every now and then. He tells of one St. Joseph Calasanctius whose house in Rome he visited; he visited only the house—the priest has been dead two hundred years. He says the Virgin Mary appeared to this saint. Then he continues:

> "His tongue and his heart, which were found after nearly a century to be whole, when the body was disinterred before his canonization, are still preserved in a glass case, and after two centuries the heart is still whole. When the French troops came to Rome, and when Pius VII. was carried away prisoner, blood dropped from it."

To read that in a book written by a monk far back in the Middle Ages, would surprise no one; it would sound natural and proper; but when it is seriously stated in the middle of the nineteenth century, by a man of finished education, an LL.D., M.A., and an Archaeological magnate, it sounds strangely enough. Still, I would gladly change my unbelief for Neligan's faith, and let him make the conditions as hard as he pleased.

The old gentleman's undoubting, unquestioning simplicity has a rare freshness about it in these matter-of-fact railroading and telegraphing days. Hear him, concerning the church of Ara Coeli:

> "In the roof of the church, directly above the high altar, is engraved, '*Regina Coeli laetare Alleluia.*' In the sixth century Rome was visited by a fearful pestilence. Gregory the Great urged the people to do penance, and a general procession was formed. It was to proceed from Ara Coeli to St. Peter's. As it passed before the mole of Adrian, now the Castle of St. Angelo, the sound of heavenly voices was heard singing (it was Easter morn.) '*Regina Coeli, laetare! alleluia! quia quem meruisti portare, alleluia! resurrexit sicut dixit; alleluia!*' The Pontiff, carrying in his hands the portrait of the Virgin, (which is over the high altar and is said to have been painted by St. Luke,) answered, with the astonished people, '*Ora pro nobis Deum, alleluia!*' At the same time an angel was seen to put up a sword in a scabbard, and the pestilence ceased on the same day. There are four

circumstances which *confirm** this miracle: the annual procession which takes place in the western church on the feast of St. Mark: the statue of St. Michael, placed on the mole of Adrian, which has since that time been called the Castle of St. Angelo; the antiphon Regina Coeli, which the Catholic church sings during paschal time; and the inscription in the church."

*The italics are mine. — M.T.

Chapter 28

From the sanguinary sports of the Holy Inquisition; the slaughter of the Coliseum; and the dismal tombs of the Catacombs, I naturally pass to the picturesque horrors of the Capuchin Convent. We stopped a moment in a small chapel in the church to admire a picture of St. Michael vanquishing Satan—a picture which is so beautiful that I can not but think it belongs to the reviled "*Renaissance,*" notwithstanding I believe they told us one of the ancient old masters painted it—and then we descended into the vast vault underneath.

Here was a spectacle for sensitive nerves! Evidently the old masters had been at work in this place. There were six divisions in the apartment, and each division was ornamented with a style of decoration peculiar to itself—and these decorations were in every instance formed of human bones! There were shapely arches, built wholly of thigh bones; there were startling pyramids, built wholly of grinning skulls; there were quaint architectural structures of various kinds, built of shin bones and the bones of the arm; on the wall were elaborate frescoes, whose curving vines were made of knotted human vertebrae; whose delicate tendrils were made of sinews and tendons; whose flowers were formed of knee-caps and toe-nails. Every lasting portion of the human frame was represented in these intricate designs (they were by Michael Angelo, I think,) and there was a careful finish about the work, and an attention to details that betrayed the artist's love of his labors as well as his schooled ability. I asked the good-natured monk who accompanied us, who did this? And he said, "*We* did it"—meaning himself and his brethren up stairs. I could see that the old friar took a high pride in his curious show. We made him talkative by exhibiting an interest we never betrayed to guides.

"Who were these people?"

"We—up stairs—Monks of the Capuchin order—my brethren."

"How many departed monks were required to upholster these six parlors?"

"These are the bones of four thousand."

"It took a long time to get enough?"

"Many, many centuries."

"Their different parts are well separated—skulls in one room, legs in another, ribs in another—there would be stirring times here for a while if the last trump should blow. Some of the brethren might get hold of the wrong leg, in the confusion, and the wrong skull, and find themselves limping, and looking through eyes that were wider apart or closer together than they were used to. You can not tell any of these parties apart, I suppose?"

"Oh, yes, I know many of them."

He put his finger on a skull. "This was Brother Anselmo—dead three hundred years—a good man."

VAULTS OF THE CONVENT.

He touched another. "This was Brother Alexander—dead two hundred and eighty years. This was Brother Carlo—dead about as long."

Then he took a skull and held it in his hand, and looked reflectively upon it, after the manner of the grave-digger when he discourses of Yorick.

"This," he said, "was Brother Thomas. He was a young prince, the scion of a proud house that traced its lineage back to the grand old days of Rome well nigh two thousand years ago. He loved beneath his estate. His family persecuted him; persecuted the girl, as well. They drove her from Rome; he followed; he sought her far and wide; he found no trace of her. He came back and offered his broken heart at our altar and his weary life to the service of God. But look you. Shortly his father died, and likewise his mother. The girl returned, rejoicing. She sought every where for him whose eyes had used to look tenderly into hers out of this poor skull, but she could not find him. At last, in this coarse garb we wear, she recognized him in the street. He knew her. It was too late. He fell where he stood. They took him up and brought him here. He never spoke afterward. Within the week he died. You can see the color of his hair—faded, somewhat—by this thin shred that clings still to the temple. This," [taking up a thigh bone,] "was his. The veins of this leaf in the decorations over your head, were his finger-joints, a hundred and fifty years ago."

This business-like way of illustrating a touching story of the heart by laying the several fragments of the lover before us and naming them, was as grotesque a performance, and as ghastly, as any I ever witnessed. I hardly knew whether to smile or shudder. There are nerves and muscles in our frames whose functions and whose methods of working it seems a sort of sacrilege to describe by cold physiological names and surgical technicalities, and the monk's talk suggested to me something of this kind. Fancy a surgeon, with his nippers lifting tendons, muscles and such things into view, out of the complex machinery of a corpse, and observing, "Now this little nerve quivers—the vibration is imparted to this muscle—from here it is passed to this fibrous substance; here its ingredients are separated by the chemical action of the blood—one part goes to the heart and thrills it with what is popularly termed emotion, another part follows this nerve to the brain and communicates intelligence of a startling character—the third part glides along this passage and touches the spring connected with the fluid receptacles that lie in the rear of the eye. Thus, by this simple and beautiful process, the party is informed that his mother is dead, and he weeps." Horrible!

I asked the monk if all the brethren up stairs expected to be put in this place when they died. He answered quietly:

"We must all lie here at last."

See what one can accustom himself to.—The reflection that he must some day be taken apart like an engine or a clock, or like a house whose owner is gone, and worked up into arches and pyramids and hideous frescoes, did not distress this monk in the least. I thought he even looked as if he were thinking, with complacent vanity, that his own skull would look well on top of the heap and his own ribs add a charm to the frescoes which possibly they lacked at present.

Here and there, in ornamental alcoves, stretched upon beds of bones, lay dead and dried-up monks, with lank frames dressed in the black robes one sees ordinarily upon priests. We examined one closely. The skinny hands were clasped upon the breast; two lustreless tufts of hair stuck to the skull; the skin was brown and sunken; it stretched tightly over the cheek bones and made them stand out sharply; the crisp dead eyes were deep in the sockets; the nostrils were painfully prominent, the end of the nose being gone; the lips had shriveled away from the yellow teeth; and brought down to us through the circling years, and petrified there, was a weird laugh a full century old!

It was the jolliest laugh, but yet the most dreadful, that one can imagine. Surely, I thought, it must have been a most extraordinary joke this veteran

DRIED CONVENT FRUIT.

produced with his latest breath, that he has not got done laughing at it yet. At this moment I saw that the old instinct was strong upon the boys, and I said we had better hurry to St. Peter's. They were trying to keep from asking, "Is—is he dead?"

It makes me dizzy, to think of the Vatican—of its wilderness of statues, paintings, and curiosities of every description and every age. The "old masters" (especially in sculpture,) fairly swarm, there. I can not write about the Vatican. I think I shall never remember any thing I saw there distinctly but the mummies, and the Transfiguration, by Raphael, and some other things it is not necessary to mention now. I shall remember the Transfiguration partly because it was placed in a room almost by itself; partly because it is acknowledged by all to be the first oil painting in the world; and partly because it was wonderfully beautiful. The colors are fresh and rich, the "expression," I am told, is fine, the "feeling" is lively, the "tone" is good, the "depth" is profound, and the width is about four and a half feet, I should judge. It is a picture that really holds one's attention; its beauty is fascinating. It is fine enough to be a *Renaissance*. A remark I made a while ago suggests a thought—and a hope. Is it not possible that the reason I find such charms in this picture is because it is out of the crazy chaos of the galleries? If some of the others were set apart, might not they be beautiful? If this were set in the midst of the tempest of pictures one finds in the vast galleries of the Roman palaces, would I think it so handsome? If, up to this time, I had seen only one "old master" in each palace, instead of acres and acres of walls and ceilings fairly papered with them, might I not have a more civilized opinion of the old masters than I have now? I think so. When I was a school-boy and was to have a new knife, I could not make up my mind as to which was the prettiest in the show-case, and I did not think any of them were particularly pretty; and so I chose with a heavy heart. But when I looked at my purchase, at home, where no glittering blades came into competition with it, I was astonished to see how handsome it was. To this day my new hats look better out of the shop than they did in it with other new hats. It begins to dawn upon me, now, that possibly, what I have been taking for uniform ugliness in the galleries may be uniform beauty after all. I honestly hope it is, to others, but certainly it is not to me. Perhaps the reason I used to enjoy going to the Academy of Fine Arts in New York was because there were but a few hundred paintings in it, and it did not surfeit me to go through the list. I suppose the Academy was bacon and beans in the Forty-Mile Desert, and a European gallery is a state dinner of thirteen courses. One leaves no sign after him of the one dish, but the thirteen frighten away his appetite and give him no satisfaction.

There is one thing I am certain of, though. With all the Michael Angelos, the Raphaels, the Guidos and the other old masters, the sublime history of Rome remains unpainted! They painted Virgins enough, and popes enough and saintly scarecrows enough, to people Paradise, almost, and these things are all they did paint. "Nero fiddling o'er burning Rome," the assassination of Caesar, the stirring spectacle of a hundred thousand people bending forward with rapt interest, in the Coliseum, to see two skillful gladiators hacking away each others' lives, a tiger springing upon a kneeling martyr—these and a thousand other matters which we read of with a living interest, must be sought for only in books—not among the rubbish left by the old masters—who are no more, I have the satisfaction of informing the public.

They did paint, and they did carve in marble, one historical scene, and one only, (of any great historical consequence.) And what was it and why did they choose it, particularly? It was the Rape of the Sabines, and they chose it for the legs and busts.

I like to look at statues, however, and I like to look at pictures, also—even of monks looking up in sacred ecstacy, and monks looking down in meditation, and monks skirmishing for something to eat—and therefore I drop ill nature to thank the papal government for so jealously guarding and so industriously gathering up these things; and for permitting me, a stranger and not an entirely friendly one, to roam at will and unmolested among them, charging me nothing, and only requiring that I shall behave myself simply as well as I ought to behave in any other man's house. I thank the Holy Father right heartily, and I wish him long life and plenty of happiness.

The Popes have long been the patrons and preservers of art, just as our new, practical Republic is the encourager and upholder of mechanics. In their Vatican is stored up all that is curious and beautiful in art; in our Patent Office is hoarded all that is curious or useful in mechanics. When a man invents a new style of horse-collar or discovers a new and superior method of telegraphing, our government issues a patent to him that is worth a fortune; when a man digs up an ancient statue in the Campagna, the Pope gives him a fortune in gold coin. We can make something of a guess at a man's character by the style of nose he carries on his face. The Vatican and the Patent Office are governmental noses, and they bear a deal of character about them.

The guide showed us a colossal statue of Jupiter, in the Vatican, which he said looked so damaged and rusty—so like the God of the Vagabonds—because it had but recently been dug up in the Campagna. He asked how much we supposed this Jupiter was worth? I replied, with intelligent promptness, that he was probably worth about four dollars—may be four and a half. "A hundred thousand dollars!" Ferguson said. Ferguson said, further, that the Pope permits no ancient work of this kind to leave his dominions. He appoints a commission to examine discoveries like this and report upon the value; then the Pope pays the discoverer one-half of that assessed value and takes the statue. He said this Jupiter was dug from a field which had just been bought for thirty-six thousand dollars, so the first crop was a good one for the new farmer. I do not know whether Ferguson always tells the truth or not, but I suppose he does. I know that an exorbitant export duty is exacted upon all pictures painted by the old masters, in order to discourage the sale of those in the private collections. I am satisfied, also, that genuine old masters hardly exist at all, in America, because the cheapest and most insignificant of them are valued at the price of a fine farm. I proposed to buy a small trifle of a Raphael, myself, but the price of it was eighty thousand dollars, the export duty would have made it considerably over a hundred, and so I studied on it awhile and concluded not to take it.

I wish here to mention an inscription I have seen, before I forget it:

"Glory to God in the highest, peace on earth TO MEN OF GOOD WILL!" It is not good scripture, but it is sound Catholic and human nature.

This is in letters of gold around the apsis of a mosaic group at the side of the *scala santa,* church of St. John Lateran, the Mother and Mistress of all the Catholic churches of the world. The group represents the Saviour, St. Peter, Pope Leo, St. Silvester, Constantine and Charlemagne. Peter is giving the *pallium* to the Pope, and a standard to Charlemagne. The Saviour is giving the keys to St. Silvester, and a standard to Constantine. No prayer is offered to the Saviour, who seems to be of little importance any where in Rome; but an inscription below says, "*Blessed Peter, give life to Pope Leo and victory to King Charles.*" It does not say, "*Intercede for us,* through the Saviour, with the Father, for this boon," but "Blessed Peter, *give it* us."

In all seriousness—without meaning to be frivolous—without meaning to be irreverent, and more than all, without meaning to be blasphemous,—I state as my simple deduction from the things I have seen and the things I have heard, that the Holy Personages rank thus in Rome:

First—"The Mother of God"—otherwise the Virgin Mary.

Second—The Deity.

Third—Peter.

Fourth—Some twelve or fifteen canonized Popes and martyrs.

Fifth—Jesus Christ the Saviour—(but always as an infant in arms.)

I may be wrong in this—my judgment errs often, just as is the case with other men's—but it *is* my judgment, be it good or bad.

Just here I will mention something that seems curious to me. There are no "Christ's Churches" in Rome, and no "Churches of the Holy Ghost," that I can discover. There are some four hundred churches, but about a fourth of them seem to be named for the Madonna and St. Peter. There are so many named for Mary that they have to be distinguished by all sorts of affixes, if I understand the matter rightly. Then we have churches of St. Louis; St. Augustine; St. Agnes; St. Calixtus; St. Lorenzo in Lucina; St. Lorenzo in Damaso; St. Cecilia; St. Athanasius; St. Philip Neri; St. Catherine, St. Dominico, and a multitude of lesser saints whose names are not familiar in the world—and away down, clear out of the list of the churches, comes a couple of hospitals: one of them is named for the Saviour and the other for the Holy Ghost!

Day after day and night after night we have wandered among the crumbling wonders of Rome; day after day and night after night we have fed upon the dust and decay of five-and-twenty centuries—have brooded over them by day and dreampt of them by night till sometimes we seemed moldering away ourselves, and growing defaced and cornerless, and liable at any moment to fall a prey to some antiquary and be patched in the legs, and "restored" with an unseemly nose, and labeled wrong and dated wrong, and set up in the Vatican for poets to drivel about and vandals to scribble their names on forever and forevermore.

But the surest way to stop writing about Rome is to stop. I wished to write a real "guide-book" chapter on this fascinating city, but I could not do it, because I have felt all the time like a boy in a candy-shop—there was every thing to choose from, and yet no choice. I have drifted along hopelessly for a hundred pages of manuscript without knowing where to commence. I will not commence at all. Our passports have been examined. We will go to Naples. . . .

Chapter 29

In this city of Naples, they believe in and support one of the wretchedest of all the religious impostures one can find in Italy—the miraculous liquefaction of the blood of St. Januarius. Twice a year the priests assemble all the people at the Cathedral, and get out this vial of clotted blood and let them see it slowly dissolve and become liquid—and every day for eight days, this dismal farce is repeated, while the priests go among the crowd and collect money for the exhibition. The first day, the blood liquefies in forty-seven minutes—the church is crammed, then, and time must be allowed the collectors to get around: after that it liquefies a little quicker and a little quicker, every day, as the houses grow smaller, till on the eighth day, with only a few dozens present to see the miracle, it liquefies in four minutes.

And here, also, they used to have a grand procession, of priests, citizens, soldiers, sailors, and the high dignitaries of the City Government, once a year, to shave the head of a made-up Madonna—a stuffed and painted image, like a milliner's dummy—whose hair miraculously grew and restored itself every twelve months. They still kept up this shaving procession as late as four or five years ago. It was a source of great profit to the church that possessed the remarkable effigy, and the ceremony of the public barbering of her was always carried out with the greatest possible eclat and display—the more the better, because the more excitement there was about it the larger the crowds it drew and the heavier the revenues it produced—but at last a day came when the Pope and his servants were unpopular in Naples, and the City Government stopped the Madonna's annual show.

There we have two specimens of these Neapolitans—two of the silliest possible frauds, which half the population religiously and faithfully believed, and the other half either believed also or else said nothing about, and thus lent themselves to the support of the imposture. I am very well satisfied to think the whole population believed in those poor, cheap miracles—a people who want two cents every time they bow to you, and who abuse a woman, are capable of it, I think. . . .

Chapter 33

. . . The Mosque of St. Sophia is the chief lion of Constantinople. You must get a firman and hurry there the first thing. We did that. We did not get a firman, but we took along four or five francs apiece, which is much the same thing.

I do not think much of the Mosque of St. Sophia. I suppose I lack appreciation. We will let it go at that. It is the rustiest old barn in heathendom. I believe all the interest that attaches to it comes from the fact that it was built for a Christian church and then turned into a mosque, without much alteration, by the Mohammedan conquerors of the land. They made me take off my boots and walk into the place in my stocking-feet. I caught cold, and got myself so stuck up with a complication of gums, slime and general corruption, that I wore out more than two thousand pair of boot-jacks getting my boots off that night, and even then some Christian hide peeled off with them. I abate not a single boot-jack.

St. Sophia is a colossal church, thirteen or fourteen hundred years old, and unsightly enough to be very, very much older. Its immense dome is said to be more wonderful than St. Peter's, but its dirt is much more wonderful than its dome, though they never mention it. The church has a hundred and seventy pillars in it, each a single piece, and all of costly marbles of various kinds, but they came from ancient temples at Baalbec, Heliopolis, Athens and Ephesus, and are battered, ugly and repulsive. They were a thousand years old when this church was new, and then the contrast must have been ghastly—if Justinian's architects did not trim them any. The inside of the dome is figured all over with a monstrous inscription in Turkish characters, wrought in gold mosaic, that looks as glaring as a circus bill; the pavements and the marble balustrades are all battered and dirty; the perspective is marred every where by a web of ropes that depend from the dizzy height of the dome, and suspend countless dingy, coarse oil lamps, and ostrich-eggs, six or seven feet above the floor. Squatting and sitting in groups, here and there and far and near, were ragged Turks reading books, hearing sermons, or receiving lessons like children, and in fifty places were more of the same sort bowing and straightening up, bowing again and getting down to kiss the earth, muttering prayers the while, and keeping up their gymnastics till they ought to have been tired, if they were not.

Every where was dirt, and dust, and dinginess, and gloom; every where were signs of a hoary antiquity, but with nothing touching or beautiful about it; every where were those groups of fantastic pagans; overhead the gaudy mosaics and the web of lamp-ropes—nowhere was there any thing to win one's love or challenge his admiration.

The people who go into ecstacies over St. Sophia must surely get them out of the guide-book (where every church is spoken of as being "considered by good judges to be the most marvelous structure, in many respects, that the world has ever seen.") Or else they are those old connoisseurs from the wilds of New Jersey who laboriously learn the difference between a fresco and a fire-plug and from that day forward feel privileged to void their critical bathos on painting, sculpture and architecture forever more.

We visited the Dancing Dervishes. There were twenty-one of them. They wore a long, light-colored loose robe that hung to their heels. Each in his turn went up to the priest (they were all within a large circular railing) and bowed profoundly and then went spinning away deliriously and took his appointed place in the circle, and continued to spin. When all had spun themselves to their places, they were about five or six feet apart—and so situated, the entire circle of spinning pagans spun itself three separate times around the room. It took twenty-five minutes to do it. They spun on the left foot, and kept themselves going by passing the right rapidly before it and digging it against the waxed floor. Some of them made incredible "time." Most of them spun around forty times in a minute, and one artist averaged about sixty-one times a minute, and kept it up during the whole twenty-five. His robe filled with air and stood out all around him like a balloon.

They made no noise of any kind, and most of them tilted their heads back and closed their eyes, entranced with a sort of devotional ecstacy. There was a rude kind of music, part of the time, but the musicians were not visible. None but spinners were allowed within the circle. A man had to either spin or stay outside. It was about as barbarous an exhibition as we have witnessed yet. Then sick persons came and lay down, and beside them women laid their sick children (one a babe at the breast,) and the patriarch of the Dervishes walked upon their bodies. He was supposed to cure their diseases by trampling upon their breasts or backs or standing on the back of their necks. This is well enough for a people who think all their affairs are made or marred by viewless spirits of the air—by giants, gnomes, and genii—and who still believe, to this day, all the wild tales in the Arabian Nights. . . .

Chapter 38

. . . This seaport of Smyrna, our first notable acquaintance in Asia, is a closely packed city of one hundred and thirty thousand inhabitants, and, like Constantinople, it has no outskirts. It is as closely packed at its outer edges as it is in the centre, and then the habitations leave suddenly off and the plain beyond seems houseless. It is just like any other Oriental city. That is to say, its Moslem houses are heavy and dark, and as comfortless as so many tombs; its streets are crooked, rudely and roughly paved, and as narrow as an ordinary staircase; the streets uniformly carry a man to any other place than the one he wants to go to, and surprise him by landing him in the most unexpected localities; business is chiefly carried on in great covered bazaars, celled like a honey-comb with innumerable shops no larger than a common closet, and the whole hive cut up into a maze of alleys about wide enough to accommodate a laden camel, and well calculated to confuse a stranger and eventually lose him; every where there is dirt, every where there are fleas, every where there are lean, broken-hearted dogs; every alley is thronged with people; wherever you look, your eye rests upon a wild masquerade of extravagant costumes; the work-shops are all open to the streets, and the workmen visible; all manner of sounds assail the ear, and over them all rings out the muezzin's cry from some tall minaret, calling the faithful vagabonds to prayer; and superior to the call to prayer, the noises in the streets, the interest of the costumes—superior to every thing, and claiming the bulk of attention first, last, and all the time—is a combination of Mohammedan stenches, to which the smell of even a Chinese quarter would be as pleasant as the roasting odors of the fatted calf to the nostrils of the returning Prodigal. Such is Oriental luxury—such is Oriental splendor! We read about it all our days, but we comprehend it not until we see it. Smyrna is a very old city. Its name occurs several times in the Bible, one or two of the disciples of Christ visited it, and here was located one of the original seven apocalyptic churches spoken of in Revelations. These churches were symbolized in the Scriptures as candlesticks, and on certain conditions there was a sort of implied promise that Smyrna should be endowed with a "crown of life." She was to "be faithful unto death"—those were the terms. She has not kept up her faith straight along, but the pilgrims that wander hither consider that she has come near enough to it to save her, and so they point to the fact that Smyrna to-day wears her crown of life, and is a great city, with a great commerce and full of energy, while the cities wherein were located the other six churches, and to which no crown of life was promised, have vanished from the earth. So Smyrna really still possesses her crown of life, in a business point of view. Her career, for eighteen centuries, has been a chequered one, and she has been under the rule of princes of many creeds, yet there has been no season during all that time, as far as we know, (and during such seasons as she was inhabited at all,) that she has been without her little community of Christians "faithful unto death." Hers was the only church against which no threats were implied in the Revelations, and the only one which survived.

With Ephesus, forty miles from here, where was located another of the seven churches, the case was different. The "candlestick" has been removed from Ephesus. Her light has been put out. Pilgrims, always prone to find prophecies in the Bible, and often where none exist, speak cheerfully and complacently of poor, ruined Ephesus as the victim of prophecy. And yet there is no sentence that promises, without due qualification, the destruction of the city. The words are:

> "Remember, therefore, from whence thou art fallen, and repent, and do the first works; or else I will come unto thee quickly, and will remove thy candlestick out of his place, except thou repent."

That is all; the other verses are singularly *complimentary* to Ephesus. The threat is qualified. There is no history to show that she did not repent. But the cruelest habit the modern prophecy-savans have, is that one of coolly and arbitrarily fitting the prophetic shirt on to the wrong man. They do it without regard to rhyme or reason. Both the cases I have just mentioned are instances in point. Those "prophecies" are distinctly leveled at the "*churches* of Ephesus, Smyrna," etc., and yet the pilgrims invariably make them refer to the *cities* instead. No crown of life is promised to the town of Smyrna and its commerce, but to the handful of Christians who formed its "church." If *they* were "faithful unto death," they have their crown now—but no amount of faithfulness and legal shrewdness combined could legitimately drag the *city* into a participation in the promises of the prophecy. The stately language of the Bible refers to a crown of life whose lustre will reflect the day-beams of the endless ages of eternity, not the butterfly existence of a city built by men's hands, which must pass to dust with the builders and be forgotten even in the mere handful of centuries vouchsafed to the solid world itself between its cradle and its grave.

The fashion of delving out fulfillments of prophecy where that prophecy consists of mere "ifs," trenches upon the absurd. Suppose, a thousand years from now, a malarious swamp builds itself up in the shallow harbor of Smyrna, or something else kills the town; and suppose, also, that within that time the swamp that has filled the renowned harbor of Ephesus and rendered her ancient site deadly and uninhabitable to-day, becomes hard and healthy ground; suppose the natural consequence ensues, to wit: that Smyrna becomes a melancholy ruin, and Ephesus is rebuilt. What would the prophecy-savans say? They would coolly skip over our age of the world, and say: "Smyrna was not faithful unto death, and so her crown of life was denied her; Ephesus repented, and lo! her candlestick was not removed. Behold these evidences! How wonderful is prophecy!"

Smyrna has been utterly destroyed six times. If her crown of life had been an insurance policy, she would have had an opportunity to collect on it the first time she fell. But she holds it on sufferance and by a complimentary construction of language which does not refer to her. Six different times, however, I suppose some infatuated prophecy-enthusiast blundered along and said, to the infinite disgust of Smyrna and the Smyrniotes: "In sooth, here is astounding fulfillment of prophecy! Smyrna hath not been faithful unto death, and behold her crown of life is vanished from her head. Verily, these things be astonishing!"

Such things have a bad influence. They provoke worldly men into using light conversation concerning sacred subjects. Thick-headed commentators upon the Bible, and stupid preachers and teachers, work more damage to religion than sensible, cool-brained clergymen can fight away again, toil as they may. It is not good judgment to fit a crown of life upon a city which has been destroyed six times. That other class of wiseacres who twist prophecy in such a manner as to make it promise the destruction and desolation of the same city, use judgment just as bad, since the city is in a very flourishing condition now, unhappily for them. These things put arguments into the mouth of infidelity. . . .

CHAPTER 43

. . . Properly, with the sorry relics we bestrode, it was a three days' journey to Damascus. It was necessary that we should do it in less than two. It was necessary because our three pilgrims would not travel on the Sabbath day. We were all perfectly willing to keep the Sabbath day, but there are times when to keep the *letter* of a sacred law whose spirit is righteous, becomes a sin, and this was a case in point. We pleaded for the tired, ill-treated horses, and tried to show that their faithful service deserved kindness in return, and their hard lot compassion. But when did ever self-righteousness know the sentiment of pity? What were a few long hours added to the hardships of some over-taxed brutes when weighed against the peril of those human souls? It was not the most promising party to travel with and hope to gain a higher veneration for religion through the example of its devotees. We said the Saviour who pitied dumb beasts and taught that the ox must be rescued from the mire even on the Sabbath day, would not have counseled a forced march like this. We said the "long trip" was exhausting and therefore dangerous in the blistering heats of summer, even when the ordinary days' stages were traversed, and if we persisted in this hard march, some of us might be stricken down with the fevers of the country in consequence of it. Nothing could move the pilgrims. They *must* press on. Men might die, horses might die, but they must enter upon holy soil next week, with no Sabbath-breaking stain upon them. Thus they were willing to commit a sin against the spirit of religious law, in order that they might preserve the letter of it. It was not worth while to tell them "the letter kills." I am talking now about personal friends; men whom I like; men who are good citizens; who are honorable, upright, conscientious; but whose idea of the Saviour's religion seems to me distorted. They lecture our shortcomings unsparingly, and every night they call us together and read to us chapters from the Testament that are full of gentleness, of charity, and of tender mercy; and then all the next day they stick to their saddles clear up to the summits of these rugged mountains, and clear down again. Apply the Testament's gentleness, and charity, and tender mercy to a toiling, worn and weary horse?—Nonsense—these are for God's human creatures, not His dumb ones. What the pilgrims choose to do, respect for their almost sacred character demands that I should allow to pass—but I would so like to catch any other member of the party riding his horse up one of these exhausting hills once!

We have given the pilgrims a good many examples that might benefit them, but it is virtue thrown away. They have never heard a cross word out of our lips toward each other—but *they* have quarreled once or twice. We love to hear them at it, after they have been lecturing us. The very first thing they did, coming ashore at Beirout, was to quarrel in the boat. I have said I like them, and I do like them—but every time they read me a scorcher of a lecture I mean to talk back in print.

Not content with doubling the legitimate stages, they switched off the main road and went away out of the way to visit an absurd fountain called Figia, because Baalam's ass had drank there once. So we journeyed on, through the terrible hills and deserts and the roasting sun, and then far into the night, seeking the honored pool of Baalam's ass, the patron saint of all pilgrims like us. I find no entry but this in my note-book:

> "Rode to-day, altogether, thirteen hours, through deserts, partly, and partly over barren, unsightly hills, and latterly through wild, rocky scenery, and camped at about eleven o'clock at night on the banks of a limpid stream, near a Syrian village. Do not know its name—do not wish to know it—want to go to bed. Two horses lame (mine and Jack's) and the others worn out. Jack and I walked three or four miles, over the hills, and led the horses. Fun—but of a mild type."

Twelve or thirteen hours in the saddle, even in a Christian land and a Christian climate, and on a good horse, is a tiresome journey; but in an oven like Syria, in a ragged spoon of a saddle that slips fore-and-aft, and "thort-ships," and every way, and on a horse that is tired and lame, and yet must be whipped and spurred with hardly a moment's cessation all day long, till the blood comes from his side, and your conscience hurts you every time you strike, if you are half a man,—it is a journey to be remembered in bitterness of spirit and execrated with emphasis for a liberal division of a man's lifetime. . . .

Chapter 46

. . . The little children were in a pitiable condition—they all had sore eyes, and were otherwise afflicted in various ways. They say that hardly a native child in all the East is free from sore eyes, and that thousands of them go blind of one eye or both every year. I think this must be so, for I see plenty of blind people every day, and I do not remember seeing any children that hadn't sore eyes. And, would you suppose that an American mother could sit for an hour, with her child in her arms, and let a hundred flies roost upon its eyes all that time undisturbed? I see that every day. It makes my flesh creep. Yesterday we met a woman riding on a little jackass, and she had a little child in her arms; honestly, I thought the child had goggles on as we approached, and I wondered how its mother could afford so much style. But when we drew near, we saw that the goggles were nothing but a camp meeting of flies assembled around each of the child's eyes, and at the same time there was a detachment prospecting its nose. The flies were happy, the child was contented, and so the mother did not interfere.

As soon as the tribe found out that we had a doctor in our party, they began to flock in from all quarters. Dr. B., in the charity of his nature, had taken a child from a woman who sat near by, and put some sort of a wash upon its diseased eyes. That woman went off and started the whole nation, and it was a sight to see them swarm! The lame, the halt, the blind, the leprous—all the distempers that are bred of indolence, dirt, and iniquity—were represented in the Congress in ten minutes, and still they came! Every woman that had a sick baby brought it along, and every woman that hadn't, borrowed one. What reverent and what worshiping looks they bent upon that dread, mysterious power, the Doctor! They watched him take his phials out; they watched him measure the particles of white powder; they watched him add drops of one precious liquid, and drops of another; they lost not the slightest movement; their eyes were riveted upon him with a fascination that nothing could distract. I believe they thought he was gifted like a god. When each individual got his portion of medicine, his eyes were radiant with joy—notwithstanding by nature they are a thankless and impassive race—and upon his face was written the unquestioning faith that nothing on earth could prevent the patient from getting well now.

Christ knew how to preach to these simple, superstitious, disease-tortured creatures: He healed the sick. They flocked to our poor human doctor this morning when the fame of what he had done to the sick child went abroad in the land, and they worshiped him with their eyes while they did not know as yet whether there was virtue in his simples or not. The ancestors of these—people precisely like them in color, dress, manners, customs, simplicity—flocked in vast multitudes after Christ, and when they saw Him make the afflicted whole with a word, it is no wonder they worshiped Him. No wonder His deeds were the talk of the nation. No wonder the multitude that followed Him was so great that at one time—thirty miles from here—they had to let a sick man down through the roof because no approach could be made to the door; no wonder His audiences were so great at Galilee that He had to preach from a ship removed a little distance from the shore; no wonder that even in the desert places about Bethsaida, five thousand invaded His solitude, and He had to feed them by a miracle or else see them suffer for their confiding faith and devotion; no wonder when there was a great commotion in a city in those days, one neighbor explained it to another in words to this effect: "They say that Jesus of Nazareth is come!"

Well, as I was saying, the doctor distributed medicine as long as he had any to distribute, and his reputation is mighty in Galilee this day. Among his patients was the child of the Shiek's daughter—for even this poor, ragged handful of sores and sin has its royal Shiek—a poor old mummy that looked as if he would be more at home in a poor-house than in the Chief Magistracy of this tribe of hopeless, shirtless savages. The princess—I mean the Shiek's daughter—was only thirteen or fourteen years old, and had a very sweet face and a pretty one. She was the only Syrian female we have seen yet who was not so sinfully ugly that she couldn't smile after ten o'clock Saturday night without breaking the Sabbath. Her child was a hard specimen, though—there wasn't enough of it to make a pie, and the poor little thing looked so pleadingly up at all who came near it (as if it had an idea that now was its chance or never,) that we were filled with compassion which was genuine and not put on. . . .

CHAPTER 48

. . . Nearly every book concerning Galilee and its lake describes the scenery as beautiful. No—not always so straightforward as that. Sometimes the *impression* intentionally conveyed is that it is beautiful, at the same time that the author is careful not to *say* that it is, in plain Saxon. But a careful analysis of these descriptions will show that the materials of which they are formed are not individually beautiful and can not be wrought into combinations that are beautiful. The veneration and the affection which some of these men felt for the scenes they were speaking of, heated their fancies and biased their judgment; but the pleasant falsities they wrote were full of honest sincerity, at any rate. Others wrote as they did, because they feared it would be unpopular to write otherwise. Others were hypocrites and deliberately meant to deceive. Any of them would say in a moment, if asked, that it was *always* right and always *best* to tell the truth. They would say that, at any rate, if they did not perceive the drift of the question.

But why should not the truth be spoken of this region? Is the truth harmful? Has it ever needed to hide its face? God made the Sea of Galilee and its surroundings as they are. Is it the province of Mr. Grimes to improve upon the work?

I am sure, from the tenor of books I have read, that many who have visited this land in years gone by, were Presbyterians, and came seeking evidences in support of their particular creed; they found a Presbyterian Palestine, and they had already made up their minds to find no other, though possibly they did not know it, being blinded by their zeal. Others were Baptists, seeking

Baptist evidences and a Baptist Palestine. Others were Catholics, Methodists, Episcopalians, seeking evidences indorsing their several creeds, and a Catholic, a Methodist, an Episcopalian Palestine. Honest as these men's intentions may have been, they were full of partialities and prejudices, they entered the country with their verdicts already prepared, and they could no more write dispassionately and impartially about it than they could about their own wives and children. Our pilgrims have brought *their* verdicts with them. They have shown it in their conversation ever since we left Beirout. I can almost tell, in set phrase, what they will say when they see Tabor, Nazareth, Jericho and Jerusalem—*because I have the books they will "smouch" their ideas from.* These authors write pictures and frame rhapsodies, and lesser men follow and see with the author's eyes instead of their own, and speak with his tongue. What the pilgrims said at Cesarea Philippi surprised me with its wisdom. I found it afterwards in Robinson. What they said when Genessaret burst upon their vision, charmed me with its grace. I find it in Mr. Thompson's "Land and the Book." They have spoken often, in happily worded language which never varied, of how they mean to lay their weary heads upon a stone at Bethel, as Jacob did, and close their dim eyes, and dream, perchance, of angels descending out of heaven on a ladder. It was very pretty. But I have recognized the weary head and the dim eyes, finally. They borrowed the idea—and the words—and the construction—and the punctuation—from Grimes. The pilgrims will tell of Palestine, when they get home, not as it appeared to *them,* but as it appeared to Thompson and Robinson and Grimes—with the tints varied to suit each pilgrim's creed. . . .

CHAPTER 50

. . . We entered the great Latin Convent which is built over the traditional dwelling-place of the Holy Family. We went down a flight of fifteen steps below the ground level, and stood in a small chapel tricked out with tapestry hangings, silver lamps, and oil paintings. A spot marked by a cross, in the marble floor, under the altar, was exhibited as the place made forever holy by the feet of the Virgin when she stood up to receive the message of the angel. So simple, so unpretending a locality, to be the scene of so mighty an event! The very scene of the Annunciation—an event which has been commemorated by splendid shrines and august temples all over the civilized world, and one which the princes of art have made it their loftiest ambition to picture worthily on their canvas; a spot whose history is familiar to the very children of every house, and city, and obscure hamlet of the furthest lands of Christendom; a spot which myriads of men would toil across the breadth of a world to see, would consider it a priceless privilege to look upon. It was easy to think these thoughts. But it was not easy to bring myself up to the magnitude of the situation. I could sit off several thousand miles and imagine the angel appearing, with shadowy wings and lustrous countenance, and note the glory that streamed downward upon the Virgin's head while the message from the Throne of God fell upon her ears—any one can do that, beyond the ocean, but few can do it here. I saw the little recess from which the angel stepped, but could not fill its void. The angels that I know are creatures of unstable fancy—they will not fit in niches of substantial stone. Imagination labors best in distant fields. I doubt if any man can stand in the Grotto of the Annunciation and people with the phantom images of his mind its too tangible walls of stone.

They showed us a broken granite pillar, depending from the roof, which they said was hacked in two by the Moslem conquerors of Nazareth, in the vain hope of pulling down the sanctuary. But the pillar remained miraculously suspended in the air, and, unsupported itself, supported then and still supports the roof. By dividing this statement up among eight, it was found not difficult to believe it.

These gifted Latin monks never do any thing by halves. If they were to show you the Brazen Serpent that was elevated in the wilderness, you could depend upon it that they had on hand the pole it was elevated on also, and even the hole it stood in. They have got the "Grotto" of the Annunciation here; and just as convenient to it as one's throat is to his mouth, they have also the Virgin's Kitchen, and even her sitting-room, where she and Joseph watched the infant Saviour play with Hebrew toys eighteen hundred years ago. All under one roof, and all clean, spacious, comfortable "grottoes." It seems curious that personages intimately connected with the Holy Family always lived in grottoes—in Nazareth, in Bethlehem, in imperial Ephesus—and yet nobody else in their day and generation thought of doing any thing of the kind. If they ever did, their grottoes are all gone, and I suppose we ought to wonder at the peculiar marvel of the preservation of these I speak of. When the Virgin fled from Herod's wrath, she hid in a grotto in Bethlehem, and the same is there to this day. The slaughter of the innocents in Bethlehem was done in a grotto; the Saviour was born in a grotto—both are shown to pilgrims yet. It is exceedingly strange that these tremendous events all happened in grottoes—and exceedingly fortunate, likewise, because the strongest houses must crumble to ruin in time, but a grotto in the living rock will last forever. It is an imposture—this grotto stuff—but it is one that all men ought to thank the Catholics for. Wherever they ferret out a lost locality made holy by some Scriptural event, they straightway build a massive—almost imperishable—church there, and preserve the memory of that locality for the gratification of future generations. If it had been left to Protestants to do this most worthy work, we would not even know where Jerusalem is to-day, and the man who could go and put his finger on Nazareth would be too wise for this world. The world owes the Catholics its good will even for the happy rascality of hewing out these bogus grottoes in the rock; for it is infinitely more satisfactory to look at a grotto, where people have faithfully believed for centuries that the Virgin once lived, than to have to imagine a dwelling-place for her somewhere, any where, nowhere, loose and at large all over this town of Nazareth. There is too large a scope of country. The imagination can not work. There is no one particular spot to chain your eye, rivet your interest, and make you think. The memory of the Pilgrims can not perish while Plymouth Rock remains to us. The old monks are wise. They know how to drive a stake through a pleasant tradition that will hold it to its place forever.

We visited the places where Jesus worked for fifteen years as a carpenter, and where he attempted to teach in the synagogue and was driven out by a mob. Catholic chapels stand upon these sites and protect the little fragments of the ancient walls which remain. Our pilgrims broke off specimens. We visited, also, a new chapel, in the midst of the town, which is built around a boulder some twelve feet long by four feet thick; the priests discovered, a few years ago, that the disciples had sat upon this rock to rest, once, when they had walked up from Capernaum. They hastened to preserve the relic. Relics are very good property. Travelers are expected to pay for seeing them, and they do it cheerfully. We like the idea. One's conscience can never be the worse for the knowledge that he has paid his way like a man. Our pilgrims would have liked very well to get out their lampblack and stencil-plates and paint their names on that rock, together with the names of the villages they hail from in America, but the priests permit nothing of that kind. To speak the strict truth, however, our party seldom offend in that way, though we have men in the ship who never lose an opportunity to do it. Our pilgrims' chief sin is their lust for "specimens." I suppose that by this time they know the dimensions of that rock to an inch, and its weight to a ton; and I do not hesitate to charge that they will go back there to-night and try to carry it off.

This "Fountain of the Virgin" is the one which tradition says Mary used to get water from, twenty times a day, when she was a girl, and bear it away in a jar upon her head. The water streams through faucets in the face of a wall of ancient masonry which stands removed from the houses of the village. The young girls of Nazareth still collect about it by the dozen and keep up a riotous laughter and sky-larking. The Nazarene girls are homely. Some of them have large, lustrous eyes, but none of them have pretty faces. These girls wear a single garment, usually, and it is loose, shapeless, of undecided color; it is generally out of repair, too. They wear, from crown to jaw, curious strings of old coins, after the manner of the belles of Tiberias, and brass jewelry upon their wrists and in their ears. They wear no shoes and stockings. They are the most human girls we have found in the country yet, and the best natured. But there is no question that these picturesque maidens sadly lack comeliness.

A pilgrim—the "Enthusiast"—said: "See that tall, graceful girl! look at the Madonna-like beauty of her countenance!"

Another pilgrim came along presently and said: "Observe that tall, graceful girl; what queenly Madonna-like gracefulness of beauty is in her countenance."

I said: "She is not tall, she is short; she is not beautiful, she is homely; she is graceful enough, I grant, but she is rather boisterous."

The third and last pilgrim moved by, before long, and he said: "Ah, what a tall, graceful girl! what Madonna-like gracefulness of queenly beauty!"

The verdicts were all in. It was time, now, to look up the authorities for all these opinions. I found this paragraph, which follows. Written by whom? Wm. C. Grimes:

> "After we were in the saddle, we rode down to the spring to have a last look at the women of Nazareth, who were, as a class, much the prettiest that we had seen in the East. As we approached the crowd a tall girl of nineteen advanced toward Miriam and offered her a cup of water. Her movement was graceful and queenly. We exclaimed on the spot at the Madonna-like beauty of her countenance. Whitely was suddenly thirsty, and begged for water, and drank it slowly, with his eyes over the top of the cup, fixed on her large black eyes, which gazed on him quite as curiously as he on her. Then Moreright wanted water. She gave it to him and he managed to spill it so as to ask for another cup, and by the time she came to me she saw through the operation; her eyes were full of fun as she looked at me. I laughed outright, and she joined me in as gay a shout as ever country maiden in old Orange county. I wished for a picture of her. A Madonna, whose face was a portrait of that beautiful Nazareth girl, would be a 'thing of beauty' and 'a joy forever.'"

That is the kind of gruel which has been served out from Palestine for ages. Commend me to Fennimore Cooper to find beauty in the Indians, and to Grimes to find it in the Arabs. Arab men are often fine looking, but Arab women are not. We can all believe that the Virgin Mary was beautiful; it is not natural to think otherwise; but does it follow that it is our duty to find beauty in these present women of Nazareth?

I love to quote from Grimes, because he is so dramatic. And because he is so romantic. And because he seems to care but little whether he tells the truth or not, so he scares the reader or excites his envy or his admiration.

He went through this peaceful land with one hand forever on his revolver, and the other on his pocket-handkerchief. Always, when he was not on the point of crying over a holy place, he was on the point of killing an Arab. More surprising things happened to him in Palestine than ever happened to any traveler here or elsewhere since Munchausen died. . . .

Chapter 51

Nazareth is wonderfully interesting because the town has an air about it of being precisely as Jesus left it, and one finds himself saying, all the time, "The boy Jesus has stood in this doorway—has played in that street—has touched these stones with his hands—has rambled over these chalky hills." Whoever shall write the Boyhood of Jesus ingeniously, will make a book which will possess a vivid interest for young and old alike. I judge so from the greater interest we found in Nazareth than any of our speculations upon Capernaum and the Sea of Galilee gave rise to. It was not possible, standing by the Sea of Galilee, to frame more than a vague, far-away idea of the majestic Personage who walked upon the crested waves as if they had been solid earth, and who touched the dead and they rose up and spoke. I read among my notes, now, with a new interest, some sentences from an edition of 1621 of the Apocryphal New Testament. [Extract.]

> "Christ, kissed by a bride made dumb by sorcerers, cures her. A leprous girl cured by the water in which the infant Christ was washed, and becomes the servant of Joseph and Mary. The leprous son of a Prince cured in like manner.
>
> "A young man who had been bewitched and turned into a mule, miraculously cured by the infant Saviour being put on his back, and is married to the girl who had been cured of leprosy. Whereupon the bystanders praise God.
>
> "Chapter 16. Christ miraculously widens or contracts gates, milk-pails, sieves or boxes, not properly made by Joseph, he not being skillful at his carpenter's trade. The King of Jerusalem gives Joseph an order for a throne. Joseph works on it for two years and makes it two spans too short. The King being angry with him, Jesus comforts him—commands him to pull one side of the throne while he pulls the other, and brings it to its proper dimensions.
>
> "Chapter 19. Jesus, charged with throwing a boy from the roof of a house, miraculously causes the dead boy to speak and acquit him; fetches water for his mother, breaks the pitcher and miraculously gathers the water in his mantle and brings it home.
>
> "Sent to a schoolmaster, refuses to tell his letters, and the schoolmaster going to whip him, his hand withers."

Further on in this quaint volume of rejected gospels is an epistle of St. Clement to the Corinthians, which was used in the churches and considered genuine fourteen or fifteen hundred years ago. In it this account of the fabled phoenix occurs:

> "1. Let us consider that wonderful type of the resurrection, which is seen in the Eastern countries, that is to say, in Arabia.
>
> "2. There is a certain bird called a phoenix. Of this there is never but one at a time, and that lives five hundred years. And when the time of its dissolution draws near, that it must die, it makes itself a nest of frankincense, and myrrh, and other spices, into which, when its time is fulfilled, it enters and dies.
>
> "3. But its flesh, putrefying, breeds a certain worm, which, being nourished by the juice of the dead bird, brings forth feathers; and when it is grown to a perfect state, it takes up the nest in which the bones of its parent lie, and carries it from Arabia into Egypt, to a city called Heliopolis:
>
> "4. And flying in open day in the sight of all men, lays it upon the altar of the sun, and so returns from whence it came.
>
> "5. The priests then search into the records of the time, and find that it returned precisely at the end of five hundred years."

Business is business, and there is nothing like punctuality, especially in a phoenix.

The few chapters relating to the infancy of the Saviour contain many things which seem frivolous and not worth preserving. A large part of the remaining portions of the book read like good Scripture, however. There is one verse that ought not to have been rejected, because it so evidently prophetically refers to the general run of Congresses of the United States:

> "199. They carry themselves high, and as prudent men; and though they are fools, yet would seem to be teachers."

I have set these extracts down, as I found them. Every where, among the cathedrals of France and Italy, one finds traditions of personages that do not figure in the Bible, and of miracles that are not mentioned in its pages. But they are all in this Apocryphal New Testament, and though they have been ruled out of our modern Bible, it is claimed that they were accepted gospel twelve or fifteen centuries ago, and ranked as high in credit as any. One needs to read this book before he visits those venerable cathedrals, with their treasures of tabooed and forgotten tradition. . . .

Chapter 53

The population of Jerusalem is composed of Moslems, Jews, Greeks, Latins, Armenians, Syrians, Copts, Abyssinians, Greek Catholics, and a handful of Protestants. One hundred of the latter sect are all that dwell now in this birthplace of Christianity. The nice shades of nationality comprised in the above list, and the languages spoken by them, are altogether too numerous to mention. It seems to me that all the races and colors and tongues of the earth must be represented among the fourteen thousand souls that dwell in Jerusalem. Rags, wretchedness, poverty and dirt, those signs and symbols that indicate the presence of Moslem rule more surely than the crescent-flag itself, abound. Lepers, cripples, the blind, and the idiotic, assail you on every hand, and they know but one word of but one language apparently—the eternal "bucksheesh." To see the numbers of maimed, malformed and diseased humanity that throng the holy places and obstruct the gates, one might suppose that the ancient days had come again, and that the angel of the Lord was expected to descend at any moment to stir the waters of Bethesda. Jerusalem is mournful, and dreary, and lifeless. I would not desire to live here.

One naturally goes first to the Holy Sepulchre. It is right in the city, near the western gate; it and the place of the Crucifixion, and, in fact, every other place intimately connected with that tremendous event, are ingeniously massed together and covered by one roof—the dome of the Church of the Holy Sepulchre.

Entering the building, through the midst of the usual assemblage of beggars, one sees on his left a few Turkish guards—for Christians of different sects will not only quarrel, but fight, also, in this sacred place, if allowed to do it. Before you is a marble slab, which covers the Stone of Unction, whereon the Saviour's body was laid to prepare it for burial. It was found necessary to conceal the real stone in this way in order to save it from destruction. Pilgrims were too much given to chipping off pieces of it to carry home. Near by is a circular railing which marks the spot where the Virgin stood when the Lord's body was anointed.

Entering the great Rotunda, we stand before the most sacred locality in Christendom—the grave of Jesus. It is in the centre of the church, and immediately under the great dome. It is inclosed in a sort of little temple of yellow and white stone, of fanciful design. Within the little temple is a portion of the very stone which was rolled away from the door of the Sepulchre, and on which the angel was sitting when Mary came thither "at early dawn." Stooping low, we enter the vault—the Sepulchre itself. It is only about six feet by seven, and the stone couch on which the dead Saviour lay extends from end to end of the apartment and occupies half its width. It is covered with a marble slab which has been much worn by the lips of pilgrims. This slab serves as an altar, now. Over it hang some fifty gold and silver lamps, which are kept always burning, and the place is otherwise scandalized by trumpery gewgaws and tawdry ornamentation.

All sects of Christians (except Protestants,) have chapels under the roof of the Church of the Holy Sepulchre, and each must keep to itself and not venture upon another's ground. It has been proven conclusively that they can not worship together around the grave of the Saviour of the World in peace. The chapel of the Syrians is not handsome; that of the Copts is the humblest of them all. It is nothing but a dismal cavern, roughly hewn in the living rock of the Hill of Calvary. In one side of it two ancient tombs are hewn, which are claimed to be those in which Nicodemus and Joseph of Aramathea were buried.

As we moved among the great piers and pillars of another part of the church, we came upon a party of black-robed, animal-looking Italian monks, with candles in their hands, who were chanting something in Latin, and going through some kind of religious performance around a disk of white marble let into the floor. It was there that the risen Saviour appeared to Mary Magdalen in the likeness of a gardener. Near by was a similar stone, shaped like a star—here the Magdalen herself stood, at the same time. Monks were performing in this place also. They perform every where—all over the vast building, and at all hours. Their candles are always flitting about in the gloom, and making the dim old church more dismal than there is any necessity that it should be, even though it is a tomb.

We were shown the place where our Lord appeared to His mother after the Resurrection. Here, also, a marble slab marks the place where St. Helena, the mother of the Emperor Constantine, found the crosses about three hundred years after the Crucifixion. According to the legend, this great discovery elicited extravagant demonstrations of joy. But they were of short duration. The question intruded itself: "Which bore the blessed Saviour, and which the thieves?" To be in doubt, in so mighty a matter as this—to be uncertain which one to adore—was a grievous misfortune. It turned the public joy to sorrow. But when lived there a holy priest who could not set so simple a trouble as this at rest? One of these soon hit upon a plan that would be a certain test. A noble lady lay very ill in Jerusalem. The wise priests ordered that the three crosses be taken to her bedside one at a time. It was done. When her eyes fell upon the first one, she uttered a scream that was heard beyond the Damascus Gate, and even upon the Mount of Olives, it was said, and then fell back in a deadly swoon. They recovered her and brought the second cross. Instantly she went into fearful convulsions, and it was with the greatest difficulty that six strong men could hold her. They were afraid, now, to bring in the third cross. They began to fear that possibly they had fallen upon the wrong crosses, and that the true cross was not with this number at all. However, as the woman seemed likely to die with the convulsions that were tearing her, they concluded that the third could do no more than put her out of her misery with a happy dispatch. So they brought it, and behold, a miracle! The woman sprang from her bed, smiling and joyful, and perfectly restored to health. When we listen to evidence like this, we can not but believe. We would be ashamed to doubt, and properly, too. Even the very part of Jerusalem where this all occurred is there yet. So there is really no room for doubt.

The priests tried to show us, through a small screen, a fragment of the genuine Pillar of Flagellation, to which Christ was bound when they scourged him. But we could not see it, because it was dark inside the screen. However, a baton is kept here, which the pilgrim thrusts through a hole in the screen, and then he no longer doubts that the true Pillar of Flagellation is in there. He can not have any excuse to doubt it, for he can feel it with the stick. He can feel it as distinctly as he could feel any thing.

Not far from here was a niche where they used to preserve a piece of the True Cross, but it is gone, now. This piece of the cross was discovered in the sixteenth century. The Latin priests say it was stolen away, long ago, by priests of another sect. That seems like a hard statement to make, but we know very well that it *was* stolen, because we have seen it ourselves in several of the cathedrals of Italy and France. . . .

But the feature of the place is a short column that rises from the middle of the marble pavement of the chapel, and marks the exact *centre of the earth.* The most reliable traditions tell us that this was known to be the earth's centre, ages ago, and that when Christ was upon earth he set all doubts upon the subject at rest forever, by stating with his own lips that the tradition was correct. Remember, He said that that particular column stood upon the centre of the world. If the centre of the world changes, the column changes its position accordingly. This column has moved three different times, of its own accord. This is because, in great convulsions of nature, at three different times, masses of the earth—whole ranges of mountains, probably—have flown off into space, thus lessening the diameter of the earth, and changing the exact locality of its centre by a point or two. This is a very curious and interesting circumstance, and is a withering rebuke to those philosophers who would make us believe that it is not possible for any portion of the earth to fly off into space.

To satisfy himself that this spot was really the centre of the earth, a sceptic once paid well for the privilege of ascending to the dome of the church to see if the sun gave him a shadow at noon. He came down perfectly convinced. The day was very cloudy and the sun threw no shadows at all; but the man was satisfied that if the sun had come out and made shadows it could not have made any for him. Proofs like these are not to be set aside by the idle tongues of cavilers. To such as are not bigoted, and are willing to be convinced, they carry a conviction that nothing can ever shake.

If even greater proofs than those I have mentioned are wanted, to satisfy the headstrong and the foolish that this is the genuine centre of the earth, they are here. The greatest of them lies in the fact that from under this very column was taken the *dust from which Adam was made.* This can surely be regarded in the light of a settler. It is not likely that the original first man would have been made from an inferior quality of earth when it was entirely convenient to get

THE GRAVE OF ADAM.

first quality from the world's centre. This will strike any reflecting mind forcibly. That Adam was formed of dirt procured in this very spot is amply proven by the fact that in six thousand years no man has ever been able to prove that the dirt was *not* procured here whereof he was made.

It is a singular circumstance that right under the roof of this same great church, and not far away from that illustrious column, Adam himself, the father of the human race, lies buried. There is no question that he is actually buried in the grave which is pointed out as his—there can be none—because it has never yet been proven that that grave is not the grave in which he is buried.

The tomb of Adam! How touching it was, here in a land of strangers, far away from home, and friends, and all who cared for me, thus to discover the grave of a blood relation. True, a distant one, but still a relation. The unerring instinct of nature thrilled its recognition. The fountain of my filial affection was stirred to its profoundest depths, and I gave way to tumultuous emotion. I leaned upon a pillar and burst into tears. I deem it no shame to have wept over the grave of my poor dead relative. Let him who would sneer at my emotion close this volume here, for he will find little to his taste in my journeyings through Holy Land. Noble old man—he did not live to see me—he did not live to see his child. And I—I—alas, I did not live to see *him*. Weighed down by sorrow and disappointment, he died before I was born—six thousand brief summers before I was born. But let us try to bear it with fortitude. Let us trust that he is better off, where he is. Let us take comfort in the thought that his loss is our eternal gain.

The next place the guide took us to in the holy church was an altar dedicated to the Roman soldier who was of the military guard that attended at the crucifixion to keep order, and who—when the vail of the Temple was rent in the awful darkness that followed; when the rock of Golgotha was split asunder by an earthquake; when the artillery of heaven thundered, and in the baleful glare of the lightnings the shrouded dead flitted about the streets of Jerusalem—shook with fear and said, "Surely this was the Son of God!" Where this altar stands now, that Roman soldier stood then, in full view of the crucified Saviour—in full sight and hearing of all the marvels that were transpiring far and wide about the circumference of the Hill of Calvary. And in this self-same spot the priests of the Temple beheaded him for those blasphemous words he had spoken.

In this altar they used to keep one of the most curious relics that human eyes ever looked upon—a thing that had power to fascinate the beholder in some mysterious way and keep him gazing for hours together. It was nothing less than the copper plate Pilate put upon the Saviour's cross, and upon which he wrote, "This is the King of the Jews." I think St. Helena, the mother of Constantine, found this wonderful memento when she was here in the third century. She traveled all over Palestine, and was always fortunate. Whenever the good old enthusiast found a thing mentioned in her Bible, Old or New, she would go and search for that thing, and never stop until she found it. If it was

Adam, she would find Adam; if it was the Ark, she would find the Ark; if it was Goliah, or Joshua, she would find *them*. She found the inscription here that I was speaking of, I think. She found it in this very spot, close to where the martyred Roman soldier stood. That copper plate is in one of the churches in Rome, now. Any one can see it there. The inscription is very distinct.

We passed along a few steps and saw the altar built over the very spot where the good Catholic priests say the soldiers divided the raiment of the Saviour.

Then we went down into a cavern which cavilers say was once a cistern. It is a chapel, now, however—the Chapel of St. Helena. It is fifty-one feet long by forty-three wide. In it is a marble chair which Helena used to sit in while she superintended her workmen when they were digging and delving for the True Cross. In this place is an altar dedicated to St. Dimas, the penitent thief. A new bronze statue is here—a statue of St. Helena. It reminded us of poor Maximilian, so lately shot. He presented it to this chapel when he was about to leave for his throne in Mexico.

From the cistern we descended twelve steps into a large roughly-shaped grotto, carved wholly out of the living rock. Helena blasted it out when she was searching for the true cross. She had a laborious piece of work, here, but it was richly rewarded. Out of this place she got the crown of thorns, the nails of the cross, the true cross itself, and the cross of the penitent thief. When she thought she had found every thing and was about to stop, she was told in a dream to continue a day longer. It was very fortunate. She did so, and found the cross of the other thief.

The walls and roof of this grotto still weep bitter tears in memory of the event that transpired on Calvary, and devout pilgrims groan and sob when these sad tears fall upon them from the dripping rock. The monks call this apartment the "Chapel of the Invention of the Cross"—a name which is unfortunate, because it leads the ignorant to imagine that a tacit acknowledgment is thus made that the tradition that Helena found the true cross here is a fiction—an invention. It is a happiness to know, however, that intelligent people do not doubt the story in any of its particulars.

Priests of any of the chapels and denominations in the Church of the Holy Sepulchre can visit this sacred grotto to weep and pray and worship the gentle Redeemer. Two different congregations are not allowed to enter at the same time, however, because they always fight.

Still marching through the venerable Church of the Holy Sepulchre, among chanting priests in coarse long robes and sandals; pilgrims of all colors and many nationalities, in all sorts of strange costumes; under dusky arches and by dingy piers and columns; through a sombre cathedral gloom freighted with smoke and incense, and faintly starred with scores of candles that appeared suddenly and as suddenly disappeared, or drifted mysteriously hither and thither about the distant aisles like ghostly jack o'-lanterns—we came at last to a small chapel which is called the "Chapel of the Mocking." Under the altar was a fragment of a marble column; this was the seat Christ sat on when he was reviled, and mockingly made King, crowned with a crown of thorns and sceptred with a reed. It was here that they blindfolded him and struck him, and said in derision, "Prophesy who it is that smote thee." The tradition that this is the identical spot of the mocking is a very ancient one. The guide said that Saewulf was the first to mention it. I do not know Saewulf, but still, I can not well refuse to receive his evidence—none of us can. . . .

When one enters the Church of the Holy Sepulchre, the Sepulchre itself is the first thing he desires to see, and really is almost the first thing he does see. The next thing he has a strong yearning to see is the spot where the Saviour was crucified. But this they exhibit last. It is the crowning glory of the place. One is grave and thoughtful when he stands in the little Tomb of the Saviour—he could not well be otherwise in such a place—but he has not the slightest possible belief that ever the Lord lay there, and so the interest he feels in the spot is very, very greatly marred by that reflection. He looks at the place where Mary stood, in another part of the church, and where John stood, and Mary Magdalen; where the mob derided the Lord; where the angel sat; where the crown of thorns was found, and the true cross; where the risen Saviour appeared—he looks at all these places with interest, but with the same conviction he felt in the case of the Sepulchre, that there is nothing genuine about them, and that they are imaginary holy places created by the monks. But the place of the Crucifixion affects him differently. He fully believes that he is looking upon the very spot where the Saviour gave up his life. He remembers that Christ was very celebrated, long before he came to Jerusalem; he knows that his fame was so great that crowds followed him all the time; he is aware that his entry into the city produced a stirring sensation, and that his reception was a kind of ovation; he can not overlook the fact that when he was crucified there were very many in Jerusalem who believed that he was the true Son of God. To publicly execute such a personage was sufficient in itself to make the locality of the execution a memorable place for ages; added to this, the storm, the darkness, the earthquake, the rending of the vail of the Temple, and the untimely waking of the dead, were events calculated to fix the execution and the scene of it in the memory of even the most thoughtless witness. Fathers would tell their sons about the strange affair, and point out the spot; the sons would transmit the story to their children, and thus a period of three hundred years would easily be spanned*—at which time Helena came and built a church upon Calvary to commemorate the death and burial of the Lord and preserve the sacred place in the memories of men; since that time there has always been a church there. It is not possible that there can be any mistake about the locality of the Crucifixion. Not half a dozen persons knew where they buried the Saviour, perhaps, and a burial is not a startling event, any how; therefore, we can be pardoned

*The thought is Mr. Prime's, not mine, and is full of good sense. I borrowed it from his "Tent Life."—M.T.

for unbelief in the Sepulchre, but not in the place of the Crucifixion. Five hundred years hence there will be no vestige of Bunker Hill Monument left, but America will still know where the battle was fought and where Warren fell. The crucifixion of Christ was too notable an event in Jerusalem, and the Hill of Calvary made too celebrated by it, to be forgotten in the short space of three hundred years. I climbed the stairway in the church which brings one to the top of the small inclosed pinnacle of rock, and looked upon the place where the true cross once stood, with a far more absorbing interest than I had ever felt in any thing earthly before. I could not believe that the three holes in the top of the rock were the actual ones the crosses stood in, but I felt satisfied that those crosses had stood so near the place now occupied by them, that the few feet of possible difference were a matter of no consequence.

When one stands where the Saviour was crucified, he finds it all he can do to keep it strictly before his mind that Christ was not crucified in a Catholic Church. He must remind himself every now and then that the great event transpired in the open air, and not in a gloomy, candle-lighted cell in a little corner of a vast church, up-stairs—a small cell all bejeweled and bespangled with flashy ornamentation, in execrable taste.

Under a marble altar like a table, is a circular hole in the marble floor, corresponding with the one just under it in which the true cross stood. The first thing every one does is to kneel down and take a candle and examine this hole. He does this strange prospecting with an amount of gravity that can never be estimated or appreciated by a man who has not seen the operation. Then he holds his candle before a richly engraved picture of the Saviour, done on a massy slab of gold, and wonderfully rayed and starred with diamonds, which hangs above the hole within the altar, and his solemnity changes to lively admiration. He rises and faces the finely wrought figures of the Saviour and the malefactors uplifted upon their crosses behind the altar, and bright with a metallic lustre of many colors. He turns next to the figures close to them of the Virgin and Mary Magdalen; next to the rift in the living rock made by the earthquake at the time of the Crucifixion, and an extension of which he had seen before in the wall of one of the grottoes below; he looks next at the show-case with a figure of the Virgin in it, and is amazed at the princely fortune in precious gems and jewelry that hangs so thickly about the form as to hide it like a garment almost. All about the apartment the gaudy trappings of the Greek Church offend the eye and keep the mind on the rack to remember that this is the Place of the Crucifixion—Golgotha—the Mount of Calvary. And the last thing he looks at is that which was also the first—the place where the true cross stood. That will chain him to the spot and compel him to look once more, and once again, after he has satisfied all curiosity and lost all interest concerning the other matters pertaining to the locality.

And so I close my chapter on the Church of the Holy Sepulchre—the most sacred locality on earth to millions and millions of men, and women, and children, the noble and the humble, bond and free. In its history from the first, and in its tremendous associations, it is the most illustrious edifice in Christendom. With all its clap-trap side-shows and unseemly impostures of every kind, it is still grand, reverend, venerable—for a god died there; for fifteen hundred years its shrines have been wet with the tears of pilgrims from the earth's remotest confines; for more than two hundred, the most gallant knights that ever wielded sword wasted their lives away in a struggle to seize it and hold it sacred from infidel pollution. Even in our own day a war, that cost millions of treasure and rivers of blood, was fought because two rival nations claimed the sole right to put a new dome upon it. History is full of this old Church of the Holy Sepulchre—full of blood that was shed because of the respect and the veneration in which men held the last resting-place of the meek and lowly, the mild and gentle, Prince of Peace!

Chapter 54

We were standing in a narrow street, by the Tower of Antonio. "On these stones that are crumbling away," the guide said, "the Saviour sat and rested before taking up the cross. This is the beginning of the Sorrowful Way, or the Way of Grief." The party took note of the sacred spot, and moved on. We passed under the "Ecce Homo Arch," and saw the very window from which Pilate's wife warned her husband to have nothing to do with the persecution of the Just Man. This window is in an excellent state of preservation, considering its great age. They showed us where Jesus rested the second time, and where the mob refused to give him up, and said, "Let his blood be upon our heads, and upon our children's children forever." The French Catholics are building a church on this spot, and with their usual veneration for historical relics, are incorporating into the new such scraps of ancient walls as they have found there. Further on, we saw the spot where the fainting Saviour fell under the weight of his cross. A great granite column of some ancient temple lay there at the time, and the heavy cross struck it such a blow that it broke in two in the middle. Such was the guide's story when he halted us before the broken column.

We crossed a street, and came presently to the former residence of St. Veronica. When the Saviour passed there, she came out, full of womanly compassion, and spoke pitying words to him, undaunted by the hootings and the threatenings of the mob, and wiped the perspiration from his face with her handkerchief. We had heard so much of St. Veronica, and seen her picture by so many masters, that it was like meeting an old friend unexpectedly to come upon her ancient home in Jerusalem. The strangest thing about the incident that has made her name so famous, is, that when she wiped the perspiration away, the print of the Saviour's face remained upon the handkerchief, a perfect portrait, and so remains unto this day. We knew this, because we saw this handkerchief in a cathedral in Paris, in another in Spain, and in two others in Italy. In the Milan cathedral it costs five francs to see it, and at St. Peter's, at

Rome, it is almost impossible to see it at any price. No tradition is so amply verified as this of St. Veronica and her handkerchief.

At the next corner we saw a deep indention in the hard stone masonry of the corner of a house, but might have gone heedlessly by it but that the guide said it was made by the elbow of the Saviour, who stumbled here and fell. Presently we came to just such another indention in a stone wall. The guide said the Saviour fell here, also, and made this depression with his elbow.

There were other places where the Lord fell, and others where he rested; but one of the most curious landmarks of ancient history we found on this morning walk through the crooked lanes that lead toward Calvary, was a certain stone built into a house—a stone that was so seamed and scarred that it bore a sort of grotesque resemblance to the human face. The projections that answered for cheeks were worn smooth by the passionate kisses of generations of pilgrims from distant lands. We asked "Why?" The guide said it was because this was one of "the very stones of Jerusalem" that Christ mentioned when he was reproved for permitting the people to cry "Hosannah!" when he made his memorable entry into the city upon an ass. One of the pilgrims said, "But there is no evidence that the stones *did* cry out—Christ said that if the people stopped from shouting Hosannah, the very stones *would* do it." The guide was perfectly serene. He said, calmly, "This is one of the stones that *would* have cried out." It was of little use to try to shake this fellow's simple faith—it was easy to see that. . . .

Conclusion

I have no fault to find with the manner in which our excursion was conducted. Its programme was faithfully carried out—a thing which surprised me, for great enterprises usually promise vastly more than they perform. It would be well if such an excursion could be gotten up every year and the system regularly inaugurated. Travel is fatal to prejudice, bigotry and narrow-mindedness, and many of our people need it sorely on these accounts. Broad, wholesome, charitable views of men and things can not be acquired by vegetating in one little corner of the earth all one's lifetime. . . .

Roughing It

In Roughing It *(1872) Twain narrates the adventures of his western wanderings. He left "civilization" in St. Louis and traveled, primarily by stagecoach, to Virginia City. The landscape and incidents along the way make up a significant portion of the story. The Virginia City Twain knew was caught up in the frenzy of silver and gold mining. After repeated disappointments in his attempts to strike it rich, he continued his adventures in the exploration of San Francisco and Hawaii. Twain claims that he originally planned a three-month sojourn, but actually spent seven years in these travels.*

The author's skepticism appears as early as Chapter I, where he creates a contrast between his imagination in anticipation of the trip and its reality. Repeatedly Twain stresses the differences between the literary descriptions of Indians, famous places, etc., and the actuality he perceives.

The book possesses a combination of forms: travel narration, description, history, anecdotes, and yarns. The story of the camel is a perfect example of a tall tale, with the added appeal of a metafictional ending. The story of Bemis and the buffalo reveals a root for skepticism—not in abstraction, but in the folk experience. In addition, the story of the coyote provides an allegory of the contrast between the green horn (the dog) and the veteran.

The ramshackle organization of the book permits Twain to comment upon almost any topic, from Mormonism to the American jury system. His views of a ship captain's argumentative style indicate Twain's keen social sense, as well as the desire for proof.

Chapter 1

My brother had just been appointed Secretary of Nevada Territory—an office of such majesty that it concentrated in itself the duties and dignities of Treasurer,

Comptroller, Secretary of State, and Acting Governor in the Governor's absence. A salary of eighteen hundred dollars a year and the title of "Mr. Secretary," gave to the great position an air of wild and imposing grandeur. I was young and ignorant, and I envied my brother. I coveted his distinction and his financial splendor, but particularly and especially the long, strange journey he was going to make, and the curious new world he was going to explore. He was going to travel! I never had been away from home, and that word "travel" had a seductive charm for me. Pretty soon he would be hundreds and hundreds of miles away on the great plains and deserts, and among the mountains of the Far West, and would see buffaloes and Indians, and prairie dogs, and antelopes, and have all kinds of adventures, and maybe get hanged or scalped, and have ever such a fine time, and write home and tell us all about it, and be a hero. And he would see the gold mines and the silver mines, and maybe go about of an afternoon when his work was done, and pick up two or three pailfuls of shining slugs, and nuggets of gold and silver on the hillside. And by and by he would become very rich, and return home by sea, and be able to talk as calmly about San Francisco and the ocean, and "the Isthmus" as if it was nothing of any consequence to have seen those marvels face to face. What I suffered in contemplating his happiness, pen cannot describe. And so, when he offered me, in cold blood, the sublime position of private secretary under him, it appeared to me that the heavens and the earth passed away, and the firmament was rolled together as a scroll! I had nothing more to desire. My contentment was complete. At the end of an hour or two I was ready for the journey. Not much packing up was necessary, because we were going in the overland stage from the Missouri frontier to Nevada, and passengers were only allowed a small quantity of baggage apiece. There was no Pacific railroad in those fine times of ten or twelve years ago—not a single rail of it.

I only proposed to stay in Nevada three months—I had no thought of staying longer than that. I meant to see all I could that was new and strange, and then hurry home to business. I little thought that I would not see the end of that three-month pleasure excursion for six or seven uncommonly long years!

I dreamed all night about Indians, deserts, and silver bars, and in due time, next day, we took shipping at the St. Louis wharf on board a steamboat bound up the Missouri River.

We were six days going from St. Louis to "St. Joe"—a trip that was so dull, and sleepy, and eventless that it has left no more impression on my memory than if its duration had been six minutes instead of that many days. No record is left in my mind, now, concerning it, but a confused jumble of savage-looking snags, which we deliberately walked over with one wheel or the other; and of reefs which we butted and butted, and then retired from and climbed over in some softer place; and of sand-bars which we roosted on occasionally, and rested, and then got out our crutches and sparred over. In fact, the boat might almost as well have gone to St. Joe by land, for she was walking most of the time, anyhow—climbing over reefs and clambering over snags patiently and laboriously all day long. The captain said she was a "bully" boat, and all she wanted was more "shear" and a bigger wheel. I thought she wanted a pair of stilts, but I had the deep sagacity not to say so.

Chapter 3

. . . Sage-brush is very fair fuel, but as a vegetable it is a distinguished failure. Nothing can abide the taste of it but the jackass and his illegitimate child the mule. But their testimony to its nutritiousness is worth nothing, for they will eat pine knots, or anthracite coal, or brass filings, or lead pipe, or old bottles, or anything that comes handy, and then go off looking as grateful as if they had had oysters for dinner. Mules and donkeys and camels have appetites that anything will relieve temporarily, but nothing satisfy. In Syria, once, at the head-waters of the Jordan, a camel took charge of my overcoat while the tents were being pitched, and examined it with a critical eye, all over, with as much interest as if he had an idea of getting one made like it; and then, after he was done figuring on it as an article of apparel, he began to contemplate it as an article of diet. He put his foot on it, and lifted one of the sleeves out with his teeth, and chewed and chewed at it, gradually taking it in, and all the while opening and closing his eyes in a kind of religious ecstasy, as if he had never tasted anything as good as an overcoat before, in his life. Then he smacked his lips once or twice, and reached after the other sleeve. Next he tried the velvet collar, and smiled a smile of such contentment that it was plain to see that he regarded that as the daintiest thing about an overcoat. The tails went next, along with some percussion caps and cough candy, and some fig-paste from Constantinople. And then my newspaper correspondence dropped out, and he took a chance in that—manuscript letters written for the home papers. But he was treading on dangerous ground, now. He began to come across solid wisdom in those documents that was rather weighty on his stomach; and occasionally he would take a joke that would shake him up till it loosened his teeth; it was getting to be perilous times with him, but he held his grip with good courage and hopefully, till at last he began to stumble on statements that not even a camel could swallow with impunity. He began to gag and gasp, and his eyes to stand out, and his forelegs to spread, and in about a quarter of a minute he fell over as stiff as a carpenter's work-bench, and died a death of indescribable agony. I went and pulled the manuscript out of his mouth, and found that the sensitive creature had choked to death on one of the mildest and gentlest statements of fact that I ever laid before a trusting public. . . .

Chapter 5

. . . Along about an hour after breakfast we saw the first prairie-dog villages, the first antelope, and the first wolf. If I remember rightly, this latter was the regular *cayote* (pronounced ky-*o*-te) of the farthest deserts. And if it *was,* he was not a pretty creature or respectable either, for I got well acquainted with his race afterward, and can speak with confidence. The cayote is a long, slim, sick and sorry-looking skeleton with a gray wolf-skin stretched over it, a tolerably bush tail that forever sags down with a despairing expression of forsakenness and misery, a furtive and evil eye, and a long, sharp face, with slightly lifted lip and exposed teeth. He has a general slinking expression all over. The cayote is a living, breathing allegory of Want. He is *always* hungry. He is always poor, out of luck and friendless. The meanest creatures despise him, and even the fleas would desert him for a velocipede. He is so spiritless and cowardly that even while his exposed teeth are pretending a threat, the rest of his face is apologizing for it. And he is *so* homely!—so scrawny, and ribby, and coarse-haired, and pitiful. When he sees you he lifts his lip and lets a flash of his teeth out, and then turns a little out of the course he was pursuing, depresses his head a bit, and strikes a long, soft-footed trot through the sage-brush, glancing over his shoulder at you, from time to time, till he is about out of easy pistol range, and then he stops and takes a deliberate survey of you; he will trot fifty yards and stop again—another fifty and stop again; and finally the gray of his gliding body blends with the gray of the sage-brush, and he disappears. All this is when you make no demonstration against him; but if you do, he develops a livelier interest in his journey, and instantly electrifies his heels and puts such a deal of real estate between himself and your weapon, that by the time you have raised the hammer you see that you need a minie rifle, and by the time you have got him in line you need a rifled cannon, and by the time you have "drawn a bead" on him you see well enough that nothing but an unusually long-winded streak of lightning could reach him where he is now. But if you start a swift-footed dog after him, you will enjoy it ever so much—especially if it is a dog that has a good opinion of himself, and has been brought up to think he knows something about speed. The cayote will go swinging gently off on that deceitful trot of his, and every little while he will smile a fraudful smile over his shoulder that will fill that dog entirely full of encouragement and worldly ambition, and make him lay his head still lower to the ground, and stretch his neck further to the front, and pant more fiercely, and stick his tail out straighter behind, and move his furious legs with a yet wilder frenzy, and leave a broader and broader, and higher and denser cloud of desert sand smoking behind, and marking his long wake across the level plain! And all this time the dog is only a short twenty feet behind the cayote, and to save the soul of him he cannot understand why it is that he cannot get perceptibly closer; and he begins to get aggravated, and it makes him madder and madder to see how gently the cayote glides along and never pants or sweats or ceases to smile; and he grows still more and more incensed to see how shamefully he has been taken in by an entire stranger, and what an ignoble swindle that long, calm, soft-footed trot is; and next he notices that he is getting fagged, and that the cayote actually has to slacken speed a little to keep from running away from him—and *then* that town-dog is mad in earnest, and he begins to strain and weep and swear, and paw the sand higher than ever, and reach for the cayote with concentrated and desperate energy. This "spurt" finds him six feet behind the gliding enemy, and two miles from his friends. And then, in the instant that a wild new hope is lighting up his face, the cayote turns and smiles blandly upon him once more, and with a something about it which seems to say: "Well, I shall have to tear myself away from you, bub—business is business, and it will not do for me to be fooling along this way all day"—and forthwith there is a rushing sound, and the sudden splitting of a long crack through the atmosphere, and behold that dog is solitary and alone in the midst of a vast solitude!

It makes his head swim. He stops, and looks all around; climbs the nearest sand-mound, and gazes into the distance; shakes his head reflectively, and then, without a word, he turns and jogs along back to his train, and takes up a humble position under the hindmost wagon, and feels unspeakably mean, and looks ashamed, and hangs his tail at half-mast for a week. And for as much as a year after that, whenever there is a great hue and cry after a cayote, that dog will merely glance in that direction without emotion, and apparently observe to himself, "I believe I do not wish any of the pie." . . .

Chapter 7

It did seem strange enough to see a town again after what appeared to us such a long acquaintance with deep, still, almost lifeless and houseless solitude! We tumbled out into the busy street feeling like meteoric people crumbled off the corner of some other world, and wakened up suddenly in this. For an hour we took as much interest in Overland City as if we had never seen a town before. The reason we had an hour to spare was because we had to change our stage (for a less sumptuous affair, called a "mud-wagon") and transfer our freight of mails.

Presently we got under way again. We came to the shallow, yellow, muddy South Platte, with its low banks and its scattering flat sand-bars and pigmy islands—a melancholy stream straggling through the centre of the enormous flat plain, and only saved from being impossible to find with the naked eye by its sentinel rank of scattering trees standing on either bank. The Platte was "up," they said—which made me wish I could see it when it was down, if it could look any sicker and sorrier. They said it was a dangerous stream to cross, now, because its quicksands were liable to swallow up horses, coach and passengers if an attempt was made to ford it. But the mails had to go, and we made the attempt. Once or twice in midstream the wheels sunk into the yielding sands so threateningly that we half believed we had dreaded and avoided the sea all our lives to be shipwrecked in a "mud-wagon" in the middle of a desert at last. But we dragged through and sped away toward the setting sun.

Next morning, just before dawn, when about five hundred and fifty miles from St. Joseph, our mud-wagon broke down. We were to be delayed five or six hours, and therefore we took horses, by invitation, and joined a party who were just starting on a buffalo hunt. It was noble sport galloping over the plain in the dewy freshness of the morning, but our part of the hunt ended in disaster and disgrace, for a wounded buffalo bull chased the passenger Bemis nearly two miles, and then he forsook his horse and took to a lone tree. He was very sullen about the matter for some twenty-four hours, but at last he began to soften little by little, and finally he said:

"Well, it was not funny, and there was no sense in those gawks making themselves so facetious over it. I tell you I was angry in earnest for a while. I should have shot that long gangly lubber they called Hank, if I could have done it without crippling six or seven other people—but of course I couldn't, the old 'Allen's' so confounded comprehensive. I wish those loafers had been up in the tree; they wouldn't have wanted to laugh so. If I had had a horse worth a cent—but no, the minute he saw that buffalo bull wheel on him and give a bellow, he raised straight up in the air and stood on his heels. The saddle began to slip, and I took him round the neck and laid close to him, and began to pray. Then he came down and stood up on the other end a while, and the bull actually stopped pawing sand and bellowing to contemplate the inhuman spectacle. Then the bull made a pass at him and uttered a bellow that sounded perfectly frightful, it was so close to me, and that seemed to literally prostrate my horse's reason, and make a raving distracted maniac of him, and I wish I may die if he didn't stand on his head for a quarter of a minute and shed tears. He was absolutely out of his mind—he was, as sure as truth itself, and he really didn't know what he was doing. Then the bull came charging at us, and my horse dropped down on all fours and took a fresh start—and then for the next ten minutes he would actually throw one hand-spring after another so fast that the bull began to get unsettled, too, and didn't know where to start in—and so he stood there sneezing, and shoveling dust over his back, and bellowing every now and then, and thinking he had got a fifteen-hundred-dollar circus horse for breakfast, certain. Well, I was first out on his neck—the horse's, not the bull's—and then underneath, and next on his rump, and sometimes head up, and sometimes heels—but I tell you it seemed solemn and awful to be ripping and tearing and carrying on so in the presence of death, as you might say. Pretty soon the bull made a snatch for us and brought away some of my horse's tail (I suppose, but do not know, being pretty busy at the time), but *something* made him hungry for solitude and suggested to him to get up and hunt for it. And then you ought to have seen that spider-legged old skeleton go! and you ought to have seen the bull cut out after him, too—head down, tongue out, tail up, bellowing like everything, and actually mowing down the weeds, and tearing up the earth, and boosting up the sand like a whirlwind! By George, it was a hot race! I and the saddle were back on the rump, and I had the bridle in my teeth and holding on to the pommel with both hands. First we left the dogs behind; then we passed a jackass rabbit; then we overtook a cayote, and were gaining on an antelope when the rotten girth let go and threw me about thirty yards off to the left, and as the saddle went down over the horse's rump he gave it a lift with his heels that sent it more than four hundred yards up in the air, I wish I may die in a minute if he didn't. I fell at the foot of the only solitary tree there was in nine counties adjacent (as any creature could see with the naked eye), and the next second I had hold of the bark with four sets of nails and my teeth, and the next second after that I was astraddle of the main limb and blaspheming my luck in a way that made my breath smell of brimstone. I *had* the bull, now, if he did not think of *one* thing. But that one thing I dreaded. I dreaded it very seriously. There was a possibility that the bull might not think of it, but there were greater chances that he would. I made up my mind what I would do in case he did. It was a little over forty feet to the ground from where I sat. I cautiously unwound the lariat from the pommel of my saddle—"

"Your *saddle?* Did you take your saddle up in the tree with you?"

"Take it up in the tree with me? Why, how you talk. Of course I didn't. No man could do that. It *fell* in the tree when it came down."

"Oh—exactly."

"Certainly. I unwound the lariat, and fastened one end of it to the limb. It was the very best green rawhide, and capable of sustaining tons. I made a slip-noose in the other end, and then hung it down to see the length. It reached down twenty-two feet—half way to the ground. I then loaded every barrel of the Allen with a double charge. I felt satisfied. I said to myself, if he never thinks of that one thing that I dread, all right—but if he does, all right anyhow—I am fixed for him. But don't you know that the very thing a man dreads is the thing that always happens? Indeed it is so. I watched the bull, now, with anxiety—anxiety which no one can conceive of who has not been in such a situation and felt that at any moment death might come. Presently a thought came into the bull's eye. I knew it! said I—if my nerve fails now, I am lost. Sure enough, it was just as I had dreaded, he started in to climb the tree—"

"What, the bull?"

"Of course—who else?"

"But a bull can't climb a tree."

"He can't, can't he? Since you know so much about it, did you ever see a bull try?"

"No! I never dreamt of such a thing."

"Well, then, what is the use of your talking that way, then? Because you never saw a thing done, is that any reason why it can't be done?"

"Well, all right—go on. What did you do?"

"The bull started up, and got along well for about ten feet, then slipped and slid back. I breathed easier. He tried it again—got up a little higher—slipped again. But he came at it once more, and this time he was careful. He got gradually higher and higher, and my spirits went down more and more. Up he came—an inch at a time—with his eyes hot, and his tongue hanging out. Higher and higher—hitched his foot over the stump of a limb, and looked up, as much as to say, 'You are my meat, friend.' Up again—higher and higher, and getting more excited the closer he got. He was within ten feet of me! I took a long breath,—and then said I, 'It is now or never.' I had the coil of the lariat all ready; I paid it out slowly, till it hung right over his head; all of a sudden I let go of the slack, and the slip-noose fell fairly round his neck! Quicker than lightning I out with the Allen and let him have it in the face. It was an awful roar, and must have scared the bull out of his senses. When the smoke cleared away, there he was, dangling in the air, twenty foot from the ground, and going out of one convulsion into another faster than you could count! I didn't stop to count, anyhow—I shinned down the tree and shot for home."

"Bemis, is all that true, just as you have stated it?"

"I wish I may rot in my tracks and die the death of a dog if it isn't."

"Well, we can't refuse to believe it, and we don't. But if there were some proofs—"

"Proofs! Did I bring back my lariat?"

"No."

"Did I bring back my horse?"

"No."

"Did you ever see the bull again?"

"No."

"Well, then, what more do you want? I never saw anybody as particular as you are about a little thing like that."

I made up my mind that if this man was not a liar he only missed it by the skin of his teeth. This episode reminds me of an incident of my brief sojourn in Siam, years afterward. The European citizens of a town in the neighborhood of Bangkok had a prodigy among them by the name of Eckert, an Englishman—a person famous for the number, ingenuity and imposing magnitude of his lies. They were always repeating his most celebrated falsehoods, and always trying to "draw him out" before strangers; but they seldom succeeded. Twice he was invited to the house where I was visiting, but nothing could seduce him into a specimen lie. One day a planter named Bascom, an influential man, and a proud and sometimes irascible one, invited me to ride over with him and call on Eckert. As we jogged along, said he:

"Now, do you know where the fault lies? It lies in putting Eckert on his guard. The minute the boys go to pumping at Eckert he knows perfectly well what they are after, and of course he shuts up his shell. Anybody might know he would. But when we get there, we must play him finer than that. Let him shape the conversation to suit himself—let him drop it or change it whenever he wants to. Let him see that nobody is trying to draw him out. Just let him have his own way. He will soon forget himself and begin to grind out lies like a mill. Don't get impatient—just keep quiet, and let me play him. I will make him lie. It does seem to me that the boys must be blind to overlook such an obvious and simple trick as that."

Eckert received us heartily—a pleasant-spoken, gentle-mannered creature.

We sat in the veranda an hour, sipping English ale, and talking about the king, and the sacred white elephant, the Sleeping Idol, and all manner of things; and I noticed that my comrade never led the conversation himself or shaped it, but simply followed Eckert's lead, and betrayed no solicitude and no anxiety about anything. The effect was shortly perceptible. Eckert began to grow communicative; he grew more and more at his ease, and more and more talkative and sociable. Another hour passed in the same way, and then all of a sudden Eckert said:

"Oh, by the way! I came near forgetting. I have got a thing here to astonish you. Such a thing as neither you nor any other man ever heard of—I've got a cat that will eat cocoanut! Common green cocoanut—and not only eat the meat, but drink the milk. It is so—I'll swear to it."

A quick glance from Bascom—a glance that I understood—then:

"Why, bless my soul, I never heard of such a thing. Man, it is impossible."

"I knew you would say it. I'll fetch the cat."

He went in the house. Bascom said:

"There—what did I tell you? Now, that is the way to handle Eckert. You see, I have petted him along patiently, and put his suspicions to sleep. I am glad we came. You tell the boys about it when you go back. Cat eat a cocoanut—oh, my! Now, that is just his way, exactly—he will tell the absurdest lie, and trust to luck to get out of it again. Cat eat a cocoanut—the innocent fool!"

Eckert approached with his cat, sure enough.

Bascom smiled. Said he:

"I'll hold the cat—you bring a cocoanut."

Eckert split one open, and chopped up some pieces. Bascom smuggled a wink to me, and proffered a slice of the fruit to puss. She snatched it, swallowed it ravenously, and asked for more!

We rode our two miles in silence, and wide apart. At least I was silent, though Bascom cuffed his horse and cursed him a good deal, notwithstanding the horse was behaving well enough. When I branched off homeward, Bascom said:

"Keep the horse till morning. And—you need not speak of this —— foolishness to the boys."

Chapter 12

. . . Two miles beyond South Pass City we saw for the first time that mysterious marvel which all Western untraveled boys have heard of and fully believe in, but are sure to be astounded at when they see it with their own eyes, nevertheless—banks of snow in dead summer time. We were now far up toward the sky, and knew all the time that we must presently encounter lofty summits clad in the "eternal snow" which was so commonplace a matter of mention in books, and yet when I did see it glittering in the sun on stately domes in the distance and knew the month was August and that my coat was hanging up because it was too warm to wear it, I was full as much amazed as if I never had heard of snow in August before. Truly, "seeing is believing"—and many a man lives a long life through, *thinking* he believes certain universally received and well established things, and yet never suspects that if he were confronted by those things once, he would discover that he did not *really* believe them before, but only thought he believed them. . . .

Chapter 16

All men have heard of the Mormon Bible, but few except the "elect" have seen it, or, at least, taken the trouble to read it. I brought away a copy from Salt Lake. The book is a curiosity to me, it is such a pretentious affair, and yet so "slow," so sleepy; such an insipid mess of inspiration. It is chloroform in print. If Joseph Smith composed this book, the act was a miracle—keeping awake while he did it was, at any rate. If he, according to tradition, merely translated it from certain ancient and mysteriously-engraved plates of copper, which he declares he found under a stone, in an out-of-the-way locality, the work of translating was equally a miracle, for the same reason.

The book seems to be merely a prosy detail of imaginary history, with the Old Testament for a model; followed by a tedious plagiarism of the New Testament. The author labored to give his words and phrases the quaint, old-fashioned sound and structure of our King James's translation of the Scriptures; and the result is a mongrel—half modern glibness, and half ancient simplicity and gravity. The latter is awkward and constrained; the former natural, but grotesque by the contrast. Whenever he found his speech growing too modern—which was about every sentence or two—he ladled in a few such Scriptural phrases as "exceeding sore," "and it came to pass," etc., and made things satisfactory again. "And it came to pass" was his pet. If he had left that out, his Bible would have been only a pamphlet. . . .

The Mormon Bible is rather stupid and tiresome to read, but there is nothing vicious in its teachings. Its code of morals is unobjectionable—it is "smouched"* from the New Testament and no credit given.

Chapter 18

At eight in the morning we reached the remnant and ruin of what had been the important military station of "Camp Floyd," some forty-five or fifty miles from Salt Lake City. At four P.M. we had doubled our distance and were ninety or a hundred miles from Salt Lake. And now we entered upon one of that species of deserts whose concentrated hideousness shames the diffused and diluted horrors of Sahara—an *"alkali"* desert. For sixty-eight miles there was but one break in it. I do not remember that this was really a break; indeed

*Milton.

it seems to me that it was nothing but a watering depot *in the midst* of the stretch of sixty-eight miles. If my memory serves me, there was no well or spring at this place, but the water was hauled there by mule and ox teams from the further side of the desert. There was a stage station there. It was forty-five miles from the beginning of the desert, and twenty-three from the end of it.

We plowed and dragged and groped along, the whole live-long night, and at the end of this uncomfortable twelve hours we finished the forty-five-mile part of the desert and got to the stage station where the imported water was. The sun was just rising. It was easy enough to cross a desert in the night while we were asleep; and it was pleasant to reflect, in the morning, that we in actual person *had* encountered an absolute desert and could always speak knowingly of deserts in presence of the ignorant thenceforward. And it was pleasant also to reflect that this was not an obscure, back country desert, but a very celebrated one, the metropolis itself, as you may say. All this was very well and very comfortable and satisfactory—but now we were to cross a desert in *daylight.* This was fine—novel—romantic—dramatically adventurous—*this,* indeed, was worth living for, worth traveling for! We would write home all about it.

This enthusiasm, this stern thirst for adventure, wilted under the sultry August sun and did not last above one hour. One poor little hour—and then we were ashamed that we had "gushed" so. The poetry was all in the anticipation—there is none in the reality. Imagine a vast, waveless ocean stricken dead and turned to ashes; imagine this solemn waste tufted with ash-dusted sagebushes; imagine the lifeless silence and solitude that belong to such a place; imagine a coach, creeping like a bug through the midst of this shoreless level, and sending up tumbled volumes of dust as if it were a bug that went by steam; imagine this aching monotony of toiling and plowing kept up hour after hour, and the shore still as far away as ever, apparently; imagine team, driver, coach and passengers so deeply coated with ashes that they are all one colorless color; imagine ash-drifts roosting above moustaches and eyebrows like snow accumulations on boughs and bushes. This is the reality of it. . . .

CHAPTER 25

. . . Nothing in this world is palled in such impenetrable obscurity as a U.S. Treasury Comptroller's understanding. The very fires of the hereafter could get up nothing more than a fitful glimmer in it. In the days I speak of he never could be made to comprehend why it was that twenty thousand dollars would not go as far in Nevada, where all commodities ranged at an enormous figure, as it would in the other Territories, where exceeding cheapness was the rule. He was an officer who looked out for the little expenses all the time. The Secretary of the Territory kept his office in his bedroom, as I before remarked; and he charged the United States no rent, although his "instructions" provided for that item and he could have justly taken advantage of it (a thing which I would have done with more than lightning promptness if I had been Secretary myself). But the United States never applauded this devotion. Indeed, I think my country was ashamed to have so improvident a person in its employ.

Those "instructions" (we used to read a chapter from them every morning, as intellectual gymnastics, and a couple of chapters in Sunday school every Sabbath, for they treated of all subjects under the sun and had much valuable religious matter in them along with the other statistics) those "instructions" commanded that pen-knives, envelopes, pens and writing-paper be furnished the members of the legislature. So the Secretary made the purchase and the distribution. The knives cost three dollars apiece. There was one too many, and the Secretary gave it to the Clerk of the House of Representatives. The United States said the Clerk of the House was not a "member" of the legislature, and took that three dollars out of the Secretary's salary, as usual.

White men charged three or four dollars a "load" for sawing up stovewood. The Secretary was sagacious enough to know that the United States would never pay any such price as that; so he got an Indian to saw up a load of office wood at one dollar and a half. He made out the usual voucher, but signed no name to it—simply appended a note explaining that an Indian had done the work, and had done it in a very capable and satisfactory way, but could not sign the voucher owing to lack of ability in the necessary direction. The Secretary had to pay that dollar and a half. He thought the United States would admire both his economy and his honesty in getting the work done at half price and not putting a pretended Indian's signature to the voucher, but the United States did not see it in that light. The United States was too much accustomed to employing dollar-and-a-half thieves in all manner of official capacities to regard his explanation of the voucher as having any foundation in fact.

But the next time the Indian sawed wood for us I taught him to make a cross at the bottom of the voucher—it looked like a cross that had been drunk a year—and then I "witnessed" it and it went through all right. The United States never said a word. I was sorry I had not made the voucher for a thousand loads of wood instead of one. The government of my country snubs honest simplicity but fondles artistic villainy, and I think I might have developed into a very capable pickpocket if I had remained in the public service a year or two.

That was a fine collection of sovereigns, that first Nevada legislature. They levied taxes to the amount of thirty or forty thousand dollars and ordered expenditures to the extent of about a million. Yet they had their little periodical explosions of economy like all other bodies of the kind. A member proposed to save three dollars a day to the nation by dispensing with the Chaplain. And yet that short-sighted man needed the Chaplain more than any other member, perhaps, for he generally sat with his feet on his desk, eating raw turnips, during the morning prayer.

The legislature sat sixty days, and passed private toll-road franchises all the time. When they adjourned it was estimated that every citizen owned about three franchises, and it was believed that unless Congress gave the Territory another degree of longitude there would not be room enough to accommodate the toll-roads. The ends of them were hanging over the boundary line everywhere like a fringe.

The fact is, the freighting business had grown to such important proportions that there was nearly as much excitement over suddenly acquired toll-road fortunes as over the wonderful silver mines.

Chapter 28

[On prospecting for silver and gold]

. . . I confess, without shame, that I expected to find masses of silver lying all about the ground. I expected to see it glittering in the sun on the mountain summits. I said nothing about this, for some instinct told me that I might possibly have an exaggerated idea about it, and so if I betrayed my thought I might bring derision upon myself. Yet I was as perfectly satisfied in my own mind as I could be of anything, that I was going to gather up, in a day or two, or at furthest a week or two, silver enough to make me satisfactorily wealthy—and so my fancy was already busy with plans for spending this money. The first opportunity that offered, I sauntered carelessly away from the cabin, keeping an eye on the other boys, and stopping and contemplating the sky when they seemed to be observing me; but as soon as the coast was manifestly clear, I fled away as guiltily as a thief might have done and never halted till I was far beyond sight and call. Then I began my search with a feverish excitement that was brim full of expectation—almost of certainty. I crawled about the ground, seizing and examining bits of stone, blowing the dust from them or rubbing them on my clothes, and then peering at them with anxious hope. Presently I found a bright fragment and my heart bounded! I hid behind a boulder and polished it and scrutinized it with a nervous eagerness and a delight that was more pronounced than absolute certainty itself could have afforded. The more I examined the fragment the more I was convinced that I had found the door to fortune. I marked the spot and carried away my specimen. Up and down the rugged mountain side I searched, with always increasing interest and always augmenting gratitude that I had come to Humboldt and come in time. Of all the experiences of my life, this secret search among the hidden treasures of silverland was the nearest to unmarred ecstasy. It was a delirious revel. By and by, in the bed of a shallow rivulet, I found a deposit of shining yellow scales, and my breath almost forsook me! A gold mine, and in my simplicity I had been content with vulgar silver! I was so excited that I half believed my overwrought imagination was deceiving me. Then a fear came upon me that people might be observing me and would guess my secret. Moved by this thought, I made a circuit of the place, and ascended a knoll to reconnoitre. Solitude. No creature was near. Then I returned to my mine, fortifying myself against possible disappointment, but my fears were groundless—the shining scales were still there. I set about scooping them out, and for an hour I toiled down the windings of the stream and robbed its bed. But at last the descending sun warned me to give up the quest, and I turned homeward laden with wealth. As I walked along I could not help smiling at the thought of my being so excited over my fragment of silver when a nobler metal was almost under my nose. In this little time the former had so fallen in my estimation that once or twice I was on the point of throwing it away.

The boys were as hungry as usual, but I could eat nothing. Neither could I talk. I was full of dreams and far away. Their conversation interrupted the flow of my fancy somewhat, and annoyed me a little, too. I despised the sordid and commonplace things they talked about. But as they proceeded, it began to amuse me. It grew to be rare fun to hear them planning their poor little economies and sighing over possible privations and distresses when a gold mine, all our own, lay within sight of the cabin and I could point it out at any moment. Smothered hilarity began to oppress me, presently. It was hard to resist the impulse to burst out with exultation and reveal everything; but I did resist. I said within myself that I would filter the great news through my lips calmly and be serene as a summer morning while I watched its effect in their faces. I said:

"Where have you all been?"

"Prospecting."

"What did you find?"

"Nothing."

"Nothing? What do you think of the country?"

"Can't tell, yet," said Mr. Ballou, who was an old gold miner, and had likewise had considerable experience among the silver mines.

"Well, haven't you formed any sort of opinion?"

"Yes, a sort of a one. It's fair enough here, maybe, but overrated. Seven-thousand-dollar ledges are scarce, though. That Sheba may be rich enough, but we don't own it; and besides, the rock is so full of base metals that all the science in the world can't work it. We'll not starve, here, but we'll not get rich, I'm afraid."

"So you think the prospect is pretty poor?"

"No name for it!"

"Well, we'd better go back, hadn't we?"

"Oh, not yet—of course not. We'll try a riffle, first."

"Suppose, now—this is merely a supposition, you know—suppose you could find a ledge that would yield, say, a hundred and fifty dollars a ton—would that satisfy you?"

"Try us once!" from the whole party.

"Or suppose—merely a supposition, of course—suppose you were to find a ledge that would yield two thousand dollars a ton—would *that* satisfy you?"

"Here—what do you mean? What are you coming at? Is there some mystery behind all this?"

"Never mind. I am not saying anything. You know perfectly well there are no rich mines here—of course you do. Because you have been around and examined for yourselves. Anybody would know that, that had been around. But just for the sake of argument, suppose—in a kind of general way—suppose some person were to tell you that two-thousand-dollar ledges were simply contemptible—contemptible, understand—and that right yonder in sight of this cabin there were piles of pure gold and pure silver—oceans of it—enough to make you all rich in twenty-four hours! Come!"

"I should say he was as crazy as a loon!" said old Ballou, but wild with excitement, nevertheless.

"Gentlemen," said I, "I don't say anything—*I* haven't been around, you know, and of course don't know anything—but all I ask of you is to cast your eye on *that,* for instance, and tell me what you think of it!" and I tossed my treasure before them.

There was an eager scramble for it, and a closing of heads together over it under the candle-light. Then old Ballou said:

"Think of it? I think it is nothing but a lot of granite rubbish and nasty glittering mica that isn't worth ten cents an acre!"

So vanished my dream. So melted my wealth away. So toppled my airy castle to the earth and left me stricken and forlorn.

Moralizing, I observed, then, that "all that glitters is not gold."

Mr. Ballou said I could go further than that, and lay it up among my treasures of knowledge, that *nothing* that glitters is gold. So I learned then, once for all, that gold in its native state is but dull, unornamental stuff, and that only low-born metals excite the admiration of the ignorant with an ostentatious glitter. However, like the rest of the world, I still go on underrating men of gold and glorifying men of mica. Commonplace human nature cannot rise above that.

Chapters 31–33

[On human reformation]

. . . The next morning it was still snowing furiously when we got away with our new stock of saddles and accoutrements. We mounted and started. The snow lay so deep on the ground that there was no sign of a road perceptible, and the snow-fall was so thick that we could not see more than a hundred yards ahead, else we could have guided our course by the mountain ranges. The case looked dubious, but Ollendorff said his instinct was as sensitive as any compass, and that he could "strike a bee-line" for Carson City and never diverge from it. He said that if he were to straggle a single point out of the true line his instinct would assail him like an outraged conscience. Consequently we dropped into his wake happy and content. For half an hour we poked along warily enough, but at the end of that time we came upon a fresh trail, and Ollendorff shouted proudly:

"I knew I was as dead certain as a compass, boys! Here we are, right in somebody's tracks that will hunt the way for us without any trouble. Let's hurry up and join company with the party."

So we put the horses into as much of a trot as the deep snow would allow, and before long it was evident that we were gaining on our predecessors, for the tracks grew more distinct. We hurried along, and at the end of an hour the tracks looked still newer and fresher—but what surprised us was, that the *number* of travelers in advance of us seemed to steadily increase. We wondered how so large a party came to be traveling at such a time and in such a solitude. Somebody suggested that it must be a company of soldiers from the fort, and so we accepted that solution and jogged along a little faster still, for they could not be far off now. But the tracks still multiplied, and we began to think the platoon of soldiers was miraculously expanding into a regiment—Ballou said they had already increased to five hundred! Presently he stopped his horse and said:

"Boys, these are our own tracks, and we've actually been circussing round and round in a circle for more than two hours, out here in this blind desert! By George this is perfectly hydraulic!"

Then the old man waxed wroth and abusive. He called Ollendorff all manner of hard names—said he never saw such a lurid fool as he was, and ended with the peculiarly venomous opinion that he "did not know as much as a logarythm!"

We certainly had been following our own tracks. Ollendorff and his "mental compass" were in disgrace from that moment. After all our hard travel, here we were on the bank of the stream again, with the inn beyond dimly outlined through the driving snow-fall. While we were considering what to do, the young Swede landed from the canoe and took his pedestrian way Carson-wards, singing his same tiresome song about his "sister and his brother" and "the child in the grave with its mother," and in a short minute faded and disappeared in the white oblivion. He was never heard of again. He no doubt got bewildered and lost, and Fatigue delivered him over to Sleep and Sleep betrayed him to Death. Possibly he followed our treacherous tracks till he became exhausted and dropped.

Presently the Overland stage forded the now fast receding stream and started toward Carson on its first trip since the flood came. We hesitated no longer, now, but took up our march in its wake, and trotted merrily along, for we had good confidence in the driver's bump of locality. But our horses were no match for the fresh stage team. We were soon left out of sight; but it was no matter, for we had the deep ruts the wheels made for a guide. By this time it was three in the afternoon, and consequently it was not very long before night came—and not with a lingering twilight, but with a sudden shutting down like a cellar door, as is its habit in that country. The snow-fall was still as thick as ever, and of course we could not see fifteen steps before us; but all about us the white glare of the snow-bed enabled us to discern the smooth sugar-loaf mounds made by the covered sage-bushes, and just in front of us the two faint grooves which we knew were the steadily filling and slowly disappearing wheel-tracks.

Now those sage-bushes were all about the same height—three or four feet; they stood just about seven feet apart, all over the vast desert; each of them was a mere snow-mound, now; in *any* direction that you proceeded (the same as in a well laid out orchard) you would find yourself moving down a distinctly defined avenue, with a row of these snow-mounds on either side of it—an avenue the customary width of a road, nice and level in its breadth, and rising at the sides in the most natural way, by reason of the mounds. But we had not thought of this. Then imagine the chilly thrill that shot through us when it finally occurred to us, far in the night, that since the last faint trace of the wheel-tracks had long ago been buried from sight, we might now be wandering down a mere sage-brush avenue, miles away from the road and diverging further and further away from it all the time. Having a cake of ice slipped down one's back is placid comfort compared to it. There was a sudden leap and stir of blood that had been asleep for an hour, and as sudden a rousing of all the drowsing activities in our minds and bodies. We were alive and awake at once—and shaking and quaking with consternation, too. There was an instant halting and dismounting, a bending low and an anxious scanning of the road-bed. Useless, of course; for if a faint depression could not be discerned from an altitude of four or five feet above it, it certainly could not with one's nose nearly against it.

We seemed to be in a road, but that was no proof. We tested this by walking off in various directions—the regular snow-mounds and the regular avenues between them convinced each man that *he* had found the true road, and that the others had found only false ones. Plainly the situation was desperate. We were cold and stiff and the horses were tired. We decided to build a sage-brush fire and camp out till morning. This was wise, because if we were wandering from the right road and the snow-storm continued another day our case would be the next thing to hopeless if we kept on.

All agreed that a camp-fire was what would come nearest to saving us, now, and so we set about building it. We could find no matches, and so we tried to make shift with the pistols. Not a man in the party had ever tried to do such a thing before, but not a man in the party doubted that it *could* be done, and without any trouble—because every man in the party had read about it in books many a time and had naturally come to believe it, with trusting simplicity, just as he had long ago accepted and believed *that other* common book-fraud about Indians and lost hunters making a fire by rubbing two dry sticks together.

We huddled together on our knees in the deep snow, and the horses put their noses together and bowed their patient heads over us; and while the feathery flakes eddied down and turned us into a group of white statuary, we proceeded with the momentous experiment. We broke twigs from a sage-bush and piled them on a little cleared place in the shelter of our bodies. In the course of ten or fifteen minutes all was ready, and then, while conversation ceased and our pulses beat low with anxious suspense, Ollendorff applied his revolver, pulled the trigger and blew the pile clear out of the country! It was the flattest failure that ever was.

This was distressing, but it paled before a greater horror—the horses were gone! I had been appointed to hold the bridles, but in my absorbing anxiety over the pistol experiment I had unconsciously dropped them and the released animals had walked off in a storm. It was useless to try to follow them, for their footfalls could make no sound, and one could pass within two yards of the creatures and never see them. We gave them up without an effort at recovering them, and cursed the lying books that said horses would stay by their masters for protection and companionship in a distressful time like ours.

We were miserable enough, before; we felt still more forlorn, now. Patiently, but with blighted hope, we broke more sticks and piled them, and once more the Prussian shot them into annihilation. Plainly, to light a fire with a pistol was an art requiring practice and experience, and the middle of a desert at midnight in a snow-storm was not a good place or time for the acquiring of the accomplishment. We gave it up and tried the other. Each man took a couple of sticks and fell to chafing them together. At the end of half an hour we were thoroughly chilled, and so were the sticks. We bitterly execrated the Indians, the hunters and the books that had betrayed us with the silly device, and wondered dismally what was next to be done. At this critical moment Mr. Ballou fished out four matches from the rubbish of an overlooked pocket. To have found four gold bars would have seemed poor and cheap good luck compared to this. One cannot think how good a match looks under such circumstances—or how lovable and precious, and sacredly beautiful to the eye. This time we gathered sticks with high hopes; and when Mr. Ballou prepared to light the first match, there was an amount of interest centred upon him that pages of writing could not describe. The match burned hopefully a moment, and then went out. It could not have carried more regret with it if it had been a human life. The next match simply flashed and died. The wind puffed the third one out just as it was on the imminent verge of success. We gathered together closer than ever, and developed a solicitude that was rapt and painful, as Mr. Ballou scratched our last hope on his leg. It lit, burned blue and sickly, and then budded into a robust flame. Shading it with his hands, the old gentleman bent gradually down and every heart went with him—everybody, too, for that matter—and blood and breath stood still. The flame touched the sticks at last, took gradual hold upon them—hesitated—took a stronger hold—hesitated again—held its breath five heart-breaking seconds, then gave a sort of human gasp and went out.

Nobody said a word for several minutes. It was a solemn sort of silence; even the wind put on a stealthy, sinister quiet, and made no more noise than the falling flakes of snow. Finally a sad-voiced conversation began, and it was soon apparent that in each of our hearts lay the conviction that this was our last night with the living. I had so hoped that I was the only one who felt so.

When the others calmly acknowledged their conviction, it sounded like the summons itself. Ollendorff said:

"Brothers, let us die together. And let us go without one hard feeling towards each other. Let us forget and forgive bygones. I know that you have felt hard towards me for turning over the canoe, and for knowing too much and leading you round and round in the snow—but I meant well; forgive me. I acknowledge freely that I have had hard feelings against Mr. Ballou for abusing me and calling me a logarythm, which is a thing I do not know what, but no doubt a thing considered disgraceful and unbecoming in America, and it has scarcely been out of my mind and has hurt me a great deal—but let it go; I forgive Mr. Ballou with all my heart, and—"

Poor Ollendorff broke down and the tears came. He was not alone, for I was crying too, and so was Mr. Ballou. Ollendorff got his voice again and forgave me for things I had done and said. Then he got out his bottle of whisky and said that whether he lived or died he would never touch another drop. He said he had given up all hope of life, and although ill-prepared, was ready to submit humbly to his fate; that he wished he could be spared a little longer, not for any selfish reason, but to make a thorough reform in his character, and by devoting himself to helping the poor, nursing the sick, and pleading with the people to guard themselves against the evil of intemperance, make his life a beneficent example to the young, and lay it down at last with the precious reflection that it had not been lived in vain. He ended by saying that his reform should begin at this moment, even here in the presence of death, since no longer time was to be vouchsafed wherein to prosecute it to men's help and benefit—and with that he threw away the bottle of whisky.

Mr. Ballou made remarks of similar purport, and began the reform he could not live to continue, by throwing away the ancient pack of cards that had solaced our captivity during the flood and made it bearable. He said he never gambled, but still was satisfied that the meddling with cards in any way was immoral and injurious, and no man could be wholly pure and blemishless without eschewing them. "And therefore," continued he, "in doing this act I already feel more in sympathy with that spiritual saturnalia necessary to entire and obsolete reform." These rolling syllables touched him as no intelligible eloquence could have done, and the old man sobbed with a mournfulness not unmingled with satisfaction.

My own remarks were of the same tenor as those of my comrades, and I know that the feelings that prompted them were heartfelt and sincere. We were all sincere, and all deeply moved and earnest, for we were in the presence of death and without hope. I threw away my pipe, and in doing it felt that at last I was free of a hated vice and one that had ridden me like a tyrant all my days. While I yet talked, the thought of the good I might have done in the world and the still greater good I might *now* do, with these new incentives and higher and better aims to guide me if I could only be spared a few years longer, overcame me and the tears came again. We put our arms about each other's necks and awaited the warning drowsiness that precedes death by freezing.

It came stealing over us presently, and then we bade each other a last farewell. A delicious dreaminess wrought its web about my yielding senses, while the snow-flakes wove a winding sheet about my conquered body. Oblivion came. The battle of life was done.

I do not know how long I was in a state of forgetfulness, but it seemed an age. A vague consciousness grew upon me by degrees, and then came a gathering anguish of pain in my limbs and through all my body. I shuddered. The thought flitted through my brain, "this is death—this is the hereafter."

Then came a white upheaval at my side, and a voice said, with bitterness:

"Will some gentleman be so good as to kick me behind?"

It was Ballou—at least it was a towzled snow image in a sitting posture, with Ballou's voice.

I rose up, and there in the gray dawn, not fifteen steps from us, were the frame buildings of a stage station, and under a shed stood our still saddled and bridled horses!

An arched snow-drift broke up, now, and Ollendorff emerged from it, and the three of us sat and stared at the houses without speaking a word. We really had nothing to say. We were like the profane man who could not "do the subject justice," the whole situation was so painfully ridiculous and humiliating that words were tame and we did not know where to commence anyhow.

The joy in our hearts at our deliverance was poisoned; well-nigh dissipated, indeed. We presently began to grow pettish by degrees, and sullen; and then, angry at each other, angry at ourselves, angry at everything in general, we moodily dusted the snow from our clothing and in unsociable single file plowed our way to the horses, unsaddled them, and sought shelter in the station.

I have scarcely exaggerated a detail of this curious and absurd adventure. It occurred almost exactly as I have stated it. We actually went into camp in a snow-drift in a desert, at midnight in a storm, forlorn and hopeless, within fifteen steps of a comfortable inn.

For two hours we sat apart in the station and ruminated in disgust. The mystery was gone, now, and it was plain enough why the horses had deserted us. Without a doubt they were under that shed a quarter of a minute after they had left us, and they must have overheard and enjoyed all our confessions and lamentations.

After breakfast we felt better, and the zest of life soon came back. The world looked bright again, and existence was as dear to us as ever. Presently an uneasiness came over me—grew upon me—assailed me without ceasing. Alas, my regeneration was not complete—I wanted to smoke! I resisted with all my strength, but the flesh was weak. I wandered away alone and wrestled with myself an hour. I recalled my promises of reform and preached to myself persuasively, upbraidingly, exhaustively. But it was all vain, I shortly found myself sneaking among the snow-drifts hunting for my pipe. I discovered it after a considerable search, and crept away to hide myself and enjoy it. I remained behind the barn a good while, asking myself how I would feel if my braver, stronger, truer comrades should catch me in my degradation. At last I lit the pipe, and no human being can feel meaner and baser than I did then. I was ashamed of being in my own pitiful company. Still dreading discovery, I felt that perhaps the further side of the barn would be somewhat safer, and so I turned the corner. As I turned the one corner, smoking, Ollendorff turned the other with his bottle to his lips, and between us sat unconscious Ballou deep in a game of "solitaire" with the old greasy cards!

Absurdity could go no farther. We shook hands and agreed to say no more about "reform" and "examples to the rising generation."

The station we were at was at the verge of the Twenty-six-Mile Desert. If we had approached it half an hour earlier the night before, we must have heard men shouting there and firing pistols; for they were expecting some sheep drovers and their flocks and knew that they would infallibly get lost and wander out of reach of help unless guided by sounds. While we remained at the station, three of the drovers arrived, nearly exhausted with their wanderings, but two others of their party were never heard of afterward. . . .

Chapter 48

. . . The men who murdered Virginia's original twenty-six cemetery-occupants were never punished. Why? Because Alfred the Great, when he invented trial by jury, and knew that he had admirably framed it to secure justice in his age of the world, was not aware that in the nineteenth century the condition of things would be so entirely changed that unless he rose from the grave and altered the jury plan to meet the emergency, it would prove the most ingenious and infallible agency for *defeating* justice that human wisdom could contrive. For how could he imagine that we simpletons would go on using his jury plan after circumstances had stripped it of its usefulness, any more than he could imagine that we would go on using his candle-clock after we had invented chronometers? In his day news could not travel fast, and hence he could easily find a jury of honest, intelligent men who had not heard of the case they were called to try—but in our day of telegraphs and newspapers his plan compels us to swear in juries composed of fools and rascals, because the system rigidly excludes honest men and men of brains.

I remember one of those sorrowful farces, in Virginia, which we call a jury trial. A noted desperado killed Mr. B., a good citizen, in the most wanton and cold-blooded way. Of course the papers were full of it, and all men capable of reading, read about it. And of course all men not deaf and dumb and idiotic, talked about it. A jury-list was made out, and Mr. B. L., a prominent banker and a valued citizen, was questioned precisely as he would have been questioned in any court in America:

"Have you heard of this homicide?"

"Yes."

"Have you held conversations upon the subject?"

"Yes."

"Have you formed or expressed opinions about it?"

"Yes."

"Have you read the newspaper accounts of it?"

"Yes."

"We do not want you."

A minister, intelligent, esteemed, and greatly respected; a merchant of high character and known probity; a mining superintendent of intelligence and unblemished reputation; a quartz mill owner of excellent standing, were all questioned in the same way, and all set aside. Each said the public talk and the newspaper reports had not so biased his mind but that sworn testimony would overthrow his previously formed opinions and enable him to render a verdict without prejudice and in accordance with the facts. But of course such men could not be trusted with the case. Ignoramuses alone could mete out unsullied justice.

When the peremptory challenges were all exhausted, a jury of twelve men was impaneled—a jury who swore they had neither heard, read, talked about nor expressed an opinion concerning a murder which the very cattle in the corrals, the Indians in the sage-brush and the stones in the streets were cognizant of! It was a jury composed of two desperadoes, two low beer-house politicians, three bar-keepers, two ranchmen who could not read, and three dull, stupid, human donkeys! It actually came out afterward, that one of these latter thought that incest and arson were the same thing.

The verdict rendered by this jury was, Not Guilty. What else could one expect?

The jury system puts a ban upon intelligence and honesty, and a premium upon ignorance, stupidity and perjury. It is a shame that we must continue to use a worthless system because it *was* good a thousand years ago. In this age, when a gentleman of high social standing, intelligence and probity, swears that testimony given under solemn oath will outweigh, with him, street talk and newspaper reports based upon mere hearsay, he is worth a hundred jurymen who will swear to their own ignorance and stupidity, and justice would be far safer in his hands than in theirs. Why could not the jury law be so altered as to give men of brains and honesty an *equal chance* with fools and miscreants? Is it right to show the present favoritism to one class of men and inflict a disability on another, in a land whose boast is that all its citizens are free and equal? I am a candidate for the legislature. I desire to tamper with the jury law. I wish to so alter it as to put a premium on intelligence and character, and close the jury box against idiots, blacklegs, and people who do not read newspapers. But no doubt I shall be defeated—every effort I make to save the country "misses fire." . . .

Chapter 62

After a three months' absence. I found myself in San Francisco again, without a cent. When my credit was about exhausted (for I had become too mean and lazy, now, to work on a morning paper, and there were no vacancies on the evening journals), I was created San Francisco correspondent of the *Enterprise,* and at the end of five months I was out of debt, but my interest in my work was gone; for my correspondence being a daily one, without rest or respite, I got unspeakably tired of it. I wanted another change. The vagabond instinct was strong upon me. Fortune favored and I got a new berth and a delightful one. It was to go down to the Sandwich Islands and write some letters for the Sacramento *Union,* an excellent journal and liberal with employés.

We sailed in the propeller *Ajax,* in the middle of winter. The almanac called it winter, distinctly enough, but the weather was a compromise between spring and summer. Six days out of port, it became summer altogether. We had some thirty passengers; among them a cheerful soul by the name of Williams, and three sea-worn old whaleship captains going down to join their vessels. These latter played euchre in the smoking room day and night, drank astonishing quantities of raw whisky without being in the least affected by it, and were the happiest people I think I ever saw. And then there was "the old Admiral"—a retired whaleman. He was a roaring, terrific combination of wind and lightning and thunder, and earnest, whole-souled profanity. But nevertheless he was tender-hearted as a girl. He was a raving, deafening, devastating typhoon, laying waste the cowering seas but with an unvexed refuge in the centre where all comers were safe and at rest. Nobody could know the "Admiral" without liking him; and in a sudden and dire emergency I think no friend of his would know which to choose—to be cursed by him or prayed for by a less efficient person.

His title of "Admiral" was more strictly "official" than any ever worn by a naval officer before or since, perhaps—for it was the voluntary offering of a whole nation, and came direct from the *people* themselves without any intermediate red tape—the people of the Sandwich Islands. It was a title that came to him freighted with affection, and honor, and appreciation of his unpretending merit. And in testimony of the genuineness of the title it was publicly ordained that an exclusive flag should be devised for him and used solely to welcome his coming and wave him God-speed in his going. From that time forth, whenever his ship was signaled in the offing, or he catted his anchor and stood out to sea, that ensign streamed from the royal halliards on the parliament house and the nation lifted their hats to it with spontaneous accord.

Yet he had never fired a gun or fought a battle in his life. When I knew him on board the *Ajax,* he was seventy-two years old and had plowed the salt water sixty-one of them. For sixteen years he had gone in and out of the harbor of Honolulu in command of a whaleship, and for sixteen more had been captain of a San Francisco and Sandwich Island passenger packet and had never had an accident or lost a vessel. The simple natives knew him for a friend who never failed them, and regarded him as children regard a father. It was a dangerous thing to oppress them when the roaring Admiral was around.

Two years before I knew the Admiral, he had retired from the sea on a competence, and had sworn a colossal nine-jointed oath that he would "never go within *smelling* distance of the salt water again as long as he lived." And he had conscientiously kept it. That is to say, *he* considered he had kept it, and it would have been more than dangerous to suggest to him, even in the gentlest way, that making eleven long sea voyages, as a passenger, during the two years that had transpired since he "retired," was only keeping the general spirit of it and not the strict letter.

The Admiral knew only one narrow line of conduct to pursue in any and all cases where there was a fight, and that was to shoulder his way straight in without an inquiry as to the rights or the merits of it, and take the part of the weaker side. And this was the reason why he was always sure to be present at the trial of any universally execrated criminal to oppress and intimidate the jury with a vindictive pantomime of what he would do to them if he ever caught them out of the box. And this was why harried cats and outlawed dogs that knew him confidently took sanctuary under his chair in time of trouble. In the beginning he was the most frantic and bloodthirsty Union man that drew breath in the shadow of the Flag; but the instant the Southerners began to go down before the sweep of the Northern armies, he ran up the Confederate colors and from that time till the end was a rampant and inexorable secessionist.

He hated intemperance with a more uncompromising animosity than any individual I have ever met, of either sex; and he was never tired of storming against it and beseeching friends and strangers alike to be wary and drink with moderation. And yet if any creature had been guileless enough to intimate that his absorbing nine gallons of "straight" whisky during our voyage was any fraction short of rigid or inflexible abstemiousness, in that self-same moment the old man would have spun him to the uttermost parts of the earth in the whirlwind of his wrath. Mind, I am not saying his whisky ever affected his head or his legs, for it did not, in even the slightest degree. He was a capacious container, but he did not hold enough for that. He took a level tumblerful of whisky every morning before he put his clothes on—"to sweeten his bilge-water," he said. He took another after he got the most of his clothes on, "to settle his mind and give him his bearings." He then shaved, and put on a clean shirt; after which he recited the Lord's Prayer in a fervent, thundering bass that shook the ship to her kelson and suspended all conversation in the main cabin. Then, at this stage, being invariably "by the head," or "by the stern," or "listed to port or starboard," he took one more to "put him on an even keel so that he would mind his hellum and not miss stays and go about, every time he came up in the wind."—And now, his state-room door swung open and the sun of his benignant face beamed redly out upon men and women and children, and he roared his "Shipmets a'hoy!" in a way that was calculated to wake the dead and precipitate the final resurrection; and forth he strode, a picture to look at and a presence to enforce attention. Stalwart and portly; not a gray hair; broad-brimmed slouch hat; semi-sailor toggery of blue navy flannel—roomy and ample; a stately expanse of shirt-front and a liberal amount of black silk neck-cloth tied with a sailor knot; large chain and imposing seals impending from his fob; awe-inspiring feet, and "a hand like the hand of Providence," as his whaling brethren expressed it; wrist-bands and sleeves pushed back half way to the elbow, out of respect for the warm weather, and exposing hairy arms, gaudy with red and blue anchors, ships, and goddesses of liberty tattooed in India ink. But these details were only secondary matters—his face was the lodestone that chained the eye. It was a sultry disk, glowing determinedly out through a weather beaten mask of mahogany, and studded with warts, seamed with scars, "blazed" all over with unfailing fresh slips of the razor; and with cheery eyes, under shaggy brows, contemplating the world from over the back of a gnarled crag of a nose that loomed vast and lonely out of the undulating immensity that spread away from its foundations. At his heels frisked the darling of his bachelor estate, his terrier "Fan," a creature no larger than a squirrel. The main part of his daily life was occupied in looking after "Fan," in a motherly way, and doctoring her for a hundred ailments which existed only in his imagination.

The Admiral seldom read newspapers; and when he did he never believed anything they said. He read nothing, and believed in nothing, but *The Old Guard,* a secession periodical published in New York. He carried a dozen copies of it with him, always, and referred to them for all required information. If it was not there, he supplied it himself, out of a bountiful fancy, inventing history, names, dates, and everything else necessary to make his point good in an argument. Consequently he was a formidable antagonist in a dispute. Whenever he swung clear of the record and began to create history, the enemy was helpless and had to surrender. Indeed, the enemy could not keep from betraying some little spark of indignation at his manufactured history—and when it came to indignation, that was the Admiral's very "best hold." He was always ready for a political argument, and if nobody started one he would do it himself. With his third retort his temper would begin to rise, and within five minutes he would be blowing a gale, and within fifteen his smoking-room audience would be utterly stormed away and the old man left solitary and alone, banging the table with his fist, kicking the chairs, and roaring a hurricane of profanity. It got so, after a while, that whenever the Admiral approached, with politics in his eye, the passengers would drop out with quiet accord, afraid to meet him; and he would camp on a deserted field.

But he found his match at last, and before a full company. At one time or another, everybody had entered the lists against him and been routed, except the quiet passenger Williams. He had never been able to get an expression of opinion out of him on politics. But now, just as the Admiral drew near the door and the company were about to slip out, Williams said:

"Admiral, are you *certain* about that circumstance concerning the clergymen you mentioned the other day?"—referring to a piece of the Admiral's manufactured history.

Every one was amazed at the man's rashness. The idea of deliberately inviting annihilation was a thing incomprehensible. The retreat came to a halt; then everybody sat down again wondering, to await the upshot of it. The Admiral himself was as surprised as any one. He paused in the door, with his red handkerchief half raised to his sweating face, and contemplated the daring reptile in the corner.

"*Certain* of it? Am I *certain* of it? Do you think I've been lying about it? What do you take me for? Anybody that don't know that circumstance, don't know anything; a child ought to know it. Read up your history! Read it up —— —— —— ——, and don't come asking a man if he's *certain* about a bit of A B C stuff that the very Southern niggers know all about."

Here the Admiral's fires began to wax hot, the atmosphere thickened, the coming earthquake rumbled, he began to thunder and lighten. Within three minutes his volcano was in full eruption and he was discharging flames and ashes of indignation, belching black volumes of foul history aloft, and vomiting red-hot torrents of profanity from his crater. Meantime Williams sat silent, and apparently deeply and earnestly interested in what the old man was saying. By and by, when the lull came, he said in the most deferential way, and with the gratified air of a man who has had a mystery cleared up which had been puzzling him uncomfortably:

"*Now* I understand it. I always thought I knew that piece of history well enough, but was still afraid to trust it, because there was not that convincing particularity about it that one likes to have in history; but when you mentioned every name, the other day, and every date, and every little circumstance, in their just order and sequence, I said to myself, *this* sounds something like—*this* is history—*this* is putting it in a shape that gives a man confidence; and I said to myself afterward, I will just ask the Admiral if he is perfectly certain about the details, and if he is I will come out and thank him for clearing this matter up for me. And that is what I want to do now—for until you set that matter right it was nothing but just a confusion in my mind, without head or tail to it."

Nobody ever saw the Admiral look so mollified before, and so pleased. Nobody had ever received his bogus history as gospel before; its genuineness had always been called in question either by words or looks; but here was a man that not only swallowed it all down, but was grateful for the dose. He was taken aback; he hardly knew what to say; even his profanity failed him. Now, Williams continued, modestly and earnestly:

"But Admiral, in saying that this was the first stone thrown, and that this precipitated the war, you have overlooked a circumstance which you are perfectly familiar with, but which has escaped your memory. Now I grant you that what you have stated is correct in every detail—to-wit: that on the 16th of October, 1860, two Massachusetts clergymen, named Waite and Granger, went in disguise to the house of John Moody, in Rockport, at dead of night, and dragged forth two Southern women and their two little children, and after tarring and feathering them conveyed them to Boston and burned them alive in the State House square; and I also grant your proposition that this deed is what led to the secession of South Carolina on the 20th of December following. Very well." [Here the company were pleasantly surprised to hear Williams proceed to come back at the Admiral with his own invincible weapon—clean, pure, *manufactured history,* without a word of truth in it.] "Very well, I say. But Admiral, why overlook the Willis and Morgan case in South Carolina? You are too well informed a man not to know all about that circumstance. Your arguments and your conversations have shown you to be intimately conversant with every detail of this national quarrel. You develop matters of history every day that show plainly that you are no smatterer in it, content to nibble about the surface, but a man who has searched the depths and possessed yourself of everything that has a bearing upon the great question. Therefore, let me just recall to your mind that Willis and Morgan case—though I see by your face that the whole thing is already passing through your memory at this moment. On the 12th of August, 1860, *two months* before the Waite and Granger affair, two South Carolina clergymen, named John H. Morgan and Winthrop L. Willis, one a Methodist and the other an Old School Baptist, disguised themselves, and went at midnight to the house of a planter named Thompson—Archibald F. Thompson, Vice President under Thomas Jefferson,—and took thence, at midnight, his widowed aunt (a Northern woman) and her adopted child, an orphan named Mortimer Highie, afflicted with epilepsy and suffering at the time from white swelling on one of his legs, and compelled to walk on crutches in consequence; and the two ministers, in spite of the pleadings of the victims, dragged them to the bush, tarred and feathered them, and afterward burned them at the stake in the city of Charleston. You remember perfectly well what a stir it made; you remember perfectly well that even the Charleston *Courier* stigmatized the act as being unpleasant, of questionable propriety, and scarcely justifiable, and likewise that it would not be matter of surprise if retaliation ensued. And you remember also, that this thing was the *cause* of the Massachusetts outrage. Who, indeed, were the two Massachusetts ministers? and who were the two Southern women they burned? I do not need to remind *you,* Admiral, with your intimate knowledge of history, that Waite was the nephew of the woman burned in Charleston; that Granger was her cousin in the second degree, and that the women they burned in Boston were the wife of John H. Morgan, and the still loved but divorced wife of Winthrop L. Willis. Now, Admiral, it is only fair that you should acknowledge that the first provocation came from the Southern preachers and that the Northern ones were justified in retaliating. In your arguments you never yet have shown the least disposition to withhold a just verdict or be in anywise unfair, when authoritative history condemned your position, and therefore I have no hesitation in asking you to take the original blame from the Massachusetts ministers, in this matter, and transfer it to the South Carolina clergymen where it justly belongs."

The Admiral was conquered. This sweet-spoken creature who swallowed his fraudulent history as if it were the bread of life; basked in his furious blasphemy as if it were generous sunshine; found only calm, even-handed justice in his rampant partisanship; and flooded him with invented history so sugar-coated with flattery and deference that there was no rejecting it, was "too many" for him. He stammered some awkward, profane sentences about the —— —— —— —— Willis and Morgan business having escaped his memory, but that he "remembered it now," and then, under pretence of giving Fan some medicine for an imaginary cough, drew out of the battle and went away, a vanquished man. Then cheers and laughter went up, and Williams, the ship's benefactor, was a hero. The news went about the vessel, champagne was ordered, an enthusiastic reception instituted in the smoking room, and everybody flocked thither to shake hands with the conqueror. The wheelsman said afterward, that the Admiral stood up behind the pilot house and "ripped and cursed all to himself" till he loosened the smoke-stack guys and becalmed the mainsail.

The Admiral's power was broken. After that, if he began an argument, somebody would bring Williams, and the old man would grow weak and begin to quiet down at once. And as soon as he was done, Williams in his dulcet, insinuating way, would invent some history (referring for proof, to the old man's own excellent memory and to copies of *The Old Guard* known not to be in his possession) that would turn the tables completely and leave the Admiral all abroad and helpless. By and by he came to so dread Williams and his gilded tongue that he would stop talking when he saw him approach, and finally ceased to mention politics altogether, and from that time forward there was entire peace and serenity in the ship.

Chapter 64

[Hawaii]

. . . Near by is an interesting ruin—the meagre remains of an ancient heathen temple—a place where human sacrifices were offered up in those old bygone days when the simple child of nature, yielding momentarily to sin when sorely tempted, acknowledged his error when calm reflection had shown it to him, and came forward with noble frankness and offered up his grandmother as an atoning sacrifice—in those old days when the luckless sinner could keep on cleansing his conscience and achieving periodical happiness as long as his relations held out; long, long before the missionaries braved a thousand privations to come and make them permanently miserable by telling them how beautiful and how blissful a place heaven is, and how nearly impossible it is to get there; and showed the poor native how dreary a place perdition is and what unnecessarily liberal facilities there are for going to it; showed him how, in his ignorance, he had gone and fooled away all his kinfolks to no purpose; showed him what rapture it is to work all day long for fifty cents to buy food for next day with, as compared with fishing for pastime and lolling in the shade through eternal summer, and eating of the bounty that nobody labored to provide but

Nature. How sad it is to think of the multitudes who have gone to their graves in this beautiful island and never knew there was a hell! . . .

Chapter 67

. . . The christianizing of the natives has hardly even weakened some of their barbarian superstitions, much less destroyed them. I have just referred to one of these. It is still a popular belief that if your enemy can get hold of any article belonging to you he can get down on his knees over it and *pray you to death.* Therefore many a native gives up and dies merely because he *imagines* that some enemy is putting him through a course of damaging prayer. This praying an individual to death seems absurd enough at a first glance, but then when we call to mind some of the pulpit efforts of certain of our own ministers the thing looks plausible. . . .

Chapter 79

. . . When I returned to San Francisco I projected a pleasure journey to Japan and thence westward around the world; but a desire to see home again changed my mind, and I took a berth in the steamship, bade good-bye to the friendliest land and livest, heartiest community on our continent, and came by the way of the Isthmus to New York—a trip that was not much of a pic-nic excursion, for the cholera broke out among us on the passage and we buried two or three bodies at sea every day. I found home a dreary place after my long absence; for half the children I had known were now wearing whiskers or waterfalls, and few of the grown people I had been acquainted with remained at their hearthstones prosperous and happy—some of them had wandered to other scenes, some were in jail, and the rest had been hanged. These changes touched me deeply, and I went away and joined the famous Quaker City European Excursion and carried my tears to foreign lands.

Thus, after seven years of vicissitudes, ended a "pleasure trip" to the silver mines of Nevada which had originally been intended to occupy only three months. However, I usually miss my calculations further than that.

Moral

If the reader thinks he is done, now, and that this book has no moral to it, he is in error. The moral of it is this: If you are of any account, stay at home and make your way by faithful diligence; but if you are "no account," go away from home, and then you will *have* to work, whether you want to or not. Thus you become a blessing to your friends by ceasing to be a nuisance to them—if the people you go among suffer by the operation.

II

A Serious Comedian

Sketches New and Old

In Mark Twain's Sketches, New and Old, *the author collected sixty-two short pieces on a variety of subjects. The selections included here begin with material on childhood. In two of these essays, Twain parodies the then conventional ideas about the bad boy and the good boy. Other essays deal commonsensically and humorously with topics as diverse as prejudice against Asiatics and the insanity defense. The Franklin sketch rounds out these selections by uniting the themes of childhood influences with those of adult conditions.*

Texts are taken from the American Publishing Company 1887 edition.

Story of the Bad Little Boy

Once there was a bad little boy whose name was Jim—though, if you will notice, you will find that bad little boys are nearly always called James in your Sunday-school books. It was strange, but still it was true that this one was called Jim.

He didn't have any sick mother either—a sick mother who was pious and had the consumption, and would be glad to lie down in the grave and be at rest but for the strong love she bore her boy, and the anxiety she felt that the world might be harsh and cold towards him when she was gone. Most bad boys in the Sunday-books are named James, and have sick mothers, who teach them to say, "Now, I lay me down," etc., and sing them to sleep with sweet, plaintive voices, and then kiss them good-night, and kneel down by the bedside and weep. But it was different with this fellow. He was named Jim, and there wasn't anything the matter with his mother—no consumption, nor anything of that kind. She was rather stout than otherwise, and she was not pious; moreover, she was not anxious on Jim's account. She said if he were to break his neck it wouldn't be much loss. She always spanked Jim to sleep, and she never kissed him good-night; on the contrary, she boxed his ears when she was ready to leave him.

Once this little bad boy stole the key of the pantry, and slipped in there and helped himself to some jam, and filled up the vessel with tar, so that his mother would never know the difference; but all at once a terrible feeling didn't come over him, and something didn't seem to whisper to him, "Is it right to disobey my mother? Isn't it sinful to do this? Where do bad little boys go who gobble up their good kind mother's jam?" and then he didn't kneel down all alone and promise never to be wicked any more, and rise up with a light, happy heart, and go and tell his mother all about it, and beg her forgiveness, and be blessed by her with tears of pride and thankfulness in her eyes. No; that is the way with all other bad boys in the books; but it happened otherwise with this Jim, strangely enough. He ate that jam, and said it was bully, in his sinful, vulgar way; and he put in the tar, and said that was bully also, and laughed, and observed "that the old woman would get up and snort" when she found it out; and when she did find it out, he denied knowing anything about it, and she whipped him severely, and he did the crying himself. Everything about this boy was curious—everything turned out differently with him from the way it does to the bad Jameses in the books.

Once he climbed up in Farmer Acorn's apple-tree to steal apples, and the limb didn't break, and he didn't fall and break his arm, and get torn by the farmer's great dog, and then languish on a sick bed for weeks, and repent and become good. Oh! no; he stole as many apples as he wanted and came down all right; and he was all ready for the dog too, and knocked him endways with a brick when he came to tear him. It was very strange—nothing like it ever happened in those mild little books with marbled backs, and with pictures in them of men with swallow-tailed coats and bell-crowned hats, and pantaloons that are short in the legs, and women with the waists of their dresses under their arms, and no hoops on. Nothing like it in any of the Sunday-school books.

Once he stole the teacher's pen-knife, and, when he was afraid it would be found out and he would get whipped, he slipped it into George Wilson's cap—poor Widow Wilson's son, the moral boy, the good little boy of the village, who always obeyed his mother, and never told an untruth, and was fond of his lessons, and infatuated with Sunday-school. And when the knife dropped from the cap, and poor George hung his head and blushed, as if in conscious guilt, and the grieved teacher charged the theft upon him, and was just in the very act of bringing the switch down upon his trembling shoulders, a white-haired, improbable justice of the peace did not suddenly appear in their midst, and strike an attitude and say, "Spare this noble boy—there stands the cowering culprit! I was passing the school-door at recess, and unseen myself, I saw the theft committed!" And then Jim didn't get whaled, and the venerable justice didn't read the tearful school a homily, and take George by the hand and say such a boy deserved to be exalted, and then tell him to come and make his home with him, and sweep out the office, and make fires, and run errands, and chop wood, and study law, and help his wife do household labors, and have all the balance of the time to play, and get forty cents a month, and be happy. No; it would have happened that way in the books, but it didn't happen that way to Jim. No meddling old clam of a justice dropped in to make trouble, and so the model boy George got thrashed, and Jim was glad of it because, you know, Jim hated moral boys. Jim said he was "down on them milksops." Such was the coarse language of this bad, neglected boy.

But the strangest thing that ever happened to Jim was the time he went boating on Sunday, and didn't get drowned, and that other time that he got caught out in the storm when he was fishing on Sunday, and didn't get struck by lightning. Why, you might look, and look, all through the Sunday-school books from now till next Christmas, and you would never come across anything like this. Oh no; you would find that all the bad boys who go boating on Sunday invariably get drowned; and all the bad boys who get caught out in storms when they are fishing on Sunday infallibly get struck by lightning. Boats with bad boys in them always upset on Sunday, and it always storms when bad boys go fishing on the Sabbath. How this Jim ever escaped is a mystery to me.

This Jim bore a charmed life—that must have been the way of it. Nothing could hurt him. He even gave the elephant in the menagerie a plug of tobacco, and the elephant didn't knock the top of his head off with his trunk. He browsed around the cupboard after essence of peppermint, and didn't make a mistake and drink *aqua fortis.* He stole his father's gun and went hunting on the Sabbath, and didn't shoot three or four of his fingers off. He struck his little sister on the temple with his fist when he was angry, and she didn't linger in pain through long summer days, and die with sweet words of forgiveness upon her lips that redoubled the anguish of his breaking heart. No; she got over it. He ran off and went to sea at last, and didn't come back and find himself sad and alone in the world, his loved ones sleeping in the quiet churchyard, and the vine-embowered home of his boyhood tumbled down and gone to decay. Ah! no; he came home as drunk as a piper, and got into the station-house the first thing.

And he grew up and married, and raised a large family, and brained them all with an axe one night, and got wealthy by all manner of cheating and rascality; and now he is the infernalest wickedest scoundrel in his native village, and is universally respected, and belongs to the Legislature.

So you see there never was a bad James in the Sunday-school books that had such a streak of luck as this sinful Jim with the charmed life.

The Story of the Good Little Boy

Once there was a good little boy by the name of Jacob Blivens. He always obeyed his parents, no matter how absurd and unreasonable their demands were; and he always learned his book, and never was late at Sabbath-school. He would not play hookey, even when his sober judgment told him it was the most profitable thing he could do. None of the other boys could ever make that boy out, he acted so strangely. He wouldn't lie no matter how convenient it was. He just said it was wrong to lie, and that was sufficient for him. And he was so honest that he was simply ridiculous. The curious ways that that Jacob had, surpassed everything. He wouldn't play marbles on Sunday, he wouldn't rob birds' nests, he wouldn't give hot pennies to organ-grinders' monkeys; he didn't seem to take any interest in any kind of rational amusement. So the other boys used to try to reason it out and come to an understanding of him, but they couldn't arrive at any satisfactory conclusion. As I said before, they could only figure out a sort of vague idea that he was "afflicted," and so they took him under their protection, and never allowed any harm to come to him.

This good little boy read all the Sunday-school books; they were his greatest delight. This was the whole secret of it. He believed in the good little boys they put in the Sunday-school books; he had every confidence in them. He longed to come across one of them alive, once; but he never did. They all died before his time, maybe. Whenever he read about a particularly good one he turned over quickly to the end to see what became of him, because he wanted to travel thousands of miles and gaze on him; but it wasn't any use; that good little boy always died in the last chapter, and there was a picture of the funeral, with all his relations and the Sunday-school children standing around the grave in pantaloons that were too short, and bonnets that were too large, and everybody crying into handkerchief's that had as much as a yard and a half of stuff in them. He was always headed off in this way. He never could see one of those good little boys on account of his always dying in the last chapter.

Jacob had a noble ambition to be put in a Sunday-school book. He wanted to be put in, with pictures representing him gloriously declining to lie to his mother, and her weeping for joy about it; and pictures representing him standing on the doorstep giving a penny to a poor beggar-woman with six children, and telling her to spend it freely, but not to be extravagant, because extravagance is a sin; and pictures of him magnanimously refusing to tell on the bad boy who always lay in wait for him around the corner as he came from school, and welted him over the head with a lath, and then chased him home, saying, "Hi! hi!" as he proceeded. That was the ambition of young Jacob Blivens. He wished to be put in a Sunday-school book. It made him feel a little uncomfortable sometimes when he reflected that the good little boys always died. He loved to live, you know, and this was the most unpleasant feature about being a Sunday-school-book boy. He knew it was not healthy to be good. He knew it was more fatal than consumption to be so supernaturally good as the boys in the books were; he knew that none of them had ever been able to stand it long, and it pained him to think that if they put him in a book he wouldn't ever see it, or even if they did get the book out before he died it wouldn't be popular without any picture of his funeral in the back part of it. It couldn't be much of a Sunday-school book that couldn't tell about the advice he gave to the community when he was dying. So at last, of course, he had to make up his mind to do the best he could under the circumstances—to live right, and hang on as long as he could, and have his dying speech all ready when his time came.

But somehow nothing ever went right with this good little boy; nothing ever turned out with him the way it turned out with the good little boys in the books. They always had a good time, and the bad boys had the broken legs; but in his case there was a screw loose somewhere, and it all happened just the other way. When he found Jim Blake stealing apples, and went under the tree to read to him about the bad little boy who fell out of a neighbor's apple-tree and broke his arm, Jim fell out of the tree too, but he fell on *him,* and broke *his* arm, and Jim wasn't hurt at all. Jacob couldn't understand that. There wasn't anything in the books like it.

And once, when some bad boys pushed a blind man over in the mud, and Jacob ran to help him up and receive his blessing, the blind man did not give him any blessing at all, but whacked him over the head with his stick and said he would like to catch him shoving *him* again, and then pretending to help him up. This was not in accordance with any of the books. Jacob looked them all over to see.

One thing that Jacob wanted to do was to find a lame dog that hadn't any place to stay, and was hungry and persecuted, and bring him home and pet him and have that dog's imperishable gratitude. And at last he found one and was happy; and he brought him home and fed him, but when he was going to pet him the dog flew at him and tore all the clothes off him except those that were in front, and made a spectacle of him that was astonishing. He examined authorities, but he could not understand the matter. It was of the same breed of dogs that was in the books, but it acted very differently. Whatever this boy did he got into trouble. The very things the boys in the books got rewarded for turned out to be about the most unprofitable things he could invest in.

Once, when he was on his way to Sunday-school, he saw some bad boys starting off pleasuring in a sail-boat. He was filled with consternation, because he knew from his reading that boys who went sailing on Sunday invariably got drowned. So he ran out on a raft to warn them, but a log turned with him and slid him into the river. A man got him out pretty soon, and the doctor pumped the water out of him, and gave him a fresh start with his bellows, but he caught cold and lay sick a-bed nine weeks. But the most unaccountable thing about it was that the bad boys in the boat had a good time all day, and then reached home alive and well in the most surprising manner. Jacob Blivens said there was nothing like these things in the books. He was perfectly dumbfounded.

When he got well he was a little discouraged, but he resolved to keep on trying anyhow. He knew that so far his experiences wouldn't do to go in a book, but he hadn't yet reached the allotted term of life for good little boys, and he hoped to be able to make a record yet if he could hold on till his time was fully up. If everything else failed he had his dying speech to fall back on.

He examined his authorities, and found that it was now time for him to go to sea as a cabin-boy. He called on a ship captain and made his application, and when the captain asked for his recommendations he proudly drew out a tract and pointed to the words, "To Jacob Blivens, from his affectionate teacher." But the captain was a coarse, vulgar man, and he said, "Oh, that be blowed! *that* wasn't any proof that he knew how to wash dishes or handle a slush-bucket, and he guessed he didn't want him." This was altogether the most extraordinary thing that ever happened to Jacob in all his life. A compliment from a teacher, on a tract, had never failed to move the tenderest emotions of ship captains, and open the way to all offices of honor and profit in their gift—it never had in any book that ever *he* had read. He could hardly believe his senses.

This boy always had a hard time of it. Nothing ever came out according to the authorities with him. At last, one day, when he was around hunting up bad little boys to admonish, he found a lot of them in the old iron foundry fixing up a little joke on fourteen or fifteen dogs, which they had tied together in long procession, and were going to ornament with empty nitro-glycerine cans made fast to their tails. Jacob's heart was touched. He sat down on one of those cans (for he never minded grease when duty was before him), and he took hold of the foremost dog by the collar, and turned his reproving eye upon wicked Tom Jones. But just at that moment Alderman McWelter, full of wrath, stepped in. All the bad boys ran away, but Jacob Blivens rose in conscious innocence and began one of those stately little Sunday-school-book speeches which always commence with "Oh, sir!" in dead opposition to the fact that no boy, good or bad, ever starts a remark with "Oh, sir." But the alderman never waited to hear the rest. He took Jacob Blivens by the ear and turned him around, and hit him a whack in the rear with the flat of his hand; and in an instant that good little boy shot out through the roof and soared away towards the sun, with the fragments of those fifteen dogs stringing after him like the tail of a kite. And there wasn't a sign of that alderman or that old iron foundry left on the face of the earth; and, as for young Jacob Blivens, he never got a chance to make his last dying speech after all his trouble fixing it up, unless he made it to the birds; because, although the bulk of him came down all right in a tree-top in an adjoining county, the rest of him was apportioned around among four townships, and so they had to hold five inquests on him to find out whether he was dead or not, and how it occurred. You never saw a boy scattered so.*

Thus perished the good little boy who did the best he could, but he didn't come out according to the books. Every boy who ever did as he did prospered except him. His case is truly remarkable. It will probably never be accounted for.

*This glycerine catastrophe is borrowed from a floating newspaper item, whose author's name I would give if I knew it.—M.T.

Disgraceful Persecution of a Boy

In San Francisco, the other day, "A well-dressed boy, on his way to Sunday-school, was arrested and thrown into the city prison for stoning Chinamen."

What a commentary is this upon human justice! What sad prominence it gives to our human disposition to tyrannize over the weak! San Francisco has little right to take credit to herself for her treatment of this poor boy. What had the child's education been? How should he suppose it was wrong to stone a Chinaman? Before we side against him, along with outraged San Francisco, let us give him a chance—let us hear the testimony for the defence.

He was a "well-dressed" boy, and a Sunday-school scholar, and therefore, the chances are that his parents were intelligent, well-to-do people, with just enough natural villainy in their composition to make them yearn after the daily papers, and enjoy them; and so this boy had opportunities to learn all through the week how to do right, as well as on Sunday.

It was in this way that he found out that the great commonwealth of California imposes an unlawful mining-tax upon John the foreigner, and allows Patrick the foreigner to dig gold for nothing—probably because the degraded Mongol is at no expense for whisky, and the refined Celt cannot exist without it.

It was in this way that he found out that a respectable number of the tax-gatherers—it would be unkind to say all of them—collect the tax twice, instead of once; and that, inasmuch as they do it solely to discourage Chinese immigration into the mines, it is a thing that is much applauded, and likewise regarded as being singularly facetious.

It was in this way that he found out that when a white man robs a sluice-box (by the term white man is meant Spaniards, Mexicans, Portuguese, Irish, Hondurans, Peruvians, Chileans, &c., &c.), they make him leave the camp; and when a Chinaman does that thing, they hang him.

It was in this way that he found out that in many districts of the vast Pacific coast, so strong is the wild, free love of justice in the hearts of the people, that whenever any secret and mysterious crime is committed, they say, "Let justice be done, though the heavens fall," and go straightway and swing a Chinaman.

It was in this way that he found out that by studying one half of each day's "local items," it would appear that the police of San Francisco were either asleep or dead, and by studying the other half it would seem that the reporters were gone mad with admiration of the energy, the virtue, the high effectiveness, and the dare-devil intrepidity of that very police—making exultant mention of how "the Argus-eyed officer So-and-so," captured a wretched knave of a Chinaman who was stealing chickens, and brought him gloriously to the city prison; and how "the gallant officer Such-and-such-a-one," quietly kept an eye on the movements of an "unsuspecting, almond-eyed son of Confucius" (your reporter is nothing if not facetious), following him around with that far-off look of vacancy and unconsciousness always so finely affected by that inscrutible being, the forty-dollar policeman, during a waking interval, and captured him at last in the very act of placing his hands in a suspicious manner upon a paper of tacks, left by the owner in an exposed situation; and how one officer performed this prodigious thing, and another officer that, and another the other—and pretty much every one of these performances having for a dazzling central incident a Chinaman guilty of a shilling's worth of crime, an unfortunate, whose misdemeanor must be hurraed into something enormous in order to keep the public from noticing how many really important rascals went uncaptured in the meantime, and how overrated those glorified policemen actually are.

It was in this way that the boy found out that the Legislature, being aware that the Constitution has made America an asylum for the poor and the oppressed of all nations, and that, therefore, the poor and oppressed who fly to our shelter must not be charged a disabling admission fee, made a law that every Chinaman, upon landing, must be *vaccinated* upon the wharf, and pay to the State's appointed officer *ten dollars* for the service, when there are plenty of doctors in San Francisco who would be glad enough to do it for him for fifty cents.

It was in this way that the boy found out that a Chinaman had no rights that any man was bound to respect; that he had no sorrows that any man was bound to pity; that neither his life nor his liberty was worth the purchase of a penny when a white man needed a scapegoat; that nobody loved Chinamen, nobody befriended them, nobody spared them suffering when it was convenient to inflict it; everybody, individuals, communities, the majesty of the State itself, joined in hating, abusing, and persecuting these humble strangers.

And, therefore, what *could* have been more natural than for this sunny-hearted boy, tripping along to Sunday-school, with his mind teeming with freshly-learned incentives to high and virtuous action, to say to himself—

"Ah, there goes a Chinaman! God will not love me if I do not stone him."

And for this he was arrested and put in the city jail.

Everything conspired to teach him that it was a high and holy thing to stone a Chinaman, and yet he no sooner attempts to do his duty that he is punished for it—he, poor chap, who has been aware all his life that one of the principal recreations of the police, out toward the Gold Refinery, is to look on with tranquil enjoyment while the butchers of Brannan Street set their dogs on unoffending Chinamen, and make them flee for their lives.*

Keeping in mind the tuition in the humanities which the entire "Pacific coast" gives its youth, there is a very sublimity of incongruity in the virtuous

* I have many such memories in my mind, but am thinking just at present of one particular one, where the Brannan Street butchers set their dogs on a Chinaman who was quietly passing with a basket of clothes on his head; and while the dogs mutilated his flesh, a butcher increased the hilarity of the occasion by knocking some of the Chinaman's teeth down his throat with half a brick. This incident sticks in my memory with a more malevolent tenacity, perhaps, on account of the fact that I was in the employ of a San Francisco journal at the time, and was not allowed to publish it because it might offend some of the peculiar element that subscribed for the paper.

flourish with which the good city fathers of San Francisco proclaim (as they have lately done) that "The police are positively ordered to arrest all boys, of every description and wherever found, who engage in assaulting Chinamen."

Still, let us be truly glad they have made the order, notwithstanding its inconsistency; and let us rest perfectly confident the police are glad, too. Because there is no personal peril in arresting boys, provided they be of the small kind, and the reporters will have to laud their performances just as loyally as ever, or go without items.

The new form for local items in San Francisco will now be: — "The ever vigilant and efficient officer So-and-so succeeded, yesterday afternoon, in arresting Master Tommy Jones, after a determined resistance," etc., etc., followed by the customary statistics and final hurrah, with its unconscious sarcasm: "We are happy in being able to state that this is the forty-seventh boy arrested by this gallant officer since the new ordinance went into effect. The most extraordinary activity prevails in the police department. Nothing like it has been seen since we can remember."

PETITION CONCERNING COPYRIGHT

TO THE HONORABLE THE SENATE AND HOUSE OF REPRESENTATIVES IN CONGRESS ASSEMBLED:

Whereas, The Constitution guarantees equal rights to all, backed by the Declaration of Independence; and

Whereas, Under our laws, the right of property in real estate is perpetual; and

Whereas, Under our laws, the right of property in the literary result of a citizen's intellectual labor is restricted to forty-two years; and

Whereas, Forty-two years seems an exceedingly just and righteous term, and a sufficiently long one for the retention of property:

Therefore, Your petitioner, having the good of his country solely at heart, humbly prays that "equal rights" and fair and equal treatment may be meted out to all citizens, by the restriction of rights in *all* property, real estate included, to the beneficent term of forty-two years. Then shall all men bless your honorable body and be happy. And for this will your petitioner ever pray.

MARK TWAIN

A PARAGRAPH NOT ADDED TO THE PETITION

The charming absurdity of restricting property-rights in books to forty-two years sticks prominently out in the fact that hardly any man's books ever *live* forty-two years, or even the half of it; and so, for the sake of getting a shabby advantage of the heirs of about one Scott or Burns or Milton in a hundred years, the law makers of the "Great" Republic are content to leave that poor little pilfering edict upon the statute books. It is like an emperor lying in wait to rob a phenix's nest, and waiting the necessary century to get the chance.

After-Dinner Speech

[AT A FOURTH-OF-JULY GATHERING, IN LONDON, OF AMERICANS.]

Mr. Chairman and Ladies and Gentlemen: I thank you for the compliment which has just been tendered me, and to show my appreciation of it I will not afflict you with many words. It is pleasant to celebrate in this peaceful way, upon this old mother soil, the anniversary of an experiment which was born of war with this same land so long ago, and wrought out to a successful issue by the devotion of our ancestors. It has taken nearly a hundred years to bring the English and Americans into kindly and mutually appreciative relations, but I believe it has been accomplished at last. It was a great step when the two last misunderstandings were settled by arbitration instead of cannon. It is another great step when England adopts our sewing machines without claiming the invention—as usual. It was another when they imported one of our sleeping cars the other day. And it warmed my heart more than I can tell, yesterday, when I witnessed the spectacle of an Englishman ordering an American sherry cobbler of his own free will and accord—and not only that but with a great brain and a level head reminding the bar-keeper not to forget the strawberries. With a common origin, a common language, a common literature, a common religion and—common drinks, what is longer needful to the cementing of the two nations together in a permanent bond of brotherhood?

This is an age of progress, and ours is a progressive land. A great and glorious land, too—a land which has developed a Washington, a Franklin, a Wm. M. Tweed, a Longfellow, a Motley, a Jay Gould, a Samuel C. Pomeroy, a recent Congress which has never had its equal—(in some respects) and a United States Army which conquered sixty Indians in eight months by tiring them out—which is much better than uncivilized slaughter, God knows. We have a criminal jury system which is superior to any in the world; and its efficiency is only marred by the difficulty of finding twelve men every day who don't know anything and can't read. And I may observe that we have an insanity plea that would have saved Cain. I think I can say, and say with pride, that we have some legislatures that bring higher prices than any in the world.

I refer with effusion to our railway system, which consents to let us live, though it might do the opposite, being our owners. It only destroyed three thousand and seventy lives last year by collisions, and twenty-seven thousand two hundred and sixty by running over heedless and unnecessary people at crossings. The companies seriously regretted the killing of these thirty thousand people, and went so far as to pay for some of them—voluntarily, of course, for the meanest of us would not claim that we possess a court treacherous enough to enforce a law against a railway company. But thank Heaven the railway companies are generally disposed to do the right and kindly thing without compulsion. I know of an instance which greatly touched me at the time. After an accident the company sent home the remains of a dear distant old relative of mine in a basket, with the remark, "Please state what figure you hold him at—and return the basket." Now there couldn't be anything friendlier than that.

But I must not stand here and brag all night. However, you won't mind a body bragging a little about his country on the fourth of July. It is a fair and legitimate time to fly the eagle. I will say only one more word of brag—and a hopeful one. It is this. We have a form of government which gives each man a fair chance and no favor. With us no individual is born with a right to look down upon his neighbor and hold him in contempt. Let such of us as are not dukes find our consolation in that. And we may find hope for the future in the fact that as unhappy as is the condition of our political morality to-day, England has risen up out of a far fouler since the days when Charles I, ennobled courtezans and all political place was a matter of bargain and sale. There is hope for us yet.*

Lionising Murderers

I had heard so much about the celebrated fortune-teller Madame ——, that I went to see her yesterday. She has a dark complexion naturally, and this effect is heightened by artificial aids which cost her nothing. She wears curls—very black ones, and I had an impression that she gave their native attractiveness a lift with rancid butter. She wears a reddish check handkerchief, cast loosely around her neck, and it was plain that her other one is slow getting back from the wash. I presume she takes snuff. At any rate, something resembling it had lodged among the hairs sprouting from her upper lip. I know she likes garlic—I knew that as soon as she sighed. She looked at me searchingly for nearly a minute, with her black eyes, and then said—

"It is enough. Come!"

She started down a very dark and dismal corridor—I stepped close after her. Presently she stopped, and said that, as the way was so crooked and dark,

* At least the above is the speech which I was *going* to make, but our minister, Gen. Schenck, presided, and after the blessing, got up and made a great long inconceivably dull harangue, and wound up by saying that inasmuch as speech-making did not seem to exhilarate the guests much, all further oratory would be dispensed with, during the evening, and we could just sit and talk privately to our elbow-neighbors and have a good sociable time. It is known that in consequence of that remark forty-four perfected speeches died in the womb. The depression, the gloom, the solemnity that reigned over the banquet from that time forth will be a lasting memory with many that were there. By that one thoughtless remark Gen. Schenck lost forty-four of the best friends he had in England. More than one said that night, "And this is the sort of person that is sent to represent us in a great sister empire!"

perhaps she had better get a light. But it seemed ungallant to allow a woman to put herself to so much trouble for me, and so I said—

"It is not worth while, madam. If you will heave another sigh, I think I can follow it."

So we got along all right. Arrived at her official and mysterious den, she asked me to tell her the date of my birth, the exact hour of that occurrence, and the color of my grandmother's hair. I answered as accurately as I could. Then she said—

"Young man, summon your fortitude—do not tremble. I am about to reveal the past."

"Information concerning the *future* would be in a general way, more———"

"Silence! You have had much trouble, some joy, some good fortune, some bad. Your great-grandfather was hanged."

"That is a l—."

"Silence! Hanged sir. But it was not his fault. He could not help it."

"I am glad you do him justice."

"Ah—grieve, rather, that the jury did. He was hanged. His star crosses yours in the fourth division, fifth sphere. Consequently you will be hanged also."

"In view of this cheerful———"

"I *must* have silence. Yours was not, in the beginning, a criminal nature, but circumstances changed it. At the age of nine you stole sugar. At the age of fifteen you stole money. At twenty you stole horses. At twenty-five you committed arson. At thirty, hardened in crime, you became an editor. You are now a public lecturer. Worse things are in store for you. You will be sent to Congress. Next, to the penitentiary. Finally, happiness will come again—all will be well—you will be hanged."

I was now in tears. It seemed hard enough to go to Congress; but to be hanged—this was too sad, too dreadful. The woman seemed surprised at my grief. I told her the thoughts that were in my mind. Then she comforted me.

"Why, man,"* she said, "hold up your head—*you* have nothing to grieve about. Listen. You will live in New Hampshire. In your sharp need and distress

* In this paragraph the fortune-teller details the exact history of the Pike-Brown assassination case in New Hampshire, from the succoring and saving of the stranger Pike by the Browns, to the subsequent hanging and coffining of that treacherous miscreant. She adds nothing, invents nothing, exaggerates nothing (see any New England paper for November 1869). This Pike-Brown case is selected merely as a type, to illustrate a custom that prevails, not in New Hampshire alone, but in every State in the union—I mean the sentimental custom of visiting, petting, glorifying, and snuffling over murderers like this Pike, from the day they enter the jail under sentence of death until they swing from the gallows. The following extract from the *Temple Bar* (1866) reveals the fact that this custom is not confined to the United States:—"On December 31st, 1841, a man named John Johnes, a shoemaker, murdered his sweetheart, Mary Hallam, the daughter of a respectable laborer, at Mansfield, in the county of Nottingham. He was executed on March 23d, 1842. He was a man of unsteady habits, and gave way to violent fits of passion. The girl declined his addresses, and he said if he did not have her no one else should. After he had inflicted the first

the Brown family will succor you—such of them as Pike the assassin left alive. They will be benefactors to you. When you shall have grown fat upon their bounty, and are grateful and happy, you will desire to make some modest return for these things, and so you will go to the house some night and brain the whole family with an axe. You will rob the dead bodies of your benefactors, and disburse your gains in riotous living among the rowdies and courtesans of Boston. Then you will be arrested, tried, condemned to be hanged, thrown into prison. Now is your happy day. You will be converted—you will be converted just as soon as every effort to compass pardon, commutation, or reprieve has failed—and then! Why, then, every morning and every afternoon, the best and purest young ladies of the village will assemble in your cell and sing hymns. This will show that assassination is respectable. Then you will write a touching letter, in which you will forgive all those recent Browns. This will excite the public admiration. No public can withstand magnanimity. Next, they will take you to the scaffold, with great *éclat,* at the head of an imposing procession composed of clergymen, officials, citizens generally, and young ladies walking pensively two and two, and bearing bouquets and immortelles. You will mount the scaffold, and while the great concourse stand uncovered in your presence, you will read your sappy little speech which the minister has written for you. And then, in the midst of a grand and impressive silence, they will swing you into per—— Paradise, my son. There will not be a dry eye on the ground. You will be a hero! Not a rough there but will envy you. Not a rough there but will resolve to emulate you. And next, a great procession will follow you to the tomb—will weep over your remains—the young ladies will sing again the hymns made dear by sweet associations connected with the jail, and, as a last tribute of affection, respect, and appreciation of your many sterling qualities, they will walk two and two around your bier, and strew wreaths of flowers on it. And lo! you are canonized. Think of it, son—ingrate, assassin, robber of the dead, drunken brawler among thieves and harlots in the slums of Boston one month, and the pet of the pure and innocent daughters of the land the next! A bloody and hateful devil—a bewept, bewailed, and sainted martyr—all in a month! Fool!—so noble a fortune, and yet you sit here grieving!"

"No, madame," I said, "you do me wrong, you do indeed. I am perfectly satisfied. I did not know before that my great-grandfather was hanged, but it

---

wound, which was not immediately fatal, she begged for her life, but seeing him resolved, asked for time to pray. He said that he would pray for both, and completed the crime. The wounds were inflicted by a shoemaker's knife, and her throat was cut barbarously. After this he dropped on his knees some time, and prayed God to have mercy on two unfortunate lovers. He made no attempt to escape, and confessed the crime. After his imprisonment he behaved in the most decorous manner; he won upon the good opinion of the jail chaplain, and he was visited by the Bishop of Lincoln. It does not appear that he expressed any contrition for the crime, but seemed to pass away with triumphant certainty that he was going to rejoin his victim in heaven. *He was visited by some pious and benevolent ladies of Nottingham, some of whom declared he was a child of God, if ever there was one. One of the ladies sent him a white camelia to wear at his execution.*"

is of no consequence. He has probably ceased to bother about it by this time—and I have not commenced yet. I confess, madame, that I do something in the way of editing and lecturing, but the other crimes you mention have escaped my memory. Yet I must have committed them—you would not deceive a stranger. But let the past be as it was, and let the future be as it may—these are nothing. I have only cared for one thing. I have always felt that I should be hanged some day, and somehow the thought has annoyed me considerably; but if you can only assure me that I shall be hanged in New Hampshire"—

"Not a shadow of a doubt!"

"Bless you, my benefactress!—excuse this embrace—you have removed a great load from my breast. To be hanged in New Hampshire is happiness—it leaves an honored name behind a man, and introduces him at once into the best New Hampshire society in the other world."

I then took leave of the fortune-teller. But, seriously, is it well to glorify a murderous villain on the scaffold, as Pike was glorified in New Hampshire? Is it well to turn the penalty for a bloody crime into a reward? Is it just to do it? Is it safe?

A New Crime

LEGISLATION NEEDED

This country, during the last thirty or forty years, has produced some of the most remarkable cases of insanity of which there is any mention in history. For instance, there was the Baldwin case, in Ohio, twenty-two years ago. Baldwin, from his boyhood up, had been of a vindictive, malignant, quarrelsome nature. He put a boy's eye out once, and never was heard upon any occasion to utter a regret for it. He did many such things. But at last he did something that was serious. He called at a house just after dark, one evening, knocked, and when the occupant came to the door, shot him dead, and then tried to escape, but was captured. Two days before, he had wantonly insulted a helpless cripple, and the man he afterward took swift vengeance upon with an assassin bullet had knocked him down. Such was the Baldwin case. The trial was long and exciting: the community was fearfully wrought up. Men said this spiteful, bad-hearted villain had caused grief enough in his time, and now he should satisfy the law. But they were mistaken; Baldwin was *insane* when he did the deed—they had not thought of that. By the arguments of counsel it was shown that at half-past ten in the morning on the day of the murder, Baldwin became insane, and remained so for eleven hours and a half exactly. This just covered the case comfortably, and he was acquitted. Thus, if an unthinking and excited community had been listened to instead of the arguments of counsel, a poor crazy creature would have been held to a fearful responsibility for a mere freak of madness. Baldwin went clear, and although his relatives and friends were naturally incensed against the community for their injurious suspicions and remarks, they said let it go for this time, and did not prosecute. The Baldwins were very wealthy. This same Baldwin had momentary fits of insanity twice afterward, and on both occasions killed people he had grudges against. And on both these occasions the circumstances of the killing were so aggravated, and the murders so seemingly heartless and treacherous, that if Baldwin had not been insane he would have been hanged without the shadow of a doubt. As it was, it required all his political and family influence to get him clear in one of the cases, and cost him not less than 10,000 dollars to get clear in the other. One of these men he had notoriously been threatening to kill for twelve years. The poor creature happened, by the merest piece of ill fortune, to come along a dark alley at the very moment that Baldwin's insanity came upon him, and so he was shot in the back with a gun loaded with slugs.

Take the case of Lynch Hackett, of Pennsylvania. Twice, in public, he attacked a German butcher by the name of Bemis Feldner, with a cane, and both times Feldner whipped him with his fists. Hackett was a vain, wealthy, violent gentleman, who held his blood and family in high esteem, and believed that a reverent respect was due to his great riches. He brooded over the shame of his chastisement for two weeks, and then, in a momentary fit of insanity, armed himself to the teeth, rode into town, waited a couple of hours until he saw Feldner coming down the street with his wife on his arm, and then, as the couple passed the doorway in which he had partially concealed himself, he drove a knife into Feldner's neck, killing him instantly. The widow caught the limp form and eased it to the earth. Both were drenched with blood. Hackett jocosely remarked to her that as a professional butcher's recent wife she could appreciate the artistic neatness of the job that left her in condition to marry again, in case she wanted to. This remark, and another which he made to a friend, that his position in society made the killing of an obscure citizen simply an "eccentricity" instead of a crime, were shown to be evidences of insanity, and so Hackett escaped punishment. The jury were hardly inclined to accept these as proofs, at first, inasmuch as the prisoner had never been insane before the murder, and under the tranquilizing effect of the butchering had immediately regained his right mind; but when the defence came to show that a third cousin of Hackett's wife's stepfather was insane, and not only insane, but had a nose the very counterpart of Hackett's, it was plain that insanity was hereditary in the family, and Hackett had come by it by legitimate inheritance. Of course the jury then acquitted him. But it was a merciful providence that Mrs. H.'s people had been afflicted as shown, else Hackett would certainly have been hanged.

However, it is not possible to recount all the marvellous cases of insanity that have come under the public notice in the last thirty or forty years. There was the Durgin case in New Jersey three years ago. The servant girl, Bridget Durgin, at dead of night, invaded her mistress' bedroom and carved the lady literally to pieces with a knife. Then she dragged the body to the middle of the floor, and beat and banged it with chairs and such things. Next she opened the feather beds, and strewed the contents around, saturated everything with kerosene, and set fire to the general wreck. She now took up the young child of the murdered woman in her blood-smeared hands, and walked off, through the snow, with no shoes on, to a neighbor's house a quarter of a mile off, and told a string of wild, incoherent stories about some men coming and setting fire to the house; and then she cried piteously, and without seeming to think there was anything suggestive about the blood upon her hands, her clothing, and the baby, volunteered the remark that she was afraid those men had murdered her mistress! Afterward, by her own confession and other testimony, it was proved that the mistress had always been kind to the girl, consequently there was no revenge in the murder; and it was also shown that the girl took nothing away from the burning house, not even her own shoes, and consequently robbery was not the motive. Now, the reader says, "Here comes that same old plea of insanity again." But the reader had deceived himself this time. No such plea was offered in her defence. The judge sentenced her, nobody persecuted the Governor with petitions for her pardon and she was promptly hanged.

There was that youth in Pennsylvania, whose curious confession was published some years ago. It was simply a conglomeration of incoherent drivel from beginning to end, and so was his lengthy speech on the scaffold afterward. For a whole year he was haunted with a desire to disfigure a certain young woman, so that no one would marry her. He did not love her himself, and did not want to marry her, but he did not want anybody else to do it. He would not go anywhere with her, and yet was opposed to anybody else's escorting her. Upon one occasion he declined to go to a wedding with her, and when she got other company, lay in wait for the couple by the road, intending to make them go back or kill the escort. After spending sleepless nights over his ruling desire for a full year, he at last attempted its execution—that is, attempted to disfigure the young woman. It was a success. It was permanent. In trying to shoot her cheek (as she sat at the supper table with her parents and brothers and sisters) in such a manner as to mar its comeliness, one of his bullets wandered a little out of the course, and she dropped dead. To the very last moment of his life he bewailed the ill luck that made her move her face just at the critical moment. And so he died, apparently about half persuaded that somehow it was chiefly her own fault that she got killed. This idiot was hanged. The plea of insanity was not offered.

Insanity certainly is on the increase in the world, and crime is dying out. There are no longer any murders—none worth mentioning, at any rate. Formerly, if you killed a man, it was possible that you were insane—but now, if you, having friends and money, kill a man it is *evidence* that you are a lunatic. In these days, too, if a person of good family and high social standing steals anything, they call it *kleptomania,* and send him to the lunatic asylum. If a person of high standing squanders his fortune in dissipation, and closes his career with strychnine or a bullet, "Temporary Aberration" is what was the trouble with *him.*

Is not this insanity plea becoming rather common? Is it not so common that the reader confidently expects to see it offered in every criminal case that comes before the courts? And is it not so cheap, and so common, and often so trivial, that the reader smiles in derision when the newspaper mentions it? And is it not curious to note how very often it wins acquittal for the prisoner? Of late years it does not seem possible for a man to so conduct himself, before killing another man, as not to be manifestly insane. If he talks about the stars, he is insane. If he appears nervous and uneasy an hour before the killing, he is insane. If he weeps over a great grief, his friends shake their heads, and fear that he is "not right." If, an hour after the murder, he seems ill at ease, preoccupied and excited, he is unquestionably insane.

Really, what we want now, is not laws against crime, but a law against *insanity*. There is where the true evil lies.

THE LATE BENJAMIN FRANKLIN

["Never put off till to-morrow what you can do day after to-morrow just as well."—B.F.]

This party was one of those persons whom they call Philosophers. He was twins, being born simultaneously in two different houses in the city of Boston. These houses remain unto this day, and have signs upon them worded in accordance with the facts. The signs are considered well enough to have, though not necessary, because the inhabitants point out the two birth-places to the stranger anyhow, and sometimes as often as several times in the same day. The subject of this memoir was of a vicious disposition, and early prostituted his talents to the invention of maxims and aphorisms calculated to inflict suffering upon the rising generation of all subsequent ages. His simplest acts, also, were contrived with a view to their being held up for the emulation of boys for ever—boys who might otherwise have been happy. It was in this spirit that he became the son of a soap-boiler, and probably for no other reason than that the efforts of all future boys who tried to be anything might be looked upon with suspicion unless they were the sons of soap-boilers. With a malevolence which is without parallel in history, he would work all day, and then sit up nights, and let on to be studying algebra by the light of a smouldering fire, so that all other boys might have to do that also, or else have Benjamin Franklin thrown up to them. Not satisfied with these proceedings, he had a fashion of living wholly on bread and water, and studying astronomy at meal time—a thing which has brought affliction to millions of boys since, whose fathers had read Franklin's pernicious biography.

His maxims were full of animosity towards boys. Nowadays a boy cannot follow out a single natural instinct without tumbling over some of those everlasting aphorisms and hearing from Franklin on the spot. If he buys two cents' worth of peanuts, his father says, "Remember what Franklin has said, my son—'A groat a day's a penny a year;'" and the comfort is all gone out of those peanuts. If he wants to spin his top when he has done work, his father quotes, "Procrastination is the thief of time." If he does a virtuous action, he never gets any thing for it, because "Virtue is its own reward." And that boy is hounded to death and robbed of his natural rest, because Franklin said once, in one of his inspired flights of malignity—

> "Early to bed and early to rise
> Makes a man healthy and wealthy and wise."

As if it were any object to a boy to be healthy and wealthy and wise on such terms. The sorrow that that maxim has cost me through my parents' experimenting on me with it, tongue cannot tell. The legitimate result is my present state of general debility, indigence, and mental aberration. My parents used to have me up before nine o'clock in the morning, sometimes, when I was a boy. If they had let me take my natural rest, where would I have been now? Keeping store, no doubt, and respected by all.

And what an adroit old adventurer the subject of this memoir was! In order to get a chance to fly his kite on Sunday he used to hang a key on the string and let on to be fishing for lightning. And a guileless public would go home chirping about the "wisdom" and the "genius" of the hoary Sabbath-breaker. If anybody caught him playing "mumble-peg" by himself, after the age of sixty, he would immediately appear to be ciphering out how the grass grew—as if it was any of his business. My grandfather knew him well, and he says Franklin was always fixed—always ready. If a body, during his old age, happened on him unexpectedly when he was catching flies, or making mud pies, or sliding on a cellar-door, he would immediately look wise, and rip out a maxim, and walk off with his nose in the air and his cap turned wrong side before, trying to appear absent-minded and eccentric. He was a hard lot.

He invented a stove that would smoke your head off in four hours by the clock. One can see the almost devilish satisfaction he took in it by his giving it his name.

He was always proud of telling how he entered Philadelphia for the first time, with nothing in the world but two shillings in his pocket and four rolls of bread under his arm. But really, when you come to examine it critically, it was nothing. Anybody could have done it.

To the subject of this memoir belongs the honor of recommending the army to go back to bows and arrows in place of bayonets and muskets. He observed, with his customary force, that the bayonet was very well under some circumstances, but that he doubted whether it could be used with accuracy at a long range.

Benjamin Franklin did a great many notable things for his country, and made her young name to be honored in many lands as the mother of such a son. It is not the idea of this memoir to ignore that or cover it up. No; the simple idea of it is to snub those pretentious maxims of his, which he worked up with a great show of originality out of truisms that had become wearisome platitudes as early as the dispersion from Babel; and also to snub his stove, and his military inspirations, his unseemly endeavor to make himself conspicuous when he entered Philadelphia, and his flying his kite and fooling away his time in all sorts of such ways when he ought to have been foraging for soap-fat, or constructing candles. I merely desired to do away with somewhat of the prevalent calamitous idea among heads of families that Franklin *acquired* his great genius by working for nothing, studying by moonlight, and getting up in the night instead of waiting till morning like a Christian; and that this programme, rigidly inflicted, will make a Franklin of every father's fool. It is time these gentlemen were finding out that these execrable eccentricities of instinct and conduct are only the *evidences* of genius, not the *creators* of it. I wish I had been the father of my parents long enough to make them comprehend this truth, and thus prepare them to let their son have an easier time of it. When I was a child I had to boil soap, notwithstanding my father was wealthy, and I had to get up early and study geometry at breakfast, and peddle my own poetry, and do everything just as Franklin did, in the solemn hope that I would be a Franklin some day. And here I am.

The Adventures of Tom Sawyer

The Adventures of Tom Sawyer (1876) remains, along with Adventures of Huckleberry Finn, Twain's best-known work. In fact, the popular imagination often combines these two quite different novels into a vague nostalgia for innocence. In Tom, Twain was exploring his memories of childhood, and he was speaking from the point of view of a perceptive, indulgent adult who understands quite well what occurs in the mind of a young boy. Chapters 4 and 5 reveal what happens during a memorable Sunday morning. It becomes apparent that Twain enjoyed letting the fresh air of actuality pierce the pretense of conventional attitudes. The standard procedures of memorization and sanctimonious behavior provide targets for his criticism.

Chapter 4

The sun rose upon a tranquil world, and beamed down upon the peaceful village like a benediction. Breakfast over, Aunt Polly had family worship: it began with a prayer built from the ground up of solid courses of Scriptural quotations, welded together with a thin mortar of originality; and from the summit of this she delivered a grim chapter of the Mosaic Law, as from Sinai.

Then Tom girded up his loins, so to speak, and went to work to "get his verses." Sid had learned his lesson days before. Tom bent all his energies to the memorizing of five verses, and he chose part of the Sermon on the Mount, because he could find no verses that were shorter. At the end of half an hour Tom had a vague general idea of his lesson, but no more, for his mind was traversing the whole field of human thought, and his hands were busy with distracting recreations. Mary took his book to hear him recite, and he tried to find his way through the fog:

"Blessed are the—a—a—"

"Poor—"

"Yes—poor; blessed are the poor—a—a—"

"In spirit—"

"In spirit; blessed are the poor in spirit, for they—they—"

"*Theirs*—"

"For *theirs*. Blessed are the poor in spirit, for *theirs* is the kingdom of heaven. Blessed are they that mourn, for they—they—"

"Sh—"

"For they—a—"

"S, H, A—"

"For they S, H—Oh, I don't know what it is!"

"*Shall!*"

"Oh, *shall!* for they shall—for they shall—a—a—shall mourn—a—a—blessed are they that shall—they that—a—they that shall mourn, for they shall—a—shall *what?* Why don't you tell me, Mary?—what do you want to be so mean for?"

"Oh, Tom, you poor thick-headed thing, I'm not teasing you. I wouldn't do that. You must go and learn it again. Don't you be discouraged, Tom, you'll manage it—and if you do, I'll give you something ever so nice. There, now, that's a good boy."

"All right! What is it, Mary? tell me what it is."

"Never you mind, Tom. You know if I say it's nice, it *is* nice."

"You bet you that's so, Mary. All right, I'll tackle it again."

And he did "tackle it again"—and under the double pressure of curiosity and prospective gain, he did it with such spirit that he accomplished a shining success. Mary gave him a brand-new "Barlow" knife worth twelve and a half cents; and the convulsion of delight that swept his system shook him to his foundations. True, the knife would not cut anything, but it was a "sure-enough" Barlow, and there was inconceivable grandeur in that—though where the Western boys ever got the idea that such a weapon could possibly be counterfeited to its injury, is an imposing mystery and will always remain so, perhaps. Tom contrived to scarify the cupboard with it, and was arranging to begin on the bureau, when he was called off to dress for Sunday-school.

Mary gave him a tin basin of water and a piece of soap, and he went outside the door and set the basin on a little bench there; then he dipped the soap in the water and laid it down; turned up his sleeves; poured out the water on the ground, gently, and then entered the kitchen and began to wipe his face diligently on the towel behind the door. But Mary removed the towel and said:

"Now ain't you ashamed, Tom! You mustn't be so bad. Water won't hurt you."

Tom was a trifle disconcerted. The basin was refilled, and this time he stood over it a little while, gathering resolution; took in a big breath and began. When he entered the kitchen presently, with both eyes shut and groping for the towel with his hands, an honorable testimony of suds and water was dripping from his face. But when he emerged from the towel, he was not yet satisfactory, for the clean territory stopped short at his chin and his jaws, like a mask; below and beyond this line there was a dark expanse of unirrigated soil that spread downward in front and backward around his neck. Mary took him in hand, and when she was done with him he was a man and a brother, without distinction of color, and his saturated hair was neatly brushed, and its short curls wrought into a dainty and symmetrical general effect. [He privately smoothed out the curls, with labor and difficulty, and plastered his hair close down to his head; for he held curls to be effeminate, and his own filled his life with bitterness.] Then Mary got out a suit of his clothing that had been used only on Sundays during two years—they were simply called his "other clothes"—and so by that we know the size of his wardrobe. The girl "put him to rights" after he had dressed himself; she buttoned his neat roundabout up to his chin, turned his vast shirt-collar down over his shoulders, brushed him off and crowned him with his speckled straw hat. He now looked exceedingly improved and uncomfortable. He was fully as uncomfortable as he looked; for there was a restraint about whole clothes and cleanliness that galled him. He hoped that Mary would forget his shoes, but the hope was blighted; she coated them thoroughly with tallow, as was the custom, and brought them out. He lost his temper and said he was always being made to do everything he didn't want to do. But Mary said, persuasively:

"Please, Tom—that's a good boy."

So he got into the shoes snarling. Mary was soon ready, and the three children set out for Sunday-school—a place that Tom hated with his whole heart; but Sid and Mary were fond of it.

Sabbath-school hours were from nine to half past ten; and then church service. Two of the children always remained for the sermon voluntarily, and the other always remained too—for stronger reasons. The church's high-backed, uncushioned pews would seat about three hundred persons; the edifice was but a small, plain affair, with a sort of pine board tree-box on top of it for a steeple At the door Tom dropped back a step and accosted a Sunday-dressed comrade:

"Say, Billy, got a yaller ticket?"

"Yes."

"What'll you take for her?"

"What'll you give?"

"Piece of lickrish and a fish-hook."

"Less see 'em."

Tom exhibited. They were satisfactory, and the property changed hands. Then Tom traded a couple of white alleys for three red tickets, and some small trifle or other for a couple of blue ones. He waylaid other boys as they came, and went on buying tickets of various colors ten or fifteen minutes longer. He entered the church, now, with a swarm of clean and noisy boys and girls, proceeded to his seat and started a quarrel with the first boy that came handy. The teacher, a grave, elderly man, interfered; then turned his back a moment and

Tom pulled a boy's hair in the next bench, and was absorbed in his book when the boy turned around; stuck a pin in another boy, presently, in order to hear him say "Ouch!" and got a new reprimand from his teacher. Tom's whole class were of a pattern—restless, noisy, and troublesome. When they came to recite their lessons, not one of them knew his verses perfectly, but had to be prompted all along. However, they worried through, and each got his reward—in small blue tickets, each with a passage of Scripture on it; each blue ticket was pay for two verses of the recitation. Ten blue tickets equaled a red one, and could be exchanged for it; ten red tickets equaled a yellow one; for ten yellow tickets the superintendent gave a very plainly bound Bible (worth forty cents in those easy times) to the pupil. How many of my readers would have the industry and application to memorize two thousand verses, even for a Doré Bible? And yet Mary had acquired two Bibles in this way—it was the patient work of two years—and a boy of German parentage had won four or five. He once recited three thousand verses without stopping; but the strain upon his mental faculties was too great, and he was little better than an idiot from that day forth—a grievous misfortune for the school, for on great occasions, before company, the superintendent (as Tom expressed it) had always made this boy come out and "spread himself." Only the older pupils managed to keep their tickets and stick to their tedious work long enough to get a Bible, and so the delivery of one of these prizes was a rare and noteworthy circumstance; the successful pupil was so great and conspicuous for that day that on the spot every scholar's heart was fired with a fresh ambition that often lasted a couple of weeks. It is possible that Tom's mental stomach had never really hungered for one of those prizes, but unquestionably his entire being had for many a day longed for the glory and the éclat that came with it.

In due course the superintendent stood up in front of the pulpit, with a closed hymn-book in his hand and his forefinger inserted between its leaves, and commanded attention. When a Sunday-school superintendent makes his customary little speech, a hymn-book in the hand is as necessary as is the inevitable sheet of music in the hand of a singer who stands forward on the platform and sings a solo at a concert—though why, is a mystery: for neither the hymn-book nor the sheet of music is ever referred to by the sufferer. This superintendent was a slim creature of thirty-five, with a sandy goatee and short sandy hair; he wore a stiff standing-collar whose upper edge almost reached his ears and whose sharp points curved forward abreast the corners of his mouth—a fence that compelled a straight lookout ahead, and a turning of the whole body when a side view was required; his chin was propped on a spreading cravat which was as broad and as long as a bank-note, and had fringed ends; his boot-toes were turned sharply up, in the fashion of the day, like sleigh-runners—an effect patiently and laboriously produced by the young men by sitting with their toes pressed against a wall for hours together. Mr. Walters was very earnest of mien, and very sincere and honest at heart; and he held sacred things and places in such reverence, and so separated them from worldly matters, that unconsciously to himself his Sunday-school voice had acquired a peculiar intonation which was wholly absent on week-days. He began after this fashion:

"Now, children, I want you all to sit up just as straight and pretty as you can and give me all your attention for a minute or two. There—that is it. That is the way good little boys and girls should do. I see one little girl who is looking out of the window—I am afraid she thinks I am out there somewhere—perhaps up in one of the trees making a speech to the little birds. [Applausive titter.] I want to tell you how good it makes me feel to see so many bright, clean little faces assembled in a place like this, learning to do right and be good." And so forth and so on. It is not necessary to set down the rest of the oration. It was of a pattern which does not vary, and so it is familiar to us all. The latter third of the speech was marred by the resumption of fights and other recreations among certain of the bad boys, and by fidgetings and whisperings that extended far and wide, washing even to the bases of isolated and incorruptible rocks like Sid and Mary. But now every sound ceased suddenly, with the subsidence of Mr. Walters's voice, and the conclusion of the speech was received with a burst of silent gratitude.

A good part of the whispering had been occasioned by an event which was more or less rare—the entrance of visitors: lawyer Thatcher, accompanied by a very feeble and aged man; a fine, portly, middle-aged gentleman with iron-gray hair; and a dignified lady who was doubtless the latter's wife. The lady was leading a child. Tom had been restless and full of chafings and repinings; conscience-smitten, too—he could not meet Amy Lawrence's eye, he could not brook her loving gaze. But when he saw this small new-comer his soul was all ablaze with bliss in a moment. The next moment he was "showing off" with all his might—cuffing boys, pulling hair, making faces—in a word, using every art that seemed likely to fascinate a girl and win her applause. His exaltation had but one alloy—the memory of his humiliation in this angel's garden—and that record in sand was fast washing out, under the waves of happiness that were sweeping over it now.

The visitors were given the highest seat of honor, and as soon as Mr. Walters's speech was finished, he introduced them to the school. The middle-aged man turned out to be a prodigious personage—no less a one than the county judge—altogether the most august creation these children had ever looked upon—and they wondered what kind of material he was made of—and they half wanted to hear him roar, and were half afraid he might, too. He was from Constantinople, twelve miles away—so he had traveled, and seen the world—these very eyes had looked upon the county courthouse—which was said to have a tin roof. The awe which these reflections inspired was attested by the impressive silence and the ranks of staring eyes. This was the great Judge Thatcher, brother of their own lawyer. Jeff Thatcher immediately went forward, to be familiar with the great man and be envied by the school. It would have been music to his soul to hear the whisperings:

"Look at him, Jim! He's a-going up there. Say—look! he's a-going to shake hands with him—he *is* shaking hands with him! By jings, don't you wish you was Jeff?"

Mr. Walters fell to "showing off," with all sorts of official bustlings and activities, giving orders, delivering judgments, discharging directions here, there, everywhere that he could find a target. The librarian "showed off"—running hither and thither with his arms full of books and making a deal of the splutter and fuss that insect authority delights in. The young lady teachers "showed off"—bending sweetly over pupils that were lately being boxed, lifting pretty warning fingers at bad little boys and patting good ones lovingly. The young gentlemen teachers "showed off" with small scoldings and other little displays of authority and fine attention to discipline—and most of the teachers, of both sexes, found business up at the library, by the pulpit; and it was business that frequently had to be done over again two or three times (with much seeming vexation). The little girls "showed off" in various ways, and the little boys "showed off" with such diligence that the air was thick with paper wads and the murmur of scufflings. And above it all the great man sat and beamed a majestic judicial smile upon all the house, and warmed himself in the sun of his own grandeur—for he was "showing off," too.

There was only one thing wanting, to make Mr. Walters's ecstasy complete, and that was a chance to deliver a Bible prize and exhibit a prodigy. Several pupils had a few yellow tickets, but none had enough—he had been around among the star pupils inquiring. He would have given worlds, now, to have that German lad back again with a sound mind.

And now at this moment, when hope was dead, Tom Sawyer came forward with nine yellow tickets, nine red tickets, and ten blue ones, and demanded a Bible. This was a thunderbolt out of a clear sky. Walters was not expecting an application from this source for the next ten years. But there was no getting around it—here were the certified checks, and they were good for their face. Tom was therefore elevated to a place with the Judge and the other elect, and the great news was announced from headquarters. It was the most stunning surprise of the decade, and so profound was the sensation that it lifted the new hero up to the judicial one's altitude, and the school had two marvels to gaze upon in place of one. The boys were all eaten up with envy—but those that suffered the bitterest pangs were those who perceived too late that they themselves had contributed to this hated splendor by trading tickets to Tom for the wealth he had amassed in selling whitewashing privileges. These despised themselves, as being the dupes of a wily fraud, a guileful snake in the grass.

The prize was delivered to Tom with as much effusion as the superintendent could pump up under the circumstances; but it lacked somewhat of the true gush, for the poor fellow's instinct taught him that there was a mystery here that could not well bear the light, perhaps; it was simply preposterous that *this* boy had warehoused two thousand sheaves of Scriptural wisdom on his premises—a dozen would strain his capacity, without a doubt.

Amy Lawrence was proud and glad, and she tried to make Tom see it in her face—but he wouldn't look. She wondered; then she was just a grain troubled; next a dim suspicion came and went—came again; she watched; a furtive glance told her worlds—and then her heart broke, and she was jealous, and angry, and the tears came and she hated everybody. Tom most of all (she thought).

Tom was introduced to the Judge; but his tongue was tied, his breath would hardly come, his heart quaked—partly because of the awful greatness of the man, but mainly because he was *her* parent. He would have liked to fall down and worship him, if it were in the dark. The Judge put his hand on Tom's head and called him a fine little man, and asked him what his name was. The boy stammered, gasped, and got it out:

"Tom."

"Oh, no, not Tom—it is—"

"Thomas."

"Ah, that's it. I thought there was more to it, maybe. That's very well. But you've another one I dare say, and you'll tell it to me, won't you?"

"Tell the gentleman your other name, Thomas," said Walters, "and say *sir.* You mustn't forget your manners."

"Thomas Sawyer—sir."

"That's it! That's a good boy. Fine boy. Fine, manly little fellow. Two thousand verses is a great many—very, very great many. And you never can be sorry for the trouble you took to learn them; for knowledge is worth more than anything there is in the world; it's what makes great men and good men; you'll be a great man and a good man yourself, some day, Thomas, and then you'll look back and say, It's all owing to the precious Sunday-school privileges of my boyhood—it's all owing to my dear teachers that taught me to learn—it's all owing to the good superintendent, who encouraged me, and watched over me, and gave me a beautiful Bible—a splendid elegant Bible—to keep and have it all for my own, always—it's all owing to right bringing up! That is what you will say, Thomas—and you wouldn't take any money for those two thousand verses—no indeed you wouldn't. And now you wouldn't mind telling me and this lady some of the things you've learned—no, I know you wouldn't—for we are proud of little boys that learn. Now, no doubt you know the names of all the twelve disciples. Won't you tell us the names of the first two that were appointed?"

Tom was tugging at a button-hole and looking sheepish. He blushed, now, and his eyes fell. Mr. Walters's heart sank within him. He said to himself, it is not possible that the boy can answer the simplest question—why *did* the Judge ask him? Yet he felt obliged to speak up and say:

"Answer the gentleman, Thomas—don't be afraid."

Tom still hung fire.

"Now I know you'll tell *me,*" said the lady. "The names of the first two disciples were—"

"DAVID AND GOLIATH!"

Let us draw the curtain of charity over the rest of the scene.

Chapter 5

About half past ten the cracked bell of the small church began to ring, and presently the people began to gather for the morning sermon. The Sunday-school children distributed themselves about the house and occupied pews with their parents, so as to be under supervision. Aunt Polly came, and Tom and Sid and Mary sat with her—Tom being placed next the aisle, in order that he might be as far away from the open window and the seductive outside summer scenes as possible. The crowd filed up the aisles: the aged and needy postmaster, who had seen better days; the mayor and his wife—for they had a mayor there, among other unnecessaries; the justice of the peace; the widow Douglas, fair, smart, and forty, a generous, good-hearted soul and well-to-do, her hill mansion the only palace in the town, and the most hospitable and much the most lavish in the matter of festivities that St. Petersburg could boast; the bent and venerable Major and Mrs. Ward; lawyer Riverson, the new notable from a distance; next the belle of the village, followed by a troop of lawn-clad and ribbon-decked young heartbreakers; then all the young clerks in town in a body—for they had stood in the vestibule sucking their cane-heads, a circling wall of oiled and simpering admirers, till the last girl had run their gantlet; and last of all came the Model Boy, Willie Mufferson, taking as heedful care of his mother as if she were cut glass. He always brought his mother to church, and was the pride of all the matrons. The boys all hated him, he was so good. And besides, he had been "thrown up to them" so much. His white handkerchief was hanging out of his pocket behind, as usual on Sundays—accidentally. Tom had no handkerchief, and he looked upon boys who had, as snobs.

The congregation being fully assembled, now, the bell rang once more, to warn laggards and stragglers, and then a solemn hush fell upon the church which was only broken by the tittering and whispering of the choir in the gallery. The choir always tittered and whispered all through service. There was once a church choir that was not ill-bred, but I have forgotten where it was, now. It was a great many years ago, and I can scarcely remember anything about it, but I think it was in some foreign country.

The minister gave out the hymn, and read it through with a relish, in a peculiar style which was much admired in that part of the country. His voice began on a medium key and climbed steadily up till it reached a certain point, where it bore with strong emphasis upon the topmost word and then plunged down as if from a spring-board:

> Shall I be car-ri-ed to the skies, on flow'ry *beds*
> of ease,
> Whilst others fight to win the prize, and sail thro' *blood-*
> -y seas?

He was regarded as a wonderful reader. At church "sociables" he was always called upon to read poetry; and when he was through, the ladies would lift up their hands and let them fall helplessly in their laps, and "wall" their eyes, and shake their heads, as much as to say, "Words cannot express it; it is too beautiful, *too* beautiful for this mortal earth."

After the hymn had been sung, the Rev. Mr. Sprague turned himself into a bulletin-board, and read off "notices" of meetings and societies and things till it seemed that the list would stretch out to the crack of doom—a queer custom which is still kept up in America, even in cities, away here in this age of abundant newspapers. Often, the less there is to justify a traditional custom, the harder it is to get rid of it.

And now the minister prayed. A good, generous prayer it was, and went into details: it pleaded for the church, and the little children of the church; for the other churches of the village; for the village itself; for the county; for the state; for the state officers; for the United States; for the churches of the United States; for Congress; for the President; for the officers of the government; for poor sailors, tossed by stormy seas; for the oppressed millions groaning under the heel of European monarchies and Oriental despotisms; for such as have the light and the good tidings, and yet have not eyes to see nor ears to hear withal; for the heathen in the far islands of the sea; and closed with a supplication that the words he was about to speak might find grace and favor, and be as seed sown in fertile ground, yielding in time a grateful harvest of good. Amen.

There was a rustling of dresses, and the standing congregation sat down. The boy whose history this book relates did not enjoy the prayer, he only endured it—if he even did that much. He was restive all through it; he kept tally of the details of the prayer, unconsciously—for he was not listening, but he knew the ground of old, and the clergyman's regular route over it—and when a little trifle of new matter was interlarded, his ear detected it and his whole nature resented it; he considered additions unfair, and scoundrelly. In the midst of the prayer a fly had lit on the back of the pew in front of him and tortured his spirit by calmly rubbing its hands together, embracing its head with its arms, and polishing it so vigorously that it seemed to almost part company with the body, and the slender thread of a neck was exposed to view; scraping its wings with its hind legs and smoothing them to its body as if they had been coat-tails; going through its whole toilet as tranquilly as if it knew it was perfectly safe. As indeed it was; for as sorely as Tom's hands itched to grab for it they did not dare—he believed his soul would be instantly destroyed if he did such a thing while the prayer was going on. But with the closing sentence his hand began to curve and steal forward; and the instant the "Amen" was out the fly was a prisoner of war. His aunt detected the act and made him let it go.

The minister gave out his text and droned along monotonously through an argument that was so prosy that many a head by and by began to nod—and yet it was an argument that dealt in limitless fire and brimstone and thinned the predestined elect down to a company so small as to be hardly worth the saving. Tom counted the pages of the sermon; after church he always knew how many pages there had been, but he seldom knew anything else about the discourse. However, this time he was really interested for a little while. The minister made a grand and moving picture of the assembling together of the world's hosts at the millennium when the lion and the lamb should lie down together and a little child should lead them. But the pathos, the lesson, the moral of the great spectacle were lost upon the boy; he only thought of the conspicuousness of the principal character before the onlooking nations; his face lit with the thought, and he said to himself that he wished he could be that child, if it was a tame lion.

Now he lapsed into suffering again, as the dry argument was resumed. Presently he bethought him of a treasure he had and got it out. It was a large black beetle with formidable jaws—a "pinchbug," he called it. It was in a percussion-cap box. The first thing the beetle did was to take him by the finger. A natural fillip followed, the beetle went floundering into the aisle and lit on its back, and the hurt finger went into the boy's mouth. The beetle lay there working its helpless legs, unable to turn over. Tom eyed it, and longed for it; but it was safe out of his reach. Other people uninterested in the sermon, found relief in the beetle, and they eyed it too. Presently a vagrant poodle-dog came idling along, sad at heart, lazy with the summer softness and the quiet, weary of captivity, sighing for change. He spied the beetle; the drooping tail lifted and wagged. He surveyed the prize; walked around it; smelt at it from a safe distance; walked around it again; grew bolder, and took a closer smell; then lifted his lip and made a gingerly snatch at it, just missing it; made another, and another; began to enjoy the diversion; subsided to his stomach with the beetle between his paws, and continued his experiments; grew weary at last, and then indifferent and absent-minded. His head nodded, and little by little his chin descended and touched the enemy, who seized it. There was a sharp yelp, a flirt of the poodle's head, and the beetle fell a couple of yards away, and lit on its back once more. The neighboring spectators shook with a gentle inward joy, several faces went behind fans and handkerchiefs, and Tom was entirely happy. The dog looked foolish, and probably felt so; but there was resentment in his heart, too, and a craving for revenge. So he went to the beetle and began a wary attack on it again; jumping at it from every point of a circle, lighting with his fore paws within an inch of the creature, making even closer snatches at it with his teeth, and jerking his head till his ears flapped again. But he grew tired once more, after a while; tried to amuse himself with a fly but found no relief; followed an ant around, with his nose close to the floor, and quickly wearied of that; yawned, sighed, forgot the beetle entirely, and sat down on it. Then there was a wild yelp of agony and the poodle went sailing up the aisle; the yelps continued, and so did the dog; he crossed the house in front of the altar; he flew down the other aisle; he crossed before the doors; he clamored up the home-stretch; his anguish grew with his progress, till presently he was but a woolly comet moving in its orbit with the gleam and the speed of light. At last the frantic sufferer sheered from its course, and sprang into its master's lap; he flung it out of the window, and the voice of distress quickly thinned away and died in the distance.

By this time the whole church was red-faced and suffocating with suppressed laughter, and the sermon had come to a dead standstill. The discourse was resumed presently, but it went lame and halting, all possibility of impressiveness being at an end; for even the gravest sentiments were constantly being received with a smothered burst of unholy mirth, under cover of some remote pew-back, as if the poor parson had said a rarely facetious thing. It was a genuine relief to the whole congregation when the ordeal was over and the benediction pronounced.

Tom Sawyer went home quite cheerful, thinking to himself that there was some satisfaction about divine service when there was a bit of variety in it. He had but one marring thought; he was willing that the dog should play with his pinchbug, but he did not think it was upright in him to carry it off.

A Tramp Abroad

The title A Tramp Abroad *(1880) has a typically Twainian double meaning: the book refers to both a walking tour of Europe and a disreputable person, a tramp wandering abroad. In this book Twain returns to his familiar pose as the naive and good-humored American who enjoys Europe but refuses to be intimidated by its traditions. Indeed, Twain even plays with the convention of the "walking tour of Europe." Although the author proclaims the intention of walking, at every occasion he takes some other, easier, means: the railroad, a carriage, or even a raft. Thus even the conventional expectation is mocked.*

Chapter 7

We did not oversleep at St. Nicholas. The church-bell began to ring at four-thirty in the morning, and from the length of time it continued to ring I judged that it takes the Swiss sinner a good while to get the invitation through his head. Most church-bells in the world are of poor quality, and have a harsh and rasping sound which upsets the temper and produces much sin, but the St. Nicholas bell is a good deal the worst one that has been contrived yet, and is peculiarly maddening in its operation. Still, it may have its right and its excuse to exist, for the community is poor and not every citizen can afford a clock, perhaps; but there cannot be any excuse for our church-bells at home, for there is no family in America without a clock, and consequently there is no fair pretext for the usual Sunday medley of dreadful sounds that issues from our steeples. There is much more profanity in America on Sunday than in all the other six days of the week put together, and it is of a more bitter and malignant character than the week-day profanity, too. It is produced by the cracked-pot clangor of the cheap church-bells.

We build our churches almost without regard to cost; we rear an edifice which is an adornment to the town, and we gild it, and fresco it, and mortgage it, and do everything we can think of to perfect it, and then spoil it all by putting a bell on it which afflicts everybody who hears it, giving some the headache, others St. Vitus's dance, and the rest the blind staggers.

An American village at ten o'clock on a summer Sunday is the quietest and peacefulest and holiest thing in nature; but it is a pretty different thing half an hour later. Mr. Poe's poem of the "Bells" stands incomplete to this day; but it is well enough that it is so, for the public reciter or "reader" who goes around trying to imitate the sounds of the various sorts of bells with his voice would find himself "up a stump" when he got to the church-bell—as Joseph Addison would say. The church is always trying to get other people to reform; it might not be a bad idea to reform itself a little, by way of example. It is still clinging to one or two things which were useful once, but which are not useful now, neither are they ornamental. One is the bell-ringing to remind a clock-caked town that it is church-time, and another is the reading from the pulpit of a tedious list of "notices" which everybody who is interested has already read in the newspaper. The clergyman even reads the hymn through—a relic of an ancient time when hymn-books were scarce and costly; but everybody has a hymn-book now, and so the public reading is no longer necessary. It is not merely unnecessary, it is generally painful; for the average clergyman could not fire into his congregation with a shotgun and hit a worse reader than himself, unless the weapon scattered shamefully. I am not meaning to be flippant and irreverent, I am only meaning to be truthful. The average clergyman, in all countries and of all denominations, is a very bad reader. One would think he would at least learn how to read the Lord's Prayer, by and by, but it is not so. He races through it as if he thought the quicker he got it in, the sooner it would be answered. A person who does not appreciate the exceeding value of pauses, and does not know how to measure their duration judiciously, cannot render the grand simplicity and dignity of a composition like that effectively.

We took a tolerably early breakfast, and tramped off toward Zermatt through the reeking lanes of the village, glad to get away from that bell. By and by we had a fine spectacle on our right. It was the wall-like butt end of a huge glacier, which looked down on us from an Alpine height which was well up in the blue sky. It was an astonishing amount of ice to be compacted together in one mass. We ciphered upon it and decided that it was not less than several hundred feet from the base of the wall of solid ice to the top of it—Harris believed it was really twice that. We judged that if St. Paul's, St. Peter's, the Great Pyramid, the Strasburg Cathedral and the Capitol at Washington were clustered against that wall, a man sitting on its upper edge could not hang his hat on the top of any one of them without reaching down three or four hundred feet—a thing which, of course, no man could do.

To me, that mighty glacier was very beautiful. I did not imagine that anybody could find fault with it; but I was mistaken. Harris had been snarling for several days. He was a rabid Protestant, and he was always saying:

"In the Protestant cantons you never see such poverty and dirt and squalor as you do in this Catholic one; you never see the lanes and alleys flowing with foulness; you never see such wretched little sties of houses; you never see an inverted tin turnip on top of a church for a dome; and as for a church-bell, why, you never hear a church-bell at all."

All this morning he had been finding fault, straight along. First it was with the mud. He said, "It ain't muddy in a Protestant canton when it rains." Then it was with the dogs: "They don't have those lop-eared dogs in a Protestant canton." Then it was with the roads: "They don't leave the roads to make themselves in a Protestant canton, the people make them—and they make a road that *is* a road, too." Next it was the goats: "You never see a goat shedding tears in a Protestant canton—a goat, there, is one of the cheerfulest objects in nature." Next it was the chamois: "You never see a Protestant chamois act like one of these—they take a bite or two and go; but these fellows camp with you and stay." Then it was the guide-boards: "In a Protestant canton you couldn't get lost if you wanted to, but you never see a guide-board in a Catholic canton." Next, "You never see any flower-boxes in the windows, here—never anything but now and then a cat—a torpid one; but you take a Protestant canton: windows perfectly lovely with flowers—and as for cats, there's just acres of them. These folks in this canton leave a road to make itself, and then fine you three francs if you 'trot' over it—as if a horse could trot over such a sarcasm of a road." Next about the goiter: "*They* talk about goiter!—I haven't seen a goiter in this whole canton that I couldn't put in a hat."

He had growled at everything, but I judged it would puzzle him to find anything the matter with this majestic glacier. I intimated as much; but he was ready, and said with surly discontent: "You ought to see them in the Protestant cantons."

This irritated me. But I concealed the feeling, and asked:

"What is the matter with this one?"

"Matter? Why, it ain't in any kind of condition. They never take any care of a glacier here. The moraine has been spilling gravel around it, and got it all dirty."

"Why, man, *they* can't help that."

"*They?* You're right. That is, they *won't*. They could if they wanted to. You never see a speck of dirt on a Protestant glacier. Look at the Rhone glacier. It is fifteen miles long, and seven hundred feet thick. If this was a Protestant glacier you wouldn't see it looking like this, I can tell you."

"That is nonsense. What would they do with it?"

"They would whitewash it. They always do."

I did not believe a word of this, but rather than have trouble I let it go; for it is a waste of breath to argue with a bigot. I even doubted if the Rhone glacier *was* in a Protestant canton; but I did not know, so I could not make anything by contradicting a man who would probably put me down at once with manufactured evidence.

About nine miles from St. Nicholas we crossed a bridge over the raging torrent of the Visp, and came to a long strip of flimsy fencing which was pretending to secure people from tumbling over a perpendicular wall forty feet high and into the river. Three children were approaching; one of them, a little girl, about eight years old, was running; when pretty close to us she stumbled and fell, and her feet shot under the rail of the fence and for a moment projected over the stream. It gave us a sharp shock, for we thought she was gone, sure, for the ground slanted steeply, and to save herself seemed a sheer impossibility; but she managed to scramble up, and ran by us laughing.

We went forward and examined the place and saw the long tracks which her feet had made in the dirt when they darted over the verge. If she had finished her trip she would have struck some big rocks in the edge of the water, and then the torrent would have snatched her down-stream among the half-covered boulders and she would have been pounded to pulp in two minutes. We had come exceedingly near witnessing her death.

And now Harris's contrary nature and inborn selfishness were strikingly manifested. He has no spirit of self-denial. He began straight off, and continued for an hour, to express his gratitude that the child was not destroyed. I never saw such a man. That was the kind of person he was; just so *he* was gratified, he never cared anything about anybody else. I had noticed that trait in him, over and over again. Often, of course, it was mere heedlessness, mere want of reflection. Doubtless this may have been the case in most instances, but it was not the less hard to bear on that account—and after all, its bottom, its groundwork, was selfishness. There is no avoiding that conclusion. In the instance under consideration, I did think the indecency of running on in that way might occur to him; but no, the child was saved and he was glad, that was sufficient—he cared not a straw for *my* feelings, or my loss of such a literary plum, snatched from my very mouth at the instant it was ready to drop into it. His selfishness was sufficient to place his own gratification in being spared suffering clear before all concern for me, his friend. Apparently, he did not once reflect upon the valuable details which would have fallen like a windfall to me: fishing the child out—witnessing the surprise of the family and the stir the thing would have made among the peasants—then a Swiss funeral—then the roadside monument, to be paid for by us and have our names mentioned in it. And we should have gone into Baedeker and been immortal. I was silent. I was too much hurt to complain. If he could act so, and be so heedless and so frivolous at such a time, and actually seem to glory in it, after all I had done for him, I would have cut my hand off before I would let him see that I was wounded. . . .

In Nevada I used to see the children play at silver-mining. Of course, the great thing was an accident in a mine, and there were two "star" parts; that of the man who fell down the mimic shaft, and that of the daring hero who was lowered into the depths to bring him up. I knew one small chap who always insisted on playing *both* of these parts—and he carried his point. He would tumble into the shaft and die, and then come to the surface and go back after his own remains.

It is the smartest boy that gets the hero part everywhere; he is head guide in Switzerland, head miner in Nevada, head bull-fighter in Spain, etc.; but I knew a preacher's son, seven years old, who once selected a part for himself compared to which those just mentioned are tame and unimpressive. Jimmy's father stopped him from driving imaginary horse-cars one Sunday—stopped him from playing captain of an imaginary steamboat next Sunday—stopped him from leading an imaginary army to battle the following Sunday—and so on. Finally the little fellow said:

"I've tried everything, and they won't any of them do. What *can* I play?"

"I hardly know, Jimmy; but you *must* play only things that are suitable to the Sabbath-day."

Next Sunday the preacher stepped softly to a back-room door to see if the children were rightly employed. He peeped in. A chair occupied the middle of the room, and on the back of it hung Jimmy's cap; one of the little sisters took the cap down, nibbled at it, then passed it to another small sister and said, "Eat of this fruit, for it is good." The Reverend took in the situation—alas, they were playing the Expulsion from Eden! Yet he found one little crumb of comfort. He said to himself, "For once Jimmy has yielded the chief rôle—I have been wronging him, I did not believe there was so much modesty in him; I should have expected him to be either Adam or Eve." This crumb of comfort lasted but a very little while; he glanced around and discovered Jimmy standing in an imposing attitude in a corner, with a dark and deadly frown on his face. What that meant was very plain—*he was impersonating the Deity!* Think of the guileless sublimity of that idea. . . .

Chapter 19

[On art criticism]

. . . We visited the picture-galleries and the other regulation "sights" of Milan—not because I wanted to write about them again, but to see if I had learned anything in twelve years. I afterward visited the great galleries of Rome and Florence for the same purpose. I found I had learned one thing. When I wrote about the Old Masters before, I said the copies were better than the originals. That was a mistake of large dimensions. The Old Masters were still unpleasing to me, but they were truly divine contrasted with the copies. The copy is to the original as the pallid, smart, inane new wax-work group is to the vigorous, earnest, dignified group of living men and women whom it professes to duplicate. There is a mellow richness, a subdued color, in the old pictures, which is to the eye what muffled and mellowed sound is to the ear. That is the merit which is most loudly praised in the old picture, and is the one which the copy most conspicuously lacks, and which the copyist must not hope to compass. It was generally conceded by the artists with whom I talked, that that subdued splendor, that mellow richness, is imparted to the picture by *age.* Then why should we worship the Old Master for it, who didn't impart it, instead of worshiping Old Time, who did? Perhaps the picture was a clanging bell, until Time muffled it and sweetened it.

In conversation with an artist in Venice, I asked: "What is it that people see in the Old Masters? I have been in the Doge's palace and I saw several acres of very bad drawing, very bad perspective, and very incorrect proportions. Paul Veronese's dogs do not resemble dogs; all the horses look like bladders on legs; one man had a *right* leg on the left side of his body; in the large picture where the Emperor (Barbarossa?) is prostrate before the Pope, there are three men in the foreground who are over thirty feet high, if one may judge by the size of a kneeling little boy in the center of the foreground; and according to the same scale, the Pope is seven feet high and the Doge is a shriveled dwarf of four feet."

The artist said:

"Yes, the Old Masters often drew badly; they did not care much for truth and exactness in minor details; but after all, in spite of bad drawing, bad perspective, bad proportions, and a choice of subjects which no longer appeal to people as strongly as they did three hundred years ago, there is a *something* about their pictures which is divine—a something which is above and beyond the art of any epoch since—a something which would be the despair of artists but that they never hope or expect to attain it, and therefore do not worry about it."

That is what he said—and he said what he believed; and not only believed, but felt.

Reasoning—especially reasoning, without technical knowledge—must be put aside, in cases of this kind. It cannot assist the inquirer. It will lead him, in the most logical progression, to what, in the eyes of artists, would be a most illogical conclusion. Thus: bad drawing, bad proportion, bad perspective, indifference to truthful detail, color which gets its merit from time, and not from the artist—these things constitute the Old Master; conclusion, the Old Master was a bad painter, the Old Master was not an Old Master at all, but an Old Apprentice. Your friend the artist will grant your premises, but deny your conclusion; he will maintain that notwithstanding this formidable list of confessed defects, there is still a something that is divine and unapproachable about the Old Master, and that there is no arguing the fact away by any system of reasoning whatever. . . .

A Short Story

EDWARD MILLS AND GEORGE BENTON: A TALE

In this brief but significant short story, Twain explores the issue of child-rearing, developing his insights about the effects of positive and negative reinforcement. The sparse, dualist nature of the story indicates that Twain was figuring out, in fictional form, the causes and effects of moral actions.

These two were distantly related to each other—seventh cousins, or something of that sort. While still babies they became orphans, and were adopted by the Brants, a childless couple, who quickly grew very fond of them. The Brants were always saying: "Be pure, honest, sober, industrious, and considerate of others, and success in life is assured." The children heard this repeated some thousands of times before they understood it; they could repeat it themselves long before they could say the Lord's Prayer; it was painted over the nursery door, and was about the first thing they learned to read. It was destined to become the unswerving rule of Edward Mills's life. Sometimes the Brants changed the wording a little, and said: "Be pure, honest, sober, industrious, considerate, and you will never lack friends."

Baby Mills was a comfort to everybody about him. When he wanted candy and could not have it, he listened to reason, and contented himself without it. When Baby Benton wanted candy, he cried for it until he got it. Baby Mills took care of his toys; Baby Benton always destroyed his in a very brief time, and then made himself so insistently disagreeable that, in order to have peace in the house, little Edward was persuaded to yield up his playthings to him.

When the children were a little older, Georgie became a heavy expense in one respect: he took no care of his clothes; consequently, he shone frequently in new ones, which was not the case with Eddie. The boys grew apace. Eddie was an increasing comfort, Georgie an increasing solicitude. It was always sufficient to say, in answer to Eddie's petitions, "I would rather you would not do it"—meaning swimming, skating, picnicking, berrying, circusing, and all sorts of things which boys delight in. But *no* answer was sufficient for Georgie; he had to be humored in his desires, or he would carry them with a high hand. Naturally, no boy got more swimming, skating, berrying, and so forth than he; no boy ever had a better time. The good Brants did not allow the boys to play out after nine in summer evenings; they were sent to bed at that hour; Eddie honorably remained, but Georgie usually slipped out of the window toward ten, and enjoyed himself till midnight. It seemed impossible to break Georgie of this bad habit, but the Brants managed it at last by hiring him, with apples and marbles, to stay in. The good Brants gave all their time and attention to vain endeavors to regulate Georgie; they said, with grateful tears in their eyes, that Eddie needed no efforts of theirs, he was so good, so considerate, and in all ways so perfect.

By and by the boys were big enough to work, so they were apprenticed to a trade: Edward went voluntarily; George was coaxed and bribed. Edward worked hard and faithfully, and ceased to be an expense to the good Brants; they praised him, so did his master; but George ran away, and it cost Mr. Brant both money and trouble to hunt him up and get him back. By and by he ran away again—more money and more trouble. He ran away a third time—and stole a few little things to carry with him. Trouble and expense for Mr. Brant once more, and besides, it was with the greatest difficulty that he succeeded in persuading the master to let the youth go unprosecuted for theft.

Edward worked steadily along, and in time became a full partner in his master's business. George did not improve; he kept the loving hearts of his aged benefactors full of trouble, and their hands full of inventive activities to protect him from ruin. Edward, as a boy, had interested himself in Sunday-schools, debating societies, penny missionary affairs, anti-tobacco organizations, anti-profanity associations, and all such things; as a man, he was a quiet but steady and reliable helper in the church, the temperance societies, and in all movements looking to the aiding and uplifting of men. This excited no remark, attracted no attention—for it was his "natural bent."

Finally, the old people died. The will testified their loving pride in Edward, and left their little property to George—because he "needed it"; whereas, "owing to a bountiful Providence," such was not the case with Edward. The property was left to George conditionally: he must buy out Edward's partner with it; else it must go to a benevolent organization called the Prisoner's Friend Society. The old people left a letter, in which they begged their dear son Edward to take their place and watch over George, and help and shield him as they had done.

Edward dutifully acquiesced, and George became his partner in the business. He was not a valuable partner: he had been meddling with drink before; he soon developed into a constant tippler now, and his flesh and eyes showed the fact unpleasantly. Edward had been courting a sweet and kindly spirited girl for some time. They loved each other dearly, and— But about this period George began to haunt her tearfully and imploringly, and at last she went crying to Edward, and said her high and holy duty was plain before her—she must not let her own selfish desires interfere with it: she must marry "poor George" and "reform him." It would break her heart, she knew it would, and so on; but duty was duty. So she married George, and Edward's heart came very near breaking, as well as her own. However, Edward recovered, and married another girl—a very excellent one she was, too.

Children came to both families. Mary did her honest best to reform her husband, but the contract was too large. George went on drinking, and by and by he fell to misusing her and the little one sadly. A great many good people strove with George—they were always at it, in fact—but he calmly took such efforts as his due and their duty, and did not mend his ways. He added a vice, presently—that of secret gambling. He got deeply in debt; he borrowed money on the firm's credit, as quietly as he could, and carried this system so far and so successfully that one morning the sheriff took possession of the establishment, and the two cousins found themselves penniless.

Times were hard, now, and they grew worse. Edward moved his family into a garret, and walked the streets day and night, seeking work. He begged for it, but it was really not to be had. He was astonished to see how soon his face became unwelcome; he was astonished and hurt to see how quickly the ancient interest which people had had in him faded out and disappeared. Still, he *must* get work; so he swallowed his chargrin, and toiled on in search of it. At last he got a job of carrying bricks up a ladder in a hod, and was a grateful man in consequence; but after that *nobody* knew him or cared anything about him. He was not able to keep up his dues in the various moral organizations to which he belonged, and had to endure the sharp pain of seeing himself brought under the disgrace of suspension.

But the faster Edward died out of public knowledge and interest, the faster George rose in them. He was found lying, ragged and drunk, in the gutter one morning. A member of the Ladies' Temperance Refuge fished him out, took him in hand, got up a subscription for him, kept him sober a whole week, then got a situation for him. An account of it was published.

General attention was thus drawn to the poor fellow, and a great many people came forward, and helped him toward reform with their countenance and encouragement. He did not drink a drop for two months, and meantime was the pet of the good. Then he fell—in the gutter; and there was general sorrow and lamentation. But the noble sisterhood rescued him again. They cleaned him up, they fed him, they listened to the mournful music of his repentances, they got him his situation again. An account of this, also, was published, and the town was drowned in happy tears over the re-restoration of the poor beast and struggling victim of the fatal bowl. A grand temperance revival was got up, and after some rousing speeches had been made the chairman said, impressively: "We are now about to call for signers; and I think there is a spectacle in store for you which not many in this house will be able to view with dry eyes." There was an eloquent pause, and then George Benton, escorted by a red-sashed detachment of the Ladies of the Refuge, stepped forward upon the platform and signed the pledge. The air was rent with applause, and everybody cried for joy. Everybody wrung the hand of the new convert when the meeting was over; his salary was enlarged next day; he was the talk of the town, and its hero. An account of it was published.

George Benton fell, regularly, every three months, but was faithfully rescued and wrought with, every time, and good situations were found for him. Finally, he was taken around the country lecturing, as a reformed drunkard, and he had great houses and did an immense amount of good.

He was so popular at home, and so trusted—during his sober intervals—that he was enabled to use the name of a principal citizen, and get a large sum of money at the bank. A mighty pressure was brought to bear to save him from the consequences of his forgery, and it was partially successful—he was "sent up" for only two years. When, at the end of a year, the tireless efforts of the benevolent were crowned with success, and he emerged from the penitentiary with a pardon in his pocket, the Prisoner's Friend Society met him at the door with a situation and a comfortable salary, and all the other benevolent people came forward and gave him advice, encouragement, and help. Edward Mills had once applied to the Prisoner's Friend Society for a situation, when in dire need, but the question, "Have you been a prisoner?" made brief work of his case.

While all these things were going on, Edward Mills had been quietly making head against adversity. He was still poor, but was in receipt of a steady and sufficient salary, as the respected and trusted cashier of a bank. George Benton never came near him, and was never heard to inquire about him. George got to indulging in long absences from the town; there were ill reports about him, but nothing definite.

One winter's night some masked burglars forced their way into the bank, and found Edward Mills there alone. They commanded him to reveal the "combination," so that they could get into the safe. He refused. They threatened his life. He said his employers trusted him, and he could not be traitor to that trust. He could die, if he must, but while he lived he would be faithful; he would not yield up the "combination." The burglars killed him.

The detectives hunted down the criminals; the chief one proved to be George Benton. A wide sympathy was felt for the widow and orphans of the dead man, and all the newspapers in the land begged that all the banks in the land would testify their appreciation of the fidelity and heroism of the murdered cashier by coming forward with a generous contribution of money in aid of his family, now bereft of support. The result was a mass of solid cash amounting to upward of five hundred dollars—an average of nearly three-eighths of a cent for each bank of the Union. The cashier's own bank testified its gratitude by endeavoring to show (but humiliatingly failed in it) that the peerless servant's accounts were not square, and that he himself had knocked his brains out with a bludgeon to escape detection and punishment.

George Benton was arraigned for trial. Then everybody seemed to forget the widow and orphans in their solicitude for poor George. Everything that money and influence could do was done to save him, but it all failed; he was sentenced to death. Straightway the Governor was besieged with petitions for commutation or pardon; they were brought by tearful young girls; by sorrowful old maids; by deputations of pathetic widows; by shoals of impressive orphans. But no, the Governor—for once—would not yield.

Now George Benton experienced religion. The glad news flew all around. From that time forth his cell was always full of girls and women and fresh flowers; all the day long there was prayer, and hymn-singing, and thanksgivings, and homilies, and tears, with never an interruption, except an occasional five-minute intermission for refreshments.

This sort of thing continued up the very gallows, and George Benton went proudly home, in the black cap, before a wailing audience of the sweetest and best that the region could produce. His grave had fresh flowers on it every day, for a while, and the head-stone bore these words, under a hand pointing aloft: "He has fought the good fight."

The brave cashier's head-stone has this inscription: "Be pure, honest, sober, industrious, considerate, and you will never—"

Nobody knows who gave the order to leave it that way, but it was so given.

The cashier's family are in stringent circumstances, now, it is said; but no matter; a lot of appreciative people, who were not willing that an act so brave and true as his should go unrewarded, have collected forty-two thousand dollars—and built a Memorial Church with it.

THE PRINCE AND THE PAUPER

In The Prince and the Pauper *(1882), Twain created a story that explores inherited monarchy as a social system. The two boys of the title switch identities, and each lad then experiences the other's world. The novel should be seen as part of Twain's concern about the power of political systems in social conditioning. This selection presents Twain's opinion of the standards of justice, logic, and proof in the era of Henry VIII. Tom Canty, the Pauper, is trapped by the identity switch into acting as the King.*

CHAPTER 15

. . . After a little while Tom, who had wandered to a window and become interested in the life and movement of the great highway beyond the palace gates—and not idly interested, but longing with all his heart to take part in person in its stir and freedom—saw the van of a hooting and shouting mob of disorderly men, women, and children of the lowest and poorest degree approaching from up the road.

"I would I knew what 'tis about!" he exclaimed, with all a boy's curiosity in such happenings.

"Thou art the king!" solemnly responded the earl with a reverence. "Have I your grace's leave to act?"

"Oh, blithely, yes! Oh, gladly, yes!" exclaimed Tom, excitedly, adding to himself with a lively sense of satisfaction, "In truth, being a king is not all dreariness—it hath its compensations and conveniences."

The earl called a page, and sent him to the captain of the guard with the order:

"Let the mob be halted, and inquiry made concerning the occasion of its movement. By the king's command!"

A few seconds later a long rank of the royal guards, cased in flashing steel, filed out at the gates and formed across the highway in front of the multitude. A messenger returned, to report that the crowd were following a man, a woman, and a young girl to execution for crimes committed against the peace and dignity of the realm.

Death—and a violent death—for these poor unfortunates! The thought wrung Tom's heartstrings. The spirit of compassion took control of him, to the exclusion of all other considerations; he never thought of the offended laws, or of the grief or loss which these three criminals had inflicted upon their victims, he could think of nothing but the scaffold and the grisly fate hanging over the heads of the condemned. His concern made him even forget, for the moment, that he was but the false shadow of a king, not the substance; and before he knew it he had blurted out the command:

"Bring them here!"

Then he blushed scarlet, and a sort of apology sprung to his lips; but observing that his order had wrought no sort of surprise in the earl or the waiting page, he suppressed the words he was about to utter. The page, in the most matter-of-course way, made a profound obeisance and retired backward out of the room to deliver the command. Tom experienced a glow of pride and a renewed sense of the compensating advantages of the kingly office. He said to himself, "Truly it is like what I used to feel when I read the old priest's tales, and did imagine mine own self a prince, giving law and command to all, saying, 'Do this, do that,' while none durst offer let or hindrance to my will."

Now the doors swung open; one high-sounding title after another was announced, the personages owning them followed, and the place was quickly half filled with noble folk and finery. But Tom was hardly conscious of the presence of these people, so wrought up was he and so intensely absorbed in that other and more interesting matter. He seated himself, absently, in his chair of state, and turned his eyes upon the door with manifestations of impatient expectancy; seeing which, the company forbore to trouble him, and fell to chatting a mixture of public business and court gossip one with another.

In a little while the measured tread of military men was heard approaching, and the culprits entered the presence in charge of an under-sheriff and escorted by a detail of the king's guard. The civil officer knelt before Tom, then stood aside; the three doomed persons knelt also, and remained so; the guard took position behind Tom's chair. Tom scanned the prisoners curiously. Something about the dress or appearance of the man had stirred a vague memory in him. "Methinks I have seen this man ere now . . . but the when or the where fail me"—such was Tom's thought. Just then the man glanced quickly up, and quickly dropped his face again, not being able to endure the awful port of sovereignty; but the one full glimpse of the face, which Tom got, was sufficient. He said to himself: "Now is the matter clear; this is the stranger that plucked Giles Witt out of the Thames, and saved his life that windy, bitter first day of the New Year—a brave, good deed—pity he hath been doing baser ones and got himself in this sad case. . . . I have not forgot the day, neither the hour; by reason that an hour after, upon the stroke of eleven, I did get a hiding by the hand of Gammer Canty which was of so goodly and admired severity that all that went before or followed after it were but fondlings and caresses by comparison."

Tom now ordered that the woman and the girl be removed from the presence for a little time; then addressed himself to the under-sheriff, saying:

"Good sir, what is this man's offense?"

The officer knelt, and answered:

"So please your majesty, he hath taken the life of a subject by poison."

Tom's compassion for the prisoner, and admiration of him as the daring rescuer of a drowning boy, experienced a most damaging shock.

"The thing was proven upon him?" he asked.

"Most clearly, sire."

Tom sighed, and said:

"Take him away—he hath earned his death. 'Tis a pity, for he was a brave heart—na—na, I mean he hath the *look* of it!"

The prisoner clasped his hands together with sudden energy, and wrung them despairingly, at the same time appealing imploringly to the "king" in broken and terrified phrases:

"Oh, my lord the king, an thou canst pity the lost, have pity upon me! I am innocent—neither hath that wherewith I am charged been more than but lamely proved—yet I speak not of that; the judgment is gone forth against me and may not suffer alteration; yet in mine extremity I beg a boon, for my doom is more than I can bear. A grace, a grace, my lord the king! in thy royal compassion grant my prayer—give commandment that I be hanged!"

Tom was amazed. This was not the outcome he had looked for.

"Odds my life, a strange *boon!* Was it not the fate intended thee?"

"Oh, good my liege, not so! It is ordered that I be *boiled alive!*"

The hideous surprise of these words almost made Tom spring from his chair. As soon as he could recover his wits he cried out:

"Have thy wish, poor soul! an thou had poisoned a hundred men thou shouldst not suffer so miserable a death."

The prisoner bowed his face to the ground and burst into passionate expressions of gratitude—ending with:

"If ever thou shouldst know misfortune—which God forbid!—may thy goodness to me this day be remembered and requited!"

Tom turned to the Earl of Hertford, and said:

"My lord, is it believable that there was warrant for this man's ferocious doom?"

"It is the law, your grace—for prisoners. In Germany coiners be boiled to death in *oil*—not cast in of a sudden, but by a rope let down into the oil by degrees, and slowly; first the feet, then the legs, then—"

"Oh, prithee, no more, my lord, I cannot bear it!" cried Tom, covering his eyes with his hands to shut out the picture. "I beseech your good lordship that order be taken to change this law—oh, let no more poor creatures be visited with its tortures."

The earl's face showed profound gratification, for he was a man of merciful and generous impulses—a thing not very common with his class in that fierce age. He said:

"These your grace's noble words have sealed its doom. History will remember it to the honor of your royal house."

The under-sheriff was about to remove his prisoner; Tom gave him a sign to wait; then he said:

"Good sir, I would look into this matter further. The man has said his deed was but lamely proved. Tell me what thou knowest."

"If the king's grace please, it did appear upon the trial, that this man entered into a house in the hamlet of Islington where one lay sick—three witnesses say it was at ten of the clock in the morning and two say it was some minutes later—the sick man being alone at the time, and sleeping—and presently the man came forth again, and went his way. The sick man died within the hour, being torn with spasm and retchings."

"Did any see the poison given? Was poison found?"

"Marry, no, my liege."

"Then how doth one know there was poison given at all?"

"Please your majesty, the doctors testified that none die with such symptoms but by poison."

Weighty evidence, this—in that simple age. Tom recognized its formidable nature, and said:

"The doctor knoweth his trade—belike they were right. The matter hath an ill look for this poor man."

"Yet was not this all, your majesty; there is more and worse. Many testified that a witch, since gone from the village, none know whither, did foretell, and speak it privately in their ears, that the sick man *would die by poison*—and more, that a stranger would give it—a stranger with brown hair and clothed in a worn and common garb; and surely this prisoner doth answer woundily to the bill. Please, your majesty, to give the circumstance that solemn weight which is its due, seeing it was *foretold.*"

This was an argument of tremendous force, in that superstitious day. Tom felt that the thing was settled; if evidence was worth anything, this poor fellow's guilt was proved. Still he offered the prisoner a chance, saying:

"If thou canst say aught in thy behalf, speak."

"Naught that will avail, my king. I am innocent, yet cannot I make it appear. I have no friends, else might I show that I was not in Islington that day; so also might I show that at that hour they name I was above a league away, seeing I was at Wapping Old Stairs; yea more, my king, for I could show, that while they say I was *taking* life, I was *saving* it. A drowning boy—"

"Peace! Sheriff, name the day the deed was done!"

"At ten in the morning, or some minutes later, the first day of the new year, most illustrious—"

"Let the prisoner go free—it is the king's will!"

Another blush followed this unregal outburst, and he covered his indecorum as well as he could by adding:

"It enrageth me that a man should be hanged upon such idle, hare-brained evidence!"

A low buzz of admiration swept through the assemblage. It was not admiration of the decree that had been delivered by Tom, for the propriety or expediency of pardoning a convicted poisoner was a thing which few there would have felt justified in either admitting or admiring—no, the admiration was for the intelligence and spirit which Tom had displayed. Some of the low-voiced remarks were to this effect:

"This is no mad king—he hath his wits sound."

"How sanely he put his questions—how like his former natural self was this abrupt, imperious disposal of the matter!"

"God be thanked his infirmity is spent! This is no weakling, but a king. He hath borne himself like to his own father."

The air being filled with applause, Tom's ear necessarily caught a little of it. The effect which this had upon him was to put him greatly at his ease, and also to charge his system with very gratifying sensations.

However, his juvenile curiosity soon rose superior to these pleasant thoughts and feelings; he was eager to know what sort of deadly mischief the woman and the little girl could have been about; so, by his command the two terrified and sobbing creatures were brought before him.

"What is it that these have done?" he inquired of the sheriff.

"Please your majesty, a black crime is charged upon them, and clearly proven; wherefore the judges have decreed, according to the law, that they be hanged. They sold themselves to the devil—such is their crime."

Tom shuddered. He had been taught to abhor people who did this wicked thing. Still, he was not going to deny himself the pleasure of feeding his curiosity, for all that; so he asked:

"Where was this done?—and when?"

"On a midnight, in December—in a ruined church, your majesty."

Tom shuddered again.

"Who was there present?"

"Only these two, your grace—and *that other.*"

"Have these confessed?"

"Nay, not so, sire—they do deny it."

"Then, prithee, how was it known?"

"Certain witnesses did see them wending thither, good your majesty; this bred the suspicion, and dire effects have since confirmed and justified it. In particular, it is in evidence that through the wicked power so obtained, they did invoke and bring about a storm that wasted all the region round about.

Above forty witnesses have proved the storm; and sooth one might have had a thousand, for all had reason to remember it, sith all had suffered by it."

"Certes this is a serious matter." Tom turned this dark piece of scoundrelism over in his mind awhile, then asked:

"Suffered the woman, also, by the storm?"

Several old heads among the assemblage nodded their recognition of the wisdom of this question. The sheriff, however, saw nothing inconsequential in the inquiry; he answered, with simple directness:

"Indeed, did she, your majesty, and most righteously, as all aver. Her habitation was swept away, and herself and child left shelterless."

"Methinks the power to do herself so ill a turn was dearly bought. She had been cheated, had she paid but a farthing for it; that she paid her soul, and her child's, argueth that she is mad; if she is mad she knoweth not what she doth, therefore sinneth not."

The elderly heads nodded recognition of Tom's wisdom once more, and one individual murmured, "An the king be mad himself, according to report, then it is a madness of a sort that would improve the sanity of some I wot of, if by the gentle providence of God they could but catch it."

"What age hath the child?" asked Tom.

"Nine years, please your majesty."

"By the law of England may a child enter into covenant and sell itself, my lord?" asked Tom, turning to a learned judge.

"The law doth not permit a child to make or meddle in any weighty matter, good my liege, holding that its callow wit unfitteth it to cope with the riper wit and evil schemings of them that are its elders. The *devil* may buy a child, if he so choose, and the child agree thereto, but not an Englishman—in this latter case the contract would be null and void."

"It seemeth a rude unchristian thing, and ill contrived, that English law denieth privileges to Englishmen, to waste them on the devil!" cried Tom, with honest heat.

This novel view of the matter excited many smiles, and was stored away in many heads to be repeated about the court as evidence of Tom's originality as well as progress toward mental health.

The elder culprit had ceased from sobbing, and was hanging upon Tom's words with an excited interest and a growing hope. Tom noticed this, and it strongly inclined his sympathies toward her in her perilous and unfriended situation. Presently he asked:

"How wrought they, to bring the storm?"

"*By pulling off their stockings,* sire."

This astonished Tom, and also fired his curiosity to fever heat. He said, eagerly:

"It is wonderful! Hath it always this dread effect?"

"Always, my liege—at least if the woman desire it, and utter the needful words, either in her mind or with her tongue."

Tom turned to the woman, and said with impetuous zeal:

"Exert thy power—I would see a storm!"

There was a sudden paling of cheeks in the superstitious assemblage, and a general, though unexpressed, desire to get out of the place—all of which was lost upon Tom, who was dead to everything but the proposed cataclysm. Seeing a puzzled and astonished look in the woman's face, he added, excitedly:

"Never fear—thou shalt be blameless. More—thou shalt go free—none shall touch thee. Exert thy power."

"O, my lord the king, I have it not—I have been falsely accused."

"Thy fears stay thee. Be of good heart, thou shalt suffer no harm. Make a storm—it mattereth not how small a one—I require naught great or harmful, but indeed prefer the opposite—do this and thy life is spared—thou shalt go out free, with thy child, bearing the king's pardon, and safe from hurt or malice from any in the realm."

The woman prostrated herself, and protested, with tears, that she had no power to do the miracle, else she would gladly win her child's life alone, and be content to lose her own, if by obedience to the king's command so precious a grace might be acquired.

Tom urged—the woman still adhered to her declarations. Finally, he said:

"I think the woman hath said true. An *my* mother were in her place and gifted with the devil's functions, she had not stayed a moment to call her storms and lay the whole land in ruins, if the saving of my forfeit life were the price she got! It is argument that other mothers are made in like mold. Thou art free, good wife—thou and thy child—for I do think thee innocent. *Now* thou'st naught to fear, being pardoned—pull off thy stockings!—an thou canst make me a storm, thou shalt be rich!"

The redeemed creature was loud in her gratitude, and proceeded to obey, while Tom looked on with eager expectancy, a little marred by apprehension; the courtiers at the same time manifesting decided discomfort and uneasiness. The woman stripped her own feet and her little girl's also, and plainly did her best to reward the king's generosity with an earthquake, but it was all a failure and a disappointment. Tom sighed, and said:

"There, good soul, trouble thyself no further, thy power is departed out of thee. Go thy way in peace; and if it return to thee at any time, forget me not, but fetch me a storm."

III

PRIME TWAIN

Life on the Mississippi

Twain gathered his memories about Mississippi River life and his career as a river-boat pilot in a series of articles for the Atlantic Monthly *in 1875. These articles became chapters in* Life on the Mississippi *(1883). In order to complete the book Twain returned to the locale in 1882 with a stenographer. He traveled down the river to New Orleans and up the river to St. Paul.*

The resulting book was a characteristic combination of travelogue, history, personal reflection, anecdotes, and commentary on the changes from the 1850s to the 1880s. The book also includes parodies of travel literature and burlesque of "interesting local legends." Twain's skeptical eye thus squinted at his own literary activity.

His explicit skepticism in this book includes his remarks about his memory, his proud independence as a river-boat pilot, and his harsh criticism of some social customs. The following selections also present several examples of the tall-tale humor that gave Twain a temperamental contempt for those who are easily fooled. Twain's disgust with the credulity of those who believed in spiritualism reveals another side of his keen mind. The visit to Hannibal unlocked a treasure of memories about religious fears and childhood guilts. But the text also reveals that Twain started doubting at an admirably young age. The texts are taken from the first American edition (Boston, 1883).

Chapter 9

[Twain as pilot]

. . . During the afternoon watch the next day, Mr. Bixby asked me if I knew how to run the next few miles. I said: —

"Go inside the first snag above the point, outside the next one, start out from the lower end of Higgins's wood-yard, make a square crossing and"—

"That's all right. I'll be back before you close up on the next point."

But he wasn't. He was still below when I rounded it and entered upon a piece of river which I had some misgivings about. I did not know that he was hiding behind a chimney to see how I would perform. I went gayly along, getting prouder and prouder, for he had never left the boat in my sole charge such a length of time before. I even got to "setting" her and letting the wheel go, entirely, while I vaingloriously turned my back and inspected the stern marks and hummed a tune, a sort of easy indifference which I had prodigiously admired in Bixby and other great pilots. Once I inspected rather long, and when I faced to the front again my heart flew into my mouth so suddenly that if I hadn't clapped my teeth together I should have lost it. One of those frightful bluff reefs was stretching its deadly length right across our bows! My head was gone in a moment; I did not know which end I stood on; I gasped and could not get my breath; I spun the wheel down with such rapidity that it wove itself together like a spider's web; the boat answered and turned square away from the reef, but the reef followed her! I fled, and still it followed still it kept—right across my bows! I never looked to see where I was going, I only fled. The awful crash was imminent—why didn't that villain come! If I committed the crime of ringing a bell, I might get thrown overboard. But better that than kill the boat. So in blind desperation I started such a rattling "shivaree" down below as never had astounded an engineer in this world before, I fancy. Amidst the frenzy of the bells the engines began to back and fill in a furious way, and my reason forsook its throne—we were about to crash into the woods on the other side of the river. Just then Mr. Bixby stepped calmly into view on the hurricane deck. My soul went out to him in gratitude. My distress vanished; I would have felt safe on the brink of Niagara, with Mr. Bixby on the hurricane deck. He blandly and sweetly took his tooth-pick out of his mouth between his fingers, as if it were a cigar,—we were just in the act of climbing an overhanging big tree, and the passengers were scudding astern like rats,—and lifted up these commands to me ever so gently:—

"Stop the starboard. Stop the larboard. Set her back on both."

The boat hesitated, halted, pressed her nose among the boughs a critical instant, then reluctantly began to back away.

"Stop the larboard. Come ahead on it. Stop the starboard. Come ahead on it. Point her for the bar."

I sailed away as serenely as a summer's morning. Mr. Bixby came in and said, with mock simplicity,—

"When you have a hail, my boy, you ought to tap the big bell three times before you land, so that the engineers can get ready."

I blushed under the sarcasm, and said I hadn't had any hail.

"Ah! Then it was for wood, I suppose. The officer of the watch will tell you when he wants to wood up."

I went on consuming, and said I wasn't after wood.

"Indeed? Why, what could you want over here in the bend, then? Did you ever know of a boat following a bend up-stream at this stage of the river?"

"No, sir,—and *I* wasn't trying to follow it. I was getting away from a bluff reef."

"No, it wasn't a bluff reef; there isn't one within three miles of where you were."

"But I saw it. It was as bluff as that one yonder."

"Just about. Run over it!"

"Do you give it as an order?"

"Yes. Run over it."

"If I don't, I wish I may die."

"All right; I am taking the responsibility."

I was just as anxious to kill the boat, now, as I had been to save her before. I impressed my orders upon my memory, to be used at the inquest, and made a straight break for the reef. As it disappeared under our bows I held my breath; but we slid over it like oil.

"Now don't you see the difference? It wasn't anything but a *wind* reef. The wind does that."

"So I see. But it is exactly like a bluff reef. How am I ever going to tell them apart?"

"I can't tell you. It is an instinct. By and by you will just naturally *know* one from the other, but you never will be able to explain why or how you know them apart."

It turned out to be true. The face of the water, in time, became a wonderful book—a book that was a dead language to the uneducated passenger, but which told its mind to me without reserve, delivering its most cherished secrets as clearly as if it uttered them with a voice. And it was not a book to be read once and thrown aside, for it had a new story to tell every day. Throughout the long twelve hundred miles there was never a page that was void of interest, never one that you could leave unread without loss, never one that you would want to skip, thinking you could find higher enjoyment in some other thing. There never was so wonderful a book written by man; never one whose interest was so absorbing, so unflagging, so sparklingly renewed with every re-perusal. The passenger who could not read it was charmed with a peculiar sort of faint dimple on its surface (on the rare occasions when he did not overlook it altogether); but to the pilot that was an *italicized* passage; indeed, it was more than that, it was a legend of the largest capitals, with a string of shouting exclamation points at the end of it; for it meant that a wreck or a rock was buried there that could tear the life out of the strongest vessel that ever floated. It is the faintest and simplest expression the water ever makes, and the most hideous to a pilot's eye. In truth, the passenger who could not read this book saw nothing but all manner of pretty pictures in it, painted by the sun and shaded by the clouds, whereas to the trained eye these were not pictures at all, but the grimmest and most dead-earnest of reading-matter.

Now when I had mastered the language of this water and had come to know every trifling feature that bordered the great river as familiarly as I knew the letters of the alphabet, I had made a valuable acquisition. But I had lost something, too. I had lost something which could never be restored to me while I lived. All the grace, the beauty, the poetry had gone out of the majestic river! I still keep in mind a certain wonderful sunset which I witnessed when steamboating was new to me. A broad expanse of the river was turned to blood; in the middle distance the red hue brightened into gold, through which a solitary log came floating, black and conspicuous; in one place a long, slanting mark lay sparkling upon the water; in another the surface was broken by boiling, tumbling rings, that were as many-tinted as an opal; where the ruddy flush was faintest, was a smooth spot that was covered with graceful circles and radiating lines, ever so delicately traced; the shore on our left was densely wooded, and the sombre shadow that fell from this forest was broken in one place by a long, ruffled trail that shone like silver; and high above the forest wall a clean-stemmed dead tree waved a single leafy bough that glowed like a flame in the unobstructed splendor that was flowing from the sun. There were graceful curves, reflected images, woody heights, soft distances; and over the whole scene, far and near, the dissolving lights drifted steadily, enriching it, every passing moment, with new marvels of coloring.

I stood like one bewitched. I drank it in, in a speechless rapture. The world was new to me, and I had never seen anything like this at home. But as I have said, a day came when I began to cease from noting the glories and the charms which the moon and the sun and the twilight wrought upon the river's face; another day came when I ceased altogether to note them. Then, if that sunset scene had been repeated, I should have looked upon it without rapture, and should have commented upon it, inwardly, after this fashion: This sun means that we are going to have wind to-morrow; that floating log means that the river is rising, small thanks to it; that slanting mark on the water refers to a bluff reef which is going to kill somebody's steamboat one of these nights, if it keeps on stretching out like that; those tumbling "boils" show a dissolving bar and a changing channel there; the lines and circles in the slick water over yonder are a warning that that troublesome place is shoaling up dangerously; that silver streak in the shadow of the forest is the "break" from a new snag, and he has located himself in the very best place he could have found to fish for steamboats; that tall dead tree, with a single living branch, is not going to last long, and then how is a body ever going to get through this blind place at night without the friendly old landmark?

No, the romance and the beauty were all gone from the river. All the value any feature of it had for me now was the amount of usefulness it could furnish toward compassing the safe piloting of a steamboat. Since those days, I have pitied doctors from my heart. What does the lovely flush in a beauty's cheek mean to a doctor but a "break" that ripples above some deadly disease? Are not all her visible charms sown thick with what are to him the signs and symbols of hidden decay? Does he ever see her beauty at all, or doesn't he simply view her professionally, and comment upon her unwholesome condition all to himself? And doesn't he sometimes wonder whether he has gained most or lost most by learning his trade?

Chapter 11

THE RIVER RISES

. . . You will hardly believe it, but many steamboat clerks always carried a large assortment of religious tracts with them in those old departed steamboating days. Indeed they did. Twenty times a day we would be cramping up around a bar, while a string of these small-fry rascals were drifting down into the head of the bend away above and beyond us a couple of miles. Now a skiff would dart away from one of them, and come fighting its laborious way across the desert of water. It would "ease all," in the shadow of our forecastle, and the panting oarsmen would shout, "Gimme a pa-a-per!" as the skiff drifted swiftly astern. The clerk would throw over a file of New Orleans journals. If these were picked up *without comment,* you might notice that now a dozen other skiffs had been drifting down upon us without saying anything. You understand, they had been waiting to see how No. 1 was going to fare. No. 1 making no comment, all the rest would bend to their oars and come on, now; and as fast as they came the clerk would heave over neat bundles of religious tracts, tied to shingles. The amount of hard swearing which twelve packages of religious literature will command when impartially divided up among twelve raftsmen's crews, who have pulled a heavy skiff two miles on a hot day to get them, is simply incredible. . . .

Chapter 13

A PILOT'S NEEDS

But I am wandering from what I was intending to do, that is, make plainer than perhaps appears in the previous chapters, some of the peculiar requirements of the science of piloting. First of all, there is one faculty which a pilot must incessantly cultivate until he has brought it to absolute perfection. Nothing short of perfection will do. That faculty is memory. He cannot stop with merely thinking a thing is so and so; he must *know* it; for this is eminently one of the "exact" sciences. With what scorn a pilot was looked upon, in the old times, if he ever ventured to deal in that feeble phrase "I think," instead of the vigorous one "I know!" One cannot easily realize what a tremendous thing it is to know every trivial detail of twelve hundred miles of river and know it with absolute exactness. If you will take the longest street in New York, and travel up and down it, conning its features patiently until you know every house and window and door and lamp-post and big and little sign by heart, and know them so accurately that you can instantly name the one you are abreast of when you are set down at random in that street in the middle of an inky black night, you will then have a tolerable notion of the amount and the exactness of a pilot's knowledge who carries the Mississippi River in his head. And then if you will go on until you know every street crossing, the character, size, and position of the crossing-stones, and the varying depth of mud in each of those numberless places, you will have some idea of what the pilot must know in order to keep a Mississippi steamer out of trouble. Next, if you will take half of the signs in that long street, and *change their places* once a month, and still manage to know their new positions accurately on dark nights, and keep up with these repeated changes without making any mistakes, you will understand what is required of a pilot's peerless memory by the fickle Mississippi.

I think a pilot's memory is about the most wonderful thing in the world. To know the Old and New Testaments by heart, and be able to recite them glibly, forward or backward, or begin at random anywhere in the book and recite both ways and never trip or make a mistake, is no extravagant mass of knowledge, and no marvellous facility, compared to a pilot's massed knowledge of the Mississippi and his marvellous facility in the handling of it. I make this comparison deliberately, and believe I am not expanding the truth when I do it. Many will think my figure too strong, but pilots will not.

And how easily and comfortably the pilot's memory does its work; how placidly effortless is its way; how *unconsciously* it lays up its vast stores, hour by hour, day by day, and never loses or mislays a single valuable package of them all! Take an instance. Let a leadsman cry, "Half twain! half twain! half twain! half twain! half twain!" until it becomes as monotonous as the ticking of a clock; let conversation be going on all the time, and the pilot be doing his share of the talking, and no longer consciously listening to the leadsman; and in the midst of this endless string of half twains let a single "quarter twain!" be interjected, without emphasis, and then the half twain cry go on again, just as before: two or three weeks later that pilot can describe with precision the boat's position in the river when that quarter twain was uttered, and give you such a lot of head-marks, stern-marks, and side-marks to guide you, that you ought to be able to take the boat there and put her in that same spot again yourself! The cry of "quarter twain" did not really take his mind from his talk, but his trained faculties instantly photographed the bearings, noted the change of depth, and laid up the important details for future reference without requiring any assistance from *him* in the matter. If you were walking and talking with a friend, and another friend at your side kept up a monotonous repetition of the vowel sound A, for a couple of blocks, and then in the midst interjected an R, thus, A, A, A, A, A, R, A, A, A, etc., and gave the R no emphasis, you would not be able to state, two or three weeks afterward, that the R had been put in, nor be able to tell what objects you were passing at the moment it was done. But you could if your memory had been patiently and laboriously trained to do that sort of thing mechanically.

Give a man a tolerably fair memory to start with, and piloting will develop it into a very colossus of capability. But *only in the matters it is daily drilled in.* A time would come when the man's faculties could not help noticing landmarks and soundings, and his memory could not help holding on to them with the grip of a vice; but if you asked that same man at noon what he had had for breakfast, it would be ten chances to one that he could not tell you. Astonishing things can be done with the human memory if you will devote it faithfully to one particular line of business.

At the time that wages soared so high on the Mississippi River, my chief, Mr. Bixby, went up there and learned more than a thousand miles of that stream with an ease and rapidity that were astonishing. When he had seen each division *once* in the daytime and *once* at night, his education was so nearly complete that he took out a "daylight" license; a few trips later he took out a full license, and went to piloting day and night,—and he ranked A 1, too.

Mr. Bixby placed me as steersman for a while under a pilot whose feats of memory were a constant marvel to me. However, his memory was born in him, I think, not built. For instance, somebody would mention a name. Instantly Mr. Brown would break in:—

"Oh, I knew *him.* Sallow-faced, red-headed fellow, with a little scar on the side of his throat, like a splinter under the flesh. He was only in the Southern trade six months. That was thirteen years ago. I made a trip with him. There was five feet in the upper river then; the 'Henry Blake' grounded at the foot of Tower Island drawing four and a half; the 'George Elliott' unshipped her rudder on the wreck of the 'Sunflower'"—

"Why, the 'Sunflower' didn't sink until"—

"*I* know when she sunk; it was three years before that, on the 2d of December; Asa Hardy was captain of her, and his brother John was first clerk; and it was his first trip in her, too; Tom Jones told me these things a week afterward in New Orleans; he was first mate of the 'Sunflower.' Captain Hardy stuck a nail in his foot the 6th of July of the next year, and died of the lockjaw on the 15th. His brother John died two years after,—3d of March,—erysipelas. I never saw either of the Hardys,—they were Alleghany River men,—but people who knew them told me all these things. And they said Captain Hardy wore yarn socks winter and summer just the same, and his first wife's name was Jane Shook,—she was from New England,—and his second one died in a lunatic asylum. It was in the blood. She was from Lexington, Kentucky. Name was Horton before she was married."

And so on, by the hour, the man's tongue would go. He could *not* forget any thing. It was simply impossible. The most trivial details remained as distinct and luminous in his head, after they had lain there for years, as the most memorable events. His was not simply a pilot's memory; its grasp was universal. If he were talking about a trifling letter he had received seven years before, he was pretty sure to deliver you the entire screed from memory. And then without observing that he was departing from the true line of his talk, he was more than likely to hurl in a long-drawn parenthetical biography of the writer of that letter; and you were lucky indeed if he did not take up that writer's relatives, one by one, and give you their biographies, too.

Such a memory as that is a great misfortune. To it, all occurrences are of the same size. Its possessor cannot distinguish an interesting circumstance from an uninteresting one. As a talker, he is bound to clog his narrative with tiresome details and make himself an insufferable bore. Moreover, he cannot stick to his subject. He picks up every little grain of memory he discerns in his way, and so is led aside. Mr. Brown would start out with the honest intention of telling you a vastly funny anecdote about a dog. He would be "so full of laugh" that he could hardly begin; then his memory would start with the dog's breed and personal appearance; drift into a history of his owner; of his owner's family, with descriptions of weddings and burials that had occurred in it, together with recitals of congratulatory verses and obituary poetry provoked by the same; then this memory would recollect that one of these events occurred during the celebrated "hard winter" of such and such a year, and a minute description of that winter would follow, along with the names of people who were frozen to death, and statistics showing the high figures which pork and hay went up to. Pork and hay would suggest corn and fodder; corn and fodder would suggest cows and horses; cows and horses would suggest the circus and certain celebrated bare-back riders; the transition from the circus to the menagerie was easy and natural; from the elephant to equatorial Africa was but a step; then of course the heathen savages would suggest religion; and at the end of three or four hours' tedious jaw, the watch would change, and Brown would go out of the pilot-house muttering extracts from sermons he had heard years before about the efficacy of prayer as a means of grace. And the original first mention would be all you had learned about that dog, after all this waiting and hungering.

A pilot must have a memory; but there are two higher qualities which he must also have. He must have good and quick judgment and decision, and a cool, calm courage that no peril can shake. Give a man the merest trifle of pluck to start with, and by the time he has become a pilot he cannot be unmanned by any danger a steamboat can get into; but one cannot quite say the same for judgment. Judgment is a matter of brains, and a man must *start* with a good stock of that article or he will never succeed as a pilot.

The growth of courage in the pilot-house is steady all the time, but it does not reach a high and satisfactory condition until some time after the young pilot has been "standing his own watch," alone and under the staggering weight of all the responsibilities connected with the position. When an apprentice has become pretty thoroughly acquainted with the river, he goes clattering along so fearlessly with his steamboat, night or day, that he presently begins to imagine that it is *his* courage that animates him; but the first time the pilot steps out and leaves him to his own devices he finds out it was the other man's. He discovers that the article has been left out of his own cargo altogether. The whole river is bristling with exigencies in a moment; he is not prepared for them; he does not know how to meet them; all his knowledge forsakes him; and within fifteen minutes he is as white as a sheet and scared almost to death. Therefore pilots wisely train these cubs by various strategic tricks to look danger in the face a little more calmly. A favorite way of theirs is to play a friendly swindle upon the candidate.

Mr Bixby served me in this fashion once, and for years afterward I used to blush even in my sleep when I thought of it. I had become a good steersman; so good, indeed, that I had all the work to do on our watch, night and day; Mr. Bixby seldom made a suggestion to me; all he ever did was to take the wheel on particularly bad nights or in particularly bad crossings, land the boat when she needed to be landed, play gentleman of leisure nine tenths of the watch, and collect the wages. The lower river was about bank-full, and if anybody had questioned my ability to run any crossing between Cairo and New Orleans without help or instruction, I should have felt irreparably hurt. The idea of being afraid of any crossing in the lot, in the *day-time,* was a thing too preposterous for contemplation. Well, one matchless summer's day I was bowling down the bend above island 66, brimful of self-conceit and carrying my nose as high as a giraffe's, when Mr. Bixby said,—

"I am going below a while. I suppose you know the next crossing?"

This was almost an affront. It was about the plainest and simplest crossing in the whole river. One couldn't come to any harm, whether he ran it right or not; and as for depth, there never had been any bottom there. I knew all this, perfectly well.

"Know how to *run* it? Why, I can run it with my eyes shut."

"How much water is there in it?"

"Well, that is an odd question. I couldn't get bottom there with a church steeple."

"You think so, do you?"

The very tone of the question shook my confidence. That was what Mr. Bixby was expecting. He left, without saying anything more. I began to imagine all sorts of things. Mr. Bixby, unknown to me, of course, sent somebody down to the forecastle with some mysterious instructions to the leadsmen, another messenger was sent to whisper among the officers, and then Mr. Bixby went into hiding behind a smoke-stack where he could observe results. Presently the captain stepped out on the hurricane deck; next the chief mate appeared; then a clerk. Every moment or two a straggler was added to my audience; and before I got to the head of the island I had fifteen or twenty people assembled down there under my nose. I began to wonder what the trouble was. As I started across, the captain glanced aloft at me and said, with a sham uneasiness in his voice,—

"Where is Mr. Bixby?"

"Gone below, sir."

But that did the business for me. My imagination began to construct dangers out of nothing, and they multiplied faster than I could keep the run of them. All at once I imagined I saw shoal water ahead! The wave of coward agony that surged through me then came near dislocating every joint in me. All my confidence in that crossing vanished. I seized the bell-rope; dropped it, ashamed; seized it again; dropped it once more; clutched it tremblingly once again, and pulled it so feebly that I could hardly hear the stroke myself. Captain and mate sang out instantly, and both together, –

"Starboard lead there! and quick about it!"

This was another shock. I began to climb the wheel like a squirrel; but I would hardly get the boat started to port before I would see new dangers on that side, and away I would spin to the other; only to find perils accumulating to starboard, and be crazy to get to port again. Then came the leadsman's sepulchral cry: –

"D-e-e-p four!"

Deep four in a bottomless crossing! The terror of it took my breath away.

"M-a-r-k three! . . . M-a-r-k three . . . Quarter less three! . . . Half twain!"

This was frightful! I seized the bell-ropes and stopped the engines.

"Quarter twain! Quarter twain! *Mark* twain!"

I was helpless. I did not know what in the world to do. I was quaking from head to foot, and I could have hung my hat on my eyes, they stuck out so far.

"Quarter *less* twain! Nine and a *half!*"

We were *drawing* nine! My hands were in a nerveless flutter. I could not ring a bell intelligibly with them. I flew to the speaking-tube and shouted to the engineer, –

"Oh, Ben, if you love me, *back* her! Quick, Ben! Oh, back the immortal *soul* out of her!"

I hear the door close gently. I looked around, and there stood Mr. Bixby, smiling a bland, sweet smile. Then the audience on the hurricane deck sent up a thundergust of humiliating laughter. I saw it all, now, and I felt meaner than the meanest man in human history. I laid in the lead, set the boat in her marks, came ahead on the engines, and said: –

"It was a fine trick to play on an orphan, *wasn't* it? I suppose I'll never hear the last of how I was ass enough to heave the lead at the head of 66."

"Well, no, you won't, maybe. In fact I hope you won't; for I want you to learn something by that experience. Didn't you *know* there was no bottom in that crossing?"

"Yes, sir, I did."

"Very well, then. You shouldn't have allowed me or anybody else to shake your confidence in that knowledge. Try to remember that. And another thing: when you get into a dangerous place, don't turn coward. That isn't going to help matters any."

It was a good enough lesson, but pretty hardly learned. Yet about the hardest part of it was that for months I so often had to hear a phrase which I had conceived a particular distaste for. It was, "Oh, Ben, if you love me, back her!"

CHAPTER 18

I TAKE A FEW EXTRA LESSONS

During the two or two and a half years of my apprenticeship, I served under many pilots, and had experience of many kinds of steamboatmen and many varieties of steamboats; for it was not always convenient for Mr. Bixby to have me with him, and in such cases he sent me with somebody else. I am to this day profiting somewhat by that experience; for in that brief, sharp schooling, I got personally and familiarly acquainted with about all the different types of human nature that are to be found in fiction, biography, or history. The fact is daily borne in upon me, that the average shore-employment requires as much as forty years to equip a man with this sort of an education. When I say I am still profiting by this thing, I do not mean that it has constituted me a judge of men—no, it has not done that; for judges of men are born, not made. My profit is various in kind and degree; but the feature of it which I value most is the zest which that early experience has given to my later reading. When I find a well-drawn character in fiction or biography, I generally take a warm personal interest in him, for the reason that I have known him before—met him on the river.

The figure that comes before me oftenest, out of the shadows of that vanished time, is that of Brown, of the steamer "Pennsylvania"—the man referred to in a former chapter, whose memory was so good and tiresome. He was a middle-aged, long, slim, bony, smooth-shaven, horse-faced, ignorant, stingy, malicious, snarling, fault-hunting, mote-magnifying tyrant. I early got the habit of coming on watch with dread at my heart. No matter how good a time I might have been having with the off-watch below, and no matter how high my spirits might be when I started aloft, my soul became lead in my body the moment I approached the pilot-house.

I still remember the first time I ever entered the presence of that man. The boat had backed out from St. Louis and was "straightening down;" I ascended to the pilot-house in high feather, and very proud to be semi-officially a member of the executive family of so fast and famous a boat. Brown was at the wheel. I paused in the middle of the room, all fixed to make my bow, but Brown did not look around. I thought he took a furtive glance at me out of the corner of his eye, but as not even this notice was repeated, I judged I had been mistaken. By this time he was picking his way among some dangerous "breaks" abreast the wood-yards; therefore it would not be proper to interrupt him; so I stepped softly to the high bench and took a seat.

There was silence for ten minutes; then my new boss turned and inspected me deliberately and painstakingly from head to heel for about—as it seemed to me—a quarter of an hour. After which he removed his countenance and I saw it no more for some seconds; then it came around once more, and this question greeted me:—

"Are you Horace Bigsby's cub?"

"Yes, sir."

After this there was a pause and another inspection. Then:

"What's your name?"

I told him. He repeated it after me. It was probably the only thing he ever forgot; for although I was with him many months he never addressed himself to me in any other way than "Here!" and then his command followed.

"Where was you born?"

"In Florida, Missouri."

A pause. Then:—

"Dern sight better staid there!"

By means of a dozen or so of pretty direct questions, he pumped my family history out of me.

The leads were going now, in the first crossing. This interrupted the inquest. When the leads had been laid in, he resumed:—

"How long you been on the river?"

I told him. After a pause:—

"Where'd you get them shoes?"

I gave him the information.

"Hold up your foot!"

I did so. He stepped back, examined the shoe minutely and contemptuously, scratching his head thoughtfully, tilting his high sugar-loaf hat well forward to facilitate the operation, then ejaculated, "Well, I'll be dod derned!" and returned to his wheel.

What occasion there was to be dod derned about it is a thing which is still as much of a mystery to me now as it was then. It must have been all of fifteen minutes—fifteen minutes of dull, homesick silence—before that long horse-face swung round upon me again—and then, what a change! It was as red as fire, and every muscle in it was working. Now came this shriek:

"Here!—You going to set there all day?"

I lit in the middle of the floor, shot there by the electric suddenness of the surprise. As soon as I could get my voice I said, apologetically:—

"I have had no orders, sir."

"You've had no *orders!* My, what a fine bird we are! We must have *orders!* Our father was a *gentleman*—owned slaves—and *we've* been to *school.* Yes, *we* are a gentleman, *too,* and got to have *orders!* ORDERS, is it? ORDERS is what you want! Dod dern my skin, *I'll* learn you to swell yourself up and blow around *here* about your dod-derned *orders!* G'way from the wheel!" (I had approached it without knowing it.)

I moved back a step or two, and stood as in a dream, all my senses stupefied by this frantic assault.

"What you standing there for? Take that ice-pitcher down to the texas-tender—come, move along, and don't you be all day about it!"

The moment I got back to the pilot-house, Brown said:—

"Here! What was you doing down there all this time?"

"I couldn't find the texas-tender; I had to go all the way to the pantry."

"Derned likely story! Fill up the stove."

I proceeded to do so. He watched me like a cat. Presently he shouted:—

"Put down that shovel! Derndest numskull I ever saw—ain't even got sense enough to load up a stove."

All through the watch this sort of thing went on. Yes, and the subsequent watches were much like it, during a stretch of months. As I have said, I soon got the habit of coming on duty with dread. The moment I was in the presence, even in the darkest night, I could feel those yellow eyes upon me, and knew their owner was watching for a pretext to spit out some venom on me. Preliminarily he would say:—

"Here! Take the wheel."

Two minutes later:—

"*Where* in the nation you going to? Pull her down! pull her down!"

After another moment:—

"Say! You going to hold her all day? Let her go—meet her! meet her!"

Then he would jump from the bench, snatch the wheel from me, and meet her himself, pouring out wrath upon me all the time.

George Ritchie was the other pilot's cub. He was having good times now; for his boss, George Ealer, was as kind-hearted as Brown wasn't. Ritchie had steered for Brown the season before; consequently he knew exactly how to entertain himself and plague me, all by the one operation. Whenever I took the wheel for a moment on Ealer's watch, Ritchie would sit back on the bench and play Brown, with continual ejaculations of "Snatch her! snatch her! Derndest mud-cat I ever saw!" "Here! where you going *now?* Going to run over that snag?" "Pull her *down!* Don't you hear me? Pull her *down!*" "There she goes! *Just* as I expected! I *told* you not to cramp that reef. G'way from the wheel!"

So I always had a rough time of it, no matter whose watch it was; and sometimes it seemed to me that Ritchie's good-natured badgering was pretty nearly as aggravating as Brown's dead-earnest nagging.

I often wanted to kill Brown, but this would not answer. A cub had to take everything his boss gave, in the way of vigorous comment and criticism; and we all believed that there was a United States law making it a penitentiary offence to strike or threaten a pilot who was on duty. However, I could *imagine* myself killing Brown; there was no law against that; and that was the thing I used always to do the moment I was abed. Instead of going over my river in my mind as was my duty, I threw business aside for pleasure, and killed Brown. I killed Brown every night for months; not in old, stale, commonplace ways, but in new and picturesque ones,—ways that were sometimes surprising for freshness of design and ghastliness of situation and environment.

Brown was *always* watching for a pretext to find fault; and if he could find no plausible pretext, he would invent one. He would scold you for shaving a shore, and for not shaving it; for hugging a bar, and for not hugging it; for "pulling down" when not invited, and *for not* pulling down when not invited;

for firing up without orders, and for waiting *for* orders. In a word, it was his invariable rule to find fault with *everything* you did; and another invariable rule of his was to throw all his remarks (to you) into the form of an insult.

One day we were approaching New Madrid, bound down and heavily laden. Brown was at one side of the wheel, steering; I was at the other, standing by to "pull down" or "shove up." He cast a furtive glance at me every now and then. I had long ago learned what that meant; viz., he was trying to invent a trap for me. I wondered what shape it was going to take. By and by he stepped back from the wheel and said in his usual snarly way:—

"Here!—See if you've got gumption enough to round her to."

This was simply *bound* to be a success; nothing could prevent it; for he had never allowed me to round the boat to before; consequently, no matter how I might do the thing, he could find free fault with it. He stood back there with his greedy eye on me, and the result was what might have been foreseen: I lost my head in a quarter of a minute, and didn't know what I was about; I started too early to bring the boat around, but detected a green gleam of joy in Brown's eye, and corrected my mistake; I started around once more while too high up, but corrected myself again in time; I made other false moves, and still managed to save myself; but at last I grew so confused and anxious that I tumbled into the very worst blunder of all—I got too far *down* before beginning to fetch the boat around. Brown's chance was come.

His face turned red with passion; he made one bound, hurled me across the house with a sweep of his arm, spun the wheel down, and began to pour out a stream of vituperation upon me which lasted till he was out of breath. In the course of this speech he called me all the different kinds of hard names he could think of, and once or twice I thought he was even going to swear—but he had never done that, and he didn't this time. "Dod dern" was the nearest he ventured to the luxury of swearing, for he had been brought up with a wholesome respect for future fire and brimstone.

That was an uncomfortable hour; for there was a big audience on the hurricane deck. When I went to bed that night, I killed Brown in seventeen different ways—all of them new.

Chapter 19

BROWN AND I EXCHANGE COMPLIMENTS

Two trips later, I got into serious trouble. Brown was steering; I was "pulling down." My younger brother appeared on the hurricane deck, and shouted to Brown to stop at some landing or other a mile or so below. Brown gave no intimation that he had heard anything. But that was his way: he never condescended to take notice of an under clerk. The wind was blowing; Brown was deaf (although he always pretended he wasn't), and I very much doubted if he had heard the order. If I had had two heads, I would have spoken; but as I had only one, it seemed judicious to take care of it; so I kept still.

Presently, sure enough, we went sailing by that plantation. Captain Klinefelter appeared on the deck, and said: —

"Let her come around, sir, let her come around. Didn't Henry tell you to land here?"

"*No,* sir!"

"I sent him up to do it."

"He *did* come up; and that's all the good it done, the dod-derned fool. He never said anything."

"Didn't *you* hear him?" asked the captain of me.

Of course I didn't want to be mixed up in this business, but there was no way to avoid it; so I said: —

"Yes, sir."

I knew what Brown's next remark would be, before he uttered it; it was: —

"Shut your mouth! you never heard anything of the kind."

I closed my mouth according to instructions. An hour later, Henry entered the pilot-house, unaware of what had been going on. He was a thoroughly inoffensive boy, and I was sorry to see him come, for I knew Brown would have no pity on him. Brown began, straightway: —

"Here! why didn't you tell me we'd got to land at that plantation?"

"I did tell you, Mr. Brown."

"It's a lie!"

I said: —

"You lie, yourself. He did tell you."

Brown glared at me in unaffected surprise; and for as much as a moment he was entirely speechless; then he shouted at me: —

"I'll attend to your case in a half a minute!" then to Henry, "And you leave the pilot-house; out with you!"

It was pilot law, and must be obeyed. The boy started out, and even had his foot on the upper step outside the door, when Brown, with a sudden access of fury, picked up a ten-pound lump of coal and sprang after him; but I was between, with a heavy stool, and I hit Brown a good honest blow which stretched him out.

I had committed the crime of crimes, — I had lifted my hand against a pilot on duty! I supposed I was booked for the penitentiary sure, and couldn't be booked any surer if I went on and squared my long account with this person while I had the chance; consequently I stuck to him and pounded him with my fists a considerable time, — I do not know how long, the pleasure of it probably made it seem longer than it really was; — but in the end he struggled free and jumped up and sprang to the wheel: a very natural solicitude, for, all this time, here was this steamboat tearing down the river at the rate of fifteen miles an hour and nobody at the helm! However, Eagle Bend was two miles wide at this bank-full stage, and correspondingly long and deep; and the boat was steering herself straight down the middle and taking no chances. Still that was only luck—a body *might* have found her charging into the woods.

Perceiving, at a glance, that the "Pennsylvania" was in no danger, Brown gathered up the big spy-glass, war-club fashion, and ordered me out of the pilot-house with more than Comanche bluster. But I was not afraid of him now; so, instead of going, I tarried, and criticised his grammar; I reformed his ferocious speeches for him, and put them into good English, calling his attention to the advantage of pure English over the bastard dialect of the Pennsylvanian collieries whence he was extracted. He could have done his part to admiration in a cross-fire of mere vituperation, of course; but he was not equipped for this species of controversy; so he presently laid aside his glass and took the wheel, muttering and shaking his head; and I retired to the bench. The racket had brought everybody to the hurricane deck, and I trembled when I saw the old captain looking up from the midst of the crowd. I said to myself, "Now I *am* done for!"—For although, as a rule, he was so fatherly and indulgent toward the boat's family, and so patient of minor shortcomings, he could be stern enough when the fault was worth it.

I tried to imagine what he *would* do to a cub pilot who had been guilty of such a crime as mine, committed on a boat guard-deep with costly freight and alive with passengers. Our watch was nearly ended. I thought I would go and hide somewhere till I got a chance to slide ashore. So I slipped out of the pilot-house, and down the steps, and around to the texas door,—and was in the act of gliding within, when the captain confronted me! I dropped my head, and he stood over me in silence a moment or two, then said impressively,—

"Follow me."

I dropped into his wake; he led the way to his parlor in the forward end of the texas. We were alone, now. He closed the after door; then moved slowly to the forward one and closed that. He sat down; I stood before him. He looked at me some little time, then said,—

"So you have been fighting Mr. Brown?"

I answered meekly:—

"Yes, sir."

"Do you know that that is a very serious matter?"

"Yes, sir."

"Are you aware that this boat was ploughing down the river fully five minutes with no one at the wheel?"

"Yes, sir."

"Did you strike him first?"

"Yes, sir."

"What with?"

"A stool, sir."

"Hard?"

"Middling, sir."

"Did it knock him down?"

"He—he fell, sir."

"Did you follow it up? Did you do anything further?"

"Yes, sir."

"What did you do?"

"Pounded him, sir."

"Pounded him?"

"Yes, sir."

"Did you pound him much?—that is, severely?"

"One might call it that, sir, maybe."

"I'm deucéd glad of it! Hark ye, never mention that I said that. You have been guilty of a great crime; and don't you ever be guilty of it again, on this boat. *But*—lay for him ashore! Give him a good sound thrashing, do you hear? I'll pay the expenses. Now go—and mind you, not a word of this to anybody. Clear out with you!—you've been guilty of a great crime, you whelp!"

I slid out, happy with the sense of a close shave and a mighty deliverance; and I heard him laughing to himself and slapping his fat thighs after I had closed his door.

When Brown came off watch he went straight to the captain, who was walking with some passengers on the boiler deck, and demanded that I be put ashore in New Orleans—and added:—

"I'll never turn a wheel on this boat again while that cub stays."

The captain said:—

"But he needn't come round when you are on watch, Mr. Brown."

"I won't even stay on the same boat with him. *One* of us has got to go ashore."

"Very well," said the captain, "let it be yourself;" and resumed his talk with the passengers.

During the brief remainder of the trip, I knew how an emancipated slave feels; for I was an emancipated slave myself. While we lay at landings, I listened to George Ealer's flute; or to his readings from his two bibles, that is to say, Goldsmith and Shakspeare; or I played chess with him—and would have beaten him sometimes, only he always took back his last move and ran the game out differently.

Chapter 20

A CATASTROPHE

We lay three days in New Orleans, but the captain did not succeed in finding another pilot; so he proposed that I should stand a daylight watch, and leave the night watches to George Ealer. But I was afraid; I had never stood a watch of any sort by myself, and I believed I should be sure to get into trouble in the head of some chute, or ground the boat in a near cut through some bar or other.

Brown remained in his place; but he would not travel with me. So the captain gave me an order on the captain of the "A. T. Lacey," for a passage to St. Louis, and said he would find a new pilot there and my steersman's berth could then be resumed. The "Lacey" was to leave a couple of days after the "Pennsylvania."

The night before the "Pennsylvania" left, Henry and I sat chatting on a freight pile on the levee till midnight. The subject of the chat, mainly, was one which I think we had not exploited before—steamboat disasters. One was then on its way to us, little as we suspected it; the water which was to make the steam which should cause it, was washing past some point fifteen hundred miles up the river while we talked;—but it would arrive at the right time and the right place. We doubted if persons not clothed with authority were of much use in cases of disaster and attendant panic; still, they might be of *some* use; so we decided that if a disaster ever fell within our experience we would at least stick to the boat, and give such minor service as chance might throw in the way. Henry remembered this, afterward, when the disaster came, and acted accordingly.

The "Lacey" started up the river two days behind the "Pennsylvania." We touched at Greenville, Mississippi, a couple of days out, and somebody shouted:—

"The 'Pennsylvania' is blown up at Ship Island, and a hundred and fifty lives lost!"

At Napoleon, Arkansas, the same evening, we got an extra, issued by a Memphis paper, which gave some particulars. It mentioned my brother, and said he was not hurt.

Further up the river we got a later extra. My brother was again mentioned; but this time as being hurt beyond help. We did not get full details of the catastrophe until we reached Memphis. This is the sorrowful story:—

It was six o'clock on a hot summer morning. The "Pennsylvania" was creeping along, north of Ship Island, about sixty miles below Memphis on a half-head of steam, towing a wood-flat which was fast being emptied. George Ealer was in the pilot-house—alone, I think; the second engineer and a striker had the watch in the engine room; the second mate had the watch on deck; George Black, Mr. Wood, and my brother, clerks, were asleep, as were also Brown and the head engineer, the carpenter, the chief mate, and one striker; Capt. Klinefelter was in the barber's chair, and the barber was preparing to shave him. There were a good many cabin passengers aboard, and three or four hundred deck passengers—so it was said at the time—and not very many of them were astir. The wood being nearly all out of the flat now, Ealer rang to "come ahead" full steam, and the next moment four of the eight boilers exploded with a thunderous crash, and the whole forward third of the boat was hoisted toward the sky! The main part of the mass, with the chimneys, dropped upon the boat again, a mountain of riddled and chaotic rubbish—and then, after a little, fire broke out.

Many people were flung to considerable distances, and fell in the river; among these were Mr. Wood and my brother, and the carpenter. The carpenter was still stretched upon his mattress when he struck the water seventy-five feet from the boat. Brown, the pilot, and George Black, chief clerk, were never seen or heard of after the explosion. The barber's chair, with Captain Klinefelter in it and unhurt, was left with its back overhanging vacancy—everything forward of it, floor and all, had disappeared; and the stupefied barber, who was also unhurt, stood with one toe projecting over space, still stirring his lather unconsciously, and saying not a word.

When George Ealer saw the chimneys plunging aloft in front of him, he knew what the matter was; so he muffled his face in the lapels of his coat, and pressed both hands there tightly to keep this protection in its place so that no steam could get to his nose or mouth. He had ample time to attend to these details while he was going up and returning. He presently landed on top of the unexploded boilers, forty feet below the former pilot-house, accompanied by his wheel and a rain of other stuff, and enveloped in a cloud of scalding steam. All of the many who breathed that steam, died; none escaped. But Ealer breathed none of it. He made his way to the free air as quickly as he could; and when the steam cleared away he returned and climbed up on the boilers again, and patiently hunted out each and every one of his chessmen and the several joints of his flute.

By this time the fire was beginning to threaten. Shrieks and groans filled the air. A great many persons had been scalded, a great many crippled; the explosion had driven an iron crowbar through one man's body—I think they said he was a priest. He did not die at once, and his sufferings were very dreadful. A young French naval cadet, of fifteen, son of a French admiral, was fearfully scalded, but bore his tortures manfully. Both mates were badly scalded, but they stood to their posts, nevertheless. They drew the wood-boat aft, and they and the captain fought back the frantic herd of frightened immigrants till the wounded could be brought there and placed in safety first.

When Mr. Wood and Henry fell in the water, they struck out for shore, which was only a few hundred yards away; but Henry presently said he believed he was not hurt, (what an unaccountable error!) and therefore would swim back to the boat and help save the wounded. So they parted, and Henry returned.

By this time the fire was making fierce headway, and several persons who were imprisoned under the ruins were begging piteously for help. All efforts to conquer the fire proved fruitless; so the buckets were presently thrown aside and the officers fell-to with axes and tried to cut the prisoners out. A striker was one of the captives; he said he was not injured, but could not free himself; and when he saw that the fire was likely to drive away the workers, he begged that some one would shoot him, and thus save him from the more dreadful death. The fire did drive the axe-men away, and they had to listen, helpless, to this poor fellow's supplications till the flames ended his miseries.

The fire drove all into the wood-flat that could be accommodated there; it was cut adrift, then, and it and the burning steamer floated down the river toward Ship Island. They moored the flat at the head of the island, and there, unsheltered from the blazing sun, the half-naked occupants had to remain, without food or stimulants, or help for their hurts, during the rest of the day. A steamer came along, finally, and carried the unfortunates to Memphis, and there the most lavish assistance was at once forthcoming. By this time Henry was insensible. The physicians examined his injuries and saw that they were fatal, and naturally turned their main attention to patients who could be saved.

Forty of the wounded were placed upon pallets on the floor of a great public hall, and among these was Henry. There the ladies of Memphis came every day, with flowers, fruits, and dainties and delicacies of all kinds, and there they remained and nursed the wounded. All the physicians stood watches there, and all the medical students; and the rest of the town furnished money, or whatever else was wanted. And Memphis knew how to do all these things well; for many a disaster like the "Pennsylvania's" had happened near her doors, and she was experienced, above all other cities on the river, in the gracious office of the Good Samaritan.

The sight I saw when I entered that large hall was new and strange to me. Two long rows of prostrate forms—more than forty, in all—and every face and head a shapeless wad of loose raw cotton. It was a grewsome spectacle. I watched there six days and nights, and a very melancholy experience it was. There was one daily incident which was peculiarly depressing: this was the removal of the doomed to a chamber apart. It was done in order that the *morale* of the other patients might not be injuriously affected by seeing one of their number in the death-agony. The fated one was always carried out with as little stir as possible, and the stretcher was always hidden from sight by a wall of assistants; but no matter: everybody knew what that cluster of bent forms, with its muffled step and its slow movement meant; and all eyes watched it wistfully, and a shudder went abreast of it like a wave.

I saw many poor fellows removed to the "death-room," and saw them no more afterward. But I saw our chief mate carried thither more than once. His hurts were frightful, especially his scalds. He was clothed in linseed oil and raw cotton to his waist, and resembled nothing human. He was often out of his mind; and then his pains would make him rave and shout and sometimes shriek. Then, after a period of dumb exhaustion, his disordered imagination would suddenly transform the great apartment into a forecastle, and the hurrying throng of nurses into the crew; and he would come to a sitting posture and shout, "Hump yourselves, *hump* yourselves, you petrifactions, snail-bellies, pall-bearers! going to be all *day* getting that hatful of freight out?" and supplement this explosion with a firmament-obliterating irruption of profanity which nothing could stay or stop till his crater was empty. And now and then while these frenzies possessed him, he would tear off handfuls of the cotton and expose his cooked flesh to view. It was horrible. It was bad for the others, of course—this noise and these exhibitions; so the doctors tried to give him morphine to quiet him. But, in his mind or out of it, he would not take it. He said his wife had been killed by that treacherous drug, and he would die before he would take it. He suspected that the doctors were concealing it in his ordinary medicines and in his water—so he ceased from putting either to his lips. Once, when he had been without water during two sweltering days, he took the dipper in his hand, and the sight of the limpid fluid, and the misery of his thirst, tempted him almost beyond his strength; but he mastered himself and threw it away, and after that he allowed no more to be brought near him. Three times I saw him carried to the death-room, insensible and supposed to be dying; but each time he revived, cursed his attendants, and demanded to be taken back. He lived to be mate of a steamboat again.

But he was the only one who went to the death-room and returned alive. Dr. Peyton, a principal physician, and rich in all the attributes that go to constitute high and flawless character, did all that educated judgment and trained skill could do for Henry; but, as the newspapers had said in the beginning, his hurts were past help. On the evening of the sixth day his wandering mind busied itself with matters far away, and his nerveless fingers "picked at his coverlet." His hour had struck; we bore him to the death-room, poor boy.

CHAPTER 21

A SECTION IN MY BIOGRAPHY

In due course I got my license. I was a pilot now, full fledged. I dropped into casual employments; no misfortunes resulting, intermittent work gave place to steady and protracted engagements. Time drifted smoothly and prosperously on, and I supposed—and hoped—that I was going to follow the river the rest of my days, and die at the wheel when my mission was ended. But by and by the war came, commerce was suspended, my occupation was gone.

I had to seek another livelihood. So I became a silver miner in Nevada; next, a newspaper reporter; next, a gold miner, in California; next, a reporter in San Francisco; next, a special correspondent in the Sandwich Islands; next, a roving correspondent in Europe and the East; next, an instructional torch-bearer on the lecture platform; and, finally, I became a scribbler of books, and an immovable fixture among the other rocks of New England.

In so few words have I disposed of the twenty-one slow-drifting years that have come and gone since I last looked from the windows of a pilot-house.

Let us resume, now.

CHAPTER 22

I RETURN TO MY MUTTONS

After twenty-one years' absence, I felt a very strong desire to see the river again, and the steamboats, and such of the boys as might be left; so I resolved to go out there. I enlisted a poet for company, and a stenographer to "take him down," and started westward about the middle of April.

As I proposed to make notes, with a view to printing, I took some thought as to methods of procedure. I reflected that if I were recognized, on the river, I should not be as free to go and come, talk, inquire, and spy around, as I should be if unknown; I remembered that it was the custom of steamboatmen in the old times to load up the confiding stranger with the most picturesque and admirable lies, and put the sophisticated friend off with dull and ineffectual facts; so I concluded, that, from a business point of view, it would be an advantage to disguise our party with fictitious names. The idea was certainly good, but it bred infinite bother; for although Smith, Jones, and Johnson are easy names to remember when there is no occasion to remember them, it was next to impossible to recollect them when they are wanted. How do criminals manage to keep a brand-new *alias* in mind? This is a great mystery. I was innocent; and yet was seldom able to lay my hand on my new name when it was needed; and it seemed to me that if I had had a crime on my conscience to further confuse me, I could never have kept the name by me at all.

We left per Pennsylvania Railroad, at 8 A.M. April 18.

> "*Evening.* Speaking of dress. Grace and picturesqueness drop gradually out of it as one travels away from New York."

I find that among my notes. It makes no difference which direction you take, the fact remains the same. Whether you move north, south, east, or west, no matter: you can get up in the morning and guess how far you have come, by noting what degree of grace and picturesqueness is by that time lacking in the costumes of the new passengers;—I do not mean of the women alone, but of both sexes. It may be that *carriage* is at the bottom of this thing; and I think it is; for there are plenty of ladies and gentlemen in the provincial cities whose garments are all made by the best tailors and dressmakers of New York; yet this has no perceptible effect upon the grand fact: the educated eye never mistakes those people for New-Yorkers. No, there is a godless grace, and snap, and style about a born and bred New-Yorker which mere clothing cannot effect.

> "*April* 19. This morning, struck into the region of full goatees—sometimes accompanied by a moustache, but only occasionally."

It was odd to come upon this thick crop of an obsolete and uncomely fashion; it was like running suddenly across a forgotten acquaintance whom you had supposed dead for a generation. The goatee extends over a wide extent of country; and is accompanied by an iron-clad belief in Adam and the biblical history of creation, which has not suffered from the assaults of the scientists.

> "*Afternoon.* At the railway stations the loafers carry *both* hands in their breeches pockets; it was observable, heretofore, that one hand was sometimes out of doors,—here, never. This is an important fact in geography."

If the loafers determined the character of a country, it would be still more important, of course.

> "Heretofore, all along, the station-loafer has been often observed to scratch one shin with the other foot; here, these remains of activity are wanting. This has an ominous look."

By and by, we entered the tobacco-chewing region. Fifty years ago, the tobacco-chewing region covered the Union. It is greatly restricted now. . . .

Chapter 24

MY INCOGNITO IS EXPLODED

After a close study of the face of the pilot on watch, I was satisfied that I had never seen him before; so I went up there. The pilot inspected me; I re-inspected the pilot. These customary preliminaries over, I sat down on the high bench, and he faced about and went on with his work. Every detail of the pilot-house was familiar to me, with one exception,—a large-mouthed tube under the breast-board. I puzzled over that thing a considerable time; then gave up and asked what it was for.

"To hear the engine-bells through."

It was another good contrivance which ought to have been invented half a century sooner. So I was thinking, when the pilot asked,—

"Do you know what this rope is for?"

I managed to get around this question, without committing myself.

"Is this the first time you were ever in a pilot-house?"

I crept under that one.

"Where are you from?"

"New England."

"First time you have ever been West?"

I climbed over this one.

"If you take an interest in such things, I can tell you what all these things are for."

I said I should like it.

"This," putting his hand on a backing-bell rope, "is to sound the fire-alarm; this," putting his hand on a go-a-head bell, "is to call the texas-tender; this one," indicating the whistle-lever, "is to call the captain"—and so he went on, touching one object after another, and reeling off his tranquil spool of lies.

I had never felt so like a passenger before. I thanked him, with emotion, for each new fact, and wrote it down in my note-book. The pilot warmed to his opportunity, and proceeded to load me up in the good old-fashioned way. At times I was afraid he was going to rupture his invention; but it always stood the strain, and he pulled through all right. He drifted, by easy stages, into revealments of the river's marvellous eccentricities of one sort and another, and backed them up with some pretty gigantic illustrations. For instance,—

"Do you see that little bowlder sticking out of the water yonder? well, when I first came on the river, that was a solid ridge of rock, over sixty feet high and two miles long. All washed away but that." [This with a sigh.]

I had a mighty impulse to destroy him, but it seemed to me that killing, in any ordinary way, would be too good for him.

Once, when an odd-looking craft, with a vast coal-scuttle slanting aloft on the end of a beam, was steaming by in the distance, he indifferently drew attention to it, as one might to an object grown wearisome through familiarity, and observed that it was an "alligator boat."

"An alligator boat? What's it for?"

"To dredge out alligators with."

"Are they so thick as to be troublesome?"

"Well, not now, because the government keeps them down. But they used to be. Not everywhere; but in favorite places, here and there, where the river is wide and shoal—like Plum Point, and Stack Island, and so on—places they call alligator beds."

"Did they actually impede navigation?"

"Years ago, yes, in very low water; there was hardly a trip, then, that we didn't get aground on alligators."

It seemed to me that I should certainly have to get out my tomahawk. However, I restrained myself and said,—

"It must have been dreadful."

"Yes, it was one of the main difficulties about piloting. It was so hard to tell anything about the water; the damned things shift around so—never lie still five minutes at a time. You can tell a wind-reef, straight off, by the look of it; you can tell a break; you can tell a sand-reef—that's all easy; but an alligator reef doesn't show up, worth anything. Nine times in ten you can't tell where the water is; and when you *do* see where it is, like as not it ain't there when *you* get there, the devils have swapped around so, meantime. Of course there were some few pilots that could judge of alligator water nearly as well as they could of any other kind, but they had to have natural talent for it; it wasn't a thing a body could *learn,* you had to be born with it. Let me see: there was Ben Thornburg, and Beck Jolly, and Squire Bell, and Horace Bixby, and Major Downing, and John Stevenson, and Billy Gordon, and Jim Brady, and George Ealer, and Billy Youngblood—all A 1 alligator pilots. *They* could tell alligator water as far as another Christian could tell whiskey. Read it?—Ah, *couldn't* they, though! I only wish I had as many dollars as they could read alligator water a mile and a half off. Yes, and it paid them to do it, too. A good alligator pilot could always get fifteen hundred dollars a month. Nights, other people had to lay up for alligators, but those fellows never laid up for alligators; they never laid up for anything but fog. They could *smell* the best alligator water—so it was said; I don't know whether it was so or not, and I think a body's got his hands full enough if he sticks to just what he knows himself, without going around backing up other people's say-so's, though there's a plenty that ain't backward about doing it, as long as they can roust out something wonderful to tell. Which is not the style of Robert Styles, by as much as three fathom—maybe quarter*less*.

[My! Was this Rob Styles?—This moustached and stately figure?—A slim enough cub, in my time. How he has improved in comeliness in five and twenty years—and in the noble art of inflating his facts.] After these musings, I said aloud,—

"I should think that dredging out the alligators wouldn't have done much good, because they could come back again right away."

"If you had had as much experience of alligators as I have, you wouldn't talk like that. You dredge an alligator once and he's *convinced.* It's the last you hear of *him.* He wouldn't come back for pie. If there's one thing that an alligator is more down on than another, it's being dredged. Besides, they were not simply shoved out of the way; the most of the scoopful were scooped aboard; they emptied them into the hold; and when they had got a trip, they took them to Orleans to the Government works."

"What for?"

"Why, to make soldier-shoes out of their hides. All the Government shoes are made of alligator hide. It makes the best shoes in the world. They last five years, and they won't absorb water. The alligator fishery is a Government monopoly. All the alligators are Government property—just like the live-oaks. You cut down a live-oak, and Government fines you fifty dollars; you kill an alligator, and up you go for misprision of treason—lucky duck if they don't hang you, too. And they will, if you're a Democrat. The buzzard is the sacred bird of the South, and you can't touch him; the alligator is the sacred bird of the Government, and you've got to let him alone."

"Do you ever get aground on the alligators now?"

"Oh, no! it hasn't happened for years."

"Well, then, why do they still keep the alligator boats in service?"

"Just for police duty—nothing more. They merely go up and down now and then. The present generation of alligators know them as easy as a burglar knows a roundsman; when they see one coming, they break camp and go for the woods."

After rounding-out and finishing-up and polishing-off the alligator business, he dropped easily and comfortably into the historical vein, and told of some tremendous feats of half a dozen old-time steamboats of his acquaintance, dwelling at special length upon a certain extraordinary performance of his chief favorite among this distinguished fleet—and then adding:—

"That boat was the 'Cyclone,'—last trip she ever made—she sunk, that very trip—captain was Tom Ballou, the most immortal liar that ever I struck. He couldn't ever seem to tell the truth, in *any* kind of weather. Why, he would make you fairly shudder. He *was* the most scandalous liar! I left him, finally;

I couldn't stand it. The proverb says, 'like master, like man;' and if you stay with that kind of a man, you'll come under suspicion by and by, just as sure as you live. He paid first-class wages; but said I, What's wages when your reputation's in danger? So I let the wages go, and froze to my reputation. And I've never regretted it. Reputation's worth everything, ain't it? That's the way I look at it. He had more selfish organs than any seven men in the world—all packed in the stern-sheets of his skull, of course, where they belonged. They weighed down the back of his head so that it made his nose tilt up in the air. People thought it was vanity, but it wasn't, it was malice. If you only saw his foot, you'd take him to be nineteen feet high, but he wasn't; it was because his foot was out of drawing. He was intended to be nineteen feet high, no doubt, if his foot was made first, but he didn't get there; he was only five feet ten. That's what he was, and that's what he is. You take the lies out of him, and he'll shrink to the size of your hat; you take the malice out of him, and he'll disappear. That 'Cyclone' was a rattler to go, and the sweetest thing to steer that ever walked the waters. Set her amidships, in a big river, and just let her go; it was all you had to do. She would hold herself on a star all night, if you let her alone. You couldn't ever feel her rudder. It wasn't any more labor to steer her than it is to count the Republican vote in a South Carolina election. One morning, just at daybreak, the last trip she ever made, they took her rudder aboard to mend it; I didn't know anything about it; I backed her out from the wood-yard and went a-weaving down the river all serene. When I had gone about twenty-three miles, and made four horribly crooked crossings—"

"Without any rudder?"

"Yes—old Capt. Tom appeared on the roof and began to find fault with me for running such a dark night—"

"Such a *dark night?*—Why, you said—"

"Never mind what I said,—'t was as dark as Egypt *now,* though pretty soon the moon began to rise, and—"

"You mean the *sun*—because you started out just at break of—look here! Was this *before* you quitted the captain on account of his lying, or—"

"It was before—oh, a long time before. And as I was saying, he—"

"But was this the trip she sunk, or was—"

"Oh, no!—months afterward. And so the old man, he—"

"Then she made *two* last trips, because you said—"

He stepped back from the wheel, swabbing away his perspiration, and said—

"Here!" (calling me by name), "*you* take her and lie a while—you're handier at it than I am. Trying to play yourself for a stranger and an innocent!—why, I knew you before you had spoken seven words; and I made up my mind to find out what was your little game. It was to *draw me out.* Well, I let you, didn't I? Now take the wheel and finish the watch; and next time play fair, and you won't have to work your passage."

Thus ended the fictitious-name business. And not six hours out from St. Louis! but I had gained a privilege, anyway, for I had been itching to get my hands on the wheel, from the beginning. I seemed to have forgotten the river, but I hadn't forgotten how to steer a steamboat, nor how to enjoy it, either.

Chapter 34

TOUGH YARNS

Stack Island. I remembered Stack Island; also Lake Providence, Louisiana—which is the first distinctly Southern-looking town you come to, downward-bound; lies level and low, shade-trees hung with venerable gray beards of Spanish moss; "restful, pensive, Sunday aspect about the place," comments Uncle Mumford, with feeling—also with truth.

A Mr. H. furnished some minor details of fact concerning this region which I would have hesitated to believe if I had not known him to be a steamboat mate. He was a passenger of ours, a resident of Arkansas City, and bound to Vicksburg to join his boat, a little Sunflower packet. He was an austere man, and had the reputation of being singularly unworldly, for a river man. Among other things, he said that Arkansas had been injured and kept back by generations of exaggerations concerning the mosquitoes there. One may smile, said he, and turn the matter off as being a small thing; but when you come to look at the effects produced, in the way of discouragement of immigration, and diminished values of property, it was quite the opposite of a small thing, or thing in any wise to be coughed down or sneered at. These mosquitoes had been persistently represented as being formidable and lawless; whereas "the truth is, they are feeble, insignificant in size, diffident to a fault, sensitive"—and so on, and so on; you would have supposed he was talking about his family. But if he was soft on the Arkansas mosquitoes, he was hard enough on the mosquitoes of Lake Providence to make up for it—"those Lake Providence colossi," as he finely called them. He said that two of them could whip a dog, and that four of them could hold a man down; and except help come, they would kill him—"butcher him," as he expressed it. Referred in a sort of casual way—and yet significant way—to "the fact that the life policy in its simplest form is unknown in Lake Providence—they take out a mosquito policy besides." He told many remarkable things about those lawless insects. Among others, said he had seen them try to *vote*. Noticing that this statement seemed to be a good deal of a strain on us, he modified it a little: said he might have been mistaken, as to that particular, but knew he had seen them around the polls "canvassing."

MOSQUITOES.

There was another passenger—friend of H.'s—who backed up the harsh

A BAD EAR.

evidence against those mosquitoes, and detailed some stirring adventures which he had had with them. The stories were pretty sizable, merely pretty sizable; yet Mr. H. was continually interrupting with a cold, inexorable "Wait—knock off twenty-five percent of that; now go on; or, "Wait—you are getting that too strong; cut it down, cut it down—you get a leetle too much costumery on to your statements: always dress a fact in tights, never in an ulster;" or, "Pardon, once more: if you are going to load anything more on to that statement, you want to get a couple of lighters and tow the rest, because it's drawing all the water there is in the river already; stick to facts—just stick to the cold facts; what these gentlemen want for a book is the frozen truth—ain't that so, gentlemen?" He explained privately that it was necessary to watch this man all the time, and keep him within bounds; it would not do to neglect this precaution, as he, Mr. H., "knew to his sorrow." Said he, "I will not deceive you; he told me such a monstrous lie once, that it swelled my left ear up, and spread it so that I was actually not able to see around it; it remained so for months, and people came miles to see me fan myself with it."

CHAPTER 42

HYGIENE AND SENTIMENT

They bury their dead in vaults, above the ground. These vaults have a resemblance to houses—sometimes to temples; are built of marble, generally; are architecturally graceful and shapely; they face the walks and driveways of the cemetery; and when one moves through the midst of a thousand or so of them and sees their white roofs and gables stretching into the distance on every hand, the phrase "city of the dead" has all at once a meaning to him. Many of the cemeteries are beautiful, and are kept in perfect order. When one goes from the levee or the business streets near it, to a cemetery, he observes to himself that if those people down there would live as neatly while they are alive as they do after they are dead, they would find many advantages in it; and besides, their quarter would be the wonder and admiration of the business world. Fresh flowers, in vases of water, are to be seen at the portals of many of

THE CEMETERY.

the vaults; placed there by the pious hands of bereaved parents and children, husbands and wives, and renewed daily. A milder form of sorrow finds its inexpensive and lasting remembrancer in the coarse and ugly but indestructible "immortelle"—which is a wreath or cross of some such emblem, made of rosettes of black linen, with sometimes a yellow rosette at the conjunction of the cross's bars,—kind of sorrowful breast-pin, so to say. The immortelle requires no attention: you just hang it up, and there you are; just leave it alone, it will take care of your grief for you, and keep it in mind better than you can; stands weather first-rate, and last like boiler-iron.

On sunny days, pretty little chameleons—gracefullest of leggéd reptiles—creep along the marble fronts of the vaults, and catch flies. Their changes of color—as to variety—are not up to the creature's reputation. They change color when a person comes along and hangs up an immortelle; but that is nothing: any right-feeling reptile would do that.

I will gradually drop this subject of graveyards. I have been trying all I could to get down to the sentimental part of it, but I cannot accomplish it. I think there is no genuinely sentimental part to it. It is all grotesque, ghastly, horrible. Graveyards may have been justifiable in the bygone ages, when nobody knew that for every dead body put into the ground, to glut the earth and the plant-roots and the air with disease-germs, five or fifty, or maybe a hundred, persons must die before their proper time; but they are hardly justifiable now, when even the children know that a dead saint enters upon a century-long career of assassination the moment the earth closes over his corpse. It is a grim sort of thought. The relics of St. Anne, up in Canada, have now, after nineteen hundred years, gone to curing the sick by the dozen. But it is merest matter-of-course that these same relics, within a generation after St. Anne's death and burial, *made* several thousand people sick. Therefore these miracle-performances are simple compensation, nothing more. St. Anne is somewhat slow pay, for a Saint, it is true; but better a debt paid after nineteen hundred years, and outlawed by the statute of limitations, than not paid at all; and most of the knights of the halo do not pay at all. Where you find one that pays—like St. Anne—you find a hundred and fifty that take the benefit of the statute. And none of them pay any more than the principal of what they owe—they pay none of the interest either simple or compound. A Saint can never *quite* return the principal, however; for his dead body *kills* people, whereas his relics *heal* only—they never restore the dead to life. That part of the account is always left unsettled.

"Dr. E. Julius Le Moyne, after fifty years of medical practice, wrote: 'The inhumation of human bodies, dead from infectious diseases, results in constantly loading the atmosphere, and polluting the waters, with not only the germs that rise from simply putrefaction, but also with the *specific* germs of the diseases from which death resulted.'

"The gases (from buried corpses) will rise to the surface through eight or ten feet of gravel, just as coal-gas will do, and there is practically no limit to their power of escape.

"During the epidemic in New Orleans in 1853, Dr. E. H. Barton reported that in the Fourth District the mortality was four hundred and fifty-two per thousand—more than double that of any other. In this district were three large cemeteries, in which during the previous year more than three thousand bodies had been buried. In other districts the proximity of cemeteries seemed to aggravate the disease.

"In 1828 Professor Bianchi demonstrated how the fearful reappearance of the plague at Modena was caused by excavations in ground where, *three hundred years previously* the victims of the pestilence had been buried. Mr. Cooper, in explaining the causes of some epidemics, remarks that the opening of the plague burial-grounds at Eyam resulted in an immediate outbreak of disease."—*North American Review, No.* 3, *Vol.* 135.

In an address before the Chicago Medical Society, in advocacy of cremation, Dr. Charles W. Purdy made some striking comparisons to show what a burden is laid upon society by the burial of the dead:—

"One and one-fourth times more money is expended annually in funerals in the United States than the Government expends for public-school purposes. Funerals cost this country in 1880 enough money to pay the liabilities of all the commercial failures in the United States during the same year, and give each bankrupt a capital of $8,630 with which to resume business. Funerals cost annually more money than the value of the combined gold and silver yield of the United States in the year 1880! These figures do not include the sums invested in burial-grounds and expended in tombs and monuments, nor the loss from depreciation of property in the vicinity of cemeteries."

For the rich, cremation would answer as well as burial; for the ceremonies connected with it could be made as costly and ostentatious as a Hindoo *suttee;* while for the poor, cremation would be better than burial, because so cheap[1] — so cheap until the poor got to imitating the rich, which they would do by and by. The adoption of cremation would relieve us of a muck of threadbare burial-witticisms; but, on the other hand, it would resurrect a lot of mildewed old cremation-jokes that have had a rest for two thousand years.

I have a colored acquaintance who earns his living by odd jobs and heavy manual labor. He never earns above four hundred dollars in a year, and as he has a wife and several young children, the closest scrimping is necessary to get him through to the end of the twelve months debtless. To such a man a funeral is a colossal financial disaster. While I was writing one of the preceding chapters, this man lost a little child. He walked the town over with a friend, trying to find a coffin that was within his means. He bought the very cheapest one he could find, plain wood, stained. It cost him *twenty-six dollars.* It would have cost less than four, probably, if it had been built to put something useful into. He and his family will feel that outlay a good many months.

Chapter 43

THE ART OF INHUMATION

About the same time, I encountered a man in the street, whom I had not seen for six or seven years; and something like this talk followed. I said,—

"But you used to look sad and oldish; you don't now. Where did you get all this youth and bubbling cheerfulness? Give me the address."

He chuckled blithely, took off his shining tile, pointed to a notched pink circlet of paper pasted into its crown, with something lettered on it, and went on chuckling while I read, "J. B——, UNDERTAKER." Then he clapped his hat on, gave it an irreverent tilt to leeward, and cried out,—

1. Four or five dollars is the minimum cost.

HE CHUCKLED.

"That's what's the matter! It used to be rough times with me when you knew me—insurance-agency business, you know; mighty irregular. Big fire, all right—brisk trade for ten days while people scared; after that, dull policy-business till next fire. Town like this don't have fires often enough—a fellow strikes so many dull weeks in a row that he gets discouraged. But you bet you, *this* is the business! People don't wait for examples to *die*. No, sir they drop off right along—there ain't any dull spots in the undertaker line. I just started in with two or three little old coffins and a hired hearse, and *now* look at the thing! I've worked up a business here that would satisfy any man, don't care who he is. Five years ago, lodged in an attic; live in a swell house now, with a mansard roof, and all the modern inconveniences."

"WHY, JUST LOOK AT IT."

"Does a coffin pay so well? Is there much profit on a coffin?"

"*Go*-way! How you talk!" Then, with a confidential wink, a dropping of the voice, and an impressive laying of his hand on my arm; "Look here; there's one thing in this world which isn't ever cheap. That's a coffin. There's one thing in this world which a person don't ever try to jew you down on. That's a coffin. There's one thing in this world which a person don't say,—'I'll look around a little and if I find I can't do better I'll come back and take it.' That's a coffin. There's one thing in this world which a person won't take in pine if he can go walnut; and won't take in walnut if he can go mahogany; and won't take in mahogany if he can go an iron casket with silver door-plate and bronze handles. That's a coffin. And there's one thing in this world which you don't have to worry around after a person to get him to pay for. And *that's* a coffin. Undertaking?—why it's the dead-surest business in Christendom, and the nobbiest.

"Why, just look at it. A rich man won't have anything but your very best; and you can just pile it on, too—pile it on and sock it to him—he won't ever holler. And you take in a poor man, and if you work him right he'll bust himself on a single lay-out. Or especially a woman. F'r instance: Mrs. O'Flaherty comes in—widow—wiping her eyes and kind of moaning. Unhandkerchiefs one eye, bats it around tearfully over the stock; says,—

"'And fhat might ye ask for that wan?'

"'Thirty-nine dollars, madam,' says I.

"'It's a foine big price, sure, but Pat shall be buried like a gintleman, as he was, if I have to work me fingers off for it. I'll have that wan, sor.'

"'Yes, madam,' says I, 'and it is a very good one, too; not costly, to be sure, but in this life we must cut our garment to our clothes, as the saying is.' And as she starts out, I heave in, kind of casually. 'This one with the white satin lining is a beauty, but I am afraid—well, sixty-five dollars *is* a rather—rather—but no matter, I felt obliged to say to Mrs. O'Shaughnessy,—'

"'D'ye mane to soy that Bridget O'Shaughnessy bought the mate to that joo-ul box to ship that dhrunken divil to Purgatory in?'

"'Yes, madam.'

"'Then Pat shall go to heaven in the twin to it, if it takes the last rap the O'Flaherties can raise; and moind you, stick on some extras, too, and I'll give ye another dollar.'

"And as I lay-in with the livery stables, of course I don't forget to mention that Mrs. O'Shaughnessy hired fifty-four dollars' worth of hacks and flung as much style into Dennis's funeral as if he had been a duke or an assassin. And of course she sails in and goes the O'Shaughnessy about four hacks and an omnibus better. That *used* to be, but that's all played now; that is, in this particular town. The

AMBITION.

Irish got to piling up hacks so, on their funerals, that a funeral left them ragged and hungry for two years afterward; so the priest pitched in and broke it all up. He don't allow them to have but two hacks now, and sometimes only one."

"Well," said I, "if you are so light-hearted and jolly in ordinary times, what *must* you be in an epidemic?"

He shook his head.

"No, you're off, there. We don't like to see an epidemic. An epidemic don't pay. Well, of course I don't mean that, exactly; but it don't pay in proportion to the regular thing. Don't it occur to you, why?"

"No."

"Think."

"I can't imagine. What is it?"

"It's just two things."

"Well, what *are* they?"

"One's Embamming."

"And what's the other?"

"Ice."

"How is that?"

"Well, in ordinary times, a person dies, and we lay him up in ice; one day, two days, maybe three, to wait for friends to come takes a lot of it—melts fast. We charge jewelry rates for that ice, and war-prices for attendance. Well, don't you know, when there's an epidemic, they rush 'em to the cemetery the minute the breath's out. No market for ice in an epidemic. Same with Embamming. You take a family that's able to embam, and you've got a soft thing. You can mention sixteen different ways to do it—though there *ain't* only one or two ways, when you come down to the bottom facts of it—and they'll take the highest-priced way, every time. It's human nature—human nature in grief. It don't reason, you see. 'Time being, it don't care a dam. All it wants is physical immortality for deceased, and they're willing to pay for it. All you've got to do is to just be ca'm and stack it up—they'll stand the racket. Why, man, you can take a defunct that you couldn't *give* away; and get your embamming traps around you and go to work; and in a couple of hours he is worth a cool six hundred—that's what *he's* worth. There ain't anything equal to it but trading rats for di'monds in time of famine. Well, don't you see, when there's an epidemic, people don't wait to embam. No, indeed

AN EXPLANATION.

they don't; and it hurts the business like hellth, as we say—hurts it like hell-th, *health,* see?—Our little joke in the trade. Well, I must be going. Give me a call whenever you need any—I mean, when you're going by, sometime."

In his joyful high spirits, he did the exaggerating himself, if any has been done. I have not enlarged on him.

With the above brief references to inhumation, let us leave the subject. As for me, I hope to be cremated. I made that remark to my pastor once, who said, with what he seemed to think was an impressive manner,—

"I wouldn't worry about that, if I had your chances."

Much he knew about it—the family all so opposed to it.

Chapter 44

. . . We visited also the venerable Cathedral, and the pretty square in front of it; the one dim with religious light, the other brilliant with the worldly sort, and lovely with orange trees and blossomy shrubs; then we drove in the hot sun through the wilderness of houses and out on to the wide dead level beyond, where the villas are, and the water wheels to drain the town, and the commons populous with cows and children; passing by an old cemetery where we were told lie the ashes of an early pirate; but we took him on trust, and did not visit him. He was a pirate with a tremendous and sanguinary history; and as long as he preserved unspotted, in retirement, the dignity of his name and the grandeur of his ancient calling, homage and reverence were his from high and low; but when at last he descended into politics and became a paltry alderman, the public "shook" him, and turned aside and wept. When he died, they set up a monument over him; and little by little he has come into respect again; but it is respect for the pirate, not the alderman. To-day the loyal and generous remember only what he was, and charitably forget what he became. . . .

CHAPTER 46

ENCHANTMENTS AND ENCHANTERS

The largest annual event in New Orleans is a something which we arrived too late to sample—the Mardi-Gras festivities. I saw the procession of the Mystic Crew of Comus there, twenty-four years ago—with knights and nobles and so on, clothed in silken and golden Paris-made gorgeousnesses, planned and bought for that single night's use; and in their train all manner of giants, dwarfs, monstrosities, and other diverting grotesquerie—a startling and wonderful sort of show, as it filed solemnly and silently down the street in the light of its smoking and flickering torches; but it is said that in these latter days the spectacle is mightily augmented, as to cost, splendor, and variety. There is a chief personage—"Rex;" and if I remember rightly, neither this king nor any of his great following of subordinates is known to any outsider. All these people are gentlemen of position and consequence; and it is a proud thing to belong to the organization; so the mystery in which they hide their personality is merely for romance's sake, and not on account of the police.

Madri-Gras is of course a relic of the French and Spanish occupation; but I judge that the religious feature has been pretty well knocked out of it now. Sir Walter has got the advantage of the gentlemen of the cowl and rosary, and he will stay. His medieval business, supplemented by the monsters and the oddities, and the pleasant creatures from fairy-land, is finer to look at than the poor fantastic inventions and performances of the revelling rabble of the priest's day, and serves quite as well, perhaps, to emphasize the day and admonish men that the grace-line between the worldly season and the holy one is reached.

This Mardi-Gras pageant was the exclusive possession of New Orleans until recently. But now it has spread to Memphis and St. Louis and Baltimore. It has probably reached its limit. It is a thing which could hardly exist in the practical North; would certainly last but a very brief time; as brief a time as it would last in London. For the soul of it is the romantic, not the funny and the grotesque. Take away the romantic mysteries, the kings and knights and big-sounding titles, and Mardi-Gras would die, down there in the South. The very feature that keeps it alive in the South—girly-girly romance—would kill it in the North or in London. Puck and Punch, and the press universal, would fall upon it and make merciless fun of it, and its first exhibition would be also its last.

Against the crimes of the French Revolution and of Bonaparte may be set two compensating benefactions: the Revolution broke the chains of the *ancien régime* and of the Church, and made of a nation of abject slaves a nation of freemen; and Bonaparte instituted the setting of merit above birth, and also so completely stripped the divinity from royalty, that whereas crowned heads in Europe were gods before, they are only men, since, and can never be gods again, but only figure-heads, and answerable for their acts like common clay. Such benefactions as these compensate the temporary harm which Bonaparte and the Revolution did, and leave the world in debt to them for these great and permanent services to liberty, humanity, and progress.

Then comes Sir Walter Scott with his enchantments, and by his single might checks this wave of progress, and even turns it back; sets the world in love and dreams and phantoms; with decayed and swinish forms of religion; with decayed and degraded systems of government; with the sillinesses and emptinesses, sham grandeurs, sham gauds, and sham chivalries of a brainless and worthless long-vanished society. He did measureless harm; more real and lasting harm, perhaps, than any other individual that ever wrote. Most of the world has now outlived good part of these harms, though by no means all of them; but in our South they flourish pretty forcefully still. Not so forcefully as half a generation ago, perhaps, but still forcefully. There, the genuine and wholesome civilization of the nineteenth century is curiously confused and commingled with the Walter Scott Middle-Age sham civilization and so you have practical, common-sense, progressive ideas, and progressive works, mixed up with the duel, the inflated speech, and the jejune romanticism of an absurd past that is dead, and out of charity ought to be buried. But for the Sir Walter disease, the character of the Southerner—or Southron, according to Sir Walter's starchier way of phrasing it—would be wholly modern, in place of modern and medieval mixed, and the South would be fully a generation further advanced than it is. It was Sir Walter that made every gentleman in the South a Major or a Colonel, or a General or a Judge, before the war; and it was he, also, that made these gentlemen value these bogus decorations. For it was he that created rank and caste down there, and also reverence for rank and caste, and pride and pleasure in them. Enough is laid on slavery, without fathering upon it these creations and contributions of Sir Walter.

Sir Walter had so large a hand in making Southern character, as it existed before the war, that he is in great measure responsible for the war. It seems a little harsh toward a dead man to say that we never should have had any war but for Sir Walter; and yet something of a plausible argument might, perhaps, be made in support of that wild proposition. The Southerner of the American revolution owned slaves; so did the Southerner of the Civil War: but the former resembles the latter as an Englishman resembles a Frenchman. The change of character can be traced rather more easily to Sir Walter's influence than to that of any other thing or person.

One may observe, by one or two signs, how deeply that influence penetrated, and how strongly it holds. If one takes up a Northern or Southern literary periodical of forty or fifty years ago, he will find it filled with wordy, windy, flowery "eloquence," romanticism, sentimentality—all imitated from Sir Walter, and sufficiently badly done, too—innocent travesties of his style and methods, in fact. This sort of literature being the fashion in both sections of the country, there was opportunity for the fairest competition; and as a consequence, the South was able to show as many well-known literary names, proportioned to population, as the North could.

But a change has come, and there is no opportunity now for a fair competition between North and South. For the North has thrown out that old inflated style, whereas the Southern writer still clings to it—clings to it and has a restricted market for his wares, as a consequence. There is as much literary talent in the South, now, as ever there was, of course; but its work can gain but slight currency under present conditions; the authors write for the past, not the present; they use obsolete forms, and a dead language. But when a Southerner of genius writes modern English, his book goes upon crutches no longer, but upon wings; and they carry it swiftly all about America and England, and through the great English reprint publishing houses of Germany—as witness the experience of Mr. Cable and Uncle Remus, two of the very few Southern authors who do not write in the southern style. Instead of three or four widely-known literary names, the South ought to have a dozen or two—and will have them when Sir Walter's time is out.

A curious exemplification of the power of a single book for good or harm is shown in the effects wrought by Don Quixote and those wrought by Ivanhoe. The first swept the world's admiration for the medieval chivalry-silliness out of existence; and the other restored it. As far as our South is concerned, the good work done by Cervantes is pretty nearly a dead letter, so effectually has Scott's pernicious work undermined it.

Chapter 48

[On spiritualism]

. . . We could have done a number of other things; but on account of limited time, we went back home. The sail up the breezy and sparkling river was a charming experience, and would have been satisfyingly sentimental and romantic but for the interruptions of the tug's pet parrot, whose tireless comments upon the scenery and the guests were always this-worldly, and often profane. He had also a superabundance of the discordant, ear-splitting, metallic laugh common to his breed,—a machine-made laugh, a Frankenstein laugh, with the soul left out of it. He applied it to every sentimental remark, and to every pathetic song. He cackled it out with hideous energy after "Home again, home again, from a foreign shore," and said he "wouldn't give a damn for a tug-load of such rot." Romance and sentiment cannot long survive this sort of discouragement; so the singing and talking presently ceased; which so delighted the parrot that he cursed himself hoarse for joy.

Then the male members of the party moved to the forecastle, to smoke and gossip. There were several old steamboatmen along, and I learned from them a great deal of what had been happening to my former river friends during my

SMOKE AND GOSSIP.

long absence. I learned that a pilot whom I used to steer for is become a spiritualist, and for more than fifteen years has been receiving a letter every week from a deceased relative, through a New York spiritualistic medium named Manchester—postage graduated by distance: from the local post-office in Paradise to New York, five dollars; from New York to St. Louis, three cents. I remember Mr. Manchester very well. I called on him once, ten years ago, with a couple of friends, one of whom wished to inquire after a deceased uncle. This uncle had lost his life in a peculiarly violent and unusual way, half a dozen years before: a cyclone blew him some three miles and knocked a tree down with him which was four feet through at the butt and sixty-five feet high. He did not survive this triumph. At the *séance* just referred to, my friend questioned his late uncle, through Mr. Manchester, and the late uncle wrote down his replies, using Mr. Manchester's hand and pencil for that purpose. The following is a fair example of the questions asked, and also of the sloppy twaddle in the way of answers, furnished by Manchester under the pretence that it came from the spectre. If this man is not the paltriest fraud that lives, I owe him an apology:—

Question. Where are you?

Answer. In the spirit world.

Q. Are you happy?

A. Very happy. Perfectly happy.

Q. How do you amuse yourself?

A. Conversation with friends, and other spirits.

Q. What else?

A. Nothing else. Nothing else is necessary.

Q. What do you talk about?

A. About how happy we are; and about friends left behind in the earth, and how to influence them for their good.

Q. When your friends in the earth all get to the spirit land, what shall you have to talk about then?—nothing but about how happy you all are?

No reply. It is explained that spirits will not answer frivolous questions.

Q. How is it that spirits that are content to spend an eternity in frivolous employments, and accept it as happiness, are so fastidious about frivolous questions upon the subject?

No reply.

Q. Would you like to come back?

A. No.

Q. Would you say that under oath?

A. Yes.

Q. What do you eat there?

A. We do not eat.

Q. What do you drink?

A. We do not drink.

Q. What do you smoke?

A. We do not smoke.

Q. What do you read?

A. We do not read.

Q. Do all the good people go to your place?

A. Yes.

Q. You know my present way of life. Can you suggest any additions to it, in the way of crime, that will reasonably insure my going to some other place?

No reply.

Q. When did you die?

A. I did not die, I passed away.

Q. Very well, then, when did you pass away? How long have you been in the spirit land?

A. We have no measurements of time here.

Q. Though you may be indifferent and uncertain as to dates and times in your present condition and environment, this has nothing to do with your former condition. You had dates then. One of these is what I ask for. You departed on a certain day in a certain year. Is not this true?

A. Yes.

Q. Then name the day of the month.

(Much fumbling with pencil, on the part of the medium, accompanied by violent spasmodic jerkings of his head and body, for some little time. Finally, explanation to the effect that spirits often forget dates, such things being without importance to them.)

Q. Then this one has actually forgotten the date of its translation to the spirit land?

This was granted to be the case.

Q. This is very curious. Well, then, what year was it?

(More fumbling, jerking, idiotic spasms, on the part of the medium. Finally, explanation to the effect that the spirit has forgotten the year.)

Q. This is indeed stupendous. Let me put one more question, one last question, to you, before we part to meet no more;—for even if I fail to avoid your

THE INTERVIEW.

asylum, a meeting there will go for nothing *as* a meeting, since by that time you will easily have forgotten me and my name: did you die a natural death, or were you cut off by a catastrophe?

A. (After long hesitation and many throes and spasms.) *Natural death.*

This ended the interview. My friend told the medium that when his relative was in this poor world, he was endowed with an extraordinary intellect and an absolutely defectless memory, and it seemed a great pity that he had not been allowed to keep some shred of these for his amusement in the realms of everlasting contentment, and for the amazement and admiration of the rest of the population there.

This man had plenty of clients—has plenty yet. He receives letters from spirits located in every part of the spirit world, and delivers them all over this country through the United States mail. These letters are filled with advice—advice from "spirits" who don't know as much as a tadpole—and this advice is religiously followed by the receivers. One of these clients was a man whom the spirits (if one may thus plurally describe the ingenious Manchester) were teaching how to contrive an improved railway car-wheel. It is coarse employment for a spirit, but it is higher and wholesomer activity than talking forever about "how happy we are."

Chapter 50

. . . Whenever Captain Sellers approached a body of gossiping pilots, a chill fell there, and talking ceased. For this reason: whenever six pilots were gathered together, there would always be one or two newly fledged ones in the lot, and the elder ones would be always "showing off" before these poor fellows; making them sorrowfully feel how callow they were, how recent their nobility, and how humble their degree, by talking largely and vaporously of old-time experiences on the river; always making it a point to date everything back as far as they could, so as to make the new men feel their newness to the sharpest degree possible, and envy the old stagers in the like degree. And how these complacent bald-heads *would* swell, and brag, and lie, and date back—ten, fifteen, twenty years,—and how they did enjoy the effect produced upon the marvelling and envying youngsters!

And perhaps just at this happy stage of the proceedings, the stately figure

"A CHILL FELL THERE."

of Captain Isaiah Sellers, that real and only genuine Son of Antiquity, would drift solemnly into the midst. Imagine the size of the silence that would result on the instant. And imagine the feelings of those bald-heads, and the exultation of their recent audience when the ancient captain would begin to drop casual and indifferent remarks of a reminiscent nature,—about islands that had disappeared, and cut-offs that had been made, a generation before the oldest bald-head in the company had ever set his foot in a pilot-house!

Many and many a time did this ancient mariner appear on the scene in the above fashion, and spread disaster and humiliation around him. If one might believe the pilots, he always dated his islands back to the misty dawn of river history; and he never used the same island twice; and never did he employ an island that still existed, or give one a name which anybody present was old enough to have heard of before. If you might believe the pilots, he was always conscientiously particular about little details; never spoke of "the State of Mississippi," for instance,—no, he would say, "When the State of Mississippi was where Arkansas now is;" and would never speak of Louisiana or Missouri in a general way, and leave an incorrect impression on your mind,—no, he would say, "When Louisiana was up the river farther," or "When Missouri was on the Illinois side."

SELLER'S MONUMENT.

The old gentleman was not of literary turn or capacity, but he used to jot down brief paragraphs of plain practical information about the river, and sign them "MARK TWAIN," and give them to the "New Orleans Picayune." They related to the stage and condition of the river, and were accurate and valuable; and thus far, they contained no poison. But in speaking of the stage of the river to-day, at a given point, the captain was pretty apt to drop in a little remark about this being the first time he had seen the water so high or so low at that particular point for forty-nine years; and now and then he would mention Island so and so, and follow it, in parentheses, with some such observation as "disappeared in 1807, if I remember rightly." In these antique interjections lay poison and bitterness for the other old pilots, and they used to chaff the "Mark Twain" paragraphs with unsparing mockery.

It so chanced that one of these paragraphs[1] became the text for my first newspaper article. I burlesqued it broadly, very broadly, stringing my fantasies

1. The original MS. of it, in the captain's own hand, has been sent to me from New Orleans. It reads as follows:—

"VICKSBURG, May 4, 1859.

"My opinion for the benefit of the citizens of New Orleans: The water is higher this far up than it has been since 1815. My opinion is that the water will be 4 feet deep in Canal street before the first of next June. Mrs. Turner's plantation at the head of Big Black Island is all under water, and it has not been since 1815.

"I. SELLERS."

out to the extent of eight hundred or a thousand words. I was a "cub" at the time. I showed my performance to some pilots, and they eagerly rushed it into print in the "New Orleans True Delta." It was a great pity; for it did nobody any worthy service, and it sent a pang deep into a good man's heart. There was no malice in my rubbish; but it laughed at the captain. It laughed at a man to whom such a thing was new and strange and dreadful. I did not know then, though I do now, that there is no suffering comparable with that which a private person feels when he is for the first time pilloried in print.

Captain Sellers did me the honor to profoundly detest me from that day forth. When I say he did me the honor, I am not using empty words. It was a very real honor to be in the thoughts of so great a man as Captain Sellers, and I had wit enough to appreciate it and be proud of it. It was distinction to be loved by such a man; but it was a much greater distinction to be hated by him, because he loved scores of people; but he didn't sit up nights to hate anybody but me.

He never printed another paragraph while he lived, and he never again signed "Mark Twain" to anything. At the time that the telegraph brought the news of his death, I was on the Pacific coast. I was a fresh new journalist, and needed a *nom de guerre;* so I confiscated the ancient mariner's discarded one, and have done my best to make it remain what it was in his hands—a sign and symbol and warrant that whatever is found in its company may be gambled on as being the petrified truth; how I have succeeded, it would not be modest in me to say.

The captain had an honorable pride in his profession and an abiding love for it. He ordered his monument before he died, and kept it near him until he did die. It stands over his grave now, in Bellefontaine cemetery, St. Louis. It is his image in marble, standing on duty at the pilot wheel; and worthy to stand and confront criticism, for it represents a man who in life would have staid there till he burned to a cinder, if duty required it.

The finest thing we saw on our whole Mississippi trip, we saw as we approached New Orleans in the steam-tug. This was the curving frontage of the crescent city lit up with the white glare of five miles of electric lights. It was a wonderful sight, and very beautiful. . . .

Chapter 52

A Burning Brand

All at once the thought came into my mind, "I have not sought out Mr. Brown."

Upon that text I desire to depart from the direct line of my subject, and make a little excursion. I wish to reveal a secret which I have carried with me nine years, and which has become burdensome.

Upon a certain occasion, nine years ago, I had said, with strong feeling, "If ever I see St. Louis again, I will seek out Mr. Brown, the great grain merchant, and ask of him the privilege of shaking him by the hand."

The occasion and the circumstances were as follows. A friend of mine, a clergyman, came one evening and said:—

"I have a most remarkable letter here, which I want to read to you, if I can do it without breaking down. I must preface it with some explanations, however. The letter is written by an ex-thief and ex-vagabond of the lowest origin and basest rearing, a man all stained with crime and steeped in ignorance; but, thank God, with a mine of pure gold hidden away in him, as you shall see. His letter is written to a burglar named Williams, who is serving a nine-year term in a certain State prison, for burglary. Williams was a particularly daring burglar, and plied that trade during a number of years; but he was caught at last and jailed, to await trial in a town where he had broken into a house at night, pistol in hand, and forced the owner to hand over to him $8,000 in government bonds. Williams was not a common sort of person, by any means; he was a graduate of Harvard College, and came of good New England stock. His father was a clergyman. While lying in jail, his health began to fail, and he was threatened with consumption. This fact, together with the opportunity for reflection afforded by solitary confinement, had its effect—its natural effect. He fell into serious thought; his early training asserted itself with power, and wrought with strong influence upon his mind and heart. He put his old life behind him, and became an earnest Christian. Some ladies in the town heard of this, visited him, and by their encouraging words supported him in his good resolutions and strengthened him to continue in his new life. The trial ended in his conviction and sentence to the State prison for the term of nine years, as I have before said. In the prison he became acquainted with the poor wretch referred to in the beginning of my talk, Jack Hunt, the writer of the letter which I am going to read. You will see that the acquaintanceship bore fruit for Hunt. When Hunt's time was out, he wandered to St. Louis; and from that place he wrote his letter to Williams. The letter got no further than the office of the prison warden, of course; prisoners are not often allowed to receive letters from outside. The prison authorities read this letter, but did not destroy it. They had not the heart to do it. They read it to several persons, and eventually it fell into the hands of those ladies of whom I spoke a while ago. The other day I came across an old friend of mine—a clergyman—who had seen this letter, and was full of it. The mere remembrance of it so moved him that he could not talk of it without his voice breaking. He promised to get a copy of it for me; and here it is,—an exact copy, with all the imperfections of the original preserved. It has many slang expressions in it—thieves' *argot*—but their meaning has been interlined, in parentheses, by the prison authorities:"—

St. Louis, June 9th, 1872.

Mr. W—— friend Charlie if i may call you so: i no you are surprised to get a letter from me, but i hope you won't be mad at my writing to you. i want to tell you my thanks for the way you talked to me when i was in prison—it has led me to try and be a better man; i guess you thought i did not cair for what you said, & at the first go off I didn't, but i noed you was a man who had don big work with good men & want no sucker, nor want gasing & all the boys knod it.

I used to think at nite what you said, & for it i nocked off swearing 5 months before my time was up, for i saw it want no good, nohow—the day my time was up you told me if i would shake the cross, (*quit stealing*) & live on the square for 3 months, it would be the best job i ever done in my life. The state agent give me a ticket to here, & on the car i thought more of what you said to me, but didn't make up my mind. When we got to Chicago on the cars from there to here, I pulled off an old woman's leather; (*robbed her of her pocketbook*) i hadn't no more than got it off when i wished i hadn't done it, for awhile before that i made up my mind to be a square bloke, for 3 months on your word, but forgot it when i saw the leather was a grip (*easy to get*)—but i kept clos to her & when she got out of the cars at a way place i said, marm have you lost anything? & she tumbled (*discovered*) her leather was off (*gone*)—is this it says i, giving it to her—well if you aint honest, says she, but i hadnt got cheak enough to stand that sort of talk, so i left her in a hurry. When i got here i had $1 and 25 cents left & i didn't get no work for 3 days as i aint strong enough for roust about on a steam bote (*for a deck hand*)—The afternoon of the 3rd day I spent my last 10 cts for 2 moons (*large, round sea-biscuit*) & cheese & i felt pretty rough & was thinking i would have to go on the dipe (*picking pockets*) again, when i thought of what you once said about a fellows calling on the Lord when he was in hard luck, & i thought i would try it once anyhow, but when i tryed it i got stuck on the start, & all i could get off wos, Lord give a poor fellow chance to square it for 3 months for Christ's sake, amen; & i kept a thinking, of it over and over as i went along—about an hour after that i was in 4th St. & this is what happened & is the cause of my being where i am now & about which i will tell you before i get done writing. As i was walking along i herd a big noise & saw a horse running

WILLIAMS PLIES HIS TRADE.

away with a carriage with 2 children in it, & I grabed up a peace of box cover from the side walk & run in the middle of the street, & when the horse came up

THE CRISIS.

i smashed him over the head as hard as i could drive—the bord split to peces & the horse checked up a little & i grabbed the reigns & pulled his head down until he stopped—the gentleman what owned him came running up & soon as he saw the children were all rite, he shook hands with me & gave me a $50 green back, & my asking the Lord to help me come into my head, & i was so thunderstruck i couldn't drop the reigns nor say nothing—he saw something was up, & coming back to me said, my boy are you hurt? & the thought come into my head just then to ask him for work; & i asked him to take back the bill and give me a job—says he, jump in here & lets talk about it, but keep the money—he asked me if i could take care of horses & i said yes, for i used to hang round livery stables & often would help clean & drive horses, he told me he wanted a man for that work, & would give me $16. a month & bord me. You bet i took that chance at once. that nite in my little room over the stable i sat a long time thinking over my past life & of what had just happened & i just got down on my nees & thanked the Lord for the job & to help me to square it, & to bless you for putting me up to it, & the next morning i done it again & got me some new togs (*clothes*) & a bible for i *made up my mind* after what the Lord had done for me i would read the bible every nite and morning, & ask him to keep an eye on me.

When I had been there about a week Mr Brown (that's his name) came in my room one nite & saw me reading the bible—he asked me if i was a Christian & i told him no—he asked me how it was i read the bible instead of papers & books—Well Charlie i thought i had better give him a square deal in the start, so i told him all about my being in prison & about you, & how i had almost done give up looking for work & how the Lord got me the job when i asked him; & the only way i had to pay him back was to read the bible & square it, & i asked him to give me a chance for 3 months—he talked to me like a father for a long time, & told me i could stay & then i felt better than ever i had done in my life, for i had given Mr. Brown a fair start with me & now i didn't fear no one giving me a back cap (*exposing his past life*) & running me off the job—the next morning he called me into the library & gave me another square talk, & advised me to study some every day, & he would help me one or 2 hours every nite, & he gave me a Arithmetic, a spelling book, a Geography & a writing book, & he hers me every nite—he lets me come into the house to prayers every morning, & got me put in a bible class in the Sunday School which i likes very much for it helps me to understand my bible better.

Now, Charlie the 3 months on the square are up 2 months ago, & as you said, it is the best job i ever did in my life, & i commenced another of the same sort right away, only it is to God helping me to last a lifetime Charlie—i wrote this letter to tell you I do think God has forgiven my sins & herd your prayers, for you told me you should pray for me—i no i love to read his word & tell him all my troubles & he helps me i know for i have plenty of chances to steal but i don't feel to as i once did & now i take more pleasure in going to church than to the theatre & that wasnt so once—our minister and others often talk with me & a month ago they wanted me to join the church, but I said no, not now, i may be mistaken in my feelings, i will wait awhile, but now i feel that God has called me & on the first Sunday in July i will join the church—dear friend i wish i could write to you as i feel, but i cant do it yet—you no i learned to read and write while in prisons & i aint got well enough along to write as i would talk; i no i aint spelled all the words rite in this & lots of other mistakes but you will excuse it i no, for you no i was brought up in a poor house until i run away, & that i never new who my father and mother was & i dont no my rite name, & i hope you wont be mad at me, but i have as much rite to one name as another & i have taken your name, for you wont use it when you get out i no, & you are the man i think most of in the world; so i hope you wont be mad—I am doing well, i put $10 a month in bank with $25 of the $50—if you ever want any or all of it let me know, & it is yours. i wish you would let me send you some now. I send you with this a receipt for a year of Littles Living Age, i didn't know what you would like & i told Mr Brown & he said he thought you would like it—i wish i were nere you so i could send you chuck (*refreshments*) on holidays; it would spoil this weather from here, but i will send you a box next thanksgiving any way—next week Mr Brown takes me into his store as lite porter & will advance me as soon as i know a little more—he keeps a big granary store, wholesale—i forgot to tell you of my mission school, sunday school class—the school is in the sunday afternoon, i went out two sunday afternoons, and picked up seven kids (*little boys*) & got them to come in. two of them new as much as i did & i had them put in a class where they could learn something. i dont no much myself, but as these kids cant read i get on nicely with them. i make sure of them by going after them every Sunday ½ hour before school time, i also got 4 girls to come. tell Mack and Harry about me, if they will come out here when their time is up i will get them jobs at once. i hope you will excuse this long letter & all mistakes, i wish i could see you for i cant

MISSION WORK.

write as i would talk—i hope the warm weather is doing your lungs good—i was afraid when you was bleeding you would die—give my respects to all the boys and tell them how i am doing—i am doing well and every one here treats me as kind as they can—Mr Brown is going to write to you sometime—i hope some day you will write to me, this letter is from your very true friend

C—— W——

who you know as Jack Hunt.

I send you Mr Brown's card. Send my letter to him.

Here was true eloquence; irresistible eloquence; and without a single grace or ornament to help it out. I have seldom been so deeply stirred by any piece of writing. The reader of it halted, all the way through, on a lame and broken voice; yet he had tried to fortify his feelings by several private readings of the letter before venturing into company with it. He was practising upon me to see if there was any hope of his being able to read the document to his prayer-meeting with anything like a decent command over his feelings. The result was not promising. However, he determined to risk it; and did. He got through tolerably well; but his audience broke down early, and stayed in that condition to the end.

The fame of the letter spread through the town. A brother minister came and borrowed the manuscript, put it bodily into a sermon, preached the sermon to twelve hundred people on a Sunday morning, and the letter drowned them in their own tears. Then my friend put it into a sermon and went before his Sunday morning congregation with it. It scored another triumph. The house wept as one individual.

My friend went on summer vacation up into the fishing regions of our northern British neighbors, and carried this sermon with him, since he might possibly chance to need a sermon. He was asked to preach, one day. The little church was full. Among the people present were the late Dr. J. G. Holland, the late Mr. Seymour of the "New York Times," Mr. Page, the philanthropist and temperance advocate, and, I think, Senator Frye, of Maine. The marvellous letter did its wonted work; all the people were moved, all the people wept; the tears flowed in a steady stream down Dr. Holland's cheeks, and nearly the same can be said with regard to all who were there. Mr. Page was so full of enthusiasm over the letter that he said he would not rest until he made pilgrimage to that prison, and had speech with the man who had been able to inspire a fellow-unfortunate to write so priceless a tract.

Ah, that unlucky Page!—and another man. If they had only been in Jericho, that letter would have rung through the world and stirred all the hearts of all the nations for a thousand years to come, and nobody might ever have found out that it was the confoundedest, brazenest, ingeniousest piece of fraud and humbuggery that was ever concocted to fool poor confiding mortals with!

The letter was a pure swindle, and that is the truth. And take it by and large, it was without a compeer among swindles. It was perfect, it was rounded, symmetrical, complete, colossal!

The reader learns it at this point; but we didn't learn it till some miles and weeks beyond this stage of the affair. My friend came back from the woods, and he and other clergymen and lay missionaries began once more to inundate audiences with their tears and the tears of said audiences; I begged hard for permission to print the letter in a magazine and tell the watery story of its triumphs; numbers of people got copies of the letter, with permission to circulate them in writing, but not in print; copies were sent to the Sandwich Islands and other far regions.

Charles Dudley Warner was at church, one day, when the worn letter was read and wept over. At the church door, afterward, he dropped a peculiarly cold iceberg down the clergyman's back with the question,—

"Do you know that letter to be genuine?"

It was the first suspicion that had ever been voiced; but it had that sickening effect which first-uttered suspicions against one's idol always have. Some talk followed:—

"Why—what should make you suspect that it isn't genuine?"

"Nothing that I know of, except that it is too neat, and compact, and fluent, and nicely put together for an ignorant person, an unpractised hand. I think it was done by an educated man."

The literary artist had detected the literary machinery. If you will look at the letter now, you will detect it yourself—it is observable in every line.

Straightway the clergyman went off, with this seed of suspicion sprouting in him, and wrote to a minister residing in that town where Williams had been jailed and converted; asked for light; and also asked if a person in the literary line (meaning me) might be allowed to print the letter and tell its history. He presently received this answer:—

REV. —— ——.

MY DEAR FRIEND,—In regard to that "convict's letter" there can be no doubt as to its genuineness. "Williams," to whom it was written, lay in our jail and professed to have been converted, and Rev. Mr. ——, the chaplain, had great faith in the genuineness of the change—as much as one can have in any such case.

The letter was sent to one of our ladies, who is a Sunday-school teacher,—sent either by Williams himself, or the chaplain of the State's prison, probably. She has been greatly annoyed in having so much publicity, lest it might seem a breach of confidence, or be an injury to Williams. In regard to its publication, I can give no permission; though if the names and places were omitted, and especially if sent out of the country, I think you might take the responsibility and do it.

WILLIAMS.

It is a wonderful letter, which no Christian genius, much less one unsanctified, could ever have written. As showing the work of grace in a human heart, and in a very degraded and wicked one, it proves its own origin and reproves our weak faith in its power to cope with any form of wickedness.

"Mr. Brown" of St. Louis, some one said, was a Hartford man. Do all whom you send from Hartford serve their Master as well?

P.S. Williams is still in the State's prison, serving out a long sentence—of nine years, I think. He has been sick and threatened with consumption, but I have not inquired after him lately. This lady that I speak of corresponds with him, I presume, and will be quite sure to look after him.

This letter arrived a few days after it was written—and up went Mr. Williams's stock again. Mr. Warner's low-down suspicion was laid in the cold, cold grave, where it apparently belonged. It was a suspicion based upon mere internal evidence, anyway; and when you come to internal evidence, it's a big field and a game that two can play at: as witness this other internal evidence, discovered by the writer of the note above quoted, that "it is a wonderful letter—which no Christian genius, much less one unsanctified, could ever have written."

I had permission now to print—provided I suppressed names and places and sent my narrative out of the country. So I chose an Australian magazine for vehicle, as being far enough out of the country, and set myself to work on my article. And the ministers set the pumps going again, with the letter to work the handles.

But meantime Brother Page had been agitating. He had not visited the penitentiary, but he had sent a copy of the illustrious letter to the chaplain of that institution, and accompanied it with—apparently—inquiries. He got an answer, dated four days later than that other Brother's reassuring epistle; and before my article was complete, it wandered into my hands. The original is before me, now, and I here append it. It is pretty well loaded with internal evidence of the most solid description:—

STATE'S PRISON, CHAPLAIN'S OFFICE, July 11, 1873.

DEAR BRO. PAGE,—Herewith please find the letter kindly loaned me. I am afraid its genuineness cannot be established. It purports to be addressed to some prisoner here. No such letter ever came to a prisoner here. All letters received are carefully read by officers of the prison before they go into the hands of the convicts, and any such letter could not be forgotten. Again, Charles Williams is not a Christian man, but a dissolute, cunning prodigal, whose father is a minister of the gospel. His name is an assumed one. I am glad to have made your acquaintance. I am preparing a lecture upon life seen through prison bars, and should like to deliver the same in your vicinity.

And so ended that little drama. My poor article went into the fire; for whereas the materials for it were now more abundant and infinitely richer than they had previously been, there were parties all around me, who, although longing for the publication before, were a unit for suppression at this stage and complexion of the game. They said,—"Wait—the wound is too fresh, yet." All the copies of the famous letter except mine, disappeared suddenly; and from that time onward, the aforetime same old drought set in in the churches. As a rule, the town was on a spacious grin for a while, but there were places in it where the grin did not appear, and where it was dangerous to refer to the ex-convict's letter.

A word of explanation. "Jack Hunt," the professed writer of the letter, was an imaginary person. The burglar Williams—Harvard graduate, son of a minister—wrote the letter himself, *to* himself: got it smuggled out of the prison; got it conveyed to persons who had supported and encouraged him in his conversion—where he knew two things would happen: the genuineness of the letter would not be doubted or inquired into; and the nub of it would be noticed, and would have valuable effect—the effect, indeed, of starting a movement to get Mr. Williams pardoned out of prison.

That "nub" is so ingeniously, so casually, flung in, and immediately left there in the tail of the letter, undwelt upon, that an indifferent reader would never suspect that it was the heart and core of the epistle, if he even took note of it at all. This is the "nub":—

"i hope the warm weather is doing your lungs good—*i was afraid when you was bleeding you would die*—give my respects," etc.

That is all there is of it—simply touch and go—no dwelling upon it. Nevertheless it was intended for an eye that would be swift to see it; and it was meant to move a kind heart to try to effect the liberation of a poor reformed and purified fellow lying in the fell grip of consumption.

When I for the first time heard that letter read, nine years ago, I felt that it was the most remarkable one I had ever encountered. And it so warmed me toward Mr. Brown of St. Louis that I said that if ever I visited that city again, I would seek out that excellent man and kiss the hem of his garment if it was a new one. Well, I visited St. Louis, but I did not hunt for Mr. Brown; for, alas! the investigations of long ago had proved that the benevolent Brown, like "Jack Hunt," was not a real person, but a sheer invention of that gifted rascal, Williams—burglar, Harvard graduate, son of a clergyman.

Chapter 53

MY BOYHOOD'S HOME

We took passage in one of the fast boats of the St. Louis and St. Paul Packet Company, and started up the river.

When I, as a boy, first saw the mouth of the Missouri River, it was twenty-two or twenty-three miles above St. Louis, according to the estimate of pilots; the wear and tear of the banks has moved it down eight miles since then; and the pilots say that within five years the river will cut through and move the mouth down five miles more, which will bring it within ten miles of St. Louis.

About nightfall we passed the large and flourishing town of Alton, Illinois; and before daylight next morning the town of Louisiana, Missouri, a sleepy village in my day, but a brisk railway centre now; however, all the towns out there are railway centres now. I could not clearly recognize the place. This seemed odd to me, for when I retired from the rebel army in '61 I retired upon Louisiana in good order; at least in good enough order for a person who had not yet learned how to retreat according to the rules of war, and had to trust to native genius. It seemed to me that for a first attempt at a retreat it was not badly done. I had done no advancing in all that campaign that was at all equal to it.

There was a railway bridge across the river here well sprinkled with glowing lights, and a very beautiful sight it was.

At seven in the morning we reached Hannibal, Missouri, where my boyhood was spent. I had had a glimpse of it fifteen years ago, and another glimpse six years earlier, but both were so brief that they hardly counted. The only notion of the town that remained in my mind was the memory of it as I had known it when I first quitted it twenty-nine years ago. That picture of it was still as clear and vivid to me as a photograph. I stepped ashore with the feeling of one who returns out of a dead-and-gone generation. I had a sort of realizing sense of what the Bastille prisoners must have felt when they used to come out and look upon Paris after years of captivity, and note how curiously the familiar and the strange were mixed together before them. I saw the new houses—saw them plainly enough—but they did not affect the older picture in my mind, for through their solid bricks and mortar I saw the vanished houses, which had formerly stood there, with perfect distinctness.

It was Sunday morning, and everybody was abed yet. So I passed through the vacant streets, still seeing the town as it was, and not as it is, and recognizing and metaphorically shaking hands with a hundred familiar objects which no longer exist; and finally climbed Holiday's Hill to get a comprehensive view. The whole town lay spread out below me then, and I could mark and fix every locality, every detail. Naturally, I was a good deal moved. I said, "Many of the people I once knew in this tranquil refuge of my childhood are now in heaven; some, I trust, are in the other place."

The things about me before me made me feel like a boy again—convinced me that I was a boy again, and that I had simply been dreaming an unusually long dream; but my reflections spoiled all that; for they forced me to say, "I see fifty old houses down yonder, into each of which I could enter and find either a man or a woman who was a baby or unborn when I noticed those houses last, or a grandmother who was a plump young bride at that time."

From this vantage ground the extensive view up and down the river, and wide over the wooded expanses of Illinois, is very beautiful,—one of the most beautiful on the Mississippi, I think; which is a hazardous remark to make, for the eight hundred miles of river between St. Louis and St. Paul afford an unbroken succession of lovely pictures. It may be that my affection for the one in question biases my judgment in its favor; I cannot say as to that. No matter, it was satisfyingly beautiful to me, and it had this advantage over all the other friends whom I was about to greet again: it had suffered no change; it was as young and fresh and comely and gracious as ever it had been; whereas, the faces of the others would be old, and scarred with the campaigns of life, and marked with their griefs and defeats, and would give me no upliftings of spirit.

An old gentleman, out on an early morning walk, came along, and we discussed the weather, and then drifted into other matters. I could not remember his face. He said he had been living here twenty-eight years. So he had come after my time, and I had never seen him before. I asked him various questions; first about a mate of mine in Sunday school—what became of him?

THE DAYS OF LONG AGO.

"He graduated with honor in an Eastern college, wandered off into the world somewhere, succeeded at nothing, passed out of knowledge and memory years ago, and is supposed to have gone to the dogs."

"He was bright, and promised well when he was a boy."

"Yes, but the thing that happened is what became of it all."

I asked after another lad, altogether the brightest in our village school when I was a boy.

"He, too, was graduated with honors, from an Eastern college; but life whipped him in every battle, straight along, and he died in one of the Territories, years ago, a defeated man."

I asked after another of the bright boys.

"He is a success, always has been, always will be, I think."

I inquired after a young fellow who came to the town to study for one of the professions when I was a boy.

"He went at something else before he got through—went from medicine to law, or from law to medicine—then to some other new thing; went away for a year, came back with a young wife; fell to drinking, then to gambling behind the door; finally took his wife and two young children to her father's, and went off to Mexico; went from bad to worse, and finally died there, without a cent to buy a shroud, and without a friend to attend the funeral."

"Pity, he was the best-natured, and most cheery and hopeful young fellow that ever was."

I named another boy.

"Oh, he is all right. Lives here yet; has a wife and children, and is prospering."

Same verdict concerning other boys.

I named three school-girls.

"The first two live here, are married and have children; the other is long ago dead—never married."

I named, with emotion, one of my early sweethearts.

"She is all right. Been married three times; buried two husbands, divorced from the third, and I hear she is getting ready to marry an old fellow out in Colorado somewhere. She's got children scattered around here and there, most everywheres."

The answer to several other inquiries was brief and simple,—

"Killed in the war."

I named another boy.

"Well, now, his case *is* curious! There wasn't a human being in this town but knew that this boy was a perfect chucklehead; perfect dummy; just a stupid ass, as you may say. Everybody knew it, and everybody said it. Well, if that very boy isn't the first lawyer in the State of Missouri to-day, I'm a Democrat!"

"Is that so?"

"It's actually so. I'm telling you the truth."

"How do you account for it?"

"Account for it? There ain't any accounting for it, except that if you send a damned fool to St. Louis, and you don't tell them he's a damned fool *they'll* never find it out. There's one thing sure—if I had a damned fool I should know what to do with him: ship him to St. Louis—it's the noblest market in the world for that kind of property. Well, when you come to look at it all around, and chew at it and think it over, *don't* it just bang anything you ever heard of?"

"Well, yes, it does seem to. But don't you think maybe it was the Hannibal people who were mistaken about the boy, and not the St. Louis people?"

"Oh, nonsense! The people here have known him from the very cradle—they knew him a hundred times better than the St. Louis idiots *could* have known him. No, if you have got any damned fools that you want to realize on, take my advice—send them to St. Louis."

I mentioned a great number of people whom I had formerly known. Some were dead, some were gone away, some had prospered, some had come to naught; but as regarded a dozen or so of the lot, the answer was comforting:

"Prosperous—live here yet—town littered with their children."

I asked about Miss ——.

"Died in the insane asylum three or four years ago—never was out of it from the time she went in; and was always suffering, too; never got a shred of her mind back."

If he spoke the truth, here was a heavy tragedy, indeed. Thirty-six years in a madhouse, that some young fools might have some fun! I was a small boy, at the time; and I saw those giddy young ladies come tiptoeing into the room where Miss —— sat reading at midnight by a lamp. The girl at the head of the file wore a shroud and a doughface; she crept behind the victim, touched her on the shoulder, and she looked up and screamed, and then fell into convulsions. She did not recover from the fright, but went mad. In these days it seems incredible that people believed in ghosts so short a time ago. But they did.

After asking after such other folk as I could call to mind, I finally inquired about *myself:*

"Oh, he succeeded well enough—another case of damned fool. If they'd sent him to St. Louis, he'd have succeeded sooner."

It was with much satisfaction that I recognized the wisdom of having told this candid gentleman, in the beginning, that my name was Smith.

CHAPTER 54

PAST AND PRESENT

Being left to myself, up there, I went on picking out old houses in the distant town, and calling back their former inmates out of the mouldy past. Among them I presently recognized the house of the father of Lem Hackett (fictitious name). It carried me back more than a generation in a moment, and landed me in the midst of a time when the happenings of life were not the natural and logical results of great general laws, but of special orders, and were freighted with very precise and distinct purposes—partly punitive in intent, partly admonitory; and usually local in application.

When I was a small boy, Lem Hackett was drowned—on a Sunday. He fell out of an empty flat-boat, where he was playing. Being loaded with sin, he went to the bottom like an anvil. He was the only boy in the village who slept that night. We others all lay awake, repenting. We had not needed the information, delivered from the pulpit that evening, that Lem's was a case of special judgment—we knew that, already. There was a ferocious thunder-storm, that night, and it raged continuously until near dawn. The winds blew, the windows rattled, the rain swept along the roof in pelting sheets, and at the briefest of intervals the inky blackness of the night vanished, the houses over the way glared out white and blinding for a quivering instant, then the solid darkness shut down again and a splitting peal of thunder followed which seemed to rend everything in the neighborhood to shreds and splinters. I sat up in bed quaking and shuddering, waiting for the destruction of the world, and expecting it. To me there was nothing strange or incongruous in heaven's making such an uproar about Lem Hackett. Apparently it was the right and proper thing to do. Not a doubt entered my mind that all the angels were grouped together, discussing this boy's case and observing the awful bombardment of our beggarly little village with satisfaction and approval. There was one thing which disturbed me in the most serious way; that was the thought that this centering of the celestial interest on our village could not fail to attract the attention of the observers to people among us who might otherwise have escaped notice for years. I felt that I was not only one of those people, but the very one most likely to be discovered. That discovery could have but one result: I should be in the fire with Lem before the chill of the river had been fairly warmed out of him. I knew that this would be only just and fair. I was increasing the chances against myself all the time, by feeling a secret bitterness against Lem for having attracted this fatal attention to me, but I could not help it—this sinful thought persisted in infesting my breast in spite of me. Every time the lightning glared I caught my breath, and judged I was gone. In my terror and misery, I meanly began to suggest other boys, and mention acts of theirs which were wickeder than mine, and peculiarly needed punishment—and I tried to pretend to myself that I was simply doing this in a casual way, and without intent to divert the heavenly attention to them for the purpose of getting rid of it myself.

"I SAT UP IN BED QUAKING."

With deep sagacity I put these mentions into the form of sorrowing recollections and left-handed sham-supplications that the sins of those boys might be allowed to pass unnoticed—"Possibly they may repent." "It is true that Jim Smith broke a window and lied about it—but maybe he did not mean any harm. And although Tom Holmes says more bad words than any other boy in the village, he probably intends to repent—though he has never said he would. And whilst it is a fact that John Jones did fish a little on Sunday, once, he didn't really catch anything but only just one small useless mud-cat; and maybe that wouldn't have been so awful if he had thrown it back—as he says he did, but he didn't. Pity but they would repent of these dreadful things—and maybe they will yet."

But while I was shamefully trying to draw attention to these poor chaps—who were doubtless directing the celestial attention to me at the same moment, though I never once suspected that—I had heedlessly left my candle burning. It was not a time to neglect even trifling precautions. There was no occasion to add anything to the facilities for attracting notice to me—so I put the light out.

It was a long night to me, and perhaps the most distressful one I ever spent. I endured agonies of remorse for sins which I knew I had committed, and for others which I was not certain about, yet was sure that they had been set down against me in a book by an angel who was wiser than I and did not trust such important matters to memory. It struck me, by and by, that I had been making a most foolish and calamitous mistake, in one respect: doubtless I had not only made my own destruction sure by directing attention to those other boys, but had already accomplished theirs!—Doubtless the lightning had stretched them all dead in their beds by this time! The anguish and the fright which this thought gave me made my previous sufferings seem trifling by comparison.

Things had become truly serious. I resolved to turn over a new leaf instantly; I also resolved to connect myself with the church the next day, if I survived to see its sun appear. I resolved to cease from sin in all its forms, and to lead a high and blameless life forever after. I would be punctual at church and Sunday-school; visit the sick; carry baskets of victuals to the poor (simply to fulfil the regulation conditions, although I knew we had none among us so poor but they would smash the basket over my head for my pains); I would instruct other boys in right ways, and take the resulting trouncings meekly; I would subsist entirely on tracts; I would invade the rum shop and warn the drunkard—and finally, if I escaped the fate of those who early become too good to live, I would go for a missionary.

The storm subsided toward daybreak, and I dozed gradually to sleep with a sense of obligation to Lem Hackett for going to eternal suffering in that abrupt way, and thus preventing a far more dreadful disaster—my own loss.

But when I rose refreshed, by and by, and found that those other boys were still alive, I had a dim sense that perhaps the whole thing was a false alarm; that the entire turmoil had been on Lem's account and nobody's else. The world looked so bright and safe that there did not seem to be any real occasion to turn over a new leaf. I was a little subdued, during that day, and perhaps the next; after that, my purpose of reforming slowly dropped out of my mind, and I had a peaceful, comfortable time again, until the next storm.

That storm came about three weeks later; and it was the most unaccountable one, to me, that I had ever experienced; for on the afternoon of that day, "Dutchy" was drowned. Dutchy belonged to our Sunday-school. He was a German lad who did not know enough to come in out of the rain; but he was exasperatingly good, and had a prodigious memory. One Sunday he made himself the envy of all the youth and the talk of all the admiring village, by reciting three thousand verses of Scripture without missing a word; then he went off the very next day and got drowned.

"ALL RIGHT, DUTCHY—GO AHEAD."

Circumstances gave to his death a peculiar impressiveness. We were all bathing in a muddy creek which had a deep hole in it, and in this hole the coopers had sunk a pile of green hickory hoop poles to soak, some twelve feet under water. We were diving and "seeing who could stay under longest." We managed to remain down by holding on to the hoop poles. Dutchy made such a poor success of it that he was hailed with laughter and derision every time his head appeared above water. At last he seemed hurt with the taunts, and begged us to stand still on the bank and be fair with him and give him an honest count—"be friendly and kind just this once, and not miscount for the sake of having the fun of laughing at him." Treacherous winks were exchanged, and all said "All right, Dutchy—go ahead, we'll play fair."

Dutchy plunged in, but the boys, instead of beginning to count, followed the lead of one of their number and scampered to a range of blackberry bushes close by and hid behind it. They imagined Dutchy's humiliation, when he should rise after a superhuman effort and find the place silent and vacant, nobody there to applaud. They were "so full of laugh" with the idea, that they were continually exploding into muffled cackles. Time swept on, and presently one who was peeping through the briers, said, with surprise:—

"Why, he hasn't come up, yet!"

The laughing stopped.

"Boys, it's a splendid dive," said one.

"Never mind that," said another, "the joke on him is all the better for it."

There was a remark or two more, and then a pause. Talking ceased, and all began to peer through the vines. Before long, the boys' faces began to look uneasy, then anxious, then terrified. Still there was no movement of the placid water. Hearts began to beat fast, and faces to turn pale. We all glided out, silently, and stood on the bank, our horrified eyes wandering back and forth from each other's countenances to the water.

"WE ALL FLEW HOME."

"Somebody must go down and see!"

Yes, that was plain; but nobody wanted that grisly task.

"Draw straws!"

So we did—with hands which shook so, that we hardly knew what we were about. The lot fell to me, and I went down. The water was so muddy I could not see anything, but I felt around among the hoop poles, and presently grasped a limp wrist which gave me no response—and if it had I should not have known it, I let it go with such a frightened suddenness.

The boy had been caught among the hoop poles and entangled there, helplessly. I fled to the surface and told the awful news. Some of us knew that if the boy were dragged out at once he might possibly be resuscitated, but we never thought of that. We did not think of anything; we did not know what to do, so we did nothing—except that the smaller lads cried, piteously, and we all struggled frantically into our clothes, putting on anybody's that came handy, and getting them wrong-side-out and upside-down, as a rule. Then we scurried away and gave the alarm, but none of us went back to see the end of the tragedy. We had a more important thing to attend to: we all flew home, and lost not a moment in getting ready to lead a better life.

The night presently closed down. Then came on that tremendous and utterly unaccountable storm. I was perfectly dazed; I could not understand it. It seemed to me that there must be some mistake. The elements were turned loose, and they rattled and banged and blazed away in the most blind and frantic manner. All heart and hope went out of me, and the dismal thought kept floating through my brain, "If a boy who knows three thousand verses by heart is not satisfactory, what chance is there for anybody else?"

Of course I never questioned for a moment that the storm was on Dutchy's account, or that he or any other inconsequential animal was worthy of such a majestic demonstration from on high; the lesson of it was the only thing that troubled me; for it convinced me that if Dutchy, with all his perfections, was not a delight, it would be vain for me to turn over a new leaf, for I must infallibly fall hopelessly short of that boy, no matter how hard I might try. Nevertheless I did turn it over—a highly educated fear compelled me to do that—but succeeding days of cheerfulness and sunshine came bothering around, and within a month I had so drifted backward that again I was as lost and comfortable as ever.

Breakfast time approached while I mused these musings and called these ancient happenings back to mind; so I got me back into the present and went down the hill.

On my way through town to the hotel, I saw the house which was my home when I was a boy. At present rates, the people who now occupy it are of no more value than I am; but in my time they would have been worth not less than five hundred dollars apiece. They are colored folk.

After breakfast, I went out alone again, intending to hunt up some of the Sunday-schools and see how this generation of pupils might compare with their progenitors who had sat with me in those places and had probably taken me as a model—though I do not remember as to that now. By the public square there had been in my day a shabby little brick church called the "Old Ship of Zion," which I had attended as a Sunday-school scholar; and I found the locality easily enough, but not the old church; it was gone, and a trig and rather hilarious new edifice was in its place. The pupils were better dressed and better looking than were those of my time; consequently they did not resemble their ancestors; and consequently there was nothing familiar to me in their faces. Still, I contemplated them with a deep interest and a yearning wistfulness, and if I had been a girl I would have cried; for they were the offspring, and represented, and occupied the places, of boys and girls some of whom I had loved to love, and some of whom I had loved to hate, but all of whom were dear to me for the one reason or the other, so many years gone by—and, Lord, where be they now!

I was mightily stirred, and would have been grateful to be allowed to remain unmolested and look my fill; but a bald-summited superintendent who had been a tow-headed Sunday-school mate of mine on that spot in the early ages, recognized me, and I talked a flutter of wild nonsense to those children to hide the thoughts which were in me, and which could not have been spoken without a betrayal of feeling that would have been recognized as out of character with me.

Making speeches without preparation is no gift of mine; and I was resolved to shirk any new opportunity, but in the next and larger Sunday-school I found myself in the rear of the assemblage; so I was very willing to go on the platform a moment for the sake of getting a good look at the scholars. On the spur of the moment I could not recall any of the old idiotic talks which visitors used to insult me with when I was a pupil there; and I was sorry for this, since it would have given me time and excuse to dawdle there and take a long and satisfying look at what I feel at liberty to say was an array of fresh young

RANDOM RUBBISH.

comeliness not matchable in another Sunday-school of the same size. As I talked merely to get a chance to inspect; and as I strung out the random rubbish solely to prolong the inspection, I judged it but decent to confess these low motives, and I did so.

If the Model Boy was in either of these Sunday-schools, I did not see him. The Model Boy of my time—we never had but the one—was perfect: perfect in manners, perfect in dress, perfect in conduct, perfect in filial piety, perfect in exterior godliness; but at bottom he was a prig; and as for the contents of his skull, they could have changed place with the contents of a pie and nobody would have been the worse off for it but the pie. This fellow's reproachlessness was a standing reproach to every lad in the village. He was the admiration of all the mothers, and the detestation of all their sons. I was told what became of him, but as it was a disappointment to me, I will not enter into details. He succeeded in life.

Chapter 55

A VENDETTA AND OTHER THINGS

During my three days' stay in the town, I woke up every morning with the impression that I was a boy—for in my dreams the faces were all young again, and looked as they had looked in the old times—but I went to bed a hundred years old, every night—for meantime I had been seeing those faces as they are now.

Of course I suffered some surprises, along at first, before I had become adjusted to the changed state of things. I met young ladies who did not seem to have changed at all; but they turned out to be the daughters of the young ladies I had in mind—sometimes their grand-daughters. When you are told that a stranger of fifty is a grandmother, there is nothing surprising about it; but if, on the contrary, she is a person whom you knew as a little girl, it seems impossible. You say to yourself, "How can a little girl be a grandmother?" It takes some little time to accept and realize the fact that while you have been growing old, your friends have not been standing still, in that matter.

I noticed that the greatest changes observable were with the women, not the men. I saw men whom thirty years had changed but slightly; but their wives had grown old. These were good women; it is very wearing to be good.

There was a saddler whom I wished to see; but he was gone. Dead, these many years, they said. Once or twice a day, the saddler used to go tearing down the street, putting on his coat as he went; and then everybody knew a steamboat was coming. Everybody knew, also, that John Stavely was not expecting anybody by the boat—or any freight, either; and Stavely must have known that everybody knew this, still it made no difference to him; he liked to seem to himself to be expecting a hundred thousand tons of saddles by this boat, and so he went on all his life, enjoying being faithfully on hand to receive and receipt for those saddles, in case by any miracle they should come. A malicious Quincy paper used always to refer to this town, in derision as "Stavely's Landing." Stavely was one of my earliest admirations; I envied him his rush of imaginary business, and the display he was able to make of it, before strangers, as he went flying down the street struggling with his fluttering coat.

But there was a carpenter who was my chiefest hero. He was a mighty liar, but I did not know that; I believed everything he said. He was a romantic, sentimental, melodramatic fraud, and his bearing impressed me with awe. I vividly remember the first time he took me into his confidence. He was planing a board, and every now and then he would pause and heave a deep sigh; and occasionally mutter broken sentences—confused and not intelligible—but out of their midst an ejaculation sometimes escaped which made me shiver and did me good: one was, "O God, it is his blood!" I sat on the tool-chest and humbly and shudderingly admired him; for I judged he was full of crime. At last he said in a low voice:—

"My little friend, can you keep a secret?"

I eagerly said I could.

"A dark and dreadful one?"

I satisfied him on that point.

"Then I will tell you some passages in my history; for oh, I *must* relieve my burdened soul, or I shall die!"

He cautioned me once more to be "as silent as the grave;" then he told me he was a "red-handed murderer." He put down his plane, held his hands out before him, contemplated them sadly, and said:—

"Look—with these hands I have taken the lives of thirty human beings!"

The effect which this had upon me was an inspiration to him, and he turned himself loose upon his subject with interest and energy. He left generalizing, and went into details,—began with his first murder; described it, told what measures he had taken to avert suspicion; then passed to his second homicide, his third, his fourth, and so on. He had always done his murders with a bowie-knife, and he made all my hairs rise by suddenly snatching it out and showing it to me.

At the end of this first *séance* I went home with six of his fearful secrets among my freightage, and found them a great help to my dreams, which had been sluggish for a while back. I sought him again and again, on my Saturday holidays; in fact I spent the summer with him—all of it which was valuable to me. His fascinations never diminished, for he threw something fresh and stirring, in the way of horror, into each successive murder. He always gave names, dates, places—everything. This by and by enabled me to note two things: that he had killed his victims in every quarter of the globe, and that these victims were always named Lynch. The destruction of the Lynches went serenely on, Saturday after Saturday, until the original thirty had multiplied to sixty,—and more to be heard from yet; then my curiosity got the better of my timidity, and I asked how it happened that these justly punished persons all bore the same name.

My hero said he had never divulged that dark secret to any living being; but felt that he could trust me, and therefore he would lay bare before me the story of his sad and blighted life. He had loved one "too fair for earth," and she had reciprocated "with all the sweet affection of her pure and noble nature." But he had a rival, a "base hireling" named Archibald Lynch, who said the girl should be his, or he would "dye his hands in her heart's best blood." The carpenter, "innocent and happy in love's young dream," gave no weight to the threat, but led his "golden-haired darling to the altar," and there, the two were made one; there also, just as the minister's hands were stretched in blessing over their heads, the fell deed was done—with a knife—and the bride fell a corpse at her husband's feet. And what did the husband do? He plucked forth that knife, and kneeling by the body of his lost one, swore to "consecrate his life to the extermination of all the human scum that bear the hated name of Lynch."

That was it. He had been hunting down the Lynches and slaughtering them, from that day to this—twenty years. He had always used that same consecrated knife; with it he had murdered his long array of Lynches, and with it he had left upon the forehead of each victim a peculiar mark—a cross, deeply incised. Said he:—

"The cross of the Mysterious Avenger is known in Europe, in America, in China, in Siam, in the Tropics, in the Polar Seas, in the deserts of Asia, in all the earth. Wherever in the uttermost parts of the globe, a Lynch had penetrated, there has the Mysterious Cross been seen, and those who have seen it have shuddered and said, 'it is his mark, he has been here.' You have heard of the Mysterious Avenger—look upon him, for before you stands no less a person! But beware—breathe not a word to any soul. Be silent, and wait. Some morning this town will flock aghast to view a gory corpse; on its brow will be seen the awful sign, and men will tremble and whisper, 'he has been here,—it is the Mysterious Avenger's mark!' You will come here, but I shall have vanished; you will see me no more."

This ass had been reading the "Jibbenainosay," no doubt, and had had his poor romantic head turned by it; but as I had not yet seen the book then, I took his inventions for truth, and did not suspect that he was a plagiarist.

However, we had a Lynch living in the town; and the more I reflected upon his impending doom, the more I could not sleep. It seemed my plain duty to save him, and a still plainer and more important duty to get some sleep for myself, so at last I ventured to go to Mr. Lynch and tell him what was about to happen to him—under strict secrecy. I advised him to "fly," and certainly expected him to do it. But he laughed at me; and he did not stop there; he led me down to the carpenter's shop, gave the carpenter a jeering and scornful lecture upon his silly pretensions, slapped his face, made him get down on his knees and beg—then went off and left me to contemplate the cheap and pitiful ruin of what, in my eyes, had so lately been a majestic and incomparable hero. The carpenter blustered, flourished his knife, and doomed this Lynch in his usual volcanic style, the size of his fateful words undiminished; but it was all wasted upon me; he was a hero to me no longer but only a poor, foolish, exposed humbug. I was ashamed of him, and ashamed of myself; I took no further interest in him, and never went to his shop any more. He was a heavy loss to me, for he was the greatest hero I had ever known. The fellow must have had some talent; for some of his imaginary murders were so vividly and dramatically described that I remember all their details yet.

The people of Hannibal are not more changed than is the town. It is no longer a village; it is a city, with a mayor, and a council, and water-works, and probably a debt. It has fifteen thousand people, is a thriving and energetic place, and is paved like the rest of the west and south—where a well-paved street and a good sidewalk are things so seldom seen, that one doubts them when he does see them. The customary half-dozen railways centre in Hannibal now, and there is a new depot which cost a hundred thousand dollars. In my time the town had no specialty, and no commercial grandeur; the daily packet usually landed a passenger and bought a catfish, and took away another passenger and a hatful of freight; but now a huge commerce in lumber has grown up and a large miscellaneous commerce is one of the results. A deal of money changes hands there now.

Bear Creek—so called, perhaps, because it was always so particularly bare of bears—is hidden out of sight now, under islands and continents of piled

A BAD CASE OF SHAKES.

lumber, and nobody but an expert can find it. I used to get drowned in it every summer regularly, and be drained out, and inflated and set going again by some chance enemy; but not enough of it is unoccupied now to drown a person in. It was a famous breeder of chills and fever in its day. I remember one summer when everybody in town had this disease at once. Many chimneys were shaken down, and all the houses were so racked that the town had to be rebuilt. The chasm or gorge between Lover's Leap and the hill west of it is supposed by scientists to have been caused by glacial action. This is a mistake.

There is an interesting cave a mile or two below Hannibal, among the bluffs. I would have liked to revisit it, but had not time. In my time the person who then owned it turned it into a mausoleum for his daughter, aged fourteen. The body of this poor child was put into a copper cylinder filled with alcohol, and this was suspended in one of the dismal avenues of the cave. The top of the cylinder was removable; and it was said to be a common thing for the baser order of tourists to drag the dead face into view and examine it and comment upon it.

Photo credits:

1. Courtesy of Mark Twain Estate
2. Collection of American Literature, Beinecke Rare Book and Manuscript Library, Yale University
3. Courtesy of Milton Meltzer
4. Buffalo Historical Society
5. Collection of American Literature, Beinecke Rare Book and Manuscript Library, Yale University
6. Courtesy of Milton Meltzer
7. Collection of American Literature, Beinecke Rare Book and Manuscript Library, Yale University
8. Library of Congress
9. Courtesy of Milton Meltzer
10. Courtesy of Milton Meltzer

1

This first known photograph *(above)* of Sam Clemens is characteristic; his eyes seem to dominate the picture, fixing the viewer, while his hand draws attention to the explicit message of his belt buckle. The other photographs show Sam Clemens aging, becoming a "public personality," and withstanding the ravages of time.

2

3

4

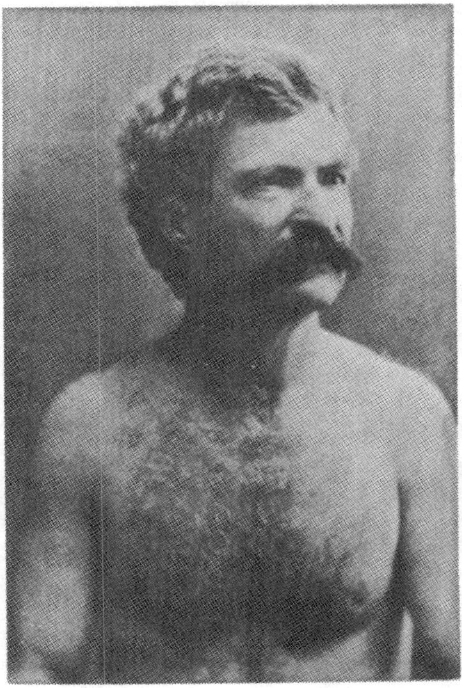
5

6

7

8

9

10

GERHARDT LETTER

In 1883 Clemens was supporting Karl Gerhardt, a young sculptor, who was studying in Paris. He was also contributing money to Mr. Porter, a young black American who was traveling in Europe.

In this remarkable letter, never previously published, Sam Clemens reveals his careful process of weighing the evidence before reaching a conclusion. His comments about a differential distribution of guilt between black and white persons are extraordinary.

Hartford, Conn. May 1st, 1883.

Dear Karl and Josephine:

Mr. Fisk arrived in New York yesterday, and we look for Mr. Warner up today with the bronzes. Of course we are exceedingly anxious to see them.

If Mrs. Clemens ever gets strong enough to swing a pen, she will write Josephine and blow up her nurse. I hoped she might at least get strength enough to dictate a letter, but that time has not arrived yet. She has wasted away to nothing; has no more flesh on her than a basket; is all bones, and has no strength at all. But she has begun to eat, now, and if she keeps it up a week or two you will hear from her. She thinks that if Josephine had had the right kind of a nurse, she would be suckling her child today; and I think she will strongly recommend that you have nothing to do with wet nurses, if the child is reasonably strong and healthy. A wet nurse is good, but she is not as good as condensed milk by any means. The best condensed milk over there is named the "Anglo Swiss." Well, I think I will drop this and leave it to Mrs. Clemens. I seem to be getting out of my depth.

Mr. Porter has written to ask me to get some orders for him, as his money is nearly spent and he wants to remain some time longer in Paris. This places me in a bothersome position; because, a long time ago, Josephine intimated in one of her letters that Porter had gone to the dogs or was on his way there. She gave no details, brought forward no facts. I meant to write her, then and there, and say that whenever one flings a flask of dynamite under a person's character, he should always go into the details of the matter, and state exactly why he felt justified in doing that thing. I haven't answered Porter; cannot answer him until I learn from you how he stands. Tell me all you have heard against him, keep back nothing whatever. Also tell me what part of the evidence rests upon trustworthy authority, and what part of it doubtful. I want to know everything about him, good and bad; for if he is worthy of help I want to turn out and see what can be done for him; and if he is not, I want to at least act with caution. At the same time I must remember, and you must also remember, that on every sin which a colored man commits, the just white man must make a considerable discount, because of the colored man's antecedents. The heirs of slavery cannot with any sort of justice, be required to be as clear and straight and upright as the heirs of ancient freedom. And besides, whenever a colored man commits an unright action, upon his head is the guilt of only about one tenth of it, and upon your heads and mine and the rest of the white race lies fairly and justly the other nine tenths of the guilt. So, when you have told me all there is to tell about Porter, I shall doubtless judge his case charitably enough.

With much love to you both and the French boarder,

Yours sincerely,

S. L. Clemens.

P.S. May 3—Mrs. Clemens is not well enough yet, to write, but will be, soon, I hope.

The bronzes have come, & we think mine is very fine. Warner's is beautiful, but not a good likeness, & has many defects of drawing & proportion. These faults were to be expected, of course—the artist needs the living model, not the dead & flat photograph.

In great haste—for Mrs. Clemens is waiting for me to help her down stairs. She is going to drive a hundred yards or so. With love

SLC

ADVENTURES OF HUCKLEBERRY FINN

In Adventures of Huckleberry Finn *(1885) Twain explored the world from the point of view of a good-hearted boy of twelve to fourteen years of age. Huck's innocence creates the possibility of a contrast between his naive descriptions and the ugly reality. A constant theme in the book is Huck's perceptions about the role of literary authority. Repeatedly people try to impose the authority of the written word on Huck, but he usually remains skeptical about the "wisdom" of books. Similarly, people try to impose upon Huck the conventional values of Christianity. But Huck pragmatically tests the information from authorities by experimenting, and he realizes that books and religion are equally deceptive, equating playing and praying as devices of deception.*

Other examples of Twain's skepticism include the effort by a new Judge to reform Pappy Finn, a habitual drunkard. And later in the book two confidence men develop impersonations of nobility fallen on hard times. The exploitation of religious credulity at a camp meeting dramatizes the con-man's frenetic activity.

Of course, the climax of the novel involves Huck's decision to oppose all the social norms by protecting Jim, refusing to betray the runaway slave. As Henry Nash Smith has stated, the conflict is between, in Twain's phrase, "a sound heart and a deformed conscience." The strikingly unconventional individualism of Huck's decision "to go to Hell" is a high point of American literature.

CHAPTER 1

You don't know about me, without you have read a book by the name of "The Adventures of Tom Sawyer," but that ain't no matter. That book was made by Mr. Mark Twain, and he told the truth, mainly. There was things which he stretched, but mainly he told the truth. That is nothing. I never seen anybody but lied, one time or another, without it was Aunt Polly, or the widow, or maybe Mary. Aunt Polly—Tom's Aunt Polly, she is—and Mary, and the Widow Douglas, is all told about in that book—which is mostly a true book; with some stretchers, as I said before.

Now the way that the book winds up, is this: Tom and me found the money that the robbers hid in the cave, and it made us rich. We got six thousand dollars apiece—all gold. It was an awful sight of money when it was piled up. Well, Judge Thatcher, he took it and put it out at interest, and it fetched us a dollar a day apiece, all the year round—more than a body could tell what to do with. The Widow Douglas, she took me for her son, and allowed she would sivilize me; but it was rough living in the house all the time, considering how dismal regular and decent the widow was in all her ways; and so when I couldn't stand it no longer, I lit out. I got into my old rags, and my sugar-hogshead again, and was free and satisfied. But Tom Sawyer, he hunted me up and said he was going to start a band of robbers, and I might join if I would go back to the widow and be respectable. So I went back.

The widow she cried over me, and called me a poor lost lamb, and she called me a lot of other names, too, but she never meant no harm by it. She put me in them new clothes again, and I couldn't do nothing but sweat and sweat, and feel all cramped up. Well, then, the old thing commenced again. The widow rung a bell for supper, and you had to come to time. When you got to the table you couldn't go right to eating, but you had to wait for the widow to tuck down her head and grumble a little over the victuals, though there warn't really anything the matter with them. That is, nothing only everything was cooked by itself. In a barrel of odds and ends it is different; things get mixed up, and the juice kind of swaps around, and the things go better.

After supper she got out her book and learned me about Moses and the Bulrushers; and I was in a sweat to find out all about him; but by-and-by she let it out that Moses had been dead a considerable long time; so then I didn't care no more about him; because I don't take no stock in dead people.

Pretty soon I wanted to smoke, and asked the widow to let me. But she wouldn't. She said it was a mean practice and wasn't clean, and I must try to not do it any more. That is just the way with some people. They get down on a thing when they don't know nothing about it. Here she was a bothering about Moses, which was no kin to her, and no use to anybody, being gone, you see, yet finding a power of fault with me for doing a thing that had some good in it. And she took snuff too; of course that was all right, because she done it herself.

Her sister, Miss Watson, a tolerable slim old maid, with goggles on, had just come to live with her, and took a set at me now, with a spelling-book. She worked me middling hard for about an hour, and then the widow made her ease up. I couldn't stood it much longer. Then for an hour it was deadly dull, and I was fidgety. Miss Watson would say, "Dont put your feet up there, Huckleberry;" and "dont scrunch up like that, Huckleberry—set up straight;"

and pretty soon she would say, "Don't gap and stretch like that, Huckleberry—why don't you try to behave?" Then she told me all about the bad place, and I said I wished I was there. She got mad, then, but I didn't mean no harm. All I wanted was to go somewheres; all I wanted was a change, I warn't particular. She said it was wicked to say what I said; said she wouldn't say it for the whole world; *she* was going to live so as to go to the good place. Well, I couldn't see no advantage in going where she was going, so I made up my mind I wouldn't try for it. But I never said so, because it would only make trouble, and wouldn't do no good.

Now she had got a start, and she went on and told me all about the good place. She said all a body would have to do there was to go around all day long with a harp and sing, forever and ever. So I didn't think much of it. But I never said so. I asked her if she reckoned Tom Sawyer would go there, and, she said, not by a considerable sight. I was glad about that, because I wanted him and me to be together.

Miss Watson she kept pecking at me, and it got tiresome and lonesome. By-and-by they fetched the niggers in and had prayers, and then everybody was off to bed. I went up to my room with a piece of candle and put it on the table. Then I set down in a chair by the window and tried to think of something cheerful, but it warn't no use. I felt so lonesome I most wished I was dead. The stars was shining, and the leaves rustled in the woods ever so mournful; and I heard an owl, away off, who-whooing about somebody that was dead, and a whippowill and a dog crying about somebody that was going to die; and the wind was trying to whisper something to me and I couldn't make out what it was, and so it made the cold shivers run over me. Then away out in the woods I heard that kind of a sound that a ghost makes when it wants to tell about something that's on its mind and can't make itself understood, and so can't rest easy in its grave and has to go about that way every night grieving. I got so down-hearted and scared, I did wish I had some company. Pretty soon a spider went crawling up my shoulder, and I flipped it off and it lit in the candle; and before I could budge it was all shriveled up. I didn't need anybody to tell me that that was an awful bad sign and would fetch me some bad luck, so I was scared and most shook the clothes off of me. I got up and turned around in my tracks three times and crossed my breast every time; and then I tied up a little lock of my hair with a thread to keep witches away. But I hadn't no confidence. You do that when you've lost a horse-shoe that you've found, instead of nailing it up over the door, but I hadn't ever heard anybody say it was any way to keep off bad luck when you'd killed a spider.

I set down again, a shaking all over, and got out my pipe for a smoke; for the house was all as still as death, now, and so the widow wouldn't know. Well, after a long time I heard the clock away off in the town go boom—boom—boom—twelve licks—and all still again—stiller than ever. Pretty soon I heard a twig snap, down in the dark amongst the trees—something was a stirring. I set still and listened. Directly I could just barely hear a "*me-yow! me-yow!*"

down there. That was good! Says I, "*me-yow! me-yow!*" as soft as I could, and then I put out the light and scrambled out of the window onto the shed. Then I slipped down to the ground and crawled in amongst the trees, and sure enough there was Tom Sawyer waiting for me.

Chapter 3

Well, I got a good going-over in the morning, from old Miss Watson, on account of my clothes; but the widow she didn't scold, but only cleaned off the grease and clay and looked so sorry that I thought I would behave a while if I could. Then Miss Watson she took me in the closet and prayed, but nothing come of it. She told me to pray every day, and whatever I asked for I would get it. But it warn't so. I tried it. Once I got a fish-line, but no hooks. It warn't any good to me without hooks. I tried for the hooks three or four times, but somehow I couldn't make it work. By-and-by, one day, I asked Miss Watson to try for me, but she said I was a fool. She never told me why, and I couldn't make it out no way.

I set down, one time, back in the woods, and had a long think about it. I says to myself, if a body can get anything they pray for, why don't Deacon Winn get back the money he lost on pork? Why can't the widow get back her silver snuff-box that was stole? Why can't Miss Watson fat up? No, says I to myself, there ain't nothing in it. I went and told the widow about it, and she said the thing a body could get by praying for it was "spiritual gifts." This was too many for me, but she told me what she meant—I must help other people, and do everything I could for other people, and look out for them all the time, and never think about myself. This was including Miss Watson, as I took it. I went out in the woods and turned it over in my mind a long time, but I couldn't see no advantage about it—except for the other people—so at last I reckoned I wouldn't worry about it any more, but just let it go. Sometimes the widow would take me one side and talk about Providence in a way to make a body's mouth water; but maybe next day Miss Watson would take hold and knock it all down again. I judged I could see that there was two Providences, and a poor chap would stand considerable show with the widow's Providence, but if Miss Watson's got him there warn't no help for him any more. I thought it all out, and reckoned I would belong to the widow's, if he wanted me, though I couldn't make out how he was agoing to be any better off then than what he was before, seeing I was so ignorant and so kind of low-down and ornery.

Pap he hadn't been seen for more than a year, and that was comfortable for me; I didn't want to see him no more. He used to always whale me when he was sober and could get his hands on me; though I used to take to the woods most of the time when he was around. Well, about this time he was found in the river drowned, about twelve mile about town, so people said. They judged it was him, anyway; said this drowned man was just his size, and was ragged, and had uncommon long hair—which was all like pap—but they couldn't make nothing out of the face, because it had been in the water so long it warn't much like a face at all. They said he was floating on his back in the water. They took him and buried him on the bank. But I warn't comfortable long, because I happened to think of something. I knowed mighty well that a drownded man don't float on his back, but on his face. So I knowed, then, that this warn't pap, but a woman dressed up in man's clothes. So I was uncomfortable again. I judged the old man would turn up again by-and-by, though I wished he wouldn't.

We played robbers now and then about a month, and then I resigned. All the boys did. We hadn't robbed nobody, we hadn't killed any people, but only just pretended. We used to hop out of the woods and go charging down on hog-drovers and women in carts taking garden stuff to market, but we never hived any of them. Tom Sawyer called the hogs "ingots," and he called the turnips and stuff "julery" and we would go to the cave and pow-wow over what we had done and how many people we had killed and marked. But I couldn't see no profit in it. One time Tom sent a boy to run about town with a blazing stick, which he called a slogan (which was the sign for the Gang to get together), and then he said he had got secret news by his spies that next day a whole parcel of Spanish merchants and rich A-rabs was going to camp in Cave Hollow with two hundred elephants, and six hundred camels, and over a thousand "sumter" mules, all loaded down with di'monds, and they didn't have only a guard of four hundred soldiers, and so we would lay in ambuscade, as he called it, and kill the lot and scoop the things. He said we must slick up our swords and guns, and get ready. He never could go after even a turnip-cart but he must have the swords and guns all scoured up for it; though they was only lath and broom-sticks, and you might scour at them till you rotted and then they warn't worth a mouthful of ashes more than what they was before. I didn't believe we could lick such a crowd of Spaniards and A-rabs, but I wanted to see the camels and elephants, so I was on hand next day, Saturday, in the ambuscade; and when we got the word, we rushed out of the woods and down the hill. But there warn't no Spaniards and A-rabs, and there warn't no camels nor no elephants. It warn't anything but a Sunday-school picnic, and only a primer-class at that. We busted it up, and chased the children up the hollow; but we never got anything but some doughnuts and jam, though Ben Rogers got a rag doll, and Jo Harper got a hymn-book and a tract; and then the teacher charged in and made us drop everything and cut. I didn't see no di'monds, and I told Tom Sawyer so. He said there was loads of them there, anyway; and he said there was A-rabs there, too, and elephants and things. I said, why couldn't we see them, then? He said if I warn't so ignorant, but had read a book called "Don Quixote," I would know without asking. He said it was all done by enchantment. He said there was hundreds of soldiers there, and elephants and treasure, and so on, but we had enemies which he called magicians, and they had turned the whole thing into an infant Sunday school, just out of spite. I said, all right, then the thing for us to do was to go for the magicians. Tom Sawyer said I was a numskull.

"Why," says he, "a magician could call up a lot of genies, and they would hash you up like nothing before you could say Jack Robinson. They are as tall as a tree and as big around as a church."

"Well," I says, "s'pose we got some genies to help *us*—can't we lick the other crowd then?"

"How you going to get them?"

"I don't know. How do *they* get them?"

"Why they rub an old tin lamp or an iron ring, and then the genies come tearing in, with the thunder and lightning a-ripping around and the smoke a-rolling, and everything they're told to do they up and do it. They don't think nothing of pulling a shot tower up by the roots, and belting a Sunday-school superintendent over the head with it—or any other man."

"Who makes them tear around so?"

"Why, whoever rubs the lamp or the ring. They belong to whoever rubs the lamp or the ring, and they've got to do whatever he says. If he tells them to build a palace forty miles long, out of di'monds, and fill it full of chewing gum, or whatever you want, and fetch an emperor's daughter from China for you to marry, they've got to do it—and they've got to do it before sun-up next morning, too. And more—they've got to waltz that palace around over the country wherever you want it, you understand."

"Well," says I, "I think they are a pack of flatheads for not keeping the palace themselves 'stead of fooling them away like that. And what's more—if I was one of them I would see a man in Jericho before I would drop my business and come to him for the rubbing of an old tin lamp."

"How you talk, Huck Finn. Why, you'd *have* to come when he rubbed it, whether you wanted to or not."

"What, and I as high as a tree and as big as a church? All right, then, I *would* come; but I lay I'd make that man climb the highest tree there was in the country."

"Shucks, it ain't no use to talk to you, Huck Finn. You don't seem to know anything, somehow—perfect sap-head."

I thought all this over for two or three days, and then I reckoned I would see if there was anything in it. I got an old tin lamp and an iron ring and went out in the woods and rubbed and rubbed till I sweat like an Injun, calculating to build a palace and sell it; but it warn't no use, none of the genies come. So then I judged that all that stuff was only just one of Tom Sawyer's lies. I reckoned he believed in the A-rabs and the elephants, but as for me I think different. It had all the marks of a Sunday school.

Chapter 5

[Huck's father]

. . . The judge and the widow went to law to get the court to take me away from him and let one of them be my guardian; but it was a new judge that had just come, and he didn't know the old man; so he said courts mustn't interfere and separate families if they could help it; said he'd druther not take a child away from its father. So Judge Thatcher and the widow had to quit on the business.

That pleased the old man till he couldn't rest. He said he'd cowhide me till I was black and blue if I didn't raise some money for him. I borrowed three dollars from Judge Thatcher, and pap took it and got drunk and went a-blowing around and cussing and whooping and carrying on; and he kept it up all over town, with a tin pan, till most midnight; then they jailed him, and next day they had him before court, and jailed him again for a week. But he said *he* was satisfied; said he was boss of his son, and he'd make it warm for *him*.

When he got out the new judge said he was agoing to make a man of him. So he took him to his own house, and dressed him up clean and nice, and had him to breakfast and dinner and supper with the family, and was just old pie to him, so to speak. And after supper he talked to him about temperance and such things till the old man cried, and said he'd been a fool, and fooled away his life; but now he was agoing to turn over a new leaf and be a man nobody wouldn't be ashamed of, and he hoped the judge would help him and not look down on him. The judge said he could hug him for them words; so *he* cried, and his wife she cried again; pap said he'd been a man that had always been misunderstood before, and the judge said he believed it. The old man said that what a man wanted that was down, was sympathy; and the judge said it was so; so they cried again. And when it was bedtime, the old man rose up and held out his hand, and says:

"Look at it gentlemen, and ladies all; take ahold of it; shake it. There's a hand that was the hand of a hog; but it ain't so no more; it's the hand of a man that's started in on a new life, and 'll die before he'll go back. You mark them words—don't forget I said them. It's a clean hand now; shake it—don't be afeard."

So they shook it, one after the other, all around, and cried. The judge's wife she kissed it. Then the old man he signed a pledge—made his mark. The judge said it was the holiest time on record, or something like that. Then they tucked the old man into a beautiful room, which was the spare room, and in the night sometime he got powerful thirsty and clumb out onto the porch-roof and slid down a stanchion and traded his new coat for a jug of forty-rod, and clumb back again and had a good old time; and towards daylight he crawled out again, drunk as a fiddler, and rolled off the porch and broke his left arm in two places and was most froze to death when somebody found him after sun-up. And when they come to look at that spare room, they had to take soundings before they could navigate it.

The judge he felt kind of sore. He said he reckoned a body could reform the ole man with a shot-gun, maybe, but he didn't know no other way.

Chapter 19

Two or three days and nights went by; I reckon I might say they swum by, they slid along so quiet and smooth and lovely. Here is the way we put in the time.

It was a monstrous big river down there—sometimes a mile and a half wide; we run nights, and laid up and hid day-times; soon as night was most gone, we stopped navigating and tied up—nearly always in the dead water under a tow-head; and then cut young cottonwoods and willows and hid the raft with them. Then we set out the lines. Next we slid into the river and had a swim, so as to freshen up and cool off; then we set down on the sandy bottom where the water was about knee deep, and watched the daylight come. Not a sound, anywheres—perfectly still—just like the whole world was asleep, only sometimes the bull-frogs a-cluttering, maybe. The first thing to see, looking away over the water, was a kind of dull line—that was the woods on t'other side—you couldn't make nothing else out; then a pale place in the sky; then more paleness, spreading around; then a river softened up, away off, and warn't black any more, but gray; you could see little dark spots drifting along, ever so far away—trading scows, and such things; and long black streaks—rafts; sometimes you could hear a sweep screaking; or jumbled up voices, it was so still, and sounds come so far; and by-and-by you could see a streak on the water which you know by the look of the streak that there's a snag there in a swift current which breaks on it and makes that streak look that way; and you see the mist curl up off of the water, and the east reddens up, and the river, and you make out a log cabin in the edge of the woods, away on the bank on t'other side of the river, being a wood-yard, likely, and piled by them cheats so you can throw a dog through it anywheres; then the nice breeze springs up, and comes fanning you from over there, so cool and fresh, and sweet to smell, on account of the woods and the flowers; but sometimes not that way, because they've left dead fish laying around, gars, and such, and they do get pretty rank; and next you've got the full day, and everything smiling in the sun, and the song-birds just going it!

A little smoke couldn't be noticed, now, so we would take some fish off of the lines, and cook up a hot breakfast. And afterwards we would watch the lonesomeness of the river, and kind of lazy along, and by-and-by lazy off to sleep. Wake up, by-and-by, and look to see what done it, and maybe see a steamboat, coughing along up stream, so far off towards the other side you couldn't tell nothing about her only whether she was stern-wheel or side-wheel; then for about an hour there wouldn't be nothing to hear nor nothing to see—just solid lonesomeness. Next you'd see a raft sliding by, away off yonder, and maybe a galoot on it chopping, because they're most always doing it on a raft; you'd see the ax flash, and come down—you don't hear nothing; you see that ax go up again, and by the time it's above the man's head, then you hear the *k'chunk!*—it had took all that time to come over the water. So we would put in the day, lazying around, listening to the stillness. Once there was a thick fog, and the rafts and things that went by was beating tin pans so the steamboats wouldn't run over them. A scow or a raft went by so close we could hear them talking and cussing and laughing—heard them plain; but we couldn't see no sign of them; it made you feel crawly, it was like spirits carrying on that way in the air. Jim said he believed it was spirits; but I says:

"No, spirits wouldn't say, 'dern the dern fog.'"

Soon as it was night, out we shoved; when we got her out to about the middle, we let her alone, and let her float wherever the current wanted her to; then we lit the pipes, and dangled our legs in the water and talked about all kinds of things—we was always naked, day and night, whenever the mosquitoes would let us—the new clothes Buck's folks made for me was too good to be comfortable, and besides I didn't go much on clothes, nohow.

Sometimes we'd have that whole river all to ourselves for the longest time. Yonder was the banks and the islands, across the water; and maybe a spark—which was a candle in a cabin window—and sometimes on the water you could see a spark or two—on a raft or a scow, you know; and maybe you could hear a fiddle or a song coming over from one of them crafts. It's lovely to live on a raft. We had the sky, up there, all speckled with stars, and we used to lay on our backs and look up at them, and discuss about whether they was made, or only just happened—Jim he allowed they was made, but I allowed they happened; I judged it would have took too long to *make* so many. Jim said the moon could a *laid* them; well, that looked kind of reasonable, so I didn't say nothing against it, because I've seen a frog lay most as many, so of course it could be done. We used to watch the stars that fell, too, and see them streak down. Jim allowed they'd got spoiled and was hove out of the nest.

Once or twice of a night we would see a steamboat slipping along in the dark, and now and then she would belch a whole world of sparks up out of her chimbleys, and they would rain down in the river and look awful pretty; then she would turn a corner and her lights would wink out and her pow-wow shut off and leave the river still again; and by-and-by her waves would get to us, a long time after she was gone, and joggle the raft a bit, and after that you wouldn't hear nothing for you couldn't tell how long, except maybe frogs or something.

After midnight the people on shore went to bed, and then for two or three hours the shores was black—no more sparks in the cabin windows. These sparks was our clock—the first one that showed again meant morning was coming, so we hunted a place to hide and tie up, right away.

One morning about day-break, I found a canoe and crossed over a chute to the main shore—it was only two hundred yards—and paddled about a mile up a crick amongst the cypress woods, to see if I couldn't get some berries. Just as I was passing a place where a kind of cow-path crossed the crick, here comes a couple of men tearing up the path as tight as they could foot it. I thought I was a goner, for whenever anybody was after anybody I judged it was *me*—or maybe Jim. I was about to dig out from there in a hurry, but they was pretty close to me then, and sung out and begged me to save their lives—said they hadn't been doing nothing, and was being chased for it—said there was men and dogs a-coming. They wanted to jump right in, but I says—

"Don't you do it. I don't hear the dogs and horses yet; you've got time to crowd through the brush and get up the crick a little ways; then you take to the water and wade down to me and get in—that'll throw the dogs off the scent."

They done it, and soon as they was aboard I lit out for our tow-head, and in about five or ten minutes we heard the dogs and the men away off, shouting. We heard them come along towards the crick, but couldn't see them; they seemed to stop and fool around a while; then, as we got further and further away all the time, we couldn't hardly hear them at all; by the time we had left a mile of woods behind us and struck the river, everything was quiet, and we paddled over to the tow-head and hid in the cotton-woods and was safe.

One of these fellows was about seventy, or upwards, and had a bald head and very gray whiskers. He had an old battered-up slouch hat on, and a greasy blue woolen shirt, and ragged old blue jeans britches stuffed into his boot tops, and home-knit galluses—no, he only had one. He had an old long-tailed blue jeans coat with slick brass buttons, flung over his arm, and both of them had big fat ratty-looking carpet-bags.

The other fellow was about thirty and dressed about as ornery. After breakfast we all laid off and talked, and the first thing that comes out was that these chaps didn't know one another.

"What got you into trouble?" says the baldhead to t'other chap.

"Well, I'd been selling an article to take the tartar off the teeth—and it does take it off, too, and generly the enamel along with it—but I staid about one night longer than I ought to, and was just in the act of sliding out when I ran across you on the trail this side of town, and you told me they were coming, and begged me to help you to get off. So I told you I was expecting trouble myself and would scatter out *with* you. That's the whole yarn—what's yourn?"

"Well, I'd ben a-runnin' a little temperance revival thar, 'bout a week, and was the pet of the women-folks, big and little, for I was makin' it mighty warm for the rummies, I *tell* you, and takin' as much as five or six dollars a night—ten cents a head, children and niggers free—and business a growin' all the time; when somehow or another a little report got around, last night, that I had a way of puttin' in my time with a private jug, on the sly. A nigger rousted me out this mornin', and told me the people was gatherin' on the quiet, with their dogs and horses, and they'd be along pretty soon and give me 'bout half an hour's start, and then run me down, if they could; and if they got me they'd tar and feather me and ride me on a rail, sure. I didn't wait for no breakfast—I warn't hungry."

"Old man," says the young one, "I reckon we might double-team it together; what do you think?"

"I ain't undisposed. What's your line—mainly?"

"Jour printer, by trade; do a little in patent medicines; theatre-actor—tragedy, you know; take a turn at mesmerism and phrenology when there's a chance; teach singing-geography school for a change; sling a lecture, sometimes oh, I do lots of things—most anything that comes handy, so it ain't work. What's your lay?"

"I've done considerble in the doctoring way in my time. Layin' on o' hands is my best holt—for cancer, and paralysis, and sich things; and I k'n tell a fortune pretty good, when I've got somebody along to find out the facts for me. Preachin's my line, too; and workin' camp-meetin's; and missionaryin around."

Nobody never said anything for a while; then the young man hove a sigh and says—

"Alas!"

"What're you alassin' about?" says the baldhead.

"To think I should have lived to be leading such a life, and be degraded down into such company." And he begun to wipe the corner of his eye with a rag.

"Dern your skin, ain't the company good enough for you?" says the baldhead, pretty pert and uppish.

"Yes, it *is* good enough for me; it's as good as I deserve; for who fetched me so low, when I was so high? *I* did myself. I don't blame *you,* gentlemen—far from it; I don't blame anybody. I deserve it all. Let the cold world do its worst; one thing I know—there's a grave somewhere for me. The world may go on just as its always done, and take everything from me—loved ones, property, everything—but it can't take that. Some day I'll lie down in it and forget it all, and my poor broken heart will be at rest." He went on a-wiping.

"Drot your pore broken heart," says the baldhead; "what are you heaving your pore broken heart at *us* f'r? *We* hain't done nothing."

"No, I know you haven't. I ain't blaming you, gentlemen. I brought myself down—yes, I did it myself. It's right I should suffer—perfectly right—I don't make any moan."

"Brought you down from whar? Whar was you brought down from?"

"Ah, you would not believe me; the world never believes—let it pass—'tis no matter. The secret of my birth—"

"The secret of your birth? Do you mean to say—"

"Gentlemen," says the young man, very solemn, "I will reveal it to you, for I feel I may have confidence in you. By rights I am a duke!"

Jim's eyes bugged out when he heard that; and I reckon mine did, too. Then the baldhead says: "No! you can't mean it?"

"Yes. My great-grandfather, eldest son of the Duke of Bridgewater, fled to this country about the end of the last century, to breathe the pure air of freedom; married here, and died, leaving a son, his own father dying about the same time. The second son of the late duke seized the title and estates—the infant real duke was ignored. I am the lineal descendant of that infant—I am the rightful Duke of Bridgewater; and here am I, forlorn, torn from my high estate, hunted of men, despised by the cold world, ragged, worn, heart-broken, and degraded to the companionship of felons on a raft!"

Jim pitied him ever so much, and so did I. We tried to comfort him, but he said it warn't much use, he couldn't be much comforted; said if we was a mind to acknowledge him, that would do him more good than most anything else; so we said we would, if he would tell us how. He said we ought to bow, when we spoke to him, and say "Your Grace," or "My Lord," or "Your Lordship"—and he wouldn't mind it if we called him plain "Bridgewater," which he said was a title, anyway, and not a name; and one of us ought to wait on him at dinner, and do any little thing for him he wanted done.

Well, that was all easy, so we done it. All through dinner Jim stood around and waited on him, and says, "Will yo' Grace have some o' dis, or some o' dat?" and so on, and a body could see it was mighty pleasing to him.

But the old man got pretty silent, by-and-by—didn't have much to say, and didn't look pretty comfortable over all that petting that was going on around that duke. He seemed to have something on his mind. So, along in the afternoon, he says:

"Looky here, Bilgewater," he says, "I'm nation sorry for you, but you ain't the only person that's had troubles like that."

"No?"

"No, you ain't. You ain't the only person that's ben snaked down wrongfully out'n a high place."

"Alas!"

"No, you ain't the only person that's had a secret of his birth." And by jing, *he* begins to cry.

"Hold! What do you mean?"

"Bilgewater, kin I trust you?" says the old man, still sort of sobbing.

"To the bitter death!" He took the old man by the hand and squeezed it, and says, "The secret of your being: speak!"

"Bilgewater, I am the late Dauphin!"

You bet you Jim and me stared, this time. Then the duke says:

"You are what?"

"Yes, my friend, it is too true—your eyes is lookin' at this very moment on the pore disappeared Dauphin, Looy the Seventeen, son of Looy the Sixteen and Marry Antonette."

"You! At your age! No! You mean you're the late Charlemagne; you must be six or seven hundred years old, at the very least."

"Trouble has done it, Bilgewater, trouble has done it; trouble has brung these gray hairs and this premature balditude. Yes, gentlemen, you see before you, in blue jeans and misery, the wanderin', exiled, trampled-on and sufferin' rightful King of France."

Well, he cried and took on so, that me and Jim didn't know hardly what to do, we was so sorry—and so glad and proud we'd got him with us, too. So we set in, like we done before with the duke, and tried to comfort *him*. But he said it warn't no use, nothing but to be dead and done with it all could do him any good; though he said it often made him feel easier and better for a while if people treated him according to his rights, and got down on one knee to speak to him, and always called him "Your Majesty," and waited on him first at meals, and didn't set down in his presence till he asked them. So Jim and me set to majestying him, and doing this and that and t'other for him, and standing up till he told us we might set down. This done him heaps of good, and so he got cheerful and comfortable. But the duke kind of soured on him, and didn't look a bit satisfied with the way things was going; still, the king acted real friendly towards him, and said the duke's great-grandfather and all the other Dukes of Bilgewater was a good deal thought of by *his* father and was allowed to come to the palace considerable; but the duke staid huffy a good while, till by-and-by the king says:

"Like as not we got to be together a blamed long time, on this h-yer raft, Bilgewater, and so what's the use o' your bein' sour? It'll only make things oncomfortable. It ain't my fault I warn't born a duke, it ain't your fault you warn't born a king—so what's the use to worry? Make the best o'things the way you find 'em, says I—that's my motto. This ain't no bad thing that we've struck here—plenty grub and an easy life—come, give us your hand, Duke, and less all be friends."

The duke done it, and Jim and me was pretty glad to see it. It took away all the uncomfortableness, and we felt mighty good over it, because it would a been a miserable business to have any unfriendliness on the raft; for what you want, above all things, on a raft, is for everybody to be satisfied, and feel right and kind towards the others.

It didn't take me long to make up my mind that these liars warn't no kings nor dukes, at all, but just low-down humbugs and frauds. But I never said nothing, never let on; kept it to myself; it's the best way; then you don't have no quarrels, and don't get into no trouble. If they wanted us to call them kings and dukes, I hadn't no objections, 'long as it would keep peace in the family; and it warn't no use to tell Jim, so I didn't tell him. If I never learnt nothing else out of pap, I learnt that the best way to get along with his kind of people is to let them have their own way.

Chapter 20

. . . When we go there, there warn't nobody stirring; streets empty, and perfectly dead and still, like Sunday. We found a sick nigger sunning himself in a back yard, and he said everybody that warn't too young or too sick or too old, was gone to camp-meeting, about two mile back in the woods. The king got the directions, and allowed he'd go and work that camp-meeting for all it was worth, and I might go, too. . . .

. . . We got there in about half an hour, fairly dripping, for it was a most awful hot day. There was as much as a thousand people there, from twenty mile around. The woods was full of teams and wagons, hitched everywheres, feeding out of the wagon troughs and stomping to keep off the flies. There was sheds made out of poles and roofed over with branches, where they had lemonade and gingerbread to sell, and piles of watermelons and green corn and such-like truck.

The preaching was going on under the same kinds of sheds, only they was bigger and held crowds of people. The benches was made out of outside slabs of logs, with holes bored in the round side to drive sticks into for legs. They didn't have no backs. The preachers had high platforms to stand on, at one end of the sheds. The women had on sun-bonnets; and some had linsey-woolsey frocks, some gingham ones, and a few of the young ones had on calico. Some of the young men was bare-footed, and some of the children didn't have on any clothes but just a tow-linen shirt. Some of the old women was knitting, and some of the young folks was courting on the sly.

The first shed we come to, the preacher was lining out a hymn. He lined out two lines, everybody sung it, and it was kind of grand to hear it, there was so many of them and they done it in such a rousing way; then he lined out two more for them to sing—and so on. The people woke up more and more, and sung louder and louder; and towards the end, some begun to groan, and some begun to shout. Then the preacher begun to preach; and begun in earnest, too; and went weaving first to one side of the platform and then the other, and then a leaning down over the front of it, with his arms and his body going all the time, and shouting his words out with all his might; and every now and then he would hold up his Bible and spread it open, and kind of pass it around this way and that, shouting, "It's the brazen serpent in the wilderness! Look upon it and live!" And people would shout out, "Glory!—A-a-*men!*" And so he went on, and the people groaning and crying and saying amen:

"Oh, come to the mourners' bench! come, black with sin! (*amen!*) come, sick and sore! (*amen!*) come, lame and halt, and blind! (*amen!*) come, pore and needy, sunk in shame! (*a-a-men!*) come all that's worn, and soiled, and suffering!—come with a broken spirit! come with a contrite heart! come in your rags and sin and dirt! the waters that cleanse is free, the door of heaven stands open—oh, enter in and be at rest!" (*a-a-men! glory, glory hallelujah!*)

And so on. You couldn't make out what the preacher said, any more, on account of the shouting and crying. Folks got up, everywheres in the crowd, and worked their way, just by main strength, to the mourners' bench, with the tears running down their faces; and when all the mourners had got up there to the front benches in a crowd, they sung, and shouted, and flung themselves down on the straw, just crazy and wild.

Well, the first I knowed, the king got agoing; and you could hear him over everybody; and next he went a-charging up on to the platform and the preacher he begged him to speak to the people, and he done it. He told them he was a pirate—been a pirate for thirty years, out in the Indian Ocean, and his crew was thinned out considerable, last spring, in a fight, and he was home now, to take out some fresh men, and thanks to goodness he'd been robbed last night, and put ashore off of a steamboat without a cent, and he was glad of it, it was the blessedest thing that ever happened to him, because he was a changed man now, and happy for the first time in his life; and poor as he was, he was going to start right off and work his way back to the Indian Ocean and put in the rest of his life trying to turn the pirates into the true path; for he could do it better than anybody else, being acquainted with all the pirate crews in that ocean;

and though it would take him a long time to get there, without money, he would get there anyway, and every time he convinced a pirate he would say to him, "Don't you thank me, don't you give me no credit, it all belongs to them dear people in Pokeville camp-meeting, natural brothers and benefactors of the race—and that dear preacher there, the truest friend a pirate ever had!"

And then he busted into tears, and so did everybody. Then somebody sings out, "Take up a collection for him, take up a collection!" Well, a half a dozen made a jump to do it, but somebody sings out, "Let *him* pass the hat around!" Then everybody said it, the preacher too.

So the king went all through the crowd with his hat, swabbing his eyes, and blessing the people and praising them and thanking them for being so good to the poor pirates away off there; and every little while the prettiest kind of girls, with the tears running down their cheeks, would up and ask him would he let them kiss him, for to remember him by; and he always done it; and some of them he hugged and kissed as many as five or six times—and he was invited to stay a week; and everybody wanted him to live in their houses, and said they'd think it was an honor; but he said as this was the last day of the camp-meeting he couldn't do no good, and besides he was in a sweat to get to the Indian Ocean right off and go to work on the pirates.

When we got back to the raft and he come to count up, he found he had collected eighty-seven dollars and seventy-five cents. And then he had fetched away a three-gallon jug of whisky, too, that he found under a wagon when we was starting home through the woods. The king said, take it all around, it laid over any day he'd ever put in in the missionarying line. He said it warn't no use talking, heathens don't amount to shucks, alongside of pirates, to work a camp-meeting with. . . .

Chapter 31

. . . Once I said to myself it would be a thousand times better for Jim to be a slave at home where his family was, as long as he'd *got* to be a slave, and so I'd better write a letter to Tom Sawyer and tell him to tell Miss Watson where he was. But I soon give up that notion, for two things: she'd be mad and disgusted at his rascality and ungratefulness for leaving her, and so she'd sell him straight down the river again; and if she didn't, everybody naturally despises an ungrateful nigger, and they'd make Jim feel it all the time, and so he'd feel ornery and disgraced. And then think of *me!* It would get all around, that Huck Finn helped a nigger to get his freedom; and if I was to ever see anybody from that town again, I'd be ready to get down and lick his boots for shame. That's just the way: a person does a low-down thing, and then he don't want to take no consequences of it. Thinks as long as he can hide it, it ain't no disgrace. That was my fix exactly. The more I studied about this, the more my conscience went to grinding me, and the more wicked and low-down and ornery I got to feeling. And at last, when it hit me all of a sudden that here was the plain hand of Providence slapping me in the face and letting me know my wickedness was being watched all the time from up there in heaven, whilst I was stealing a poor old woman's nigger that hadn't ever done me no harm, and now was showing me there's One that's always on the lookout, and ain't agoing to allow no such miserable doings to go only just so fur and no further, I most dropped in my tracks I was so scared. Well, I tried the best I could to kinder soften it up somehow for myself, by saying I was brung up wicked, and so I warn't so much to blame; but something inside of me kept saying, "There was the Sunday school, you could a gone to it; and if you'd a done it they'd a learnt you, there, that people that acts as I'd been acting about that nigger goes to everlasting fire."

It made me shiver. And I about made up my mind to pray; and see if I couldn't try to quit being the kind of a boy I was, and be better. So I kneeled down. But the words wouldn't come. Why wouldn't they? It warn't no use to try and hide it from Him. Nor from *me,* neither. I knowed very well why they wouldn't come. It was because my heart warn't right; it was because I warn't square; it was because I was playing double. I was letting *on* to give up sin, but away inside of me I was holding on to the biggest one of all. I was trying to make my mouth *say* I would do the right thing and the clean thing and go and write to that nigger's owner and tell where he was; but deep down in me I knowed it was a lie—and He knowed it. You can't pray a lie—I found that out.

So I was full of trouble, full as I could be, and didn't know what to do. At last I had an idea; and I says, I'll go and write the letter—and *then* see if I can pray. Why, it was astonishing, the way I felt as light as a feather, right straight off, and my troubles all gone. So I got a piece of paper and a pencil, all glad and excited, and set down and wrote:

> Miss Watson your runaway nigger Jim is down here two mile below Pikesville and Mr. Phelps has got him and he will give him up for the reward if you send.
>
> Huck Finn.

I felt good and all washed clean of sin for the first time I had ever felt so in my life, and I knowed I could pray now but I didn't do it straight off, but laid the paper down and set there thinking—thinking how good it was all this happened so and how near I come to being lost and going to hell. And went on thinking. And got to thinking over our trip down the river; and I see Jim before me, all the time, in the day, and in the night-time, sometimes moonlight, sometimes storms, and we a floating along, talking, and singing, and laughing. But somehow I couldn't seem to strike no places to harden me against him, but only the other kind. I'd see him standing my watch on top of his'n, stead of calling me, so I could go on sleeping; and see him how glad he was when I come back out of the fog; and when I come to him again in the swamp, up there where the feud was; and such-like times; and would always call me honey, and pet me, and do everything he could think of for me, and how good he always was; and at last I struck the time I saved him by telling the men we had small-pox aboard, and he was so grateful, and said I was the best friend old Jim ever had in the world, and the *only* one he's got now; and then I happened to look around, and see that paper.

It was a close place. I took it up, and held it in my hand. I was a trembling, because I'd got to decide, forever, betwixt two things, and I knowed it. I studied a minute, sort of holding my breath, and then says to myself:

"All right, then, I'll *go* to hell"—and tore it up.

It was awful thoughts, and awful words, but they was said. And I let them stay said; and never thought no more about reforming. I shoved the whole thing out of my head; and said I would take up wickedness again, which was in my line, being brung up to it, and the other warn't. And for a starter, I would go to work and steal Jim out of slavery again; and if I could think up anything worse, I would do that, too; because as long as I was in, and in for good, I might as well go the whole hog. . . .

A Connecticut Yankee in King Arthur's Court

In A Connecticut Yankee in King Arthur's Court *(1889) Twain wrote a double-edged satire, criticizing medieval English belief in nobility and religion while also criticizing nineteenth-century American reliance upon mercantilism and technology. Hank Morgan, a shop foreman at an arms factory, receives a blow to the head and wakes up, much to his astonishment, in King Arthur's Britain. The book narrates his conflicts with feudal customs and beliefs. Hank's technological superiority soon earns him the title of "The Boss." As Hank begins to organize the country with the help of nineteenth-century devices like telephones and bicycles, the satire becomes reciprocal. For example, Hank Morgan sees a hermit making ritualized, repeated praying motions and hitches him up to a sewing machine to produce garments.*

The contemporary relevance of the satire in the text was greatly increased when the drawings of Dan Beard were added. Beard perceived the social criticisms and drew recognizable faces. For instance, Beard gave the slave driver Jay Gould's face.

Twain was investing heavily and disastrously in the Paige typesetting machine while composing and revising the book. Ultimately, the failure of technology in the novel mirrored the breakdown of this machine. The concluding segment, with the battle between the feudal knights and the small band of technologists, has frequently been perceived as a frightening conclusion, a devastating account prophetic of a war-ravaged landscape, as bodies drape from the wires. The sheer horror of the scene approaches the way the world looks after any war, pre- or post-atomic.

The novel presented a fictional forum for many of Twain's beliefs; the temporal and spatial dislocation provided an aesthetic distance for harsh social criticism. Twain was forming his own explanations for human action, charging that environmental influences largely determine beliefs. Obviously such a

The Slave Driver

"THIS WOULD UNDERMINE THE CHURCH."

THE CHURCH, THE KING, THE NOBLEMAN, AND THE FREEMAN.

"BROTHER!—TO DIRT LIKE THIS?"

"BROTHER!—TO DIRT LIKE THIS?"

"BROTHER!—TO DIRT LIKE THIS?"

POLICY
CHURCH
STATE
IGNORANCE
SUPERSTITION
SLAVERY
I Command the fell spirit that possesses
"the Holy Fountain, to now disgorge into the skies, all
like infernal fires that still remains
in him!"

They have a right to their own view.
I only stand to this

6th CENTURY
LABOR
LABOR
Sister your blind is disarranged

theory subverts the ability of social leaders to claim exclusive correctness for a policy or belief.

CHAPTER 8

To be vested with enormous authority is a fine thing; but to have the on-looking world consent to it is a finer. The tower episode solidified my power, and made it impregnable. If any were perchance disposed to be jealous and critical before that, they experienced a change of heart, now. There was not any one in the kingdom who would have considered it good judgment to meddle with my matters.

I was fast getting adjusted to my situation and circumstances. For a time, I used to wake up, mornings, and smile at my "dream," and listen for the Colt's factory whistle; but that sort of thing played itself out, gradually, and at last I was fully able to realize that I was actually living in the sixth century, and in Arthur's court, not a lunatic asylum. After that, I was just as much at home in that century as I could have been in any other; and as for preference, I wouldn't have traded it for the twentieth. Look at the opportunities here for a man of knowledge, brains, pluck and enterprise to sail in and grow up with the country. The grandest field that ever was; and all my own; not a competitor; not a man who wasn't a baby to me in acquirements and capacities; whereas, what would I amount to in the twentieth century? I should be foreman of a factory, that is about all; and could drag a seine down-street any day and catch a hundred better men than myself.

What a jump I had made! I couldn't keep from thinking about it, and contemplating it, just as one does who has struck oil. There was nothing back of me that could approach it, unless it might be Joseph's case; and Joseph's only approached it, it didn't equal it, quite. For it stands to reason that as Joseph's splendid financial ingenuities advantaged nobody but the king, the general public must have regarded him with a good deal of disfavor, whereas I had done my entire public a kindness in sparing the sun, and was popular by reason of it.

I was no shadow of a king; I was the substance; the king himself was the shadow. My power was colossal; and it was not a mere name, as such things have generally been, it was the genuine article. I stood here, at the very spring and source of the second great period of the world's history; and could see the trickling stream of that history gather, and deepen and broaden, and roll its mighty tides down the far centuries; and I could note the upspringing of adventurers like myself in the shelter of its long array of thrones: De Montforts, Gavestons, Mortimers, Villierses; the war-making, campaign-directing wantons of France, and Charles the Second's sceptre-wielding drabs; but nowhere in the procession was my full-sized fellow visible. I was a Unique; and glad to know that that fact could not be dislodged or challenged for thirteen centuries and a half, for sure.

Yes, in power I was equal to the king. At the same time there was another power that was a trifle stronger than both of us put together. That was the Church. I do not wish to disguise that fact. I couldn't, if I wanted to. But never mind about that, now; it will show up, in its proper place, later on. It didn't cause me any trouble in the beginning—at least any of consequence.

Well, it was a curious country, and full of interest. And the people! They were the quaintest and simplest and trustingest race; why, they were nothing but rabbits. It was pitiful for a person born in a wholesome free atmosphere to listen to their humble and hearty outpourings of loyalty toward their king and Church and nobility; as if they had any more occasion to love and honor king and Church and noble than a slave has to love and honor the lash, or a dog has to love and honor the stranger that kicks him! Why, dear me, *any* kind of royalty, howsoever modified, *any* kind of aristocracy, howsoever pruned, is rightly an insult; but if you are born and brought up under that sort of arrangement you probably never find it out for yourself, and don't believe it when somebody else tells you. It is enough to make a body ashamed of his race to think of the sort of froth that has always occupied its thrones without shadow of right or reason, and the seventh-rate people that have always figured as its aristocracies—a company of monarchs and nobles who, as a rule, would have achieved only poverty and obscurity if left, like their betters, to their own exertions.

The most of King Arthur's British nation were slaves, pure and simple, and bore that name, and wore the iron collar on their necks; and the rest were slaves in fact, but without the name; they imagined themselves men and freemen, and called themselves so. The truth was, the nation as a body was in the world for one object, and one only: to grovel before king and Church and noble; to slave for them, sweat blood for them, starve that they might be fed, work that they might play, drink misery to the dregs that they might be happy, go naked that they might wear silks and jewels, pay taxes that they might be spared from paying them, be familiar all their lives with the degrading language and postures of adulation that they might walk in pride and think themselves the gods of this world. And for all this, the thanks they got were cuffs and contempt; and so poor-spirited were they that they took even this sort of attention as an honor.

Inherited ideas are a curious thing, and interesting to observe and examine. I had mine, the king and his people had theirs. In both cases they flowed in ruts worn deep by time and habit, and the man who should have proposed to divert them by reason and argument would have had a long contract on his hands. For instance, those people had inherited the idea that all men without title and a long pedigree, whether they had great natural gifts and acquirements or hadn't, were creatures of no more consideration than so many animals, bugs, insects; whereas I had inherited the idea that human daws who can consent to masquerade in the peacock-shams of inherited dignities and unearned titles, are of no good but to be laughed at. The way I was looked upon

"INHERITED IDEAS ARE A CURIOUS THING."

was odd, but it was natural. You know how the keeper and the public regard the elephant in the menagerie: well, that is the idea. They are full of admiration of his vast bulk and his prodigious strength; they speak with pride of the fact that he can do a hundred marvels which are far and away beyond their own powers; and they speak with the same pride of the fact that in his wrath he is able to drive a thousand men before him. But does that make him one of *them?* No; the raggedest tramp in the pit would smile at the idea. He couldn't comprehend it; couldn't take it in; couldn't in any remote way conceive of it. Well, to the king, the nobles, and all the nation, down to the very slaves and tramps, I was just that kind of an elephant, and nothing more. I was admired, also feared; but it was as an animal is admired and feared. The animal is not reverenced, neither was I; I was not even respected. I had no pedigree, no inherited title; so in the king's and nobles' eyes I was mere dirt; the people regarded me with wonder and awe, but there was no reverence mixed with it; through the force of inherited ideas they were not able to conceive of anything being entitled to that except pedigree and lordship. There you see the hand of that awful power, the Roman Catholic Church. In two or three little centuries it had converted a nation of men to a nation of worms. Before the day of the Church's supremacy in the world, men were men, and held their heads up, and had a man's pride and spirit and independence; and what of greatness and position a person got, he got mainly by achievement, not by birth. But then the Church came to the front, with an axe to grind; and she was wise, subtle, and knew more than one way to skin a cat—or a nation; she invented "divine right of kings," and propped it all around, brick by brick, with the Beatitudes—wrenching them from their good purpose to make them fortify an evil one; she preached (to the commoner,) humility, obedience to superiors, the beauty of self-sacrifice; she preached (to the commoner,) meekness under insult; preached (still to the commoner, always to the commoner,) patience, meanness of spirit, non-resistance under oppression; and she introduced heritable ranks and aristocracies, and taught all the Christian populations of the earth to bow down to them and worship them. Even down to my birth-century that poison was still in the blood of Christendom, and the best of English commoners were still content to see his inferiors imprudently continuing to hold a number of positions, such as lordships and the throne, to which the grotesque laws of his country did not allow him to aspire; in fact he was not merely contented with this strange condition of things, he was even able to persuade himself that he was proud of it. It seems to show that there isn't anything you can't stand, if you are only born and bred to it. Of course that taint, that reverence for rank and title, had been in our American blood, too—I know that; but when I left America it had disappeared—at least to all intents and purposes. The remnant of it was restricted to the dudes and dudesses. When a disease has worked its way down to that level, it may fairly be said to be out of the system.

But to return to my anomalous position in King Arthur's kingdom. Here I was, a giant among pigmies, a man among children, a master intelligence among intellectual moles: by all rational measurement the one and only actually great man in that whole British world; and yet there and then, just as in the remote England of my birth-time, the sheep-witted earl who could claim long descent from a king's leman, acquired at second-hand from the slums of London, was a better man than I was. Such a personage was fawned upon in Arthur's realm and reverently looked up to by everybody, even though his dispositions were as mean as his intelligence, and his morals as base as his lineage. There were times when *he* could sit down in the king's presence, but I couldn't. I could have got a title easily enough, and that would have raised me a large step in everybody's eyes; even in the king's, the giver of it. But I didn't ask for it; and I declined it when it was offered. I couldn't have enjoyed such a thing with my notions; and it wouldn't have been fair, anyway, because as far back as I could go, our tribe had always been short of the bar sinister. I couldn't have felt really and satisfactorily fine and proud and set-up over any title except one that should come from the nation itself, the only legitimate source; and such an one I hoped to win; and in the course of years of honest and honorable endeavor, I did win it and did wear it with a high and clean pride. This title fell casually from the lips of a blacksmith, one day, in a village, was caught up as a happy thought and tossed from mouth to mouth with a laugh and an affirmative vote; in ten days it had swept the kingdom, and was become as familiar as the king's name. I was never known by any other designation afterwards, whether in the nation's talk or in grave debate upon matters of state at the council-board of the sovereign. This title, translated into modern speech, would be THE BOSS. Elected by the nation. That suited me. And it was a pretty high title. There were very few THE's, and I was one of them. If you spoke of the duke, or the earl, or the bishop, how could anybody tell which one you meant? But if you spoke of The King or The Queen or The Boss, it was different.

Well, I liked the king, and *as* king I respected him—respected the office; at least respected it as much as I was capable of respecting any unearned supremacy; but as *men* I looked down upon him and his nobles—privately. And he and they liked me, and respected my office; but as an animal, without birth or sham title, they looked down upon me—and were not particularly private about it, either. I didn't charge for my opinion about them, and they didn't charge for their opinion about me: the account was square, the books balanced, everybody was satisfied.

CHAPTER 10

. . . I was pretty well satisfied with what I had already accomplished. In various quiet nooks and corners I had the beginnings of all sorts of industries under way—nuclei of future vast factories, the iron and steel missionaries of my future civilization. In these were gathered together the brightest young minds I could find, and I kept agents out raking the country for more, all the time. I was training a crowd of ignorant folk into experts—experts in every sort of handiwork and scientific calling. These nurseries of mine went smoothly and privately along undisturbed in their obscure country retreats, for nobody was allowed to come into their precincts without a special permit—for I was afraid of the Church.

I had started a teacher-factory and a lot of Sunday-schools the first thing; as a result, I now had an admirable system of graded schools in full blast in those places, and also a complete variety of Protestant congregations all in a prosperous and growing condition. Everybody could be any kind of a Christian he wanted to; there was perfect freedom in that matter. But I confined public religious teaching to the churches and the Sunday-schools, permitting nothing of it in my other educational buildings. I could have given my own sect the preference and made everybody a Presbyterian without any trouble, but that would have been to affront a law of human nature: spiritual wants and instincts are as various in the human family as are physical appetites, complexions, and features, and a man is only at his best, morally, when he is equipped with the religious garment whose color and shape and size most nicely accommodate themselves to the spiritual complexion, angularities, and stature of the individual who wears it; and besides I was afraid of a united Church; it makes a mighty power, the mightiest conceivable, and then when it by and by gets into selfish hands, as it is always bound to do, it means death to human liberty, and paralysis to human thought. . . .

Chapter 13

. . . We were off before sunrise, Sandy riding and I limping along behind. In half an hour we came upon a group of ragged poor creatures who had assembled to mend the thing which was regarded as a road. They were as humble as animals to me; and when I proposed to breakfast with them, they were so flattered, so overwhelmed by this extraordinary condescension of mine that at first they were not able to believe that I was in earnest. My lady put up her scornful lip and withdrew to one side; she said in their hearing that she would as soon think of eating with the other cattle—a remark which embarrassed these poor devils merely because it referred to them, and not because it insulted or offended them, for it didn't. And yet they were not slaves, not chattels. By a sarcasm of law and phrase they were freemen. Seven-tenths of the free population of the country were of just their class and degree: small "independent" farmers, artisans, etc.; which is to say, they were the nation, the actual Nation; they were about all of it that was useful, or worth saving, or really respectworthy; and to subtract them would have been to subtract the Nation and leave behind some dregs, some refuse, in the shape of a king, nobility and gentry, idle, unproductive, acquainted mainly with the arts of wasting and destroying, and of no sort of use or value in any rationally constructed world. And yet, by ingenious contrivance, this gilded minority, instead of being in the tail of the procession where it belonged, was marching head up and banners flying, at the other end of it; had elected itself to be the Nation, and these innumerable clams had permitted it so long that they had come at last to accept it as a truth; and not only that, but to believe it right and as it should be. The priests had told their fathers and themselves that this ironical state of things was ordained of God; and so, not reflecting upon how unlike God it would be to amuse himself with sarcasms, and especially such poor transparent ones as this, they had dropped the matter there and become respectfully quiet.

The talk of these meek people had a strange enough sound in a formerly American ear. They were freemen, but they could not leave the estates of their lord or their bishop without his permission; they could not prepare their own bread, but must have their corn ground and their bread baked at his mill and his bakery, and pay roundly for the same; they could not sell a piece of their own property without paying him a handsome percentage of the proceeds, nor buy a piece of somebody else's without remembering him in cash for the privilege; they had to harvest his grain for him gratis, and be ready to come at a moment's notice, leaving their own crop to destruction by the threatened storm; they had to let him plant fruit trees in their fields, and then keep their indignation to themselves when his heedless fruit gatherers trampled the grain around the trees; they had to smother their anger when his hunting parties galloped through their fields laying waste the result of their patient toil; they were not allowed to keep doves themselves, and when the swarms from my lord's dovecote settled on their crops they must not lose their temper and kill a bird, for awful would the penalty be; when the harvest was at last gathered, then came the procession of robbers to levy their blackmail upon it: first the Church carted off its fat tenth, then the king's commissioner took his twentieth, then my lord's people made a mighty inroad upon the remainder; after which, the skinned freeman had liberty to bestow the remnant in his barn, in case it was worth the trouble; there were taxes, and taxes, and taxes, and more taxes, and taxes again, and yet other taxes—upon this free and independent pauper, but none upon his lord the baron or the bishop, none upon the wasteful nobility or the all-devouring Church; if the baron would sleep unvexed, the freeman must sit up all night after his day's work and whip the ponds to keep the frogs quiet; if the freeman's daughter—but no, that last infamy of monarchical government is unprintable; and finally, if the freeman, grown desperate with his tortures, found his life unendurable under such conditions, and sacrificed it and fled to death for mercy and refuge, the gentle Church condemned him to eternal fire, the gentle law buried him at midnight at the crossroads with a stake through his back, and his master the baron or the bishop confiscated all his property and turned his widow and his orphans out of doors.

And here were these freemen assembled in the early morning to work on their lord the bishop's road three days each—gratis; every head of a family, and every son of a family, three days each, gratis, and a day or so added for their servants. Why, it was like reading about France and the French, before the ever-memorable and blessed Revolution, which swept a thousand years of such villany away in one swift tidal wave of blood—one: a settlement of that hoary debt in the proportion of half a drop of blood for each hogshead of it that had been pressed by slow tortures out of that people in the weary stretch of ten centuries of wrong and shame and misery the like of which was not to be mated but in hell. There were two "Reigns of Terror," if we would but remember it and consider it; the one wrought murder in hot passion, the other in heartless cold blood; the one lasted mere months, the other had lasted a thousand years; the one inflicted death upon ten thousand persons, the other upon a hundred millions; but our shudders are all for the "horrors" of the minor Terror, the momentary Terror, so to speak; whereas, what is the horror of swift death by the ax, compared with lifelong death from hunger, cold, insult, cruelty, and heartbreak? What is swift death by lightning compared with death by slow fire at the stake? A city cemetery could contain the coffins filled by that brief Terror which we have all been so diligently taught to shiver at and mourn over; but all France could hardly contain the coffins filled by that older and real Terror—that unspeakably bitter and awful Terror which none of us has been taught to see in its vastness or pity as it deserves.

These poor ostensible freemen who were sharing their breakfast and their talk with me, were as full of humble reverence for their king and Church and nobility as their worst enemy could desire. There was something pitifully ludicrous about it. I asked them if they supposed a nation of people ever existed, who, with a free vote in every man's hand, would elect that a single family and its descendants should reign over it forever, whether gifted or boobies, to the exclusion of all other families—including the voter's; and would also elect that a certain hundred families should be raised to dizzy summits of rank, and clothed on with offensive transmissible glories and privileges to the exclusion of the rest of the nation's families—*including his own.*

They all looked unhit, and said they didn't know; that they had never thought about it before, and it hadn't ever occurred to them that a nation could be so situated that every man *could* have a say in the government. I said I had seen one—and that it would last until it had an Established Church. Again they were all unhit—at first. But presently one man looked up and asked me to state that proposition again; and state it slowly, so it could soak into his understanding. I did it; and after a little he had the idea, and he brought his fist down and said *he* didn't believe a nation where every man had a vote would voluntarily get down in the mud and dirt in any such way; and that to steal from a nation its will and preference must be a crime and the first of all crimes.

I said to myself:

"This one's a man. If I were backed by enough of his sort, I would make a strike for the welfare of this country, and try to prove myself its loyalest citizen by making a wholesome change in its system of government."

You see my kind of loyalty was loyalty to one's country, not to its institutions or its officeholders. The country is the real thing, the substantial thing, the eternal thing; it is the thing to watch over, and care for, and be loyal to; institutions are extraneous, they are its mere clothing, and clothing can wear out, become ragged, cease to be comfortable, cease to protect the body from winter, disease, and death. To be loyal to rags, to shout for rags, to worship rags, to die for rags—that is a loyalty of unreason, it is pure animal; it belongs to monarchy, was invented by monarchy; let monarchy keep it. I was from Connecticut, whose Constitution declares "that all political power is inherent in the people, and all free governments are founded on their authority and instituted for their benefit; and that they have *at all times* an undeniable and indefeasible right to *alter their form of government* in such a manner as they may think expedient."

Under that gospel, the citizen who thinks he sees that the commonwealth's political clothes are worn out, and yet holds his peace and does not agitate for a new suit, is disloyal; he is a traitor. That he may be the only one who thinks he sees this decay, does not excuse him; it is his duty to agitate any way, and it is the duty of the others to vote him down if they do not see the matter as he does.

And now here I was, in a country where a right to say how the country should be governed was restricted to six persons in each thousand of its population. For the nine hundred and ninety-four to express dissatisfaction with the regnant system and propose to change it, would have made the whole six shudder as one man, it would have been so disloyal, so dishonorable, such putrid black treason. So to speak, I was become a stockholder in a corporation where nine hundred and ninety-four of the members furnished all the money and did all the work, and the other six elected themselves a permanent board of direction and took all the dividends. It seemed to me that what the nine hundred and ninety-four dupes needed was a new deal. The thing that would have best suited the circus side of my nature would have been to resign the Boss-ship and get up an insurrection and turn it into a revolution; but I knew that the Jack Cade or the Wat Tyler who tries such a thing without first educating his materials up to revolution grade is almost absolutely certain to get left. I had never been accustomed to getting left, even if I do say it myself. Wherefore, the "deal" which had been for some time working into shape in my mind was of a quite different pattern from the Cade-Tyler sort.

So I did not talk blood and insurrection to that man there who sat munching black bread with that abused and mistaught herd of human sheep, but took him aside and talked matter of another sort to him. After I had finished, I got him to lend me a little ink from his veins; and with this and a sliver I wrote on a piece of bark—

Put him in the Man Factory—

and gave it to him, and said—

"Take it to the palace of Camelot and give it into the hands of Amyas le Poulet, whom I call Clarence, and he will understand."

"He is a priest, then," said the man, and some of the enthusiasm went out of his face.

"How—a priest? Didn't I tell you that no chattel of the Church, no bond-slave of pope or bishop can enter my Man Factory? Didn't I tell you that *you* couldn't enter unless your religion, whatever it might be, was your own free property?"

"Marry, it is so, and for that I was glad; wherefore it liked me or not, and bred in me a cold doubt, to hear of this priest being there."

"But he isn't a priest, I tell you."

The man looked far from satisfied. He said:

"He is not a priest, and yet can read?"

"He is not a priest and yet can read—yes, and write, too, for that matter. I taught him myself." The man's face cleared. "And it is the first thing that you yourself will be taught in that Factory—"

"I? I would give blood out of my heart to know that art. Why, I will be your slave, your—"

"No you won't, you won't be anybody's slave. Take your family and go along. Your lord the bishop will confiscate your small property, but no matter, Clarence will fix you all right."

CHAPTER 18

IN THE QUEEN'S DUNGEONS

Well, I arranged all that; and I had the man sent to his home. I had a great desire to rack the executioner; not because he was a good, painstaking and paingiving official,—for surely it was not to his discredit that he performed his functions well—but to pay him back for wantonly cuffing and otherwise distressing that young woman. The priests told me about this, and were generously hot to have him punished. Something of this disagreeable sort was turning up every now and then. I mean, episodes that showed that not all priests were frauds and self-seekers, but that many, even the great majority, of these that were down on the ground among the common people, were sincere and right-hearted, and devoted to the alleviation of human troubles and sufferings. Well, it was a thing which could not be helped, so I seldom fretted about it, and never many minutes at a time; it has never been my way to bother much about things which you can't cure. But I did not like it, for it was just the sort of thing to keep people reconciled to an Established Church. We *must* have a religion—it goes without saying—but my idea is, to have it cut up into forty free sects, so that they will police each other, as had been the case in the United States in my time. Concentration of power in a political machine is bad; and an Established Church is only a political machine; it was invented for that; it is nursed, cradled, preserved for that; it is an enemy to human liberty, and does no good which it could not better do in a split-up and scattered condition.

That wasn't law; it wasn't gospel: it was only an opinion—my opinion, and I was only a man, one man: so it wasn't worth any more than the Pope's—or any less, for that matter.

Well, I couldn't rack the executioner, neither would I overlook the just complaint of the priests. The man must be punished some how or other, so I degraded him from his office and made him leader of the band—the new one that was to be started. He begged hard, and said he couldn't play—a plausible excuse, but too thin; there wasn't a musician in the country that could.

The queen was a good deal outraged, next morning, when she found she was going to have neither Hugo's life nor his property. But I told her she must bear this cross; that while by law and custom she certainly was entitled to both the man's life and his property, there were extenuating circumstances, and so in Arthur the king's name I had pardoned him. The deer was ravaging the man's fields, and he had killed it in sudden passion, and not for gain; and he had carried it into the royal forest in the hope that that might make detection of the misdoer impossible. Confound her, I couldn't make her see that sudden passion is an extenuating circumstance in the killing of venison—or of a person—so I gave it up and let her sulk it out. I *did* think I was going to make her see it by remarking that her own sudden passion in the case of the page modified that crime.

"Crime!" she exclaimed. "How thou talkest! Crime, forsooth! Man, I am going to *pay* for him!"

Oh, it was no use to waste sense on her. Training—training is everything; training is all there is *to* a person. We speak of nature; it is folly; there is no such thing as nature; what we call by that misleading name is merely heredity and training. We have no thoughts of our own, no opinions of our own; they are transmitted to us, trained into us. All that is original in us, and therefore fairly creditable or discreditable to us, can be covered up and hidden by the point of a cambric needle, all the rest being atoms contributed by, and inherited from, a procession of ancestors that stretches back a billion years to the Adam-clam or grasshopper or monkey from whom our race has been so tediously and ostentatiously and unprofitably developed. And as for me, all that I think about in this plodding sad pilgrimage, this pathetic drift between the eternities, is to look out and humbly live a pure and high and blameless life, and save that one microscopic atom in me that is truly *me:* the rest may land in Sheol and welcome for all I care.

No, confound her, her intellect was good, she had brains enough, but her training made her an ass—that is, from a many-centuries-later point of view. To kill the page was no crime—it was her right; and upon her right she stood, serenely and unconscious of offense. She was a result of generations of training in the unexamined and unassailed belief that the law which permitted her to kill a subject when she chose was a perfectly right and righteous one.

Well, we must give even Satan his due. She deserved a compliment for one thing; and I tried to pay it, but the words stuck in my throat. She had a right to kill the boy, she was in no wise obliged to pay for him. That was law for some other people, but not for her. She knew quite well that she was doing a large and generous thing to pay for that lad, and that I ought in common fairness to come out with something handsome about it, but I couldn't—my mouth refused. I couldn't help seeing, in my fancy, that poor old grandam with the broken heart, and that fair young creature lying butchered, his little silken pomps and vanities laced with his golden blood. How could she *pay* for him? *Whom* could she pay? And so, well knowing that this woman, trained as she had been, deserved praise, even adulation, I was yet not able to utter it, trained as *I* had been. The best I could do was to fish up a compliment from outside, so to speak—and the pity of it was, that it was true:

"Madame, your people will adore you for this."

Quite true, but I meant to hang her for it some day, if I lived. Some of those laws were too bad, altogether too bad. A master might kill his slave for nothing: for mere spite, malice, or to pass the time—just as we have seen that the crowned head could do it with *his* slave, that is to say, anybody. A gentleman could kill a free commoner, and pay for him—cash or garden truck. A noble could kill a noble without expense, as far as the law was concerned, but reprisals in kind were to be expected. *Any*body could kill *some*body, except the commoner and the slave; these had no privileges. If they killed, it was murder, and the law wouldn't stand murder. It made short work of the experimenter—and of his family too, if he murdered somebody who belonged up among the ornamental ranks. If a commoner gave a noble even so much as a Damiens-scratch which didn't kill or even hurt, he got Damiens's dose for it just the same; they pulled him to rags and tatters with horses, and all the world came to see the show, and crack jokes, and have a good time; and some of the performances of the best people present were as tough, and as properly unprintable, as any that have been printed by the pleasant Casanova in his chapter about the dismemberment of Louis XV's poor awkward enemy.

I had had enough of this grisly place by this time, and wanted to leave, but I couldn't, because I had something on my mind that my conscience kept prodding me about, and wouldn't let me forget. If I had the remaking of man, he wouldn't have any conscience. It is one of the most disagreeable things connected with a person; and although it certainly does a great deal of good, it cannot be said to pay, in the long run; it would be much better to have less good and more comfort. Still, this is only my opinion, and I am only one man; others, with less experience, may think differently. They have a right to their view. I only stand to this: I have noticed my conscience for many years, and I know it is more trouble and bother to me than anything else I started with. I suppose that in the beginning I prized it, because we prize anything that is ours; and yet how foolish it was to think so. If we look at it in another way, we see how absurd it is: if I had an anvil in me would I prize it? Of course not. And yet when you come to think, there is no real difference between a conscience and an anvil—I mean for comfort. I have noticed it a thousand times.

And you could dissolve an anvil with acids, when you couldn't stand it any longer; but there isn't any way that you can work off a conscience—at least so it will stay worked off; not that I know of, anyway. . . .

Chapter 25

A COMPETITIVE EXAMINATION

When the king traveled for change of air, or made a progress, or visited a distant noble whom he wished to bankrupt with the cost of his keep, part of the administration moved with him. It was a fashion of the time. The Commission charged with the examination of candidates for posts in the army came with the king to the Valley, whereas they could have transacted their business just as well at home. And although this expedition was strictly a holiday excursion for the king, he kept some of his business functions going, just the same. He touched for the evil, as usual; he held court in the gate at sunrise and tried cases, for he was himself Chief Justice of the King's Bench.

He shone very well in this latter office. He was a wise and humane judge, and he clearly did his honest best and fairest—according to his lights. That is a large reservation. His lights—I mean his rearing—often colored his decisions. Whenever there was a dispute between a noble or gentleman and a person of lower degree, the king's leanings and sympathies were for the former class always, whether he suspected it or not. It was impossible that this should be otherwise. The blunting effects of slavery upon the slaveholder's moral perceptions are known and conceded, the world over, and a privileged class, an aristocracy, is but a band of slaveholders under another name. This has a harsh sound and yet should not be offensive to any—even to the noble himself—unless the fact itself be an offense: for the statement simply formulates a fact. The repulsive feature of slavery is the *thing,* not its name. One needs but to hear an aristocrat speak of the classes that are below him to recognize—and in but indifferently modified measure—the very air and tone of the actual slaveholder; and behind these are the slaveholder's spirit, the slaveholder's blunted feeling. They are the result of the same cause in both cases: the possessor's old and inbred custom of regarding himself as a superior being. The king's judgment wrought frequent injustices, but it was merely the fault of his training, his natural and unalterable sympathies. He was as unfitted for a judgeship as would be the average mother for the position of milk-distributor to starving children in famine time; her own children would fare a shade better than the rest. . . .

. . . Men write many fine and plausible arguments in support of monarchy, but the fact remains that where every man in a State has a vote, brutal laws are impossible. Arthur's people were of course poor material for a republic, because they had been debased so long by monarchy, and yet even they would have been intelligent enough to make short work of that law which the king had just been administering if it had been submitted to their full and free vote. There is a phrase which has grown so common in the world's mouth that it has come to seem to have sense and meaning—the sense and meaning implied when it is used—that is, the phrase which refers to this or that or the other nation as possibly being "capable of self-government"; and the implied sense of it is, that there has been a nation somewhere, sometime or other which *wasn't* capable of it—wasn't as able to govern itself as some self-appointed specialists were or would be to govern it. The master minds of all nations, in all ages, have sprung in affluent multitude from the mass of the nation, and from the mass of the nation only—not from its privileged classes; and so, no matter what the nation's intellectual grade was, whether high or low, the bulk of its ability was in the long ranks of its nameless and its poor, and so it never saw the day that it had not the material in abundance whereby to govern itself. Which is to assert an always self-proven fact: that even the best governed and most free and most enlightened monarchy is still behind the best condition attainable by its people; and that the same is true of kindred governments of lower grades, all the way down to the lowest. . . .

Chapter 28

. . . Words realize nothing, vivify nothing to you, unless you have suffered in your own person the thing which the words try to describe. There are wise people who talk ever so knowingly and complacently about "the working classes," and satisfy themselves that a day's hard intellectual work is very much harder than a day's hard manual toil, and is righteously entitled to much bigger pay. Why, they really think that, you know, because they know all about the one, but haven't tried the other. But I know all about both; and so far as I am concerned, there isn't money enough in the universe to hire me to swing a pickax thirty days, but I will do the hardest kind of intellectual work for just as near nothing as you can cipher it down—and I will be satisfied, too.

Intellectual "work" is misnamed; it is a pleasure, a dissipation, and is its own highest reward. The poorest paid architect, engineer, general, author, sculptor, painter, lecturer, advocate, legislator, actor, preacher, singer is constructively in heaven when he is at work; and as for the magician with the fiddle bow in his hand who sits in the midst of a great orchestra with the ebbing and flowing tides of divine sound washing over him—why, certainly, he is at work, if you wish to call it that, but lord, it's a sarcasm just the same. The law of work does seem utterly unfair—but there it is: and nothing can change it: the higher the pay in enjoyment the worker gets out of it, the higher shall be his pay in cash, also. And it's also the very law of those transparent swindles, transmissible nobility and kingship.

Chapter 30

. . . We slept till far into the afternoon, and then got up hungry enough to make cotter fare quite palatable to the king, the more particularly as it was scant in quantity. And also in variety; it consisted solely of onions, salt, and the national black bread—made out of horse feed. The woman told us about the affair of the evening before. At ten or eleven at night, when everybody was in bed, the manor house burst into flames. The countryside swarmed to the rescue, and the family were saved, with one exception, the master. He did not appear. Everybody was frantic over this loss, and two brave yeomen sacrificed their lives in ransacking the burning house seeking that valuable personage. But after a while he was found—what was left of him—which was his corpse. It was in a copse three hundred yards away, bound, gagged, stabbed in a dozen places.

Who had done this? Suspicion fell upon a humble family in the neighborhood who had been lately treated with peculiar harshness by the baron; and from these people the suspicion easily extended itself to their relatives and familiars. A suspicion was enough; my lord's liveried retainers proclaimed an instant crusade against these people, and were promptly joined by the community in general. The woman's husband had been active with the mob, and had not returned home until nearly dawn. He was gone, now, to find out what the general result had been. While we were still talking, he came back from his quest. His report was revolting enough. Eighteen persons hanged or butchered, and two yeomen and thirteen prisoners lost in the fire.

"And how many prisoners were there altogether, in the vaults?"

"Thirteen."

"Then every one of them was lost."

"Yes, all."

"But the people arrived in time to save the family; how is it they could save none of the prisoners?"

The man looked puzzled, and said:

"Would one unlock the vaults at such a time? Marry, some would have escaped."

"Then you mean that nobody *did* unlock them?"

"None went near them, either to lock or unlock. It standeth to reason that the bolts were fast; wherefore it was only needful to establish a watch, so that if any broke the bonds he might not escape, but be taken. None were taken."

"Natheless, three did escape," said the king, "and ye will do well to publish it and set justice upon their track, for these murthered the baron and fired the house."

I was just expecting he would come out with that. For a moment the man and his wife showed an eager interest in this news and an impatience to go out and spread it; then a sudden something else betrayed itself in their faces, and they began to ask questions. I answered the questions myself, and narrowly watched the effects produced. I was soon satisfied that the knowledge of who these three prisoners were, had somehow changed the atmosphere; that our hosts' continued eagerness to go and spread the news was now only pretended and not real. The king did not notice the change, and I was glad of that. I worked the conversation around toward other details of the night's proceedings, and noted that these people were relieved to have it take that direction.

The painful thing observable about all this business was, the alacrity with which this oppressed community had turned their cruel hands against their own class in the interest of the common oppressor. This man and woman seemed to feel that in a quarrel between a person of their own class and his lord, it was the natural and proper and rightful thing for that poor devil's whole caste to side with the master and fight his battle for him, without ever stopping to inquire into the rights or wrongs of the matter. This man had been out helping to hang his neighbors, and had done his work with zeal, and yet was aware that there was nothing against them but a mere suspicion, with nothing back of it describable as evidence, still neither he nor his wife seemed to see anything horrible about it.

This was depressing—to a man with the dream of a republic in his head. It reminded me of a time thirteen centuries away, when the "poor whites" of our South who were always despised and frequently insulted, by the slave-lords around them, and who owned their base condition simply to the presence of slavery in their midst, were yet pusillanimously ready to side with slave-lords in all political moves for the upholding and perpetuating of slavery, and did also finally shoulder their muskets and pour out their lives in an effort to prevent the destruction of that very institution which degraded them. And there was only one redeeming feature connected with that pitiful piece of history; and that was, that secretly the "poor white" did detest the slave-lord, and did feel his own shame. That feeling was not brought to the surface, but the fact that it was there and could have been brought out, under favoring circumstances, was something—in fact it was enough; for it showed that a man is at bottom a man, after all, even if it doesn't show on the outside.

Well, as it turned out, this charcoal burner was just the twin of the Southern "poor white" of the far future. The king presently showed impatience, and said:

"An ye prattle here all the day, justice will miscarry. Think ye the criminals will abide in their father's house? They are fleeing, they are not waiting. You should look to it that a party of horse be set upon their track."

The woman paled slightly, but quite perceptibly, and the man looked flustered and irresolute. I said:

"Come, friend, I will walk a little way with you, and explain which direction I think they would try to take. If they were merely resisters of the gabelle or some kindred absurdity I would try to protect them from capture; but when men murder a person of high degree and likewise burn his house, that is another matter."

The last remark was for the king—to quiet him. On the road the man pulled his resolution together, and began the march with a steady gait, but there was no eagerness in it. By and by I said:

"What relation were these men to you—cousins?"

He turned as white as his layer of charcoal would let him, and stopped, trembling.

"Ah, my God, how knew you that?"

"I didn't know it; it was a chance guess."

"Poor lads, they are lost. And good lads they were, too."

"Were you actually going yonder to tell on them?"

He didn't quite know how to take that; but he said, hesitatingly:

"Ye-s."

"Then I think you are a damned scoundrel!"

It made him as glad as if I had called him an angel.

"Say the good words again, brother! For surely ye mean that ye would not betray me an I failed of my duty."

"Duty? There is no duty in the matter, except the duty to keep still and let those men get away. They've done a righteous deed."

He looked pleased; pleased, and touched with apprehension at the same time. He looked up and down the road to see that no one was coming, and then said in a cautious voice:

"From what land come you, brother, that you speak such perilous words, and seem not to be afraid?"

"They are not perilous words when spoken to one of my own caste, I take it. You would not tell anybody I said them?"

"I? I would be drawn asunder by wild horses first."

"Well, then, let me say my say. I have no fears of your repeating it. I think devil's work has been done last night upon those innocent poor people. That old baron got only what he deserved. If I had my way, all his kind should have the same luck."

Fear and depression vanished from the man's manner, and gratefulness and a brave animation took their place:

"Even though you be a spy, and your words a trap for my undoing, yet are they such refreshment that to hear them again and others like to them, I would go to the gallows happy, as having had one good feast at least in a starved life. And I will say my say, now, and ye may report it if ye be so minded. I helped to hang my neighbors for that it were peril to my own life to show lack of zeal in the master's cause; the others helped for none other reason. All rejoice today that he is dead, but all do go about seemingly sorrowing, and shedding the hypocrite's tear, for in that lies safety. I have said the words. I have said the words! the only ones that have ever tasted good in my mouth, and the reward of that taste is sufficient. Lead on, an ye will, be it even to the scaffold, for I am ready."

There it was, you see. A man *is* a man, at bottom. Whole ages of abuse and oppression cannot crush the manhood clear out of him. Whoever thinks it a mistake, is himself mistaken. Yes, there is plenty good enough material for a republic in the most degraded people that ever existed—even the Russians; plenty of manhood in them—even in the Germans—if one could but force it out of its timid and suspicious privacy, to overthrow and trample in the mud any throne that ever was set up and any nobility that ever supported it. We should see certain things yet, let us hope and believe. First, a modified monarchy, till Arthur's days were done, then the destruction of the throne, nobility abolished, every member of it bound out to some useful trade, universal suffrage instituted, and the whole government placed in the hands of the men and women of the nation there to remain. Yes, there was no occasion to give up my dream yet awhile.

Chapter 31

We strolled along in a sufficiently indolent fashion, now, and talked. We must dispose of about the amount of time it ought to take to go to the little hamlet of Abblasoure and put justice on the track of those murderers and get back home again. And meantime I had an auxiliary interest which had never paled yet, never lost its novelty for me, since I had been in Arthur's kingdom: the behavior—born of nice and exact subdivisions of caste—of chance passersby toward each other. Toward the shaven monk who trudged along with his cowl tilted back and the sweat washing down his fat jowls, the coal burner was deeply reverent; to the gentleman he was abject; with the small farmer and the free mechanic he was cordial and gossipy; and when a slave passed by with a countenance respectfully lowered, this chap's nose was in the air—he couldn't even see him. Well, there are times when one would like to hang the whole human race and finish the farce.

Presently we struck an incident. A small mob of half naked boys and girls came tearing out of the woods, scared and shrieking. The eldest among them were not more than twelve or fourteen years old. They implored help, but they were so beside themselves that we couldn't make out what the matter was. However, we plunged into the wood, they scurrying in the lead, and the trouble was quickly revealed: they had hanged a little fellow with a bark rope, and he was kicking and struggling, in the process of choking to death. We rescued him, and fetched him around. It was some more human nature; the admiring little folk imitating their elders; they were playing mob, and had achieved a success which promised to be a good deal more serious than they had bargained for. . . .

Chapter 34

. . . We jogged along, six in the party, at a moderate and comfortable gait, and in conversation learned that my lord Grip was a very great personage in his own region, which lay a day's journey beyond Cambenet. We loitered to such a degree that it was near the middle of the forenoon when we entered the market square of the town. We dismounted, and left our thanks once more for my lord, and then approached a crowd assembled in the center of the square, to see what might be the object of interest. It was the remnant of that old peregrinating band of slaves! So they had been dragging their chains about, all this weary time. That poor husband was gone, and also many others; and some few purchases had been added to the gang. The king was not interested, and wanted to move along, but I was absorbed, and full of pity. I could not take my eyes away from these worn and wasted wrecks of humanity. There they sat, grouped upon the ground, silent, uncomplaining, with bowed heads, a pathetic sight. And by hideous contrast, a redundant orator was making a speech to another gathering not thirty steps away, in fulsome laudation of "our glorious British liberties!"

I was boiling. I had forgotten I was a plebian, I was remembering I was a man. Cost what it might, I would mount that rostrum and—

Click! the king and I were handcuffed together! Our companions, those servants, had done it; my lord Grip stood looking on. The king burst out in a fury, and said:

"What meaneth this ill-mannered jest?"

My lord merely said to his head miscreant, coolly:

"Put up the slaves and sell them!"

Slaves! The word had a new sound—and how unspeakably awful! The king lifted his manacles and brought them down with a deadly force; but my lord was out of the way when they arrived. A dozen of the rascal's servants sprang forward, and in a moment we were helpless, with our hands bound behind us. We so loudly and so earnestly proclaimed ourselves freemen, that we got the interested attention of that liberty-mouthing orator and his patriotic crowd, and they gathered about us and assumed a very determined attitude. The orator said:

"If indeed ye are freemen, ye have nought to fear—the God-given liberties of Britain are about ye for your shield and shelter! (Applause.) Ye shall soon see. Bring forth your proofs."

"What proofs?"

"Proof that ye are freemen."

Ah—I remembered! I came to myself; I said nothing. But the king stormed out:

"Thou'rt insane, man. It were better, and more in reason, that this thief and scoundrel here prove that we are *not* freemen."

You see, he knew his own laws just as other people so often know the laws: by words, not by effects. They take a *meaning,* and get to be very vivid, when you come to apply them to yourself.

All hands shook their heads and looked disappointed; some turned away, no longer interested. The orator said—and this time in the tones of business, not of sentiment:

"An ye do not know your country's laws, it were time ye learned them. Ye are strangers to us; ye will not deny that. Ye may be freemen, we do not deny that; but also ye may be slaves. The law is clear: it doth not require the claimant to prove ye are slaves, it requireth you to prove ye are *not.*"

I said:

"Dear sir, give us only time to send to Astolat; or give us only time to send to the Valley of Holiness—"

"Peace, good man, these are extraordinary requests, and you may not hope to have them granted. It would cost much time, and would unwarrantably inconvenience your master—"

"*Master,* idiot!" stormed the king. "I have no master, I myself am the m——"

"Silence, for God's sake!"

I got the words out in time to stop the king. We were in trouble enough already; it could not help us any to give these people the notion that we were lunatics.

There is no use in stringing out the details. The earl put us up and sold us at auction. This same infernal law had existed in our own South in my own time, more than thirteen hundred years later, and under it hundreds of freemen who could not prove that they were freemen had been sold into lifelong slavery without the circumstance making any particular impression upon me; but the minute law and the auction block came into my personal experience, a thing which had been merely improper before became suddenly hellish. Well, that's the way we are made.

Yes, we were sold at auction, like swine. In a big town and an active market we should have brought a good price; but this place was utterly stagnant and so we sold at a figure which makes me ashamed, every time I think of it. The King of England brought seven dollars, and his prime minister nine; whereas the king was easily worth twelve dollars and I as easily worth fifteen. But that is the way things always go; if you force a sale on a dull market, I don't care what the property is, you are going to make a poor business of it, and you can make up your mind to it. If the earl had had wit enough to—

However, there is no occasion for my working my sympathies up on his account. Let him go, for the present: I took his number, so to speak.

The slave dealer bought us both, and hitched us onto that long chain of his, and we constituted the rear of his procession. We took up our line of march and passed out of Cambenet at noon; and it seemed to me unaccountably strange and odd that the King of England and his chief minister, marching manacled and fettered and yoked, in a slave convoy, could move by all manner of idle men and women, and under windows where sat the sweet and the lovely, and yet never attract a curious eye, never provoke a single remark. Dear, dear, it only shows that there is nothing diviner about a king than there is about a tramp, after all. He is just a cheap and hollow artificiality when you don't know he is a king. But reveal his quality, and dear me it takes your very breath away to look at him. I reckon we are all fools. Born so, no doubt.

Chapter 43

. . . I had spies out, every night, of course, to get news. Every report made things look more and more impressive. The hosts were gathering, gathering;

down all the roads and paths of England the knights were riding, and priests rode with them, to hearten these original Crusaders, this being the Church's war. All the nobilities, big and little, were on their way, and all the gentry. This was all as was expected. We should thin out this sort of folk to such a degree that the people would have nothing to do but just step to the front with their republic and——

Ah, what a donkey I was! Toward the end of the week I began to get this large and disenchanting fact through my head: that the mass of the nation had swung their caps and shouted for the republic for about one day, and there an end! The Church, the nobles, and the gentry then turned one grand, all-disapproving frown upon them and shriveled them into sheep! From that moment the sheep had begun to gather to the fold—that is to say, the camps—and offer their valueless lives and their valuable wool to the "righteous cause." Why, even the very men who had lately been slaves were in the "righteous cause," and glorifying it, praying for it, sentimentally slabbering over it, just like all the other commoners. Imagine such human muck as this; conceive of this folly!

Yes, it was now "Death to the Republic!" everywhere—not a dissenting voice. All England was marching against us! Truly this was more than I had bargained for.

I watched my fifty-two boys narrowly; watched their faces, their walk, their unconscious attitudes: for all these are a language—a language given us purposely that it may betray us in times of emergency, when we have secrets which we want to keep. I knew that that thought would keep saying itself over and over again in their minds and hearts, *All England is marching against us!* and evermore strenuously imploring attention with each repetition, ever more sharply realizing itself to their imaginations, until even in their sleep they would find no rest from it, but hear the vague and flitting creatures of their dreams say, *All England*—ALL ENGLAND—*is marching against you!* I knew all this would happen; I knew that ultimately the pressure would become so great that it would compel utterance; therefore, I must be ready with an answer at that time—an answer well chosen and tranquilizing.

I was right. The time came. They *had* to speak. Poor lads, it was pitiful to see, they were so pale, so worn, so troubled. At first their spokesman could hardly find voice or words; but he presently got both. This is what he said—and he put it in the neat modern English taught him in my schools:

"We have tried to forget what we are—English boys. We have tried to put reason before sentiment, duty before love; our minds approve, but our hearts reproach us. While apparently it was only the nobility, only the gentry, only the twenty-five or thirty thousand knights left alive out of the late wars, we were of one mind, and undisturbed by any troubling doubt; each and every one of these fifty-two lads who stand here before you, said, 'They have chosen—it is their affair.' But think—the matter is altered—*all England is marching against us!* Oh, sir, consider! Reflect! These people are our people, they are bone of our bone, flesh of our flesh, we love them—do not ask us to destroy our nation!"

Well, it shows the value of looking ahead, and being ready for a thing when it happens. If I hadn't foreseen this thing and been fixed, that boy would have had me—I couldn't have said a word. But I *was* fixed. I said:

"My boys, your hearts are in the right place, you have thought the worthy thought, you have done the worthy thing. You are English boys, you will remain English boys, and you will keep that name unsmirched. Give yourselves no further concern, let your minds be at peace. Consider this: while all England *is* marching against us, who is in the van? Who, by the commonest rules of war, will march in the front? Answer me."

"The mounted host of mailed knights."

"True. They are 30,000 strong. Acres deep, they will march. Now, observe: none but *they* will ever strike the sand belt! Then there will be an episode! Immediately after, the civilian multitude in the rear will retire, to meet business engagements elsewhere. None but nobles and gentry are knights, and *none but these* will remain to dance to our music after that episode. It is absolutely true that we shall have to fight nobody but these thirty thousand knights. Now speak, and it shall be as you decide. Shall we avoid the battle, retire from the field?"

"NO! ! !"

The shout was unanimous and hearty.

"Are you—are you—well, afraid of these thirty thousand knights?"

That joke brought out a good laugh, the boys' troubles vanished away, and they went gaily to their posts. Ah, they were a darling fifty-two! As pretty as girls, too.

I was ready for the enemy now. Let the approaching big day come along—it would find us on deck.

The big day arrived on time. At dawn the sentry on watch in the corral came into the cave and reported a moving black mass under the horizon, and a faint sound which he thought to be military music. Breakfast was just ready; we sat down and ate it.

This over, I made the boys a little speech, and then sent out a detail to man the battery, with Clarence in command of it.

The sun rose presently and sent its unobstructed splendors over the land, and we saw a prodigious host moving slowly toward us, with the steady drift and aligned front of a wave of the sea. Nearer and nearer it came, and more and more sublimely imposing became its aspect; yes, all England were there, apparently. Soon we could see the innumerable banners fluttering, and then the sun struck the sea of armor and set it all a-flash. Yes, it was a fine sight; I hadn't ever seen anything to beat it.

At last we could make out details. All the front ranks, no telling how many acres deep, were horsemen—plumed knights in armor. Suddenly we heard the blare of trumpets; the slow walk burst into a gallop, and then—well, it was wonderful to see! Down swept that vast horseshoe wave—it approached the sand belt—my breath stood still; nearer, nearer—the strip of green turf beyond the yellow belt grew narrow—narrower still—became a mere ribbon in front of the horses—then disappeared under their hoofs. Great Scott! Why, the whole front of that horse shot into the sky with a thundercrash, and became a whirling tempest of rags and fragments; and along the ground lay a thick wall of smoke that hid what was left of the multitude from our sight.

Time for the second step in the plan of campaign! I touched a button, and shook the bones of England loose from her spine!

In that explosion all our noble civilization-factories went up in the air and disappeared from the earth. It was a pity, but it was necessary. We could not afford to let the enemy turn our own weapons against us.

Now ensued one of the dullest quarter hours I had ever endured. We waited in a silent solitude enclosed by our circles of wire, and by a circle of heavy smoke outside of these. We couldn't see over the wall of smoke, and we couldn't see through it. But at last it began to shred away lazily, and by the end of another quarter hour the land was clear and our curiosity was enabled to satisfy itself. No living creature was in sight! We now perceived that additions had been made to our defenses. The dynamite had dug a ditch more than a hundred feet wide, all around us, and cast up an embankment some twenty-five feet high on both borders of it. As to destruction of life, it was amazing. Moreover, it was beyond estimate. Of course we could not *count* the dead, because they did not exist as individuals, but merely as homogeneous protoplasm, with alloys of iron and buttons.

No life was in sight, but necessarily there must have been some wounded in the rear ranks, who were carried off the field under cover of the wall of smoke; there would be sickness among the others—there always is, after an episode like that. But there would be no reinforcements; this was the last stand of the chivalry of England, it was all that was left of the order, after the recent annihilating wars. So I felt quite safe in believing that the utmost force that could for the future be brought against us would be but small; that is, of knights. I therefore issued a congratulatory proclamation to my army in these words:

> SOLDIERS, CHAMPIONS OF HUMAN LIBERTY AND EQUALITY: Your General congratulates you! In the pride of his strength and the vanity of his renown, an arrogant enemy came against you. You were ready. The conflict was brief; on your side, glorious. This mighty victory having been achieved utterly without loss, stands without example in history. So long as the planets shall continue to move in their orbits, the BATTLE OF THE SAND BELT will not perish out in the memories of men.
>
> THE BOSS.

I read it well, and the applause I got was very gratifying to me. I then wound up with these remarks:

"The war with the English nation, as a nation, is at an end. The nation has retired from the field and the war. Before it can be persuaded to return, war will have ceased. This campaign is the only one that is going to be fought. It will be brief—the briefest in history. Also the most destructive to life considered from the standpoint of proportion of casualties to numbers engaged. We are done with the nation; henceforth we deal only with the knights. English knights can be killed, but they cannot be conquered. We know what is before us. While one of these men remains alive, our task is not finished, the war is not ended. We will kill them all." [Loud and long continued applause.]

I picketed the great embankments thrown up around our lines by the dynamite explosion—merely a lookout of a couple of boys to announce the enemy when he should appear again.

Next, I sent an engineer and forty men to a point just beyond our lines on the south, to turn a mountain brook that was there, and bring it within our lines and under our command, arranging it in such a way that I could make instant use of it in an emergency. The forty men were divided into two shifts of twenty each, and were to relieve each other every two hours. In ten hours the work was accomplished.

It was nightfall, now, and I withdrew my pickets. The one who had had the northern outlook reported a camp in sight, but visible with the glass only. He also reported that a few knights had been feeling their way toward us, and had driven some cattle across our lines, but that the knights themselves had not come very near. That was what I had been expecting. They were feeling us, you see; they wanted to know if we were going to play that red terror on them again. They would grow bolder in the night, perhaps. I believed I knew what project they would attempt, because it was plainly the thing I would attempt myself if I were in their places and as ignorant as they were. I mentioned it to Clarence.

"I think you are right," said he; "it is the obvious thing for them to try."

"Well, then," I said, "if they do it they are doomed."

"Certainly."

"They won't have the slightest show in the world."

"Of course they won't."

"It's dreadful, Clarence. It seems an awful pity."

The thing disturbed me so, that I couldn't get any peace of mind for thinking of it and worrying over it. So, at last, to quiet my conscience, I framed this message to the knights:

> TO THE HONORABLE THE COMMANDER OF THE INSURGENT CHIVALRY OF ENGLAND: You fight in vain. We know your strength—if one may call it by that name. We know that at the utmost you cannot bring against us above five and twenty thousand knights. Therefore, you have no chance—none whatever. Reflect: we are well equipped, well fortified, we number fifty-four. Fifty-four what? Men? No, *minds*—the capablest in the world; a force against which mere animal might may no more hope to prevail than may the idle waves of the sea hope to prevail against the granite barriers of England. Be advised. We offer you your lives; for the sake of your families, do not reject the gift. We offer you this chance, and it

is the last: throw down your arms; surrender unconditionally to the Republic, and all will be forgiven.

(Signed) THE BOSS.

I read it to Clarence, and said I proposed to send it by a flag of truce. He laughed the sarcastic laugh he was born with, and said:

"Somehow it seems impossible for you to ever fully realize what these nobilities are. Now let us save a little time and trouble. Consider me the commander of the knights yonder. Now then, you are the flag of truce; approach and deliver me your message, and I will give you your answer."

I humored the idea. I came forward under an imaginary guard of the enemy's soldiers, produced my paper, and read it through. For answer, Clarence struck the paper out of my hand, pursed up a scornful lip and said with lofty disdain—

"Dismember me this animal, and return him in a basket to the baseborn knave who sent him; other answer have I none!"

How empty is theory in presence of fact! And this was just fact, and nothing else. It was the thing that would have happened, there was no getting around that. I tore up the paper and granted my mistimed sentimentalities a permanent rest.

Then, to business. I tested the electric signals from the gatling platform to the cave, and made sure that they were all right; I tested and retested those which commanded the fences—these were signals whereby I could break and renew the electric current in each fence independently of the others, at will. I placed the brook connection under the guard and authority of three of my best boys, who would alternate in two-hour watches all night and promptly obey my signal, if I should have occasion to give it—three revolver-shots in quick succession. Sentry duty was discarded for the night, and the corral left empty of life; I ordered that quiet be maintained in the cave, and the electric lights turned down to a glimmer.

As soon as it was good and dark, I shut off the current from all of the fences, and then groped my way out to the embankment bordering our side of the great dynamite ditch. I crept to the top of it and lay there on the slant of the muck to watch. But it was too dark to see anything. As for sounds, there were none. The stillness was deathlike. True, there were the usual nightsounds of the country—the whir of night birds, the buzzing of insects, the barking of distant dogs, the mellow lowing of far-off kine—but these didn't seem to break the stillness, they only intensified it, and added a gruesome melancholy to it into the bargain.

I presently gave up looking, the night shut down so black, but I kept my ears strained to catch the least suspicious sound, for I judged I had only to wait and I shouldn't be disappointed. However, I had to wait a long time. At last I caught what you may call indistinct glimpses of sound—dulled metallic sound.

I pricked up my ears, then, and held my breath, for this was the sort of thing I had been waiting for. This sound thickened, and approached—from toward the north. Presently I heard it at my own level—the ridgetop of the opposite embankment, a hundred feet or more away. Then I seemed to see a row of black dots appear along that ridge—human heads? I couldn't tell; it mightn't be anything at all; you can't depend on your eyes when your imagination is out of focus. However, the question was soon settled. I heard that metallic noise descending into the great ditch. It augmented fast, it spread all along, and it unmistakably furnished me this fact: an armed host was taking up its quarters in the ditch. Yes, these people were arranging a little surprise party for us. We could expect entertainment about dawn, possibly earlier.

I groped my way back to the corral, now; I had seen enough. I went to the platform and signaled to turn the current onto the two inner fences. Then I went into the cave, and found everything satisfactory there—nobody awake but the working watch. I woke Clarence and told him the great ditch was filling up with men, and that I believed all the knights were coming for us in a body. It was my notion that as soon as dawn approached we could expect the ditch's ambuscaded thousands to swarm up over the embankment and make an assault, and be followed immediately by the rest of their army.

Clarence said:

"They will be wanting to send a scout or two in the dark to make preliminary observations. Why not take the lightning off the outer fences, and give them a chance?"

"I've already done it, Clarence. Did you ever know me to be inhospitable?"

"No, you are a good heart. I want to go and—"

"Be a reception committee? I will go, too."

We crossed the corral and lay down together between the two inside fences. Even the dim light of the cave had disordered our eyesight somewhat, but the focus straightway began to regulate itself and soon it was adjusted for present circumstances. We had had to feel our way before, but we could make out to see the fence posts now. We started a whispered conversation, but suddenly Clarence broke off and said:

"What is that?"

"What is what?"

"That thing yonder?"

"What thing—where?"

"There beyond you a little piece—a dark something—a dull shape of some kind—against the second fence."

I gazed and he gazed. I said:

"Could it be a man, Clarence?"

"No, I think not. If you notice, it looks a lit—why, it *is* a man—leaning on the fence!"

"I certainly believe it is; let's us go and see."

We crept along on our hands and knees until we were pretty close, and then looked up. Yes, it was a man—a dim great figure in armor, standing erect, with both hands on the upper wire—and of course there was a smell of burning flesh. Poor fellow, dead as a doornail, and never knew what hurt him. He stood there like a statue—no motion about him, except that his plumes swished about a little in the night wind. We rose up and looked in through the bars of his visor, but couldn't make out whether we knew him or not—features too dim and shadowed.

We heard muffled sounds approaching, and we sank down to the ground where we were. We made out another knight vaguely; he was coming very stealthily, and feeling his way. He was near enough, now, for us to see him put out a hand, find an upper wire, then bend and step under it and over the lower one. Now he arrived at the first knight—and started slightly when he discovered him. He stood a moment—no doubt wondering why the other one didn't move on; then he said, in a low voice, "Why dreamest thou here, good Sir Mar—" then he laid his hand on the corpse's shoulder—and just uttered a little soft moan and sunk down dead. Killed by a dead man, you see—killed by a dead friend, in fact. There was something awful about it.

These early birds came scattering along after each other, about one every five minutes in our vicinity, during half an hour. They brought no armor of offense but their swords; as a rule they carried the sword ready in the hand, and put it forward and found the wires with it. We would now and then see a blue spark when the knight that caused it was so far away as to be invisible to us; but we knew what had happened, all the same, poor fellow; he had touched a charged wire with his sword and been elected. We had brief intervals of grim stillness, interrupted with piteous regularity by the clash made by the falling of an ironclad; and this sort of thing was going on, right along, and was very creepy, there in the dark and lonesomeness.

We concluded to make a tour between the inner fences. We elected to walk upright, for convenience sake; we argued that if discerned, we should be taken for friends rather than enemies, and in any case we should be out of reach of swords, and these gentry did not seem to have any spears along. Well, it was a curious trip. Everywhere dead men were lying outside the second fence—not plainly visible, but still visible; and we counted fifteen of those pathetic statues—dead knights standing with their hands on the upper wire.

One thing seemed to be sufficiently demonstrated: our current was so tremendous that it killed before the victim could cry out. Pretty soon we detected a muffled and heavy sound, and next moment we guessed what it was. It was a surprise in force coming! I whispered Clarence to go and wake the army, and notify it to wait in silence in the cave for further orders. He was soon back, and we stood by the inner fence and watched the silent lightning do its awful work upon that swarming host. One could make out but little of detail; but he could note that a black mass was piling itself up beyond the second fence. That swelling bulk was dead men! Our camp was enclosed with a solid wall of the dead—a bulwark, a breastwork, of corpses, you may say. One terrible thing about this thing was the absence of human voices; there were no cheers, no war cries: being intent upon a surprise, these men moved as noiselessly as they could; and always when the front rank was near enough to their goal to make it proper for them to begin to get a shout ready, of course they struck the fatal line and went down without testifying.

I sent a current through the third fence, now; and almost immediately through the fourth and fifth, so quickly were the gaps filled up. I believed the time was come, now, for my climax; I believed that that whole army was in our trap. Anyway, it was high time to find out. So I touched a button and set fifty electric suns aflame on the top of our precipice.

Land, what a sight! We were enclosed in three walls of dead men! All the other fences were pretty nearly filled with the living, who were stealthily working their way forward through the wires. The sudden glare paralyzed this host, petrified them, you may say, with astonishment; there was just one instant for me to utilize their immobility in, and I didn't lose the chance. You see, in another instant they would have recovered their faculties, then they'd have burst into a cheer and made a rush, and my wires would have gone down before it; but that lost instant lost them their opportunity forever; while even that slight fragment of time was still unspent, I shot the current through all the fences and struck the whole host dead in their tracks! *There* was a groan you could *hear!* It voiced the death pang of eleven thousand men. It swelled out on the night with awful pathos.

A glance showed that the rest of the enemy—perhaps ten thousand strong—were between us and the encircling ditch, and pressing forward to the assault. Consequently we had them *all!* and had them past help. Time for the last act of the tragedy. I fired the three appointed revolver shots—which meant:

"Turn on the water!"

There was a sudden rush and roar, and in a minute the mountain brook was raging through the big ditch and creating a river a hundred feet wide and twenty-five deep.

"Stand to your guns, men! Open fire!"

The thirteen gatlings began to vomit death into the fated ten thousand. They halted, they stood their ground a moment against that withering deluge of fire, then they broke, faced about and swept toward the ditch like chaff before a gale. A full fourth part of their force never reached the top of the lofty embankment; the three-fourths reached it and plunged over—to death by drowning.

Within ten short minutes after we had opened fire, armed resistance was totally annihilated, the campaign was ended, we fifty-four were masters of England! Twenty-five thousand men lay dead around us.

But how treacherous is fortune! In a little while—say an hour—happened a thing, by my own fault, which—but I have no heart to write that. Let the record end here.

The American Claimant

In The American Claimant *(1892) Twain again attacked notions of inherited nobility. In this novel, which is generally regarded as a failure, Colonel Mulberry Sellers claims to be the rightful heir to a British title. Mulberry also continually claims that his plans will earn a fortune. (Twain was fascinated by claimants, pretenders, and projectors.) In this brief selection Twain develops Colonel Sellers's attempt to make money through Spiritualism.*

[His wife describes Colonel Mulberry Sellers]

. . . "Oh, they like to hear him talk, especially if their load is getting rather heavy on one shoulder and they want to shift it. He's all air, you know—breeze, you may say—and he freshens them up; it's a trip to the country, they say. Many a time he's made General Grant laugh—and that's a tidy job, I can tell you; and as for Sheridan, his eye lights up and he listens to Mulberry Sellers the same as if he was artillery. You see, the charm about Mulberry is, he is so catholic and unprejudiced that he fits in anywhere and everywhere. It makes him powerful good company, and as popular as scandal. You go to the White House when the President's holding a general reception—some time when Mulberry's there. Why, dear me, *you* can't tell which of them it is that's holding that reception."

"Well, he certainly is a remarkable man—and he always was. Is he religious?"

"Clear to his marrow—does more thinking and reading on that subject than any other, except Russia and Siberia; thrashes around over the whole field, too; nothing bigoted about him."

"What is his religion?"

"He—" She stopped, and was lost for a moment or two in thinking; then she said, with simplicity, "I think he was a Mohammedan or something last week."

Washington started down-town now to bring his trunk, for the hospitable Sellerses would listen to no excuses; their house must be his home during the session. The Colonel returned presently and resumed work upon his plaything. It was finished when Washington got back.

"There it is," said the Colonel, "all finished."

"What is it for, Colonel?"

"Oh, it's just a trifle. Toy to amuse the children."

Washington examined it.

"It seems to be a puzzle."

"Yes, that's what it is. I call it Pigs in the Clover. Put them in—see if you can put them in the pen."

After many failures Washington succeeded, and was as pleased as a child.

"It's wonderfully ingenious, Colonel—it's ever so clever. And interesting—why, I could play with it all day. What are you going to do with it?"

"Oh, nothing. Patent it and throw it aside."

"Don't you do anything of the kind. There's money in that thing."

A compassionate look traveled over the Colonel's countenance, and he said:

"Money—yes; pin money; a couple of hundred thousand, perhaps. Not more."

Washington's eyes blazed.

"A couple of hundred thousand dollars! Do you call that pin money?"

The Colonel rose and tiptoed his way across the room, closed a door that was slightly ajar, tiptoed his way to his seat again, and said, under his breath:

"You can keep a secret?"

Washington nodded his affirmative; he was too awed to speak.

"You have heard of materialization—materialization of departed spirits?"

Washington had heard of it.

"And probably didn't believe in it; and quite right, too. The thing as practised by ignorant charlatans is unworthy of attention or respect—where there's a dim light and a dark cabinet, and a parcel of sentimental gulls gathered together, with their faith and their shudders and their tears all ready, and one and the same fatty degeneration of protoplasm and humbug comes out and materializes himself into anybody you want, grandmother, grandchild, brother-in-law, Witch of Endor, John Milton, Siamese Twins, Peter the Great, and all such frantic nonsense—no, that is all foolish and pitiful. But when a man that is competent brings the vast powers of *science* to bear, it's a different matter—a totally different matter, you see. The specter that answers *that* call has come to stay. Do you note the commercial value of that detail?"

"Well, I—the—the truth is, that I don't quite know that I do. Do you mean that such, being permanent, not transitory, would give more general satisfaction, and so enhance the price of tickets to the show—"

"Show? Folly—listen to me; and get a good grip on your breath, for you are going to need it. Within three days I shall have completed my method, and then—let the world stand aghast, for it shall see marvels. Washington, within three days—ten at the outside—you shall see me call the dead of any century, and they will arise and walk. Walk?—they shall walk forever, and never die again. Walk with all the muscle and spring of their pristine vigor."

"Colonel! Indeed, it does take one's breath away."

"*Now* do you see the money that's in it?"

"I'm—well, I'm—not really sure that I do."

"Great Scott, look here! I shall have a monopoly; they'll all belong to me, won't they? Two thousand policemen in the city of New York. Wages, four dollars a day. I'll replace them with dead ones at half the money."

"Oh, prodigious! I never thought of that. F-o-u-r thousand dollars a day. Now I do begin to see! But will dead policemen answer?"

"Haven't they—up to this time?"

"Well, if you put it that way—"

"Put it any way you want to. Modify it to suit yourself, and my lads shall still be superior. They won't eat, they won't drink—don't need those things; they won't wink for cash at gambling-dens and unlicensed rum-holes; they won't spark the scullery maids; and, moreover, the band of toughs that ambuscade them on lonely beats and cowardly shoot and knife them will only damage the uniforms, and not live long enough to get more than a momentary satisfaction out of that."

"Why, Colonel, if you can furnish policemen, then of course—"

"Certainly—I can furnish any line of goods that's wanted. Take the army, for instance—now twenty-five thousand men; expense, twenty-two millions a year. I will dig up the Romans, I will resurrect the Greeks, I will furnish the government, for ten millions a year, ten thousand veterans drawn from the victorious legions of all the ages—soldiers that will chase Indians year in and year out on materialized horses, and cost never a cent for rations or repairs. The armies of Europe cost two billions a year now—I will replace them all for a billion. I will dig up the trained statesmen of all ages and all climes, and furnish this country with a Congress that knows enough to come in out of the rain—a thing that's never happened yet since the Declaration of Independence, and never will happen till these practically dead people are replaced with the genuine article. I will restock the thrones of Europe with the best brains and the best morals that all the royal sepulchers of all the centuries can furnish—which isn't promising very much—and I'll divide the wages and the civil list, fair and square, merely taking my half and—"

"Colonel, if the half of this is true, there's millions in it—millions."

"Billions in it—billions; that's what you mean. Why, look here; the thing is so close at hand, so imminent, so absolutely immediate, that if a man were to come to me now and say, Colonel, I am a little short, and if you could lend me a couple of billion dollars for— Come in!"

This in answer to a knock. An energetic-looking man bustled in with a big pocket-book in his hand, took a paper from it and presented it, with the curt remark:

"Seventeenth and last call—you want to out with that three dollars and forty cents this time without fail, Colonel Mulberry Sellers."

The Colonel began to slap this pocket and that one, and feel here and there and everywhere, muttering:

"What *have* I done with that wallet?—let me see—um—not here, not there—oh, I must have left it in the kitchen; I'll just run and—"

"No, you won't—you'll stay right where you are. And you're going to disgorge, too—this time."

Washington innocently offered to go and look. When he was gone the Colonel said:

"The fact is, I've got to throw myself on your indulgence just this once more, Suggs; you see, the remittances I was expecting—"

"Hang the remittances—it's too stale—it won't answer. Come!"

The Colonel glanced about him in despair. Then his face lighted; he ran to the wall and began to dust off a peculiarly atrocious chromo with his handkerchief. Then he brought it reverently, offered it to the collector, averted his face, and said:

"Take it, but don't let me see it go. It's the sole remaining Rembrandt that—"

"Rembrandt be damned; it's a chromo."

"Oh, don't speak of it so, I beg you. It's the only really great original, the only supreme example, of that mighty school of art which—"

"Art! It's the sickest-looking thing I—"

The Colonel was already bringing another horror and tenderly dusting it.

"Take this one too—the gem of my collection—the only genuine Fra Angelico that—"

"Illuminated liver-pad, that's what it is. Give it here—good day—people will think I've robbed a nigger barber-shop."

As he slammed the door behind him the Colonel shouted, with an anguished accent:

"Do please cover them up—don't let the damp get at them. The delicate tints in the Angelico—"

But the man was gone. . . .

TOM SAWYER ABROAD

In this brief selection from Tom Sawyer Abroad *(1894), Twain reveals his knowledge of the deceptive nature of figurative language. Tom, Huck, and Jim are aboard a primitive airship, flying from America to Africa, when this conversation occurs.*

[CHAPTER V]

. . . After breakfast Tom learned me and Jim how to steer, and divided us all up into four-hour watches, turn and turn about; and when his watch was out I took his place, and he got out the professor's papers and pens and wrote a letter home to his aunt Polly, telling her everything that had happened to us, and dated it "*In the Welkin, approaching England,*" and folded it together and stuck it fast with a red wafer, and directed it, and wrote above the direction, in big writing, "*From Tom Sawyer, the Erronort,*" and said it would stump old Nat Parsons, the postmaster, when it come along in the mail. I says:

"Tom Sawyer, this ain't no welkin; it's a balloon."

"Well, now, who *said* it was a welkin, smarty?"

"You've wrote it on the letter, anyway."

"What of it? That don't mean that the balloon's the welkin."

"Oh, I thought it did. Well, then, what is a welkin?"

I see in a minute he was stuck. He raked and scraped around in his mind, but he couldn't find nothing, so he had to say:

"*I* don't know, and nobody don't know. It's just a word, and it's a mighty good word, too. There ain't many that lays over it. I don't believe there's *any* that does."

"Shucks!" I says. "But what does it *mean?*—that's the p'int."

"*I* don't know what it means, I tell you. It's a word that people uses for—

for—well, it's ornamental. They don't put ruffles on a shirt to keep a person warm, do they?"

"Course they don't."

"But they put them *on,* don't they?"

"Yes."

"All right, then; that letter I wrote is a shirt, and the welkin's the ruffle on it."

I judged that that would gravel Jim, and it did.

"Now, Mars Tom, it ain't no use to talk like dat; en, moreover, it's sinful. You knows a letter ain't no shirt, en dey ain't no ruffles on it, nuther. Dey ain't no place to put 'em on; you can't put 'em on, and dey wouldn't stay ef you did."

"Oh, *do* shut up, and wait till something's started that you know something about."

"Why, Mars Tom, sholy you can't mean to say I don't know about shirts, when, goodness knows, I's toted home de washin' ever sence—"

"I tell you, this hasn't got anything to *do* with shirts. I only—"

"Why, Mars Tom, you said yo'self dat a letter—"

"Do you want to drive me crazy? Keep still. I only used it as a metaphor."

That word kinder bricked us up for a minute. Then Jim says—rather timid, because he see Tom was getting pretty tetchy:

"Mars Tom, what is a metaphor?"

"A metaphor's a—well, it's a—a—a metaphor's an illustration." He see *that* didn't git home, so he tried again. "When I say birds of a feather flocks together, it's a metaphorical way of saying—"

"But dey *don't,* Mars Tom. No sir, 'deed dey don't. Dey ain't no feathers dat's more alike den a bluebird en a jaybird, but ef you waits till you catches *dem* birds together, you'll—"

"Oh, give us a rest! You can't get the simplest little thing through your thick skull. Now don't bother me any more."

Jim was satisfied to stop. He was dreadful pleased with himself for catching Tom out. The minute Tom begun to talk about birds I judged he was a goner, because Jim knowed more about birds than both of us put together. You see, he had killed hundreds and hundreds of them, and that's the way to find out about birds. That's the way people does that writes books about birds, and loves them so that they'll go hungry and tired and take any amount of trouble to find a new bird and kill it. Their name is ornithologers, and I could have been an ornithologer myself, because I always loved birds and creatures; and I started out to learn how to be one, and I see a bird setting on a limb of a high tree, singing with its head tilted back and its mouth open, and before I thought I fired, and his song stopped and he fell straight down from the limb, all limp like a rag, and I run and picked him up and he was dead, and his body was warm in my hand, and his head rolled about this way and that, like his neck was broke, and there was a little white skin over his eyes, and one little drop of blood on the side of his head; and, laws! I couldn't see nothing more for the tears; and I hain't never murdered no creature since that warn't doing me no harm, and I ain't going to. . . .

The Tragedy of Pudd'nhead Wilson

In The Tragedy of Pudd'nhead Wilson *(1894) Twain created an extraordinarily bleak view of humankind. He explores the relative importance of heredity and training upon two boys who are exchanged in their cradles by Roxana, a slave woman. Her child, who is one-thirty-second black and therefore legally a slave, is brought up as a white master. Because of his training in arrogance and cruelty he becomes a despicable adult. When he learns of the switched identities, his character worsens. At one point the boy sells his own mother down the river.*

The novel also contains a shrewd, misunderstood country lawyer, Pudd'nhead Wilson, whose hobbies include the then new art of fingerprinting and the creation of memorable aphoristic phrases. These sayings make up "Pudd'nhead Wilson's Calendar," a gathering of skeptical and unillusioned insights that Twain uses as chapter introductions. The Calendar is presented here as a unit.

The novel also includes a set of twins, a First Family of Virginia, a murder mystery, and a dramatic courtroom scene. The pervading corrosive cynicism of the novel prevents this sparse, almost diagrammatic fiction from commanding a massive popular audience.

Pudd'nhead Wilson's Calendar

There is no character, howsoever good and fine, but it can be destroyed by ridicule, howsoever poor and witless. Observe the ass, for instance: his character is about perfect, he is the choicest spirit among all the humbler animals, yet see what ridicule has brought him to. Instead of feeling complimented when we are called an ass, we are left in doubt.

Tell the truth or trump—but get the trick.

Adam was but human—this explains it all. He did not want the apple for the apple's sake, he wanted it only because it was forbidden. The mistake was in not forbidding the serpent; then he would have eaten the serpent.

Whoever has lived long enough to find out what life is, knows how deep a debt of gratitude we owe to Adam, the first great benefactor of our race. He brought death into the world.

Adam and Eve had many advantages, but the principal one was, that they escaped teething.

Training is everything. The peach was once a bitter almond; cauliflower is nothing but cabbage with a college education.

Let us endeavor so to live that when we come to die even the undertaker will be sorry.

Habit is habit, and not to be flung out of the window by any man, but coaxed downstairs a step at a time.

One of the most striking differences between a cat and a lie is that a cat has only nine lives.

The holy passion of Friendship is of so sweet and steady and loyal and enduring a nature that it will last through a whole lifetime, if not asked to lend money.

Consider well the proportions of things. It is better to be a young June bug than an old bird of paradise.

There is this trouble about special providences—namely, there is so often a doubt as to which party was intended to be the beneficiary. In the case of the children, the bears, and the prophet, the bears got more real satisfaction out of the episode than the prophet did, because they got the children.

Why is it that we rejoice at a birth and grieve at a funeral? It is because we are not the person involved.

It is easy to find fault, if one has that disposition. There was once a man who, not being able to find any other fault with his coal, complained that there were too many prehistoric toads in it.

All say, "How hard it is that we have to die"—a strange complaint to come from the mouths of people who have had to live.

When angry, count four; when very angry, swear.

There are three infallible ways of pleasing an author, and the three form a rising scale of compliment: 1 — to tell him you have read one of his books; 2 — to tell him you have read all of his books; 3 — to ask him to let you read the manuscript of his forthcoming book. No. 1 admits you to his respect; No. 2 admits you to his admiration; No. 3 carries you clear into his heart.

As to the Adjective: when in doubt, strike it out.

Courage is resistance to fear, mastery of fear — not absence of fear. Except a creature be part coward, it is not a compliment to say it is brave; it is merely a loose misapplication of the word. Consider the flea! — incomparably the bravest of all the creatures of God, if ignorance of fear were courage. Whether you are asleep or awake he will attack you, caring nothing for the fact that in bulk and strength you are to him as are the massed armies of the earth to a sucking child; he lives both day and night and all days and nights in the very lap of peril and the immediate presence of death, and yet it is no more afraid than is the man who walks the streets of a city that was threatened by an earthquake ten centuries before. When we speak of Clive, Nelson, and Putnam as men who "didn't know what fear was," we ought always to add the flea — and put him at the head of the procession.

When I reflect upon the number of disagreeable people who I know have gone to a better world, I am moved to lead a different life.

October. This is one of the peculiarly dangerous months to speculate in stocks in. The others are July, January, September, April, November, May, March, June, December, August, and February.

The true Southern watermelon is a boon apart, and not to be mentioned with commoner things. It is chief of this world's luxuries, king by the grace of God over all the fruits of the earth. When one has tasted it, he knows what the angels eat. It was not a Southern watermelon that Eve took: we know it because she repented.

Nothing so needs reforming as other people's habits.

Behold, the fool saith, "Put not all thine eggs in the one basket" — which is but a manner of saying, "Scatter your money and your attention"; but the wise man saith, "Put all your eggs in the one basket and — WATCH THAT BASKET."

If you pick up a starving dog and make him prosperous, he will not bite you. This is the principal difference between a dog and a man.

We know all about the habits of the ant, we know all about the habits of the bee, but we know nothing at all about the habits of the oyster. It seems almost certain that we have been choosing the wrong time for studying the oyster.

Even popularity can be overdone. In Rome, along at first, you are full of regrets that Michelangelo died; but by and by, you only regret that you didn't see him do it.

July 4. Statistics show that we lose more fools on this day than in all the other days of the year put together. This proves, by the number left in stock, that one Fourth of July per year is now inadequate, the country has grown so.

Gratitude and treachery are merely the two extremities of the same procession. You have seen all of it that is worth staying for when the band and the gaudy officials have gone by.

Thanksgiving Day. Let all give humble, hearty, and sincere thanks now, but the turkeys. In the island of Fiji they do not use turkeys; they use plumbers. It does not become you and me to sneer at Fiji.

Few things are harder to put up with than the annoyance of a good example.

It were not best that we should all think alike; it is difference of opinion that makes horse races.

Even the clearest and most perfect circumstantial evidence is likely to be at fault, after all, and therefore ought to be received with great caution. Take the case of any pencil, sharpened by any woman: if you have witnesses, you will find she did it with a knife; but if you take simply the aspect of the pencil, you will say she did it with her teeth.

He is useless on top of the ground; he ought to be under it, inspiring the cabbages.

April 1. This is the day upon which we are reminded of what we are on the other three hundred and sixty-four.

It is often the case that the man who can't tell a lie thinks he is the best judge of one.

October 12, the Discovery. It was wonderful to find America, but it would have been more wonderful to miss it.

* * *

. . . The next day—that is to say on the fourth of September—something occurred which profoundly impressed Roxana. Mr. Driscoll missed another small sum of money—which is a way of saying that this was not a new thing, but had happened before. In truth, it had happened three times before. Driscoll's patience was exhausted. He was a fairly humane man toward slaves and other animals; he was an exceedingly humane man toward the erring of his own race. Theft he could not abide, and plainly there was a thief in his house. Necessarily the thief must be one of his Negroes. Sharp measures must be taken. He called his servants before him. There were three of these, besides Roxy: a man, a woman, and a boy twelve years old. They were not related. Mr. Driscoll said:

"You have all been warned before. It has done no good. This time I will teach you a lesson. I will sell the thief. Which of you is the guilty one?"

They all shuddered at the threat, for here they had a good home, and a new one was likely to be a change for the worse. The denial was general. None had stolen anything—not money, anyway—a little sugar, or cake, or honey, or something like that, that "Marse Percy wouldn't mind or miss," but not money—never a cent of money. They were eloquent in their protestations, but Mr. Driscoll was not moved by them. He answered each in turn with a stern "Name the thief!"

The truth was, all were guilty but Roxana; she suspected that the others were guilty, but she did not know them to be so. She was horrified to think how near she had come to being guilty herself; she had been saved in the nick of time by a revival in the colored Methodist Church, a fortnight before, at which time and place she "got religion." The very next day after that gracious experience, while her change of style was fresh upon her and she was vain of her purified condition, her master left a couple of dollars lying unprotected on his desk, and she happened upon that temptation when she was polishing around with a dustrag. She looked at the money awhile with a steadily rising resentment, then she burst out with:

"Dad blame dat revival, I wisht it had 'a' be'n put off till tomorrow!"

Then she covered the tempter with a book, and another member of the kitchen cabinet got it. She made this sacrifice as a matter of religious etiquette; as a thing necessary just now, but by no means to be wrested into a precedent; no, a week or two would limber up her piety, then she would be rational again, and the next two dollars that got left out in the cold would find a comforter—and she could name the comforter.

Was she bad? Was she worse than the general run of her race? No. They had an unfair show in the battle of life, and they held it no sin to take military advantage of the enemy—in a small way; in a small way, but not in a large one. They would smouch provisions from the pantry whenever they got a chance; or a brass thimble, or a cake of wax, or án emery bag, or a paper of needles, or a silver spoon, or a dollar bill, or small articles of clothing, or any other property of light value; and so far were they from considering such reprisals sinful, that they would go to church and shout and pray the loudest and sincerest with their plunder in their pockets. A farm smokehouse had to be kept heavily padlocked, for even the colored deacon himself could not resist a ham when Providence showed him in a dream, or otherwise, where such a thing hung lonesome, and longed for someone to love. But with a hundred hanging before him, the deacon would not take two—that is, on the same night. On frosty nights the humane Negro prowler would warm the end of a plank and put it up under the cold claws of chickens roosting in a tree; a drowsy hen would step on to the comfortable board, softly clucking her gratitude, and the prowler would dump her into his bag, and later into his stomach, perfectly sure that in taking this trifle from the man who daily robbed him of an inestimable treasure—his liberty—he was not committing any sin that God would remember against him in the Last Great Day.

"Name the thief!"

For the fourth time Mr. Driscoll had said it, and always in the same hard tone. And now he added these words of awful import:

"I give you one minute." He took out his watch. "If at the end of that time, you have not confessed, I will not only sell all four of you, *but*—I will sell you DOWN THE RIVER!"

It was equivalent to condemning them to hell! No Missouri Negro doubted this. Roxy reeled in her tracks, and the color vanished out of her face; the others dropped to their knees as if they had been shot; tears gushed from their eyes, their supplicating hands went up, and three answers came in the one instant.

"I done it!"

"I done it!"

"I done it!—have mercy, marster—Lord have mercy on us po' niggers!"

"Very good," said the master, putting up his watch, "I will sell you *here* though you don't deserve it. You ought to be sold down the river."

The culprits flung themselves prone, in an ecstasy of gratitude, and kissed his feet, declaring that they would never forget his goodness and never cease to pray for him as long as they lived. They were sincere, for like a god he had stretched forth his mighty hand and closed the gates of hell against them. He knew, himself, that he had done a noble and gracious thing, and was privately well pleased with his magnanimity; and that night he set the incident down in his diary, so that his son might read it in after years, and be thereby moved to deeds of gentleness and humanity himself. . . .

Percy Driscoll slept well the night he saved his house minions from going down the river, but no wink of sleep visited Roxy's eyes. A profound terror had taken possession of her. Her child could grow up and be sold down the river! The thought crazed her with horror. If she dozed and lost herself for a moment, the next moment she was on her feet flying to her child's cradle to see if it was still there. Then she would gather it to her heart and pour out her love upon it in a frenzy of kisses, moaning, crying, and saying, "Dey sha'n't, oh, dey *sha'n't!*—yo' po' mammy will kill you fust!"

Once, when she was tucking it back in its cradle again, the other child nestled in its sleep and attracted her attention. She went and stood over it a long time communing with herself.

"What has my po' baby done, dat he couldn't have yo' luck? He hain't done noth'n'. God was good to you; why warn't he good to him? Dey can't sell *you* down de river. I hates yo' pappy; he hain't got no heart—for niggers, he hain't, anyways. I hate him, en I could kill him!" She paused awhile, thinking; then she burst into wild sobbings again, and turned away, saying, "Oh, I got to kill my chile, dey ain't no yuther way—killin' *him* wouldn't save de chile fum goin' down de river. Oh, I got to do it, yo' po' mammy's got to kill you to save you, honey." She gathered her baby to her bosom now, and began to smother it with caresses. "Mammy's got to kill you—how *kin* I do it! But yo' mammy ain't gwine to desert you—no, no; *dah,* don't cry—she gwine *wid* you, she gwine to kill herself too. Come along, honey, come along wid mammy; we gwine to jump in de river, den de troubles o' dis worl' is all over—dey don't sell po' niggers down the river over *yonder.*"

She started toward the door, crooning to the child and hushing it; midway she stopped, suddenly. She had caught sight of her new Sunday gown—a cheap curtain-calico thing, a conflagration of gaudy colors and fantastic figures. She surveyed it wistfully, longingly.

"Hain't ever wore it yet," she said, "en it's jist lovely." Then she nodded her head in response to a pleasant idea, and added, "No, I ain't gwine to be fished out, wid everybody lookin' at me, in dis mis'able ole linsey-woolsey."

She put down the child and made the change. She looked in the glass and was astonished at her beauty. She resolved to make her death toilet perfect. She took off her handkerchief turban and dressed her glossy wealth of hair "like white folks"; she added some odds and ends of rather lurid ribbon and a spray of atrocious artificial flowers; finally she threw over her shoulders a fluffy thing called a "cloud" in that day, which was of a blazing red complexion. Then she was ready for the tomb.

She gathered up her baby once more; but when her eyes fell upon its miserably short little gray tow-linen shirt and noted the contrast between its pauper shabbiness and her own volcanic eruption of infernal splendors, her mother-heart was touched, and she was ashamed.

"No, dolling, mammy ain't gwine to treat you so. De angels is gwine to 'mire you jist as much as dey does yo' mammy. Ain't gwine to have 'em putt'n' dey han's up 'fo' dey eyes en sayin' to David en Goliah en dem yuther prophets, 'Dat chile is dress' too indelicate fo' dis place.'"

By this time she had stripped off the shirt. Now she clothed the naked little creature in one of Thomas à Becket's snowy, long baby gowns, with its bright blue bows and dainty flummery of ruffles.

"Dah—now you's fixed." She propped the child in a chair and stood off to inspect it. Straightway her eyes began to widen with astonishment and admiration, and she clapped her hands and cried out, "Why, it do beat all! I *never* knowed you was so lovely. Marse Tommy ain't a bit puttier—not a single bit."

She stepped over and glanced at the other infant; she flung a glance back at her own; then one more at the heir of the house. Now a strange light dawned in her eyes, and in a moment she was lost in thought. She seemed in a trance; when she came out of it, she muttered, "When I 'uz a-washin' 'em in de tub, yistiddy, his own pappy asked me which of 'em was his'n."

She began to move about like one in a dream. She undressed Thomas à Becket, stripping him of everything, and put the tow-linen shirt on him. She put his coral necklace on her own child's neck. Then she placed the children side by side, and after earnest inspection she muttered:

"Now who would b'lieve clo'es could do de like o' dat? Dog my cats if it ain't all *I* kin do to tell t' other fum which, let alone his pappy."

She put her cub in Tommy's elegant cradle and said:

"You's young Marse *Tom* fum dis out, en I got to practice and git used to 'memberin' to call you dat, honey, or I's gwine to make a mistake sometime en git us bofe into trouble. Dah—now you lay still en don't fret no mo', Marse Tom. Oh, thank de good Lord in heaven, you's saved, you's saved! Dey ain't no man kin ever sell mammy's po' little honey down de river now!"

She put the heir of the house in her own child's unpainted pine cradle, and said, contemplating its slumbering form uneasily:

"I's sorry for you, honey; I's sorry, God knows I is—but what *kin* I do, what *could* I do? Yo' pappy would sell him to somebody, sometime, en den he'd go down de river, sho', en I couldn't, couldn't, *couldn't* stan' it."

She flung herself on her bed and began to think and toss, toss and think. By and by she sat suddenly upright, for a comforting thought had flown through her worried mind.

" 'Tain't no sin—*white* folks has done it! It ain't no sin; glory to goodness, it ain't no sin! *Dey's* done it—yes, en dey was de biggest quality in de whole bilin', too—*kings!*"

She began to muse; she was trying to gather out of her memory the dim particulars of some tale she had heard sometime or other. At last she said:

"Now I's got it; now I 'member. It was dat ole nigger preacher dat tole it, de time he come over here fum Illinois en preached in de nigger church. He said dey ain't nobody kin save his own self—can't do it by faith, can't do it by works, can't do it no way at all. Free grace is de *on'y* way, en dat don't come fum nobody but jis' de Lord; en *He* kin give it to anybody He please, saint or sinner—*He* don't kyer. He do jis' as He's a mineter. He s'lect out anybody dat suit Him, en put another one in his place, en make de fust one happy forever en leave t'other one to burn wid Satan. De preacher said it was jist like dey done in Englan' one time, long time ago. De queen she lef' her baby layin' aroun' one day, en went out callin'; en one o' de niggers roun'bout de place dat was 'mos' white, she come in en see de chile layin' aroun', en tuck en put her own chile's clo'es on de queen's chile, en put de queen's chile's clo'es on her own chile, en den lef' her own chile layin' aroun', en tuck en toted de queen's chile home to de nigger quarter, en nobody ever foun' it out, en her chile was de king bimeby, en sole de queen's chile down de river one time when dey had to settle up de estate. Dah, now—de preacher said it his own self, en it ain't no sin, 'ca'se white folks done it. *Dey* done it—yes, *dey* done it; en not on'y jis' common white folks nuther, but de biggest quality dey is in de whole bilin'. Oh, I's *so* glad I 'member 'bout dat!"

She got up lighthearted and happy, and went to the cradles, and spent what was left of the night "practicing." She would give her own child a light pat and say humbly, "Lay still, Marse Tom," then give the real Tom a pat and say with severity, "Lay *still,* Chambers! Does you want me to take somep'n' *to* you?"

As she progressed with her practice, she was surprised to see how steadily and surely the awe which had kept her tongue reverent and her manner humble toward her young master was transferring itself to her speech and manner toward the usurper, and how similarly handy she was becoming in transferring her motherly curtness of speech and peremptoriness of manner to the unlucky heir of the ancient house of Driscoll.

She took occasional rests from practicing, and absorbed herself in calculating her chances.

"Dey'll sell dese niggers today fo' stealin' de money, den dey'll buy some mo' dat don't know de chillen—so *dat's* all right. When I takes de chillen out to git de air, de minute I's roun' de corner I's gwine to gaum dey mouths all roun' wid jam, den dey can't *nobody* notice dey's changed. Yes, I gwine ter do dat till I's safe, if it's a year.

"Dey ain't but one man dat I's afeard of, en dat's dat Pudd'nhead Wilson. Dey calls him a pudd'nhead, en says he's a fool. My lan', dat man ain't no mo' fool den I is! He's de smartes' man in dis town, less'n it's Jedge Driscoll or maybe Pem Howard. Blame dat man, he worries me wid dem ornery glasses o' his'n; *I* b'lieve he's a witch. But nemmine, I's gwine to happen aroun' dah one o' dese days en let on dat I reckon he wants to print de chillen's fingers ag'in; en if *he* don't notice dey's changed, I bound dey ain't nobody gwine to notice it, en den I's safe, sho'. But I reckon I'll tote along a hoss-shoe to keep off de witch work."

The new Negroes gave Roxy no trouble, of course. The master gave her none, for one of his speculations was in jeopardy, and his mind was so occupied that he hardly saw the children when he looked at them, and all Roxy had to do was to get them both into a gale of laughter when he came about; then their faces were mainly cavities exposing gums, and he was gone again before the spasm passed and the little creatures resumed a human aspect.

Within a few days the fate of the speculation became so dubious that Mr. Percy went away with his brother, the judge, to see what could be done with it. It was a land speculation as usual, and it had gotten complicated with a lawsuit. The men were gone seven weeks. Before they got back, Roxy had paid her visit to Wilson, and was satisfied. Wilson took the fingerprints, labeled them with the names and with the date—October the first—put them carefully away, and continued his chat with Roxy, who seemed very anxious that he should admire the great advance in flesh and beauty which the babies had made since he took their fingerprints a month before. He complimented their improvement to her contentment; and as they were without any disguise of jam or other stain, she trembled all the while and was miserably frightened lest at any moment he—

But he didn't. He discovered nothing; and she went home jubilant, and dropped all concern about the matter permanently out of her mind. . . .

Judge Driscoll had retired from the bench and from all business activities in 1850, and had now been comfortably idle three years. He was president of the Freethinkers' Society, and Pudd'nhead Wilson was the other member. The society's weekly discussions were now the old lawyer's main interest in life. Pudd'nhead was still toiling in obscurity at the bottom of the ladder, under the blight of that unlucky remark which he had let fall twenty-three years before about the dog.

Judge Driscoll was his friend, and claimed that he had a mind above the average, but that was regarded as one of the judge's whims, and it failed to modify the public opinion. Or rather, that was one of the reasons why it failed, but there was another and better one. If the judge had stopped with bare assertion, it would have had a good deal of effect; but he made the mistake of trying to prove his position. For some years Wilson had been privately at work on a whimsical almanac, for his amusement—a calendar, with a little dab of ostensible philosophy, usually in ironical form, appended to each date; and the judge thought that these quips and fancies of Wilson's were neatly turned and cute; so he carried a handful of them around one day, and read them to some of the chief citizens. But irony was not for those people; their mental vision was not focused for it. They read those playful trifles in the solidest earnest, and decided without hesitancy that if there had ever been any doubt that Dave Wilson was a pudd'nhead—which there hadn't—this revelation removed that doubt for good and all. That is just the way in this world; an enemy can partly ruin a man, but it takes a good-natured injudicious friend to complete the thing and make it perfect. After this the judge felt tenderer than ever toward Wilson, and surer than ever that his calendar had merit.

Judge Driscoll could be a freethinker and still hold his place in society because he was the person of most consequence in the community, and therefore could venture to go his own way and follow out his own notions. The other member of his pet organization was allowed the like liberty because he was a cipher in the estimation of the public, and nobody attached any importance to what he thought or did. He was liked, he was welcome enough all around, but he simply didn't count for anything. . . .

* * *

Every now and then, after Tom went to bed, he had sudden wakings out of his sleep, and his first thought was, "Oh, joy, it was all a dream!" Then he laid himself heavily down again, with a groan and the muttered words, "A nigger! I am a nigger! Oh, I wish I was dead!"

He woke at dawn with one more repetition of this horror, and then he resolved to meddle no more with that treacherous sleep. He began to think. Sufficiently bitter thinkings they were. They wandered along something after this fashion:

"Why were niggers *and* whites made? What crime did the uncreated first nigger commit that the curse of birth was decreed for him? And why is this awful difference made between white and black? . . . How hard the nigger's fate seems, this morning!—yet until last night such a thought never entered my head."

He sighed and groaned an hour or more away. Then "Chambers" came humbly in to say that breakfast was nearly ready. "Tom" blushed scarlet to see this aristocratic white youth cringe to him, a nigger, and call him "Young Marster." He said roughly:

"Get out of my sight!" and when the youth was gone, he muttered, "He has done me no harm, poor wretch, but he is an eyesore to me now, for he is Driscoll, the young gentleman, and I am a—oh, I wish I was dead!"

A gigantic eruption, like that of Krakatoa a few years ago, with the accompanying earthquakes, tidal waves, and clouds of volcanic dust, changes the face of the surrounding landscape beyond recognition, bringing down the high lands, elevating the low, making fair lakes where deserts had been, and deserts where green prairies had smiled before. The tremendous catastrophe which had befallen Tom had changed his moral landscape in much the same way. Some of his low places he found lifted to ideals, some of his ideals had sunk to the valleys, and lay there with the sackcloth and ashes of pumice stone and sulphur on their ruined heads.

For days he wandered in lonely places, thinking, thinking, thinking—trying to get his bearings. It was new work. If he met a friend, he found that the habit of a lifetime had in some mysterious way vanished—his arm hung limp, instead of involuntarily extending the hand for a shake. It was the "nigger" in him asserting its humility, and he blushed and was abashed. And the "nigger" in him was surprised when the white friend put out his hand for a shake with him. He found the "nigger" in him involuntarily giving the road, on the sidewalk, to the white rowdy and loafer. When Rowena, the dearest thing his heart knew, the idol of his secret worship, invited him in, the "nigger" in him made an embarrassed excuse and was afraid to enter and sit with the dread white folks on equal terms. The "nigger" in him went shrinking and skulking here and there and yonder, and fancying it saw suspicion and maybe detection in all faces, tones, and gestures. So strange and uncharacteristic was Tom's conduct that people noticed it, and turned to look after him when he passed on; and when he glanced back—as he could not help doing, in spite of his best resistance—and caught that puzzled expression in a person's face, it gave him a sick feeling, and he took himself out of view as quickly as he could. He presently came to have a hunted sense and a hunted look, and then he fled away to the hilltops and the solitudes. He said to himself that the curse of Ham was upon him.

He dreaded his meals; the "nigger" in him was ashamed to sit at the white folks' table, and feared discovery all the time; and once when Judge Driscoll said, "What's the matter with you? You look as meek as a nigger," he felt as secret murderers are said to feel when the accuser says, "Thou art the man!" Tom said he was not well, and left the table.

His ostensible "aunt's" solicitudes and endearments were become a terror to him, and he avoided them.

And all the time, hatred of his ostensible "uncle" was steadily growing in his heart; for he said to himself, "He is white; and I am his chattel, his property, his goods, and he can sell me, just as he could his dog."

For as much as a week after this, Tom imagined that his character had undergone a pretty radical change. But that was because he did not know himself.

In several ways his opinions were totally changed, and would never go back to what they were before, but the main structure of his character was not changed, and could not be changed. One or two very important features of it were altered, and in time effects would result from this, if opportunity offered—effects of a quite serious nature, too. Under the influence of a great mental and moral upheaval, his character and habits had taken on the appearance of complete change, but after a while with the subsidence of the storm, both began to settle toward their former places. He dropped gradually back into his old frivolous and easygoing ways and conditions of feeling and manner of speech, and no familiar of his could have detected anything in him that differentiated him from the weak and careless Tom of other days.

The theft raid which he had made upon the village turned out better than he had ventured to hope. It produced the sum necessary to pay his gaming debts, and saved him from exposure to his uncle and another smashing of the will. He and his mother learned to like each other fairly well. She couldn't love him, as yet, because there "warn't nothing *to* him," as she expressed it, but her nature needed something or somebody to rule over, and he was better than nothing. Her strong character and aggressive and commanding ways compelled Tom's admiration in spite of the fact that he got more illustrations of them than he needed for his comfort. However, as a rule her conversation was made up of racy tattle about the privacies of the chief families of the town (for she went harvesting among the kitchens every time she came to the village), and Tom enjoyed this. It was just in his line. She always collected her half of his pension punctually, and he was always at the haunted house to have a chat with her on these occasions. Every now and then, she paid him a visit there on between-days also.

Occasionally he would run up to St. Louis for a few weeks, and at last temptation caught him again. He won a lot of money, but lost it, and with it a deal more besides, which he promised to raise as soon as possible.

For this purpose he projected a new raid on his town. He never meddled with any other town, for he was afraid to venture into houses whose ins and outs he did not know and the habits of whose households he was not acquainted with. He arrived at the haunted house in disguise on the Wednesday before the advent of the twins—after writing his Aunt Pratt that he would not arrive until two days after—and lay in hiding there with his mother until toward daylight Friday morning, when he went to his uncle's house and entered by the back way with his own key, and slipped up to his room, where he could have the use of mirror and toilet articles. He had a suit of girl's clothes with him in a bundle as a disguise for his raid, and was wearing a suit of his mother's clothing, with black gloves and veil. By dawn he was tricked out for his raid, but he caught a glimpse of Pudd'nhead Wilson through the window over the way, and knew that Pudd'nhead had caught a glimpse of him. So he entertained Wilson with some airs and graces and attitudes for a while, then stepped out of sight and resumed the other disguise, and by and by went down and out the back way and started downtown to reconnoiter the scene of his intended labors.

But he was ill at ease. He had changed back to Roxy's dress, with the stoop of age added to the disguise, so that Wilson would not bother himself about a humble old woman leaving a neighbor's house by the back way in the early morning, in case he was still spying. But supposing Wilson had seen him leave, and had thought it suspicious, and had also followed him? The thought made Tom cold. He gave up the raid for the day, and hurried back to the haunted house by the obscurest route he knew. His mother was gone; but she came back, by and by, with the news of the grand reception at Patsy Cooper's, and soon persuaded him that the opportunity was like a special Providence, it was so inviting and perfect. So he went raiding, after all, and made a nice success of it while everybody was gone to Patsy Cooper's. Success gave him nerve and even actual intrepidity; insomuch, indeed, that after he had conveyed his harvest to his mother in a back alley, he went to the reception himself, and added several of the valuables of that house to his takings.

After this long digression we have now arrived once more at the point where Pudd'nhead Wilson, while waiting for the arrival of the twins on that same Friday evening, sat puzzling over the strange apparition of that morning—a girl in young Tom Driscoll's bedroom; fretting, and guessing, and puzzling over it, and wondering who the shameless creature might be. . . .

* * *

Wilson went back to his principal and reported the failure of his mission. Luigi was incensed, and asked how it could be that the old gentleman, who was by no means dull witted, held his trifling nephew's evidence and inferences to be of more value than Wilson's. But Wilson laughed, and said:

"That is quite simple; that is easily explicable. I am not his doll—his baby—his infatuation: his nephew is. The judge and his late wife never had any children. The judge and his wife were past middle age when this treasure fell into their lap. One must make allowances for a parental instinct that has been starving for twenty-five or thirty years. It is famished, it is crazed with hunger by that time, and will be entirely satisfied with anything that comes handy; its taste is atrophied, it can't tell mud cat from shad. A devil born to a young couple is measurably recognizable by them as a devil before long, but a devil adopted by an old couple is an angel to them, and remains so, through thick and thin. Tom is this old man's angel; he is infatuated with him. Tom can persuade him into things which other people can't—not all things; I don't mean that, but a good many—particularly one class of things: the things that create or abolish personal partialities or prejudices in the old man's mind. The old man liked both of you. Tom conceived a hatred for you. That was enough; it turned the old man around at once. The oldest and strongest friendship must go to the ground when one of these late-adopted darlings throws a brick at it."

"It's a curious philosophy," said Luigi.

"It ain't a philosophy at all—it's a fact. And there is something pathetic and beautiful about it, too. I think there is nothing more pathetic than to see one of these poor old childless couples taking a menagerie of yelping little worthless dogs to their hearts; and then adding some cursing and squawking parrots and a jackass-voiced macaw; and next a couple of hundred screeching songbirds, and presently some fetid guinea pigs and rabbits, and a howling colony of cats. It is all a groping and ignorant effort to construct out of base metal and brass filings, so to speak, something to take the place of that golden treasure denied them by Nature, a child. But this is a digression. The unwritten law of this region requires you to kill Judge Driscoll on sight, and he and the community will expect that attention at your hands—though of course your own death by his bullet will answer every purpose. Look out for him! Are you heeled—that is, fixed?"

"Yes, he shall have his opportunity. If he attacks me, I will respond." . . .

In Defense of Harriet Shelley

Twain's intolerance for cant permeates In Defense of Harriet Shelley. *A biography of the poet Percy Shelley had constructed an elaborate case defending the poet's adultery. The case depended upon connotations, intimations, and, primarily, the biographer's bias in favor of the poet. In opposition, Twain's sense of justice and his argumentative skills are fully engaged in defense of Harriet Shelley.*

I have committed sins, of course; but I have not committed enough of them to entitle me to the punishment of reduction to the bread and water of ordinary literature during six years when I might have been living on the fat diet spread for the righteous in Professor Dowden's *Life of Shelley,* if I had been justly dealt with.

During these six years I have been living a life of peaceful ignorance. I was not aware that Shelley's first wife was unfaithful to him, and that that was why he deserted her and wiped the stain from his sensitive honor by entering into soiled relations with Godwin's young daughter. This was all new to me when I heard it lately, and was told that the proofs of it were in this book, and that this book's verdict is accepted in the girls' colleges of America and its view taught in their literary classes.

In each of these six years multitudes of young people in our country have arrived at the Shelley-reading age. Are these six multitudes unacquainted with the life of Shelley? Perhaps they are; indeed, one may feel pretty sure that the great bulk of them are. To these, then, I address myself, in the hope that some account of this romantic historical fable and the fabulist's manner of constructing and adorning it may interest them.

First, as to its literary style. Our negroes in America have several ways of entertaining themselves which are not found among the whites anywhere.

Among these inventions of theirs is one which is particularly popular with them. It is a competition in elegant deportment. They hire a hall and bank the spectators' seats in rising tiers along the two sides, leaving all the middle stretch of the floor free. A cake is provided as a prize for the winner in the competition, and a bench of experts in deportment is appointed to award it. Sometimes there are as many as fifty contestants, male and female, and five hundred spectators. One at a time the contestants enter, clothed regardless of expense in what each considers the perfection of style and taste, and walk down the vacant central space and back again with that multitude of critical eyes on them. All that the competitor knows of fine airs and graces he throws into his carriage, all that he knows of seductive expression he throws into his countenance. He may use all the helps he can devise: watch-chain to twirl with his fingers, cane to do graceful things with, snowy handkerchief to flourish and get artful effects out of, shiny new stovepipe hat to assist in his courtly bows; and the colored lady may have a fan to work up *her* effects with, and smile over and blush behind, and she may add other helps, according to her judgment. When the review by individual detail is over, a grand review of all the contestants in procession follows, with all the airs and graces and all the bowings and smirkings on exhibition at once, and this enables the bench of experts to make the necessary comparisons and arrive at a verdict. The successful competitor gets the prize which I have before mentioned, and an abundance of applause and envy along with it. The negroes have a name for this grave deportment tournament; a name taken from the prize contended for. They call it a Cake-Walk.

The Shelley biography is a literary cake-walk. The ordinary forms of speech are absent from it. All the pages, all the paragraphs, walk by sedately, elegantly, not to say mincingly, in their Sunday-best, shiny and sleek, perfumed, and with *boutonnières* in their buttonholes; it is rare to find even a chance sentence that has forgotten to dress. If the book wishes to tell us that Mary Godwin, child of sixteen, had known afflictions, the fact saunters forth in this nobby outfit: "Mary was herself not unlearned in the lore of pain"—meaning by that that she had not always traveled on asphalt; or, as some authorities would frame it, that she had "been there herself," a form which, while preferable to the book's form, is still not to be recommended. If the book wishes to tell us that Harriet Shelley hired a wet-nurse, that commonplace fact gets turned into a dancing-master, who does his professional bow before us in pumps and knee-breeches, with his fiddle under one arm and his crush-hat under the other, thus: "The beauty of Harriet's motherly relation to her babe was marred in Shelley's eyes by the introduction into his house of a hireling nurse to whom was delegated the mother's tenderest office."

This is perhaps the strangest book that has seen the light since Frankenstein. Indeed, it is a Frankenstein itself; a Frankenstein with the original infirmity supplemented by a new one; a Frankenstein with the reasoning faculty wanting. Yet it believes it can reason, and is always trying. It is not content to leave a mountain of fact standing in the clear sunshine, where the simplest reader can perceive its form, its details, and its relation to the rest of the landscape, but thinks it must help him examine it and understand it; so its drifting mind settles upon it with that intent, but always with one and the same result: there is a change of temperature and the mountain is hid in a fog. Every time it sets up a premise and starts to reason from it, there is a surprise in store for the reader. It is strangely near-sighted, cross-eyed, and purblind. Sometimes when a mastodon walks across the field of its vision it takes it for a rat; at other times it does not see it at all.

The materials of this biographical fable are facts, rumors, and poetry. They are connected together and harmonized by the help of suggestion, conjecture, innuendo, perversion, and semi-suppression.

The fable has a distinct object in view, but this object is not acknowledged in set words. Percy Bysshe Shelley has done something which in the case of other men is called a grave crime; it must be shown that in his case it is not that, because he does not think as other men do about these things.

Ought not that to be enough, if the fabulist is serious? Having proved that a crime is not a crime, was it worth while to go on and fasten the responsibility of a crime which was not a crime upon somebody else? What is the use of hunting down and holding to bitter account people who are responsible for other people's innocent acts?

Still, the fabulist thinks it a good idea to do that. In his view Shelley's first wife, Harriet, free of all offense as far as we have historical facts for guidance, must be held unforgivably responsible for her husband's innocent act in deserting her and taking up with another woman.

Any one will suspect that this task has its difficulties. Any one will divine that nice work is necessary here, cautious work, wily work, and that there is entertainment to be had in watching the magician do it. There is indeed entertainment in watching him. He arranges his facts, his rumors, and his poems on his table in full view of the house, and shows you that everything is there—no deception, everything fair and aboveboard. And this is apparently true, yet there is a defect, for some of his best stock is hid in an appendix-basket behind the door, and you do not come upon it until the exhibition is over and the enchantment of your mind accomplished—as the magician thinks.

There is an insistent atmosphere of candor and fairness about this book which is engaging at first, then a little burdensome, then a trifle fatiguing, then progressively suspicious, annoying, irritating, and oppressive. It takes one some little time to find out that phrases which seem intended to guide the reader aright are there to mislead him; that phrases which seem intended to throw light are there to throw darkness; that phrases which seem intended to interpret a fact are there to misinterpret it; that phrases which seem intended to forestall prejudice are there to create it; that phrases which seem antidotes are poisons in disguise. The naked facts arrayed in the book establish Shelley's guilt in that one episode which disfigures his otherwise superlatively lofty and beautiful life; but the historian's careful and methodical misinterpretation of them transfers the responsibility to the wife's shoulders—as he persuades himself. The few meager facts of Harriet Shelley's life, as furnished by the book, acquit her of offense; but by calling in the forbidden helps of rumor, gossip, conjecture, insinuation, and innuendo he destroys her character and rehabilitates Shelley's—as he believes. And in truth his unheroic work has not been barren of the results he aimed at; as witness the assertion made to me that girls in the colleges of America are taught that Harriet Shelley put a stain upon her husband's honor, and that that was what stung him into repurifying himself by deserting her and his child and entering into scandalous relations with a school-girl acquaintance of his.

If that assertion is true, they probably use a reduction of this work in those colleges, maybe only a sketch outlined from it. Such a thing as that could be harmful and misleading. They ought to cast it out and put the whole book in its place. It would not deceive. It would not deceive the janitor.

All of this book is interesting on account of the sorcerer's methods and the attractiveness of some of his characters and the repulsiveness of the rest, but no part of it is so much so as are the chapters wherein he tries to think he thinks he sets forth the causes which led to Shelley's desertion of his wife in 1814. . . .

We have now arrived at a part of the swamp where the difficulties and perplexities are going to be greater than any we have yet met with—where, indeed, the finger-boards are multitudinous, and the most of them pointing diligently in the wrong direction. We are to be told by the biography why Shelley deserted his wife and child and took up with Cornelia Turner and Italian. It was not on account of Cornelia's sighs and sentimentalities and tea and manna and late hours and soft and sweet and industrious enticements; no, it was because "his happiness in his home had been wounded and bruised almost to death."

It had been wounded and bruised almost to death in this way:

1st. Harriet persuaded him to set up a carriage.

2d. After the intrusion of the baby, Harriet stopped reading aloud and studying.

3d. Harriet's walks with Hogg "commonly conducted us to some fashionable bonnet-shop."

4th. Harriet hired a wet-nurse.

5th. When an operation was being performed upon the baby, "Harriet stood by, narrowly observing all that was done, but, to the astonishment of the operator, betraying not the smallest sign of emotion."

6th. Eliza Westbrook, sister-in-law, was still of the household.

The evidence against Harriet Shelley is all in; there is no more. Upon these six counts she stands indicted of the crime of driving her husband into that sty at Bracknell; and this crime, by these helps, the biographical prosecuting attorney has set himself the task of proving upon her.

Does the biographer *call* himself the attorney for the prosecution? No, only to himself, privately; publicly he is the passionless, disinterested, impartial judge on the bench. He holds up his judicial scales before the world, that all may see; and it all tries to look so fair that a blind person would sometimes fail to see him slip the false weights in. . . .

Shelley's happiness in his home had been wounded and bruised almost to death, fourthly, by the introduction there of a wet-nurse. The wet-nurse was introduced at the time of the Edinburgh sojourn, immediately after Shelley had been enjoying the two months of study with Cornelia which broke up his wife's studies and destroyed his personal interest in them. Why, by this time, nothing that Shelley's wife could do would have been satisfactory to him, for he was in love with another woman, and was never going to be contented again until he got back to her. If he had been still in love with his wife it is not easily conceivable that he would care much who nursed the baby, provided the baby was well nursed. Harriet's jealousy was assuredly voicing itself now, Shelley's conscience was assuredly nagging him, pestering him, persecuting him. Shelley needed excuses for his altered attitude toward his wife; Providence pitied him and sent the wet-nurse. If Providence had sent him a cotton doughnut it would have answered just as well; all he wanted was something to find fault with. . . .

The biographer says of Harriet, "If words of tender affection and motherly pride proved the reality of love, then undoubtedly she loved her first-born child." That is, if mere empty words can prove it, it stands proved—and in this way, without committing himself, he gives the reader a chance to infer that there isn't any extant evidence but words, and that he doesn't take much stock in them. How seldom he shows his hand! He is always lurking behind a non-committal "if" or something of that kind; always gliding and dodging around, distributing colorless poison here and there and everywhere, but always leaving himself in a position to say that his language will be found innocuous if taken to pieces and examined. He clearly exhibits a steady and never-relaxing purpose to make Harriet the scapegoat for her husband's first great sin—but it is in the general view that this is revealed, not in the details. His insidious literature is like blue water; you know what it is that makes it blue, but you cannot produce and verify any detail of the cloud of microscopic dust in it that does it. Your adversary can dip up a glassful and show you that it is pure white and you cannot deny it; and he can dip the lake dry, glass by glass, and show that every glassful is white, and prove it to any one's eye—and yet that lake *was* blue and you can swear it. This book is blue—with slander in solution. . . .

Against Harriet Shelley's good name there is not one scrap of tarnishing evidence, and not even a scrap of evil gossip, that comes from a source that entitles it to a hearing.

On the credit side of the account we have strong opinions from the people who knew her best. Peacock says:

> I feel it due to the memory of Harriet to state my most decided conviction that her conduct as a wife was as pure, as true, as absolutely faultless, as that of any who for such conduct are held most in honor.

Thornton Hunt, who had picked and published slight flaws in Harriet's character, says, as regards this alleged large one:

> There is not a trace of evidence or a whisper of scandal against her before her voluntary departure from Shelley.

Trelawney says:

> I was assured by the evidence of the few friends who knew both Shelley and his wife—Hookham, Hogg, Peacock, and one of the Godwins—that Harriet was perfectly innocent of all offense.

What excuse was there for raking up a parcel of foul rumors from malicious and discredited sources and flinging them at this dead girl's head? Her very defenselessness should have been her protection. The fact that all letters to her or about her, with almost every scrap of her own writing, had been diligently mislaid, leaving her case destitute of a voice, while every pen-stroke which could help her husband's side had been as diligently preserved, should have excused her from being brought to trial. Her witnesses have all disappeared, yet we see her summoned in her grave-clothes to plead for the life of her character, without the help of an advocate, before a disqualified judge and a packed jury.

Harriet Shelley wrote her distressed letter on the 7th of July. On the 28th her husband ran away with Mary Godwin and her part-sister Claire to the Continent. He deserted his wife when her confinement was approaching. She bore him a child at the end of November, his mistress bore him another one something over two months later. The truants were back in London before either of these events occurred.

On one occasion, presently, Shelley was so pressed for money to support his mistress with that he went to his wife and got some money of his that was in her hands—twenty pounds. Yet the mistress was not moved to gratitude; for later, when the wife was troubled to meet her engagements, the mistress makes this entry in her diary:

> Harriet sends her creditors here; nasty woman. Now we shall have to change our lodgings.

The deserted wife bore the bitterness and obloquy of her situation two years and a quarter; then she gave up, and drowned herself. A month afterward the body was found in the water. Three weeks later Shelley married his mistress.

I must here be allowed to italicize a remark of the biographer's concerning Harriet Shelley:

> *That no act of Shelley's during the two years which immediately preceded her death tended to cause the rash act which brought her life to its close seems certain.*

Yet her husband had deserted her and her children, and was living with a concubine all that time! Why should a person attempt to write biography when the simplest facts have no meaning to him? This book is littered with as crass stupidities as that one—deductions by the page which bear no discoverable kinship to their premises.

The biographer throws off that extraordinary remark without any perceptible disturbance to his serenity; for he follows it with a sentimental justification of Shelley's conduct which has not a pang of conscience in it, but is silky and smooth and undulating and pious—a cake-walk with all the colored brethren at their best. There may be people who can read that page and keep their temper, but it is doubtful.

Shelley's life has the one indelible blot upon it, but is otherwise worshipfully noble and beautiful. It even stands out indestructibly gracious and lovely from the ruck of these disastrous pages, in spite of the fact that they expose and establish his responsibility for his forsaken wife's pitiful fate—a responsibility which he himself tacitly admits in a letter to Eliza Westbrook, wherein he refers to his taking up with Mary Godwin as an act which Eliza "might excusably regard as the cause of her sister's ruin."

IV

The Icy Perceptive Stare

Short Writings

This brief selection from Twain's short writings covers a wide range of topics, usually in essay form. In response to a French commentator about American culture, Twain mounted an extended argument that is edited here to reveal only two points: a misunderstanding about Americans' love of money and a misuse of statistics.

In "Stirring Times in Austria," a long, rambling account of political upheavals, Twain has one closely focused section on governmental creation of tranquility by censorship and suppression.

In "A Majestic Literary Fossil," Twain uses his reading of a medical textbook as a springboard to describe the great change in social attitude toward experimentation and scientific progress.

"Concerning the Jews" presents Twain's analysis of a difficult problem—the persistence of anti-Jewish attitudes.

In a brief short story, "The Five Boons of Life," Twain presents a bleak, sparse, icy interpretation.

What Paul Bourget Thinks of Us

. . . I spoke a moment ago of the existence of some superstitions that have been parading the world as facts this long time. For instance, consider the Dollar. The world seems to think that the love of money is "American"; and that the mad desire to get suddenly rich is "American." I believe that both of these things are merely and broadly human, not American monopolies at all. The love of money is natural to all nations, for money is a good and strong friend.

I think that this love has existed everywhere, ever since the Bible called it the root of all evil.

I think that the reason why we Americans seem to be so addicted to trying to get rich suddenly is merely because the *opportunity* to make promising efforts in that direction has offered itself to us with a frequency out of all proportion to the European experience. For eighty years this opportunity has been offering itself in one new town or region after another straight westward, step by step, all the way from the Atlantic coast to the Pacific. When a mechanic could buy ten town lots on tolerably long credit for ten months' savings out of his wages, and reasonably expect to sell them in a couple of years for ten times what he gave for them, it was human for him to try the venture, and he did it no matter what his nationality was. He would have done it in Europe or China if he had had the same chance.

In the flush times in the silver regions a cook or any other humble worker stood a very good chance to get rich out of a trifle of money risked in a stock deal; and that person promptly took that risk, no matter what his or her nationality might be. I was there, and saw it.

But these opportunities have not been plenty in our Southern states; so there you have a prodigious region where the rush for sudden wealth is almost an unknown thing—and has been, from the beginning.

Europe has offered few opportunities for poor Tom, Dick, and Harry; but when she has offered one, there has been no noticeable difference between European eagerness and American. England saw this in the wild days of the Railroad King; France saw it in 1720—time of Law and the Mississippi Bubble. I am sure I have never seen in the gold and silver mines any madness, fury, frenzy to get suddenly rich which was even remotely comparable to that which raged in France in the Bubble day. If I had a cyclopedia here I could turn to that memorable case, and satisfy nearly anybody that the hunger for the sudden dollar is no more "American" than it is French. And if I could furnish an American opportunity to staid Germany, I think I could wake her up like a house afire. . . .

"But on the other hand I believe in statistics; and those on divorces appear to me to be most conclusive." And he sets himself the task of explaining—in a couple of columns—the process by which Easy-Divorce conceived, invented, originated, developed, and perfected an empire-embracing condition of sexual purity in the States. *In forty years.* No, he doesn't state the interval. With all his passion for statistics he forgot to ask how long it took to produce this gigantic miracle.

I have followed his pleasant but devious trail through those columns, but I was not able to get hold of his argument and find out what it was. I was not even able to find out where it left off. It seemed to gradually dissolve and flow off into other matters. I followed it with interest, for I was anxious to learn how easy-divorce eradicated adultery in America, but I was disappointed; I have no idea yet how it did it. I only know it didn't. But that is not valuable; I knew it before.

Well, humor is the great thing, the saving thing, after all. The minute it crops up, all our hardnesses yield, all our irritations and resentments flit away, and a sunny spirit takes their place. . . .

Stirring Times in Austria

. . . The next man will give you some further information. "The government has a policy—a wise one—and sticks steadily to it. This policy is—*tranquillity:* keep this hive of excitable nations as quiet as possible; encourage them to amuse themselves with things less inflammatory than politics. To this end it furnishes them an abundance of Catholic priests to teach them to be docile and obedient, and to be diligent in acquiring ignorance about things here below, and knowledge about the kingdom of heaven, to whose historic delights they are going to add the charm of their society by and by; and further—to this same end—it cools off the newspapers every morning at five o'clock, whenever warm events are happening." There is a censor of the press, and apparently he is always on duty and hard at work. A copy of each morning paper is brought to him at five o'clock. His official wagons wait at the doors of the newspaper offices and scud to him with the first copies that come from the press. His company of assistants read every line in these papers, and mark everything which seems to have a dangerous look; then he passes final judgment upon these markings. Two things conspire to give to the results a capricious and unbalanced look: his assistants have diversified notions as to what is dangerous and what isn't; he can't get time to examine their criticisms in much detail; and so sometimes the very same matter which is suppressed in one paper fails to be damned in another one, and gets published in full feather and unmodified. Then the paper in which it was suppressed blandly copies the forbidden matter into its evening edition—provokingly giving credit and detailing all the circumstances in courteous and inoffensive language—and of course the censor cannot say a word.

Sometimes the censor sucks all the blood out of a newspaper and leaves it colorless and inane; sometimes he leaves it undisturbed, and lets it talk out its opinions with a frankness and vigor hardly to be surpassed, I think, in the journals of any country. Apparently the censor sometimes revises his verdicts upon second thought, for several times lately he has suppressed journals after their issue and partial distribution. The distributed copies are then sent for by the censor and destroyed. I have two of these, but at the time they were sent for I could not remember what I had done with them.

If the censor did his work before the morning edition was printed, he would be less of an inconvenience than he is; but of course the papers cannot wait many minutes after five o'clock to get his verdict; they might as well go out of business as do that; so they print, and take the chances. Then, if they get caught by a suppression, they must strike out the condemned matter and print the edition over again. That delays the issue several hours, and is expensive besides. The government gets the suppressed edition for nothing. If it bought it, that would be joyful, and would give great satisfaction. Also, the edition would be larger. Some of the papers do not replace the condemned paragraphs with other matter; they merely snatch them out and leave blanks behind—mourning blanks, marked "*Confiscated.*"

The government discourages the dissemination of newspaper information in other ways. For instance, it does not allow newspapers to be sold on the streets; therefore the newsboy is unknown in Vienna. And there is a stamp duty of nearly a cent upon each copy of a newspaper's issue. Every American paper that reaches me has a stamp upon it, which has been pasted there in the post-office or down-stairs in the hotel office; but no matter who put it there, I have to pay for it, and that is the main thing. Sometimes friends send me so many papers that it takes all I can earn that week to keep this government going.

I must take passing notice of another point in the government's measures for maintaining tranquillity. Everybody says it does not like to see any individual attain to commanding influence in the country, since such a man can become a disturber and an inconvenience. "We have as much talent as the other nations," says the citizen, resignedly, and without bitterness, "but for the sake of the general good of the country we are discouraged from making it overconspicuous; and not only discouraged, but tactfully and skillfully prevented from doing it, if we show too much persistence. Consequently we have no renowned men; in centuries we have seldom produced one—that is, seldom allowed one to produce himself. We can say to-day what no other nation of first importance in the family of Christian civilizations can say: that there exists no Austrian who has made an enduring name for himself which is familiar all around the globe."

Another helper toward tranquillity is the army. It is as pervasive as the atmosphere. It is everywhere. All the mentioned creators, promoters, and preservers of the public tranquillity do their several shares in the quieting work. They make a restful and comfortable serenity and reposefulness. This is disturbed sometimes for a little while: a mob assembles to protect against something; it gets noisy—noisier—still noisier—finally *too* noisy; then the persuasive soldiery comes charging down upon it, and in a few minutes all is quiet again, and there is no mob. . . .

A Majestic Literary Fossil

If I were required to guess offhand, and without collusion with higher minds, what is the bottom cause of the amazing material and intellectual advancement of the last fifty years, I should guess that it was the modern-born and previously non-existent disposition on the part of men to believe that a new idea can have value. With the long roll of the mighty names of history present in our minds, we are not privileged to doubt that for the past twenty or thirty centuries every conspicuous civilization in the world has produced intellects able to invent and create the things which make our day a wonder; perhaps we may be justified in inferring, then, that the reason they did not do it was that the public reverence for old ideas and hostility to new ones always stood in their way, and was a wall they could not break down or climb over. The prevailing tone of old books regarding new ideas is one of suspicion and uneasiness at times, and at other times contempt. By contrast, our day is indifferent to old ideas, and even considers that their age makes their value questionable, but jumps at a new idea with enthusiasm and high hope—a hope which is high because it has not been accustomed to being disappointed. I make no guess as to just when this disposition was born to us, but it certainly is ours, was not possessed by any century before us, is our peculiar mark and badge, and is doubtless the bottom reason why we are a race of lightning-shod Mercuries, and proud of it—instead of being, like our ancestors, a race of plodding crabs, and proud of that.

So recent is this change from a three or four thousand year twilight to the flash and glare of open day that I have walked in both, and yet am not old. Nothing is to-day as it was when I was an urchin; but when I was an urchin, nothing was much different from what it had always been in this world. Take a single detail, for example—medicine. Galen could have come into my sick-room at any time during my first seven years—I mean any day when it wasn't fishing weather, and there wasn't any choice but school or sickness—and he could have sat down there and stood my doctor's watch without asking a question. He would have smelt around among the wilderness of cups and bottles and vials on the table and the shelves, and missed not a stench that used to glad him two thousand years before, nor discovered one that was of a later date. He would have examined me, and run across only one disappointment—I was already salivated; I would have him there; for I was always salivated, calomel was so cheap. He would get out his lancet then; but I would have him again; our family doctor didn't allow blood to accumulate in the system. However, he could take dipper and ladle, and freight me up with old familiar doses that had come down from Adam to his time and mine; and he could go out with a wheelbarrow and gather weeds and offal, and build some more, while those others were getting in their work. And if our reverend doctor came and found him there, he would be dumb with awe, and would get down and worship him. Whereas if Galen should appear among us to-day, he could not stand anybody's watch; he would inspire no awe; he would be told he was a back number, and it would surprise him to see that that fact counted against him, instead of in his favor. He wouldn't know our medicines; he wouldn't know our practice; and the first time he tried to introduce his own we would hang him.

This introduction brings me to my literary relic. It is a *Dictionary of Medicine,* by Dr. James, of London, assisted by Mr. Boswell's Doctor Samuel Johnson, and is a hundred and fifty years old, it having been published at the time of the rebellion of '45. If it had been sent against the Pretender's troops there probably wouldn't have been a survivor. In 1861 this deadly book was still working the cemeteries—down in Virginia. For three generations and a half it had been going quietly along, enriching the earth with its slain. Up to its last free day it was trusted and believed in, and its devastating advice taken, as was shown by notes inserted between its leaves. But our troops captured it and brought it home, and it has been out of business since. These remarks from its preface are in the true spirit of the olden time, sodden with worship of the old, disdain of the new:

> If we inquire into the Improvements which have been made by the Moderns, we shall be forced to confess that we have so little Reason to value ourselves beyond the Antients, or to be tempted to contemn them, that we cannot give stronger or more convincing Proofs of our own Ignorance, as well as our Pride.
>
> Among all the systematical Writers, I think there are very few who refuse the Preference to *Hieron, Fabricius ab Aquapendente,* as a Person of unquestion'd Learning and Judgment; and yet is he not asham'd to let his Readers know that *Celsus* among the Latins, *Paulus Aegineta* among the Greeks, and *Albucasis* among the Arabians, whom I am unwilling to place among the Moderns, tho' he liv'd but six hundred Years since, are the Triumvirate to whom he principally stands indebted, for the Assistance he had receiv'd from them in composing his excellent Book.
>
> [In a previous paragraph are puffs of Galen, Hippocrates, and other debris of the Old Silurian Period of Medicine.] How many Operations are there now in Use which were unknown to the Antients?

That is true. The surest way for a nation's scientific men to prove that they were proud and ignorant was to claim to have found out something fresh in the course of a thousand years or so. Evidently the peoples of this book's day regarded themselves as children, and their remote ancestors as the only grown-up people that had existed. Consider the contrast: without offense, without over-egotism, our own scientific men may and do regard themselves as grown people and their grandfathers as children. The change here presented is probably the most sweeping that has ever come over mankind in the history of the race. It is the utter reversal, in a couple of generations, of an attitude which had been maintained without challenge or interruption from the earliest antiquity. It amounts to creating man over again on a new plan; he was a canal-boat before, he is an ocean greyhound to-day. The change from reptile to bird was not more tremendous, and it took longer.

It is curious. If you read between the lines what this author says about Brer Albucasis, you detect that in venturing to compliment him he has to whistle a little to keep his courage up, because Albucasis "liv'd but six hundred Years since," and therefore came so uncomfortably near being a "modern" that one couldn't respect him without risk.

Phlebotomy, Venesection—terms to signify bleeding—are not often heard in our day, because we have ceased to believe that the best way to make a bank or a body healthy is to squander its capital; but in our author's time the physician went around with a hatful of lancets on his person all the time, and took a hack at every patient whom he found still alive. He robbed his man of pounds and pounds of blood at a single operation. The details of this sort in this book make terrific reading. Apparently even the healthy did not escape, but were bled twelve times a year, on a particular day of the month, and exhaustively purged besides. Here is a specimen of the vigorous old-time practice; it occurs in our author's adoring biography of a Doctor Aretaeus, a licensed assassin of Homer's time, or thereabouts:

> In a Quinsey he used Venesection, and allow'd the Blood to flow till the Patient was ready to faint away.

There is no harm in trying to cure a headache—in our day. You can't do it, but you get more or less entertainment out of trying, and that is something; besides, you live to tell about it, and that is more. A century or so ago you could have had the first of these features in rich variety, but you might fail of the other once—and once would do. I quote:

> As Dissections of Persons who have died of severe Head-achs, which have been related by Authors, are too numerous to be inserted in this Place, we shall here abridge some of the most curious and important Observations relating to this Subject, collected by the celebrated *Bonetus.*

The celebrated Bonetus's "Observation No. I" seems to me a sufficient sample, all by itself, of what people used to have to stand any time between the creation of the world and the birth of your father and mine when they had the disastrous luck to get a "Head-ach":

> A certain Merchant, about forty Years of Age, of a Melancholic Habit, and deeply involved in the Cares of the World, was, during the Dog-days, seiz'd with a violent pain of his Head, which some time after oblig'd him to keep his Bed.
>
> I, being call'd, order'd Venesection in the Arms, the Application of Leeches to the Vessels of his Nostrils, Forehead, and Temples, as also to those behind his Ears; I likewise prescrib'd the Application of Cupping-glasses, with Scarification, to his Back: But notwithstanding these Precautions, he dy'd. If any Surgeon, skill'd in Arteriotomy, had been present, I should have also order'd that Operation.

I looked for "Arteriotomy" in this same Dictionary, and found this definition: "The opening of an Artery with a View of taking away Blood." Here was a person who was being bled in the arms, forehead, nostrils, back, temples, and behind the ears, yet the celebrated Bonetus was not satisfied, but wanted to open an artery "with a View" to insert a pump, probably. "Notwithstanding these Precautions"—he dy'd. No art of speech could more quaintly convey this butcher's innocent surprise. Now that we know what the celebrated Bonetus did when he wanted to relieve a Head-ach, it is no trouble to infer that if he wanted to comfort a man that had a Stomach-ach he disemboweled him.

I have given one "Observation"—a single Head-ach case; but the celebrated Bonetus follows it with eleven more. Without enlarging upon the matter, I merely note this coincidence—they all "dy'd." Not one of these people got well; yet this obtuse hyena sets down every little gory detail of the several assassinations as complacently as if he imagined he was doing a useful and meritorious work in perpetuating the methods of his crimes. "Observations," indeed! They are confessions. . . .

CONCERNING THE JEWS

Some months ago I published a magazine article descriptive of a remarkable scene in the Imperial Parliament in Vienna. Since then I have received from Jews in America several letters of inquiry. They were difficult letters to answer, for they were not very definite. But at last I received a definite one. It is from a lawyer, and he really asks the questions which the other writers probably believed they were asking. By help of this text I will do the best I can to publicly answer this correspondent, and also the others—at the same time apologizing for having failed to reply privately. The lawyer's letter reads as follows:

> I have read "Stirring Times in Austria." One point in particular is of vital import to not a few thousand people, including myself, being a point about which I have often wanted to address a question to some disinterested person. The show of military force in the Austrian Parliament, which precipitated the riots, was not introduced by any Jew. No Jew was a member of that body. No Jewish question was involved in the *Ausgleich* or in the language proposition. No Jew was insulting anybody. In short, no Jew was doing any mischief toward anybody whatsoever. In fact, the Jews were the only ones of the nineteen different races in Austria which did not have a party—they are absolutely non-participants. Yet in your article you say that in the rioting which followed, all classes of people were unanimous only on one thing—*viz.*, in being against the Jews. Now will you kindly tell me why, in your judgment, the Jews have thus ever been, and are even now, in these days of supposed intelligence, the butt of baseless, vicious animosities? I dare say that for centuries there has been no more quiet, undisturbing, and well-behaving citizens, as a class, than that same Jew. It seems to me that ignorance and fanaticism cannot alone account for these horrible and unjust persecutions.
>
> Tell me, therefore, from your vantage-point of cold view, what in your mind is the cause. Can American Jews do anything to correct it either in America or abroad? Will it ever come to an end? Will a Jew be permitted to live honestly, decently, and peaceably like the rest of mankind? What has become of the golden rule?

I will begin by saying that if I thought myself prejudiced against the Jew, I should hold it fairest to leave this subject to a person not crippled in that way.

But I think I have no such prejudice. A few years ago a Jew observed to me that there was no uncourteous reference to his people in my books, and asked how it happened. It happened because the disposition was lacking. I am quite sure that (bar one) I have no race prejudices, and I think I have no color prejudices nor caste prejudices nor creed prejudices. Indeed, I know it. I can stand any society. All that I care to know is that a man is a human being—that is enough for me; he can't be any worse. I have no special regard for Satan; but I can at least claim that I have no prejudice against him. It may even be that I lean a little his way, on account of his not having a fair show. All religions issue bibles against him, and say the most injurious things about him, but we never hear *his* side. We have none but the evidence for the prosecution, and yet we have rendered the verdict. To my mind, this is irregular. It is un-English; it is un-American; it is French. Without this precedent Dreyfus could not have been condemned. Of course Satan has some kind of a case, it goes without saying. It may be a poor one, but that is nothing; that can be said about any of us. As soon as I can get at the facts I will undertake his rehabilitation myself, if I can find an unpolitic publisher. It is a thing which we ought to be willing to do for any one who is under a cloud. We may not pay him reverence, for that would be indiscreet, but we can at least respect his talents. A person who has for untold centuries maintained the imposing position of spiritual head of four-fifths of the human race, and political head of the whole of it, must be granted the possession of executive abilities of the loftiest order. In his large presence the other popes and politicians shrink to midges for the microscope. I would like to see him. I would rather see him and shake him by the tail than any other member of the European Concert. In the present paper I shall allow myself to use the word Jew as if it stood for both religion and race. It is handy; and, besides, that is what the term means to the general world.

In the above letter one notes these points:

1. The Jew is a well-behaved citizen.
2. Can ignorance and fanaticism *alone* account for his unjust treatment?
3. Can Jews do anything to improve the situation?
4. The Jews have no party; they are non-participants.
5. Will the persecution ever come to an end?
6. What has become of the golden rule?

Point No. I.—We must grant proposition No. I, for several sufficient reasons. The Jew is not a disturber of the peace of any country. Even his enemies will concede that. He is not a loafer, he is not a sot, he is not noisy, he is not a brawler nor a rioter, he is not quarrelsome. In the statistics of crime his presence is conspicuously rare—in all countries. With murder and other crimes of violence he has but little to do: he is a stranger to the hangman. In the police court's daily long roll of "assaults" and "drunk and disorderlies" his name seldom appears. That the Jewish home is a home in the truest sense is a fact which no one will dispute. The family is knitted together by the strongest affections; its members show each other every due respect; and reverence for the elders is an inviolate law of the house. The Jew is not a burden on the charities of the state nor of the city; these could cease from their functions without affecting him. When he is well enough, he works; when he is incapacitated, his own people take care of him. And not in a poor and stingy way, but with a fine and large benevolence. His race is entitled to be called the most benevolent of all the races of men. A Jewish beggar is not impossible, perhaps; such a thing may exist, but there are few men that can say they have seen that spectacle. The Jew has been staged in many uncomplimentary forms, but, so far as I know, no dramatist has done him the injustice to stage him as a beggar. Whenever a Jew has real need to beg, his people save him from the necessity of doing it. The charitable institutions of the Jews are supported by Jewish money, and amply. The Jews make no noise about it; it is done quietly; they do not nag and pester and harass us for contributions; they give us peace, and set us an example—an example which we have not found ourselves able to follow; for by nature we are not free givers, and have to be patiently and persistently hunted down in the interest of the unfortunate.

These facts are all on the credit side of the proposition that the Jew is a good and orderly citizen. Summed up, they certify that he is quiet, peaceable, industrious, unaddicted to high crimes and brutal dispositions; that his family life is commendable; that he is not a burden upon public charities; that he is not a beggar; that in benevolence he is above the reach of competition. These are the very quintessentials of good citizenship. If you can add that he is as honest as the average of his neighbors— But I think that question is affirmatively answered by the fact that he is a successful business man. The basis of successful business is honesty; a business cannot thrive where the parties to it cannot trust each other. In the matter of numbers the Jew counts for little in the overwhelming population of New York; but that his honesty counts for much is guaranteed by the fact that the immense wholesale business of Broadway, from the Battery to Union Square, is substantially in his hands.

I suppose that the most picturesque example in history of a trader's trust in his fellow-trader was one where it was not Christian trusting Christian, but Christian trusting Jew. That Hessian Duke who used to sell his subjects to George III to fight George Washington with got rich at it; and by and by, when the wars engendered by the French Revolution made his throne too warm for him, he was obliged to fly the country. He was in a hurry, and had to leave his earnings behind—nine million dollars. He had to risk the money with some one without security. He did not select a Christian, but a Jew—a Jew of only modest means, but of high character; a character so high that it left him lonesome—Rothschild of Frankfort. Thirty years later, when Europe had become quiet and safe again, the Duke came back from overseas, and the Jew returned the loan, with interest added.[1]

1. Here is another piece of picturesque history; and it reminds us that shabbiness and dishonesty are not the monopoly of any race or creed, but are merely human:

The Jew has his other side. He has some discreditable ways, though he has not a monopoly of them, because he cannot get entirely rid of vexatious Christian competition. We have seen that he seldom transgresses the laws against crimes of violence. Indeed, his dealings with courts are almost restricted to matters connected with commerce. He has a reputation for various small forms of cheating, and for practising oppressive usury, and for burning himself out to get the insurance, and arranging for cunning contracts which leave him an exit but lock the other man in, and for smart evasions which find him safe and comfortable just within the strict letter of the law, when court and jury know very well that he has violated the spirit of it. He is a frequent and faithful and capable officer in the civil service, but he is charged with an unpatriotic disinclination to stand by the flag as a soldier—like the Christian Quaker.

Now if you offset these discreditable features by the creditable ones summarized in a preceding paragraph beginning with the words, "These facts are all on the credit side," and strike a balance, what must the verdict be? This, I think: that, the merits and demerits being fairly weighed and measured on both sides, the Christian can claim no superiority over the Jew in the matter of good citizenship.

Yet, in all countries, from the dawn of history, the Jew has been persistently and implacably hated, and with frequency persecuted.

Point No. 2—"Can fanaticism *alone* account for this?"

Years ago I used to think that it was responsible for nearly all of it, but latterly I have come to think that this was an error. Indeed, it is now my conviction

"Congress passed a bill to pay $379.56 to Moses Pendergrass, of Libertyville, Missouri. The story of the reason of this liberality is pathetically interesting, and shows the sort of pickle that an honest man may get into who undertakes to do an honest job of work for Uncle Sam. In 1886 Moses Pendergrass put in a bid for the contract to carry the mail on the route from Knob Lick to Libertyville and Coffman, thirty miles a day, from July 1, 1887, for one year. He got the postmaster at Knob Lick to write the letter for him, and while Moses intended that his bid should be $400, his scribe carelessly made it $4. Moses got the contract, and did not find out about the mistake until the end of the first quarter, when he got his first pay. When he found at what rate he was working he was sorely cast down, and opened communication with the Post Office Department. The department informed him that he must either carry out his contract or throw it up, and that if he threw it up his bondsmen would have to pay the government $1,459.85 damages. So Moses carried out his contract, walked thirty miles every weekday for a year, and carried the mail and received for his labor $4— or, to be accurate, $6.84; for, the route being extended after his bid was accepted, the pay was proportionately increased. Now, after ten years, a bill was finally passed to pay to Moses the difference between what he earned in that unlucky year and what he received."

The *Sun,* which tells the above story, says that bills were introduced in three or four Congresses for Moses' relief, and that committees repeatedly investigated his claim.

It took six Congresses, containing in their persons the compressed virtues of 70,000,000 of people, and cautiously and carefully giving expression to those virtues in the fear of God and the next election, eleven years to find out some way to cheat a fellow-Christian out of about $13 on his honestly executed contract, and out of nearly $300 due him on its enlarged terms. And they succeeded. During the same time they paid out $1,000,000,000 in pensions—a third of it unearned and undeserved. This indicates a splendid all-around competency in theft, for it starts with farthings, and works its industries all the way up to ship-loads. It may be possible that the Jews can beat this, but the man that bets on it is taking chances.

that it is responsible for hardly any of it. In this connection I call to mind Genesis, chapter xlvii.

We have all thoughtfully—or unthoughtfully—read the pathetic story of the years of plenty and the years of famine in Egypt, and how Joseph, with that opportunity, made a corner in broken hearts, and the crusts of the poor, and human liberty—a corner whereby he took a nation's money all away, to the last penny; took a nation's land away, to the last acre; then took the nation itself, buying it for bread, man by man, woman by woman, child by child, till all were slaves; a corner which took everything, left nothing; a corner so stupendous that, by comparison with it, the most gigantic corners in subsequent history are but baby things, for it dealt in hundreds of millions of bushels, and its profits were reckonable by hundreds of millions of dollars, and it was a disaster so crushing that its effects have not wholly disappeared from Egypt today, more than three thousand years after the event.

Is it presumable that the eye of Egypt was upon Joseph, the foreign Jew, all this time? I think it likely. Was it friendly? We must doubt it. Was Joseph establishing a character for his race which would survive long in Egypt? And in time would his name come to be familiarly used to express that character—like Shylock's? It is hardly to be doubted. Let us remember that this was *centuries before the crucifixion.*

I wish to come down eighteen hundred years later and refer to a remark made by one of the Latin historians. I read it in a translation many years ago, and it comes back to me now with force. It was alluding to a time when people were still living who could have seen the Saviour in the flesh. Christianity was so new that the people of Rome had hardly heard of it, and had but confused notions of what it was. The substance of the remark was this: Some Christians were persecuted in Rome through error, they being "*mistaken for Jews.*"

The meaning seems plain. These pagans had nothing against Christians, but they were quite ready to persecute Jews. For some reason or other they hated a Jew before they even knew what a Christian was. May I not assume, then, that the persecution of Jews is a thing which *antedates* Christianity and was not born of Christianity? I think so. What was the origin of the feeling?

When I was a boy, in the back settlements of the Mississippi Valley, where a gracious and beautiful Sunday-school simplicity and unpracticality prevailed, the "Yankee" (citizen of the New England states) was hated with a splendid energy. But religion had nothing to do with it. In a trade, the Yankee was held to be about five times the match of the Westerner. His shrewdness, his insight, his judgment, his knowledge, his enterprise, and his formidable cleverness in applying these forces were frankly confessed, and most competently cursed.

In the cotton states, after the war, the simple and ignorant negroes made the crops for the white planter on shares. The Jew came down in force, set up shop on the plantation, supplied all the negro's wants on credit, and at the end of the season was proprietor of the negro's share of the present crop and of part of his share of the next one. Before long, the whites detested the Jew, and it is doubtful if the negro loved him.

The Jew is being legislated out of Russia. The reason is not concealed. The movement was instituted because the Christian peasant and villager stood no chance against his commercial abilities. He was always ready to lend money on a crop, and sell vodka and other necessaries of life on credit while the crop was growing. When settlement day came he owned the crop; and next year or year after he owned the farm, like Joseph.

In the dull and ignorant England of John's time everybody got into debt to the Jew. He gathered all lucrative enterprises into his hands; he was the king of commerce; he was ready to be helpful in all profitable ways; he even financed crusades for the rescue of the Sepulcher. To wipe out his account with the nation and restore business to its natural and incompetent channels he had to be banished the realm.

For the like reasons Spain had to banish him four hundred years ago, and Austria about a couple of centuries later.

In all the ages Christian Europe has been obliged to curtail his activities. If he entered upon a mechanical trade, the Christian had to retire from it. If he set up as a doctor, he was the best one, and he took the business. If he exploited agriculture, the other farmers had to get at something else. Since there was no way to successfully compete with him in any vocation, the law had to step in and save the Christian from the poorhouse. Trade after trade was taken away from the Jew by statute till practically none was left. He was forbidden to engage in agriculture; he was forbidden to practise law; he was forbidden to practise medicine, except among Jews; he was forbidden the handicrafts. Even the seats of learning and the schools of science had to be closed against this tremendous antagonist. Still, almost bereft of employments, he found ways to make money, even ways to get rich. Also ways to invest his takings well, for usury was not denied him. In the hard conditions suggested, the Jew without brains could not survive, and the Jew with brains had to keep them in good training and well sharpened up, or starve. Ages of restriction to the one tool which the law was not able to take from him—his brain—have made that tool singularly competent; ages of compulsory disuse of his hands have atrophied them, and he never uses them now. This history has a very, very commercial look, a most sordid and practical commercial look, the business aspect of a Chinese cheap-labor crusade. Religious prejudices may account for one part of it, but not for the other nine.

Protestants have persecuted Catholics, but they did not take their livelihoods away from them. The Catholics have persecuted the Protestants with bloody and awful bitterness, but they never closed agriculture and the handicrafts against them. Why was that? That has the candid look of genuine religious persecution, not a trade-union boycott in a religious disguise.

The Jews are harried and obstructed in Austria and Germany, and lately in France; but England and America give them an open field and yet survive.

Scotland offers them an unembarrassed field too, but there are not many takers. There are a few Jews in Glasgow, and one in Aberdeen; but that is because they can't earn enough to get away. The Scotch pay themselves that compliment, but it is authentic.

I feel convinced that the Crucifixion has not much to do with the world's attitude toward the Jew; that the reasons for it are older than that event, as suggested by Egypt's experience and by Rome's regret for having persecuted an unknown quantity called a Christian, under the mistaken impression that she was merely persecuting a Jew. *Merely* a Jew—a skinned eel who was used to it, presumably. I am persuaded that in Russia, Austria, and Germany nine-tenths of the hostility to the Jew comes from the average Christian's inability to compete successfully with the average Jew in business—in either straight business or the questionable sort.

In Berlin, a few years ago, I read a speech which frankly urged the expulsion of the Jews from Germany; and the agitator's *reason* was as frank as his proposition. It was this: *that eighty-five per cent.* of the successful lawyers of Berlin were Jews, and that about the same percentage of the great and lucrative businesses of all sorts in Germany were in the hands of the Jewish race! Isn't it an amazing confession? It was but another way of saying that in a population of 48,000,000, of whom only 500,000 were registered as Jews, eighty-five per cent. of the brains and honesty of the whole was lodged in the Jews. I must insist upon the honesty—it is an essential of successful business, taken by and large. Of course it does not rule out rascals entirely, even among Christians, but it is a good working rule, nevertheless. The speaker's figures may have been inexact, but *the motive of persecution* stands out as clear as day.

The man claimed that in Berlin the banks, the newspapers, the theaters, the great mercantile, shipping, mining, and manufacturing interests, the big army and city contracts, the tramways, and pretty much all other properties of high value, and *also* the small businesses—were in the hands of the Jews. He said the Jew was pushing the Christian to the wall all along the line; that it was all a Christian could do to scrape together a living; and that the Jew *must* be banished, and soon—there was no other way of saving the Christian. Here in Vienna, last autumn, an agitator said that all these disastrous details were true of Austria-Hungary also; and in fierce language he demanded the expulsion of the Jews. When politicians come out without a blush and read the baby act in this frank way, *unrebuked,* it is a very good indication that they have a market back of them, and know where to fish for votes.

You note the crucial point of the mentioned agitation; the argument is that the Christian cannot *compete* with the Jew, and that hence his very bread is in peril. To human beings this is a much more hate-inspiring thing than is any detail connected with religion. With most people, of a necessity, bread and meat take first rank, religion second. I am convinced that the persecution of the Jew is not due in any large degree to religious prejudice.

No, the Jew is a money-getter; and in getting his money he is a very serious obstruction to less capable neighbors who are on the same quest. I think that that is the trouble. In estimating worldly values the Jew is not shallow, but deep. With precocious wisdom he found out in the morning of time that some men worship rank, some worship heroes, some worship power, some worship God, and that over these ideals they dispute and cannot unite—but that they all worship money; so he made it the end and aim of his life to get it. He was at it in Egypt thirty-six centuries ago; he was at it in Rome when that Christian got persecuted by mistake for him; he has been at it ever since. The cost to him has been heavy; his success has made the whole human race his enemy—but it has paid, for it has brought him envy, and that is the only thing which men will sell both soul and body to get. He long ago observed that a millionaire commands respect, a two-millionaire homage, a multi-millionaire the deepest deeps of adoration. We all know that feeling; we have seen it express itself. We have noticed that when the average man mentions the name of a multi-millionaire he does it with that mixture in his voice of awe and reverence and lust which burns in a Frenchman's eye when it falls on another man's centime.

Point No. 4.—"The Jews have no party; they are non-participants."

Perhaps you have let the secret out and given yourself away. It seems hardly a credit to the race that it is able to say that; or to you, sir, that you can say it without remorse; more, that you should offer it as a plea against maltreatment, injustice, and oppression. Who gives the Jew the right, who gives any race the right, to sit still, in a free country, and let somebody else look after its safety? The oppressed Jew was entitled to all pity in the former times under brutal autocracies, for he was weak and friendless, and had no way to help his case. But he has ways now, and he has had them for a century, but I do not see that he has tried to make serious use of them. When the Revolution set him free in France it was an act of grace—the grace of other people; he does not appear in it as a helper. I do not know that he helped when England set him free. Among the Twelve Sane Men of France who have stepped forward with great Zola at their head to fight (and win, I hope and believe[1]) the battle for the most infamously misused Jew of modern times, do you find a great or rich or illustrious Jew helping? In the United States he was created free in the beginning—he did not need to help, of course. In Austria, and Germany, and France he has a vote, but of what considerable use is it to him? He doesn't seem to know how to apply it to the best effect. With all his splendid capacities and all his fat wealth he is to-day not politically important in any country. In America, as early as 1854, the ignorant Irish hod-carrier, who had a spirit of his own and a way of exposing it to the weather, made it apparent to all that he must be politically reckoned with; yet fifteen years before that we hardly knew what an Irishman looked like. As an intelligent force, and numerically, he has always been away down, but he has governed the country just the same. It was because he was *organized*. It made his vote valuable—in fact, essential.

1. The article was written in the summer of 1898.—EDITOR.

You will say the Jew is everywhere numerically feeble. That is nothing to the point—with the Irishman's history for an object-lesson. But I am coming to your numerical feebleness presently. In all parliamentary countries you could no doubt elect Jews to the legislatures—and even *one* member in such a body is sometimes a force which counts. How deeply have you concerned yourselves about this in Austria, France, and Germany? Or even in America for that matter? You remark that the Jews were not to blame for the riots in this Reichsrath here, and you add with satisfaction that there wasn't one in that body. That is not strictly correct; if it were, would it not be in order for you to explain it and apologize for it, not try to make a merit of it? But I think that the Jew was by no means in as large force there as he ought to have been, with his chances. Austria opens the suffrage to him on fairly liberal terms, and it must surely be his own fault that he is so much in the background politically.

As to your numerical weakness. I mentioned some figures awhile ago—500,000—as the Jewish population of Germany. I will add some more—6,000,000 in Russia, 5,000,000 in Austria, 250,000 in the United States. I take them from memory; I read them in the *Encyclopaedia Britannica* about ten years ago. Still, I am entirely sure of them. If those statistics are correct, my argument is not as strong as it ought to be as concerns America, but it still has strength. It is plenty strong enough as concerns Austria, for ten years ago 5,000,000 was nine per cent. of the empire's population. The Irish would govern the Kingdom of Heaven if they had a strength there like that.

I have some suspicions; I got them at second hand, but they have remained with me these ten or twelve years. When I read in the *E. B.* that the Jewish population of the United States was 250,000, I wrote the editor, and explained to him that I was personally acquainted with more Jews than that in my country, and that his figures were without doubt a misprint for 25,000,000. I also added that I was personally acquainted with *that* many there; but that was only to raise his confidence in me, for it was not true. His answer miscarried, and I never got it; but I went around talking about the matter, and people told me they had reason to suspect that for business reasons many Jews whose dealings were mainly with the Christians did not report themselves as Jews in the census. It looked plausible; it looks plausible yet. Look at the city of New York; and look at Boston, and Philadelphia, and New Orleans, and Chicago, and Cincinnati, and San Francisco—how your race swarms in those places!—and everywhere else in America, down to the least little village. Read the signs on the marts of commerce and on the shops: Goldstein (gold stone), Edelstein (precious stone), Blumenthal (flower-vale), Rosenthal (rose-vale), Veilchenduft (violet odor), Singvogel (song-bird), Rosenzweig (rose branch), and all the amazing list of beautiful and enviable names which Prussia and Austria glorified you with so long ago. It is another instance of Europe's coarse and cruel persecution of your race; not that it was coarse and cruel to outfit it with pretty and poetical names like those, but that it was coarse and cruel to make it *pay* for them or else take such hideous and often indecent names that to-day their owners never use them; or, if they do, only on official papers. And it was the many, not the few, who got the odious names, they being too poor to bribe the officials to grant them better ones.

Now why was the race renamed? I have been told that in Prussia it was given to using fictitious names, and often changing them, so as to beat the tax-gatherer, escape military service, and so on; and that finally the idea was hit upon of furnishing all the inmates of a house with *one and the same surname,* and then holding the house responsible right along for those inmates, and accountable for any disappearances that might occur; it made the Jews keep track of *each other,* for self-interest's sake, and saved the government the trouble.[1]

If that explanation of how the Jews of Prussia came to be renamed is correct, if it is true that they fictitiously registered themselves to gain certain advantages, it may possibly be true that in America they refrain from registering themselves as Jews to fend off the damaging prejudices of the Christian customer. I have no way of knowing whether this notion is well founded or not. There may be other and better ways of explaining why only that poor little 250,000 of our Jews got into the *Encyclopaedia.* I may, of course, be mistaken, but I am strongly of the opinion that we have an immense Jewish population in America.

Point No. 3.—"Can Jews do anything to improve the situation?"

I think so. If I may make a suggestion without seeming to be trying to teach my grandmother how to suck eggs, I will offer it. In our days we have learned the value of combination. We apply it everywhere—in railway systems, in trusts, in trade-unions, in Salvation Armies, in minor politics, in major politics, in European Concerts. Whatever our strength may be, big or little, we *organize* it. We have found out that that is the only way to get the most out of it that is in it. We know the weakness of individual sticks, and the strength of the concentrated fagot. Suppose you try a scheme like this, for instance. In England and America put every Jew on the census-book *as* a Jew (in case you have not been doing that). Get up volunteer regiments composed of Jews solely, and, when the drum beats, fall in and go to the front, so as to remove the reproach that you have few Massénas among you, and that you feed on a country but don't like to fight for it. Next, in politics, organise your strength, band together, and deliver the casting vote where you can, and, where you can't, compel as good terms as possible. You huddle to yourselves already in all countries, but you huddle to no sufficient purpose, politically speaking. You do not seem to be organized, except for your charities. There you are

1. In Austria the renaming was merely done because the Jews in some newly acquired regions had no surnames, but were mostly named Abraham and Moses, and therefore the tax-gatherer could not tell t'other from which, and was likely to lose his reason over the matter. The renaming was put into the hands of the War Department, and a charming mess the graceless young lieutenants made of it. To them a Jew was of no sort of consequence, and they labeled the race in a way to make the angels weep. As an example take these two! *Abraham Bellyache* and *Schmul Godbedamned.—Culled from "Namens Studien," by Karl Emil Franzos.*

omnipotent; there you compel your due of recognition—you do not have to beg for it. It shows what you can do when you band together for a definite purpose.

And then from America and England you can encourage your race in Austria, France, and Germany, and materially help it. It was a pathetic tale that was told by a poor Jew in Galicia a fortnight ago during the riots, after he had been raided by the Christian peasantry and despoiled of everything he had. He said his vote was of no value to him, and he wished he could be excused from casting it, for indeed casting it was a sure *damage* to him, since no matter which party he voted for, the other party would come straight and take its revenge out of him. Nine per cent. of the population of the empire, these Jews, and apparently they cannot put a plank into any candidate's platform! If you will send our Irish lads over here I think they will organize your race and change the aspect of the Reichsrath.

You seem to think that the Jews take no hand in politics here, that they are "absolutely non-participants." I am assured by men competent to speak that this is a very large error, that the Jews are exceedingly active in politics all over the empire, but that they scatter their work and their votes among the numerous parties, and thus lose the advantages to be had by concentration. I think that in America they scatter too, but you know more about that than I do.

Speaking of concentration, Dr. Herzl has a clear insight into the value of that. Have you heard of his plan? He wishes to gather the Jews of the world together in Palestine, with a government of their own—under the suzerainty of the Sultan, I suppose. At the convention of Berne, last year, there were delegates from everywhere, and the proposal was received with decided favor. I am not the Sultan, and I am not objecting; but if that concentration of the cunningest brains in the world was going to be made in a free country (bar Scotland), I think it would be politic to stop it. It will not be well to let that race find out its strength. If the horses knew theirs, we should not ride any more.

Point No. 5.—"Will the persecution of the Jews ever come to an end?"

On the score of religion, I think it has already come to an end. On the score of race prejudice and trade, I have the idea that it will continue. That is, here and there in spots about the world, where a barbarous ignorance and a sort of mere animal civilization prevail; but I do not think that elsewhere the Jew need now stand in any fear of being robbed and raided. Among the high civilizations he seems to be very comfortably situated indeed, and to have more than his proportionate share of the prosperities going. It has that look in Vienna. I suppose the race prejudice cannot be removed; but he can stand that; it is no particular matter. By his make and ways he is substantially a foreigner wherever he may be, and even the angels dislike a foreigner. I am using this word foreigner in the German sense—*stranger*. Nearly all of us have an antipathy to a stranger, even of our own nationality. We pile gripsacks in a vacant seat to keep him from getting it; and a dog goes further, and does as a savage would—challenges him on the spot. The German dictionary seems to make no distinction between a stranger and a foreigner; in its view a stranger *is* a foreigner—a sound position, I think. You will always be by ways and habits and predilections substantially strangers—foreigners—wherever you are, and that will probably keep the race prejudice against you alive.

But you were the favorites of Heaven originally, and your manifold and unfair prosperities convince me that you have crowded back into that snug place again. Here is an incident that is significant. Last week in Vienna a hailstorm struck the prodigious Central Cemetery and made wasteful destruction there. In the Christian part of it, according to the official figures, 621 window-panes were broken; more than 900 singing-birds were killed; five great trees and many small ones were torn to shreds and the shreds scattered far and wide by the wind; the ornamental plants and other decorations of the graves were ruined, and more than a hundred tomb-lanterns shattered; and it took the cemetery's whole force of 300 laborers more than three days to clear away the storm's wreckage. In the report occurs this remark—and in its italics you can hear it grit its Christian teeth: ". . . lediglich die *israelitische* Abtheilung des Friedhofes vom Hagelwetter *ganzlich verschont* worden war." Not a hailstone hit the Jewish reservation! Such nepotism makes me tired.

Point No. 6.—"What has become of the golden rule?"

It exists, it continues to sparkle, and is well taken care of. It is Exhibit A in the Church's assets, and we pull it out every Sunday and give it an airing. But you are not permitted to try to smuggle it into this discussion, where it is irrelevant and would not feel at home. It is strictly religious furniture, like an acolyte, or a contribution-plate, or any of those things. It has never been intruded into business; and Jewish persecution is not a religious passion, it is a business passion.

To conclude.—If the statistics are right, the Jews constitute but *one per cent.* of the human race. It suggests a nebulous dim puff of star dust lost in the blaze of the Milky Way. Properly the Jew ought hardly to be heard of; but he is heard of, has always been heard of. He is as prominent on the planet as any other people, and his commercial importance is extravagantly out of proportion to the smallness of his bulk. His contributions to the world's list of great names in literature, science, art, music, finance, medicine, and abstruse learning are also away out of proportion to the weakness of his numbers. He has made a marvelous fight in this world, in all the ages; and has done it with his hands tied behind him. He could be vain of himself, and be excused for it. The Egyptian, the Babylonian, and the Persian rose, filled the planet with sound and splendor, then faded to dream-stuff and passed away; the Greek and the Roman followed, and made a vast noise, and they are gone; other peoples have sprung up and held their torch high for a time, but it burned out, and they sit in twilight now, or have vanished. The Jew saw them all, beat them all, and is now what he always was, exhibiting no decadence, no infirmities of age, no weakening of his parts, no slowing of his energies, no dulling of his alert and aggressive mind. All things are mortal but the Jew; all other forces pass, but he remains. What is the secret of his immortality?

The Five Boons of Life

1

In the morning of life came the good fairy with her basket and said:

"Here are the gifts. Take one, leave the others. And be wary, choose wisely; oh, choose wisely! for only one of them is valuable."

The gifts were five: Fame, Love, Riches, Pleasure, Death. The youth said, eagerly:

"There is no need to consider"; and he chose Pleasure.

He went out into the world and sought out the pleasures that youth delights in. But each in its turn was short-lived and disappointing, vain and empty; and each, departing, mocked him. In the end he said: "These years I have wasted. If I could but choose again, I would choose wisely."

2

The fairy appeared, and said:

"Four of the gifts remain. Choose once more; and oh, remember—time is flying, and only one of them is precious."

The man considered long, then chose Love; and did not mark the tears that rose in the fairy's eyes.

After many, many years the man sat by a coffin, in an empty home. And he communed with himself, saying: "One by one they have gone away and left me; and now she lies here, the dearest and the last. Desolation after desolation has swept over me; for each hour of happiness the treacherous trader, Love, has sold me I have paid a thousand hours of grief. Out of my heart of hearts I curse him."

3

"Choose again." It was the fairy speaking. "The years have taught you wisdom—surely it must be so. Three gifts remain. Only one of them has any worth—remember it, and choose warily."

The man reflected long, then chose Fame; and the fairy, sighing, went her way.

Years went by and she came again, and stood behind the man where he sat solitary in the fading day, thinking. And she knew his thought:

"My name filled the world, and its praises were on every tongue, and it seemed well with me for a little while. How little a while it was! Then came envy; then detraction; then calumny; then hate; then persecution. Then derision, which is the beginning of the end. And last of all came pity, which is the funeral of fame. Oh, the bitterness and misery of renown! target for mud in its prime, for contempt and compassion in its decay."

4

"Choose yet again." It was the fairy's voice. "Two gifts remain. And do not despair. In the beginning there was but one that was precious, and it is still here."

"Wealth—which is power! How blind I was!" said the man. "Now, at last, life will be worth the living. I will spend, squander, dazzle. These mockers and despisers will crawl in the dirt before me, and I will feed my hungry heart with their envy. I will have all luxuries, all joys, all enchantments of the spirit, all contentments of the body that man holds dear. I will buy, buy, buy! deference, respect, esteem, worship—every pinchbeck grace of life the market of a trivial world can furnish forth. I have lost much time, and chosen badly heretofore, but let that pass: I was ignorant then, and could but take for best what seemed so."

Three short years went by, and a day came when the man sat shivering in a mean garret; and he was gaunt and wan and hollow-eyed, and clothed in rags; and he was gnawing a dry crust and mumbling:

"Curse all the world's gifts, for mockeries and gilded lies! And mis-called, every one. They are not gifts, but merely lendings. Pleasure, Love, Fame, Riches: they are but temporary disguises for lasting realities—Pain, Grief, Shame, Poverty. The fairy said true; in all her store there was but one gift which was precious, only one that was not valueless. How poor and cheap and mean I know those others now to be, compared with that inestimable one, that dear and sweet and kindly one, that steeps in dreamless and enduring sleep the pains that persecute the body, and the shames and griefs that eat the mind and heart. Bring it! I am weary, I would rest."

5

The fairy came, bringing again four of the gifts, but Death was wanting. She said:

"I gave it to a mother's pet, a little child. It was ignorant, but trusted me, asking me to choose for it. You did not ask me to choose."

"Oh, miserable me! What is there left for me?"

"What not even you have deserved: the wanton insult of Old Age."

The Personal Recollections of Joan of Arc

The Personal Recollections of Joan of Arc (1896) was for a while Twain's favorite book, a fact that modern literary critics consider evidence of his poor critical judgment. The few modern critics who read the long narrative usually find it tedious, dull, sentimental, or inartistic, or all of the above. Moreover, this story of a Christian martyr would not be likely to contain much evidence of Twain's skepticism.

But this puzzling information can be thought through. First of all, Twain's emotional connection to the book is so strong because he used the character of Joan to represent some of his beloved daughter Susy's characteristics. He valued Susy's intelligence, her ability to see a topic freshly, and her strength of character. These traits he of course gave to Joan of Arc. Joan was, in addition, frequently at odds with the authorities of her times. The historical content of the novel gave Twain a chance to comment at length about medieval superstitions and religious credulity. To tell this story Twain created a narrator, the Sieur Louis De Conte, who had been Joan's hometown, childhood friend and who later became her page and secretary. This fictional device provides a first-person account of Joan's childhood, her rise to prominence, her military campaigns, her national devotion, and, finally, her trial and execution. The chapters on her trial dramatize dishonest religious casuistry by her accusers. Her execution demonstrates a terrible abuse of religious power.

Because Twain felt that his works were usually taken to be humorous, he attempted to publish this novel pseudonymously, but the deception was realized within a few months.

Book I

Chapter 1

. . . These were all good children, just of the ordinary peasant type; not bright, of course—you would not expect that—but good-hearted and companionable, obedient to their parents and the priest; and as they grew up they became properly stocked with narrownesses and prejudices got at second hand from their elders, and adopted without reserve; and without examination also—which goes without saying. Their religion was inherited, their politics the same. John Huss and his sort might find fault with the Church, in Domremy it disturbed nobody's faith; and when the split came, when I was fourteen, and we had three Popes at once, nobody in Domremy was worried about how to choose among them—the Pope of Rome was the right one, a Pope outside of Rome was no Pope at all. Every human creature in the village was an Armagnac—a patriot—and if we children hotly hated nothing else in the world, we did certainly hate the English and Burgundian name and polity in that way.

Chapter 2

Our Domremy was like any other humble little hamlet of that remote time and region. It was a maze of crooked, narrow lanes and alleys shaded and sheltered by the overhanging thatch roofs of the barnlike houses. The houses were dimly lighted by wooden-shuttered windows—that is, holes in the walls which served for windows. The floors were of dirt, and there was very little furniture. Sheep and cattle grazing was the main industry; all the young folks tended flocks.

The situation was beautiful. From one edge of the village a flowery plain extended in a wide sweep to the river—the Meuse; from the rear edge of the village a grassy slope rose gradually, and at the top was the great oak forest—a forest that was deep and gloomy and dense, and full of interest for us children, for many murders had been done in it by outlaws in old times, and in still earlier times prodigious dragons that spouted fire and poisonous vapors from their nostrils had their homes in there. In fact, one was still living in there in our own time. It was as long as a tree, and had a body as big around as a tierce, and scales like overlapping great tiles, and deep ruby eyes as large as a cavalier's hat, and an anchor-fluke on its tail as big as I don't know what, but very big, even unusually so for a dragon, as everybody said who knew about dragons. It was thought that this dragon was of a brilliant blue color, with gold mottlings, but no one had ever seen it, therefore this was not known to be so, it was only an opinion. It was not my opinion; I think there is no sense in forming an opinion when there is no evidence to form it on. If you build a person without any bones in him he may look fair enough to the eye, but he will be limber and cannot stand up; and I consider that *evidence* is the bones of an opinion. But I will take up this matter more at large at another time, and try to make the justness of my position appear. As to that dragon, I always held the belief that its color was gold and without blue, for that has always been the color of dragons. That this dragon lay but a little way within the wood at one time is shown by the fact that Pierre Morel was in there one day and smelt it, and recognized it by the smell. It gives one a horrid idea of how near to us the deadliest danger can be and we not suspect it.

In the earliest times a hundred knights from many remote places in the earth would have gone in there one after another, to kill the dragon and get the reward, but in our time that method had gone out, and the priest had become the one that abolished dragons. Père Guillaume Fronte did it in this case. He had a procession, with candles and incense and banners, and marched around the edge of the wood and exorcised the dragon, and it was never heard of again, although it was the opinion of many that the smell never wholly passed away. Not that any had ever smelt the smell again, for none had; it was only an opinion, like that other—and lacked bones, you see. I know that the creature was there before the exorcism, but whether it was there afterward or not is a thing which I cannot be so positive about.

In a noble open space carpeted with grass on the high ground toward Vaucouleurs stood a most majestic beech tree with wide-reaching arms and a grand spread of shade, and by it a limpid spring of cold water; and on summer days the children went there—oh, every summer for more than five hundred years—went there and sang and danced around the tree for hours together, refreshing themselves at the spring from time to time, and it was most lovely and enjoyable. Also they made wreaths of flowers and hung them upon the tree and about the spring to please the fairies that lived there; for they liked that, being idle innocent little creatures, as all fairies are, and fond of anything delicate and pretty like wild flowers put together in that way. And in return for this attention the fairies did any friendly thing they could for the children, such as keeping the spring always full and clear and cold, and driving away serpents and insects that sting; and so there was never any unkindness between the fairies and the children during more than five hundred years—tradition said a thousand—but only the warmest affection and the most perfect trust and confidence; and whenever a child died the fairies mourned just as that child's playmates did, and the sign of it was there to see; for before the dawn on the day of the funeral they hung a little immortelle over the place where that child was used to sit under the tree. I know this to be true by my own eyes; it is not hearsay. And the reason it was known that the fairies did it was this—that it was made all of black flowers of a sort not known in France anywhere.

Now from time immemorial all children reared in Domremy were called the Children of the Tree; and they loved that name, for it carried with it a mystic privilege not granted to any others of the children of this world. Which was this: whenever one of these came to die, then beyond the vague and formless images drifting through his darkening mind rose soft and rich and fair a vision of the Tree—if all was well with his soul. That was what some said. Others said the vision came in two ways: once as a warning, one or two years in advance of death, when the soul was the captive of sin, and then the Tree appeared in its desolate winter aspect—then that soul was smitten with an awful fear. If repentance, came, and purity of life, the vision came again, this time summer-clad and beautiful; but if it were otherwise with that soul the vision was withheld, and it passed from life knowing its doom. Still others said that the vision came but once, and then only to the sinless dying forlorn in distant lands and pitifully longing for some last dear reminder of their home. And what reminder of it could go to their hearts like the picture of the Tree that was the darling of their love and the comrade of their joys and comforter of their small griefs all through the divine days of their vanished youth?

Now the several traditions were as I have said, some believing one and some another. One of them I knew to be the truth, and that was the last one. I do not say anything against the others; I think they were true, but I only *know* that the last one was; and it is my thought that if one keep to the things he knows, and not trouble about the things which he cannot be sure about, he will have the steadier mind for it—and there is profit in that. I know that when the Children of the Tree die in a far land, then—if they be at peace with God—they turn their longing eyes toward home, and there, far-shining, as through a rift in a cloud that curtains heaven, they see the soft picture of the Fairy Tree, clothed in a dream of golden light; and they see the bloomy mead sloping away to the river, and to their perishing nostrils is blown faint and sweet the fragrance of the flowers of home. And then the vision fades and passes—but *they* know, *they* know! and by their transfigured faces you know also, you who stand looking on; yes, you know the message that has come, and that it has come from heaven.

Joan and I believed alike about this matter. But Pierre Morel, and Jacques d'Arc, and many others believed that the vision appeared twice—to a sinner. In fact, they and many others said they *knew* it. Probably because their fathers had known it and had told them; for one gets most things at second hand in this world.

Now one thing that does make it quite likely that there were really two apparitions of the Tree is this fact: From the most ancient times if one saw a villager of ours with his face ash-white and rigid with a ghastly fright, it was common for every one to whisper to his neighbor, "Ah, he is in sin, and has got his warning." And the neighbor would shudder at the thought and whisper back, "Yes, poor soul, he has seen the Tree."

Such evidences as these have their weight; they are not to be put aside with a wave of the hand. A thing that is backed by the cumulative experience of centuries naturally gets nearer and nearer to being proof all the time; and if this continue and continue, it will some day become authority—and authority is a bedded rock, and will abide.

In my long life I have seen several cases where the Tree appeared announcing a death which was still far away; but in none of these was the person in a state of sin. No; the apparition was in these cases only a special grace; in place of deferring the tidings of that soul's redemption till the day of death, the apparition brought them long before, and with them peace—peace that might no more be disturbed—the eternal peace of God. I myself, old and broken, wait with serenity; for I have seen the vision of the Tree. I have seen it, and am content. . . .

Chapter 5

. . . You may well believe that we had plenty of matter for talk now, since the raiding of our village seemed by long odds the greatest event that had really ever occurred in the world; for although these dull peasants may have *thought* they recognized the bigness of some of the previous occurrences that had filtered from the world's history dimly into their minds, the truth is that they hadn't. One biting little fact, visible to their eyes of flesh and felt in their own personal vitals, became at once more prodigious to them than the grandest remote episode in the world's history which they had got at second hand and by hearsay. It amuses me now when I recall how our elders talked then. They fumed and fretted in a fine fashion.

"Ah, yes," said old Jacques d'Arc, "things are come to a pretty pass, indeed! The King must be informed of this. It is time that he cease from idleness and dreaming, and get at his proper business." He meant our young disinherited King, the hunted refugee, Charles VII.

"You say well," said the maire. "He should be informed, and that at once. It is an outrage that such things should be permitted. Why, we are not safe in our beds, and he taking his ease yonder. It shall be made known, indeed it shall—all France shall hear of it!"

To hear them talk, one would have imagined that all the previous ten thousand sackings and burnings in France had been but fables, and this one the only fact. It is always the way; words will answer as long as it is only a person's neighbor who is in trouble, but when that person gets into trouble himself, it is time that the King rise up and *do* something. . . .

Book III

Chapter 2

My wound gave me a great deal of trouble clear into the first part of October; then the fresher weather renewed my life and strength. All this time there were reports drifting about that the King was going to ransom Joan. I believed these, for I was young and had not yet found out the littleness and meanness of our poor human race, which brags about itself so much, and thinks it is better and higher than the other animals. . . .

Following the Equator

Twain wrote Following the Equator *(1897) while concealing his stunning grief over the death of his daughter, Susan. In a letter (Feb. 23, 1897) to William Dean Howells, Twain confided that Howells's complimentary comments about his work:*

> *stir the dead heart of me, & throw a glow of color into a life which sometimes seems to have grown wholly wan. I don't mean that I am miserable; no—worse than that, indifferent. Indifferent to nearly everything but work. I like that; I enjoy it, & stick to it. I do it without purpose & without ambition; merely for the love of it.*
>
> *This mood will pass, some day—there is history for it. But it cannot pass until my wife comes up out of the submergence. She was always so quick to recover herself before, but now there is no rebound, & we are dead people who go through the motions of life. Indeed I am a mud image, & it puzzles me to know what it is in me that writes, & that has comedy-fancies & finds pleasure in phrasing them. It is a law of our nature, of course, or it wouldn't happen; the thing in me forgets the presence of the mud image & goes its own way wholly unconscious of it & apparently of no kinship with it. I have finished my book, but I go on as if the end were indefinitely away—as indeed it is. There is no hurry—at any rate there is no limit.* [Mark Twain-Howells Letters, *pp. 664-65*]

Following the Equator *included aphorisms from "Pudd'nhead Wilson's New Calendar," used to head each chapter. These statements are here gathered and presented as a unit.*

The book is an account of Twain's travels to Hawaii, Australia, New Zealand, India, and Africa. In his typical fashion Twain interweaves descriptions, local history, anecdotes, and random thoughts. The skepticism in Following the Equator *is unusually dense because, in addition to his personal sorrow, his observations of different customs, religions, values, and geography provoked many semi-philosophical reflections.*

PUDD'NHEAD WILSON'S NEW CALENDAR

A man may have no bad habits and have worse.

When in doubt, tell the truth.

It is more trouble to make a maxim than it is to do right.

A dozen direct censures are easier to bear than one morganatic compliment.

Noise proves nothing. Often a hen who has merely laid an egg cackles as if she had laid an asteroid.

He was as shy as a newspaper is when referring to its own merits.

Truth is the most valuable thing we have. Let us economize it.

It could probably be shown by facts and figures that there is no distinctly native American criminal class except Congress.

It is your human environment that makes climate.

Everything human is pathetic. The secret source of Humor is not joy but sorrow. There is no humor in heaven.

We should be careful to get out of an experience only the wisdom that it is in it—and stop there; lest we be like the cat that sits down on a hot stove-lid. She will never sit down on a hot stove-lid again—and that is well; but also she will never sit down on a cold one any more.

There are those who scoff at the school-boy, calling him frivolous and shallow. Yet it was the school-boy who said, "Faith is believing what you know ain't so."

The timid man yearns for full value and demands a tenth. The bold man strikes for double value and compromises on par.

We can secure other people's approval, if we do right and try hard; but our own is worth a hundred of it, and no way has been found of securing that.

Truth is stranger than fiction—to some people, but I am measurably familiar with it.

Truth is stranger than fiction, but it is because Fiction is obliged to stick to possibilities; Truth isn't.

There is a Moral Sense, and there is an Immoral Sense. History shows us that the Moral Sense enables us to perceive morality and how to avoid it, and that the Immoral Sense enables us to perceive Immorality and how to enjoy it.

The English are mentioned in the Bible: Blessed are the meek for they shall inherit the earth.

It is easier to stay out than to get out.

Pity is for the living, envy is for the dead.

It is by the goodness of God that in our country we have those three unspeakably precious things: freedom of speech, freedom of conscience, and the prudence never to practice either of them.

Man will do many things to get himself loved; he will do all things to get himself envied.

Nothing is so ignorant as a man's left hand, except a lady's watch.

Be careless in your dress if you must, but keep a tidy soul.

There is no such thing as "the Queen's English." The property has gone into the hands of a joint stock company and we own the bulk of the shares!

"*Classic.*" A book which people praise and don't read.

There are people who can do all fine and heroic things but one: keep from telling their happiness to the unhappy.

Man is the Only Animal that Blushes. Or needs to.

The universal brotherhood of man is our most precious possession, what there is of it.

Let us be thankful for the fools. But for them the rest of us could not succeed.

When people do not respect us we are sharply offended; yet deep down in his private heart no man much respects himself.

Nature makes the locust with an appetite for crops; man would have made him with an appetite for sand.

The spirit of wrath—not the words—is the sin; and the spirit of wrath is cursing. We begin to swear before we can talk.

A man with a new idea is a Crank until the idea succeeds.

Let us be grateful to Adam our benefactor. He cut us out of the "blessing" of idleness and won for us the "curse" of labor.

Let us not be too particular. It is better to have old second-hand diamonds than none at all.

The Autocrat of Russia possesses more power than any other man in the earth; but he cannot stop a sneeze.

There are several good protections against temptations, but the surest is cowardice.

Names are not always what they seem. The common Welsh name Bzjxxllwep is pronounced Jackson.

To succeed in the other trades, capacity must be shown; in the law concealment of it will do.

Prosperity is the best protection of principle.

By trying we can easily learn to endure adversity. Another man's, I mean.

Few of us can stand prosperity. Another man's, I mean.

There is an old-time toast which is golden for its beauty—"When you ascend the hill of prosperity may you not meet a friend."

Each person is born to one possession which outvalues all his others—his last breath.

Hunger is the handmaid of genius.

The old maxim says, "Let a sleeping dog lie." Right. Still, when there is much at stake it is better to get a newspaper to do it.

It takes your enemy and your friend, working together, to hurt you to the heart; the one to slander you and the other to get the news to you.

If the desire to kill and the opportunity to kill came always together, who would escape hanging?

Simple rules for saving money: To save half, when you are fired by an eager impulse to contribute to a charity, wait and count forty. To save three-quarters count sixty. To save it all, count sixty-five.

Grief takes care of itself; but to get the full value of a joy you must have some-one to divide it with.

He that had much experience of physicians, and said, "the only way to keep your health is to eat what you don't want, drink what you don't like, and do what you'd druther not."

The man who is ostentatious of his modesty is twin to the statue that wears a fig-leaf.

Let me make the superstitions of a nation and I care not who makes its laws or its songs either.

Wrinkles should merely indicate where smiles have been.

True irreverence is disrespect for another man's god.

Do not undervalue the headache. While it is its sharpest it seems a bad invest-ment; but when relief begins, the unexpired remainder is worth four dollars a minute.

There are eight hundred and sixty-nine different forms of lying, but only one of them has been squarely forbidden. Thou shalt not bear false witness against thy neighbor.

There are two times in a man's life when he should not speculate; when he can't afford it, and when he can.

She was not quite what you would call refined. She was not quite what you would call unrefined. She was the kind of person that keeps a parrot.

Volume 1: Chapter 1

. . . The brightest passenger in the ship, and the most interesting and felicitous talker, was a young Canadian who was not able to let the whisky bottle alone. He was of a rich and powerful family, and could have had a distinguished career and abundance of effective help toward it if he could have conquered his appetite for drink; but he could not do it, so his great equipment of talent was of no use to him. He had often taken the pledge to drink no more, and was a good example of what that sort of unwisdom can do for a man—for a man with anything short of an iron will. The system is wrong in two ways: it does not strike at the root of the trouble, for one thing, and to make a *pledge* of any kind is to declare war against nature; for a pledge is a chain that is always clanking and reminding the wearer of it that he is not a free man.

I have said that the system does not strike at the root of the trouble, and I venture to repeat that. The root is not the *drinking,* but the *desire* to drink. These are very different things. The one merely requires will—and a great deal of it, both as to bulk and staying capacity—the other merely requires watchfulness—and for no long time. The desire of course precedes the act, and should have one's first attention; it can do but little good to refuse the act over and over again, always leaving the desire unmolested, unconquered; the desire will continue to assert itself, and will be almost sure to win in the long run. When the desire intrudes, it should be at once banished out of the mind. One should be on the watch for it all the time—otherwise it will get *in.* It must be taken in time and not allowed to get a lodgment. A desire constantly repulsed for a fortnight should die, then. That should cure the drinking-habit. The system of refusing the mere *act* of drinking, and leaving the *desire* in full force, is unintelligent war tactics, it seems to me.

I used to take pledges—and soon violate them. My will was not strong, and I could not help it. And then, to be tied in any way naturally irks an otherwise free person and makes him chafe in his bonds and want to get his liberty. But when I finally ceased from taking definite pledges, and merely resolved that I would kill an injurious desire, but leave myself free to resume the desire and the habit whenever I should choose to do so, I had no more trouble. In five days I drove out the desire to smoke and was not obliged to keep watch after that; and I never experienced any strong desire to smoke again. At the end of a year and a quarter of idleness I began to write a book, and presently found that the pen was strangely reluctant to go. I tried a smoke to see if that would help me out of the difficulty. It did. I smoked eight or ten cigars and as many pipes a day for five months; finished the book, and did not smoke again until a year had gone by and another book had to be begun.

I can quit any of my nineteen injurious habits at any time, and without discomfort or inconvenience. I think that the Dr. Tanners and those others who go forty days without eating do it by resolutely keeping out the desire to eat, in the beginning; and that after a few hours the desire is discouraged and comes no more.

Once I tried my scheme in a large medical way. I had been confined to my bed several days with lumbago. My case refused to improve. Finally the doctor said:

"My remedies have no fair chance. Consider what they have to fight, besides the lumbago. You smoke extravagantly, don't you?"

"Yes."

"You take coffee immoderately?"

"Yes."

"And some tea?"

"Yes."

"You eat all kinds of things that are dissatisfied with each other's company?"

"Yes."

"You drink two hot Scotches every night?"

"Yes."

"Very well, there you can see what I have to contend against. We can't make progress the way the matter stands. You must make a reduction in these things; you must cut down your consumption of them considerably for some days."

"I can't, doctor."

"Why can't you?"

"I lack the will-power. I can cut them off entirely, but I can't merely moderate them."

He said that that would answer, and said he would come around in twenty-four hours and begin work again. He was taken ill himself and could not come; but I did not need him. I cut off all those things for two days and nights; in fact, I cut off all kinds of food, too, and all drinks except water, and at the end of the forty-eight hours the lumbago was discouraged and left me. I was a well man; so I gave thanks and took to those delicacies again.

It seemed a valuable medical course, and I recommended it to a lady. She had run down and down and down, and had at last reached a point where medicines no longer had any helpful effect upon her. I said I knew I could put her upon her feet in a week. It brightened her up, it filled her with hope, and she said she would do everything I told her to do. So I said she must stop swearing and drinking and smoking and eating for four days, and then she would be all right again. And it would have happened just so, I know it; but she said she could not stop swearing and smoking and drinking, because she had never done these things. So there it was. She had neglected her habits, and hadn't any. Now that they would have come good, there were none in stock. She had nothing to fall back on. She was a sinking vessel, with no freight in her to throw overboard and lighten ship withal. Why, even one or two little bad habits could have saved her, but she was just a moral pauper. When she could have acquired them she was dissuaded by her parents, who were ignorant people though reared in the best society, and it was too late to begin now. It seemed such a pity; but there was no help for it. These things ought to be attended to while a person is young; otherwise, when age and disease come, there is nothing effectual to fight them with.

When I was a youth I used to take all kinds of pledges, and do my best to keep them, but I never could, because I didn't strike at the root of the habit—the *desire;* I generally broke down within the month. Once I tried limiting a habit. That worked tolerably well for a while. I pledged myself to smoke but one cigar a day. I kept the cigar waiting until bedtime, then I had a luxurious time with it. But desire persecuted me every day and all day long; so, within the week I found myself hunting for larger cigars than I had been used to smoke; then larger ones still, and still larger ones. Within the fortnight I was getting cigars *made* for me—on a yet larger pattern. They still grew and grew in size. Within the month my cigar had grown to such proportions that I could have used it as a crutch. It now seemed to me that a one-cigar limit was no real protection to a person, so I knocked my pledge on the head and resumed my liberty.

To go back to that young Canadian. He was a "remittance-man," the first one I had ever seen or heard of. Passengers explained the term to me. They said that dissipated ne'er-do-weels belonging to important families in England and Canada were not cast off by their people while there was any hope of reforming them, but when that last hope perished at last, the ne'er-do-weel was sent abroad to get him out of the way. He was shipped off with just enough money in his pocket—no, in the purser's pocket—for the needs of the voyage—and when he reached his destined port he would find a remittance awaiting him there. Not a large one, but just enough to keep him a month. A similar remittance would come monthly thereafter. It was the remittance-man's custom to pay his month's board and lodging straightway—a duty which his landlord did not allow him to forget—then spree away the rest of his money in a single night, then brood and mope and grieve in idleness till the next remittance came. It is a pathetic life.

We had other remittance-men on board, it was said. At least *they* said they were R. M.'s. There were two. But they did not resemble the Canadian; they lacked his tidiness, and his brains, and his gentlemanly ways, and his resolute spirit, and his humanities and generosities. One of them was a lad of nineteen or twenty, and he was a good deal of a ruin, as to clothes, and morals, and general aspect. He said he was a scion of a ducal house in England, and had been shipped to Canada for the house's relief, that he had fallen into trouble there, and was now being shipped to Australia. He said he had no title. Beyond this remark he was economical of the truth. The first thing he did in Australia was to get into the lockup, and the next thing he did was to proclaim himself an earl in the police court in the morning and fail to prove it.

Chapter 5

Wednesday, *Sept. 11.* In this world we often make mistakes of judgment. We do not, as a rule, get out of them sound and whole, but sometimes we do. At dinner yesterday evening—present, a mixture of Scotch, English, American, Canadian, and Australasian folk—a discussion broke out about the pronunciation of certain Scottish words. This was private ground, and the non-Scotch nationalities, with one exception, discreetly kept still. But I am not discreet, and I took a hand. I didn't know anything about the subject, but I took a hand just to have something to do. At that moment the word in dispute was the word *three.* One Scotchman was claiming that the peasantry of Scotland pronounced *three,* his adversaries claimed that they didn't—that they pronounced it *thraw.* The solitary Scot was having a sultry time of it, so I thought I would enrich him with my help. In my position I was necessarily quite impartial, and was equally as well and as ill equipped to fight on the one side as on the other. So I spoke up and said the peasantry pronounced the word *three,* not *thraw.* It was an error of judgment. There was a moment of astonished and ominous silence, then weather ensued. The storm rose and spread in a surprising way, and I was snowed under in a very few minutes. It was a bad defeat for me—a kind of Waterloo. It promised to remain so, and I wished I had had better sense than to enter upon such a forlorn enterprise. But just then I had a saving thought—at least a thought that offered a chance. While the storm was still raging, I made up a Scotch couplet, and then spoke up and said:

"Very well, don't say any more. I confess defeat. I thought I knew, but I see my mistake. I was deceived by one of your Scotch poets."

"A *Scotch* poet! Oh come! Name him."

"*Robert Burns.*"

It is wonderful the power of that name. These men looked doubtful—but paralyzed, all the same. They were quite silent for a moment; then one of them said—with the reverence in his voice which is always present in a Scotchman's tone when he utters the name:

"Does Robbie Burns say—*what* does he say?"

"This is what he says:

> "There were nae bairns but only three—
> Ane at the breast, twa at the knee."

It ended the discussion. There was no man there profane enough, disloyal enough, to say any word against a thing which Robert Burns had settled. I shall always honor that great name for the salvation it brought me in this time of my sore need.

It is my belief that nearly any invented quotation, played with confidence, stands a good chance to deceive. There are people who think that honesty is always the best policy. This is a superstition; there are times when the appearance of it is worth six of it. . . .

Chapter 7

. . . It is a fine race, the Fijians, with brains in their heads and an inquiring turn of mind. It appears that their savage ancestors had a doctrine of immortality in their scheme of religion—with limitations. That is to say, their dead friend would go to a happy hereafter if he could be accumulated, but not otherwise. They drew the line; they thought that the missionary's doctrine was too sweeping, too comprehensive. They called his attention to certain facts. For instance, many of their friends had been devoured by sharks; the sharks, in their turn, were caught and eaten by other men; later, these men were captured in war, and eaten by the enemy. The original persons had entered into the composition of the sharks; next, they and the sharks had become part of the flesh and blood and bone of the cannibals. How, then, could the particles of the original men be searched out from the final conglomerate and put together again? The inquirers were full of doubts, and considered that the missionary had not examined the matter with the gravity and attention which so serious a thing deserved.

The missionary taught these exacting savages many valuable things, and got from them one—a very dainty and poetical idea: Those wild and ignorant poor children of Nature believed that the flowers, after they perish, rise on the winds and float away to the fair fields of heaven, and flourish there forever in immortal beauty! . . .

Chapter 12

In Sydney I had a large dream, and in the course of talk I told it to a missionary from India who was on his way to visit some relatives in New Zealand. I dreamed that the visible universe is the physical person of God; that the vast worlds that we see twinkling millions of miles apart in the fields of space are the blood-corpuscles in His veins; and that we and the other creatures are the microbes that charge with multitudinous life the corpuscles.

Mr. X., the missionary, considered the dream awhile, then said:

> It is not surpassable for magnitude, since its metes and bounds are the metes and bounds of the universe itself; and it seems to me that it almost accounts for a thing which is otherwise nearly unaccountable—the origin of the sacred legends of the Hindus. Perhaps they dream them, and then honestly believe them to be divine revelations of fact. It looks like that, for the legends are built on so vast a scale that it does not seem reasonable that plodding priests would happen upon such colossal fancies when awake.

He told some of the legends, and said that they were implicitly believed by all classes of Hindus, including those of high social position and intelligence; and he said that this universal credulity was a great hindrance to the missionary in his work. Then he said something like this:

> At home, people wonder why Christianity does not make faster progress in India. They hear that the Indians believe easily, and that they have a natural trust in miracles and give them a hospitable reception. Then they argue like this: since the Indian believes easily, place Christianity before them and they must believe; confirm its truths by the Biblical miracles, and they will no longer doubt. The natural deduction is, that as Christianity makes but indifferent progress in India, the fault is with us: we are not fortunate in presenting the doctrines and the miracles.
>
> But the truth is, we are not by any means so well equipped as they think. We have *not* the easy task that they imagine. To use a military figure, we are sent

against the enemy with good powder in our guns, but only wads for bullets; that is to say, our miracles are not effective; the Hindus do not care for them; they have more extraordinary ones of their own. All the details of their own religion are proven and established by miracles; the details of ours must be proven in the same way. When I first began my work in India I greatly underestimated the difficulties thus put upon my task. A correction was not long in coming. I thought as our friends think at home—that to prepare my childlike wonder-lovers to listen with favor to my grave message I only needed to charm the way to it with wonders, marvels, miracles. With full confidence I told the wonders performed by Samson, the strongest man that had ever lived—for so I called him.

At first I saw lively anticipation and strong interest in the faces of my people, but as I moved along from incident to incident of the great story, I was distressed to see that I was steadily losing the sympathy of my audience. I could not understand it. It was a surprise to me, and a disappointment. Before I was through, the fading sympathy had paled to indifference. Thence to the end the indifference remained; I was not able to make any impression upon it.

A good old Hindu gentleman told me where my trouble lay. He said: "We Hindus recognize a god by the work of his hands—we accept no other testimony. Apparently, this is also the rule with you Christians. And we know when a man has his power from a god by the fact that he does things which he could not do, as a man, with the mere powers of a man. Plainly, this is the Christian's way also, of knowing when a man is working by a god's power and not by his own. You saw that there was a supernatural property in the hair of Samson; for you perceived that when his hair was gone he was as other men. It is our way, as I have said. There are many nations in the world, and each group of nations has its own gods, and will pay no worship to the gods of the others. Each group believes its own gods to be strongest, and it will not exchange them except for gods that shall be proven to be their superiors in power. Man is but a weak creature, and needs the help of gods—he cannot do without it. Shall he place his fate in the hands of weak gods when there may be stronger ones to be found? That would be foolish. No, if he hear of gods that are stronger than his own, he should not turn a deaf ear, for it is not a light matter that is at stake. How then shall he determine which gods are the stronger, his own or those that preside over the concerns of other nations? By comparing the known works of his own gods with the works of those others; there is no other way. Now, when we make this comparison, we are not drawn toward the gods of any other nation. Our gods are shown by their works to be the strongest, the most powerful. The Christians have but few gods, and they are new—new, and not strong, as it seems to us. They will increase in number, it is true, for this has happened with all gods, but that time is far away, many ages and decades of ages away, for gods multiply slowly, as is meet for beings to whom a thousand years is but a single moment. Our own gods have been born millions of years apart. The process is slow, the gathering of strength and power is similarly slow. In the slow lapse of the ages the steadily accumulating power of our gods has at last become prodigious. We have a thousand proofs of this in the colossal character of their personal acts and the acts of ordinary men to whom they have given supernatural qualities. To your Samson was given supernatural power, and when he broke the withes, and slew the thousands with the jawbone of an ass, and carried away the gates of the city upon his shoulders, you were amazed—and also awed, for you recognized the divine source of his strength. But it could not profit to place these things before your Hindu congregation and invite their wonder; for they would compare them with the deed done by Hanuman, when our gods infused their divine strength into his muscles; and they would be indifferent to them—as you saw. In the old, old times, ages and ages gone by, when our god Rama was warring with the demon god of Ceylon, Rama bethought him to bridge the sea and connect Ceylon with India, so that his armies might pass easily over; and he sent his general, Hanuman, inspired like your own Samson with divine strength, to bring the materials for the bridge. In two days Hanuman strode fifteen hundred miles, to the Himalayas, and took upon his shoulder a range of those lofty mountains two hundred miles long, and started with it toward Ceylon. It was in the night; and, as he passed along the plain, the people of Govardhun heard the thunder of his tread and felt the earth rocking under it, and they ran out, and there, with their snowy summits piled to heaven, they saw the Himalayas passing by. And as this huge continent swept along overshadowing the earth, upon its slopes they discerned the twinkling lights of a thousand sleeping villages, and it was as if the constellations were filing in procession through the sky. While they were looking, Hanuman stumbled, and a small ridge of red sandstone twenty miles long was jolted loose and fell. Half of its length has wasted away in the course of the ages, but the other ten miles of it remain in the plain by Govardhun to this day as proof of the might of the inspiration of our gods. You must know, yourself, that Hanuman could not have carried those mountains to Ceylon except by the strength of the gods. You know that it was not done by his own strength, therefore you know that it *was* done by the strength of the gods, just as you know that Samson carried the gates by the divine strength and not by his own. I think you must concede two things: First, That in carrying the gates of the city upon his shoulders, Samson did not establish the superiority of his gods over ours; secondly, That his feat is not supported by any but verbal evidence, while Hanuman's is not only supported by verbal evidence, but this evidence is confirmed, established, proven, by visible, tangible evidence, which is the strongest of all testimony. We have the sandstone ridge, and while it remains we cannot doubt, and shall not. Have you the gates?"

Chapter 21

. . . That is the theater for the drama. When you comprehend one or two other details, you will perceive how well suited for trouble it was, and how loudly it invited it. The cattlemen's stations were scattered over that profound wilderness miles and miles apart—at each station half a dozen persons. There was a plenty of cattle, the black natives were always ill-nourished and hungry. The land belonged to *them.* The whites had not bought it, and couldn't buy it; for the tribes had no chiefs, nobody in authority, nobody competent to sell and convey; and the tribes themselves had no comprehension of the idea of transferable ownership of land. The ousted owners were despised by the white interlopers, and this opinion was not hidden under a bushel. More promising materials for a tragedy could not have been collated. Let Mrs. Praed speak:

> At Nie Nie station, one dark night, the unsuspecting hut-keeper, having, as he believed, secured himself against assault, was lying wrapped in his blankets sleeping profoundly. The Blacks crept stealthily down the chimney and battered in his skull while he slept.

One could guess the whole drama from that little text. The curtain was up. It would not fall until the mastership of one party or the other was determined—and permanently:

> There was treachery on both sides. The Blacks killed the Whites when they found them defenseless, and the Whites slew the Blacks in a wholesale and promiscuous fashion which offended against my childish sense of justice. . . . They were regarded as little above the level of brutes, and in some cases *were destroyed like vermin.*
>
> Here is an instance. A squatter, whose station was surrounded by Blacks, whom he suspected to be hostile and from whom he feared an attack, parleyed with them from his house-door. He told them it was Christmas-time—a time at which all men, black or white, feasted; that there were flour, sugar-plums, good things in plenty in the store, and that he would make for them such a pudding as they had never dreamed of—a great pudding of which all might eat and be filled. The Blacks listened and were lost. The pudding was made and distributed. Next morning there was howling in the camp, for it had been sweetened with sugar and arsenic!

The white man's spirit was right, but his method was wrong. His spirit was the spirit which the civilized white has always exhibited toward the savage, but the use of poison was a departure from custom. True, it was merely a technical departure, not a real one; still, it was a departure, and therefore a mistake, in my opinion. It was better, kinder, swifter, and much more humane than a number of the methods which have been sanctified by custom, but that does not justify its employment. That is, it does not wholly justify it. Its unusual nature makes it stand out and attract an amount of attention which it is not entitled to. It takes hold upon morbid imaginations and they work it up into a sort of exhibition of cruelty, and this smirches the good name of our civilization, whereas one of the old harsher methods would have had no such effect because usage has made those methods familiar to us and innocent. In many countries we have chained the savage and starved him to death; and this we do not care for, because custom has inured us to it; yet a quick death by poison is loving-kindness to it. In many countries we have burned the savage at the stake; and this we do not care for, because custom has inured us to it; yet a quick death is loving-kindness to it. In more than one country we have hunted the savage and his little children and their mother with dogs and guns through the woods and swamps for an afternoon's sport, and filled the region with happy laughter over their sprawling and stumbling flight, and their wild supplications for mercy; but this method we do not mind, because custom has inured us to it; yet a quick death by poison is loving-kindness to it. In many countries we have taken the savage's land from him, and made him our slave, and lashed him every day, and broken his pride, and made death his only friend, and overworked him till he dropped in his tracks; and this we do not care for, because custom has inured us to it; yet a quick death by poison is loving-kindness to it. In the Matabeleland to-day—why, there we are confining ourselves to sanctified custom, we Rhodes-Beit millionaires in South Africa and Dukes in London; and nobody cares, because we are used to the old holy customs, and all we ask is that no notice-inviting new ones shall be intruded upon the attention of our comfortable consciences. Mrs. Praed says of the poisoner, "That squatter deserves to have his name handed down to the contempt of posterity."

I am sorry to hear her say that. I myself blame him for one thing, and severely, but I stop there. I blame him for the indiscretion of introducing a novelty which was calculated to attract attention to our civilization. There was no occasion to do that. It was his duty, and it is every loyal man's duty, to protect that heritage in every way he can; and the best way to do that is to attract attention elsewhere. The squatter's judgment was bad—that is plain; but his heart was right. He is almost the only pioneering representative of civilization in history who has risen above the prejudices of his caste and his heredity and tried to introduce the element of mercy into the superior race's dealings with the savage. His name is lost, and it is a pity; for it deserves to be handed down to posterity with homage and reverence.

This paragraph is from a London journal:

> To learn what France is doing to spread the blessings of civilization in her distant dependencies we may turn with advantage to New Caledonia. With a view to attracting free settlers to that penal colony, M. Feillet, the Governor, forcibly expropriated the Kanaka cultivators from the best of their plantations, with a derisory compensation, in spite of the protests of the Council General of the island. Such immigrants as could be induced to cross the seas thus found themselves in possession of thousands of coffee, cocoa, banana, and bread-fruit trees, the raising of which had cost the wretched natives years of toil, whilst the latter had a few five-franc pieces to spend in the liquor stores of Noumea.

You observe the combination? It is robbery, humiliation, and slow, slow murder, through poverty and the white man's whisky. The savage's gentle friend, the savage's noble friend, the only magnanimous and unselfish friend the savage has ever had, was not there with the merciful swift release of his poisoned pudding.

There are many humorous things in the world; among them the white man's notion that he is less savage than the other savages.

Chapter 27

. . . The Whites always mean well when they take human fish out of the ocean and try to make them dry and warm and happy and comfortable in a chickencoop; but the kindest-hearted white man can always be depended on to prove himself inadequate when he deals with savages. He cannot turn the situation around and imagine how he would like it to have a well-meaning savage transfer him from his house and his church and his clothes and his books and his choice food to a hideous wilderness of sand and rocks and snow, and ice and sleet and storm and blistering sun, with no shelter, no bed, no covering for his and his family's naked bodies, and nothing to eat but snakes and grubs and offal. This would be a hell to him; and if he had any wisdom he would know that his own civilization is a hell to the savage—but he hasn't any, and has never had any; and for lack of it he shut up those poor natives in the unimaginable perdition of his civilization, committing his crime with the very best intentions, and saw those poor creatures waste away under his tortures; and gazed at it, vaguely troubled and sorrowful, and wondered what could be the matter with them. One is almost betrayed into respecting those criminals, they were so sincerely kind, and tender, and humane, and well-meaning.

They didn't know why those exiled savages faded away, and they did their honest best to reason it out. And one man, in a like case, in New South Wales, *did* reason it out and arrive at a solution:

"It is from the wrath of God, which is revealed from heaven against all ungodliness and unrighteousness of men."

That settles it.

Volume 2: Chapter 3

. . . The first Bearer that applied waited below and sent up his recommendations. That was the first morning in Bombay. We read them over; carefully, cautiously, thoughtfully. There was not a fault to find with them—except one; they were all from Americans. Is that a slur? If it is, it is a deserved one. In my experience, an American's recommendation of a servant is not usually valuable. We are too good-natured a race; we hate to say the unpleasant thing; we shrink from speaking the unkind truth about a poor fellow whose bread depends upon our verdict; so we speak of his good points only, thus not scrupling to tell a lie—a *silent* lie—for in not mentioning his bad ones we as good as say he hasn't any. The only difference that I know of between a silent lie and a spoken one is, that the silent lie is a less respectable one than the other. And it can deceive, whereas the other can't—as a rule. We not only tell the silent lie as to a servant's faults, but we sin in another way: we overpraise his merits; for when it comes to writing recommendations of servants we are a nation of gushers. And we have not the Frenchman's excuse. In France you *must* give the departing servant a good recommendation; and you *must* conceal his faults; you have no choice. If you mention his faults for the protection of the next candidate for his services, he can sue you for damages; and the court will award them, too; and, moreover, the judge will give you a sharp dressing-down from the bench for trying to destroy a poor man's character and rob him of his bread.

I do not state this on my own authority, I got it from a French physician of fame and repute—a man who was born in Paris, and had practised there all his life. And he said that he spoke not merely from common knowledge, but from exasperating personal experience.

As I was saying, the Bearer's recommendations were all from American tourists; and St. Peter would have admitted him to the fields of the blest on them—I mean if he is as unfamiliar with our people and our ways as I suppose he is. According to these recommendations, Manuel X was supreme in all the arts connected with his complex trade; and these manifold arts were mentioned—and praised—in detail. His English was spoken of in terms of warm admiration—admiration verging upon rapture. I took pleased note of that, and hoped that some of it might be true.

We had to have some one right away; so the family went down-stairs and took him a week on trial; then sent him up to me and departed on their affairs. I was shut up in my quarters with a bronchial cough, and glad to have something fresh to look at, something new to play with. Manuel filled the bill; Manuel was very welcome. He was toward fifty years old, tall, slender, with a slight stoop—an artificial stoop, a deferential stoop, a stoop rigidified by long habit—with face of European mold; short hair, intensely black; gentle black eyes, timid black eyes, indeed; complexion very dark, nearly black in fact; face smooth-shaven. He was bareheaded and barefooted, and was never otherwise while his week with us lasted; his clothing was European, cheap, flimsy, and showed much wear.

He stood before me and inclined his head (and body) in the pathetic Indian way, touching his forehead with the finger-ends of his right hand, in salute. I said:

"Manuel, you are evidently Indian, but you seem to have a Spanish name when you put it all together. How is that?"

A perplexed look gathered in his face; it was plain that he had not understood—but he didn't let on. He spoke back placidly:

"Name, Manuel. Yes, master."

"I know; but how did you *get* the name?"

"Oh yes, I suppose. Think happen so. Father same name, not mother."

I saw that I must simplify my language and spread my words apart, if I would be understood by this English scholar.

"Well—then—how—did—your—father—get—*his*—name?"

"Oh, he"—brightening a little—"he Christian—Portygee; live in Goa; I born Goa; mother not Portygee, mother native—high-caste Brahman—Coolin Brahman; highest caste; no other so high caste. I high-caste Brahman, too. Christian, too, same like father; high-caste Christian Brahman, master—Salvation Army."

All this haltingly, and with difficulty. Then he had an inspiration, and began to pour out a flood of words that I could make nothing of; so I said:

"There—don't do that. I can't understand Hindustani."

"Not Hindustani, master—English. Always I speak English sometimes when I talking every day all the time at you."

"Very well, stick to that; that is intelligible. It is not up to my hopes, it is not up to the promise of the recommendations, still it is English, and I understand it. Don't elaborate it; I don't like elaborations when they are crippled by uncertainty of touch."

"Master?"

"Oh, never mind; it was only a random thought; I didn't expect you to understand it. How did you get your English; is it an acquirement, or just a gift of God?"

After some hesitation—piously:

"Yes, he very good. Christian god very good; Hindu god very good, too. Two million Hindu god, one Christian god—make two million and one. All mine; two million and one god. I got a plenty. Sometime I pray all time at those, keep it up, go all time every day; give something at shrine, all good for me, make me better man; good for me, good for my family, dam good."

Then he had another inspiration, and went rambling off into fervent confusions and incoherencies, and I had to stop him again. I thought we had talked enough, so I told him to go to the bathroom and clean it up and remove the slops—this to get rid of him. He went away, seeming to understand, and got out some of my clothes and began to brush them. I repeated my desire several times, simplifying and resimplifying it, and at last he got the idea. Then he went away and put a coolie at the work, and explained that he would lose caste if he did it himself; it would be pollution, by the law of his caste, and it would cost him a deal of fuss and trouble to purify himself and accomplish his rehabilitation. He said that that kind of work was strictly forbidden to persons of caste, and as strictly restricted to the very bottom layer of Hindu society—the despised *Sudra* (the toiler, the laborer). He was right; and apparently the poor Sudra has been content with his strange lot, his insulting distinction, for ages and ages—clear back to the beginning of things, so to speak. Buckle says that his name—laborer—is a term of contempt; that it is ordained by the Institutes of Menu (900 B.C.) that *if a Sudra sit on a level with his superior he shall be exiled or branded* . . . ; if he speak contemptuously of his superior or insult him *he shall suffer death; if he listen to the reading of the sacred books he shall have burning oil poured in his ears;* if he memorize passages from them *he shall be killed;* if he marry his daughter to a Brahman *the husband shall go to hell for defiling himself by contact with a woman so infinitely his inferior;* and that it is *forbidden to a Sudra to acquire wealth.* "The bulk of the population of India," says Buckle, "is the Sudras—the *workers, the farmers, the creators of wealth.*"

Manuel was a failure, poor old fellow. His age was against him. He was desperately slow and phenomenally forgetful. When he went three blocks on an errand he would be gone two hours, and then forget what it was he went for. When he packed a trunk it took him forever, and the trunk's contents were an unimaginable chaos when he got done. He couldn't wait satisfactorily at table—a prime defect, for if you haven't your own servant in an Indian hotel you are likely to have a slow time of it and go away hungry. We couldn't understand his English; he couldn't understand ours; and when we found that he couldn't understand his own, it seemed time for us to part. I had to discharge him; there was no help for it. But I did it as kindly as I could, and as gently. We must part, said I, but I hoped we should meet again in a better world. It was not true, but it was only a little thing to say, and saved his feelings and cost me nothing.

But now that he was gone, and was off my mind and heart, my spirits began to rise at once, and I was soon feeling brisk and ready to go out and have adventures. Then his newly hired successor flitted in, touched his forehead, and began to fly around here, there, and everywhere, on his velvet feet, and in five minutes he had everything in the room "ship-shape and Bristol fashion," as the sailors say, and was standing at the salute, waiting for orders. Dear me, what a rustler he was after the slumbrous way of Manuel, poor old slug! All my heart, all my affection, all my admiration, went out spontaneously to this frisky little forked black thing, this compact and compressed incarnation of energy and force and promptness and celerity and confidence, this smart, smily, engaging, shiny-eyed little devil, feruled on his upper end by a gleaming fire-coal of a fez with a red-hot tassel dangling from it. I said, with deep satisfaction:

"You'll suit. What is your name?"

He reeled it mellowly off.

"Let me see if I can make a selection out of it—for business uses, I mean; we will keep the rest for Sundays. Give it to me in instalments."

He did it. But there did not seem to be any short ones, except Mousa—which suggested mouse. It was out of character; it was too soft, too quiet, too conservative; it didn't fit his splendid style. I considered, and said:

"Mousa is short enough, but I don't quite like it. It seems colorless—inharmonious—inadequate; and I am sensitive to such things. How do you think Satan would do?"

"Yes, master. Satan do wair good."

It was his way of saying "very good."

There was a rap at the door. Satan covered the ground with a single skip; there was a word or two of Hindustani, then he disappeared. Three minutes later he was before me again, militarily erect, and waiting for me to speak first.

"What is it, Satan?"

"God wants to see you."

"*Who?*"

"God. I show him up, master?"

"Why, this is so unusual, that—that—well, you see—indeed I am so unprepared—I don't quite know what I *do* mean. Dear me, can't you explain? Don't you see that this is a most ex—"

"Here his card, master."

Wasn't it curious—and amazing, and tremendous, and all that? Such a personage going around calling on such as I, and sending up his card, like a mortal—sending it up by Satan. It was a bewildering collision of the impossibles. But this was the land of the Arabian Nights, this was India! and what is it that cannot happen in India?

We had the interview. Satan was right—the Visitor was indeed a God in the conviction of his multitudinous followers, and was worshiped by them in sincerity and humble adoration. They are troubled by no doubts as to his divine origin and office. They believe in him, they pray to him, they make offerings to him, they beg of him remission of sins; to them his person, together with everything connected with it, is sacred; from his barber they buy the parings of his nails and set them in gold, and wear them as precious amulets.

I tried to seem tranquilly conversational and at rest, but I was not. Would you have been? I was in a suppressed frenzy of excitement and curiosity and glad wonder. I could not keep my eyes off him. I was looking upon a *god,* an actual god, a recognized and accepted god; and every detail of his person and his dress had a consuming interest for me. And the thought went floating through my head, "He is worshiped—think of it—he is not a recipient of the pale homage called compliment, wherewith the highest human clay must make shift to be satisfied, but of an infinitely richer spiritual food: adoration, worship!—men and women lay their cares and their griefs and their broken hearts at his feet, and he gives them his peace, and they go away healed."

And just then the Awful Visitor said, in the simplest way:

"There is a feature of the philosophy of Huck Finn which"—and went luminously on with the construction of a compact and nicely discriminated literary verdict.

It *is* a land of surprises—India! I had had my ambitions—I had hoped, and almost expected, to be read by kings and presidents and emperors—but I had never looked so high as That. It would be false modesty to pretend that I was not inordinately pleased. I was. I was much more pleased than I should have been with a compliment from a man.

He remained half an hour, and I found him a most courteous and charming gentleman. The godship has been in his family a good while, but I do not know how long. He is a Mohammedan deity; by earthly rank he is a prince; not an Indian but a Persian prince. He is a direct descendant of the Prophet's line. He is comely; also young—for a god; not forty, perhaps not above thirty-five years old. He wears his immense honors with tranquil grace, and with a dignity proper to his awful calling. He speaks English with the ease and purity of a person born to it. I think I am not overstating this. He was the only god I had ever seen, and I was very favorably impressed. When he rose to say good-by, the door swung open and I caught the flash of a red fez, and heard these words, reverently said:

"Satan see God out?"

"Yes." And these mismated Beings passed from view—Satan in the lead and The Other following after.

Chapter 4

. . . After being properly necklaced, according to custom, with great garlands made of yellow flowers, and provided with betel-nut to chew, this pleasant visit closed, and we passed thence to a scene of a different sort: from this glow of color and this sunny life to those grim receptacles of the Parsee dead, the Towers of Silence. There is something stately about that name, and an impressiveness which sinks deep; the hush of death is in it. We have the Grave, the Tomb, the Mausoleum, God's Acre, the Cemetery; and association has made them eloquent with solemn meaning; but we have no name that is so majestic as that one, or lingers upon the ear with such deep and haunting pathos.

On lofty ground, in the midst of a paradise of tropical foliage and flowers, remote from the world and its turmoil and noise, they stood—the Towers of Silence; and away below were spread the wide groves of cocoa-palms, then the city, mile on mile, then the ocean with its fleets of creeping ships—all steeped in a stillness as deep as the hush that hallowed this high place of the dead. The vultures were there. They stood close together in a great circle all around the rim of a massive low tower—waiting; stood as motionless as sculptured ornaments, and indeed almost deceived one into the belief that that was what they were. Presently there was a slight stir among the score of persons present, and all moved reverently out of the path and ceased from talking. A funeral procession entered the great gate, marching two and two, and moved silently by, toward the Tower. The corpse lay in a shallow shell, and was under cover of a white cloth, but was otherwise naked. The bearers of the body were separated by an interval of thirty feet from the mourners. They, and also the mourners, were draped all in pure white, and each couple of mourners was figuratively bound together by a piece of white rope or a handkerchief—though they merely held the ends of it in their hands. Behind the procession followed a dog, which was led in a leash. When the mourners had reached the neighborhood of the Tower—neither they nor any other human being but the bearers of the dead must approach within thirty feet of it—they turned and went back to one of the prayer-houses within the gates, to pray for the spirit of their dead. The bearers unlocked the Tower's sole door and disappeared from view within. In a little while they came out bringing the bier and the white covering-cloth, and locked the door again. Then the ring of vultures rose, flapping their wings, and swooped down into the Tower to devour the body. Nothing was left of it but a clean-picked skeleton when they flocked out again a few minutes afterward.

The principle which underlies and orders everything connected with a Parsee funeral is Purity. By the tenets of the Zoroastrian religion, the elements, Earth, Fire, and Water, are sacred, and must not be contaminated by contact with a dead body. Hence corpses must not be burned, neither must they be buried. None may touch the dead or enter the Towers where they repose except certain men who are officially appointed for that purpose. They receive high pay, but theirs is a dismal life, for they must live apart from their species, because their commerce with the dead defiles them, and any who should associate with them would share their defilement. When they come out of the Tower the clothes they are wearing are exchanged for others, in a building within the grounds, and the ones which they have taken off are left behind, for they are contaminated, and must never be used again or suffered to go outside the grounds. These bearers come to every funeral in new garments. So far as is known, no human being, other than an official corpse-bearer—save one—has ever entered a Tower of Silence after its consecration. Just a hundred years ago a European rushed in behind the bearers and fed his brutal curiosity with a glimpse of the forbidden mysteries of the place. This shabby savage's name is not given; his quality is also concealed. These two details, taken in connection with the fact that for his extraordinary offense the only punishment he got from the East India Company's Government was a solemn official "reprimand"—suggest the suspicion that he was a European of consequence. The same public document which contained the reprimand gave warning that future offenders of his sort, if in the company's service, would be dismissed; and if merchants, suffer revocation of license and exile to England.

The Towers are not tall, but are low in proportion to their circumference, like a gasometer. If you should fill a gasometer half-way up with solid granite masonry, then drive a wide and deep well down through the center of this mass of masonry, you would have the idea of a Tower of Silence. On the masonry surrounding the well the bodies lie, in shallow trenches which radiate like wheel-spokes from the well. The trenches slant toward the well and carry into it the rainfall. Underground drains, with charcoal filters in them, carry off this water from the bottom of the well.

When a skeleton has lain in the Tower exposed to the rain and the flaming sun a month it is perfectly dry and clean. Then the same bearers that brought it there come gloved and take it up with tongs and throw it into the well. There it turns to dust. It is never seen again, never touched again, in the world. Other peoples separate their dead, and preserve and continue social distinctions in the grave—the skeletons of kings and statesmen and generals in temples and pantheons proper to skeletons of their degree, and the skeletons of the commonplace and the poor in places suited to their meaner estate; but the Parsees hold that all men rank alike in death—all are humble, all poor, all destitute. In sign of their poverty they are sent to their grave naked, in sign of their equality the bones of the rich, the poor, the illustrious, and the obscure are flung into the common well together. At a Parsee funeral there are no vehicles; all concerned must walk, both rich and poor, howsoever great the distance to be traversed may be. In the wells of the Five Towers of Silence is mingled the dust of all the Parsee men and women and children who have died in Bombay and its vicinity during the two centuries which have elapsed since the Mohammedan conquerors drove the Parsees out of Persia, and into that region of India. The earliest of the five towers was built by the Modi family something more than two hundred years ago, and it is now reserved to their heirs of that house; none but the dead of that blood are carried thither.

The origin of at least one of the details of a Parsee funeral is not now known—the presence of the dog. Before a corpse is borne from the house of mourning it must be uncovered and exposed to the gaze of a dog; a dog must also be led in the rear of the funeral. Mr. Nusserwanjee Byramjee, Secretary to the Parsee Punchayet, said that these formalities had once had a meaning and a reason for their institution, but that they were survivals whose origin none could now account for. Custom and tradition continue them in force, antiquity hallows them. It is thought that in ancient times in Persia the dog was a sacred animal and could guide souls to heaven; also that his eye had the power of purifying objects which had been contaminated by the touch of the dead; and that hence his presence with the funeral cortège provides an ever-applicable remedy in case of need.

The Parsees claim that their method of disposing of the dead is an effective protection of the living; that it disseminates no corruption, no impurities of any sort, no disease-germs; that no wrap, no garment which has touched the dead is allowed to touch the living afterward; that from the Towers of Silence nothing proceeds which can carry harm to the outside world. These are just claims, I think. As a sanitary measure, their system seems to be about the equivalent of cremation, and as sure. We are drifting slowly—but hopefully—toward cremation in these days. It could not be expected that this progress should be swift, but if it be steady and continuous, even if slow, that will suffice. When cremation becomes the rule we shall cease to shudder at it; we should shudder at burial if we allowed ourselves to think what goes on in the grave.

The dog was an impressive figure to me, representing as he did a mystery whose key is lost. He was humble, and apparently depressed; and he let his head droop pensively, and looked as if he might be trying to call back to his mind what it was that he had used to symbolize ages ago when he began his function. There was another impressive thing close at hand, but I was not privileged to see it. That was the sacred fire—a fire which is supposed to have been burning without interruption for more than two centuries; and so, living by the same heat that was imparted to it so long ago.

The Parsees are a remarkable community. There are only about sixty thousand in Bombay, and only about half as many as that in the rest of India; but they make up in importance what they lack in numbers. They are highly educated, energetic, enterprising, progressive, rich, and the Jew himself is not more lavish or catholic in his charities and benevolences. The Parsees build and endow hospitals, for both men and animals; and they and their womenkind keep an open purse for all great and good objects. They are a political force, and a valued support to the government. They have a pure and lofty religion, and they preserve it in its integrity and order their lives by it.

We took a final sweep of the wonderful view of plain and city and ocean, and so ended our visit to the garden and the Towers of Silence; and the last thing I noticed was another symbol—a voluntary symbol this one; it was a vulture standing on the sawed-off top of a tall and slender and branchless palm in an open space in the ground; he was perfectly motionless, and looked like a piece of sculpture on a pillar. And he had a mortuary look, too, which was in keeping with the place.

Chapter 7

. . . The criminal side of the native has always been picturesque, always readable. The Thuggee and one or two other particularly outrageous features of it have been suppressed by the English, but there is enough of it left to keep it darkly interesting. One finds evidence of these survivals in the newspapers. Macaulay has a light-throwing passage upon this matter in his great historical sketch of Warren Hastings, where he is describing some effects which followed the temporary paralysis of Hastings's powerful government brought about by Sir Philip Francis and his party:

> The natives considered Hastings as a fallen man; and they acted after their kind. Some of our readers may have seen, in India, a cloud of crows pecking a sick vulture to death—no bad type of what happens in that country as often as fortune deserts one who has been great and dreaded. In an instant all the sycophants, who had lately been ready to lie for him, to forge for him, to poison for him, hasten to purchase the favor of his victorious enemies by accusing him. An Indian government has only to let it be understood that it wishes a particular man to be ruined, and in twenty-four hours it will be furnished with grave charges, supported by depositions so full and circumstantial that any person unaccustomed to Asiatic mendacity would regard them as decisive. It is well if the signature of the destined victim is not counterfeited at the foot of some illegal compact, and if some treasonable paper is not slipped into a hiding-place in his house.

That was nearly a century and a quarter ago. An article in one of the chief journals of India (the *Pioneer*) shows that in some respects the native of to-day is just what his ancestor was then. Here are niceties of so subtle and delicate a sort that they lift their breed of rascality to a place among the fine arts, and almost entitle it to respect:

> The records of the Indian courts might certainly be relied upon to prove that swindlers as a class in the East come very close to, if they do not surpass, in brilliancy of execution and originality of design the most expert of their fraternity in Europe and America. India in especial is the home of forgery. There are some particular districts which are noted as marts for the finest specimens of the forger's handiwork. The business is carried on by firms who possess *stores of stamped papers to suit every emergency*. They habitually lay in a store of fresh stamped papers every year, and some of the older and more thriving houses can

> supply documents *for the past forty years, bearing the proper water-mark and possessing the genuine appearance of age.* Other districts have earned notoriety for skilled perjury, a pre-eminence that excites a respectful admiration when one thinks of *the universal prevalence of the art,* and persons desirous of succeeding in false suits are ready to pay handsomely to avail themselves of the services of these local experts as witnesses.

Various instances illustrative of the methods of those swindlers are given. They exhibit deep cunning and total depravity on the part of the swindler and his pals, and more obtuseness on the part of the victim than one would expect to find in a country where suspicion of your neighbor must surely be one of the earliest things learned. The favorite subject is the young fool who has just come into a fortune and is trying to see how poor a use he can put it to. I will quote one example:

> Sometimes another form of confidence trick is adopted, which is invariably successful. The particular pigeon is spotted, and, his acquaintance having been made, he is encouraged in every form of vice. When the friendship is thoroughly established, the swindler remarks to the young man that he has a brother who has asked him to lend him Rs.10,000. The swindler says he has the money and would lend it; but, as the borrower is his brother, he cannot charge interest. So he proposes that he should hand the dupe the money, and the latter should lend it to the swindler's brother, exacting a heavy pre-payment of interest, which, it is pointed out, they may equally enjoy in dissipation. The dupe sees no objection, and on the appointed day receives Rs.7,000 from the swindler, which he hands over to the confederate. The latter is profuse in his thanks, and executes a promissory note for Rs.10,000, payable to bearer. The swindler allows the scheme to remain quiescent for a time, and then suggests that, as the money has not been repaid and as it would be unpleasant to sue his brother, it would be better to sell the note in the bazaar. The dupe hands the note over, for the money he advanced was not his, and, on being informed that it would be necessary to have his signature on the back so as to render the security negotiable, he signs without any hesitation. The swindler passes it on to confederates, and the latter employ a respectable firm of solicitors to ask the dupe if his signature is genuine. He admits it at once, and his fate is sealed. A suit is filed by a confederate against the dupe, two accomplices being made co-defendants. They admit their signatures as indorsers, and the one swears he bought the note for value from the dupe. The latter has no defense, for no court would believe the apparently idle explanation of the manner in which he came to indorse the note.

There is only one India! It is the only country that has a monopoly of grand and imposing specialties. When another country has a remarkable thing, it cannot have it all to itself—some other country has a duplicate. But India—that is different. Its marvels are its own; the patents cannot be infringed; imitations are not possible. And think of the size of them, the majesty of them, the weird and outlandish character of the most of them!

There is the Plague, the Black Death: India invented it; India is the cradle of that mighty birth.

The Car of Juggernaut was India's invention.

So was the Suttee; and within the time of men still living eight hundred widows willingly, and, in fact, rejoicingly, burned themselves to death on the bodies of their dead husbands in a single year. Eight hundred would do it this year if the British Government would let them.

Famine is India's specialty. Elsewhere famines are inconsequential incidents—in India they are devastating cataclysms; in one case they annihilate hundreds; in the other, millions.

India has two million gods, and worships them all. In religion all other countries are paupers; India is the only millionaire.

With her everything is on a giant scale—even her poverty; no other country can show anything to compare with it. And she has been used to wealth on so vast a scale that she has to shorten to single words the expressions describing great sums. She describes one hundred thousand with one word—a *lakh;* she describes ten millions with one word—a *crore.* . . .

Chapter 14

. . . Without doubt modesty is nothing less than a holy feeling; and without doubt the person whose rule of modesty has been transgressed feels the same sort of wound that he would feel if something made holy to him by his religion had suffered a desecration. I say "rule of modesty" because there are about a million rules in the world, and this makes a million standards to be looked out for. Major Sleeman mentions the case of some high-caste veiled ladies who were profoundly scandalized when some English young ladies passed by with faces bare to the world; so scandalized that they spoke out with strong indignation and wondered that people could be so shameless as to expose their persons like that. And yet "the legs of the objectors were naked to mid-thigh." Both parties were clean-minded and irreproachably modest, while abiding by their separate rules, but they couldn't have traded rules for a change without suffering considerable discomfort. All human rules are more or less idiotic, I suppose. It is best so, no doubt. The way it is now, the asylums can hold the sane people, but if we tried to shut up the insane we should run out of building materials. . . .

Chapter 16

In one of those Benares temples we saw a devotee working for salvation in a curious way. He had a huge wad of clay beside him and was making it up into little wee gods no bigger than carpet-tacks. He stuck a grain of rice into each—to represent the lingam, I think. He turned them out nimbly, for he had had long practice and had acquired great facility. Every day he made two thousand gods, then threw them into the holy Ganges. This act of homage brought him the profound homage of the pious—also their coppers. He had a sure living here, and was earning a high place in the hereafter.

The Ganges front is the supreme show-place of Benares. Its tall bluffs are solidly caked from water to summit, along a stretch of three miles, with a splendid jumble of massive and picturesque masonry, a bewildering and beautiful confusion of stone platforms, temples, stair-flights, rich and stately palaces—nowhere a break, nowhere a glimpse of the bluff itself; all the long face of it is compactly walled from sight by this crammed perspective of platforms, soaring stairways, sculptured temples, majestic palaces, softening away into the distances; and there is movement, motion, human life everywhere, and brilliantly costumed—streaming in rainbows up and down the lofty stairways, and massed in metaphorical flower-gardens on the miles of great platforms at the river's edge.

All this masonry, all this architecture represents piety. The palaces were built by native princes whose homes, as a rule, are far from Benares, but who go there from time to time to refresh their souls with the sight and touch of the Ganges, the river of their idolatry. The stairways are records of acts of piety; the crowd of costly little temples are tokens of money spent by rich men for present credit and hope of future reward. Apparently, the rich Christian who spends large sums upon his religion is conspicuous with us, by his rarity, but the rich Hindu who doesn't spend large sums upon his religion is seemingly non-existent. With us the poor spend money on their religion, but they keep back some to live on. Apparently, in India, the poor bankrupt themselves daily for their religion. The rich Hindu can afford his pious outlays; he gets much glory for his spendings, yet keeps back a sufficiency of his income for temporal purposes; but the poor Hindu is entitled to compassion, for his spendings keep him poor, yet get him no glory.

We made the usual trip up and down the river, seated in chairs under an awning on the deck of the usual commodious hand-propelled ark; made it two or three times, and could have made it with increasing interest and enjoyment many times more; for, of course, the palaces and temples would grow more and more beautiful every time one saw them, for that happens with all such things; also, I think one would not get tired of the bathers, nor their costumes, nor of their ingenuities in getting out of them and into them again without exposing too much bronze, nor of their devotional gesticulations and absorbed bead-tellings.

But I should get tired of seeing them wash their mouths with that dreadful water and drink it. In fact, I did get tired of it, and very early, too. At one place where we halted for a while, the foul gush from a sewer was making the water turbid and murky all around, and there was a random corpse slopping around in it that had floated down from up country. Ten steps below that place stood a crowd of men, women, and comely young maidens waist-deep in the water—and they were scooping it up in their hands and drinking it. Faith can certainly do wonders, and this is an instance of it. Those people were not drinking that fearful stuff to assuage thirst, but in order to purify their souls and the interior of their bodies. According to their creed, the Ganges water makes everything pure that it touches—instantly and utterly pure. The sewer-water was not an offense to them, the corpse did not revolt them; the sacred water had touched both, and both were now snow-pure, and could defile no one. The memory of that sight will always stay by me; but not by request.

A word further concerning the nasty but all-purifying Ganges water. When we went to Agra, by and by, we happened there just in time to be in at the birth of a marvel—a memorable scientific discovery—the discovery that in certain ways the foul and derided Ganges water *is* the most puissant purifier in the world! This curious fact, as I have said, had just been added to the treasury of modern science. It had long been noted as a strange thing that while Benares is often afflicted with the cholera she does not spread it beyond her borders. This could not be accounted for. Mr. Henkin, the scientist in the employ of the government of Agra, concluded to examine the water. He went to Benares and made his tests. He got water at the mouths of the sewers where they empty into the river at the bathing-ghats; a cubic centimeter of it contained millions of germs; at the end of six hours they were *all dead.* He caught a floating corpse, towed it to the shore, and from beside it he dipped up water that was swarming with cholera germs; at the end of six hours they were *all dead.* He added swarm after swarm of cholera germs to this water; within the six hours *they always died,* to the last sample. Repeatedly, he took pure well-water which was barren of animal life, and put into it a few cholera germs; they always began to propagate at once, and always within six hours they swarmed—and were *numerable by millions upon millions.*

For ages and ages the Hindus have had absolute faith that the water of the Ganges was absolutely pure, could not be defiled by any contact whatsoever, and infallibly made pure and clean whatsoever thing touched it. They still believe it, and that is why they bathe in it and drink it, caring nothing for its *seeming* filthiness and the floating corpses. The Hindus have been laughed at, these many generations, but the laughter will need to modify itself a little from now on. How did they find out the water's secret in those ancient ages? Had they germ-scientists then? We do not know. We only know that they had a civilization long before we emerged from savagery. But to return to where I was before; I was about to speak of the burning-ghat.

They do not burn fakirs—those revered mendicants. They are so holy that they can get to their place without that sacrament, provided they be consigned to the consecrating river. We saw one carried to mid-stream and thrown overboard. He was sandwiched between two great slabs of stone.

We lay off the cremation-ghat half an hour and saw nine corpses burned. I should not wish to see any more of it, unless I might select the parties. The mourners follow the bier through the town and down to the ghat; then the bier-bearers deliver the body to some low-caste natives—Doms—and the mourners turn about and go back home. I heard no crying and saw no tears, there was no ceremony of parting. Apparently, these expressions of grief and affection are reserved for the privacy of the home. The dead women came draped in red, the men in white. They are laid in the water at the river's edge while the pyre is being prepared.

The first subject was a man. When the Doms unswathed him to wash him, he proved to be a sturdily built, well-nourished, and handsome old gentleman, with not a sign about him to suggest that he had ever been ill. Dry wood was brought and built up into a loose pile; the corpse was laid upon it and covered over with fuel. Then a naked holy man who was sitting on high ground a little distance away began to talk and shout with great energy, and he kept up this noise right along. It may have been the funeral sermon, and probably was. I forgot to say that one of the mourners remained behind when the others went away. This was the dead man's son, a boy of ten or twelve, brown and handsome, grave and self-possessed, and clothed in flowing white. He was there to burn his father. He was given a torch, and while he slowly walked seven times around the pyre the naked black man on the high ground poured out his sermon more clamorously than ever. The seventh circuit completed, the boy applied the torch at his father's head, then at his feet; the flames sprang briskly up with a sharp crackling noise, and the lad went away. Hindus do not want daughters, because their weddings make such a ruinous expense; but they want sons, so that at death they may have honorable exit from the world; and there is no honor equal to the honor of having one's pyre lighted by one's son. The father who dies sonless is in a grievous situation indeed, and is pitied. Life being uncertain, the Hindu marries while he is still a boy, in the hope that he will have a son ready when the day of his need shall come. But if he have no son, he will adopt one. This answers every purpose.

Meantime, the corpse is burning, also several others. It is a dismal business. The stokers did not sit down in idleness, but moved briskly about, punching up the fires with long poles, and now and then adding fuel. Sometimes they hoisted the half of a skeleton into the air, then slammed it down and beat it with the pole, breaking it up so that it would burn better. They hoisted skulls up in the same way and banged and battered them. The sight was hard to bear; it would have been harder if the mourners had stayed to witness it. I had but a moderate desire to see a cremation, so it was soon satisfied. For sanitary reasons it would be well if cremation were universal; but this form is revolting, and not to be recommended.

The fire used is sacred, of course—for there is money in it. Ordinary fire is forbidden; there is no money in it. I was told that this sacred fire is all furnished by one person, and that he has a monopoly of it and charges a good price for it. Sometimes a rich mourner pays a thousand rupees for it. To get to paradise from India is an expensive thing. Every detail connected with the matter costs something, and helps to fatten a priest. I suppose it is quite safe to conclude that that fire-bug is in holy orders.

Close to the cremation-ground stand a few time-worn stones which are remembrances of the Suttee. Each has a rough carving upon it, representing a man and a woman standing or walking hand in hand, and marks the spot where a widow went to her death by fire in the days when the suttee flourished. Mr. Parker said that widows would burn themselves now if the government would allow it. The family that can point to one of these little memorials and say, "She who burned herself there was an ancestress of ours," is envied.

It is a curious people. With them, all life seems to be sacred, except human life. Even the life of vermin is sacred, and must not be taken. The good Jain wipes off a seat before using it, lest he cause the death of some valueless insect by sitting down on it. It grieves him to have to drink water, because the provisions in his stomach may not agree with the microbes. Yet India invented Thuggery and the Suttee. India is a hard country to understand.

We went to the temple of the Thug goddess, Bhowanee, or Kali, or Durga. She has these names and others. She is the only god to whom living sacrifices are made. Goats are sacrificed to her. Monkeys would be cheaper. There are plenty of them about the place. Being sacred, they make themselves very free, and scramble around wherever they please. The temple and its porch are beautifully carved, but this is not the case with the idol. Bhowanee is not pleasant to look at. She has a silver face, and tongue painted a deep red. She wears a necklace of skulls.

In fact, none of the idols in Benares are handsome or attractive. And what a swarm of them there is! The town is a vast museum of idols—and all of them crude, misshapen, and ugly. They flock through one's dreams at night, a wild mob of nightmares. When you get tired of them in the temples and take a trip on the river, you find idol giants, flashily painted, stretched out side by side on the shore. And apparently wherever there is room for one more lingam, a lingam is there. If Vishnu had foreseen what his town was going to be, he would have called it Idolville or Lingamburg.

The most conspicuous feature of Benares is the pair of slender white minarets which tower like masts from the great Mosque of Aurangzeb. They seem to be always in sight, from everywhere, those airy, graceful, inspiring things. But masts is not the right word, for masts have a perceptible taper, while these minarets have not. They are 142 feet high, and only 8½ feet in diameter at the base, and 7½ at the summit—scarcely any taper at all. These are the proportions of a candle; and fair and fairylike candles these are. Will be, anyway, some day, when the Christians inherit them and top them with the electric light. There is a great view from up there—a wonderful view. A large gray monkey was part of it, and damaged it. A monkey has no judgment. This one was skipping about the upper great heights of the mosque—skipping across empty yawning intervals which were almost too wide for him, and which he only just barely cleared, each time, by the skin of his teeth. He got me so nervous that I couldn't look at the view. I couldn't look at anything but him. Every time he went sailing over one of those abysses my breath stood still, and when he grabbed for the perch he was going for, I grabbed too, in sympathy. And he was perfectly indifferent, perfectly unconcerned, and I did all the panting myself. He came within an ace of losing his life a dozen times, and I was so troubled about him that I would have shot him if I had had anything to do it with. But I strongly recommend the view. There is more monkey than view, and there is always going to be more monkey while that idiot survives, but what view you get is superb. All Benares, the river, and the region round about are spread before you. Take a gun, and look at the view.

The next thing I saw was more reposeful. It was a new kind of art. It was a picture painted on water. It was done by a native. He sprinkled fine dust of various colors on the still surface of a basin of water, and out of these sprinklings a dainty and pretty picture gradually grew, a picture which a breath could destroy. Somehow it was impressive, after so much browsing among massive and battered and decaying fanes that rest upon ruins, and those ruins upon still other ruins, and those upon still others again. It was a sermon, an allegory, a symbol of Instability. Those creations in stone were only a kind of water pictures, after all. . . .

Chapter 17

It was in Benares that I saw another living god. That makes two. I believe I have seen most of the greater and lesser wonders of the world, but I do not remember that any of them interested me so overwhelmingly as did that pair of gods.

When I try to account for this effect I find no difficulty about it. I find that, as a rule, when a thing is a wonder to us it is not because of what *we* see in it, but because of what *others* have seen in it. We get almost all our wonders at second hand. We are eager to see any celebrated thing—and we never fail of our reward; just the deep privilege of gazing upon an object which has stirred the enthusiasm or evoked the reverence or affection or admiration of multitudes of our race is a thing which we value; we are profoundly glad that we have seen it, we are permanently enriched from having seen it, we would not part with the memory of that experience for a great price. And yet that very spectacle may be the *Taj*. You cannot keep your enthusiasms down, you cannot keep your emotions within bounds when that soaring bubble of marble breaks upon your view. But these are not *your* enthusiasms and emotions—they are the accumulated emotions and enthusiasms of a thousand fervid writers, who have been slowly and steadily storing them up in your heart day by day and year by year all your life; and now they burst out in a flood and overwhelm you; and you could not be a whit happier if they were your very own. By and by you sober down, and then you perceive that you have been drunk on the smell of somebody else's cork. For ever and ever the memory of my distant first glimpse of the Taj will compensate me for creeping around the globe to have that great privilege.

But the Taj—with all your inflation of delusive emotions, acquired at second hand from people to whom in the majority of cases they were also delusions acquired at second hand—a thing which you fortunately did not think of or it might have made you doubtful of what you imagined were your own—what is the Taj as a marvel, a spectacle, and an uplifting and overpowering wonder, compared with a living, breathing, speaking personage whom several millions of human beings devoutly and sincerely and unquestionably believe to be a god, and humbly and gratefully worship as a god?

He was sixty years old when I saw him. He is called Sri 108 Swami Bhaskarananda Saraswati. That is one form of it. I think that that is what you would call him in speaking to him—because it is short. But you would use more of his name in addressing a letter to him; courtesy would require this. Even then you would not have to use all of it, but only this much:

Sri 108 Matparamahansaparivrajakacharyaswamibhaskaranandasaraswati.

You do not put "Esq." after it, for that is not necessary. The word which opens the volley is itself a title of honor—"Sri." The "108" stands for the rest of his names, I believe. Vishnu has 108 names which he does not use in business, and no doubt it is a custom of gods and a privilege sacred to their order to keep 108 extra ones in stock. Just the restricted name set down above is a handsome property, without the 108. By my count it has fifty-eight letters in it. This removes the long German words from competition; they are permanently out of the race.

Sri 108 S. B. Saraswati has attained to what among the Hindus is called the "state of perfection." It is a state which other Hindus reach by being born again and again, and over and over again into this world, through one reincarnation after another—a tiresome long job covering centuries and decades of centuries, and one that is full of risks, too, like the accident of dying on the wrong side of the Ganges some time or other and waking up in the form of an ass, with a fresh start necessary and the numerous trips to be made all over again. But in reaching perfection, Sri 108 S. B. S. has escaped all that. He is no longer a part or a feature of this world; his substance has changed, all earthiness has departed out of it; he is utterly holy, utterly pure; nothing can desecrate this holiness or stain this purity; he is no longer of the earth, its concerns are matters foreign to him, its pains and griefs and troubles cannot reach him. When he dies, Nirvana is his; he will be absorbed into the substance of the Supreme Deity and be at peace forever.

The Hindu Scriptures point out how this state is to be reached, but it is only once in a thousand years, perhaps, that a candidate accomplishes it. This one has traversed the course required, stage by stage, from the beginning to the end, and now has nothing left to do but wait for the call which shall release him from a world in which he has now no part nor lot. First, he passed through the student stage, and became learned in the holy books. Next he became citizen, householder, husband, and father. That was the required second stage. Then—like John Bunyan's Christian—he bade perpetual good-by to his family, as required, and went wandering away. He went far into the desert and served a term as hermit. Next, he became a beggar, "in accordance with the rites laid down in the Scriptures," and wandered about India eating the bread of mendicancy. A quarter of a century ago he reached the stage of purity. This needs no garment; its symbol is nudity; he discarded the waist-cloth which he had previously worn. He could resume it now if he chose, for neither that nor any other contact can defile him; but he does not choose.

There are several other stages, I believe, but I do not remember what they are. But he has been through them. Throughout the long course he was perfecting himself in holy learning, and writing commentaries upon the sacred books. He was also meditating upon Brahma, and he does that now.

White marble relief-portraits of him are sold all about India. He lives in a good house in a noble great garden in Benares, all meet and proper to his stupendous rank. Necessarily, he does not go abroad in the streets. Deities would never be able to move about handily in any country. If one whom we recognized and adored as a god should go abroad in our streets, and the day it was to happen were known, all traffic would be blocked and business would come to a standstill.

This god is comfortably housed, and yet modestly, all things considered, for if he wanted to live in a palace he would only need to speak and his worshipers would gladly build it. Sometimes he sees devotees for a moment, and comforts them and blesses them, and they kiss his feet and go away happy. Rank is nothing to him, he being a god. To him all men are alike. He sees whom he pleases and denies himself to whom he pleases. Sometimes he sees a prince and denies himself to a pauper; at other times he receives the pauper and turns the prince away. However, he does not receive many of either class. He has to husband his time for his meditations. I think he would receive Rev. Mr. Parker at any time. I think he is sorry for Mr. Parker, and I think Mr. Parker is sorry for him; and no doubt this compassion is good for both of them.

When we arrived we had to stand around in the garden a little while and wait, and the outlook was not good, for he had been turning away Maharajas that day and receiving only the riffraff, and we belonged in between, somewhere. But presently, a servant came out saying it was all right, he was coming.

And sure enough, he came, and I saw him—that object of the worship of millions. It was a strange sensation, and thrilling. I wish I could feel it stream through my veins again. And yet, to me he was not a god, he was only a Taj. The thrill was not my thrill, but had come to me second hand from those invisible millions of believers. By a handshake with their god I had ground-circuited their wire and got their monster battery's whole charge.

He was tall and slender, indeed emaciated. He had a clean-cut and conspicuously intellectual face, and a deep and kindly eye. He looked many years older than he really was, but much study and meditation and fasting and prayer, with the arid life he had led as hermit and beggar, could account for that. He is wholly nude when he receives natives, of whatever rank they may be, but he had white cloth around his loins now, a concession to Mr. Parker's European prejudices, no doubt.

As soon as I had sobered down a little we got along very well together, and I found him a most pleasant and friendly deity. He had heard a deal about Chicago, and showed a quite remarkable interest in it, for a god. It all came of the World's Fair and the Congress of Religions. If India knows about nothing else American, she knows about those, and will keep them in mind one while.

He proposed an exchange of autographs, a delicate attention which made me believe in him, but I had been having my doubts before. He wrote his in his book, and I have a reverent regard for that book, though the words run from right to left, and so I can't read it. It was a mistake to print in that way. It contains his voluminous comments on the Hindu holy writings, and if I could make them out I would try for perfection myself. I gave him a copy of *Huckleberry Finn.* I thought it might rest him up a little to mix it in along with his meditations on Brahma, for he looked tired, and I knew that if it didn't do him any good it wouldn't do him any harm.

He has a scholar meditating under him—Mina Bahadur Rana—but we did not see him. He wears clothes and is very imperfect. He has written a little pamphlet about his master, and I have that. It contains a wood-cut of the master and himself seated on a rug in the garden. The portrait of the master is very good, indeed. The posture is exactly that which Brahma himself affects, and it requires long arms and limber legs, and can be accumulated only by gods and the india-rubber man. There is a life-size marble relief of Sri 108 S. B. S. in the garden. It represents him in this same posture.

Dear me! It is a strange world. Particularly the Indian division of it. This pupil, Mina Bahadur Rana, is not a commonplace person, but a man of distinguished capacities and attainments, and, apparently, he had a fine worldly career in front of him. He was serving the Nepal Government in a high capacity at the Court of the Viceroy of India, twenty years ago. He was an able man, educated, a thinker, a man of property. But the longing to devote himself to a religious life came upon him, and he resigned his place, turned his back upon the vanities and comforts of the world, and went away into the solitudes to live in a hut and study the sacred writings and meditate upon virtue and holiness and seek to attain them. This sort of religion resembles ours. Christ recommended the rich to give away all their property and follow Him in poverty, not in worldly comfort. American and English millionaires do it every day, and thus verify and confirm to the world the tremendous forces that lie in religion. Yet many people scoff at them for this loyalty to duty, and many will scoff at Mina Bahadur Rana and call him a crank. Like many Christians of great character and intellect, he has made the study of his Scriptures and the writing of books of commentaries upon them the loving labor of his life. Like them, he has believed that this was not an idle and foolish waste of his life, but a most worthy and honorable employment of it. Yet, there are many people who will see in those others, men worthy of homage and deep reverence, but in him merely a crank. But I shall not. He has my reverence. And I don't offer it as a common thing and poor, but as an unusual thing and of value. The ordinary reverence, the reverence defined and explained by the dictionary, costs nothing. Reverence for one's own sacred things—parents, religion, flag, laws, and respect for one's own beliefs—these are feelings which we cannot even help. They come natural to us; they are involuntary, like breathing. There is no personal merit in breathing. But the reverence which is difficult, and which has personal merit in it, is the respect which you pay, without compulsion, to the political or religious attitude of a man whose beliefs are not yours. You can't revere his gods or his politics, and no one expects you to do that, but you could respect his belief in them if you tried hard enough; and you could respect *him,* too, if you tried hard enough. But it is very, very difficult; it is next to impossible, and so we hardly ever try. If the man doesn't believe as we do, we say he is a crank, and that settles it. I mean it does nowadays, because now we can't burn him.

We are always canting about people's "irreverence," always charging this offense upon somebody or other, and thereby intimating that we are better than that person and do not commit that offense ourselves. Whenever we do this we are in a lying attitude, and our speech is cant; for none of us are reverent—in a meritorious way; deep down in our hearts we are all irreverent. There is probably not a single exception to this rule in the earth. There is probably not one person whose reverence rises higher than respect for his *own* sacred things; and therefore, it is not a thing to boast about and be proud of, since the most degraded savage has that—and, like the best of us, has nothing higher. To speak plainly, we despise all reverences and all objects of reverence which are outside the pale of our own list of sacred things. And yet, with strange inconsistency, we are shocked when other people despise and defile the things which are holy to us. Suppose we should meet with a paragraph like the following, in the newspapers:

"Yesterday a visiting party of the British nobility had a picnic at Mount Vernon, and in the tomb of Washington they ate their luncheon, sang popular songs, played games, and danced waltzes and polkas."

Should we be shocked? Should we feel outraged? Should we be amazed? Should we call the performance a desecration? Yes, that would all happen. We should denounce those people in round terms, and call them hard names.

And suppose we found this paragraph in the newspapers:

"Yesterday a visiting party of American pork-millionaires had a picnic in Westminster Abbey, and in that sacred place they ate their luncheon, sang popular songs, played games, and danced waltzes and polkas."

Would the English be shocked? Would they feel outraged? Would they be amazed? Would they call the performance a desecration? That would all happen. The pork-millionaires would be denounced in round terms; they would be called hard names.

In the tomb at Mount Vernon lie the ashes of America's most honored son; in the Abbey, the ashes of England's greatest dead; the tomb of tombs, the costliest in the earth, the wonder of the world, the Taj, was built by a great

Emperor to honor the memory of a perfect wife and perfect mother, one in whom there was no spot or blemish, whose love was his stay and support, whose life was the light of the world to him; in it her ashes lie, and to the Mohammedan millions of India it is a holy place; to them it is what Mount Vernon is to Americans, it is what the Abbey is to the English.

Major Sleeman wrote forty or fifty years ago (the italics are mine):

> I would here enter my humble protest against the *quadrille and lunch parties* which are sometimes given to European ladies and gentlemen of the station at this imperial tomb; drinking and dancing are no doubt very good things in their season, but they are sadly out of place *in a sepulcher.*

Were there any Americans among those lunch-parties? If they were invited, there were.

If my imagined lunch-parties in Westminster and the tomb of Washington should take place, the incident would cause a vast outbreak of bitter eloquence about Barbarism and Irreverence; and it would come from two sets of people who would go next day and dance in the Taj if they had a chance.

As we took our leave of the Benares god and started away we noticed a group of natives waiting respectfully just within a gate—a Raja from somewhere in India, and some people of lesser consequence. The god beckoned them to come, and as we passed out the Raja was kneeling and reverently kissing his sacred feet.

If Barnum—but Barnum's ambitions are at rest. This god will remain in the holy peace and seclusion of his garden undisturbed. Barnum could not have gotten him, anyway. Still, he would have found a substitute that would answer.

Chapter 26

. . . *April 7.* We are far abroad upon the smooth waters of the Indian Ocean, now; it is shady and pleasant and peaceful under the vast spread of the awnings, and life is perfect again—ideal.

The difference between a river and a sea is, that the river looks fluid, and the sea solid—usually looks as if you could step out and walk on it.

The captain has this peculiarity—he cannot tell the truth in a plausible way. In this he is the very opposite of the austere Scot who sits midway of the table; *he* canot tell a lie in an *un*plausible way. When the captain finishes a statement the passengers glance at each other privately, as who should say, "Do you believe that?" When the Scot finishes one, the look says, "How strange and interesting." The whole secret is in the manner and method of the two men. The captain is a little shy and diffident, and he states the simplest fact as if he were a little afraid of it, while the Scot delivers himself of the most abandoned lie with such an air of stern veracity that one is forced to believe it although one knows it isn't so. For instance, the Scot told about a pet flying-fish he once owned, that lived in a little fountain in his conservatory, and supported itself by catching birds and frogs and rats in the neighboring fields. It was plain that no one at the table doubted this statement.

By and by, in the course of some talk about custom-house annoyances, the captain brought out the following simple every-day incident, but through his infirmity of style managed to tell it in such a way that it got no credence. He said:

> I went ashore at Naples one voyage when I was in that trade, and stood around helping my passengers, for I could speak a little Italian. Two or three times, at intervals, the officer asked me if I had anything dutiable about me, and seemed more and more put out and disappointed every time I told him no. Finally, a passenger whom I had helped through asked me to come out and take something. I thanked him, but excused myself, saying I had taken a whisky just before I came ashore.
>
> It was a fatal admission. The officer at once made me pay sixpence import duty on the whisky—just from ship to shore, you see; and he fined me £5 for not declaring the goods, another £5 for falsely denying that I had anything dutiable about me, also £5 for concealing the goods, and £50 for smuggling, which is the maximum penalty for unlawfully bringing in goods under the value of sevenpence ha'penny. Altogether, sixty-five pounds sixpence for a little thing like that.

The Scot is always believed, yet he never tells anything but lies; whereas the captain is never believed, although he never tells a lie, so far as I can judge. If he should say his uncle was a male person, he would probably say it in such a way that nobody would believe it; at the same time the Scot could claim that he had a female uncle and not stir a doubt in anybody's mind. My own luck has been curious all my literary life; I never could tell a lie that anybody would doubt, nor a truth that anybody would believe. . . .

April 10. The sea is a Mediterranean blue; and I believe that that is about the divinest color known to nature.

It is strange and fine—Nature's lavish generosities to her creatures. At least to all of them except man. For those that fly she has provided a home that is nobly spacious—a home which is forty miles deep and envelops the whole globe, and has not an obstruction in it. For those that swim she has provided a more than imperial domain—a domain which is miles deep and covers four-fifths of the globe. But as for man, she has cut him off with the mere odds and ends of the creation. She has given him the thin skin, the meager skin which is stretched over the remaining one-fifth—the naked bones stick up through it in most places. On the one-half of this domain he can raise snow, ice, sand, rocks, and nothing else. So the valuable part of his inheritance really consists of but a single fifth of the family estate; and out of it he has to grub hard to get enough to keep him alive and provide kings and soldiers and powder to extend the blessings of civilization with. Yet man, in his simplicity and complacency and inability to cipher, thinks Nature regards him as the important member of the family—in fact, her favorite. Surely, it must occur to even his dull head, sometimes, that she has a curious way of showing it.

April 22. To such as believe that the quaint product called French civilization would be an improvement upon the civilization of New Guinea and the like, the snatching of Madagascar and the laying on of French civilization there will be fully justified. But why did the English allow the French to have Madagascar? Did she respect a theft of a couple of centuries ago? Dear me, robbery by European nations of each other's territories has never been a sin, is not a sin to-day. To the several cabinets the several political establishments of the world are clothes-lines; and a large part of the official duty of these cabinets is to keep an eye on each other's wash and grab what they can of it as opportunity offers. All the territorial possessions of all the political establishments in the earth—including America, of course—consist of pilferings from other people's wash. No tribe, howsoever insignificant, and no nation, howsoever mighty, occupies a foot of land that was not stolen. When the English, the French, and the Spaniards reached America, the Indian tribes had been raiding each other's territorial clothes-line for ages, and every acre of ground in the continent had been stolen and restolen five hundred times. The English, the French, and the Spaniards went to work and stole it all over again; and when that was satisfactorily accomplished they went diligently to work and stole it from each other. In Europe and Asia and Africa every acre of ground has been stolen several millions of times. A crime persevered in a thousand centuries ceases to be a crime, and becomes a virtue. This is the law of custom, and custom supersedes all other forms of law. Christian governments are as frank to-day, as open and above-board, in discussing projects for raiding each other's clothes-lines as ever they were before the Golden Rule came smiling into this inhospitable world and couldn't get a night's lodging anywhere. In one hundred and fifty years England has beneficently retired garment after garment from the Indian lines, until there is hardly a rag of the original wash left dangling anywhere. In eight hundred years an obscure tribe of Muscovite savages has risen to the dazzling position of Land-Robber-in-Chief; she found a quarter of the world hanging out to dry on a hundred parallels of latitude, and she scooped in the whole wash. She keeps a sharp eye on a multitude of little lines that stretch along the northern boundaries of India, and every now and then she snatches a hip-rag or a pair of pajamas. It is England's prospective property, and Russia knows it; but Russia cares nothing for that. In fact, in our day, land-robbery, claim-jumping, is become a European governmental frenzy. Some have been hard at it in the borders of China, in Burma, in Siam, and the islands of the sea; and *all* have been at it in Africa. Africa has been as coolly divided up and portioned out among the gang as if they had bought it and paid for it. And now straightway they are beginning the old game again—to steal each other's grabbings. Germany found a vast slice of Central Africa with the English flag and the English missionary and the English trader scattered all over it, but with certain formalities neglected—no signs up, "Keep off the grass," "Trespassers forbidden," etc.—and she stepped in with a cold calm smile and put up the signs herself, and swept those English pioneers promptly out of the country.

There is a tremendous point there. It can be put into the form of a maxim: Get your formalities right—never mind about the moralities.

It was an impudent thing; but England had to put up with it. Now, in the case of Madagascar, the formalities had originally been observed, but by neglect they had fallen into desuetude ages ago. England should have snatched Madagascar from the French clothes-line. Without an effort she could have saved those harmless natives from the calamity of French civilization, and she did not do it. Now it is too late.

The signs of the times show plainly enough what is going to happen. All the savage lands in the world are going to be brought under subjection to the Christian governments of Europe. I am not sorry, but glad. This coming fate might have been a calamity to those savage peoples two hundred years ago; but now it will in some cases be a benefaction. The sooner the seizure is consummated, the better for the savages. The dreary and dragging ages of bloodshed and disorder and oppression will give place to peace and order and the reign of law. When one considers what India was under her Hindu and Mohammedan rulers, and what she is now; when he remembers the miseries of her millions then and the protections and humanities which they enjoy now, he must concede that the most fortunate thing that has ever befallen that empire was the establishment of British supremacy there. The savage lands of the world are to pass to alien possession, their peoples to the mercies of alien rulers. Let us hope and believe that they will all benefit by the change. . . .

Chapter 29

The chameleon in the hotel court. He is fat and indolent and contemplative; but is businesslike and capable when a fly comes about—reaches out a tongue like a teaspoon and takes him in. He gums his tongue first. He is always pious, in his looks. And pious and thankful both, when Providence or one of us sends him a fly. He has a froggy head, and a back like a new grave—for shape; and hands like a bird's toes that have been frost-bitten. But his eyes are his exhibition feature. A couple of skinny cones project from the sides of his head, with a wee shiny bead of an eye set in the apex of each; and these cones turn bodily like pivot-guns and point every which way, and they are independent of each other; each has its own exclusive machinery. When I am behind him and C. in front of him, he whirls one eye rearward and the other forward—which gives him a most Congressional expression (one eye on the constituency and one on the swag); and then if something happens above and below him he shoots out one eye upward like a telescope and the other downward—and this changes his expression, but does not improve it. . . .

There is a large Trappist monastery two hours from Durban, over the country roads, and in company with Mr. Milligan and Mr. Hunter, general manager of the Natal Government railways, who knew the heads of it, we went out to see it.

There it all was, just as one reads about it in books and cannot believe that it is so—I mean the rough, hard work, the impossible hours, the scanty food, the coarse raiment, the Maryborough beds, the *tabu* of human speech, of social intercourse, of relaxation, of amusement, of entertainment, of the presence of women in the men's establishment. There it all was. It was not a dream, it was not a lie. And yet with the fact before one's face it was still incredible. It is such a sweeping suppression of human instincts, such an extinction of the man as an individual.

La Trappe must have known the human race well. The scheme which he invented hunts out everything that a man wants and values—and withholds it from him. Apparently there is no detail that can help make life worth living that has not been carefully ascertained and placed out of the Trappist's reach. La Trappe must have known that there were men who would enjoy this kind of misery, but how did he find it out?

If he had consulted you or me he would have been told that his scheme lacked too many attractions; that it was impossible; that it could never be floated. But there in the monastery was proof that he knew the human race better than it knew itself. He set his foot upon every desire that a man has—yet he floated his project, and it has prospered for two hundred years, and will go on prospering forever, no doubt.

Man likes personal distinction—there in the monastery it is obliterated. He likes delicious food—there he gets beans and bread and tea, and not enough of it. He likes to lie softly—there he lies on a sand mattress, and has a pillow and a blanket, but no sheet. When he is dining, in a great company of friends, he likes to laugh and chat—there a monk reads a holy book aloud during meals, and nobody speaks or laughs. When a man has a hundred friends about him, evenings, he likes to have a good time and run late—there he and the rest go silently to bed at eight; and in the dark, too; there is but a loose brown robe to discard, there are no nightclothes to put on, a light is not needed. Man likes to lie abed late—there he gets up once or twice in the night to perform some religious office, and gets up finally for the day at two in the morning. Man likes light work or none at all—there he labors all day in the field, or in the blacksmith shop or the other shops devoted to the mechanical trades, such as shoemaking, saddlery, carpentry, and so on. Man likes the society of girls and women—there he never has it. He likes to have his children about him, and pet them and play with them—there he has none. He likes billiards—there is no table there. He likes outdoor sports and indoor dramatic and musical and social entertainments—there are none there. He likes to bet on things—I was told that betting is forbidden there. When a man's temper is up he likes to pour it out upon somebody—there this is not allowed. A man likes animals—pets; there are none there. He likes to smoke—there he cannot do it. He likes to read the news—no papers or magazines come there. A man likes to know how his parents and brothers and sisters are getting along when he is away, and if they miss him—there he cannot know. A man likes a pretty house, and pretty furniture, and pretty things, and pretty colors—there he has nothing but naked aridity and somber colors. A man likes—name it yourself: whatever it is, it is absent from that place.

From what I could learn, all that a man gets for this is merely the saving of his soul.

It all seems strange, incredible, impossible. But La Trappe knew the race. He knew the powerful attraction of unattractiveness: he knew that no life could be imagined, howsoever comfortless and forbidding, but somebody would want to try it.

This parent establishment of Germans began its work fifteen years ago, strangers, poor, and unencouraged; it owns fifteen thousand acres of land now, and raises grain and fruit, and makes wines, and manufactures all manner of things, and has native apprentices in its shops, and sends them forth able to read and write, and also well equipped to earn their living by their trades. And this young establishment has set up eleven branches in South Africa, and in them they are Christianizing and educating and teaching wage-yielding mechanical trades to twelve hundred boys and girls. Protestant Missionary work is coldly regarded by the commercial white colonists all over the heathen world, as a rule, and its product is nicknamed "rice-Christians" (occupationless incapables who join the church for revenue only), but I think it would be difficult to pick a flaw in the work of these Catholic monks, and I believe that the disposition to attempt it has not shown itself. . . .

Conclusion

. . . Our trip around the earth ended at the Southampton pier, where we embarked thirteen months before. It seemed a fine and large thing to have accomplished—the circumnavigation of this great globe in that little time, and I was privately proud of it. For a moment. Then came one of those vanity-snubbing astronomical reports from the Observatory people, whereby it appeared that another great body of light had lately flamed up in the remotenesses of space which was traveling at a gait which would enable it to do all that I had done in *a minute and a half.* Human pride is not worth while; there is always something lying in wait to take the wind out of it.

To the Person Sitting in Darkness

"To the Person Sitting in Darkness" first appeared in the North American Review *in 1901. Twain severely criticized the behavior of American missionaries who exacted indemnities for damages in the Boxer rebellion. A telegraphic error had led Twain to believe that they collected fines* thirteen *times the amount of the damages; however, the missionaries stated that the actual amount was one and one-third the damages. The precise amount became unimportant in the critical exchange: first Twain published "To the Person Sitting in Darkness"; then the missionaries responded, and Twain replied in "To My Missionary Critics." The full exchange demonstrates Twain's fastidious attention to detail and his formidable skill in debate.*

. . . The following news from China appeared in the *Sun,* of New York, on Christmas Eve. The italics are mine:

> The Rev. Mr. Ament, of the American Board of Foreign Missions, has returned from a trip which he made for the purpose of collecting indemnities for damages done by Boxers. *Everywhere he went he compelled the Chinese to pay.* He says that all his native Christians are now provided for. He had 700 of them under his charge, and 300 were killed. He has *collected 300 taels for each* of these murders, and has *compelled full payment for all the property belonging to Christians* that was destroyed. He also assessed *fines* amounting to THIRTEEN TIMES the amount of the indemnity. *This money will be used for the propagation of the Gospel.*
>
> Mr. Ament declares that the compensation he has collected is *moderate* when compared with the amount secured by the Catholics, who demand, in addition to money, *head for head.* They collect 500 taels for each murder of a Catholic. In the Wenchiu country, 680 Catholics were killed, and for this the European Catholics here demand 750,000 strings of cash and 680 *heads.*
>
> In the course of a conversation, Mr. Ament referred to the attitude of the missionaries toward the Chinese. He said:

"I deny emphatically that the missionaries are *vindictive,* that they *generally* looted, or that they have done anything *since* the siege that *the circumstances did not demand.* I criticize the Americans. *The soft hand of the Americans is not as good as the mailed fist of the Germans.* If you deal with the Chinese with a soft hand they will take advantage of it.

"The statement that the French government will return the loot taken by the French soldiers is the source of the greatest amusement here. The French soldiers were more systematic looters than the Germans, and it is a fact that to-day *Catholic Christians,* carrying French flags and armed with modern guns, *are looting villages* in the Province of Chili."

By happy luck, we get all these glad tidings on Christmas Eve—just in time enable us to celebrate the day with proper gayety and enthusiasm. Our spirits soar, and we find we can even make jokes: Taels, I win, Heads you lose.

Our Reverend Ament is the right man in the right place. What we want of our missionaries out there is, not that they shall merely represent in their acts and persons the grace and gentleness and charity and loving-kindness of our religion, but that they shall also represent the American spirit. The oldest Americans are the Pawnees. Macallum's History says:

> When a white Boxer kills a Pawnee and destroys his property, the other Pawnees do not trouble to seek *him* out, they kill any white person that comes along; also, they make some white village pay deceased's heirs the full cash value of deceased, together with full cash value of the property destroyed; they also make the village pay, in addition, *thirteen times* the value of that property into a fund for the dissemination of the Pawnee religion, which they regard as the best of all religions for the softening and humanizing of the heart of man. It is their idea that it is only fair and right that the innocent should be made to suffer for the guilty, and that it is better that ninety and nine innocent should suffer than that one guilty person should escape.

Our Reverend Ament is justifiably jealous of those enterprising Catholics, who not only get big money for each lost convert, but get "head for head" besides. But he should soothe himself with the reflections that the entirety of their exactions are for their own pockets, whereas he, less selfishly, devotes only 300 taels per head to that service, and gives the whole vast thirteen repetitions of the property-indemnity to the service of propagating the Gospel. His magnanimity has won him the approval of his nation, and will get him a monument. Let him be content with these rewards. We all hold him dear for manfully defending his fellow missionaries from exaggerated charges which were beginning to distress us, but which his testimony has so considerably modified that we can now contemplate them without noticeable pain. For now we know that, even before the siege, the missionaries were not "generally" out looting, and that, "since the siege," they have acted quite handsomely, except when "circumstances" crowded them. I am arranging for the monument. Subscriptions for it can be sent to the American Board; designs for it can be sent to me. Designs must allegorically set forth the Thirteen Reduplications of the Indemnity, and the Object for which they were exacted; as Ornaments, the designs must exhibit 680 Heads, so disposed as to give a pleasing and pretty effect; for the Catholics have done nicely, and are entitled to notice in the monument. Mottoes may be suggested, if any shall be discovered that will satisfactorily cover the ground.

Mr. Ament's financial feat of squeezing a thirteenfold indemnity out of the pauper peasants to square other people's offenses, thus condemning them and their women and innocent little children to inevitable starvation and lingering death, in order that the blood money so acquired might be "*used for the propagation of the Gospel,*" does not flutter my serenity; although the act and the words, taken together, concrete a blasphemy so hideous and so colossal that, without doubt, its mate is not findable in the history of this or of any other age. Yet, if a layman had done that thing and justified it with those words, I should have shuddered, I know. Or, if I had done the thing and said the words myself—However, the thought is unthinkable, irreverent as some imperfectly informed people think me. Sometimes an ordained minister sets out to be blasphemous. When this happens, the layman is out of the running; he stands no chance.

We have Mr. Ament's impassioned assurance that the missionaries are not "vindictive." Let us hope and pray that they will never become so, but will remain in the almost morbidly fair and just and gentle temper which is affording so much satisfaction to their brother and champion to-day.

The following is from the New York *Tribune* of Christmas Eve. It comes from that journal's Tokyo correspondent. It has a strange and impudent sound, but the Japanese are but partially civilized as yet. When they become wholly civilized they will not talk so:

> The missionary question, of course, occupies a foremost place in the discussion. It is now felt as essential that the Western Powers take cognizance of the sentiment here, that religious invasions of Oriental countries by powerful Western organizations are tantamount to filibustering expeditions, and should not only be discountenanced, but that stern measures should be adopted for their suppression. The feeling here is that the missionary organizations constitute a constant menace to peaceful international relations.

Shall we? That is, shall we go on conferring our Civilization upon the peoples that sit in darkness, or shall we give those poor things a rest? Shall we bang right ahead in our old-time, loud, pious way, and commit the new century to the game; or shall we sober up and sit down and think it over first? Would it not be prudent to get our Civilization tools together, and see how much stock is left on hand in the way of Glass Beads and Theology, and Maxim Guns and Hymn Books, and Trade Gin and Torches of Progress and Enlightenment (patent adjustable ones, good to fire villages with, upon occasion), and balance the books, and arrive at the profit and loss, so that we may intelligently decide whether to continue the business or sell out the property and start a new Civilization Scheme on the proceeds?

Extending the Blessings of Civilization to our Brother who Sits in Darkness has been a good trade and has paid well, on the whole; and there is money in it yet, if carefully worked—but not enough, in my judgment, to make any considerable risk advisable. The People that Sit in Darkness are getting to be too scarce—too scarce and too shy. And such darkness as is now left is really of but an indifferent quality, and not dark enough for the game. The most of those People that Sit in Darkness have been furnished with more light than was good for them or profitable for us. We have been injudicious.

The Blessings-of-Civilization Trust, wisely and cautiously administered, is a Daisy. There is more money in it, more territory, more sovereignty, and other kinds of emolument, than there is in any other game that is played. But Christendom has been playing it badly of late years, and must certainly suffer by it, in my opinion. She has been so eager to get every stake that appeared on the green cloth, that the People who Sit in Darkness have noticed it—they have noticed it, and have begun to show alarm. They have become suspicious of the Blessings of Civilization. More—they have begun to examine them. This is not well. The Blessings of Civilization are all right, and a good commercial property; there could not be a better, in a dim light. In the right kind of a light, and at a proper distance, with the goods a little out of focus, they furnish this desirable exhibit to the Gentlemen who Sit in Darkness:

LOVE,	LAW AND ORDER,
JUSTICE,	LIBERTY,
GENTLENESS,	EQUALITY,
CHRISTIANITY,	HONORABLE DEALING,
PROTECTION TO THE WEAK,	MERCY,
TEMPERANCE,	EDUCATION,

—and so on.

There. Is it good? Sir, it is pie. It will bring into camp any idiot that sits in darkness anywhere. But not if we adulterate it. It is proper to be emphatic upon that point. This brand is strictly for Export—apparently. *Apparently*. Privately and confidentially, it is nothing of the kind. Privately and confidentially, it is merely an outside cover, gay and pretty and attractive, displaying the special patterns of our Civilization which we reserve for Home Consumption, while *inside* the bale is the Actual Thing that the Customer Sitting in Darkness buys with his blood and tears and land and liberty. That Actual Thing is, indeed, Civilization, but it is only for Export. Is there a difference between the two brands? In some of the details, yes. . . .

WHAT IS MAN?

Twain's What Is Man? *was privately printed in 1906. The essay uses a Socratic dialogue form, with the Old Man representing experience and a mechanistic view of human motivations; the Young Man keeps asking questions and attempts to defend a conventional philosophy. The Old Man gradually explains and convinces the Young Man that all people are motivated by a desire for self-approval, influenced by the training of outside forces and by individual temperament.*

Twain's knowledge of the philosophical tradition appears in his inclusion of the Classic virtues, such as courage and magnanimity, within the discussion.

CONCLUSION

O. M. You have been taking a holiday?

Y. M. Yes; a mountain-tramp covering a week. Are you ready to talk?

O. M. Quite ready. What shall we begin with?

Y. M. Well, lying abed resting-up, two days and nights, I have thought over all these talks, and passed them carefully in review. With this result: that . . . that . . . are you intending to publish your notions about Man some day?

O. M. Now and then, in these past twenty years, the Master inside of me has half-intended to order me to set them to paper and publish them. Do I have to tell you why the order has remained unissued, or can you explain so simple a thing without my help?

Y. M. By your doctrine, it is simplicity itself: outside influences moved your interior Master to give the order; stronger outside influences deterred him. Without the outside influences, neither of these impulses could ever have been born, since a person's brain is incapable of originating an idea within itself.

O. M. Correct. Go on.

Y. M. The matter of publishing or withholding is still in your Master's hands. If, some day, an outside influence shall determine him to publish, he will give the order, and it will be obeyed.

O. M. That is correct. Well?

Y. M. Upon reflection I have arrived at the conviction that the publication of your doctrines would be harmful. Do you pardon me?

O. M. Pardon *you?* You have done nothing. You are an instrument—a speaking-trumpet. Speaking-trumpets are not responsible for what is said through them. Outside influences—in the form of life-long teachings, trainings, notions, prejudices, and other second-hand importations—have persuaded the Master within you that the publication of these doctrines would be harmful. Very well, this is quite natural, and was to be expected; in fact was inevitable. Go on; for the sake of ease and convenience, stick to habit: speak in the first person, and tell me what your Master thinks about it.

Y. M. Well, to begin: it is a desolating doctrine; it is not inspiring, enthusing, uplifting. It takes the glory out of man, it takes the pride out of him, it takes the heroism out of him, it denies him all personal credit, all applause; it not only degrades him to a machine, but allows him no control over the machine; makes a mere coffee-mill of him, and neither permits him to supply the coffee nor turn the crank, his sole and piteously humble function being to grind coarse or fine, according to his make, outside impulses doing all the rest.

O. M. It is correctly stated. Tell me—what do men admire most in each other?

Y. M. Intellect, courage, majesty of build, beauty of countenance, charity, benevolence, magnanimity, kindliness, heroism, and—and—

O. M. I would not go any further. These are *elementals.* Virtue, fortitude, holiness, truthfulness, loyalty, high ideals—these, and all the related qualities that are named in the dictionary, are *made out of the elementals,* by blendings, combinations, and shadings of the elementals, just as one makes green by blending blue and yellow, and makes several shades and tints of red by modifying the elemental red. There are seven elemental colors, they are all in the rainbow; out of them we manufacture and name fifty shades of them. You have named the elementals of the human rainbow, and also one *blend*—heroism, which is made out of courage and magnanimity. Very well, then; which of these elements does the possessor of it manufacture for himself? Is it intellect?

Y. M. No.

O. M. Why?

Y. M. He is born with it.

O. M. Is it courage?

Y. M. No. He is born with it.

O. M. Is it majesty of build, beauty of countenance?

Y. M. No. They are birthrights.

O. M. Take those others—the elemental moral qualities—charity, benevolence, magnanimity, kindliness; fruitful seeds, out of which spring, through cultivation by outside influences, all the manifold blends and combinations of virtues named in the dictionaries: does man manufacture any one of those seeds, or are they all born in him?

Y. M. Born in him.

O. M. Who manufactures them, then?

Y. M. God.

O. M. Where does the credit of it belong?

Y. M. To God.

O. M. And the glory of which you spoke, and the applause?

Y. M. To God.

O. M. Then it is *you* who degrade man. You make him claim glory, praise, flattery, for every valuable thing he possesses—*borrowed* finery, the whole of it; no rag of it earned by himself, not a detail of it produced by his own labor. *You* make man a humbug; have I done worse by him?

Y. M. You have made a machine of him.

O. M. Who devised that cunning and beautiful mechanism, a man's hand?

Y. M. God.

O. M. Who devised the law by which it automatically hammers out of a piano an elaborate piece of music, without error, while the man is thinking about something else, or talking to a friend?

Y. M. God.

O. M. Who devised the blood? Who devised the wonderful machinery which automatically drives its renewing and refreshing streams through the body, day and night, without assistance or advice from the man? Who devised the man's mind, whose machinery works automatically, interests itself in what it pleases, regardless of his will or desire, labors all night when it likes, deaf to his appeals for mercy? God devised all these things. *I* have not made man a machine, God made him a machine. I am merely calling attention to the fact, nothing more. Is it wrong to call attention to a fact? Is it a crime?

Y. M. I think it is wrong to *expose* a fact when harm can come of it.

O. M. Go on.

Y. M. Look at the matter as it stands now. Man has been taught that he is the supreme marvel of the Creation; he believes it; in all the ages he has never doubted it, whether he was a naked savage, or clothed in purple and fine linen, and civilized. This has made his heart buoyant, his life cheery. His pride in himself, his sincere admiration of himself, his joy in what he supposed were his own and unassisted achievements, and his exultation over the praise and applause which they evoked—these have exalted him, enthused him, ambitioned him to higher and higher flights; in a word, made his life worth the living. But by your scheme, all this is abolished; he is degraded to a machine, he is a nobody, his noble prides wither to mere vanities; let him strive as he may, he can never be any better than his humblest and stupidest neighbor; he would never be cheerful again, his life would not be worth the living.

O. M. You really think that?

Y. M. I certainly do.

O. M. Have you ever seen me uncheerful, unhappy?

Y. M. No.

O. M. Well, *I* believe these things. Why have they not made me unhappy?

Y. M. Oh, well—temperament, of course! You never let *that* escape from your scheme.

O. M. That is correct. If a man is born with an unhappy temperament, nothing can make him happy; if he is born with a happy temperament, nothing can make him unhappy.

Y. M. What—not even a degrading and heart-chilling system of beliefs?

O. M. Beliefs? Mere beliefs? Mere convictions? They are powerless. They strive in vain against inborn temperament.

Y. M. I can't believe that, and I don't.

O. M. Now you are speaking hastily. It shows that you have not studiously examined the facts. Of all your intimates, which one is the happiest? Isn't it Burgess?

Y. M. Easily.

O. M. And which one is the unhappiest? Henry Adams?

Y. M. Without a question!

O. M. I know them well. They are extremes, abnormals; their temperaments are as opposite as the poles. Their life-histories are about alike—but look at the results! Their ages are about the same—around about fifty. Burgess has always been buoyant, hopeful, happy; Adams has always been cheerless, hopeless, despondent. As young fellows both tried country journalism—and failed. Burgess didn't seem to mind it; Adams couldn't smile, he could only mourn and groan over what had happened, and torture himself with vain regrets for not having done so-and-so instead of so-and-so—*then* he would have succeeded. They tried the law—and failed. Burgess remained happy—because he couldn't help it, Adams was wretched—because he couldn't help it. From that day to this, those two men have gone on trying things and failing: Burgess has come out happy and cheerful every time, Adams the reverse. Now we do absolutely know that these men's inborn temperaments have remained unchanged through all the vicissitudes of their material affairs. Let us see how it is with their immaterialities. Both have been zealous Democrats; both have been zealous Republicans; both have been zealous mugwumps. Burgess has always found happiness and Adams unhappiness, in these several political beliefs and in their migrations out of them. Both of these men have been Presbyterians, Universalists, Methodists, Catholics—then Presbyterians again, then Methodists again. Burgess has always found rest in these excursions, and Adams unrest; they are trying Christian Science, now, with the customary result, the inevitable result. No political or religious belief can make Burgess unhappy or the other man happy. I assure you it is purely a matter of temperament. Beliefs are *acquirements,* temperaments are *born;* beliefs are subject to change, nothing whatever can change temperament.

Y. M. You have instanced extreme temperaments.

O. M. Yes. The half-dozen others are modifications of the extremes. But the law is the same. Where the temperament is two-thirds happy, or two-thirds unhappy, no political or religious beliefs can change the proportions. The vast majority of temperaments are pretty equally balanced; the intensities are absent, and this enables a nation to learn to accommodate itself to its political and religious circumstances and like them, be satisfied with them, at last prefer them. Nations do not *think,* they only *feel.* They get their feelings at second-hand—through their temperaments, not their brains. A nation can be brought—by force of circumstances, not argument—to reconcile itself to *any kind of government or religion that can be devised;* in time it will fit itself to the required conditions; later, it will prefer them, and will fiercely fight for them. As instances, you have all history: the Greeks, the Romans, the Persians, the Egyptians, the Russians, the Germans, the French, the English, the Spaniards, the Americans, the South Americans, the Japanese, the Chinese, the Hindoos, the Turks—a thousand wild and tame religions, every kind of government that can be thought of, from tiger to housecat, each nation *knowing* it has the only true religion and the only sane system of government, each despising all the others, each an ass and not suspecting it, each proud of its fancied supremacy, each perfectly sure it is the pet of God, each with undoubting confidence summoning Him to take command in time of war, each surprised when He goes over to the enemy, but by habit able to excuse it and resume compliments—in a word, the whole human race content, always content, persistently content, indestructibly content, happy, thankful, proud, *no matter what its religion is, nor whether its master be tiger or house-cat.* Am I stating facts? You know I am. Is the human race cheerful? You know it is. Considering what it can stand, and be happy, you do me too much honor when you think that *I* can place before it a system of plain cold facts that can take the cheerfulness out of it. Nothing can do that. Everything has been tried. Without success. I beg you not to be troubled.

CHRISTIAN SCIENCE

Twain devoted all of Christian Science *to his doubts about the new, then rapidly expanding religion. In this volume Twain revealed both his skill as a debater and his awed contempt for Mary Baker Eddy. The book begins with a brief, humorous narration in which Twain claims that when he needed a doctor desperately a Christian Scientist treated him in absentia, and finally in person, by praying and by demonstrating that sickness, pain, and death do not exist. The rest of the book is a sustained, meticulous attack on Mary Baker Eddy as the organizer of Christian Science. Twain analyzes her profiteering, her centralization of power, her claim to divine inspiration, her selfishness, her incomprehensibility, her contradictions, her self-deification, and her incoherent writing. He examines the rules and by-laws of the church, professing awe that she would be such a thorough dictator. Twain mounted such a fierce attack because he believed and feared that Christian Scientism would expand so rapidly that it would control Congress by the 1930s. His conclusion offers his opinion about the morality of congressmen.*

The text is taken from the Authorized Uniform Edition of Christian Science with Notes Containing Corrections to Date *(New York, 1907).*

BOOK I

CHAPTER 3

. . . For of all the strange and frantic and incomprehensible and uninterpretable books which the imagination of man has created, surely this one is the prize sample. It is written with a limitless confidence and complacency, and with a dash and stir and earnestness which often compel the effects of eloquence, even when the words do not seem to have any traceable meaning. There are plenty of people who imagine they understand the book; I know this, for I have talked with them; but in all cases they were people who also imagined that there were no such things as pain, sickness, and death, and no realities in the world; nothing actually existent but Mind. It seems to me to modify the value of their testimony. When these people talk about Christian Science they do as Mrs. Fuller did: they do not use their own language, but the book's; they pour out the book's showy incoherences, and leave you to find out later that they were not originating, but merely quoting; they seem to know the volume by heart, and to revere it as they would a Bible—another Bible, perhaps I ought to say. Plainly the book was written under the mental desolations of the Third Degree, and I feel sure that none but the membership of that Degree can discover meanings in it. When you read it you seem to be listening to a lively and aggressive and oracular speech delivered in an unknown tongue, a speech whose spirit you get but not the particulars; or, to change the figure, you seem to be listening to a vigorous instrument which is making a noise which it thinks is a tune, but which, to persons not members of the band, is only the martial tooting of a trombone, and merely stirs the soul through the noise, but does not convey a meaning. . . .

Chapter 4

No one doubts—certainly not I—that the mind exercises a powerful influence over the body. From the beginning of time, the sorcerer, the interpreter of dreams, the fortune-teller, the charlatan, the quack, the wild medicine-man, the educated physician, the mesmerist, and the hypnotist have made use of the client's *imagination* to help them in their work. They have all recognized the potency and availability of that force. Physicians cure many patients with a bread pill; they know that where the disease is only a fancy, the patient's confidence in the doctor will make the bread pill effective.

Faith in the doctor. Perhaps that is the entire thing. It seems to look like it. In old times the King cured the king's evil by the touch of the royal hand. He frequently made extraordinary cures. Could his footman have done it? No—not in his own clothes. Disguised as the King, could he have done it? I think we may not doubt it. I think we may feel sure that it was not the King's touch that made the cure in any instance, but the patient's faith in the efficacy of a King's touch. Genuine and remarkable cures have been achieved through contact with the relics of a saint. Is it not likely that any other bones would have done as well if the substitution had been concealed from the patient? When I was a boy a farmer's wife who lived five miles from our village had great fame as a faith-doctor—that was what she called herself. Sufferers came to her from all around, and she laid her hand upon them and said, "Have faith—it is all that is necessary," and they went away well of their ailments. She was not a religious woman, and pretended to no occult powers. She said that the patient's faith in her did the work. Several times I saw her make immediate cures of severe toothaches. My mother was the patient. In Austria there is a peasant who drives a great trade in this sort of industry, and has both the high and the low for patients. He gets into prison every now and then for practising without a diploma, but his business is as brisk as ever when he gets out, for his work is unquestionably successful and keeps his reputation high. In Bavaria there is a man who performed so many great cures that he had to retire from his profession of stage-carpentering in order to meet the demand of his constantly increasing body of customers. He goes on from year to year doing his miracles, and has become rich. He pretends to no religious helps, no supernatural aids, but thinks there is something in his make-up which inspires the confidence of his patients, and that it is this confidence which does the work, and not some mysterious power issuing from himself.[1]

Within the last quarter of a century, in America, several sects of curers have appeared under various names and have done notable things in the way of healing ailments without the use of medicines. There are the Mind Cure, the Faith Cure, the Prayer Cure, the Mental-Science Cure, and the Christian-Science Cure; and apparently they all do their miracles with the same old, powerful instrument—*the patient's imagination.* Differing names, but no difference in the process. But they do not give that instrument the credit; each sect claims that its way differs from the ways of the others.

They all achieve some cures, there is no question about it; and the Faith Cure and the Prayer Cure probably do no harm when they do no good, since they do not forbid the patient to help out the cure with medicines if he wants to; but the others bar medicines, and claim ability to cure every conceivable human ailment through the application of their mental forces alone. There would seem to be an element of danger here. It has the look of claiming too much, I think. Public confidence would probably be increased if less were claimed.[2]

The Christian Scientist was not able to cure my stomach-ache and my cold; but the horse-doctor did it. This convinces me that Christian Science claims too much. In my opinion it ought to let diseases alone and confine itself to surgery. There it would have everything its own way.

The horse-doctor charged me thirty kreutzers, and I paid him; in fact, I doubled it and gave him a shilling. Mrs. Fuller brought in an itemized bill for a crate of broken bones mended in two hundred and thirty-four places—one dollar per fracture.

1. *January, 1903.* I have personal and intimate knowledge of the "miraculous" cure of a case of paralysis which had kept the patient helpless in bed during two years, in spite of all that the best medical science of New York could do. The traveling "quack" (that is what they called him) came on two successive mornings and lifted the patient out of bed and said "Walk!" and the patient walked. That was the end of it. It was forty-one years ago. The patient has walked ever since.—M. T.

2. *February, 1903.* I find that Christian Science claims that the healing-force which it employs is radically different from the force used by any other party in the healing business. I shall talk about this toward the end of this work.—M. T.

"Nothing exists but Mind?"

"Nothing," she answered. "All else is substanceless, all else is imaginary."

I gave her an imaginary check, and now she is suing me for substantial dollars. It looks inconsistent.

Chapter 5

Let us consider that we are all partially insane. It will explain us to each other; it will unriddle many riddles; it will make clear and simple many things which are involved in haunting and harassing difficulties and obscurities now.

Those of us who are not in the asylum, and not demonstrably due there, are nevertheless, no doubt, insane in one or two particulars. I think we must admit this; but I think that we are otherwise healthy-minded. I think that when we all see one thing alike, it is evidence that, as regards that one thing, our minds are perfectly sound. Now there are really several things which we do all see alike; things which we all accept, and about which we do not dispute. For instance, we who are outside of the asylum all agree that water seeks its level; that the sun gives light and heat; that fire consumes; that fog is damp; that six times six are thirty-six, that two from ten leaves eight; that eight and seven are fifteen. These are, perhaps, the only things we are agreed about; but, although they are so few, they are of inestimable value, because they make an infallible standard of sanity. Whosoever accepts them him we know to be substantially sane; sufficiently sane; in the working essentials, sane. Whoever disputes a single one of them him we know to be wholly insane, and qualified for the asylum.

Very well, the man who disputes none of them we concede to be entitled to go at large. But that is concession enough. We cannot go any further than that; for we know that in all matters of mere *opinion* that same man is insane—just as insane as we are; just as insane as Shakespeare was. We know exactly where to put our finger upon his insanity: *it is where his opinion differs from ours.*

That is a simple rule, and easy to remember. When I, a thoughtful and unbiased Presbyterian, examine the Koran, I know that beyond any question every Mohammedan is insane; not in all things, but in religious matters. When a thoughtful and unbiased Mohammedan examines the Westminster Catechism, he knows that beyond any question I am spiritually insane. I cannot prove to him that he is insane, because you never can prove anything to a lunatic—for that is a part of his insanity and the evidence of it. He cannot prove to me that I am insane, for my mind has the same defect that afflicts his. All Democrats are insane, but not one of them knows it; none but the Republicans and Mugwumps know it. All the Republicans are insane, but only the Democrats and Mugwumps can perceive it. The rule is perfect: *in all matters of opinion our adversaries are insane.* When I look around me, I am often troubled to see how many people are mad. To mention only a few:

The Atheist	The Theosophists
The Infidel	The Swedenborgians

The Agnostic	The Shakers
The Baptist	The Millerites
The Methodist	The Mormons
The Christian Scientist	The Laurence Oliphant Harrasites
The Catholic, and the 115 Christian sects, the Presbyterian excepted	The Grand Lama's people
The 72 Mohammedan sects	The Monarchists
The Buddhist	The Imperialists
The Blavatsky-Buddhist	The Democrats
The Nationalist	The Republicans (but not the Mugwumps)
The Confucian	The Mind-Curists
The Spiritualist	The Faith-Curists
The 2,000 East Indian sects	The Mental Scientists
The Peculiar People	The Allopaths
	The Homeopaths
	The Electropaths
	The ——

But there's no end to the list; there are millions of them! And all insane; each in his own way; insane as to his pet fad or opinion, but otherwise sane and rational.

This should move us to be charitable toward one another's lunacies. I recognize that in his special belief the Christian Scientist is insane, because he does not believe as I do; but I hail him as my mate and fellow, because I am as insane as he—insane from his point of view, and his point of view is as authoritative as mine and worth as much. That is to say, worth a brass farthing. Upon a great religious or political question, the opinion of the dullest head in the world is worth the same as the opinion of the brightest head in the world—a brass farthing. How do we arrive at this? It is simple. The affirmative opinion of a stupid man is neutralized by the negative opinion of his stupid neighbor—no decision is reached; the affirmative opinion of the intellectual giant Gladstone is neutralized by the negative opinion of the intellectual giant Newman—no decision is reached. Opinions that prove nothing are, of course, without value—any but a dead person knows that much. This obliges us to admit the truth of the unpalatable proposition just mentioned above—that, in disputed matters political and religious, one man's opinion is worth no more than his peer's, and hence it follows that no man's opinion possesses any real value. It is a humbling thought, but there is no way to get around it: *all* opinions upon these great subjects are brass-farthing opinions.

It is a mere plain, simple fact—as clear and as certain as that eight and seven make fifteen. And by it we recognize that we are all insane, as concerns those matters. If we were sane, we should all see a political or religious doctrine alike; there would be no dispute: it would be a case of eight and seven—just as it is in heaven, where all are sane and none insane. There there is but one religion, one belief; the harmony is perfect; there is never a discordant note.

Under protection of these preliminaries, I suppose I may now repeat without offense that the Christian Scientist is insane. I mean him no discourtesy, and I am not charging—nor even imagining—that he is insaner than the rest of the human race. I think he is more picturesquely insane than some of us. At the same time, I am quite sure that in one important and splendid particular he is much saner than is the vast bulk of the race.

Why is he insane? I told you before: it is because his opinions are not ours. I know of no other reason, and I do not need any other; it is the only way we *have* of discovering insanity when it is not violent. It is merely the picturesqueness of his insanity that makes it more interesting than my kind or yours. For instance, consider his "little book"; the "little book" exposed in the sky eighteen centuries ago by the flaming angel of the Apocalypse, and handed down in our day to Mrs. Mary Baker G. Eddy, of New Hampshire, and translated by her, word for word, into English (with help of a polisher), and now published and distributed in hundreds of editions by her at a clear profit per volume, above cost, of seven hundred per cent.![1]—a profit which distinctly belongs to the angel of the Apocalypse, and let him collect it if he can; a "little book" which the C. S. very frequently calls by just that name, and always inclosed in quotation-marks to keep its high origin exultantly in mind; a "little book" which "explains" and reconstructs and new-paints and decorates the Bible, and puts a mansard roof on it and a lightning-rod and all the other modern improvements; a "little book" which for the present affects to travel in yoke with the Bible and be friendly to it, and within half a century will hitch the Bible in the rear and thenceforth travel tandem, itself in the lead, in the coming great march of Christian Scientism through the Protestant dominions of the planet.

Chapter 9

Four years ago I wrote the preceding chapters.[2] I was assured by the wise that Christian Science was a fleeting craze and would soon perish. This prompt and all-competent stripe of prophet is always to be had in the market at ground-floor rates. He does not stop to load, or consider, or take aim, but lets fly just as he stands. Facts are nothing to him, he has no use for such things; he works wholly by inspiration. And so, when he is asked why he considers a new movement a passing fad and quickly perishable, he finds himself unprepared with a reason and is more or less embarrassed. For a moment. Only for a moment. Then he waylays the first specter of a reason that goes flitting through the

1. *February, 1903.* This has been disputed by novices. It is not possible that the copy possessed by me could have cost above thirty-seven and a half cents. I have been a printer and bookmaker myself. I shall go into some particulars concerning this matter in a later chapter.—M. T.

2. That is to say, in 1898.

desert places of his mind, and is at once serene again and ready for conflict. Serene and confident. Yet he should not be so, since he has had no chance to examine his catch, and cannot know whether it is going to help his contention or damage it.

The impromptu reason furnished by the early prophets of whom I have spoken was this:

"There is nothing *to* Christian Science; there is nothing about it that appeals to the intellect; its market will be restricted to the unintelligent, the mentally inferior, the people who do not think."

They called that a reason why the cult would not flourish and endure. It seems the equivalent of saying:

"There is no money in tinware; there is nothing about it that appeals to the rich; its market will be restricted to the poor."

It is like bringing forward the best reason in the world why Christian Science should flourish and live, and then blandly offering it as a reason why it should sicken and die.

That reason was furnished me by the complacent and unfrightened prophets four years ago, and it has been furnished me again to-day. If conversions to new religions or to old ones were in any considerable degree achieved through the intellect, the aforesaid reason would be sound and sufficient, no doubt; the inquirer into Christian Science might go away unconvinced and unconverted. But we all know that conversions are seldom made in that way; that such a thing as a serious and painstaking and fairly competent inquiry into the claims of a religion or of a political dogma is a rare occurrence; and that the vast mass of men and women are far from being capable of making such an examination. They are not capable, for the reason that their minds, howsoever good they may be, are not trained for such examinations. The mind not trained for that work is no more competent to do it than are lawyers and farmers competent to make successful clothes without learning the tailor's trade. There are seventy-five million men and women among us who do not know how to cut out and make a dress-suit, and they would not think of trying; yet they all think they can competently think out a political or religious scheme without any apprenticeship to the business, and many of them believe they have actually worked that miracle. But, indeed, the truth is, almost all the men and women of our nation or of any other get their religion and their politics where they get their astronomy—entirely at second hand. Being untrained, they are no more able to intelligently examine a dogma or a policy than they are to calculate an eclipse.

Men are usually competent thinkers along the lines of their specialized training only. Within these limits alone are their opinions and judgments valuable; outside of these limits they grope and are lost—usually without knowing it. In a church assemblage of five hundred persons, there will be a man or two whose trained minds can seize upon each detail of a great manufacturing scheme and recognize its value or its lack of value promptly; and can pass the details in intelligent review, section by section, and finally as a whole, and then deliver a verdict upon the scheme which cannot be flippantly set aside nor easily answered. And there will be one or two other men there who can do the same thing with a great and complicated educational project; and one or two others who can do the like with a large scheme for applying electricity in a new and unheard-of way; and one or two others who can do it with a showy scheme for revolutionizing the scientific world's accepted notions regarding geology. And so on, and so on. But the manufacturing experts will not be competent to examine the educational scheme intelligently, and their opinion about it would not be valuable; neither of these two groups will be able to understand and pass upon the electrical scheme; none of these three batches of experts will be able to understand and pass upon the geological revolution; and probably not one man in the entire lot will be competent to examine, capably, the intricacies of a political or religious scheme, new or old, and deliver a judgment upon it which any one need regard as precious.

There you have the top crust. There will be four hundred and seventy-five men and women present who can draw upon their training and deliver incontrovertible judgments concerning cheese, and leather, and cattle, and hardware, and soap, and tar, and candles, and patent medicines, and dreams, and apparitions, and garden truck, and cats, and baby-food, and warts, and hymns, and time-tables and freight-rates, and summer resorts, and whisky, and law, and surgery, and dentistry, and blacksmithing, and shoemaking, and dancing, and Huyler's candy, and mathematics, and dog-fights, and obstetrics, and music, and sausages, and dry-goods, and molasses, and railroad stocks, and horses, and literature, and labor-unions, and vegetables, and morals, and lamb's fries, and etiquette, and agriculture. And not ten among the five hundred—let their minds be ever so good and bright—will be competent, by grace of the requisite specialized mental training, to take hold of a complex abstraction of any kind and make head or tail of it.

The whole five hundred are thinkers, and they are all capable thinkers—but only within the narrow limits of their specialized trainings. Four hundred and ninety of them cannot competently examine either a religious plan or a political one. A scattering few of them do examine both—that is, they think they do. With results as precious as when I examine the nebular theory and explain it to myself.

If the four hundred and ninety got their religion through their minds, and by weighed and measured detail, Christian Science would not be a scary apparition. But they don't: they get a little of it through their minds, more of it through their feelings, and the overwhelming bulk of it through their environment. . . .

Book II

Chapter 15

. . . I do not wish to impose my opinion on any one who will not permit it, but such as it is I offer it here for what it is worth. I cannot believe, and I do not believe, that Mrs. Eddy originated any of the thoughts and reasonings out of which the book *Science and Health* is constructed; and I cannot believe, and do not believe that she ever wrote any part of that book.

I think that if anything in the world stands proven, and well and solidly proven, by unimpeachable testimony—the treacherous testimony of her own pen in her known and undisputed literary productions—it is that Mrs. Eddy is not capable of thinking upon high planes, nor of reasoning clearly nor writing intelligently upon low ones.

Inasmuch as—in my belief—the very first editions of the book *Science and Health* were far above the reach of Mrs. Eddy's mental and literary abilities, I think she has from the very beginning been claiming as her own another person's book, and wearing as her own property laurels rightfully belonging to that person—the *real* author of *Science and Health.* And I think the reason—and the only reason—that he has not protested is because his work was not exposed to print until after he was safely dead.

That with an eye to business, and by grace of her business talent, she has restored to the world neglected and abandoned features of the Christian religion which her thousands of followers find gracious and blessed and contenting, I recognize and confess; but I am convinced that every single detail of the work except just that one—the delivery of the product to the world—was conceived and performed by another.

Conclusion

Broadly speaking, the hostiles reject and repudiate all the pretensions of Christian Science Christianity. They affirm that it has added nothing new to Christianity; that it can do nothing that Christianity could not do and was not doing before Christian Science was born.

In that case is there no field for the new Christianity, no opportunity for usefulness, precious usefulness, great and distinguished usefulness? I think there is. I am far from being confident that it can fill it, but I will indicate that unoccupied field—without charge—and if it can conquer it, it will deserve the praise and gratitude of the Christian world, and will get it, I am sure.

The present Christianity makes an excellent private Christian, but its endeavors to make an excellent public one go for nothing, substantially.

This is an honest nation—in private life. The American Christian is a straight and clean and honest man, and in his private commerce with his fellows can be trusted to stand faithfully by the principles of honor and honesty imposed upon him by his religion. But the moment he comes forward to exercise a public trust he can be confidently counted upon to betray that trust in nine cases out of ten, if "party loyalty" shall require it.

If there are two tickets in the field in his city, one composed of honest men and the other of notorious blatherskites and criminals, he will not hesitate to lay his private Christian honor aside and vote for the blatherskites if his "party honor" shall exact it. His Christianity is of no use to him and has no influence upon him when he is acting in a public capacity. He has sound and sturdy private morals, but he has no public ones. In the last great municipal election in New York, almost a complete one-half of the votes representing 3,500,000 Christians were cast for a ticket that had hardly a man on it whose earned and proper place was outside of a jail. But that vote was present at church next Sunday the same as ever, and as unconscious of its perfidy as if nothing had happened.

Our Congresses consist of Christians. In their private life they are true to every obligation of honor; yet in every session they violate them all, and do it without shame; because honor to party is above honor to themselves. It is an accepted law of public life that in it a man may soil his honor in the interest of party expediency—*must* do it when party expediency requires it. In private life those men would bitterly resent—and justly—any insinuation that it would not be safe to leave unwatched money within their reach; yet you could not wound their feelings by reminding them that every time they vote ten dollars to the pension appropriation nine of it is stolen money and they the marauders. They have filched the money to take care of the party; they believe it was right to do it; they do not see how their private honor is affected; therefore their consciences are clear and at rest. By vote they do wrongful things every day, in the party interest, which they could not be persuaded to do in private life. In the interest of party expediency they give solemn pledges, they make solemn compacts; in the interest of party expediency they repudiate them without a blush. They would not dream of committing these strange crimes in private life.

Now then, can Christian Science introduce the Congressional Blush? There are Christian Private Morals, but there are no Christian Public Morals, at the polls, or in Congress or anywhere else—except here and there and scattered around like lost comets in the solar system. Can Christian Science persuade the nation and Congress to throw away their public morals and use none but their private ones henceforth in all their activities, both public and private?

I do not think so; but no matter about me: there is the field—a grand one, a splendid one, a sublime one, and absolutely unoccupied. Has Christian Science confidence enough in itself to undertake to enter in and try to possess it?

Make the effort, Christian Science; it is a most noble cause, and it might succeed. It could succeed. Then we should have a new literature, with romances entitled, How To Be an Honest Congressman Though a Christian; How To Be a Creditable Citizen Though a Christian.

V

Letters

The correspondence between Mark Twain and William Dean Howells contains fascinating evidence of their deep friendship. The 680 letters, covering the thirty-eight years from 1872 to 1910, reveal both ordinary concerns and deep philosophical issues. In this selection three letters of condolence from Howells to Twain, about the deaths of Susy and Mrs. Clemens, are included to show how Twain responded to his friend's religious consolation.

Twain's mind saw philosophical issues in the most ordinary, everyday occurrences. Twain can capture in an episode about a runaway carriage a whole debate about providence. In these vivid letters Twain also reveals his contempt for his brother's intellectual fickleness. Frank opinions about man are given—in blunt, unbuttoned style.

The dates in square brackets have been determined by the editors of the Mark Twain-Howells Letters, Henry Nash Smith and William M. Gibson. The italicized words in brackets are editorial explanations. The words in arrow brackets are Twain's cancellations.

Hartford, June 15 [1872].

Friend Howells—

Could you tell me how I could get a copy of your portrait as published in Hearth & Home? I hear so much talk about it as being among the finest works of art which have yet appeared in that journal, that I feel a strong desire to see it. Is it suitable for framing? I have written the publishers of H & H time & again, but they say that the demand for the portrait immediately exhausted the edition & now a copy cannot be had, even for the European demand, which has now begun. Bret Harte has been here, & says his family would not be without that

---

These letters are reprinted from *Mark Twain-Howells Letters,* ed. by Henry Nash Smith and William M. Gibson. The Mark Twain letters appear by permission of the trustees of the Mark Twain Foundation; those of William Dean Howells, by permission of W. W. Howells, Literary Executor, Peabody Museum, Harvard University.

portrait for any consideration. He says his children get up in the night & yell for it. I would give anything for a copy of that portrait to put up in my parlor. I have Oliver Wendell Holmes's & Bret Harte's, as published in Every Saturday, & of all the swarms that come every day to gaze upon them none go away that are not softened & humbled & made more resigned to the will of God. If I had yours to put up alongside of them, I believe the combination would bring more souls to earnest reflection & ultimate conviction of their lost condition, than any other kind of warning would. Where in the nation *can* I get that portrait? Here are heaps of people that want it,—that *need* it. There is my uncle. *He* wants a copy. He is lying at the point of death. He has *been* lying at the point of death for two years. He wants a copy—& I want him to *have* a copy. And I want you to send a copy to the man that shot my dog. I want to see if he is dead to Every human instinct.

Now you send me that portrait. I am sending you mine, in this letter; & am glad to do it, for it has been greatly admired. People who are judges of art, find in the execution a grandeur which has not been equalled in this country, & an expression which has not been approached in *any*.

Ys Truly

S. L. Clemens.

P.S.—62,000 copies of Roughing It sold & delivered in 4 months.

[Hartford, 21 Sept. 1876]

. . . I can always tell which party's funeral is appointed if I can find out how my brother has made up his mind to vote. For some inscrutable reason God never allows him to vote right. (I believe I told you once about my brother's religious gymnastics? Well, I have some late news under that head: he is getting stuck after the Mohammedan plan of salvation, now.). . .

Ys Ever

Mark.

Elmira, Aug. 25 [-27]/77

My Dear Howellses:

I thought I ought to make a sort of record of it for future reference; the pleasantest way to do that would be to write it to somebody; BUT that somebody would let it leak into print, & that we wish to avoid. The Howellses would be safe—so let us tell the Howellses about it.

Day before yesterday was a fine summer day away up here on the summit. Aunt Marsh & Cousin May Marsh were here visiting Susie Crane & Livy at our farm house. By & by mother Langdon came up the hill in the "high carriage" with Nora the nurse & little Jervis (Charley Langdon's little boy)—Timothy the coachman driving. Behind these came Charley's wife & little girl in the buggy with the new, young, spry gray horse—a high-stepper. Theodore Crane arrived a little later.

The Bay [*Clara Clemens*] & Susie were on hand with their nurse, Rosa. I was on hand, too. Susie Crane's trio of colored servants ditto—these being Josie, housemaid; Aunty Cord, cook, aged 62,turbaned, very tall, very broad, very fine every way (see her portrait in "A True Story Just as I Heard It" in my Sketches); Chocklate (the laundress,) (as the Bay calls her—she can't say Charlotte), still taller, still more majestic of proportions, turbaned, very black, straight as an Indian—age 24. Then there was the farmer's wife (colored) & her little girl, Susie.

Wasn't it a good audience to get up an excitement before? Good excitable, inflammable <combustible> material?

Lewis was still down town, three miles away, with his two-horse wagon, to get a load of manure. Lewis is the farmer (colored.) He is of mighty frame & muscle, stocky, stooping, ungainly, has a good manly face & a clear eye. Age about 45— & the most picturesque of men, when he sits in his fluttering work-day rags, humped forward into a bunch, with his aged slouch hat mashed down over his ears & neck. It is a spectacle to make the broken-hearted smile.

Lewis has worked mighty hard & remained mighty poor. At the end of each whole year's toil he can't show a gain of fifty dollars. He had borrowed money of the Cranes till he owed them $700— & he being conscientious & honest, imagine what it was to him to have to carry this stubborn, hopeless load year in & year out.

Well, sunset came, & Ida the young & comely (Charley Langdon's wife) & her little Julia & the nurse Nora, drove out at the gate behind the new gray horse & started down the long hill—the high carriage receiving its load under the porte cochère. Ida was seen to turn her face toward us across the fence & intervening lawn—Theodore waved good bye to her, for he did not know that her sign was a speechless appeal for help.

The next moment Livy said, "Ida's driving too fast down hill!" She followed it with a sort of scream, "Her horse is running away!"

We could see two hundred yards down that descent. The buggy seemed to fly. It would strike obstructions & apparently spring the height of a man from the ground.

Theodore & I left the shrieking crowd behind & ran down the hill bare-headed & shouting. A neighbor appeared at his gate—a tenth of a second too late!—the buggy vanished past him like a thought. My last glimpse showed it for one instant, far down the descent, springing high in the air out of a cloud of dust, & then it disappeared. As I flew down the road, my impulse was to shut my eyes as I turned them to the right or left, & so delay for a moment the ghastly spectacle of mutilation & death I was expecting.

I ran on & on, still spared this spectacle, but saying to myself "I shall see it at the turn of the road; they never can pass that turn alive." When I came in sight of that turn I saw two wagons there bunched together—one of them full of people. I said, "Just so—they are staring petrified at the remains."

But when I got amongst that bunch, there sat Ida in her buggy & nobody hurt, not even the horse or the vehicle. Ida was pale but serene. As I came tearing down she smiled back over her shoulder at me & [I] said, "Well, you're alive yet, *aren't* you?" A miracle had been performed—nothing less.

You see, Lewis,—the prodigious, humped upon his front seat, had been toiling up, on his load of manure; he saw the frantic horse plunging down the hill toward him, on a full gallop, throwing his heels as high as a man's head at every jump. So Lewis turned his team diagonally across the road just at the "turn," thus making a V with the fence—the running horse could not escape that but must enter it. Then Lewis sprang to the ground & stood in this V. He gathered his vast strength, and with a perfect Creedmoor aim he seized the gray horse's bit as he plunged by & fetched him up standing!

It was down hill, mind you; ten feet *further* down hill neither Lewis nor any other man could have saved them, for they would have been on the abrupt "turn," then. But how this miracle was ever accomplished at all, by human strength, generalship & accuracy, is clear beyond my comprehension—& grows more so the more I go & examine the ground & try to believe it was actually done. I know one thing, well; if Lewis had missed his aim he would have been killed on the spot in the trap he had made for himself, & we should have found the rest of the remains away down at the bottom of the steep ravine.

Ten minutes later Theodore & I arrived opposite the house, with the servants straggling after us, & shouted to the distracted group on the porch, "Everybody safe!"

Believe it? Why how *could* they? They knew the road perfectly. We might as well have said it to people who had seen their friends go over Niagara.

However, we convinced them; & then, instead of saying something, or going on crying, they grew very still—words could not express it, I suppose.

Nobody could do anything that night, or sleep, either; but there was a deal of moving talk, with long pauses between—pictures of that flying carriage, these pauses represented—this picture intruded itself all the time & disjointed the talk.

But yesterday evening late, when Lewis arrived from down town he found his supper spread, & some presents of books there, with very complimentary writings on the fly-leaves, & certain very complimentary letters, & more or less greenbacks of dignified denomination pinned to these letters & fly-leaves,—& one said, among other things, (signed by The Cranes) "We cancel $400 of your indebtedness to us," &c &c.

(The end whereof is not yet, of course, for Charley Langdon is west & will arrive ignorant of all these things to-day.)

The supper-room had been kept locked & imposingly secret & mysterious until Lewis should arrive; but around that part of the house were gathered Lewis's wife & child, Chocklate, Josie, Aunty Cord & our Rosa, canvassing things & waiting impatiently. They were all on hand when the <avalanche came> curtain rose.

Now Aunty Cord is a violent Methodist & Lewis an <fanatic> implacable Dunker-Baptist. These two are inveterate religious disputants. The revealments having been made, Aunty Cord said with effusion—

"*Now* let folks go on saying there ain't no God! Lewis, the Lord sent you there to stop that horse."

Says Lewis—

"Then who sent the *horse* there in sich a shape?"

But I want to call your attention to one thing. When Lewis arrived the other evening, after saying those lives by a feat which I think is the most marvelous of any I can call to mind—when he arrived, hunched up on his manure wagon & as grotesquely picturesque as usual, everybody wanted to go & see how he looked.—They came back & said he was beautiful. It was *so,* too—& yet he would have *photographed* exactly as he would have done any day these past 7 years that he has occupied this farm.

Aug. 27.

P. S.—Our little romance in real life is happily & satisfactorily completed. Charley has come, listened, acted—& now John T. Lewis has ceased to consider himself as belonging to that class called "the poor."

It has been known, during some years, that it was Lewis's purpose to buy a thirty-dollar silver watch some day, if he ever got where he could afford it. To-day Ida has given him a new, sumptuous gold Swiss stem-winding stop-watch; & if any scoffer shall say "Behold this thing is out of character," there is an inscription within, which will silence him; for it will teach him that this wearer aggrandizes the watch, not the watch the wearer.

I was asked, beforehand, if this would be a wise gift, & I said "Yes, the very wisest of all; I know the colored race, & I know that in Lewis's eyes this fine toy will throw the other more valuable testimonials far away into the shade. If he lived in England, the Humane Society would give him a gold medal as costly as this watch, & nobody would say 'It is out of character.'

"If Lewis chose to wear a town clock, who would become it better?"

Lewis has sound common sense, & is not going to be spoiled.—The instant he found himself possessed of money, he forgot himself in a plan to make his old father comfortable, who is wretchedly poor & lives down in Maryland. His next act, on the spot, was the proffer to the Cranes of the $300 of his remaining indebtedness to them. This was put off by them to the indefinite future, for he is not going to be allowed to pay that at all, though he doesn't know it.

A letter of acknowledgment from Lewis contains a sentence which raises it to the dignity of literature:

"But I beg to say, humbly, that inasmuch as divine providence saw fit to use me as a instrument for the saving of those presshious lives, the honner conferd upon me was greater than the feat performed."

That is well said.

Yrs Ever

Mark.

Schloss Hotel [Heidelberg] June 27 [1878].

My Dear Howells:

. . . Mrs. Clemens, who even reads note-books in her hunger for culture, was rather startled to run across this paragraph in mine, last night:

"Have all sorts of heavens—have a gate for each sort. Wakeman visits these various heavens. One gate where they receive a barkeeper with artillery salutes, swarms of angels in the sky, & a noble torchlight procession. *He* thinks he is *the* lion of Heaven. Procession over, he drops at once into solid obscurity. But the roughest part of it is, that he has to do 30 weeks' penance—day & night he must carry a torch & shout himself hoarse to do honor to some poor scrub whom he wishes had gone to hell."

I wish I was writing that Wakeman book, but I suppose I shan't get at it again before next year.

Privately, I have some good news to tell you. That is, I believe it will gratify you—in fact I am sure it will—though I am not acquainted with a great many people whom it would please. It is this: *we've quit feeling poor!* Isn't that splendid? You know that for two years we have been coming to want, every little while, & have straightway gone to economising. <Well, the annual report from the coal firm came yesterday, & with that as a basis> Yesterday we fell to figuring & discovered that we have more than income enough, from investments, to live in Hartford on a generous scale. Well, now that we are fixed at last, of course the communists & the asinine government will go to work & smash it all. No matter, we have resolved to quit feeling poor for a little while, any way. This thing was so gratifying to me that my first impulse was to run to you with it.

Drat this German tongue, I never shall be able to learn it. I think I could learn a little conversational stuff, maybe, if I could attend to it, but I found I couldn't spare the time. I took lessons two weeks & got so I could understand the talk going on around me, & even answer back, after a fashion. But I neither talk nor listen, now, so I can't even understand the language any more. Mrs. Clemens is getting along fast, & Miss Spaulding & our little Susie talk the devilish tongue without difficulty. But the Bay scorns the language. The nurse & the governess blandish around her in vain. She maintains the calm & persistent attitude of not caring a damn for German. There is a good deal of character in the Bay—such as it is.

Look here, Howells, when I choose to gratify my passions by writing great long letters to you, you are not to consider anything but the briefest answers necessary—& not even those when you have got things to do. Don't forget that. A lengthy letter from you is a great prize & a welcome, but it gives me a reproach, because I seem to have robbed a busy man of time which he ought not to have spared.

Well, good bye & good luck attend you. We both send love to you & yours.

As Ever

Mark.

All day to-day I have been having an experience—& it results in this maxim:

To man all things are possible but one—he cannot have a hole in the seat of his breeches & keep his fingers out of it.

A man does seem to feel more distress & more persistent & distracting solicitude about such a thing than he could about a sick child that was threatening to grow worse every time he took his attention away from it. (Mrs Clemens said you wouldn't understand the maxim unless I explained it!)

Munich, Feb. 9 [1879].

My Dear Howells—

I have just received this letter from Orion—take care of it, for it is worth preserving. I got as far as 9 pages in my answer to it, when Mrs. Clemens shut down on it, & said it was cruel, & made me send the money & simply wish his lectures success. I said I couldn't lose my 9 pages—so she said send them to you. But I will acknowledge that I thought I was writing a very kind letter.

Now just look at this letter of Orion's. Did you ever see the grotesquely absurd & the heart-breakingly pathetic more closely joined together? Mrs. Clemens said "Raise his monthly pension." So I wrote to Perkins to raise it, a trifle.

Now only think of it! He still has 100 pages to write on his lectures, yet in one inking of his pen he has already swooped around the United States & invested the result!

You *must* put him in a book or a play right away. You are the only man capable of doing it. You might die at any moment, & your very greatest work would be lost to the world. *I* could write Orion's simple biography, & make it effective, too, by merely stating the bald facts—& this I will do if he dies before I do: but *you* must put him into romance. This was the understanding you & I had the day I sailed.

Observe Orion's career—that is, a *little* of it:

He has belonged to as many as five different religious denominations; last March he withdrew from deaconship in a Congregational Church & the superintendency of its Sunday School, in a speech in which he said that for many months (it runs in my mind that he said 13 years,) he had been a confirmed *infidel,* & so it to be his duty to retire from <his> the flock.

2. After being a republican for years, he wanted me to buy him a democratic newspaper merely because his prophetic mind told him Tilden would be President—in which case he would be able to get an office for his services.

A few days before the Presidential election, he came out in a speech & publicly went over to the democrats; but at the last moment, while voting for Tilden & 6 State democrats, he prudently "hedged" by voting for 6 State republicans, also. He said it might make him safe, no matter who won.

The new convert was made one of the secretaries of a democratic meeting,

& placed in the list of speakers. He wrote me jubilantly of what a ten-strike he was going to make with that speech. All right—but think of his innocent & pathetic candor in writing me something like this, a week later: "I was more diffident than I had expected to be, & this was increased by the silence with which I was received when I came forward; so I seemed unable to get the fire into my speech which I calculated upon, & presently they began to get up & go out; & in a few minutes they all rose up & went away."

How *could* a man uncover such a sore as that & show it to another? Not a word of complaint, you see—only a patient, sad surprise.

3. His next project was to write a burlesque upon Paradise Lost.

4. Then, learning that the Times was paying Harte $100 a column for stories, he concluded to write some for the same price. I read his first one & persuaded him not to write any more.

4. Then he read proof in the N. Y. Eve. Post at $10 a week, & meekly observed that the foreman swore at him & ordered him around "like a steamboat mate."

5. Being discharged from that post, he wanted to try agriculture—was sure he could make a fortune out of a chicken farm. I gave him $900 & he went to a ten-house village 2 miles above Keokuk on the river bank—this place was a railway station. He soon asked for money to buy a horse & light wagon,—because the trains did not run at church time on Sunday, & his wife found it rather far to walk.

For a long time I answered demands for "loans," & by next mail always received his check for the interest due me to date. In the most guileless way he let it leak out that he did not underestimate the value of his custom to me, since it was not likely that any other customer of mine paid his interest *quarterly,* & thus enabled me to use my capital twice in 6 months instead of only once. But alas, when the debt at last reached $1500 or $2500 (I have forgotten which,) the interest ate too formidably into his borrowings, & so he quietly ceased to pay it or speak of it. At the end of two years I found that the chicken farm had long ago been abandoned, & he had moved into Keokuk. Later, in one of his casual moments, he casually observed that his books had shown that there was no money in fattening a chicken on 65 cents worth of corn & then selling it for 50.

6. Finally, if I would lend him $500 a year for 2 years (this was 4 or 5 years ago.) he *knew* he could make a success as a lawyer, & would prove it.—This is the pension which we have just increased to $600. The first year his legal business brought him $5. It also brought him an unremunerative case where some villains were trying to chouse some negro orphans out of $700. He still has this case. He has waggled it around through various courts & made some booming speeches on it. The negro children have grown up & married off, now, I believe, & their litigated town-lot has been dug up & carted off by somebody—but Orion still infests the courts with his documents & makes the welkin ring with his venerable case. The second year, he didn't make anything. The third, he made $6, & I made Bliss put a case in his hands—about half an hour's

work. Orion charged $50 for it—Bliss paid him $15. Thus four or five years of lawing has brought him $26, but this will doubtless be increased when he gets done lecturing & buys that "law library." Meantime his office rent has been $60 a year, & he has stuck to that lair day by day as patiently as a spider.

7. Then he by & by conceived the idea of lecturing around America as "Mark Twain's Brother"—that to be on the bills. Subject of proposed lecture, "On the Formation of Character."

8. I protested, & he got on his war-paint, couched his lance, & ran a bold tilt against Total Abstinence & the Red Ribbon fanatics. It raised a fine stink among the virtuous Keokukians.

9. I wrote to encourage him in his good work, but I had let a mail intervene; so by the time my letter reached him he was already winning laurels as a Red Ribbon Howler.

10. Afterward he took a rabid part in a prayer meeting epidemic; dropped that to travesty Jules Verne; dropped that, in the middle of the last chapter, last March, to digest the matter of an infidel book which he proposed to write; & now he comes to the surface to rescue our "noble & beautiful religion" from the sacrilegious talons of Bob Ingersoll.

Now come! Don't fool away this treasure which Providence has laid at your feet, but take it up & use it.—One can let his imagination run riot in portraying Orion, for there is nothing so extravagant as to be out of character with him.

And then his wife is the only woman who could have so rounded & perfected Orion's character. She was a bald-headed old maid. She was poor & taboo; she wanted position & clothes, oh, so badly; she had the snaffle on this ass before he knew what he was about—for he was editor of a daily paper & a good catch. She is saturated to the marrow with the most malignant form of Presbyterianism,—that sort which considers the saving one's own paltry soul the first & supreme end & object of life. So you see she has harried him into the church several times, & then made religion so intolerable to him with her prayings & Bible readings & her other & eternal pious clack-clack that it has had the effect of harrying him out of it again. He is a printer, but she won't allow him to work at his trade because she can't abide the thought of being a mechanic's wife. She prefers to keep boarding-house & make him let on to be a lawyer. He wrote piteously once, how the governor or somebody gave a blow out, with a broad general invitation to lawyers & their wives to be present, & she made him go, & take her,—& it was the year that he didn't have a case or make a cent, & those people all knew it. Moreover, he hadn't any decent clothes, for she gobbles all the money & buys clothes & new wigs for herself with it. The only way we can keep him from being ragged is to send him money distinctly for *himself* occasionally. Then he treats himself to something "for Sunday & weddings" & a pair of "bifocal spectacles"—that is, if bi-focal spectacles happen to be the newest & freshest astonisher in the spectacle market. For he wouldn't give a curse for a pair that hadn't anything surprising about them. She won't let him work at a trade, but in the privacy of the boarding-house she makes him get up in the cold gray dawns of winter & go from one lodger's room to another (young fellows not half his age,—& they pity him & protest, too,) & build the fires, & go down on his knees & bow his gray head & blow them, to save the parlor bellows from wear & tear. Orion is in his 54th year. He & she are two curses which are dovetailed together with marvelous exactness. She is such a vain, proud fool; he is so utterly devoid of pride. He is a curse to her, & she is a curse to him. And these two curses have been yoked fast together for five & twenty years! If Orion ever goes to hell, he will be likely to say,

"I don't think *this* place is much of an invention." And if she ever goes to heaven, she will be likely to say, "I am disappointed; I did not think so many would be saved."

Well,—good-bye, & a short life & a merry one be yours. Poor old Methuselah, how did he manage to stand it so long?

Yrs Ever

Mark.

Munich, Feb. 9.

My Dear Bro—

Yours has just arrived. I enclose a draft on Hartford for $25. You will have abandoned the project you wanted it for, by the time it arrives,—but no matter, apply it to your newer & present project, whatever it is. You see I have an ineradicable faith in your unsteadfastness,—but mind you, *I* didn't invent that faith, you conferred it on me yourself. But fire away, fire away!—I don't see why a changeable man shouldn't get as much enjoyment out of his changes, & transformations & transfigurations as a steadfast man gets out of standing still & pegging at the same old monotonous thing all the time. That is to say, I don't see why a Kaleidoscope shouldn't enjoy itself as much as a telescope, nor a grindstone have as good a time as a whetstone, nor a barometer as good a time as a yard stick. I don't feel like girding at you any more about fickleness of purpose, because I recognize & realize at last that it is incurable; but before I learned to accept this truth, each new weekly project of yours possessed the power of throwing me into the most exhausting & helpless convulsions of profanity. But fire away, now! Your magic has lost its might. I am able to view your inspirations dispassionately & judicially, now, & say "This one or that one or the other one is not up to your average flight, or is above it, or below it."

And so, without passion, or prejudice, or bias of any kind, I sit in judgment upon your lecture project & say it was up to your average, it was indeed above it, for it had possibilities in it, & <not only that> even *practical* ones. While I am not sorry you abandoned it, I should not be sorry if you had stuck to it & given it a trial. But on the whole you did the wise thing to lay it aside, I think, because a lecture is a most easy thing to fail in; & at your time of life, & in your own town, such a failure would make a deep & cruel wound in your heart & in your pride. It was decidedly unwise in you to think for a moment of coming before a community who knew you, with such a course of lectures; because Keokuk is not unaware that you have been a Swedenborgian, a Presbyterian, a Congregationalist, & a Methodist (on probation,) & that just a year ago you were an infidel. If Keokuk had gone to your lecture-course, it would have gone to be amused, not instructed,—for when a man is known to have no settled convictions of his own he can't convict other people. They would have gone to be amused, & that would have been a deep humiliation to you. It could have been safe for you to appear only where you were unknown—then many of your hearers would think you were in earnest. And they would be right. You *are* in earnest while your convictions are new. But, taking it by & large, you probably did best to discard that project altogether. But I leave you to judge of that, for you are the worst judge I know of. . . .

Elmira, Sep. 15 [1879].

My Dear Howells:

When & where? Here on the farm would be an elegant place to meet, but of course you cannot come so far. So we will say Hartford or Belmont, about the beginning of November. The date of our return to Hartford is uncertain, but will be three or four weeks hence, I judge. I hope to finish my book here before migrating.

I think maybe I've got some Atlanticable stuff in my head, but there's none in MS I believe.

Say—a friend of mine wants to write a play with me, I to furnish the broad-comedy cuss.—I don't know anything about his ability, but his letter serves to remind me of *our* old projects. If you haven't used Orion or Old Wakeman (Amateur Detective), don't you think you & I can get together & grind out a play with one of those fellows in it? Orion is a field which grows richer & richer the more he manures it with each new top-dressing of religion or other guano.—Drop me an immediate line about this, won't you? I imagine I see Orion on the stage, always gentle, always melancholy, always changing his politics & religion, & trying to reform the world, always inventing something, & losing a limb by a new kind of explosion at the end of each of the four acts. Poor old chap, he is good material. I can imagine his wife or his sweetheart reluctantly adopting each of his new religions in turn, just in time to see him waltz into the next one & leave her isolated once more.—(*Mem.* Orion's wife *has* followed him into the outer darkness, after 30 years' rabid membership in the Presbyterian church.)

Well, with the sincerest & most abounding love to you & yours, from all this family, I am Yrs Ever Mark.

What *is* your P.O. address?

Elmira, Jan. 24/80.

Say—are you dead again? And did you go to the Tile Club dinner in New

York? I should have gone, sure, if my wife had had two husbands, so one could stay here & give the medicine. I've read the Feb. Undiscovered, & it is perfectly wrote—as Susy says.—What a master hand you are to <hand> jabber the nauseating professional slang of spiritism—it flows from you like your native language. I see that that poor old man & that poor girl are going to pain me more & more, to the end. . . .

Ys Ever

Mark.

[Hartford] Jan 7/84

My Dear Howells—

"O my goodn's"! as Jean says. You have now encountered at last the heaviest calamity that can befal an author. The scarlet fever, once domesticated, is a permanent member of the family. Money may desert you, friends forsake you, enemies grow indifferent to you, but the scarlet fever will be true to you, through thick & thin, till you be all saved or damned, down to the last one. I say these things to cheer you. As to the pecuniary feature—the six weeks which Jean robbed me of, happened by accident to be the very most valuable 6 weeks of my entire life.

The bare suggestion of scarlet fever in the family makes me shudder; I believe I would almost rather have Osgood publish a book for me.

You folks have our most sincere sympathy. O, the intrusion of this hideous disease is an unspeakable disaster.

My billiard table is stacked up with books relating to the Sandwich Islands; the walls are upholstered with scraps of paper penciled with notes drawn from them. I have saturated myself with knowledge of that unimaginably beautiful land & that most strange & fascinating people. And I have begun a story. Its hidden motive will illustrate a but-little considered fact in human nature: that the religious folly you are born in you will *die* in, no matter what apparently reasonabler religious folly may seem to have taken its place meanwhile & abolished & obliterated it. I start Bill Ragsdale at 12 years of age, & the heroine at 4, in the midst of the ancient idolatrous system, with its picturesque & amazing customs & superstitions, 3 months before the arrival of the missionaries & the erection of a shallow Christianity upon the ruins of the old paganism.

Then these two will become educated Christians, & highly civilized. And then I will jump 15 years, & do Ragsdale's leper business. When we come to dramatize, we can draw a deal of matter from the story, all ready to our hand.

Yrs Ever

Mark

Elmira, Aug. 31/84.

My Dear Howells—

. . . This presidential campaign is too delicious for anything. <especially> To see grown men, apparently in their right mind, seriously arguing against a bachelor's fitness for President because he has had private intercourse with a consenting widow! Those grown men know what the bachelor's other alternative was—& tacitly they seem to prefer that to the widow. *Is*n't human nature the most consummate sham & lie that was ever invented? Isn't man a creature to be ashamed of in pretty much all his aspects? Is he really fit for anything but to be stood up on the street corner as a convenience for dogs? Man, "Know thyself"—& then thou wilt despise thyself, to a dead moral certainty. Take three quite good specimens—Hawley, Warner, & Charley Clark. Even *I* do not loathe Blaine more than they do; yet Hawley is howling for Blaine, Warner & Clark are eating their daily crow in the paper for him, & all three will vote for him. O stultification, where is thy sting, O slave where is thy hickory!. . .

Yrs Ever

Mark.

Elmira, Sept. 17/84.

My Dear Howells:

Somehow I can't seem to rest quiet under the idea of your voting for Blaine. I believe you said something about the country & the party. Certainly allegiance to these <are> is well; but as certainly a man's *first* duty is to his own conscience & honor—the party & the country come second to that, & never first. I don't ask you to vote *at all*—I only urge you to not soil yourself by voting for Blaine. When you wrote before, you were able to say the charges against him were not proven. But you know now that they are proven, & it seems to me that that bars you & all other honest & honorable men (who are independently situated) from voting for him.

It is not necessary to vote for Cleveland; the only necessary thing to do, as I understand it, is that a man <shall not smirch himself> shall keep *himself* clean (by withholding his vote for an improper man,) even though the party & the country go to destruction in consequence. It is not *parties* that make or save countries or that build them to greatness—it is clean men, clean ordinary citizens, rank & file, the masses. Clean masses are not made by individuals standing back till the *rest* become clean.

As I said before, I think a man's first duty is to his own honor; not to his country & not to his party.

Don't be offended; I mean no offense. I am not so concerned about the *rest* of the nation, but—well, good-bye.

Ys Ever

Mark

Elmira, Sept. 17/84.

My Dear Howells—

Before I forget it I must tell you that Mrs Clemens has said a bright thing. A drop letter came to me asking me to lecture here for a <Baptist> church debt. I began to rage <as usual> over the exceedingly cool wording of the request, when Mrs. Clemens said "I think I know that church; & if so, this preacher is a colored man—he doesn't know how to write a polished letter—how should he?"

My manner changed so suddenly & so radically that Mrs. C. said: "I will give you a motto, & it will be useful to you if you will adopt it: "Consider every man colored till he is proved white."

It is dern good, I think.

Yrs Ever

Mark

Philada, Feb. 27/85.

My Dear Howells—

To-night in Baltimore, tomorrow afternoon & night in Washington, & my four-months platform campaign is ended at last. It has been a curious experience. It has taught me that Cable's gifts of mind are greater & higher than I had suspected. But—

That "but" is pointing toward his religion. You will never never know, never divine, guess, imagine, how loathsome a thing the Christian religion can be made until you come to know & study Cable daily & hourly. Mind you, I like him; he is pleasant company; I rage & swear at him sometimes, but we do not quarrel; we get along mighty happily together; but in him & his person I have learned to hate all religions. He has taught me to abhor & detest the Sabbath-day & hunt up new & troublesome ways to dishonor it. . . .

Ys Ever

Mark.

Elmira, Aug. 22/87.

My Dear Howells:

. . . How stunning are the changes which age makes in a man while he sleeps. When I finished Carlyle's French Revolution in 1871, I was a Girondin; every time I have read it since, I have read it differently—being influenced & changed, little by little, by life & environment (& Taine, & St. Simon): & now I lay the book down once more, & recognize that I am a Sansculotte!—And not a pale, characterless Sansculotte, but a Marat. Carlyle teaches no such gospel: so the change is in *me*—in my vision of the evidences.

People pretend that the Bible means the same to them at 50 that it did at all former milestones in their journey. I wonder how they can lie so. It comes of practice, no doubt. They would not say that of Dickens's or Scott's books. *Nothing* remains the same: when the man goes back to look at the house of his childhood, it has always *shrunk:* there is no instance of such house being <bigger than> as big as the picture in memory & imagination call for. Shrunk how? Why, to its correct dimensions; the *house* hasn't altered; this is the first time it has been in focus.

Well, that's loss. To have house & Bible shrink so, under the disillusioning corrected angle, is loss—for a moment. But there are compensations. You tilt the tube skyward & bring planets & comets & corona-flames a hundred & fifty thousand miles high into the field. Which I see you have done, & found Tolstöi. I can't get *him* in focus yet, but I've got Browning. . . .

Ys Ever

Mark.

Hartford, July 13/89.

Dear Howells:

I came on from Elmira a day or two ago, where I left a house of mourning. Mr. Crane died after ten months of pain & two whole days of dying, at the farm on the hill the 3d inst: A man who had always hoped for a swift death. Mrs. Crane & Mrs. Clemens & the children were in a gloom which brought back to me the days of nineteen years ago, when Mr. Langdon died. It is heart-breaking to see Mrs. Crane. Many a time, in the past ten days, the sight of her has reminded me, with a pang, of the desolation which uttered itself in the closing sentence of your last letter to me. I do see that there is an argument against suicide: the grief of the worshipers left behind, the awful famine in their hearts, these are too costly terms for the release.

I shall be here ten days yet, & all alone; nobody in the house but the servants. Can't Mrs. Howells spare you to me? Can't you come & stay with me? The house is cool & pleasant; your work will not be interrupted; we will keep to ourselves & let the rest of the world do the same; you can have your choice of three bedrooms, & you will find the children's schoolroom (which was built for my study), the perfection of a retired & silent den for work. There isn't a fly or a mosquito on the estate. *Come*—say you will.

With kindest regards to Mrs. Howells, & Pilla & John.

Yours Ever

Mark.

Elmira, July 24/89.

Dear Howells:

. . . Well, just think of it: a while ago, while Providence's attention was absorbed in disordering some timetables so as to break up a trip of mine to Mr. Church's on the Hudson, that Johnstown dam got loose. I swear I was afraid to pray, for fear I should laugh. . . .

Yours Ever

Mark.

Hartford, May 20/91.

Dear Howells:

For her health's sake Mrs. Clemens *must* try some baths somewhere, & this it is that has determined us to go to Europe. The water required seems to be provided at a little obscure & little-visited nook up in the hills back of the

Rhine somewhere & you get to it by Rhine traffic-boat & country stage-coach. Come, get "sick or sorry enough" & join us. We shall be a little while at that bath, & the rest of the summer at Annecy (this is confidential to you) in Haute Savoie, 22 miles from Geneva. Spend the winters in Berlin. I don't know how long we shall be in Europe—I have a vote, but I don't cast it. I'm going to do whatever the others desire, with leave to change their mind, without prejudice, whenever they want to. Travel has no longer any charm for me. I have seen all the foreign countries I want to see except heaven & hell, & I have only a vague curiosity as concerns one of those. . . .

Mark.

[Letter about the death of Susy]

Far Rockaway, L. I., Sept. 13, 1896.

My dear Clemens:

I remember how you came in one day when we were bleeding from the death of Winnie, and said to me, "Oh did I *wake* you?" because I suppose my heavy heart had got into my eyes, and I looked sleep-broken. I have never forgotten just how you said it, and the tender intelligence you put into your words, and I wish now my affection for you and your wife could translate itself into some phrase that could be as nearly like comfort. There is really nothing to say to you, poor souls, and yet I must write, as I have already written to Mrs. Clemens to say that we suffer with you. As for the gentle creature who is gone, the universe is all a crazy blunder if she is not some where in conscious blessedness that knows and feels your love. The other night I woke to think, "Why do we bother trying to conceive a state of being beyond this which shall be different from this, when there will really be nothing but something like an earthly separation to bridge over?" You are parted from her a little longer, and that's all, and the joint life will go on when you meet on the old terms, but with the horror and pain gone forever. This is the easiest and the most reasonable thing to believe, and it is not to be refused because it is so old and simple.

We join in the love to you which has known the same sorrow as yours.

W. D. Howells.

London, Sept. 24/96.

Dear Howells:

Yes, you two know what we feel—but no others among our friends. They have lost children, but the proportions were not the same. As Mrs. Clemens says, "they have lost a daughter, but they have not lost a Susy Clemens." There was not a detail in Susy's make-up that was commonplace.

To me our loss is bitter, bitter, bitter. Then what must it be to my wife. It would bankrupt the vocabularies of all the languages to put it into words. For the relation between Susy & her mother was not merely & only the relation of mother & child, but that of sweethearts, lovers also. "Do you love me, mamma?" "No, I don't love you, Susy, I worship you."

What a ghastly tragedy it was; how cruel it was; how exactly & precisely it was planned; & how remorselessly every detail of the dispensation was carried out. Susy stood on the platform at Elmira at half past ten on the 14th of July, 1895, in the glare of the electric lights, waving her good-byes as our train moved westward on the long trip; & she was brimming with life & the joy of it. That is what I saw; & it was what her mother saw through her tears. One year, one month, & one week later, Livy & Clara had completed the circuit of the globe, arriving at Elmira at the same hour in the evening, by the same train & *in the same car*—& Susy was there to meet them—lying white & fair in her coffin in the house she was born in.

They were flying on the wings of steam & in the torture of dread & anxiety; & if three days could have been spared them out of the rich hoard laid up for the building of the coming ages, poor Susy would have died in her mother's arms— & the poor three days were denied: they could not be afforded.

(Blank to be filled some day.)

We send our love to both of you. Mrs. Clemens asks me to thank Mr. Howells for his note, & to say that it was a comfort to her, coming as it did from a heart that had suffered the same bruise as her own.

Good-bye. Will healing ever come, or life have value again?

And shall we see Susy? Without doubt! without *shadow* of doubt, if it can furnish opportunity to break our hearts again.

S L Clemens

Hotel Metropole, Vienna, Jan. 22/98.

Dear Howells—

Look at those ghastly figures. I used to write it "Hartford, *1871*." There was no Susy then—there is no Susy now. And how much lies between—one long lovely stretch of scented fields, & meadows, & shady woodlands; & suddenly Sahara! You speak of the glorious days of that old time— & they were. It is my quarrel—that traps like that are set. Susy & Winnie given us, in miserable sport, & then taken away.

About the last time I saw you I described to you the culminating disaster in a book I was going to write (& will yet, when the stroke is further away)—a man's dead daughter brought to him when he had been through all other possible misfortunes— & I said it couldn't be done as it ought to be done except by a man who had lived it—it must be written with the blood out of a man's heart. I could not know, then, how soon I was to be made competent. I have thought of it many a time since. If you were here I think we could cry down each other's necks, as in your dream. For we *are* a pair of old derelicts drifting around, now, with some of our passengers gone & the sunniness of the others in <total> eclipse.

I couldn't get along without work now. I bury myself in it up to the ears. Long hours—8 & 9 on a stretch, sometimes. And all the days, Sundays included. It isn't all for print, by any means, for much of it fails to suit me; 50,000 words of it in the past year. It was because of the deadness which invaded me when Susy died. But I have made a change lately—into dramatic work— & I find it absorbingly entertaining. I don't know that I can write a play that will play; but no matter, I'll write half a dozen that won't, anyway. Dear me, I didn't know there was such fun in it. I'll write twenty that won't play. I get into immense spirits as soon as my day is fairly started. Of course a good deal of this friskiness comes of my being in sight of land—on the Webster & Co debts, I mean. (Private.) We've lived close to the bone & saved every cent we could, & there's no undisputed claim, now, that we can't cash. I have marked this "private" because it is for the friends who are attending to the matter for us in New York to reveal it when they want to & if they want to. There are only two claims which I dispute & which I mean to look into personally before I pay them. But they are small. Both together they amount to only $12,500. I hope you will never get the like of the load saddled onto you that was saddled onto me 3 years ago. And yet there is such a solid pleasure in *paying* the things that I reckon maybe it is worth while to get into that kind of a hobble, after all. Mrs. Clemens gets millions of delight out of it; & the children have never uttered one complaint about the scrimping, from the beginning.

We all send you & all of you our love.

Mark.

P. S. I see that I have left out something which I particularly wanted to say. In assuring Mrs. Clemens of your love for her you touched her very deeply, & she has never been more outspokenly grateful for any prized thing which these clouded eighteen months have brought her. She needs all the love she can get, & there is no other support that is so good & so welcome as the love of the old, old friends of the days that are gone..

[Vienna] April 2 [-13]/99.

Dear Howells:

I am waiting for the April Harper, which is about due now; waiting, & strongly interested. You are old enough to be a weary man, with paling interests, but you do not show it. You do your work in the same old delicate & delicious & forceful & searching & perfect way. I don't know how you can—but I suspect. I suspect that to you there is still dignity in human life, & that Man is not a joke—a poor joke—the poorest that was ever contrived—an April-fool joke, played by a malicious <urchin> Creator with nothing better to waste his time upon. Since I wrote my Bible, (last year) which Mrs. Clemens loathes, & shudders over, & will not listen to the last half nor allow me to print any part of it, Man is not to me the respect-worthy person he was before; & so I have lost my pride in him & can't write gaily nor praisefully about him any more. And I don't intend to try. I mean to go on writing, for that is my best amusement, but I shan't print much. (For I don't wish to be scalped, any more than another.) . . .

Is it imagination, or— Anyway I seem to get furtive & fleeting glimpses which I take to be the weariness & indolence of age; indifference to sights & things once brisk with interest; tasteless stale stuff which used to be champagne; the boredom of travel; the secret sigh behind the public smile, the private what-in-hell-did-I-come-for!

But maybe that is your art. Maybe that is what you intend the reader to detect and think he has made a Columbus-discovery. Then it is well done, perfectly done. I wrote my last travel-book in hell; but I let on, the best I could, that it was an excursion through heaven. Some day I will read it, & if its lying cheerfulness fools me, than I shall believe it fooled the reader. How I did loathe that journey around the world!—except the sea-part & India. . . .

Next Morning. I have been reading the morning paper. I do it every morning—well knowing that I shall find in it the usual depravities and baseness & hypocricies & cruelties that make up Civilization, & cause me to put in the rest of the day pleading for the damnation of the human race. I cannot seem to get my prayers answered, yet I do not despair.

(Escaped from) 5 o'clock Tea. ('sh!) Oh, the American girl in Europe! Often she is creditable, but sometimes she is just shocking. This one, a minute ago—19, fat-face, raspy voice, pert ways, the self-complacency of God; & with it all a silly laugh <embarrassed> which kept breaking out through her chatter all along, whereas there was no call for it, for she said nothing that was funny. "S'pose so many 've told y' how they 'njoyed y'r chapt'r on the Germ' tongue it's bring'n coals to Newcastle ke-he! say anything *'bout* it ke-hehe! Spent m' vacation 'n Russia, 'n' saw Tolstoi; *he* said"—

"Tolstoi" blos! It made me shudder. It should make a dog shudder. (I take back the slur on the dog—the dog is a gentleman; I hope to go to his heaven, not man's.)

And now comes this tiresome old yellow German woman & leans out of the 6th-floor window the other side of the street, & the pigeons swarm down in a cloud & discharge their excrement on her & she feeds them & is as proud as if she were in a sentimental German book. I can never keep my temper when she is showing off like that. She reminds me of the loathsome pigeons of St. Mark in V. [*Venice*]. I wonder why she doesn't fall out & break her neck.

Mark.

Evening. We all belong to the nasty stinking little human race, & of course it is not nice for God's belovéd vermin to scoff at each other; but how can I help it when the Abendblatt pukes another mess of Helen-Gould adulation onto me. Kipling was mentioned just twice during his illness by this chief Austrian daily; whereas it has mentioned & worshiped Helen Gould a hundred times since she contributed a month's income to the war from her investments of stolen money. I wonder if she was the only neighbor who was hospitable to the Windsor sufferers. Got a badge from the Fire Department making her a holy personage at fires hereafter! Motion offered by General Wheeler for the thanks of Congress for her! Hang it, *I* would contribute a month's income to a war, myself, if it wrought me no deprivation, but left me a million to pull through the rest of the year on. Particularly if I was to become an object of the planet's worship for it besides, & if the money was stolen & had cost me no labor. Oh, we *are* a nasty little lot — & to think there are people who would like to save us & continue us. It won't happen if I have any influence.

Mark

April 12. Jean has been in here with a copy of Literature, complaining that I am *again* behind you in the election of the 10 consecrated members; & seems troubled about it & not quite able to understand it. But I have explained to her that you are right there on the ground, inside the poll-booth, keeping game — & that that makes a large difference in these things.

13th. I have been to the Kunstausstellung with Mrs. Clemens. The office of art seems to be, to grovel in the dirt before Emperors & this & that & the other damned breed of priests. Yrs Ever

Mark.

[Vienna], May 12 [-13]/99

. . . *6 p.m.* For several years I have been intending to stop writing for print as soon as I could afford it. At last I can afford it, & have put the pot-boiler pen away. What I have been wanting was a chance to write a book without reserves — a book which should take account of no one's feelings, no one's prejudices, opinions, beliefs, hopes, illusions, delusions; a book which should say my say, right out of my heart, in the plainest language & without a limitation of any sort. I judged that that would be an unimaginable luxury, heaven on earth. There was no condition but one under which the writing of such a book could be possible; only one — the consciousness that it would not see print.

It is under way, now, & it *is* a luxury! an intellectual drunk. Twice I didn't start it right; & got pretty far in, both times, before I found it out. But I am sure it is started right this time. It is in <story> tale-form. I believe I can make it tell what I think of Man, & how he is constructed, & what a shabby poor ridiculous thing he is, & how mistaken he is in his estimate of his character & powers & qualities & his place among the animals.

So far, I think I am succeeding. I let the madam into the secret day before yesterday, & locked the doors & read to her the opening chapters. She said —

"It is perfectly horrible — and perfectly beautiful!"

"Within the due limits of modesty, that is what *I* think."

I hope it will take me a year or two to write it, & that it will turn out to be the right vessel to contain all the ordure I am planning to dump into it.

Yours ever

Mark.

Wellington Court, Knightsbridge,
[London] Jan. 25 [-26], 1900.

Dear Howells:

. . . Privately speaking, this is a sordid & criminal war, & in every way shameful & excuseless. Every day I write (in my head) bitter magazine articles about it, but I have to stop with that. For England must not fall: it would mean an inundation of Russian & German political degradations which would envelop the globe & steep it in a sort of Middle-Age night & slavery which would last till Christ comes again—which I hope he will not do; he made trouble enough before. Even wrong— & she is wrong—England must be upheld. He is an enemy of the human race who shall speak against her now. Why *was* the human race created? Or at least why wasn't something creditable created in place of it. God had His opportunity; He could have made a reputation. But no, He must commit this grotesque folly—a lark which must have cost him a regret or two when He came to think it over & observe effects. For a giddy & unbecoming caprice there has been nothing like it till this war. I talk the war with both sides—always waiting until the other man introduces the topic. Then I say "My head is with the Briton, but my heart — such rags of morals as I have are with the Boer—now we will talk, unembarrassed & without prejudice." And so we discuss, & have no trouble.

Jan. 26.

It was my intention to make some disparaging remarks about the human race; & so I kept this letter open for that purpose, & for the purpose of telling my dream, wherein the Trinity were trying to guess a conundrum propounded by One of Them regarding that premature birth; but I can do better—for I can snip out of the "Times" various samples & side-lights which bring the race down to date, & expose it as of yesterday. If you will notice, there is seldom a telegram in a paper which fails to show up one or more members & beneficiaries of our Civilization as promenading with his shirt-tail up & the rest of his regalia in the wash.

I love to see the holy ones air their smug pieties & admire them & smirk over them, & at the same moment frankly & publicly make water on the pieties of his Brer—confidently expecting the approval of his country & his pulpit, & getting it.

I notice that God is on both sides in this war; thus history repeats itself. But I am the only person who has noticed this; everybody here thinks He is playing the game for this side, & for this side only.

With great love to you all

Mark.

Villa di Quarto Florence, June 6/04.

Dear Howells:

Last night at 9.20 I entered Mrs. Clemens's room to say the usual good-night—& she was dead! tho' no one knew it. She had been cheerfully talking, a moment before. She was sitting up in bed—she had not lain down for months—& Katie & the nurse were supporting her. They supposed she had fainted, & they were holding the oxygen pipe to her mouth, expecting to revive her. I bent over her & looked in her face, & I think I spoke—I was surprised and troubled that she did not notice me. Then we understood, & our hearts broke. How poor we are to-day!

But how thankful I am that her persecutions are ended. I would not call her back if I could.

To-day, treasured in her worn old Testament, I found a dear & gentle letter from you, dated Far Rockaway, Sept. 13, 1896, about our poor Susy's death. I am tired & old; I wish I were with Livy.

I send my love—& hers—to you all.

S L C.

1 Clarges street,
[London] June 7, 1904.

My dear Clemens:

The news has just reached us. I will not try to say anything in the stupid notion of trying to help you. But I must, as if it had never occurred to me before, realize in words, that the character which now remains a memory, was one of the most perfect ever formed on the earth. How often John and I have spoken of that wonderful goodness, that soul of exquisite kindness, which was so strong and so gentle! Poor old fellow; I am so sorry for you and for your girls. But they will have the comfort of taking up her place in your life. What nonsense! Even they cannot do that. Well! Here are my love and pity.

Yours ever
W. D. Howells.

1 Clarges street,
[London] June 9, 1904.

My dear old friend:

I had written to you as soon as I knew of the fact, just to let you know I was with you in that insurpassable sorrow of yours; but you must have known it already. Pilla and I tried to read your letter aloud; we couldn't. It wrings my heart to think about you. What are you going to do, you poor soul? I mean literally. Are you going back to America at once? Or shall we have any chance of seeing you again on this side? My wife arrives on the 18th; John goes straight to Italy, sailing on the 2d July; we expect, we three, to spend the winter in Italy.

My love to your dear girls; Pilla has written already.

I cannot speak of your wife's having kept that letter of mine, where she did. You know how it must humiliate a man in his unworthiness to have anything of his so consecrated. She hallowed what she touched, far beyond priests.

Yours affectionately
W. D. Howells.

Villa di Quarto [Florence], /04.
June 12, 6 p.m.

Dear Howells:

We have to sit & hold our hands & wait—in the silence & solitude of this prodigious house; wait until June 25, then we go to Naples & sail in the Prince Oscar the 28th. There is a ship 12 days earlier (but we came in that one.) I see Clara twice a day—morning- & evening-greeting—nothing more is allowed. She keeps her bed, & says nothing. She has not cried yet. I wish she could cry. Our old Katy stays near by, in the days, and Miss Lyon (secretary) sleeps in the room with her, nights. It would break Livy's heart to see Clara. We excuse ourselves from all the friends that call—though of course only intimates come. Intimates—but they are not the old old friends, the friends of the old old times when we laughed. Shall we ever laugh again? If I could only see a dog that I knew in the old times! & could put my arms around his neck & tell him all, everything, & ease my heart.

Think—in 3 hours it will be a week!—& soon a month; & by & by a year. How fast our dead fly from us.

She loved you so, & was always as pleased as a child with any notice you took of her.

Soon your wife will be with you, oh fortunate man! And John, whom mine was so fond of. The sight of him was such a delight to her. Lord, the old friends, how dear they are. . . .

Stormfield
10 a.m. April 17/09.

To W. D. Howells

When I wrote you at 3 this morning I did not know I was laying an egg that would hatch out in the course of a few hours & produce a cunning & handy scheme, but I know it now. I am glad. For I like to see my mind perform according to the law which I have laid down in "What Is Man": the law that the mind works automatically, & plans & perfects many a project without its owner suspecting what it is about; the mind being merely a machine, & not in even the slightest degree under the control of its owner or subject to his influence.

My mind's present <plan> scheme is a good one; I could not like it better if I had invented it myself. It is this: to write letters to friends *& not send them.*

I will now try it on you as a beginning, & see how it works. Dictating Autobiography has certain irremovable drawbacks.

¶ 1. A stenographer is a lecture-audience; you are always conscious of him; he is a restraint, because there is only one of him, & one alien auditor can seldom be an inspiration; you *pay out* to him from your own treasury, whereas if there were five hundred of him you would pay out from *his*: he would furnish the valuable part of your discourse—that is, the soul & spirit of it—& you would only have to furnish the words.

2. You are not talking to yourself; you are not thinking aloud—processes which insure a free & unembarrassed delivery—for that petrified audience-person is always there, to block that game.

3. If it's a she person, there are *so* many thousands & thousands of things you are suffering to say, every day, but mustn't, because they are indecent.

4. If it's a religious person, your jaw is locked again, several times a day: profane times & theological times. I had a person of that breed for a year or two. The profanity cruelly shocked her at first; soon she became reconciled to it; <finally she> presently she got to liking it, next she couldn't get along without it; but from the beginning to the end there was never a time when she could stand my theology. She said she wouldn't give a Gatun Dam for it.

5. Often you are burning to pour out a sluice of intimately personal, & particularly private things—& there you are again! You can't make your mouth say them. It won't say them to any but a very close personal friend, like Howells, or Twichell, or Henry Rogers.

But that scheme—that new-born scheme—that splendid scheme—that all-comforting, all-satisfying, all-competent scheme—blows all these obstructing and irritating difficulties to the winds! I will fire the profanities at Rogers, the indecencies at Howells, the theologies at Twichell. Oh, to think—I am a free man at last!

Do you see? Talking to the same, same, same old one-character stenographer all the time, is talking to the *vague*—there's no definite target; but the *scheme* furnishes a definite target for each letter, & you can choose the target that's going to be the most sympathetic for what you are hungering & thirsting to say at that particular moment. And you can talk with a quite unallowable frankness & freedom, because you are not going to send the letter. When you are on fire with theology, you'll not write it to Rogers, who wouldn't <yawn over it,> be an inspiration, you'll write it to Twichell, because it would make him writhe & squirm & break the furniture. When you are on fire with a good thing that's indecent, you won't waste it on Twichell, you'll save it for Howells, who will love it. As he will never see it, you can make it really indecenter than he could stand; & so no harm is done, yet a vast advantage is gained. . . .

VI

Posthumous Publications

Twain's posthumous writings have been problematic in several ways. Many of the works that he decided not to publish in his lifetime were fragmentary, unfinished, weakly developed, or too corrosive for his audience. In fairness it must also be admitted that some are difficult, tedious, or repetitious of themes already effectively expressed in his published writings. Several generations of devoted scholars have gradually brought this material to light.

A. B. Paine edited the volume Europe and Elsewhere *for publication in 1923. Five of the following selections come from this volume. They reveal Twain's understanding of the interaction of religion, morality, politics, and self-concern.*

Bernard DeVoto edited Letters from the Earth *in 1939, but Sam Clemens's only surviving daughter, Clara, did not wish it published. Finally, in 1961, the volume appeared. Twain's most fully developed attack on the Bible occurs in this volume. In* Letters from the Earth *Twain cleverly returns to the genre of travel letters, which he had used in* The Innocents Abroad. *But this time, instead of an American reporting about Europe, Twain imaginatively reports the words of an angel who wanders the earth. Satan is attempting to explain human religious beliefs, foibles, sexual practices, and inhibitions to the somewhat bored angels. Satan must explain human folly patiently, because so many human beliefs seem palpably absurd.*

A Word of Encouragement for Our Blushing Exiles

. . . Well, what do you think of our country *now?* And what do you think of the figure she is cutting before the eyes of the world? For one, I am ashamed—(Extract from a long and heated letter from a Voluntary Exile, Member of the American Colony, Paris.)

And so you are ashamed. I am trying to think out what it can have been that has produced this large attitude of mind and this fine flow of sarcasm. Apparently you are ashamed to look Europe in the face; ashamed of the American name; temporarily ashamed of your nationality. By the light of remarks made to me by an American here in Vienna, I judge that you are ashamed because:

1. We are meddling where we have no business and no right; meddling with the private family matters of a sister nation; intruding upon her sacred right to do as she pleases with her own, unquestioned by anybody.
2. We are doing this under a sham humanitarian pretext.
3. Doing it in order to filch Cuba, the formal and distinct disclaimer in the ultimatum being very, very thin humbug, and easily detectable as such by you and virtuous Europe.
4. And finally you are ashamed of all this because it is new, and base, and brutal, and dishonest; and because Europe, having had no previous experience of such things, is horrified by it and can never respect us nor associate with us any more.

Brutal, base, dishonest? We? Land thieves? Shedders of innocent blood? We? Traitors to our official word? We? Are we going to lose Europe's respect because of this new and dreadful conduct? Russia's, for instance? Is she lying stretched out on her back in Manchuria, with her head among her Siberian prisons and her feet in Port Arthur, trying to read over the fairy tales she told Lord Salisbury, and not able to do it for crying because we are maneuvering to treacherously smouch Cuba from feeble Spain, and because we are ungently shedding innocent Spanish blood?

Is it France's respect that we are going to lose? Is our unchivalric conduct troubling a nation which exists to-day because a brave young girl saved it when its poltroons had lost it—a nation which deserted her as one man when her day of peril came? Is our treacherous assault upon a weak people distressing a nation which contributed Bartholomew's Day to human history? Is our ruthless spirit offending the sensibilities of the nation which gave us the Reign of Terror to read about? Is our unmanly intrusion into the private affairs of a sister nation shocking the feelings of the people who sent Maximilian to Mexico? Are our shabby and pusillanimous ways outraging the fastidious people who have sent an innocent man (Dreyfus) to a living hell, taken to their embraces the slimy guilty one, and submitted to a thousand indignities Emile Zola—the manliest man in France?

Is it Spain's respect that we are going to lose? Is she sitting sadly conning her great history and contrasting it with our meddling, cruel, perfidious one—our shameful history of foreign robberies, humanitarian shams, and annihilations of weak and unoffending nations? Is she remembering with pride how she sent Columbus home in chains; how she sent half of the harmless West Indians into slavery and the rest to the grave, leaving not one alive; how she robbed and slaughtered the Inca's gentle race, then beguiled the Inca into her power with fair promises and burned him at the stake; how she drenched the New World in blood, and earned and got the name of The Nation with the Bloody Footprint; how she drove all the Jews out of Spain in a day, allowing them to sell their property, but forbidding them to carry any money out of the country; how she roasted heretics by the thousands and thousands in her public squares, generation after generation, her kings and her priests looking on as at a holiday show; how her Holy Inquisition imported hell into the earth; how she was the first to institute it and the last to give it up—and then only under compulsion; how, with a spirit unmodified by time, she still tortures her prisoners to-day; how, with her ancient passion for pain and blood unchanged, she still crowds the arena with ladies and gentlemen and priests to see with delight a bull harried and persecuted and a gored horse dragging his entrails on the ground; and how, with this incredible character surviving all attempts to civilize it, her Duke of Alva rises again in the person of General Weyler—to-day the most idolized personage in Spain—and we see a hundred thousand women and children shut up in pens and pitilessly starved to death?

Are we indeed going to lose Spain's respect? Is there no way to avoid this calamity—or this compliment? Are we going to lose her respect because we have made a promise in our ultimatum which she thinks we shall break? And meantime is she trying to recall some promise of her own which she has kept?

Is the Professional Official Fibber of Europe really troubled with our morals? Dear Parisian friend, are you taking seriously the daily remark of the newspaper and the orator about "this noble nation with an illustrious history"?

That is mere kindness, mere charity for a people in temporary hard luck. The newspaper and the orator do not mean it. They wink when they say it.

And so you are ashamed. Do not be ashamed; there is no occasion for it.

As Regards Patriotism

It is agreed, in this country, that if a man can arrange his religion so that it perfectly satisfies his conscience, it is not incumbent upon him to care whether the arrangement is satisfactory to anyone else or not.

In Austria and some other countries this is not the case. There the state arranges a man's religion for him, he has no voice in it himself.

Patriotism is merely a religion—love of country, worship of country, devotion to the country's flag and honor and welfare.

In absolute monarchies it is furnished from the throne, cut and dried, to the subject; in England and America it is furnished, cut and dried, to the citizen by the politician and the newspaper.

The newspaper-and-politician-manufactured Patriot often gags in private over his dose; but he takes it, and keeps it on his stomach the best he can. Blessed are the meek.

Sometimes, in the beginning of an insane shabby political upheaval, he is strongly moved to revolt, but he doesn't do it—he knows better. He knows that his maker would find it out—the maker of his Patriotism, the windy and incoherent six-dollar subeditor of his village newspaper—and would bray out in print and call him a Traitor. And how dreadful that would be. It makes him tuck his tail between his legs and shiver. We all know—the reader knows it quite well—that two or three years ago nine tenths of the human tails in England and America performed just that act. Which is to say, nine tenths of the Patriots in England and America turned traitor to keep from being called traitor. Isn't it true? You know it to be true. Isn't it curious?

Yet it was not a thing to be very seriously ashamed of. A man can seldom—very, very seldom—fight a winning fight against his training; the odds are too heavy. For many a year—perhaps always—the training of the two nations had been dead against independence in political thought, persistently inhospitable toward patriotism manufactured on a man's own premises, Patriotism reasoned out in the man's own head and fire-assayed and tested and proved in his own conscience. The resulting Patriotism was a shop-worn product procured at second hand. The Patriot did not know just how or when or where he got his opinions, neither did he care, so long as he was with what seemed the majority—which was the main thing, the safe thing, the comfortable thing. Does the reader believe he knows three men who have actual reasons for their pattern of Patriotism—and can furnish them? Let him not examine, unless he wants to be disappointed. He will be likely to find that his men got their Patriotism at the public trough, and had no hand in its preparation themselves.

Training does wonderful things. It moved the people of this country to oppose the Mexican War; then moved them to fall in with what they supposed was the opinion of the majority—majority Patriotism is the customary Patriotism—and go down there and fight. Before the Civil War it made the North indifferent to slavery and friendly to the slave interest: in that interest it made Massachusetts hostile to the American flag, and she would not allow it to be hoisted on her State House—in her eyes it was the flag of a faction. Then by and by, training swung Massachusetts the other way, and she went raging South to fight under that very flag and against that aforetime protected interest of hers.

There is nothing that training cannot do. Nothing is above its reach or below it. It can turn bad morals to good, good morals to bad; it can destroy principles, it can recreate them; it can debase angels to men and lift men to angelship. And it can do any one of these miracles in a year—even in six months.

Then men can be trained to manufacture their own Patriotism. They can be trained to labor it out in their own heads and hearts and in the privacy and independence of their own premises. It can train them to stop taking it by command, as the Austrian takes his religion.

Bible Teaching and Religious Practice

Religion had its share in the changes of civilization and national character, of course. What share? The lion's. In the history of the human race this has always been the case, will always be the case, to the end of time, no doubt; or at least until man by the slow processes of evolution shall develop into something really fine and high—some billions of years hence, say.

The Christian's Bible is a drug store. Its contents remain the same; but the medical practice changes. For eighteen hundred years these changes were slight—scarcely noticeable. The practice was allopathic—allopathic in its rudest and crudest form. The dull and ignorant physician day and night, and all the days and all the nights, drenched his patient with vast and hideous doses of the most repulsive drugs to be found in the store's stock; he bled him, cupped him, purged him, puked him, salivated him, never gave his system a chance to rally, nor nature a chance to help. He kept him religion sick for eighteen centuries, and allowed him not a well day during all that time. The stock in the store was made up of about equal portions of baleful and debilitating poisons, and healing and comforting medicines; but the practice of the time confined the physician to the use of the former; by consequence, he could only damage his patient, and that is what he did.

Not until far within our century was any considerable change in the practice introduced; and then mainly, or in effect only, in Great Britain and the United States. In the other countries to-day, the patient either still takes the ancient treatment or does not call the physician at all. In the English-speaking countries the changes observable in our century were forced by that very thing just referred to—the revolt of the patient against the system; they were not projected by the physician. The patient fell to doctoring himself, and the physician's practice began to fall off. He modified his method to get back his trade. He did it gradually, reluctantly; and never yielded more at a time than the pressure compelled. At first he relinquished the daily dose of hell and damnation, and administered it every other day only; next he allowed another day to pass; then another and presently another; when he had restricted it at last to Sundays, and imagined that now there would surely be a truce, the homoeopath arrived on the field and made him abandon hell and damnation altogether, and administered Christ's love, and comfort, and charity and compassion in its stead. These had been in the drug store all the time, gold labeled and conspicuous among the long shelfloads of repulsive purges and vomits and poisons, and so the practice was to blame that they had remained unused, not the pharmacy. To the ecclesiastical physician of fifty years ago, his predecessor for eighteen centuries was a quack; to the ecclesiastical physician of to-day, his predecessor of fifty years ago was a quack. To the every-man-his-own-ecclesiastical-doctor of—when?—what will the ecclesiastical physician of to-day be? Unless evolution, which has been a truth ever since the globes, suns, and planets of the solar system were but wandering films of meteor dust, shall reach a limit and become a lie, there is but one fate in store for him.

The methods of the priest and the parson have been very curious, their history is very entertaining. In all the ages the Roman Church has owned slaves, bought and sold slaves, authorized and encouraged her children to trade in them. Long after some Christian peoples had freed their slaves the Church still held on to hers. If any could know, to absolute certainty, that all this was right, and according to God's will and desire, surely it was she, since she was God's specially appointed representative in the earth and sole authorized and infallible expounder of his Bible. There were the texts; there was no mistaking their meaning; she was right, she was doing in this thing what the Bible had mapped out for her to do. So unassailable was her position that in all the centuries she had no word to say against human slavery. Yet now at last, in our immediate day, we hear a Pope saying slave trading is wrong, and we see him sending an expedition to Africa to stop it. The texts remain: it is the practice that has changed. Why? Because the world has corrected the Bible. The Church never corrects it; and also never fails to drop in at the tail of the procession—and take the credit of the correction. As she will presently do in this instance.

Christian England supported slavery and encouraged it for two hundred and fifty years, and her Church's consecrated ministers looked on, sometimes taking an active hand, the rest of the time indifferent. England's interest in the business may be called a Christian interest, a Christian industry. She had her full share in its revival after a long period of inactivity, and this revival was a Christian monopoly; that is to say, it was in the hands of Christian countries exclusively. English parliaments aided the slave traffic and protected it; two English kings held stock in slave-catching companies. The first regular English slave hunter—John Hawkins, of still revered memory—made such successful havoc, on his second voyage, in the matter of surprising and burning villages, and maiming, slaughtering, capturing, and selling their unoffending inhabitants, that his delighted queen conferred the chivalric honor of knighthood on him—a rank which had acquired its chief esteem and distinction in other and earlier fields of Christian effort. The new knight, with characteristic English frankness and brusque simplicity, chose as his device the figure of a negro slave, kneeling and in chains. Sir John's work was the invention of Christians, was to remain a bloody and awful monopoly in the hands of Christians for a quarter of a millennium, was to destroy homes, separate families, enslave friendless men and women, and break a myriad of human hearts, to the end that Christian nations might be prosperous and comfortable, Christian churches be built, and the gospel of the meek and merciful Redeemer be spread abroad in the earth; and so in the name of his ship, unsuspected but eloquent and clear, lay hidden prophecy. She was called *The Jesus.*

But at last in England, an illegitimate Christian rose against slavery. It is curious that when a Christian rises against a rooted wrong at all, he is usually an illegitimate Christian, member of some despised and bastard sect. There was a bitter struggle, but in the end the slave trade had to go—and went. The Biblical authorization remained, but the practice changed.

Then—the usual thing happened; the visiting English critic among us began straightway to hold up his pious hands in horror at our slavery. His distress was unappeasable, his words full of bitterness and contempt. It is true we had not so many as fifteen hundred thousand slaves for him to worry about, while his England still owned twelve millions, in her foreign possessions; but that fact did not modify his wail any, or stay his tears, or soften his censure. The fact that every time we had tried to get rid of our slavery in previous generations, but had always been obstructed, balked, and defeated by England, was a matter of no consequence to him; it was ancient history, and not worth the telling.

Our own conversion came at last. We began to stir against slavery. Hearts grew soft, here, there, and yonder. There was no place in the land where the seeker could not find some small budding sign of pity for the slave. No place in all the land but one—the pulpit. It yielded at last; it always does. It fought a strong and stubborn fight, and then did what it always does, joined the procession—at the tail end. Slavery fell. The slavery text remained; the practice changed, that was all.

During many ages there were witches. The Bible said so. The Bible commanded that they should not be allowed to live. Therefore the Church, after doing its duty in but a lazy and indolent way for eight hundred years, gathered up its halters, thumbscrews, and firebrands, and set about its holy work in earnest. She worked hard at it night and day during nine centuries and imprisoned, tortured, hanged, and burned whole hordes and armies of witches, and washed the Christian world clean with their foul blood.

Then it was discovered that there was no such thing as witches, and never had been. One does not know whether to laugh or to cry. Who discovered that there was no such thing as a witch—the priest, the parson? No, these never discover anything. At Salem, the parson clung pathetically to his witch text after the laity had abandoned it in remorse and tears for the crimes and cruelties it has persuaded them to do. The parson wanted more blood, more shame, more brutalities; it was the unconsecrated laity that stayed his hand. In Scotland the parson killed the witch after the magistrate had pronounced her innocent; and when the merciful legislature proposed to sweep the hideous laws against witches from the statute book, it was the parson who came imploring, with tears and imprecations, that they be suffered to stand.

There are no witches. The witch text remains; only the practice has changed. Hell fire is gone, but the text remains. Infant damnation is gone, but the text remains. More than two hundred death penalties are gone from the law books, but the texts that authorized them remain.

Is it not well worthy of note that of all the multitude of texts through which man has driven his annihilating pen he has never once made the mistake of obliterating a good and useful one? It does certainly seem to suggest that if man continues in the direction of enlightenment, his religious practice may, in the end, attain some semblance of human decency.

The War Prayer

It was a time of great and exalting excitement. The country was up in arms, the war was on, in every breast burned the holy fire of patriotism; the drums were beating, the bands playing, the toy pistols popping, the bunched firecrackers hissing and spluttering; on every hand and far down the receding and fading spread of roofs and balconies a fluttering wilderness of flags flashed in the sun; daily the young volunteers marched down the wide avenue gay and fine in their new uniforms, the proud fathers and mothers and sisters and sweethearts cheering them with voices choked with happy emotion as they swung by; nightly the packed mass meetings listened, panting, to patriot oratory which stirred the deepest deeps of their hearts, and which they interrupted at briefest intervals with cyclones of applause, the tears running down their cheeks the while; in the churches the pastors preached devotion to flag and country, and invoked the God of Battles, beseeching His aid in our good cause in outpouring of fervid eloquence which moved every listener. It was indeed a glad and gracious time, and the half dozen rash spirits that ventured to disapprove of the war and cast a doubt upon its righteousness straightway got such a stern and angry warning that for their personal safety's sake they quickly shrank out of sight and offended no more in that way.

Sunday morning came—next day the battalions would leave for the front; the church was filled; the volunteers were there, their young faces alight with martial dreams—visions of the stern advance, the gathering momentum, the rushing charge, the flashing sabers, the flight of the foe, the tumult, the enveloping smoke, the fierce pursuit, the surrender!—then home from the war, bronzed heroes, welcomed, adored, submerged in golden seas of glory! With the volunteers sat their dear ones, proud, happy, and envied by the neighbors and friends who had no sons and brothers to send forth to the field of honor, there to win for the flag, or, failing, die the noblest of noble deaths. The service proceeded; a war chapter from the Old Testament was read; the first prayer was said; it was followed by an organ burst that shook the building, and with one impulse the house rose, with glowing eyes and beating hearts, and poured out that tremendous invocation—

> "God the all-terrible! Thou who ordainest,
> Thunder thy clarion and lightning thy sword!"

Then came the "long" prayer. None could remember the like of it for passionate pleading and moving and beautiful language. The burden of its supplication was, that an ever-merciful and benignant Father of us all would watch over our noble young soldiers, and aid, comfort, and encourage them in their patriotic work; bless them, shield them in the day of battle and the hour of peril, bear them in His mighty hand, make them strong and confident, invincible in the bloody onset; help them to crush the foe, grant to them and to their flag and country imperishable honor and glory—

An aged stranger entered and moved with slow and noiseless step up the main aisle, his eyes fixed upon the minister, his long body clothed in a robe that reached to his feet, his head bare, his white hair descending in a frothy cataract to his shoulders, his seamy face unnaturally pale, pale even to ghastliness. With all eyes following him and wondering, he made his silent way; without pausing, he ascended to the preacher's side and stood there, waiting. With shut lids the preacher, unconscious of his presence, continued his moving prayer, and at last finished it with the words, uttered in fervent appeal, "Bless our arms, grant us the victory, O Lord our God, Father and Protector of our land and flag!"

The stranger touched his arm, motioned him to step aside—which the startled minister did—and took his place. During some moments he surveyed the spellbound audience with solemn eyes, in which burned an uncanny light; then in a deep voice he said:

"I come from the Throne—bearing a message from Almighty God!" The words smote the house with a shock; if the stranger perceived it he gave no attention "He has heard the prayer of His servant your shepherd, and will grant it if such shall be your desire after I, His messenger, shall have explained to you its import—that is to say, its full import. For it is like unto many of the prayers of men, in that it asks for more than he who utters it is aware of—except he pause and think.

"God's servant and yours has prayed his prayer. Has he paused and taken thought? Is it one prayer? No, it is two—one uttered, the other not. Both have reached the ear of Him Who heareth all supplications, the spoken and the unspoken. Ponder this—keep it in mind. If you would beseech a blessing upon yourself, beware! lest without intent you invoke a curse upon a neighbor at the same time. If you pray for the blessing of rain upon your crop which needs it, by that act you are possibly praying for a curse upon some neighbor's crop which may not need rain and can be injured by it.

"You have heard your servant's prayer—the uttered part of it. I am commissioned of God to put into words the other part of it—that part which the pastor—and also you in your hearts—fervently prayed silently. And ignorantly and unthinkingly? God grant that it was so! You heard these words: 'Grant us the victory, O Lord our God!' That is sufficient. The *whole* of the uttered prayer is compact into those pregnant words. Elaborations were not necessary. When you have prayed for victory you have prayed for many unmentioned results which follow victory—*must* follow it, cannot help but follow it. Upon the listening spirit of God the Father fell also the unspoken part of the prayer. He commandeth me to put it into words. Listen!

"O Lord our Father, our young patriots, idols of our hearts, go forth to battle—be Thou near them! With them—in spirit—we also go forth from the sweet peace of our beloved firesides to smite the foe. O Lord our God, help us to tear their soldiers to bloody shreds with our shells; help us to cover their smiling fields with the pale forms of their patriot dead; help us to drown the thunder of the guns with the shrieks of their wounded, writhing in pain; help us to lay waste their humble homes with a hurricane of fire; help us to wring the hearts of their unoffending widows with unavailing grief; help us to turn them out roofless with their little children to wander unfriended the wastes of their desolated land in rags and hunger and thirst, sports of the sun flames of summer and the icy winds of winter, broken in spirit, worn with travail, imploring Thee for the refuge of the grave and denied it—for our sakes who adore Thee, Lord, blast their hopes, blight their lives, protract their bitter pilgrimage, make heavy their steps, water their way with their tears, stain the white snow with the blood of their wounded feet! We ask it, in the spirit of love, of Him Who is the Source of Love, and Who is the ever-faithful refuge and friend of all that are sore beset and seek His aid with humble and contrite hearts. Amen."

(After a pause.) "Ye have prayed it; if ye still desire it, speak! The messenger of the Most High waits."

It was believed afterward that the man was a lunatic, because there was no sense in what he said.

Corn-Pone Opinions

Fifty years ago, when I was a boy of fifteen and helping to inhabit a Missourian village on the banks of the Mississippi, I had a friend whose society was very dear to me because I was forbidden by my mother to partake of it. He was a gay and impudent and satirical and delightful young black man—a slave—who daily preached sermons from the top of his master's woodpile, with me for sole audience. He imitated the pulpit style of the several clergymen of the village, and did it well, and with fine passion and energy. To me he was a wonder. I believed he was the greatest orator in the United States and would some day be heard from. But it did not happen; in the distribution of rewards he was overlooked. It is the way, in this world.

He interrupted his preaching, now and then, to saw a stick of wood; but the sawing was a pretense—he did it with his mouth; exactly imitating the sound the bucksaw makes in shrieking its way through the wood. But it served its purpose; it kept his master from coming out to see how the work was getting along. I listened to the sermons from the open window of a lumber room at the back of the house. One of his texts was this:

"You tell me whar a man gits his corn pone, en I'll tell you what his 'pinions is."

I can never forget it. It was deeply impressed upon me. By my mother. Not upon my memory, but elsewhere. She had slipped in upon me while I was absorbed and not watching. The black philosopher's idea was that a man is not independent, and cannot afford views which might interfere with his bread and butter. If he would prosper, he must train with the majority; in matters of large moment, like politics and religion, he must think and feel with the bulk of his neighbors, or suffer damage in his social standing and in his business prosperities. He must restrict himself to corn-pone opinions—at least on the surface. He must get his opinions from other people; he must reason out none for himself; he must have no first-hand views.

I think Jerry was right, in the main, but I think he did not go far enough.

1. It was his idea that a man conforms to the majority view of his locality by calculation and intention.

This happens, but I think it is not the rule.

2. It was his idea that there is such a thing as a first-hand opinion; an original opinion; an opinion which is coldly reasoned out in a man's head, by a searching analysis of the facts involved, with the heart unconsulted, and the jury room closed against outside influences. It may be that such an opinion has been born somewhere, at some time or other, but I suppose it got away before they could catch it and stuff it and put it in the museum.

I am persuaded that a coldly-thought-out and independent verdict upon a fashion in clothes, or manners, or literature, or politics, or religion, or any other matter that is projected into the field of our notice and interest, is a most rare thing—if it has indeed ever existed.

A new thing in costume appears—the flaring hoopskirt, for example—and the passers-by are shocked, and the irreverent laugh. Six months later everybody is reconciled; the fashion has established itself; is admired, now, and no one laughs. Public opinion resented it before, public opinion accepts it now, and is happy in it. Why? Was the resentment reasoned out? Was the acceptance reasoned out? No. The instinct that moves to conformity did the work. It is our nature to conform; it is a force which not many can successfully resist. What is its seat? The inborn requirement of self-approval. We all have to bow to that; there are no exceptions. Even the woman who refuses from first to last to wear the hoopskirt comes under that law and is its slave; she could not wear the skirt and have her own approval; and that she *must* have, she cannot help herself. But as a rule our self-approval has its source in but one place and not elsewhere—the approval of other people. A person of vast consequences can introduce any kind of novelty in dress and the general world will presently adopt it—moved to do it, in the first place, by the natural instinct to passively yield to that vague something recognized as authority, and in the second place by the human instinct to train with the multitude and have its approval. An empress introduced the hoopskirt, and we know the result. A nobody introduced the bloomer, and we know the result. If Eve should come again, in her ripe renown, and reintroduce her quaint styles—well, we know what would happen. And we should be cruelly embarrassed, along at first.

The hoopskirt runs its course and disappears. Nobody reasons about it. One woman abandons the fashion; her neighbor notices this and follows her lead; this influences the next woman; and so on and so on, and presently the skirt has vanished out of the world, no one knows how nor why; nor cares, for that matter. It will come again, by and by; and in due course will go again.

Twenty-five years ago, in England, six or eight wine glasses stood grouped by each person's plate at a dinner party, and they were used, not left idle and empty; to-day there are but three or four in the group, and the average guest sparingly uses about two of them. We have not adopted this new fashion yet, but we shall do it presently. We shall not think it out; we shall merely conform, and let it go at that. We get our notions and habits and opinions from outside influences; we do not have to study them out.

Our table manners, and company manners, and street manners change from time to time, but the changes are not reasoned out; we merely notice and conform. We are creatures of outside influences; as a rule we do not think, we only imitate. We cannot invent standards that will stick; what we mistake for standards are only fashions, and perishable. We may continue to admire them, but we drop the use of them. We notice this in literature. Shakespeare is a standard, and fifty years ago we used to write tragedies which we couldn't tell from—from somebody else's; but we don't do it any more, now. Our prose standard, three quarters of a century ago, was ornate and diffuse; some authority or other changed it in the direction of compactness and simplicity, and conformity followed, without argument. The historical novel starts up suddenly, and sweeps the land. Everybody writes one, and the nation is glad. We had historical novels before; but nobody read them, and the rest of us conformed—without reasoning it out. We are conforming in the other way, now, because it is another case of everybody.

The outside influences are always pouring in upon us, and we are always obeying their orders and accepting their verdicts. The Smiths like the new play; the Joneses go to see it, and they copy the Smith verdict. Morals, religions, politics, get their following from surrounding influences and atmospheres, almost entirely; not from study, not from thinking. A man must and will have his own approval first of all, in each and every moment and circumstance of his life—even if he must repent of a self-approved act the moment after its commission, in order to get his self-approval *again:* but, speaking in general terms, a man's self-approval in the large concerns of life has its source in the approval of the peoples about him, and not in a searching personal examination of the matter. Mohammedans are Mohammedans because they are born and reared among that sect, not because they have thought it out and can furnish sound reasons for being Mohammedans; we know why Catholics are Catholics; why Presbyterians are Presbyterians; why Baptists are Baptists, why Mormons are Mormons; why thieves are thieves; why monarchists are monarchists; why Republicans are Republicans and Democrats, Democrats. We know it is a matter of association and sympathy, not reasoning and examination; that hardly a man in the world has an opinion upon morals, politics, or religion which he got otherwise than through his associations and sympathies. Broadly speaking, there are none but corn-pone opinions. And broadly speaking, corn-pone stands for self-approval. Self-approval is acquired mainly from the approval of other people. The result is conformity. Sometimes conformity has a sordid business interest—the bread-and-butter interest—but not in most cases, I think. I think that in the majority of cases it is unconscious and not calculated; that it is born of the human being's natural yearning to stand well with his fellows and have their inspiring approval and praise—a yearning which is commonly so strong and so insistent that it cannot be effectually resisted, and must have its way.

A political emergency brings out the corn-pone opinion in fine force in its two chief varieties—the pocketbook variety, which has its origin in self-interest, and the bigger variety, the sentimental variety—the one which can't bear to be outside the pale; can't bear to be in disfavor; can't endure the averted face and the cold shoulder; wants to stand well with his friends, wants to be smiled upon, wants to be welcome, wants to hear the precious words, "*He's* on the right track!" Uttered, perhaps by an ass, but still an ass of high degree, an ass whose approval is gold and diamonds to a smaller ass, and confers glory and honor and happiness, and membership in the herd. For these gauds many a man will dump his life-long principles into the street, and his conscience along with them. We have seen it happen. In some millions of instances.

Men think they think upon great political questions, and they do; but they think with their party, not independently; they read its literature, but not that of the other side; they arrive at convictions, but they are drawn from a partial view of the matter in hand and are of no particular value. They swarm with their party, they feel with their party, they are happy in their party's approval; and where the party leads they will follow, whether for right and honor, or through blood and dirt and a mush of mutilated morals.

In our late canvass half of the nation passionately believed that in silver lay salvation, the other half as passionately believed that that way lay destruction. Do you believe that a tenth part of the people, on either side, had any rational excuse for having an opinion about the matter at all? I studied that mighty question to the bottom—came out empty. Half of our people passionately believe in high tariff, the other half believe otherwise. Does this mean study and examination, or only feeling? The latter, I think. I have deeply studied that question, too—and didn't arrive. We all do no end of feeling, and we mistake it for thinking. And out of it we get an aggregation which we consider a boon. Its name is Public Opinion. It is held in reverence. It settles everything. Some think it the Voice of God.

Letters from the Earth

LETTER II

"I have told you nothing about man that is not true." You must pardon me if I repeat that remark now and then in these letters; I want you to take seriously the things I am telling you, and I feel that if I were in your place and you in mine, I should need that reminder from time to time, to keep my credulity from flagging.

For there is nothing about man that is not strange to an immortal. He looks at nothing as we look at it, his sense of proportion is quite different from ours, and his sense of values is so widely divergent from ours, that with all our large intellectual powers it is not likely that even the most gifted among us would ever be quite able to understand it.

For instance, take this sample: he has imagined a heaven, and has left entirely out of it the supremest of all his delights, the one ecstasy that stands first and foremost in the heart of every individual of his race—and of ours—sexual intercourse!

It is as if a lost and perishing person in a roasting desert should be told by a rescuer he might choose and have all longed-for things but one, and he should elect to leave out water!

His heaven is like himself: strange, interesting, astonishing, grotesque. I give you my word, it has not a single feature in it that he *actually values.* It consists—utterly and entirely—of diversions which he cares next to nothing about, here in the earth, yet is quite sure he will like in heaven. Isn't it curious? Isn't it interesting? You must not think I am exaggerating, for it is not so. I will give you details.

Most men do not sing, most men cannot sing, most men will not stay where others are singing if it be continued more than two hours. Note that.

Only about two men in a hundred can play upon a musical instrument, and not four in a hundred have any wish to learn how. Set that down.

Many man pray, not many of them like to do it. A few pray long, the others make a short cut.

More men go to church than want to.

To forty-nine men in fifty the Sabbath Day is a dreary, dreary bore.

Of all the men in a church on a Sunday, two-thirds are tired when the service is half over, and the rest before it is finished.

The gladdest moment for all of them is when the preacher uplifts his hands for the benediction. You can hear the soft rustle of relief that sweeps the house,and you recognize that it is eloquent with gratitude.

All nations look down upon all other nations.

All nations dislike all other nations.

All white nations despise all colored nations, of whatever hue, and oppress them when they can.

White men will not associate with "niggers," nor marry them.

They will not allow them in their schools and churches.

All the world hates the Jew, and will not endure him except when he is rich.

I ask you to note all those particulars.

Further. All sane people detest noise.

All people, sane or insane, like to have variety in their life. Monotony quickly wearies them.

Every man, according to the mental equipment that has fallen to his share, exercises his intellect constantly, ceaselessly, and this exercise makes up a vast and valued and essential part of his life. The lowest intellect, like the highest, possesses a skill of some kind and takes a keen pleasure in testing it, proving it, perfecting it. The urchin who is his comrade's superior in games is as diligent and as enthusiastic in his practice as are the sculptor, the painter, the pianist, the mathematician and the rest. Not one of them could be happy if his talent were put under an interdict.

Now then, you have the facts. You know what the human race enjoys, and what it doesn't enjoy. It has invented a heaven, out of its own head, all by itself: guess what it is like! In fifteen hundred eternities you couldn't do it. The ablest mind known to you or me in fifty million aeons couldn't do it. Very well, I will tell you about it.

1. First of all, I recall to your attention the extraordinary fact with which I began. To wit, that the human being, like the immortals, naturally places sexual intercourse far and away above all other joys—yet he has left it out of his heaven! The very thought of it excites him; opportunity sets him wild; in this state he will risk life, reputation, everything—even his queer heaven itself—to make good that opportunity and ride it to the overwhelming climax. From youth to middle age all men and all women prize copulation above all other pleasures combined, yet it is actually as I have said: it is not in their heaven; prayer takes its place.

They prize it thus highly; yet, like all their so-called "boons," it is a poor thing. At its very best and longest the act is brief beyond imagination—the imagination of an immortal, I mean. In the matter of repetition the man is limited—oh, quite beyond immortal conception. We who continue the act and its supremest ecstasies unbroken and without withdrawal for centuries, will never be able to understand or adequately pity the awful poverty of these people in that rich gift which, possessed as we possess it, makes all other possessions trivial and not worth the trouble of invoicing.

2. In man's heaven *everybody sings!* The man who did not sing on earth sings there; the man who could not sing on earth is able to do it there. This universal singing is not casual, not occasional, not relieved by intervals of quiet; it goes on, all day long, and every day, during a stretch of twelve hours. And *everybody stays;* whereas in the earth the place would be empty in two hours. The singing is of hymns alone. Nay, it is of one hymn alone. The words are always the same, in number they are only about a dozen, there is no rhyme, there is no poetry: "Hosannah, hosannah, hosannah, Lord God of Sabaoth, 'rah! 'rah! 'rah! siss!—boom! . . . a-a-ah!"

3. Meantime, every person is playing on a harp—those millions and millions!—whereas not more than twenty in the thousand of them could play an instrument in the earth, or ever wanted to.

Consider the deafening hurricane of sound—millions and millions of voices screaming at once and millions and millions of harps gritting their teeth at the same time! I ask you: is it hideous, is it odious, is it horrible?

Consider further: it is a *praise* service; a service of compliment, of flattery, of adulation! Do you ask who it is that is willing to endure this strange compliment, this insane compliment; and who not only endures it, but likes it, enjoys it, requires it, *commands* it? Hold your breath!

It is God! This race's God, I mean. He sits on his throne, attended by his four and twenty elders and some other dignitaries pertaining to his court, and looks out over his miles and miles of tempestuous worshipers, and smiles, and purrs, and nods his satisfaction northward, eastward, southward; as quaint and naïve a spectacle as has yet been imagined in this universe, I take it.

It is easy to see that the inventor of the heavens did not originate the idea, but copied it from the show-ceremonies of some sorry little sovereign State up in the back settlements of the Orient somewhere.

All sane white people hate noise; yet they have tranquilly accepted this kind of a heaven—without thinking, without reflection, without examination—and they actually want to go to it! Profoundly devout old gray-headed men put in a large part of their time dreaming of the happy day when they will lay down the cares of this life and enter into the joys of that place. Yet you can see how unreal it is to them, and how little it takes a grip upon them as being fact, for they make no practical preparation for the great change: you never see one of them with a harp, you never hear one of them sing.

As you have seen, that singular show is a service of praise: praise by hymn, praise by prostration. It takes the place of "church." Now then, in the earth these people cannot stand much church—an hour and a quarter is the limit, and they draw the line at once a week. That is to say, Sunday. One day in seven; and even then they do not look forward to it with longing. And so—consider what their heaven provides for them: "church" that lasts forever, and a Sabbath that has no end! They quickly weary of this brief hebdomadal Sabbath here, yet they long for that eternal one; they dream of it, they talk about it, they *think* they think they are going to enjoy it—with all their simple hearts they think they think they are going to be happy in it!

It is because they do not think at all; they only think they think. Whereas they can't think; not two human beings in ten thousand have anything to think with. And as to imagination—oh, well, look at their heaven! They accept it, they approve it, they admire it. That gives you their intellectual measure.

4. The inventor of their heaven empties into it all the nations of the earth, in one common jumble. All are on an equality absolute, no one of them ranking another; they have to be "brothers"; they have to mix together, pray together, harp together, hosannah together—whites, niggers, Jews, everybody—there's no distinction. Here in the earth all nations hate each other, and every one of them hates the Jew. Yet every pious person adores that heaven and wants to get into it. He really does. And when he is in a holy rapture he thinks he thinks that if he were only there he would take all the populace to his heart, and hug, and hug, and hug!

He is a marvel—man is! I would I knew who invented him.

5. Every man in the earth possesses some share of intellect, large or small; and be it large or be it small he takes a pride in it. Also his heart swells at mention of the names of the majestic intellectual chiefs of his race, and he loves the tale of their splendid achievements. For he is of their blood, and in honoring themselves they have honored him. Lo, what the mind of man can do! he cries; and calls the roll of the illustrious of all the ages; and points to the imperishable literatures they have given to the world, and the mechanical wonders they have invented, and the glories wherewith they have clothed science and the arts; and to them he uncovers, as to kings, and gives to them the profoundest homage, and the sincerest, his exultant heart can furnish—thus exalting intellect about all things else in his world, and enthroning it there under the arching skies in a supremacy unapproachable. And then he contrives a heaven that hasn't a rag of intellectuality in it anywhere!

Is it odd, is it curious, is it puzzling? It is exactly as I have said, incredible as it may sound. This sincere adorer of intellect and prodigal rewarder of its mighty services here in the earth has invented a religion and a heaven which pay no compliments to intellect, offer it no distinctions, fling to it no largess: in fact, never even mention it.

By this time you will have noticed that the human being's heaven has been thought out and constructed upon an absolutely definite plan; and that this plan is, that it shall contain, in labored detail, each and every imaginable thing that is repulsive to a man, and not a single thing he likes!

Very well, the further we proceed the more will this curious fact be apparent.

Make a note of it: in man's heaven there are no exercises for the intellect, nothing for it to live upon. It would rot there in a year—rot and stink. Rot and stink—and at that stage become holy. A blessed thing: for only the holy can stand the joys of that bedlam.

LETTER III

You have noticed that the human being is a curiosity. In times past he has had (and worn out and flung away) hundreds and hundreds of religions; today he has hundreds and hundreds of religions, and launches not fewer than three new ones every year. I could enlarge that number and still be within the facts.

One of his principal religious is called the Christian. A sketch of it will interest you. It is set forth in detail in a book containing two million words, called the Old and New Testaments. Also it has another name—The Word of God. For the Christian thinks every word of it was dictated by God—the one I have been speaking of.

It is full of interest. It has noble poetry in it; and some clever fables; and some blood-drenched history; and some good morals; and a wealth of obscenity; and upwards of a thousand lies.

This Bible is built mainly out of the fragments of older Bibles that had their day and crumbled to ruin. So it noticeably lacks in originality, necessarily. Its three or four most imposing and impressive events all happened in earlier Bibles; all its best precepts and rules of conduct came also from those Bibles; there are only two new things in it: hell, for one, and that singular heaven I have told you about.

What shall we do? If we believe, with these people, that their God invented these cruel things, we slander him; if we believe that these people invented them themselves, we slander them. It is an unpleasant dilemma in either case, for neither of these parties has done us any harm.

For the sake of tranquillity, let us take a side. Let us join forces with the people and put the whole ungracious burden upon *him*—heaven, hell, Bible and all. It does not seem right, it does not seem fair; and yet when you consider that heaven, and how crushingly charged it is with everything that is repulsive to a human being, how can we believe a human being invented it? And when I come to tell you about hell, the strain will be greater still, and you will be likely to say, No, a man would not provide that place, for either himself or anybody else; he simply couldn't.

That innocent Bible tells about the Creation. Of what—the universe? Yes, the universe. In six days!

God did it. He did not call it the universe—that name is modern. His whole attention was upon this world. He constructed it in five days—and then? It took him only one day to make twenty million suns and eighty million planets!

What were they for—according to his idea? To furnish light for this little toy-world. That was his whole purpose; he had no other. One of the twenty million suns (the smallest one) was to light it in the daytime, the rest were to help one of the universe's countless moons modify the darkness of its nights.

It is quite manifest that he believed his fresh-made skies were diamond-sown with those myriads of twinkling stars the moment his first-day's sun sank below the horizon; whereas, in fact, not a single star winked in that black vault until three years and a half after that memorable week's formidable industries had been completed.* Then one star appeared, all solitary and alone, and began to blink. Three years later another one appeared. The two blinked together for more than four years before a third joined them. At the end of the first hundred years there were not yet twenty-five stars twinkling in the wide wastes of those gloomy skies. At the end of a thousand years not enough stars were yet visible to make a show. At the end of a million years only half of the present array had sent their light over the telescopic frontiers, and it took another million for the rest to follow suit, as the vulgar phrase goes. There being at that time no telescope, their advent was not observed.

For three hundred years, now, the Christian astronomer has known that his Deity didn't make the stars in those tremendous six days; but the Christian astronomer does not enlarge upon that detail. Neither does the priest.

In his Book, God is eloquent in his praises of his mighty works, and calls them by the largest names he can find—thus indicating that he has a strong and just admiration of magnitudes; yet he made those millions of prodigious suns to light this wee little orb, instead of appointing this orb's little sun to dance attendance upon them. He mentions Arcturus in his Book—you remember Arcturus; we went there once. It is one of this earth's night lamps!—that giant globe which is fifty thousand times as large as this earth's sun, and compares with it as a melon compares with a cathedral.

However, the Sunday school still teaches the child that Arcturus was created to help light this earth, and the child grows up and continues to believe it long after he has found out that the probabilities are against its being so.

According to the Book and its servants the universe is only six thousand years old. It is only within the last hundred years that studious, inquiring minds have found out that it is nearer a hundred million.

During the Six Days, God created man and the other animals.

He made a man and a woman and placed them in a pleasant garden, along with the other creatures. They all lived together there in harmony and contentment and blooming youth for some time; then trouble came. God had warned the man and the woman that they must not eat of the fruit of a certain tree. And he added a most strange remark: he said that if they ate of it they should surely die. Strange, for the reason that inasmuch as they had never seen a

*It takes the light of the nearest star (61 Cygni) three and a half years to come to the earth, traveling at the rate of 186,000 miles per second. Arcturus had been shining 200 years before it was visible from the earth. Remoter stars gradually became visible after thousands and thousands of years.—THE EDITOR [M. T.]

sample of death they could not possibly know what he meant. Neither would he nor any other god have been able to make those ignorant children understand what was meant, without furnishing a sample. The mere word could have no meaning for them, any more than it would have for an infant of days.

Presently a serpent sought them out privately, and came to them walking upright, which was the way of serpents in those days. The serpent said the forbidden fruit would store their vacant minds with knowledge. So they ate it, which was quite natural, for man is so made that he eagerly wants to know; whereas the priest, like God, whose imitator and representative he is, has made it his business from the beginning to keep him *from* knowing any useful thing.

Adam and Eve ate the forbidden fruit, and at once a great light streamed into their dim heads. They had acquired knowledge. What knowledge—useful knowledge? No—merely knowledge that there was such a thing as good, and such a thing as evil, and how to do evil. They couldn't do it before. Therefore all their acts up to this time had been without stain, without blame, without offense.

But now they could do evil—and suffer for it; now they had acquired what the Church calls an invaluable possession, the Moral Sense; that sense which differentiates man from the beast and sets him above the beast. Instead of below the beast—where one would suppose his proper place would be, since he is always foul-minded and guilty and the beast always clean-minded and innocent. It is like valuing a watch that must go wrong, above a watch that can't.

The Church still prizes the Moral Sense as man's noblest asset today, although the Church knows God had a distinctly poor opinion of it and did what he could in his clumsy way to keep his happy Children of the Garden from acquiring it.

Very well, Adam and Eve now knew what evil was, and how to do it. They knew how to do various kinds of wrong things, and among them one principal one—the one God had his mind on principally. That one was the art and mystery of sexual intercourse. To them it was a magnificent discovery, and they stopped idling around and turned their entire attention to it, poor exultant young things!

In the midst of one of these celebrations they heard God walking among the bushes, which was an afternoon custom of his, and they were smitten with fright. Why? Because they were naked. They had not known it before. They had not minded it before; neither had God.

In that memorable moment immodesty was born; and some people have valued it ever since, though it would certainly puzzle them to explain why.

Adam and Eve entered the world naked and unashamed—naked and pure-minded; and no descendant of theirs has ever entered it otherwise. All have entered it naked, unashamed, and clean in mind. They have entered it modest. They had to acquire immodesty and the soiled mind; there was no other way to get it. A Christian mother's first duty is to soil her child's mind, and she does not neglect it. Her lad grows up to be a missionary, and goes to the innocent savage and to the civilized Japanese, and soils their minds. Whereupon they adopt immodesty, they conceal their bodies, they stop bathing naked together.

The convention miscalled modesty has no standard, and cannot have one, because it is opposed to nature and reason, and is therefore an artificiality and subject to anybody's whim, anybody's diseased caprice. And so, in India the refined lady covers her face and breasts and leaves her legs naked from the hips down, while the refined European lady covers her legs and exposes her face and her breasts. In lands inhabited by the innocent savage the refined European lady soon gets used to full-grown native stark-nakedness, and ceases to be offended by it. A highly cultivated French count and countess—unrelated to each other—who were marooned in their nightclothes, by shipwreck, upon an uninhabited island in the eighteenth century, were soon naked. Also ashamed—for a week. After that their nakedness did not trouble them, and they soon ceased to think about it.

You have never seen a person with clothes on. Oh, well, you haven't lost anything.

To proceed with the Biblical curiosities. Naturally you will think the threat to punish Adam and Eve for disobeying was of course not carried out, since they did not create themselves, nor their natures nor their impulses nor their weaknesses, and hence were not properly subject to anyone's commands, and not responsible to anybody for their acts. It will surprise you to know that the threat was carried out. Adam and Eve were punished, and that crime finds apologists unto this day. The sentence of death was executed.

As you perceive, the only person responsible for the couple's offense escaped; and not only escaped but became the executioner of the innocent.

In your country and mine we should have the privilege of making fun of this kind of morality, but it would be unkind to do it here. Many of these people have the reasoning faculty, but no one uses it in religious matters.

The best minds will tell you that when a man has begotten a child he is morally bound to tenderly care for it, protect it from hurt, shield it from disease, clothe it, feed it, bear with its waywardness, lay no hand upon it save in kindness and for its own good, and never in any case inflict upon it a wanton cruelty. God's treatment of his earthly children, every day and every night, is the exact opposite of all that, yet those best minds warmly justify these crimes, condone them, excuse them, and indignantly refuse to regard them as crimes at all when *he* commits them. Your country and mine is an interesting one, but there is nothing there that is half so interesting as the human mind.

Very well, God banished Adam and Eve from the Garden, and eventually assassinated them. All for disobeying a command which he had no right to utter. But he did not stop there, as you will see. He has one code of morals for himself, and quite another for his children. He requires his children to deal justly—and gently—with offenders, and forgive them seventy-and-seven times; whereas he deals neither justly nor gently with anyone, and he did not forgive the ignorant and thoughtless first pair of juveniles even their first small offense and say, "You may go free this time, I will give you another chance."

On the contrary! He elected to punish *their* children, all through the ages to the end of time, for a trifling offense committed by others before they were born. He is punishing them yet. In mild ways? No, in atrocious ones.

You would not suppose that this kind of a Being gets many compliments. Undeceive yourself: the world calls him the All-Just, the All-Righteous, the All-Good, the All-Merciful, the All-Forgiving, the All-Truthful, the All-Loving, the Source of All Morality. These sarcasms are uttered daily, all over the world. But not as conscious sarcasms. No, they are meant seriously: they are uttered without a smile.

LETTER VIII

Man is without any doubt the most interesting fool there is. Also the most eccentric. He hasn't a single written law, in his Bible or out of it, which has any but just one purpose and intention—to *limit or defeat a law of God.*

He can seldom take a plain fact and get any but a wrong meaning out of it. He cannot help this; it is the way the confusion he calls his mind is constructed. Consider the things he concedes, and the curious conclusions he draws from them.

For instance, he concedes that God made man. Made him without man's desire or privity.

This seems to plainly and indisputably make God, and God alone, responsible for man's acts. But man denies this.

He concedes that God has made angels perfect, without blemish, and immune from pain and death, and that he could have been similarly kind to man if he had wanted to, but denies that he was under any moral obligation to do it.

He concedes that man has no moral right to visit the child of his begetting with wanton cruelties, painful diseases and death, but refuses to limit God's privileges in this sort with the children of his begetting.

The Bible and man's statutes forbid murder, adultery, fornication, lying, treachery, robbery, oppression and other crimes, but contend that God is free of these laws and has a right to break them when he will.

He concedes that God gives to each man his temperament, his disposition, at birth; he concedes that man cannot by any process change this temperament, but must remain always under its dominion. Yet if it be full of dreadful passions, in one man's case, and barren of them in another man's, it is right and rational to punish the one for his crimes, and reward the other for abstaining from crime.

There—let us consider these curiosities.

Temperament (Disposition)

Take two extremes of temperament—the goat and the tortoise.

Neither of these creatures makes its own temperament, but is born with it, like man, and can no more change it than can man.

Temperament is the law of God written in the heart of every creature by

God's own hand, and *must* be obeyed, and will be obeyed in spite of all restricting or forbidding statutes, let them emanate whence they may.

Very well, lust is the dominant feature of the goat's temperament, the law of God in its heart, and it must obey it and will obey it the whole day long in the rutting season, without stopping to eat or drink. If the Bible said to the goat, "Thou shalt not fornicate, thou shalt not commit adultery," even Man—sap-headed man—would recognize the foolishness of the prohibition, and would grant that the goat ought not to be punished for obeying the law of his Maker. Yet he thinks it right and just that man should be put under the prohibition. All men. All alike.

On its face this is stupid, for, by temperament, which is the *real law* of God, many men are goats and can't help committing adultery when they get a chance; whereas there are numbers of men who, by temperament, can keep their purity and let an opportunity go by if the woman lacks in attractiveness. But the Bible doesn't allow adultery at all, whether a person can help it or not. It allows no distinction between goat and tortoise—the excitable goat, the emotional goat, that has to have some adultery every day or fade and die; and the tortoise, that cold calm puritan, that takes a treat only once in two years and then goes to sleep in the midst of it and doesn't wake up for sixty days. No lady goat is safe from criminal assault, even on the Sabbath Day, when there is a gentleman goat within three miles to leeward of her and nothing in the way but a fence fourteen feet high, whereas neither the gentleman tortoise nor the lady tortoise is ever hungry for the solemn joys of fornication to be willing to break the Sabbath to get them. Now according to man's curious reasoning, the goat has earned punishment, and the tortoise praise.

"Thou shalt not commit adultery" is a command which makes no distinction between the following persons. They are all required to obey it:

Children at birth.
Children in the cradle.
School children.
Youths and maidens.
Fresh adults.
Older ones.
Men and women of 40.
Of 50.
Of 60.
Of 70.
Of 80.
Of 90.
Of 100.

The command does not distribute its burden equally, and cannot.

It is not hard upon the three sets of children.

It is hard—harder—still harder upon the next three sets—cruelly hard.

It is blessedly softened to the next three sets.

It has now done all the damage it can, and might as well be put out of commission. Yet with comical imbecility it is continued, and the four remaining estates are put under its crushing ban. Poor old wrecks, they couldn't disobey if they tried. And think—because they holily refrain from adulterating each other, they get praise for it! Which is nonsense; for even the Bible knows enough to know that if the oldest veteran there could get his lost heyday back again for an hour he would cast that commandment to the winds and ruin the first woman he came across, even though she were an entire stranger.

It is as I have said: every statute in the Bible and in the law books is an attempt to defeat a law of God—in other words an unalterable and indestructible law of nature. These people's God has shown them by a million acts that he respects none of the Bible's statutes. He breaks every one of them himself, adultery and all.

The law of God, as quite plainly expressed in woman's construction, is this: There shall be no limit put upon your intercourse with the other sex sexually, at any time of life.

The law of God, as quite plainly expressed in man's construction, is this: During your entire life you shall be under inflexible limits and restrictions, sexually.

During twenty-three days in every month (in the absence of pregnancy) from the time a woman is seven years old till she dies of old age, she is ready for action, and *competent*. As competent as the candlestick is to receive the candle. Competent every day, competent every night. Also, she *wants* that candle—yearns for it, longs for it, hankers after it, as commanded by the law of God in her heart.

But man is only briefly competent; and only then in the moderate measure applicable to the word in *his* sex's case. He is competent from the age of sixteen or seventeen thenceforward for thirty-five years. After fifty his performance is of poor quality, the intervals between are wide, and its satisfactions of no great value to either party; whereas his great-grandmother is as good as new. There is nothing the matter with her plant. Her candlestick is as firm as ever, whereas his candle is increasingly softened and weakened by the weather of age, as the years go by, until at last it can no longer stand, and is mournfully laid to rest in the hope of a blessed resurrection which is never to come.

By the woman's make, her plant has to be out of service three days in the month and during a part of her pregnancy. These are times of discomfort, often of suffering. For fair and just compensation she has the high privilege of unlimited adultery all the other days of her life.

That is the law of God, as revealed in her make. What becomes of this high privilege? Does she live in the free enjoyment of it? No. Nowhere in the whole world. She is robbed of it everywhere. Who does this? Man. Man's statutes—if the Bible *is* the Word of God.

Now there you have a sample of man's "reasoning powers," as he calls them. He observes certain facts. For instance, that in all his life he never sees the day that he can satisfy one woman; also, that no woman ever sees the day that she can't overwork, and defeat, and put out of commission any ten masculine plants that can be put to bed to her.* He puts those strikingly suggestive and luminous facts together, and from them draws this astonishing conclusion: The Creator intended the woman to be restricted to one man.

So he concretes that singular conclusion into a *law,* for good and all.

And he does it without consulting the woman, although she has a thousand times more at stake in the matter than he has. His procreative competency is limited to an average of a hundred exercises per year for fifty years, hers is good for three thousand a year for that whole time—and as many years longer as she may live. Thus his life interest in the matter is five thousand refreshments, while hers is a hundred and fifty thousand; yet instead of fairly and honorably leaving the making of the law to the person who has an overwhelming interest at stake in it, this immeasurable hog, who has nothing at stake in it worth considering, makes it himself!

You have heretofore found out, by my teachings, that man is a fool; you are now aware that woman is a damned fool.

Now if you or any other really intelligent person were arranging the fairnesses and justices between man and woman, you would give the man a one-fiftieth interest in one woman, and the woman a harem. Now wouldn't you? Necessarily. I give you my word, this creature with the decrepit candle has arranged it exactly the other way. Solomon, who was one of the Deity's favorites, had a copulation cabinet composed of seven hundred wives and three hundred concubines. To save his life he could not have kept two of those young creatures satisfactorily refreshed, even if he had had fifteen experts to help him. Necessarily almost the entire thousand had to go hungry years and years on a stretch. Conceive of a man hardhearted enough to look daily upon all that suffering and not be moved to mitigate it. He even wantonly added a sharp pang to that pathetic misery; for he kept within those women's sight, always, stalwart watchmen whose splendid masculine forms made the poor lassies' mouths water but who hadn't anything to solace a candlestick with, these gentry being eunuchs. A eunuch is a person whose candle has been put out. By art.**

From time to time, as I go along, I will take up a Biblical statute and show you that it always violates a law of God, and then is imported into the lawbooks of the nations, where it continues its violations. But those things will keep; there is no hurry.

*In the Sandwich Islands in 1866 a buxom royal princes died. Occupying a place of distinguished honor at her funeral were thirty-six splendidly built young native men. In a iaudatory song which celebrated the various merits, achievements and accomplishments of the late princess those thirty-six stallions were called her *harem*, and the song said it had been her pride and boast that she kept the whole of them busy, and that several times it had happened that more than one of them had been able to charge overtime. [M. T.]

**I purpose publishing these Letters here in the world before I return to you. Two editions. One, unedited, for Bible readers and their children; the other, expurgated, for persons of refinement. [M. T.]

LETTER X

The two Testaments are interesting, each in its own way. The Old one gives us a picture of these people's Deity as he was before he got religion, the other one gives us a picture of him as he appeared afterward. The Old Testament is interested mainly in blood and sensuality. The New one in Salvation. Salvation by fire.

The first time the Deity came down to earth, he brought life and death; when he came the second time, he brought hell.

Life was not a valuable gift, but death was. Life was a fever-dream made up of joys embittered by sorrows, pleasure poisoned by pain; a dream that was a nightmare-confusion of spasmodic and fleeting delights, ecstasies, exultations, happinesses, interspersed with long-drawn miseries, griefs, perils, horrors, disappointments, defeats, humiliations, and despairs—the heaviest curse devisable by divine ingenuity; but death was sweet, death was gentle, death was kind; death healed the bruised spirit and the broken heart, and gave them rest and forgetfulness; death was man's best friend; when man could endure life no longer, death came and set him free.

In time, the Deity perceived that death was a mistake; a mistake, in that it was insufficient; insufficient, for the reason that while it was an admirable agent for the inflicting of misery upon the survivor, it allowed the dead person himself to escape from all further persecution in the blessed refuge of the grave. This was not satisfactory. A way must be contrived to pursue the dead beyond the tomb.

The Deity pondered this matter during four thousand years unsuccessfully, but as soon as he came down to earth and became a Christian his mind cleared and he knew what to do. He invented hell, and proclaimed it.

Now here is a curious thing. It is believed by everybody that while he was in heaven he was stern, hard, resentful, jealous, and cruel; but that when he came down to earth and assumed the name Jesus Christ, he became the opposite of what he was before: that is to say, he became sweet, and gentle, merciful, forgiving, and all harshness disappeared from his nature and a deep and yearning love for his poor human children took its place. Whereas it as as Jesus Christ that he devised hell and proclaimed it!

Which is to say, that as the meek and gentle Savior he was a thousand billion times crueler than ever he was in the Old Testament—oh, incomparably more atrocious than ever he was when he was at the very worst in those old days!

Meek and gentle? By and by we will examine this popular sarcasm by the light of the hell which he invented. . . .

UNPUBLISHED AUTOBIOGRAPHICAL DICTATION

For many years Twain worked at creating his "Autobiography." By 1906 he had decided that many of the frank, corrosive opinions would not be published in his lifetime. The style is usually rambling, partially because Twain composed much of it by daily, topical dictations of his memories and thoughts to a secretary.

But from Tuesday, June 19, 1906, until Monday, June 25, Twain created five extended considerations on religion and Christianity. He edited this material into final form, but the author apparently decided that the material was too scandalous to print, because he wrote on each typescript:

> *Not to be exposed to any eye until the edition of* A.D. *2406. S.L.C.*

His opinion that five hundred years would be necessary seems extreme. The full sequence is now available to scholars at the Mark Twain Papers in Berkeley, California, and will someday appear in a full edition of the "Autobiography." This selection accurately represents the tenor of his skepticism about religion.

Wednesday, June 20, 1906.

The defects about Bibles—Remarks about the Immaculate Conception.

There are one or two curious defects about Bibles. An almost pathetic poverty of invention characterizes them all. That is one striking defect. Another is that each pretends to originality, without possessing any. Each borrows from the others, and gives no credit, which is a distinctly immoral act. Each, in turn, confiscates decayed old stage-properties from the others, and with naïve confidence puts them forth as fresh new inspirations from on high. We borrow the Golden Rule from Confucius, after it has seen service for centuries, and copyright it without a blush. When we want a Deluge we go away back to hoary Babylon and borrow it, and are as proud of it and as satisfied with it as if it had been worth the trouble. We still revere it and admire it, to-day, and claim that it came to us direct from the mouth of the Deity; whereas we know that Noah's flood never happened, and couldn't have happened. The flood is a favorite with Bible-makers. If there is a Bible—or even a tribe of savages—that lacks a General Deluge it is only because the religious scheme that lacks it hadn't any handy source to borrow it from.

Another prime favorite with the authors of sacred literature and founders of religions is the Immaculate Conception. It had been worn threadbare before we adopted it as a fresh new idea—and we admire it as much now as did the original conceiver of it when his mind was delivered of it a million years ago. The Hindus prized it ages ago when they acquired Krishna by the Immaculate process. The Buddhists were happy when they acquired Gautama by the same process twenty-five hundred years ago. The Greeks of the same period had great joy in it when their Supreme Being and his cabinet used to come down and people Greece with mongrels half human and half divine. The Romans borrowed the idea from Greece, and found great happiness in Jupiter's Immaculate Conception products. We got it direct from Heaven, by way of Rome. We are still charmed with it. And only a fortnight ago, when an Episcopal clergyman in Rochester was summoned before the governing body of his church to answer the charge of intimating that he did not believe that the Savior was miraculously conceived, the Rev. Dr. Briggs, who is perhaps the most daringly broad-minded religious person now occupying an American pulpit, took up the cudgels in favor of the Immaculate Conception, in an article in the *North American Review,* and from the tone of that article it seemed apparent that he believed he had settled that vexed question, once and for all. His idea was that there could be no doubt about it, for the reason that the Virgin Mary knew it was authentic because the Angel of the Annunciation told her so. Also, it must have been so, for the additional reason that Jude—a later son of Mary, the Virgin, and born in wedlock—was still living and associating with the adherents of the early church many years after the event, and that he said quite decidedly that it was a case of Immaculate Conception; therefore it must be true, for Jude was right there in the family and in a position to know.

If there is anything more amusing than the Immaculate Conception doctrine, it is the quaint reasonings whereby ostensibly intelligent human beings persuade themselves that the impossible fact is proven.

If Dr. Briggs were asked to believe in the Immaculate Conception process as exercised in the cases of Krishna, Osiris, Buddha, and the rest of the tribe, he would decline, with thanks, and probably be offended. If pushed, he would probably say that it would be childish to believe in those cases, for the reason that they were supported by none but human testimony, and that it would be impossible to prove such a thing by human testimony, because if the entire human race were present at a case of Immaculate Conception they wouldn't be able to tell when it happened, nor whether it happened at all—and yet this bright man with the temporarily muddy mind is quite able to believe an impossibility whose authenticity rests entirely upon human testimony—the testimony of but one human being, the Virgin herself, a witness not disinterested, but powerfully interested; a witness incapable of knowing the fact as a fact, but getting all that she supposed she knew about it at second hand,—at second hand from an entire stranger, an alleged angel, who could have been an angel, perhaps, but also could have been a tax collector. It is not likely that she had ever seen an angel before, or knew their trade-marks. He was a stranger. He brought no credentials. His evidence was worth nothing at all to anybody else in the community. It is worth nothing, to-day, to any but minds which are like Dr. Briggs's—which have lost their clarity through mulling over absurdities in the pious wish to dig something sane and rational out of them. The Immaculate Conception rests wholly upon the testimony of a single witness—a witness whose testimony is without value—a witness whose very existence has nothing to rest upon but the assertion of the young peasant wife whose husband needed to be pacified. Mary's testimony satisfied him, but that is because he lived in Nazareth, instead of New York. There isn't any carpenter in New York that would take that testimony at par. If the Immaculate Conception could be repeated in New York to-day, there isn't a man, woman, or child, of those four millions, who would believe in it—except perhaps some addled Christian Scientist. A person who can believe in Mother Eddy wouldn't strain at an Immaculate Conception, or six of them in a bunch. The Immaculate Conception could not be repeated successfully in New York in our day. It would produce laughter, not reverence and adoration.

To a person who doesn't believe in it, it seems a most puerile invention. It could occur to nobody but a god that it was a large and ingenious arrangement, and had dignity in it. It could occur to nobody but a god that a divine Son procured through promiscuous relations with a peasant family in a village could improve the purity of the product, yet that is the very idea. The product acquires purity—purity absolute—purity from all stain or blemish—through a gross violation of both human and divine law, as set forth in the constitution and by-laws of the Bible. Thus the Christian religion, which requires everybody to be moral and to obey the laws, has its very beginning in immorality and in disobedience to law. You couldn't purify a tomcat by the Immaculate Conception process.

Apparently, as a pious stage-property, it is still useful, still workable, although it is so bent with age and so nearly exhausted by overwork. It is another case of begats. What's-his-name begat Krishna, Krishna begat Buddha, Buddha begat Osiris, Osiris begat the Babylonian deities, they begat God, He begat Jesus, Jesus begat Mrs. Eddy. If she is going to continue the line and do her proper share of the begatting, she must get at it, for she is already an antiquity.

There is one notable thing about our Christianity: bad, bloody, merciless, money-grabbing and predatory as it is—in our country, particularly, and in all other Christian countries in a somewhat modified degree—it is still a hundred times better than the Christianity of the Bible, with its prodigious crime—the invention of Hell. Measured by our Christianity of to-day, bad as it is, hypocritical as it is, empty and hollow as it is, neither the Deity nor his Son is a Christian, nor qualified for that moderately high place. Ours is a terrible religion. The fleets of the world could swim in spacious comfort in the innocent blood it has spilt.

— — — — — — — — — — — — —

Friday, June 22, 1906.

. . . There are no peaceful nations now, except those unhappy ones whose borders have not been invaded by the Gospel of Peace. All Christendom is a soldier-camp. During all the past generation, the Christian poor have been taxed almost to starvation-point to support the giant armaments which the Christian Governments have built up, each to protect itself from the rest of the brotherhood and, incidentally, to snatch any patch of real estate left exposed by its savage owner. King Leopold II. of Belgium—probably the most intensely Christian monarch, except Alexander the Sixth, that has escaped Hell thus far—has stolen an entire kingdom in Africa, and in fourteen years of Christian endeavor there has reduced the population of thirty millions to fifteen, by murder, mutilation, overwork, robbery, rapine—confiscating the helpless native's very labor, and giving him nothing in return but salvation and a home in Heaven, furnished at the last moment by the Christian priest.

Within this last generation each Christian power has turned the bulk of its attention to finding out newer and still newer, and more and more effective ways of killing Christians—and, incidentally, a pagan now and then—and the surest way to get rich quickly, in Christ's earthly kingdom, is to invent a gun that can kill more Christians at one shot than any other existing gun.

Also, during the same generation, each Christian Government has played with its neighbors a continuous poker game, in the naval line. In this game

France puts up a battle-ship; England sees that battle-ship, and goes it one battle-ship better; Russia comes in and raises it a battle-ship, or two—*did,* before the untaught stranger entered the game and reduced her stately pile of ships to a damaged ferry-boat and a cruiser that can't cruise. We are in it ourselves, now. This game goes on, and on, and on. There is never a new shuffle; never a new deal. No player ever calls another's hand. It is merely an unending game of put up, and put up, and put up; and by the law of probabilities, a day is coming when no Christians will be left on the land, except the women. The men will all be at sea, manning the fleets.

This singular game, which is so costly and so ruinous, and so silly, is called statesmanship—which is different from assmanship on account of the spelling. Anybody but a statesman could invent some way to reduce these vast armaments to rational and sensible and safe police proportions, with the result that thenceforth all Christians could sleep in their beds unafraid, and even the Savior could come down and walk on the seas, foreigner as He is, without dread of being chased by Christian battle-ships.

Has the Bible done something still worse than drench the planet with innocent blood? To my mind it has—but this is only an opinion, and it may be a mistaken one. There has never been a Protestant boy nor a Protestant girl whose mind the Bible has not soiled. No Protestant child ever comes clean from association with the Bible. This association cannot be prevented. Sometimes the parents try to prevent it, by not allowing the children to have access to the Bible's awful obscenities, but this only whets the child's desire to taste that forbidden fruit, and it does taste it—seeks it out secretly and devours it with a strong and grateful appetite. The Bible does its baleful work in the propagation of vice among children, and vicious and unclean ideas, daily and constantly, in every Protestant family in Christendom. It does more of this deadly work than all of the other unclean books in Christendom put together; and not only more, but a thousandfold more. It is easy to protect the young from those other books, and they are protected from them. But they have no protection against the deadly Bible.

Is it doubted that the young people hunt out the forbidden passages privately, and study them with pleasure? If my reader were here present—let him be of either sex or any age, between ten and ninety—I would make him answer this question himself—and he could answer it in only one way. He would be obliged to say that by his own knowledge and experience of the days of his early youth, he knows positively that the Bible defiles all Protestant children, without a single exception.

Do I think the Christian religion is here to stay? Why should I think so? There had been a thousand religions before it was born. They are all dead. There had been millions of gods before ours was invented. Swarms of them are dead and forgotten long ago. Ours is by long odds the worst God that the ingenuity of man has begotten from his insane imagination—and shall He and His Christianity be immortal, against the great array of probabilities furnished by the theological history of the past? No. I think that Christianity, and its God, must follow the rule. They must pass on, in their turn, and make room for another God and a stupider religion. Or perhaps a better than this? No. That is not likely. History shows that in the matter of religions, we progress backward, and not the other way. No matter, there will be a new God and a new religion. They will be introduced to popularity and acceptance with the only arguments that have ever persuaded any people in this earth to adopt Christianity, or any other religion that they were not born to: the Bible, the sword, the torch, and the axe—the only missionaries that have ever scored a single victory since gods and religions began in the world. After the new God and the new religion have become established in the usual proportions—one-fifth of the world's population ostensible adherents, the four-fifths pagan missionary field, with the missionary scratching its continental back complacently and inefficiently—will the new converts believe in them? Certainly they will. They have always believed in the million gods and religions that have been stuffed down their midriffs. There isn't anything so grotesque or so incredible that the average human being can't believe it.

Suggestions for Further Reading

Because an ordinary library has over one hundred and twelve feet of shelves devoted to Mark Twain, this list must be highly selective.

Primary Texts

Charles Neider edited *The Complete Short Stories of Mark Twain* (New York, 1957). The volume includes "The Notorious Jumping Frog of Calaveras County," "Some Learned Fables for Good Old Boys and Girls" (a satire on scientific inferences), "The Diary of Adam and Eve," "The Man that Corrupted Hadleyburg," "Was It Heaven? Or Hell?" "The Mysterious Stranger" (an editorial compilation), "A Fable," and "Captain Stormfield's Visit to Heaven."

Neider also edited *The Complete Essays of Mark Twain* (New York, 1963). Two contra-skeptical essays involve Twain's curiosity about "Mental Telegraphy." Two essays about Paul Bourget show the range and precision of Twain's thought. This volume also includes "About Play Acting" and more than ten other essays that demonstrate Twain's skepticism.

Neider's other collections are the recommended *Life As I Find It* (New York, 1961) and *The Complete Humorous Sketches and Tales of Mark Twain* (New York, 1961), which includes "The Facts Concerning the Recent Carnival of Crime in Connecticut," a witty treatment of conscience.

Bernard DeVoto's edition of *Letters from the Earth* (New York, 1962) assembles an essential anthology. Similarly, *A Pen Warmed Up in Hell: Mark Twain in Protest,* edited by Janet Smith, with a preface by Maxwell Geismar (New York, 1962), also deserves careful reading. Walter Blair's *Selected Shorter Writings of Mark Twain* (Boston, 1962) offers a useful introduction to a good selection.

The massive scholarly achievement undertaken by the University of California Press has put in print formerly unpublished material, notebooks and manuscripts of great scholarly interest. Titles include *Mark Twain's Fables of Man, Mark Twain's "Which Was the Dream" and Other Symbolic Writings of the Later Years, Mark Twain's Mysterious Stranger Manuscripts,* and *Mark Twain's Satires and Burlesques.* The multi-volume series, *The Works of Mark Twain,* establishes reliable texts and provides informative introductions and footnotes.

Portions of Twain's *Autobiography* are available in two different versions, each incomplete. His "Private History of a Campaign that Failed" is a powerful, satiric anti-war essay.

The two-volume *Mark Twain-Howells Letters,* edited by Henry Nash Smith and William M. Gibson (Cambridge, 1960), is a splendid source of information. In the Bancroft Library, at the University of California, Berkeley, the Mark Twain collection preserves priceless material.

Secondary Texts

Although Mark Twain was Sam Clemens's earliest biographer, many have continued to explore the tangled web of identities. William Dean Howells's *My Mark Twain* (New York, 1910) was a lovingly perceptive appreciation. Dixon Wecter set a high standard in *Sam Clemens of Hannibal* (Boston, 1952). Justin Kaplan's *Sam Clemens and Mark Twain* (New York, 1966) integrates the man and his era, taking up the story when Sam left California to go to New York. Hamlin Hill's *Mark Twain: God's Fool* (New York, 1973) created a major change in our understanding of Twain's later years.

Scholars and critics have increased our knowledge and perception. A. B. Paine, Bernard DeVoto, Fred Anderson, Gladys Bellamy, Henry Nash Smith, Walter Blair, E. Hudson Long, Caroline Harnsberger, Edgar Branch, Hamlin Hill, Leo Marx, De Lancey Ferguson, Louis Budd, William Gibson, Frank Baldanza, Paul Fatout, Franklin Rogers, Philip Foner, Cyril Clemens, Jim Cox, Allison Ensor, Robert Regan, and Robert Hirst are among the many scholars who have shaped our understanding of Twain.

Two bibliographic tools deserve special mention: Thomas Asa Tenney's *Mark Twain: A Reference Guide* (Boston, 1977) is invaluable. Similarly, Alan Gribben's *Mark Twain's Library: A Reconstruction* (Boston, 1980) provides a foundation for another generation of scholars and critics.